Art& Agenda

POLITICAL ART AND ACTIVISM

gestalten

GREGOR JANSEN & ROBERT KLANTEN

PREFACE

Political art has had a significant place in art history ever since the French Revolution and romanticism. The political emphasis of the Age of Enlightenment extended to the aesthetic sphere. And from the beginning of postmodernism in the 1960s, art's political aspect has expanded in several different directions; in turn, challenging the monopolization of politics by the state, its organs of power, the parties, and their organizations. Politics is presently generally understood to mean the regulation of "basic activities" in all areas of social life—a situation that allows nonpolitically cultural or artistic areas of social activity to mix with politicized activities. It is this generalization of "the political" that has opened the way for an autonomous left-wing culture.

The word politics derives from the Latin term *politica, politicus* (of the state; of or relating to citizens), and the Greek term *politiká* (of the city). In the city-states of ancient Greece, the word described all activities, objects, and issues that concerned the community, or the pólis, as a whole—although today the term inevitably makes us think of political policing. *Politiká*, then, should be literally translated as "things that concern the city"—and "politics" in a similar sense to the Roman concept *of res publica*, from which the modern term "republic," derives. The use of the term "politics" as the title of a major work by Aristotle—*Politiká*—is highly significant in etymological terms; Aristotle considered rhetoric one of the seven *artes liberales* (as opposed to the craft-oriented and less artistic *artes mechanicae*) that characterized the free citizens who did not have to work for their daily bread—a luxury that politicians insist on to this day; except that today, after leaving public service, they promptly switch to the (free) market economy in order to appear worthy of their political influence in monetary terms.

A *res publica* is a public matter rather than a "thing" in isolation; but a "thing" in a context, which is subject to specific circumstances. But who speaks for this "thing"? Who takes up a position, or an opposition? And is speech always essential? The answer is yes—at least in the democratic state model, which depends on freedom of speech and on parliamentary discussions (and sometimes on nonparliamentary opposition), and on where and when "matters" and "things" are discussed. It is interesting that there is a German website that goes by the name RESpublica. It is used by a Munich communication agency that strives to create advertising campaigns that get everyone talking about the featured products. This, however, fails to take into account the style and form of communication in aesthetic terms—as rhetoric, or as the crafting of the message's formulation and manner of expression.

Quite apart from the communications and advertising companies that flourish all over the planet, promising to package their clients' message in bite-size pieces, the "product aesthetics critical analysis" label has existed in research circles since the 1970s. More recently, in 2004, the French sociologist and philosopher Bruno Latour gave the title *Making Things Public: Atmospheres of Democracy* to both an exhibition and a book he had authored. With the most significant concept—the "matter," the *res publica*—in mind, he raised issues that went beyond a purely parliamentary babble that deals only in "things."

Latour wrote that "the political" as expounded by him did not exclude scientific and artistic representation strategies. His new concept of the political expanded "political representation techniques" to include science and art, changing the focus on to the context in which things are formed. He states in an introductory text to the "Making Things Public" exhibition at ZKM in Karlsruhe: "Instead of searching for more democracy only in the realm of professional politics, we draw attention to the new atmospheric conditions of democracy, to a complex set of technologies, interfaces, platforms, networks, and media that allow things to become public. In other words, we go back to the things of nature, of people, and of art that constitute the political, and ask what these things actually are. We ask how things come about and are made public. What are public things, res publica? A republic?"

To edit a book about political art that is intended as a comprehensive survey of the present age, as this book is, means setting oneself to Latour's challenge. It also poses the question: How were the artists in the book chosen? Was there a democratic selection process, a referendum, or some other similar procedure? Was it the usual party affiliations or family ties—ultimately the political sleaze of inclusion and exclusion—that took hold, in this context in the form of postcolonial theory, and was it that the effect of this nepotism willfully left a number of nonaffiliated individuals out in the cold? After all, one can assume that the political is constituted as a specific communication space, which means that aside from the forms and media of political communication, it has boundaries that regulate who enters this space. Deciding who can take part in the communication process and in what manner, however, results from the drawing of boundaries, which always takes place at a structural and semantic level.

This book is an investigation of the interactions between politics, art, and activism. During political art's growing pains—and influenced by the widespread protests of 1968—this social movement announced its hostility to pictures, rejecting both the new figurative panel paintings, as well as abstract

BRUNO LATOUR

"THE NEW CONCEPT OF THE POLITICAL PRESENTED HERE DOES NOT TURN A BLIND EYE TO THE REPRESENTATIONAL STRATEGIES OF ART AND SCIENCE. ON THE CONTRARY, IT EXTENDS THE PREVIOUS TECHNIQUES OF POLITICAL REPRESENTATION BY ADDING ART AND SCIENCE TO THEM. INSTEAD OF SEARCHING FOR MORE DEMOCRACY ONLY IN THE REALM OF PROFESSIONAL POLITICS, WE DRAW ATTENTION TO THE NEW ATMOSPHERIC CONDITIONS OF DEMOCRACY, TO A COMPLEX SET OF TECHNOLOGIES, INTERFACES, PLATFORMS, NETWORKS, AND MEDIA THAT ALLOW THINGS TO BECOME PUBLIC. IN OTHER WORDS, WE GO BACK TO THE THINGS OF NATURE, OF PEOPLE AND OF ART THAT CONSTITUTE THE POLITICAL AND ASK WHAT THESE THINGS ACTUALLY ARE. WE ASK HOW THINGS COME ABOUT AND ARE MADE PUBLIC. WHAT ARE PUBLIC THINGS, RES PUBLICAE? A REPUBLIC?"

modernism, as bourgeois. The expansion of the concept of art, which was accelerated during this period, and which included both fluxus and Viennese actionism, resulted in ephemeral art forms such as Body Art, happenings, and performances becoming established as new forms of expression. In 1972 all of this culminated in the revolutionary documenta 5: Befragung der Realität—Bildwelten heute (Questioning Reality—Pictorial Worlds Today), which was curated by Harald Szeemann. With the birth of institutional criticism, which suspected every form of representation as an instrument of domination, art was torn from the context of museums. It gradually became clear that localized campaigns incorporating both the surroundings and the audience, combined with documentation on film and on canvas (action painting) and, finally, media coverage, were the most effective ways of formulating a particular cause or issue, crystallizing it as an artwork and bringing it into the space outside the museum. Creating radical pictures ensured wide distribution of political art by the media; this principle is particularly conspicuous in the protest movements of the 1970s, and in the use of the media by certain organizations in the immediate context of a radicalized gender debate that includes Greenpeace and the women's movement.

But let us move on to *political art*! What might it be, and what does it represent? How is it expressed compared with its opposite: *nonpolitical art*? Is it, in the classical sense of the word, "political": that is, art created by an artist who does not have to create art to earn a living? Or are there other definitions? While political art may not be tainted with commercial considerations to the extent that nonpolitical art is, this is far from being the case. The most recent Kassel documenta, documenta 12 held in 2007, was scrupulous in maintaining its independence from the market, but even so it was not acting any more politically or nonpolitically than the average citizen does in exercising his or her freedom of decision. This is the sad reality of a system without power, that is, one that does not permit the power to make decisions. Because the power to actually implement anything (to make or to effect things) will always lie with the market in any case, whether it is the art market or the economy that is under discussion. Politicians, as the assistants or marionettes of the economy, are actually freer than this; their role in speaking for "things" at least gives them a certain state power, albeit without conscience! And wasn't Catherine David's documenta X—with its simple but highly expressive title, *Politics/Poetics*—an unequalled example of the combination of text and image, and of politically motivated art (both in the exhibition itself and in the associated book)?

The development of modernism, including modern art, is shot through with a belief in progress—an ideology of progress whose aims are not, in fact, political, and indeed are inherently nonpolitical. The reason for this lies in the modernist artist's claim to autonomy, and of emphasizing free existence: freedom as a human being, as an artist, and as a citizen. The Danish-German painter Asmus Jacob Carstens could be described as the first free artist; in a letter to the Berliner Akademie in 1796, he put it like this: "I wish to inform Your Excellencies that I do not belong to the Berliner Akademie, but to humanity… I can only develop myself here, among the best artworks in the world, and I will go on to justify myself to the world to the best of my powers.… My abilities were entrusted to me by God; I must be a conscientious steward of them, so that when the day comes and I have to give an account, I am not forced to say: Lord, I took the talent that you gave me and buried it in Berlin."

ASMUS JACOB CARSTENS

"I WISH TO INFORM YOUR EXCELLENCIES THAT I DO NOT BELONG TO THE BERLINER AKADEMIE, BUT TO HUMANITY [...] I CAN ONLY DEVELOP MYSELF HERE, AMONG THE BEST ARTWORKS IN THE WORLD, AND I WILL GO ON TO JUSTIFY MYSELF TO THE WORLD TO THE BEST OF MY POWERS. [...] MY ABILITIES WERE ENTRUSTED TO ME BY GOD; I MUST BE A CONSCIENTIOUS STEWARD OF THEM, SO THAT WHEN THE DAY COMES AND I HAVE TO GIVE AN ACCOUNT, I AM NOT FORCED TO SAY: LORD, I TOOK THE TALENT THAT YOU GAVE ME AND BURIED IT IN BERLIN."

Is political art free *per se* today—after a 200-year progressive modernization process, is it so differentiated that it has now become a postmodern symbol and reference system, sufficiently provocative, but no longer able to claim any political relevance? Is the political art of today, for example, art that deals in things that are of interest to the police? Or, to refer to the "ting" or "thing"—the ancient place of meeting and governing assembly of the Germanic and Nordic tribes, which forms the root of many German words such as stipulation, negotiation, and examination—art in which intervention, participation, and specific location play a central role? The general opinion is that anything expressed in public, any art in a public form, that is, in a public space, must be deemed political. Jürgen Habermas once spoke of the reasonable justification of norms, even if master and man have always held different opinions on the matter, which was substantiated by Thomas Locher in terms of Hegelian dialectics.

Art, if we consider it as a broad and inclusive generic term for creative acts, is a medium which, in the process of being received by people and anticipated on a visual, aesthetic, or indeed artistic level in other media, is—or can be—reinterpreted or rejected. So it is a question of demanding a political dimension, and here we are speaking of it in the best sense of the word, of reclaiming it, because generally all that is created is seemingly political art in which the division between political rhetoric and concrete artistic performance is glossed over.

For example, Ai Weiwei from Peking, China, who was born in 1957, is an artist whose sculptures, installations, videos, and happenings generally have a political impetus, and relate to, or can be related to, specific problematic issues in today's China. These works have, at least potentially, a major impact in the West as "human rights art." His exhibitions all over the world and his fame, give him a voice in the media that is not good news for the Chinese state because it allows democratic western systems, whether politics or art, to criticize and question the power of the Chinese Communist Party system. The views he expresses on his blogs and on Twitter are thorns in the side of "Big Brother."

Art in a democracy is less political than art in a dictatorship. Reflecting on this fact, German art critic and sociologist Walter Grasskamp described the democratic political form as "non-aesthetic democracy" in 1992. He went on to explain that in Mexico and Cuba, across the continent of Africa, and in Russia and China, there are many states in which the production conditions for art are very difficult. In the West, the art in question has been and continues to be persistently lionized as an expression of political will and the fight for survival. Irene and Peter Ludwig's collection in the Suermondt-Ludwig Museum in Aachen with its numerous bequests, is a good example of this enthusiastically received direction in figurative art; and the first "global art history" in the 1950s acknowledged it by describing abstract art as a *western* model of freedom. This, however, also calls to mind the suppression of abstraction and of expressionism by the National Socialists in Germany, and by Fascists in Italy, Spain, Russia, and elsewhere—which found its most extreme expression in the term "degenerate art," and which exploited the concept of the will to power as symbolized by a "pure" Aryan figurative and primitive art style for propaganda purposes, disseminating an ideal of beauty borrowed from classical art. The same is true of music.

THOMAS LOCHER
Base and Abyss
1997, 81 Aluminium plates, engraving
Every plate 48×48×0.8 cm
Total size 7.68×5.28 cm

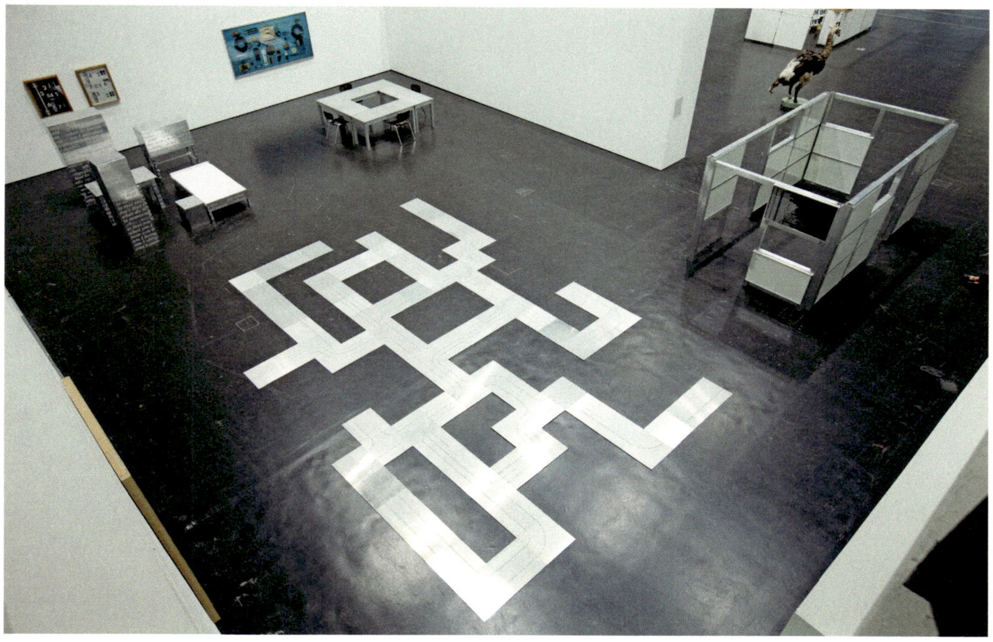

To take another example, there is an art of politics just as there is an art of cooking, or of making wine, but how does politics relate to art? Let us examine the wonderful gestures and declarations of Willy Brandt and John F. Kennedy: one an image, the other a message. The famous kneeling gesture took place on December 7, 1970, after German chancellor Willy Brandt signed a treaty normalizing relations between the Federal Republic of Germany and the People's Republic of Poland in Warsaw. The Warsaw Treaty established the Oder-Neisse Line as the western boundary of Poland, removing the possibility of either state making territorial claims. Brandt's visit was transformed into a turning point in the history of German–Polish relations by a wholly unexpected gesture. During the laying of a wreath at a monument to the victims of the German National Socialists on the site of the Warsaw Ghetto, Brandt suddenly sank to his knees. Just over a year later, he was awarded the Nobel Peace Prize.

On July 26, 1963, American president John F. Kennedy was in Berlin, standing in front of the Schöneberg town hall and making a speech to the population of the divided city. In the wake of the building of the wall, and in the shadow of the East–West conflict, hundreds of thousands of people gathered there, hopeful and expectant. Kennedy's visit to Berlin was a powerfully symbolic display of resolve, and his message, delivered in German—"Ich bin ein Berliner" (I am a Berliner)—was unforgettable. Once upon a time, to be a citizen of Rome meant belonging to a world power within which established laws and rules applied. In the 1960s, the president of a world power—America—declared his affiliation to a divided city, nearly two years after the wall between East and West Germany was erected, affirming certain rights for both the included and the excluded. Five months later, Kennedy was shot in Dallas.

It is crucial to the significance of both events that they took place in public, and that both of these events, which shaped the history of the countries involved, had a presence in the media. This reveals a crucial feature of political messages—and of political art.

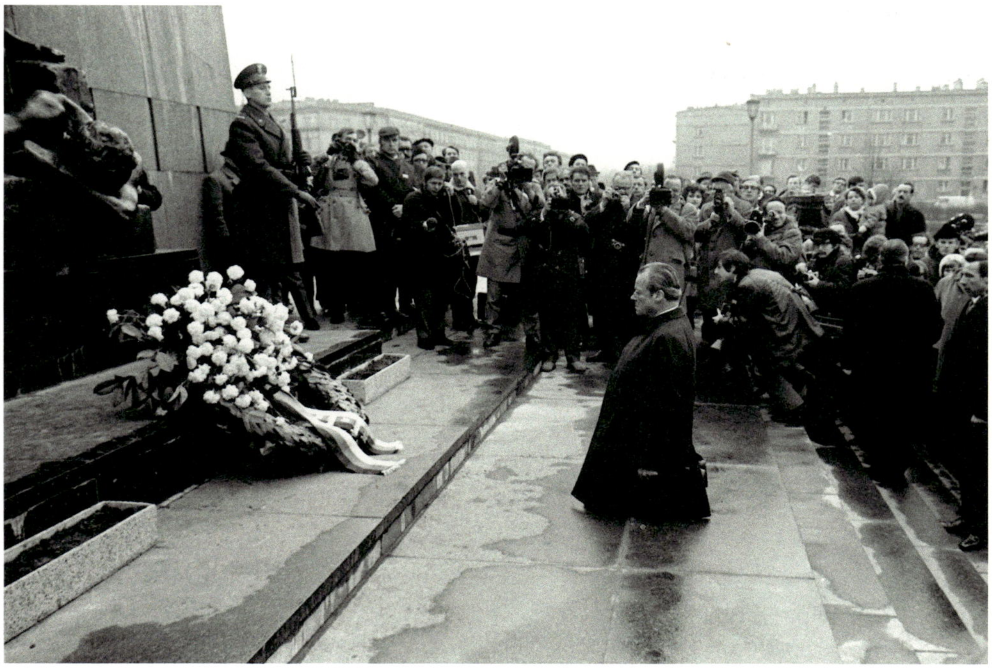

After German chancellor Willy Brandt laid a wreath down at a monument to the Warsaw Ghetto Uprising, he surprisingly—and to all appearances spontaneously—knelt in a gesture of humility and penance.
(Fotoagentur Sven Simon)

To take another example, was Joseph Beuys a political artist, because, in installing permanent sculptural works, he spoke of "social sculpture"? Or did he become political in 1979, when was among the 500 founders of the Die Grünen (the German Green party) and ran for election to the European Parliament as a member of that party? Was his impressive campaign *7,000 Eichen—Stadtverwaldung statt Stadtverwaltung" (7,000 Oaks—Municipal Afforestation Instead of Municipal Government)* an artistic or a political act? The surprising answer is that it was both. In 1982, the artist had pieces of basalt piled up in a heap at documenta 7 so that in five years (at documenta 8 in 1987) he could set up those basalt columns next to newly-planted trees in urban spaces. No other artwork was such a challenge or such a life's work, or was rooted so intensively and sustainably in the topographical, social, and climatic structure of the city of Kassel; no other artwork demanded such permanent active care, and changed the (ecological) self-consciousness of Kassel's citizens and of others. As the artwork (the heap of basalt pillars) vanished, a "forest" of political will toward municipal afforestation instead of municipal government was created. Art becomes politics, and political action is art.

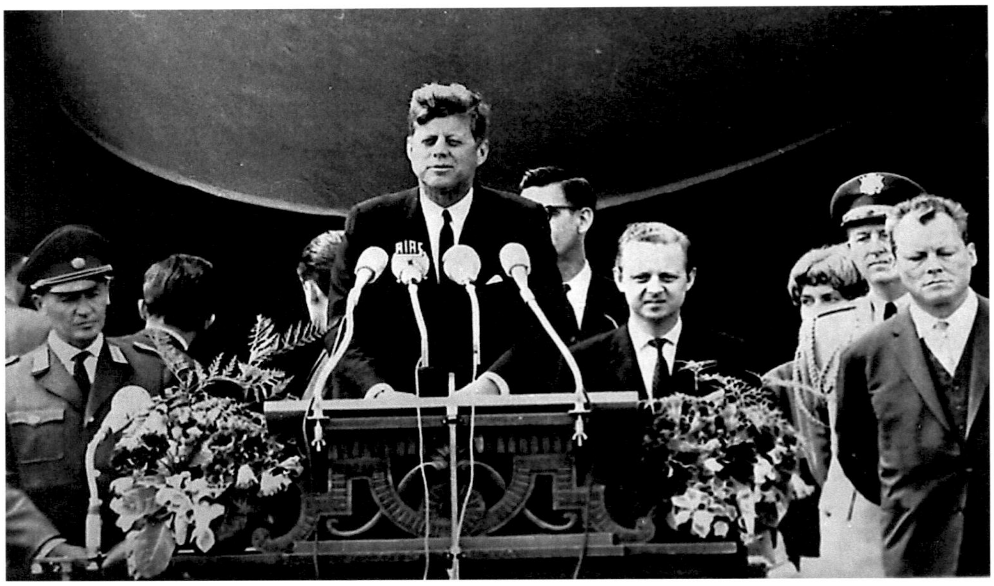

President John F. Kennedy delivers his famous "Ich bin ein Berliner" speech in front of the city hall in West Berlin concerning the Berlin Wall, June 26, 1963. At far right is the mayor of West Berlin, Willy Brandt. (AP Photo)

Another aesthetic phenomenon is the choice of certain formal techniques or strategies. Just as in media coverage of politicians making pointing gestures to symbolize the will and ability to make decisions, there are forms of artistic expression in which political agitation or criticism is revealed in a less-affirmative way. Since the painters of the French Revolution, painting's role in the political sphere has more or less run its course. Today it is textual artworks or Street Art that harbor political thoughts, or to which political thoughts are ascribed. Since John Heartfield, is collage the primary way of making statements that criticize institutions, or is it a medium like any other? For a long time painting was the central medium for politically motivated art. However, today it has been replaced by photography and video.

It only remains for us to note the contextual factors that will not escape attentive observers in the case of political art, or of what is supposed to be political art. This type of art practice takes place primarily in public space, and it draws its pictorial vocabulary from propaganda campaign techniques such as collages, banners, and texts—its message is a message, sometimes in the sense of a poster slogan.

It is easy to compare political art with propaganda, realism, critical, campaign, and activist art, but this does not take into account its *res publica*—its relevance to the wider public. It is always "context art" that relates to a certain set of circumstances; it is the result of artistic research into public affairs. However, in this it is not necessarily different from abstract formalism or from art produced for the art market, which has been increasingly praised for its political content in the past few years. Ultimately, it is the consumer, the recipient, who decides how political political art really is, or can potentially be, and what its radius of impact is. This point was made by Marcel Duchamp at the Convention of the American Federation of Arts held in Houston, Texas in 1957, at a time when the concept of art was being challenged: "All in all, the creative act is not performed by the artist alone; the spectator brings the work in contact with the external world by deciphering and interpreting its inner qualification and thus adds his contribution to the creative act. This becomes even more obvious when posterity gives a final verdict and sometimes rehabilitates forgotten artists."

This book is a significant contribution to the discussion of this "public matter." It envisages a different form of public to the art itself, and allows a discussion and enables comparisons that were previously impossible—albeit comparisons that can never be objective or fact-based, and a discussion whose selection criteria admit no democracy or claim to comprehensiveness. Visual art undoubtedly has social significance, but, regardless of this, at present it is hardly educational and hardly a political force in our society, and generally confines itself to a nonpolitical environmental consciousness. Contradiction is not merely a welcome, but is also an integral addition to this "annual report," as it is an essential part of any "public matter."

My doctor recently said that a doctor's natural enemy is a teacher. A teacher finds out what illness he has on Wikipedia, and then tells the doctor what medicine to prescribe. The distribution and democratization of knowledge gives amateurs more power in terms of the public sphere, allowing them to question and criticize the experts and their practices. In a similar way, the visual art of today tells the politicians the ways in which they should change the world, something artists have absorbed from more intelligent commentators—and possibly from the theater directors Claus Peymann, Frank Castorf, and Christoph Schlingensief. Artists are filled with Hegelian self-understanding, believing they have a pure heart and the necessary (theoretical) knowledge to change local conditions—but, alas, little time.

"ALL IN ALL, THE CREATIVE ACT IS NOT PERFORMED BY THE ARTIST ALONE; THE SPECTATOR BRINGS THE WORK IN CONTACT WITH THE EXTERNAL WORLD BY DECIPHERING AND INTERPRETING ITS INNER QUALIFICATION AND THUS ADDS HIS CONTRIBUTION TO THE CREATIVE ACT. THIS BECOMES EVEN MORE OBVIOUS WHEN POSTERITY GIVES A FINAL VERDICT AND SOMETIMES REHABILITATES FORGOTTEN ARTISTS."

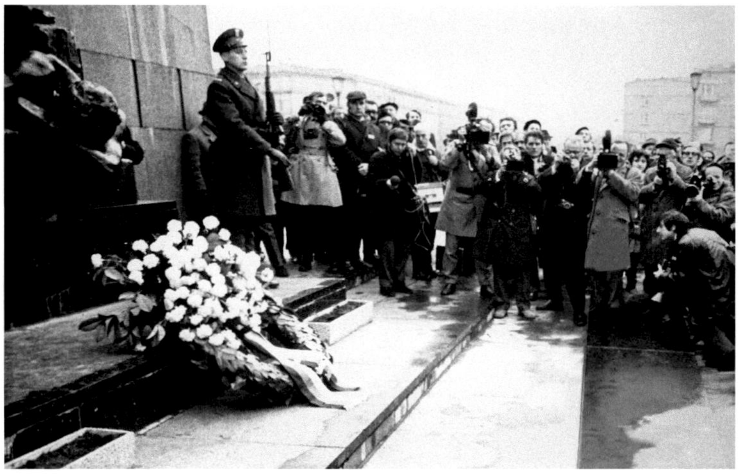

MICHAEL SCHIRNER
BYE BYE, WAR70
2006–2009, Digigraphie by Epson, Courtesy the artist

THE COM-MERCIAL ASPECT

TABLE OF CONTENTS

INTRODUCTION

In our consumer-oriented world, it seems almost impossible to ignore advertising and avoid succumbing to the desire to buy, buy, buy. Commerce, after all, defines a large part of our lives. When the pop art movement emerged in the 1950s, art turned its attention to the worlds of advertising and consumerism for the first time. While pop art saw itself as an integral part of industrial consumer culture, it also cast it in a critical light. By drawing on the visual language of this mass culture and setting it in new contexts, pop artists revealed the banality of a world driven by consumerist desires. Today's artists use similar strategies. U.S. artist Ron English [see p. 32], for example, exploits the language of advertising. At first glance, his large-format works don't seem any different from the billboard advertising that peppers highways, streets, and buildings; closer inspection reveals that they are actually subversive works of art.

Although the same first glance often makes it seem as if artists are examining business and consumerism, their focus is frequently elsewhere. They consciously use their strategies and mechanisms to refer to something completely different. Many use sophisticated design to hide brutal truths behind polished product aesthetics. An installation by U.S. artist Walter Robinson [see p. 22] carries the harmless, almost charming name *Kinder Blitz*. But the work has a shock in store for viewers when they realize that the colorful shapes are actually bombs. Murray Gaylard [see p. 33] and Thomas Sachs [see p. 38] explore questions of identity in their work, and Sachs, like many of his contemporaries, also addresses how our obsession with brands is defining our era. This also includes the co-opting of brands and the commercialization of public spaces that often goes along with it. The Spanish artist duo 0100101110101101.org [see p. 44] devises striking campaigns to illustrate these ideas, while the Danish-Norwegian duo Elmgreen and Dragset [see p. 46] built a detailed but non-functioning Prada boutique in the middle of the Texas desert.

The fashion world is also the focus of Zoë Sheehan Saldaña's [see p. 36] work. Her *Shopdropping* series involved producing handsewn replicas of mass-produced items and smuggling them into the U.S. chains where the originals came from. The Spanish duo PSJM [see p. 40] also finds ways of visualizing the issue of cheap products, giving particular attention to child labor and globalization. Jota Castro [see p. 16], a former diplomat, uses his art to explore financial markets and is particularly interested in how the financial crisis affected the fates of small investors. And the work of Italian artist Filippo Minelli [see p. 12] illustrates our dependency on the internet and our fading connection to reality. His *Google world* series reflects on Google's global dominance by pasting the logo onto some of the remotest spots in the world.

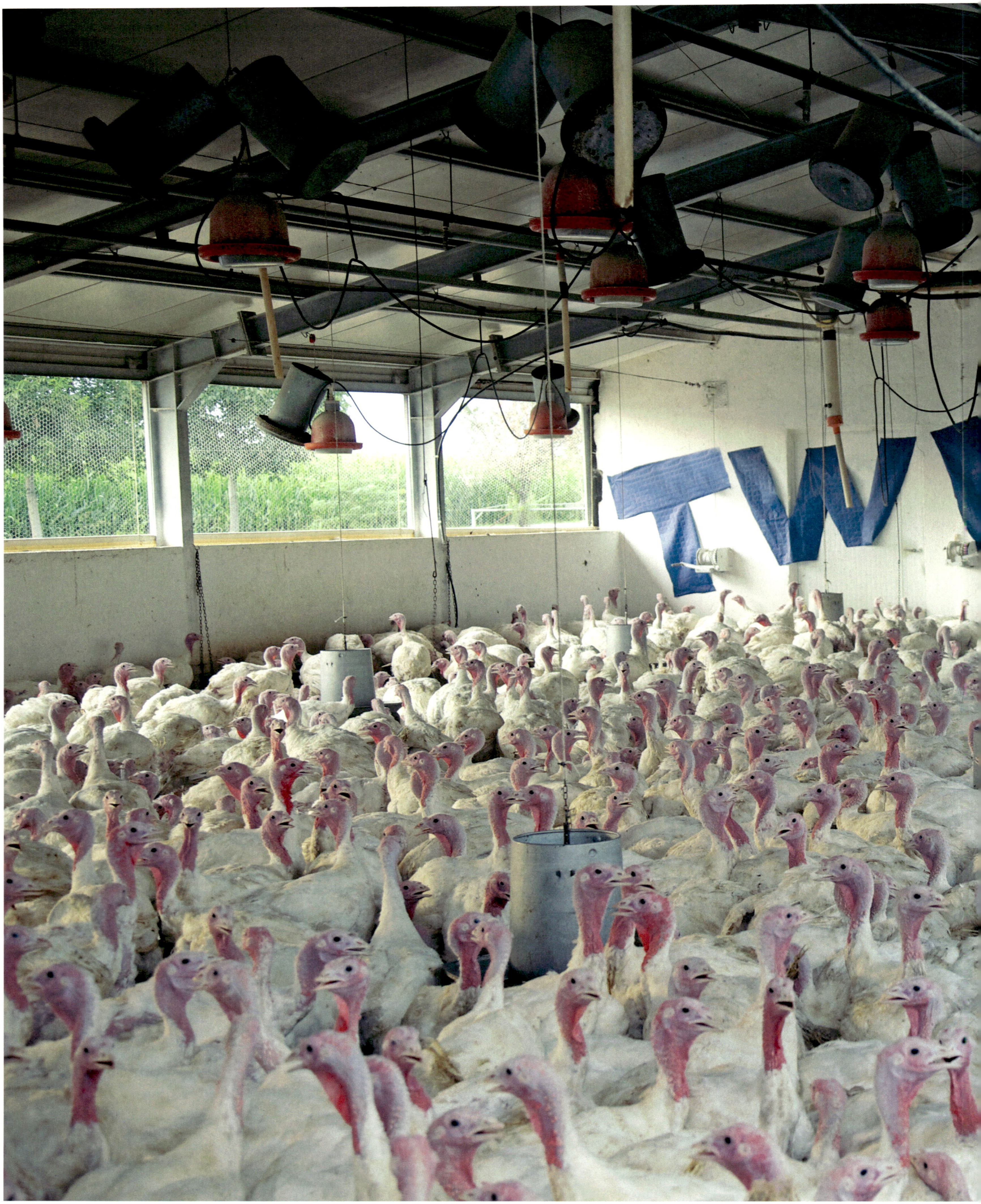
TW

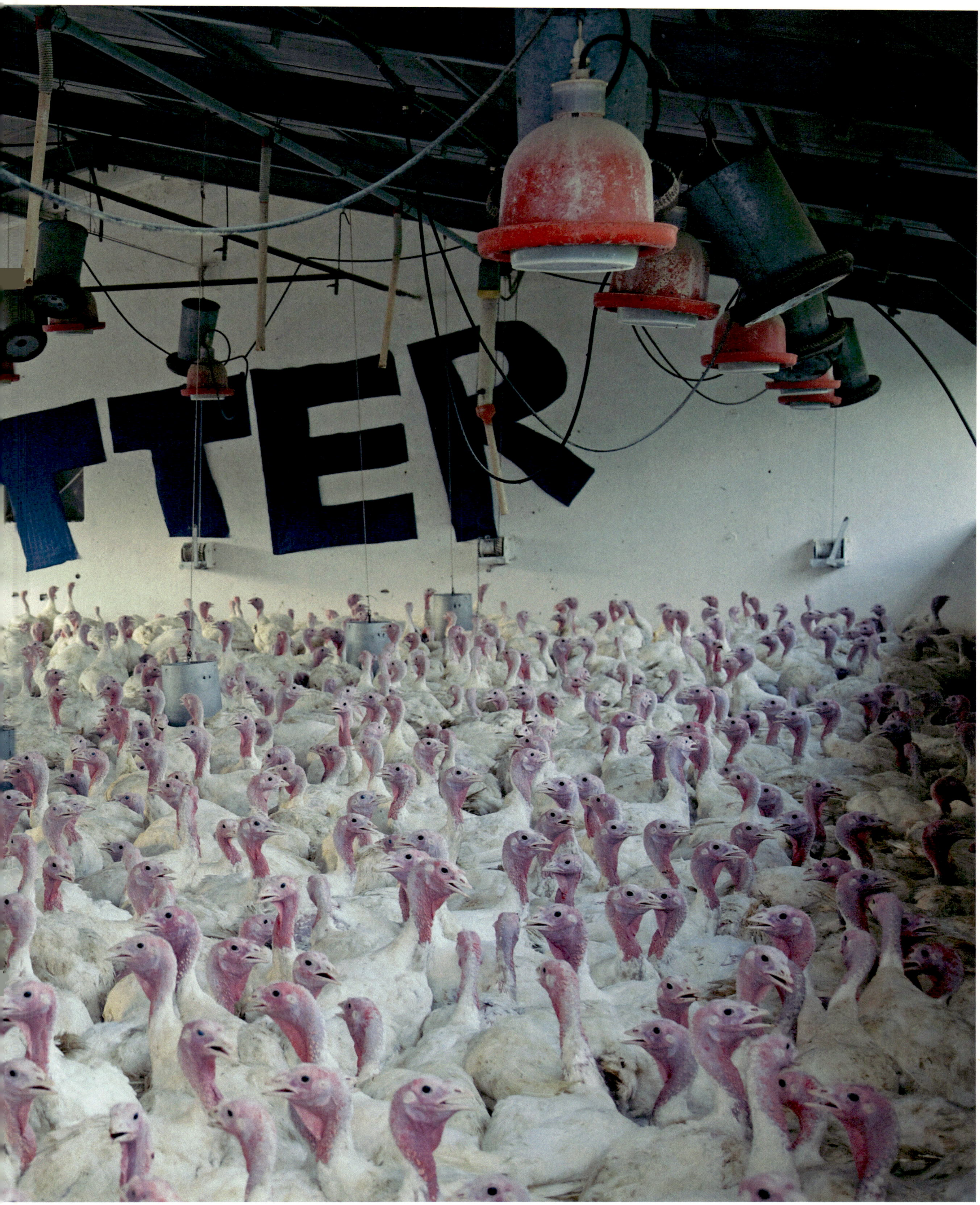
TER

FILIPPO MINELLI

1 (previous spread)
Contradictions
2010, Brescia, Italy
Courtesy Andrea Danesi
2
Flags
2009, Sarajevo, Bosnia and Herzegovina
3
Contradictions
2007, Bamako, Mali
4
Google world
2008, Beijing, China
5
Google world
2008, Paris, France

"I'll just google that"; "Yes I know, I read it on Twitter, and I've seen the photo on her Facebook page." Day-to-day living without the internet has become unthinkable; we do not notice how much of our everyday actions and communication are dependent on search engines and virtual networks. Reality and virtual worlds sometimes seem almost inextricably intertwined—and this is the inspiration for Filippo Minelli's (* 1983) land art. The Italian artist's work addresses web 2.0 technologies, and the idea that they are slowly but surely superseding reality. Since 2008, he has been traveling round the world, sticking the striking logos of the internet sites that have such an impact on us, on everything he comes across. "Users are pushed to live the abstraction from reality in an intense way. They often experience technologies only as an idea, and sometimes without even knowing their real functions. And this aspect works for the social networks, too. The idealization connected with these experiences provokes a small but important detachment from the perception of reality, and what I want to do by writing the names of anything connected with the 2.0 life we are living in the slums of the Third World, is to point out the gap between the reality we still live in and the ephemeral world of technologies." The artist left behind a variety of logos in major European cities, landscapes from South America to South Africa, in Kathmandu, in the heart of the Himalayas, and in the slums of Southeast Asia. The stylized logo names of Google, Twitter, and Facebook now appear on underground rail lines, on rocks, and in churches—all over the real world. But, at the end of the day, hasn't the real world already been conquered by Google, Facebook, and co.? With applications such as Google Earth, Google Street View, and Google Maps, the virtual world of the search engine approximates ever more closely to our real world. Minelli draws attention to this media phenomenon—the omnipresence of Google—by inventing his own apps and, for instance, sticking "Google Answers" on a church pew in Notre Dame in Paris and "Google Great Walls" on the Great Wall of China. In his series *Confrontation*, on the other hand, he challenges the boundaries between the real and virtual worlds in a very realistic way. He does this, for example, by painting "MySpace" on the simple huts of slums or by applying "Twitter" on the wall of a feed lot for turkeys.

2

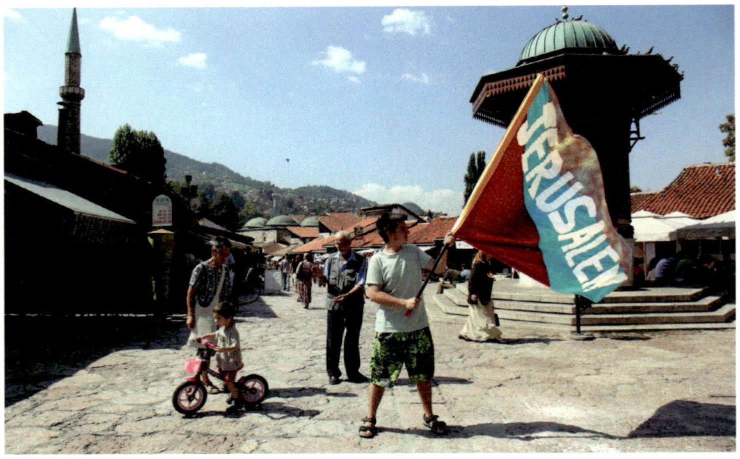

3

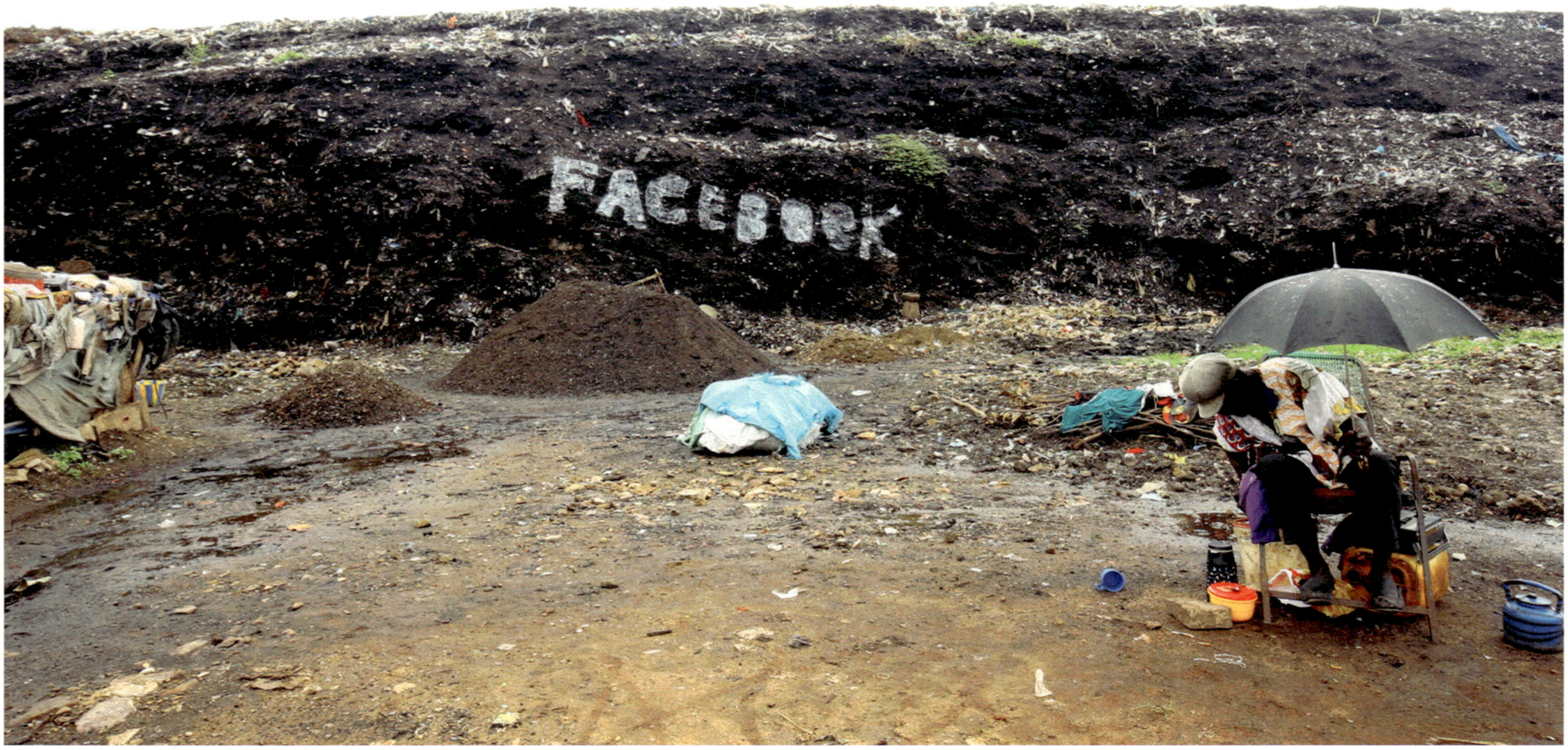

4

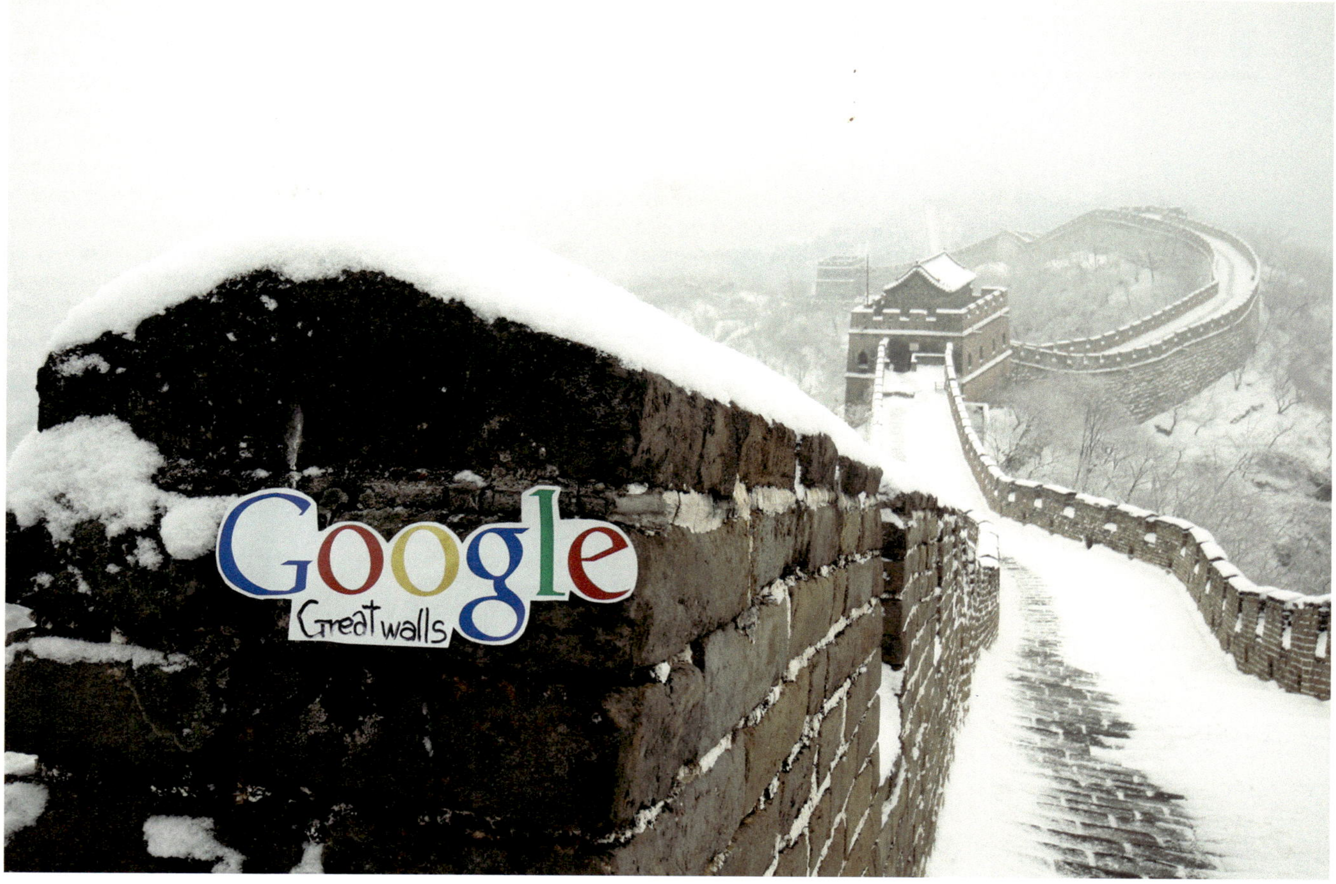

5

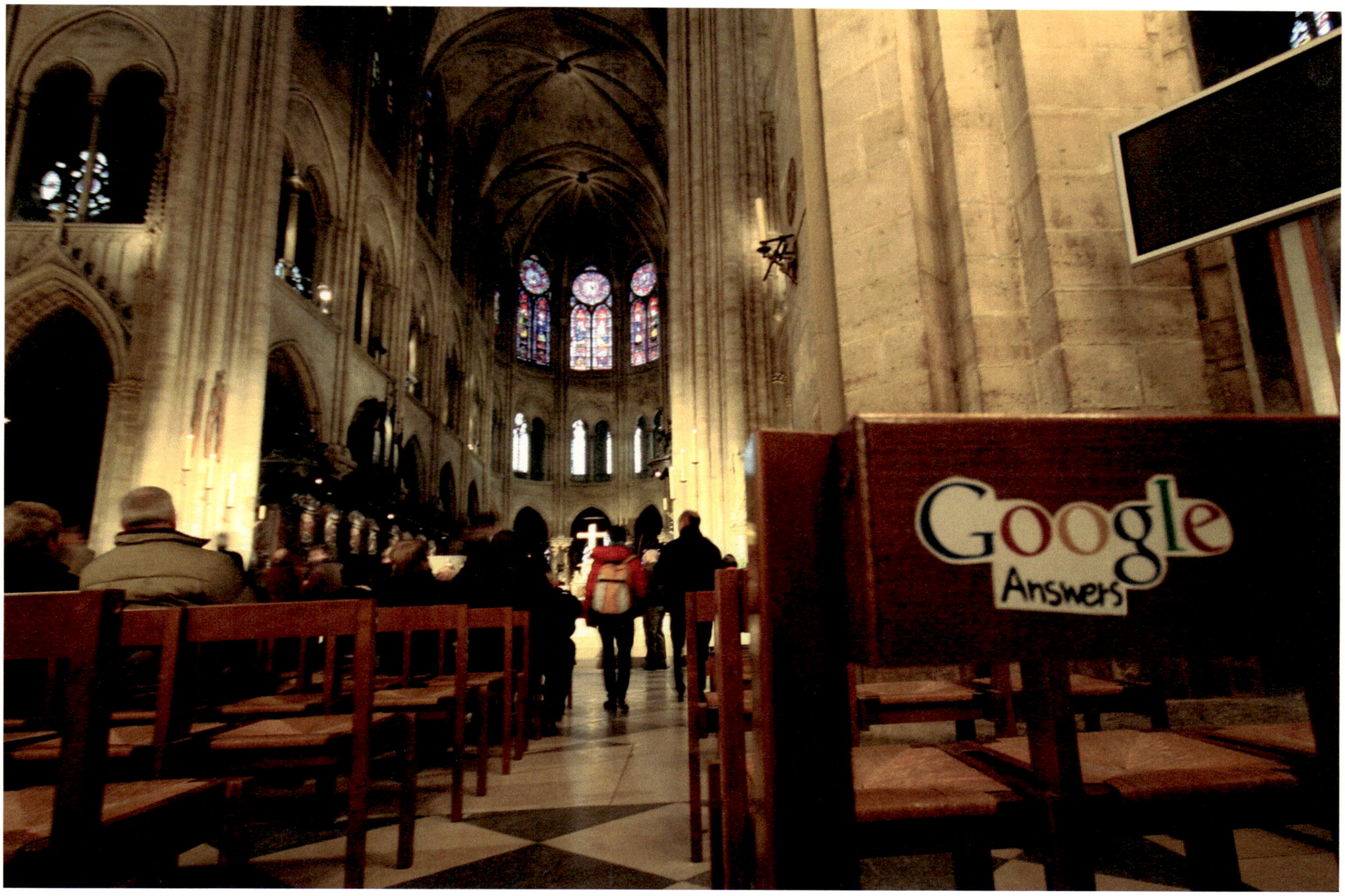

JOTA CASTRO

1
Mortgage
2009, One dollar bills, rope variable dimensions Courtesy the artist and Galerie Barbara Thumm, Berlin
2
500 Ways
2007, Plastic boat, coins, and wood, Courtesy the artist and Umberto di Marino, Naples
3
Amazonas
2009, Wood and toilet paper Variable dimensions, Courtesy the artist and Galerie Barbara Thumm, Berlin
4 (next spread)
China
2006, Courtesy the artist and Umberto di Marino, Naples

Born in Peru and now living in Brussels, Jota Castro (* 1965) initiated his career in diplomacy at the United Nations and at the European Union; a career that he left in the late 1990s in order to devote himself to pursuing an activist form of art. Castro considers his education as a lawyer and his experience in diplomacy and political science as necessary training to becoming an artist. The work is overtly political, utilizing various mediums including sculpture, installation, objects, and video to address environmental issues, poverty, social injustice, corporate greed, and inequality. Although politically poignant, the work is not dry; humor and political satire are embedded in his practice.

Castro feels that all art is sincerely political. In 2009 he presented a work titled, *Amazonas,* in which he re-created a forest using toilet paper and wooden poles. The stacks of pastel-colored toilet paper resemble the leafless trees, which are the product of the slash and burn techniques used in deforestation. The bright, unnatural colors recall a fake forest or candy-land-like setting, where the inhabitants live in denial and everything is all right. The artist equates the treatment of the rainforest to the daily use of toilet paper: "*Amazonas* is just like toilet paper. We use it, some even abuse it, we do not think so much about it, it is there for our convenience, and some people take it for granted. But it will not last forever."

In the work titled, *Mortgage,* 2009, he created a hangman's noose using rope and dollar bills. This work clearly and effectively addresses the global financial crisis brought on by the collapse of mortgage-backed loans in the United States. The work is directed not only at the irresponsible behavior of the banks and government regulators, which allows easy credit to swell debt, creating a financial bubble, but also at those who suffered the most, namely homeowners. Although many banks were bailed out of the crisis through government relief efforts, many homeowners have been left destitute, losing their homes with no form of effective relief in sight. Jota Castro continues his critique of financial and economic policies in a very simple work titled, *China,* 2009. A selection of shoes, all made in China, where the majority of the world's shoes are now manufactured, are arranged to spell the word, "China." This work addresses two main issues: The first is the immense trade deficits that nations are incurring with China due to the fact that this country is manufacturing and exporting a disproportionate amount of the world's goods. The second issue is the abusive tactics this nation is using to gain and sustain an economic advantage, such as the wholesale manufacturing of pirated goods, as well as the artificial valuation of the Chinese currency, the renminbi, against other currencies in order to maintain a competitive edge in the costs of production.

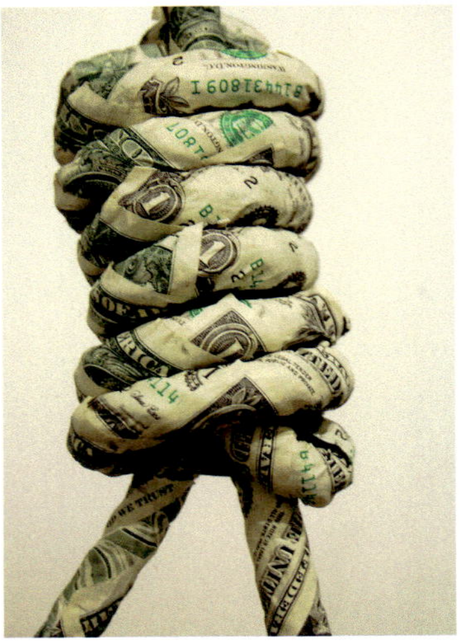

1
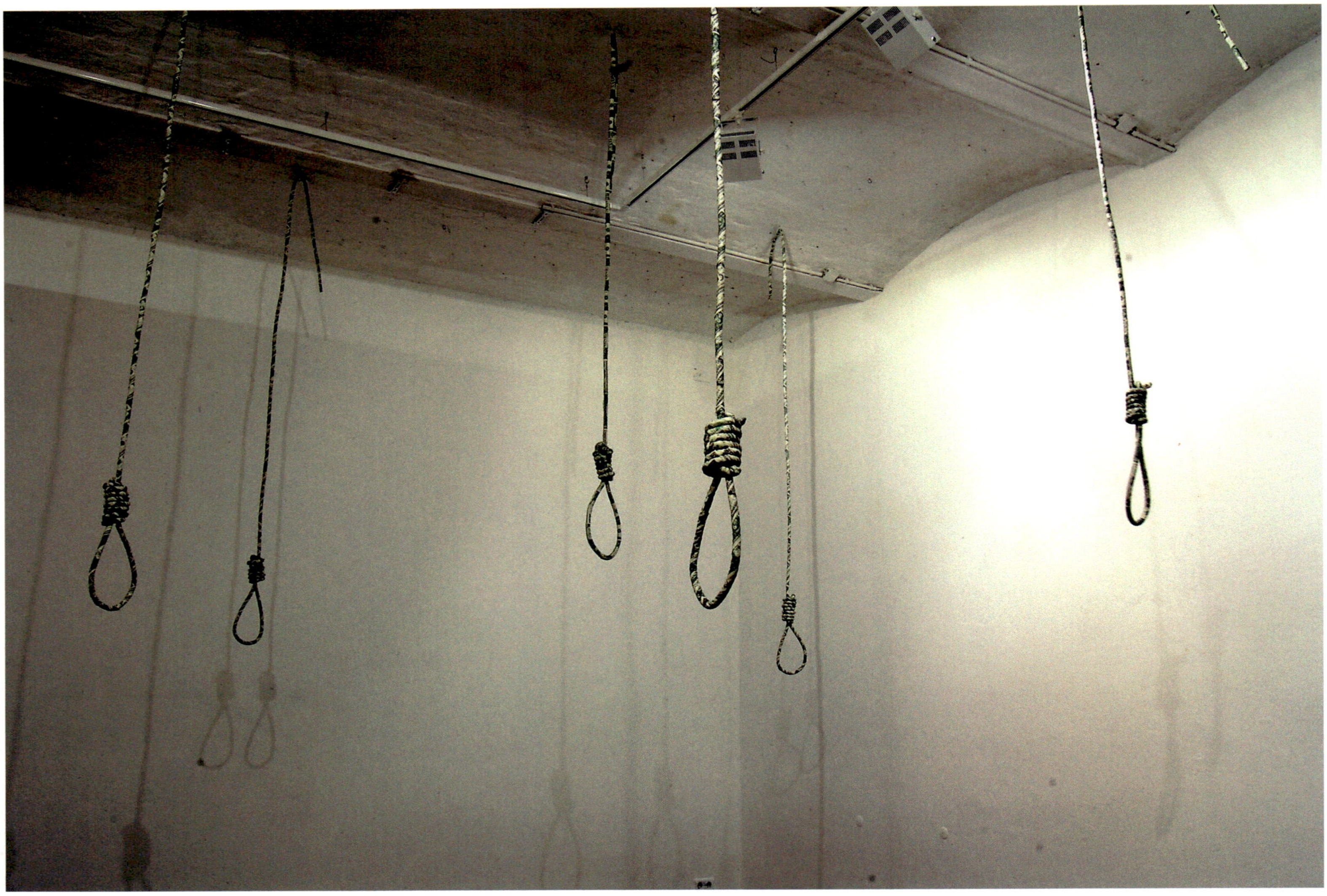

2

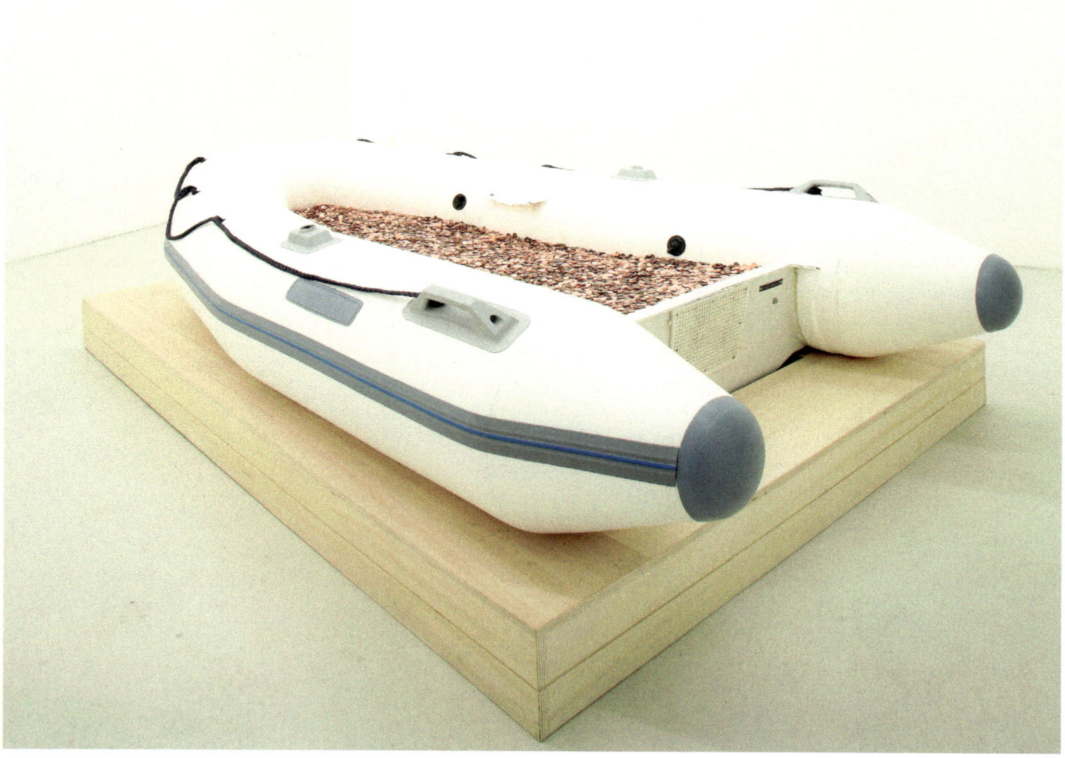

3

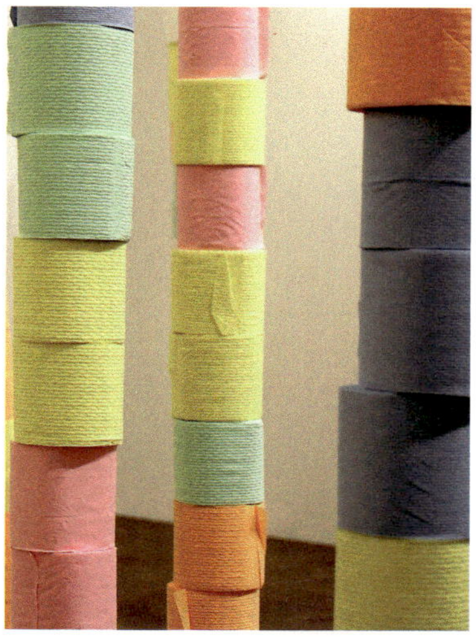

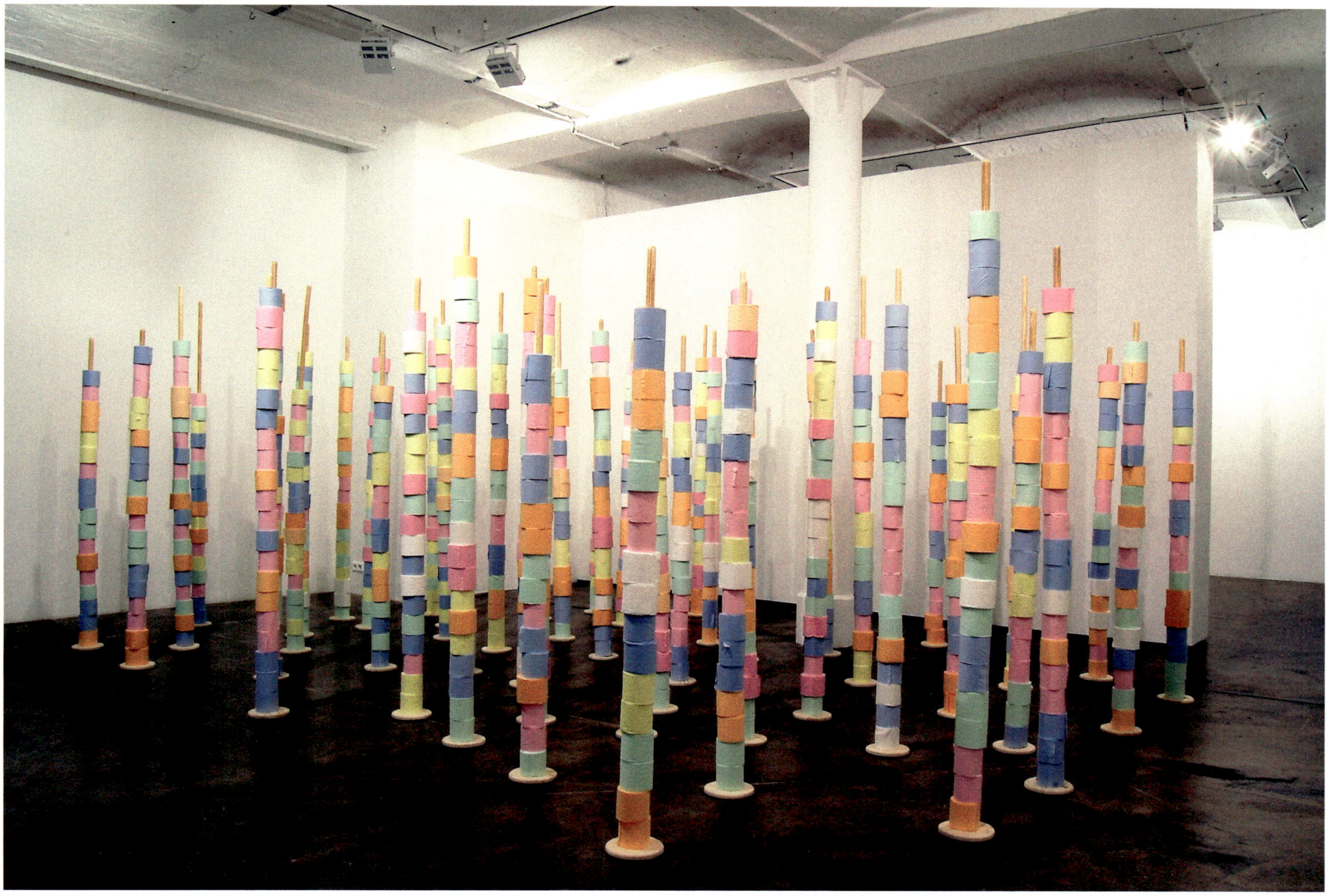

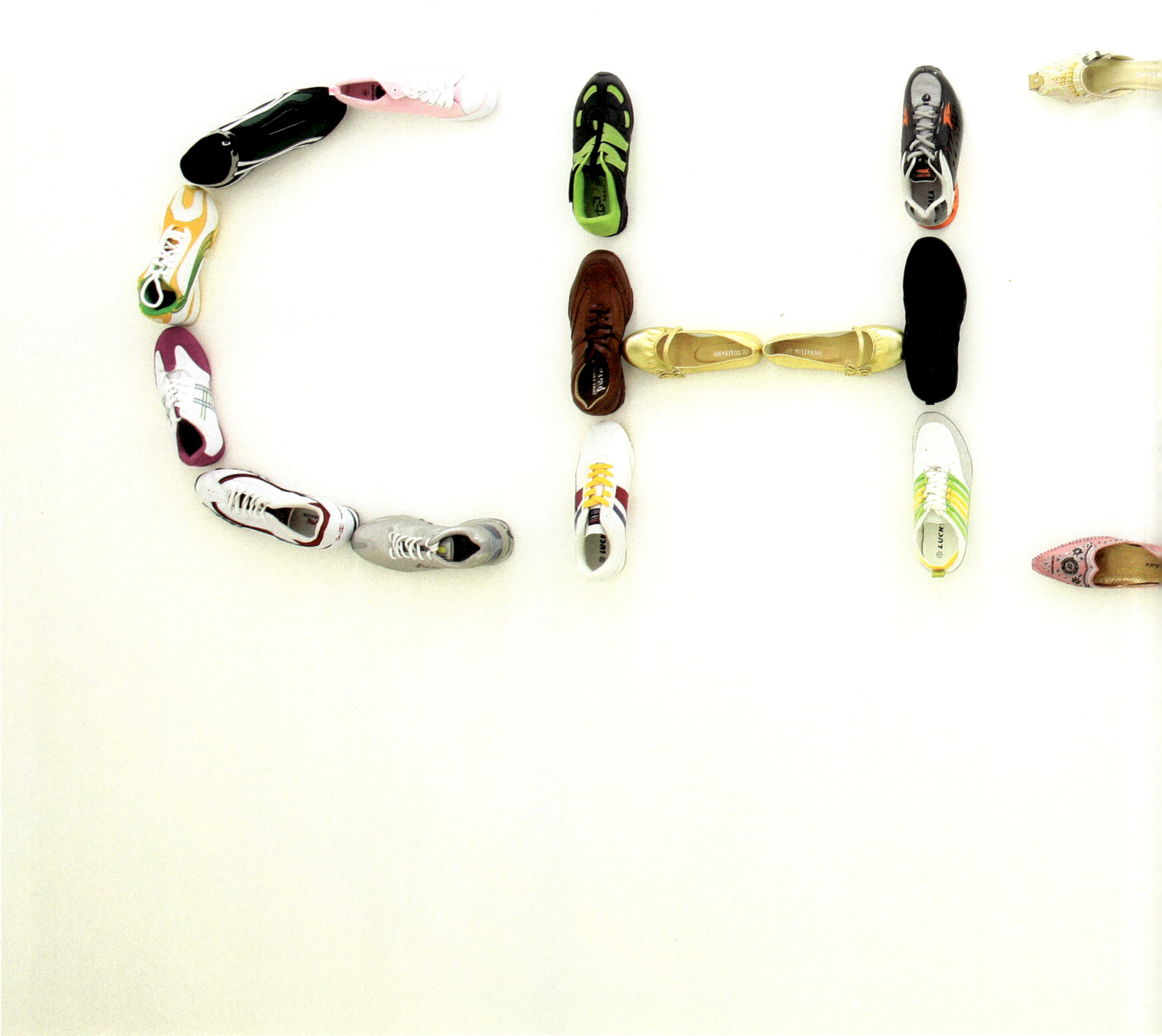

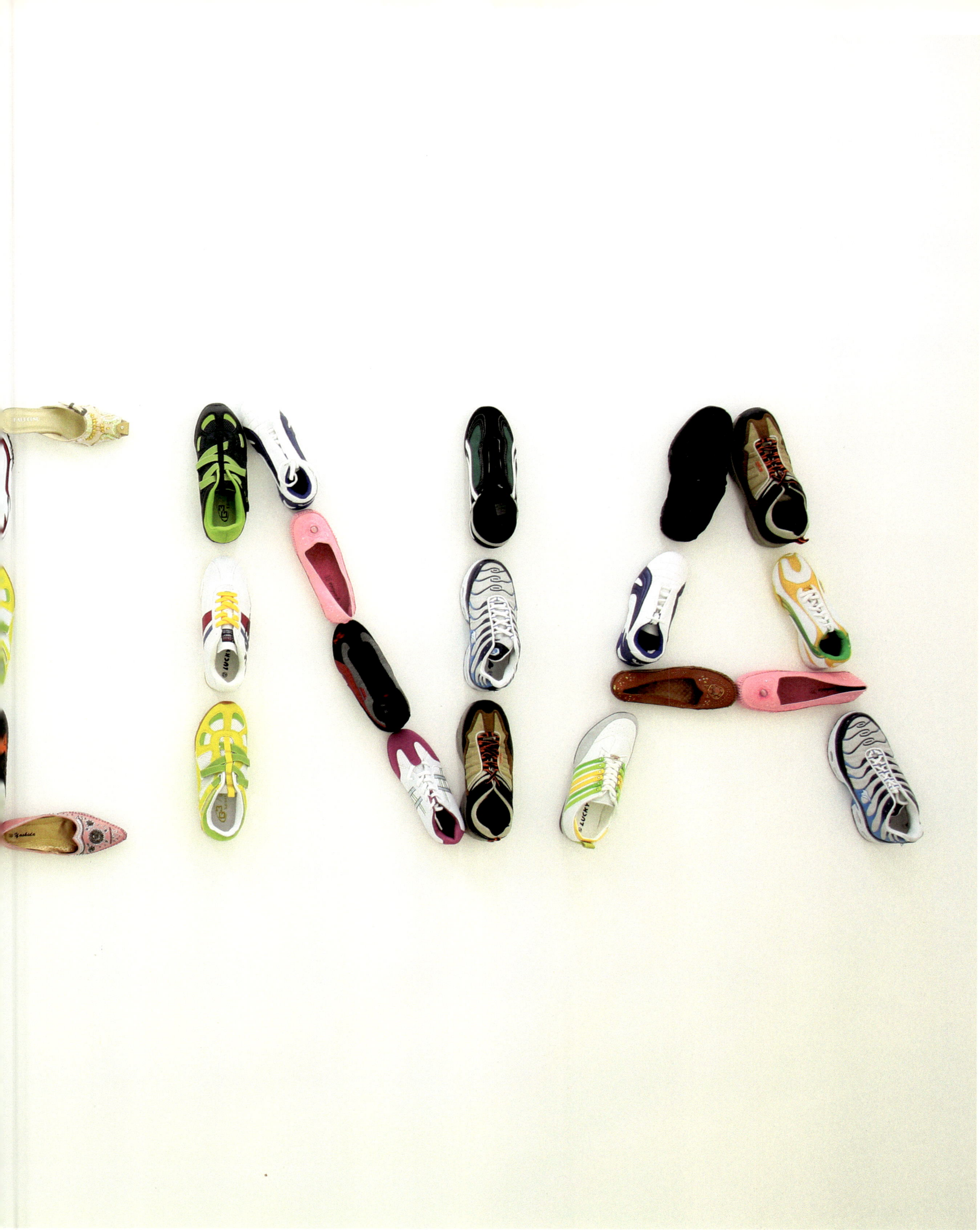

WASTE

The skeleton crawling on the floor and, with its last gesture, reaching out with the right hand to grasp something—perhaps its last handhold—is quite shocking and quite apart from its position and its brilliant whiteness, quite disconcerting. The perfection of the design is attractive, making the shock of seeing it up close all the stronger. After all, this skeleton is not made from porcelain or a similar material—it is made of countless plastic forks, knives, and spoons, which are joined together in a minute, painstaking process with glue and wire. These disposable pieces of cutlery are thrown away in vast numbers every day. Five graphics and photography graduates from Kingston University, Ashley Maine, Laura Bowman, Jamie Breach, Elliott Mariess, and Lewis Woolner, had the idea of creating an artwork from these articles of trash. Their goal was to create an ironic but shocking connection between the addiction to snacks in our culture and the problem of world hunger. *Waste* is the title they chose for their work, which has been awarded the 2009 Digital and Analog Design Award (D&DA).

Waste
2009, Plastic cutlery

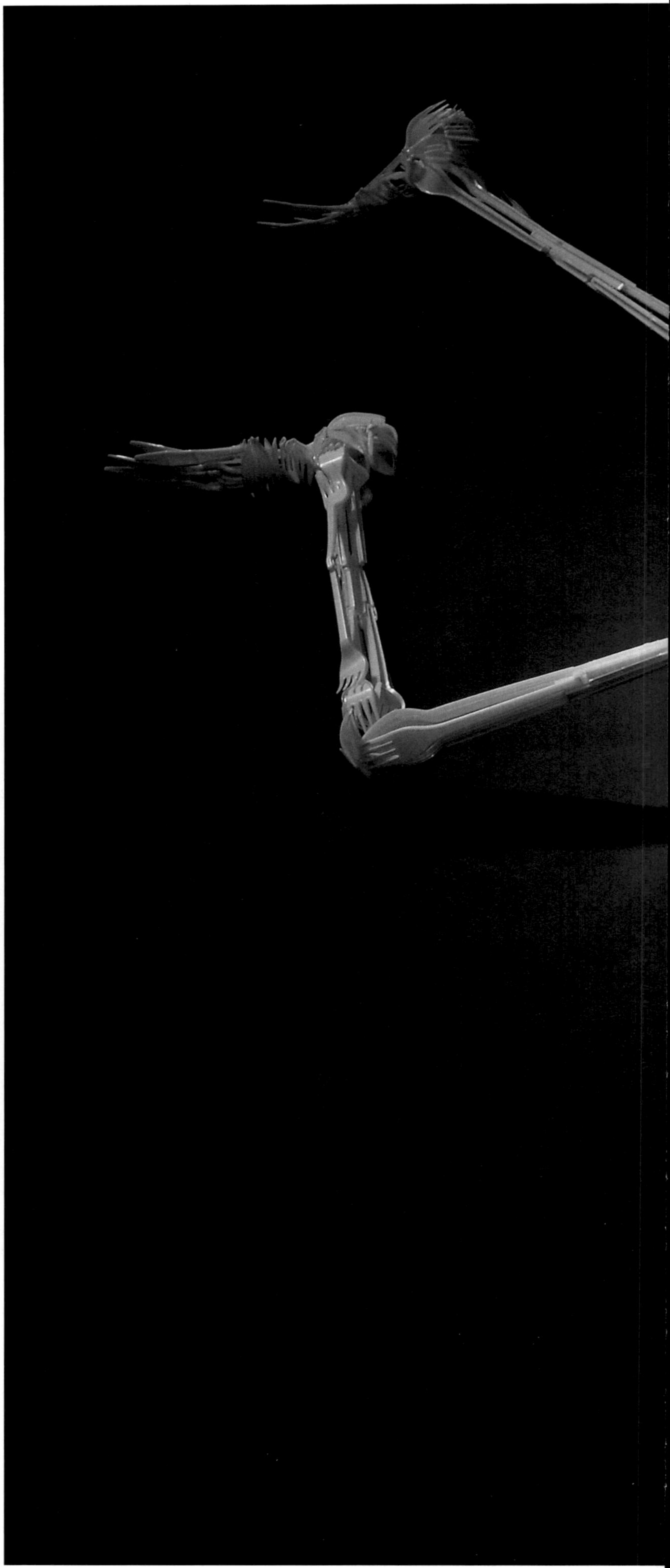

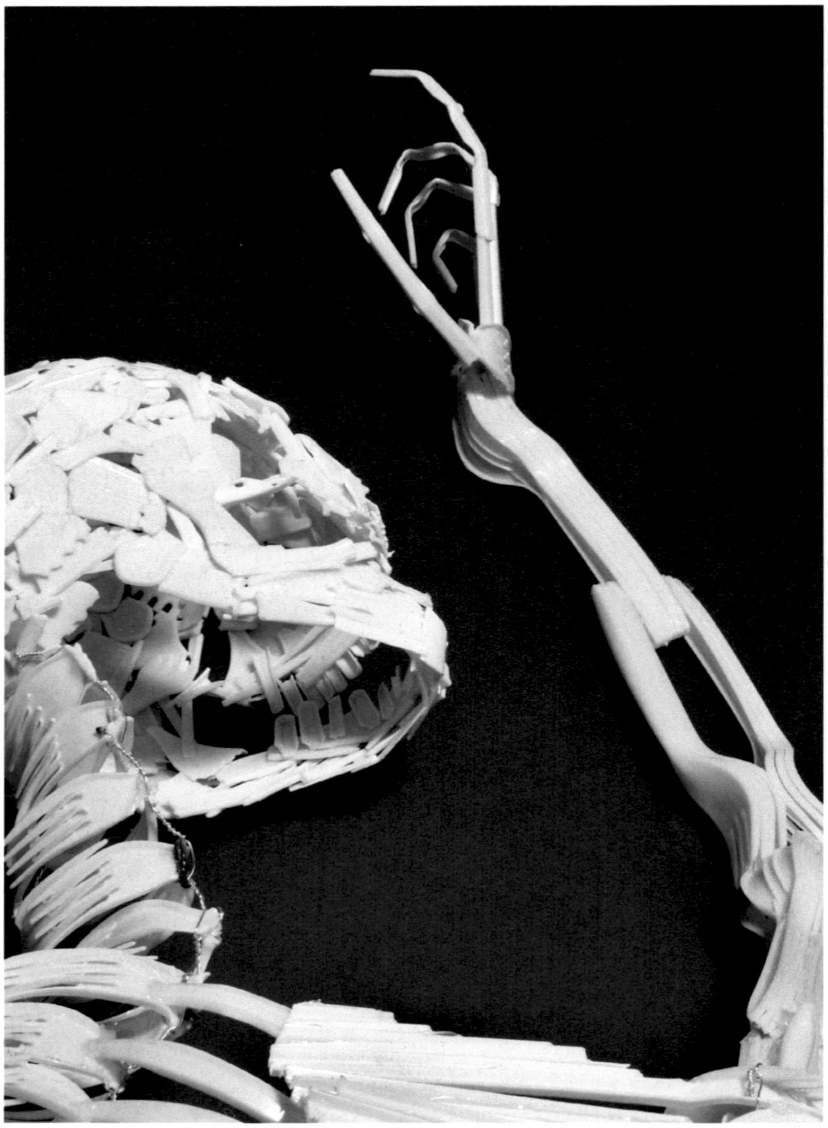

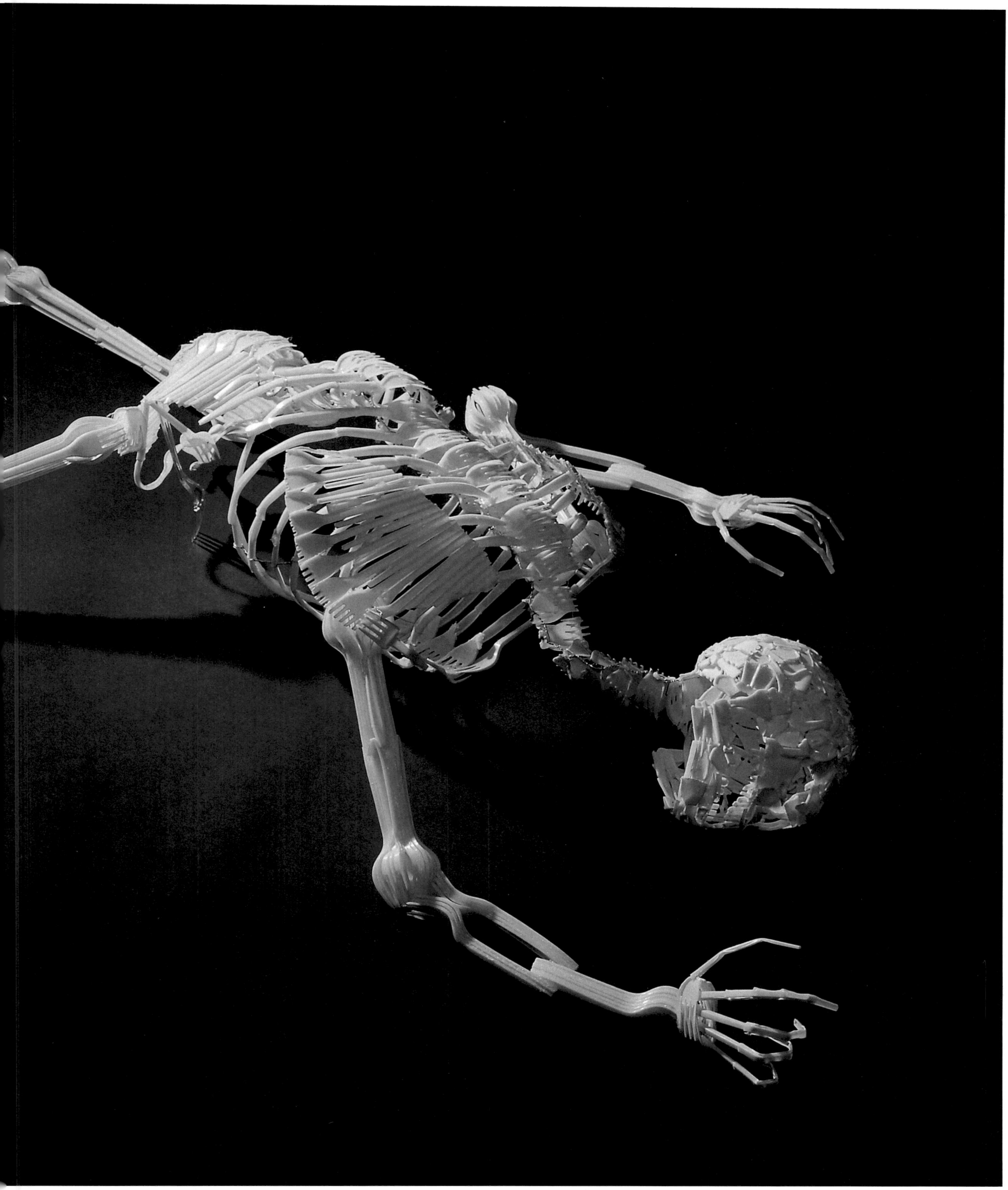

WALTER ROBINSON

1
Hunter-Gatherer
2006, USA, Wood, epoxy, steel, feathers
2
Spin
2007, USA, Wood, steel, epoxy, metalflake
Courtesy Catharine Clark Gallery, San Francisco and Charlie James Gallery, Los Angeles
3
Red Ink/Kinder Blitz
2006, USA, Wood, cotton rag paper, ink, epoxy
Courtesy Catharine Clark Gallery, San Francisco and Charlie James Gallery, Los Angeles
4
Civics Lesson
2008, USA, Wood, plaster
5
Hybrid
2009, USA, Wood, plastic, steel, rubber, iron paint, rust patina

Photos by Phocasso/John Wilson White

The sculptures and installations of artist and art critic Walter Robinson (* 1950) from San Francisco, have an aura of color and shine. However, their pleasant appearance is deceptive, and their pastel-colored outer shell can hide a highly ironic message as the artwork *Civics Lesson,* 2008, goes to show. It consists of giant pencils with erasers in the shape of John F. Kennedy's head. On them are alternating phrases: "ask what you," "can do for you," etc. This is the artist's elegant travesty of Kennedy's famous phrase "Ask not what your country can do for you—ask what you can do for your country." The artist has his own good reasons for choosing this well-known phrase: "Using text and the strategies of appropriation, conflation, and dislocation, I uncover the subconscious and biological human imperatives hidden beneath social, political, religious, and capitalist packaging."

The tree-shaped air fresheners, made of metal (and therefore scentless), are a further example of mimicry. On them is written the word "Napalm." The artist deliberately echoes the readily appealing designs that fill our colorful consumerist world: "I consciously use seductive surfaces and saturated colors—the same tropes employed by advertising—to draw my audience into examining their relationship to consumer culture and its effect on the environment and world events." In works like *Hunter-Gatherer,* 2006, in which two pumas are shot with arrows, he goes a step further and uses the logo of the well-known sportswear manufacturer. "In an effort to destabilize the power of the product logos that surround us, I tweak their scale or context, or combine them in disjunctive pairs. Sometimes I re-stage twenty-first century geopolitical events, using childhood icons to provoke the shock of corrupted innocence." For instance, he shows us a helicopter growing out of Pinocchio's long nose. The title of this artwork, *Spin,* 2007, suggests that it is about how explanations of military actions are concocted as part of an image strategy. The installation *Red Ink,* 2006, initially looks like a toy for playing at schools. What is being taught is not child's play, but a clear political statement by the American artist. The large stamp for stamping a facsimile of an old classroom map of the world is solid bright red, and at first glance its outline is clearly the outline of the United States. However, something doesn't seem quite right. The artist has left out the few liberal states around the periphery of the United States (whose political color is designated as blue). A closer look at the colorful objects that fall from the ceiling—harmlessly entitled *Kinder Blitz,* 2006, reveals them as bombs.

1

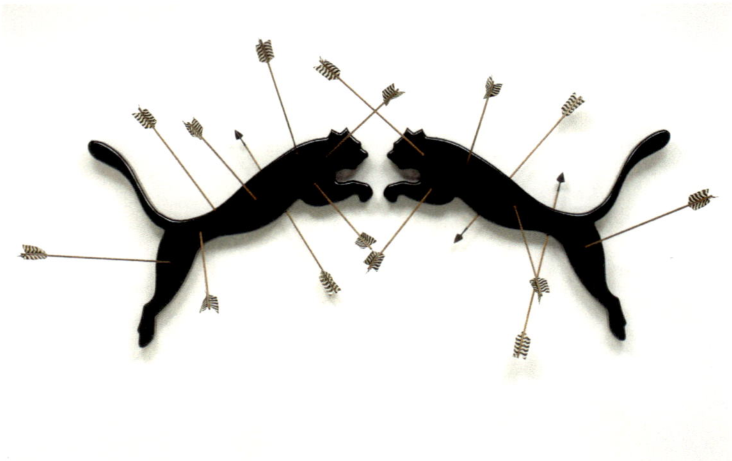

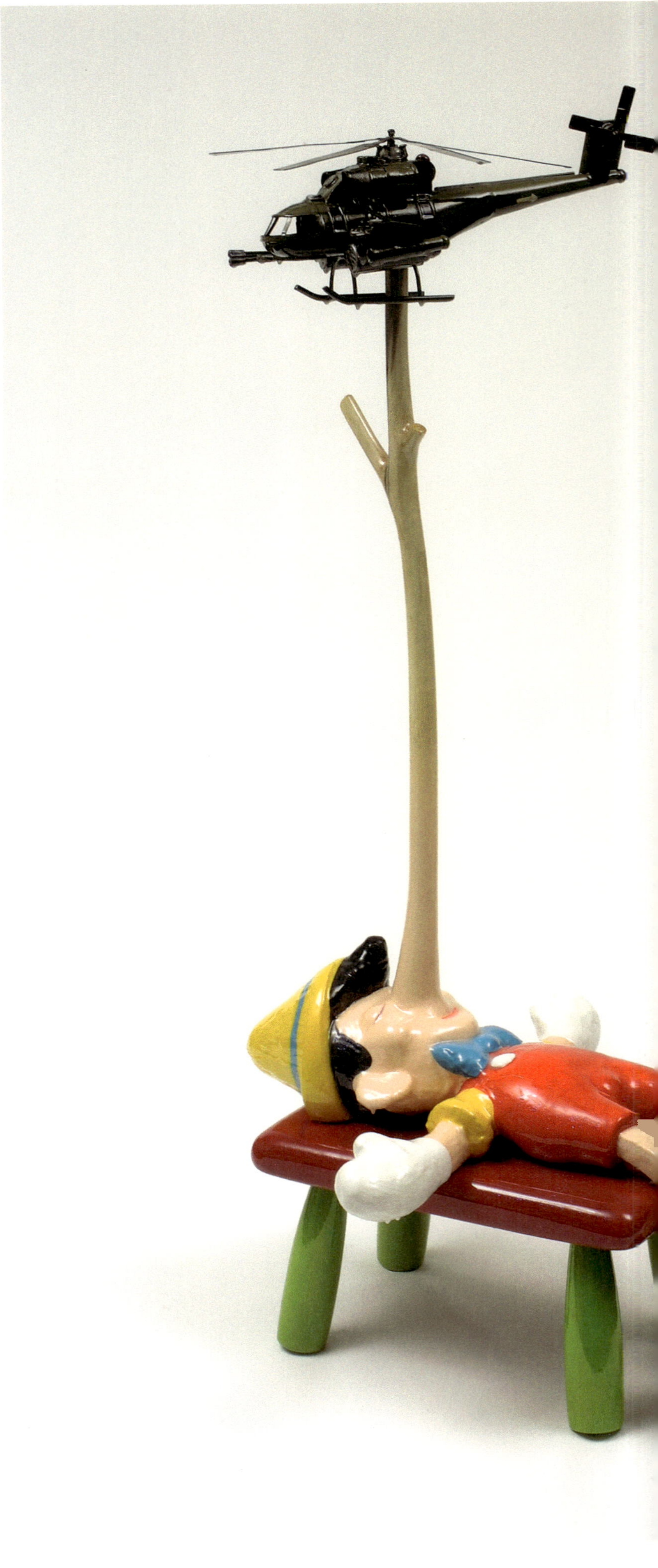

2

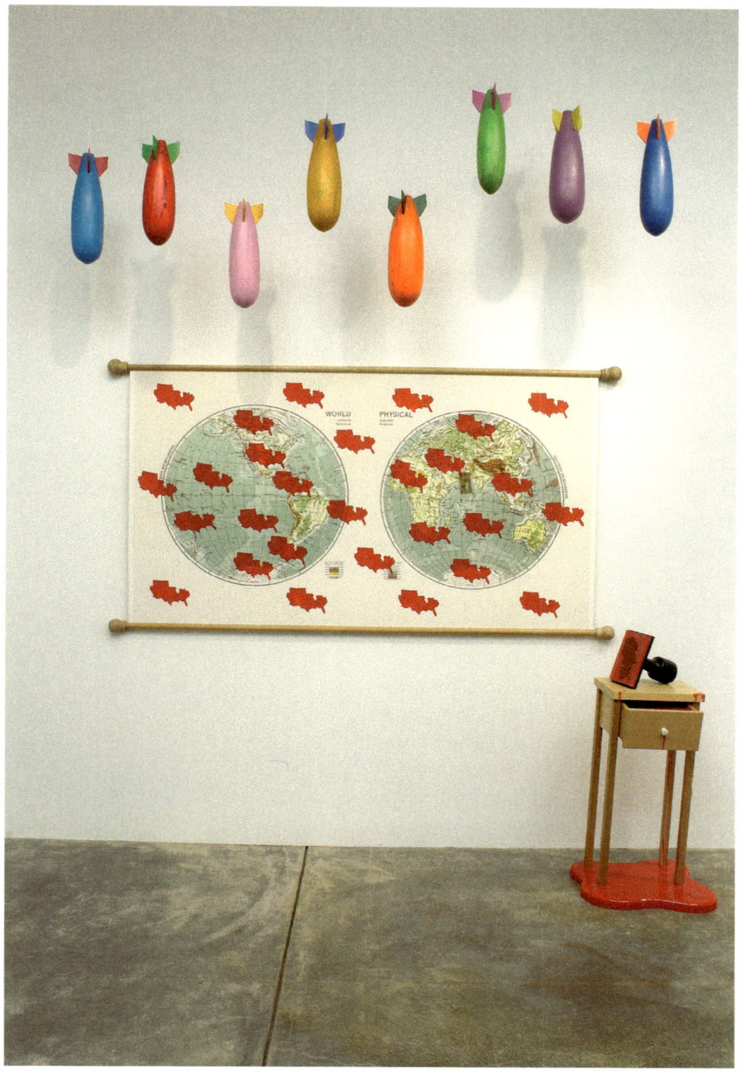
WORLD
PHYSICAL

3

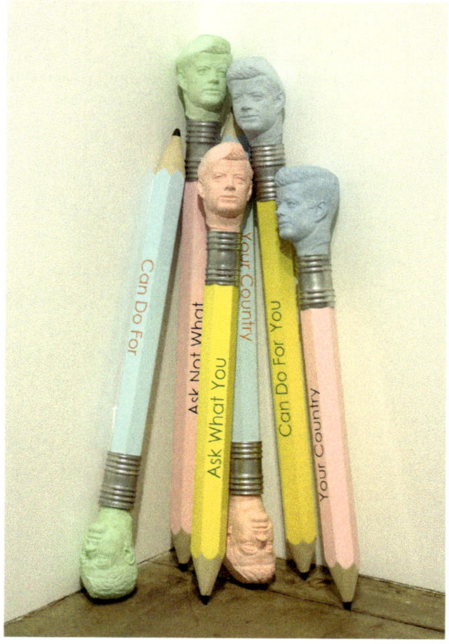
Can Do For
Ask Not What
Ask What You
Your Country
Can Do For You
Your Country

4

5

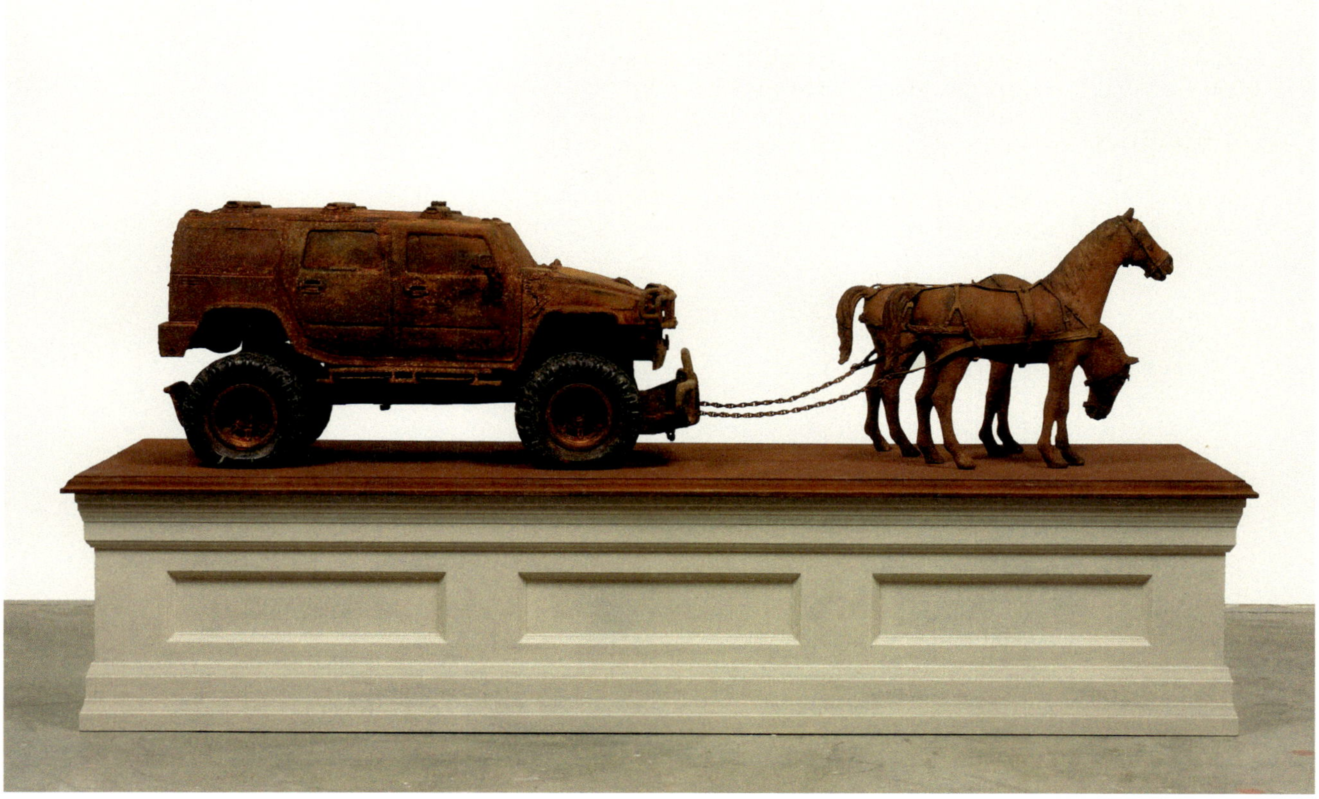

EUGENIO MERINO

1
Always
2007, Epoxy, Coca-Cola light cans
2
Fat Rat
2007, Painted resin, fast-food trash
3
Redecorate Your Life
2010, Silicone, polyester, cardboard, blanket, clothes, IKEA catalog, plastic bag
4
Still Staying Alive
2007, Silicone, polyester, human hair, carpet, clothes, and accessories.

How far should art go? When is art still art and when is it trash? With the realistic and trashy sculptures he exhibits at the annual art fairs—the ARCO in Madrid, for instance—the Spanish sculptor Eugenio Merino (* 1975) from Madrid, regularly provokes questions like these. He is considered their enfant terrible, and is guaranteed to provide an art fair scandal. In 2009, he presented a life-size wax figure of Damien Hirst in a glass case, his face smeared with blood, holding a pistol to his temple. The artist called his provocative shock artwork *4 the Love of Go(l)d,* a reference to Hirst's famous diamond skull, which appears as a picture on the figure's T-shirt. Merino is referring to the fact that Hirst's skull, set with 8,601 diamonds, is currently the most expensive artwork in the world. The only way Hirst could exceed the target price it reached at auction—74 million euros—would be by killing himself and thereby automatically increasing the value of his work. The Spanish artist says that he does not hate Hirst—in fact, he admires him. Yet at the same time he parodies his artwork with his series of macabre skulls. Perhaps what Merino is really concerned about is the issue of whether and to what extent an artist can be more interested in the money than in the art? This was certainly what many art critics thought when confronted by his doubles of Hirst's artwork. After all, the enterprising Briton directly sold artworks at a high-profile auction in 2008 and not through a gallery at Sotheby's in the usual fashion. Merino's sculpture *Stairway to Heaven,* 2010, also ventures into controversial territory. This life-size sculpture shows the devotions practiced by three world religions: a Muslim kneels with his forehead on the ground and a praying Christian stands on his back while an Orthodox Jew, in turn, stands on the Christian figure's shoulders. Next to the figures, Merino presents an erect machine gun with a menorah, a seven-branched candlestick, rising from its barrel. A written criticism of the art fair's directors by the Israeli embassy, which was quoted in the *Yediot Aharonot* newspaper, stated that values such as freedom of art or freedom of expression are sometimes "only masks for prejudices, stereotypes, and provocation for its own sake. The offensive message transmitted by this item is made no less painful by the fact that it is made under the guise of art." The artist defended his work by saying that it reflected "the idea of coexisting religions," all of which seek God, and that the message of the sculpture was therefore positive and optimistic. *Stairway to Heaven* was purchased by a Belgian woman for her private art collection for 45,000 euros on the first day of the art fair.

Is Merino's work crude provocation or a pithy and intentionally trashy interpretation of certain discussions in the media? Is Merino's Osama Bin Laden dancing (in classic John Travolta fashion) to "Staying Alive" on a Persian rug a transference of the regular headlines suggesting that this terrorist figure, wanted all over the world, is still alive? Works such as *Redecorate Your Life,* 2010, which shows a homeless person who has covered himself with an IKEA box and seems to have fallen asleep while reading an IKEA magazine, show that in spite of his cynicism, the artist has not lost touch with reality.

2

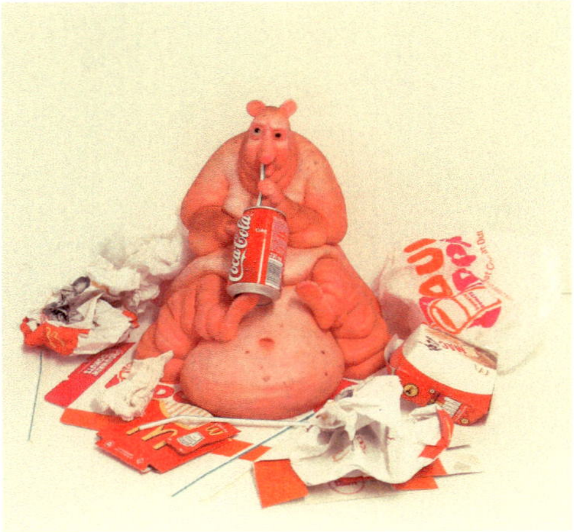

1

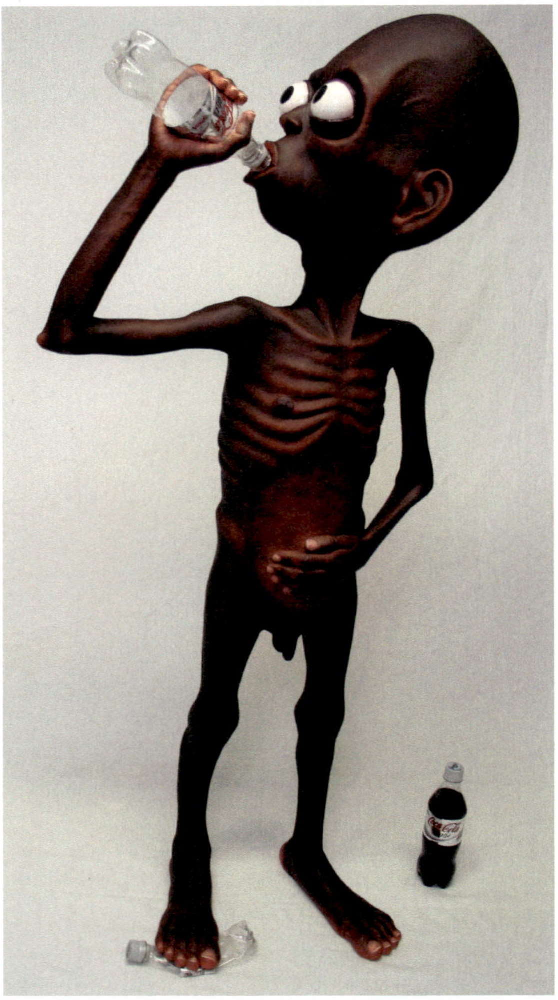

3

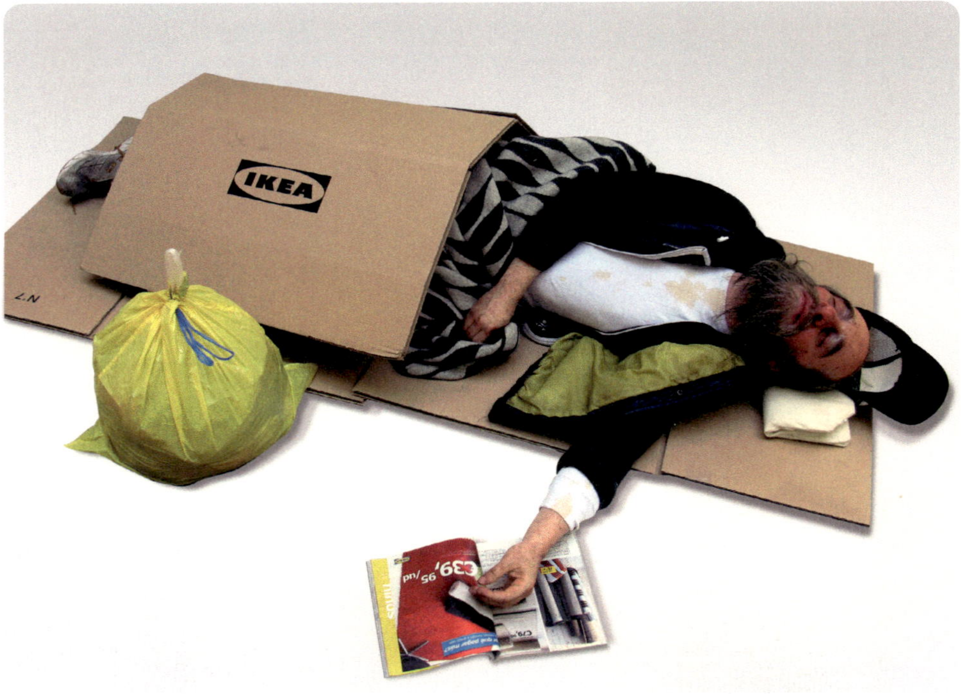

Redecorate your life

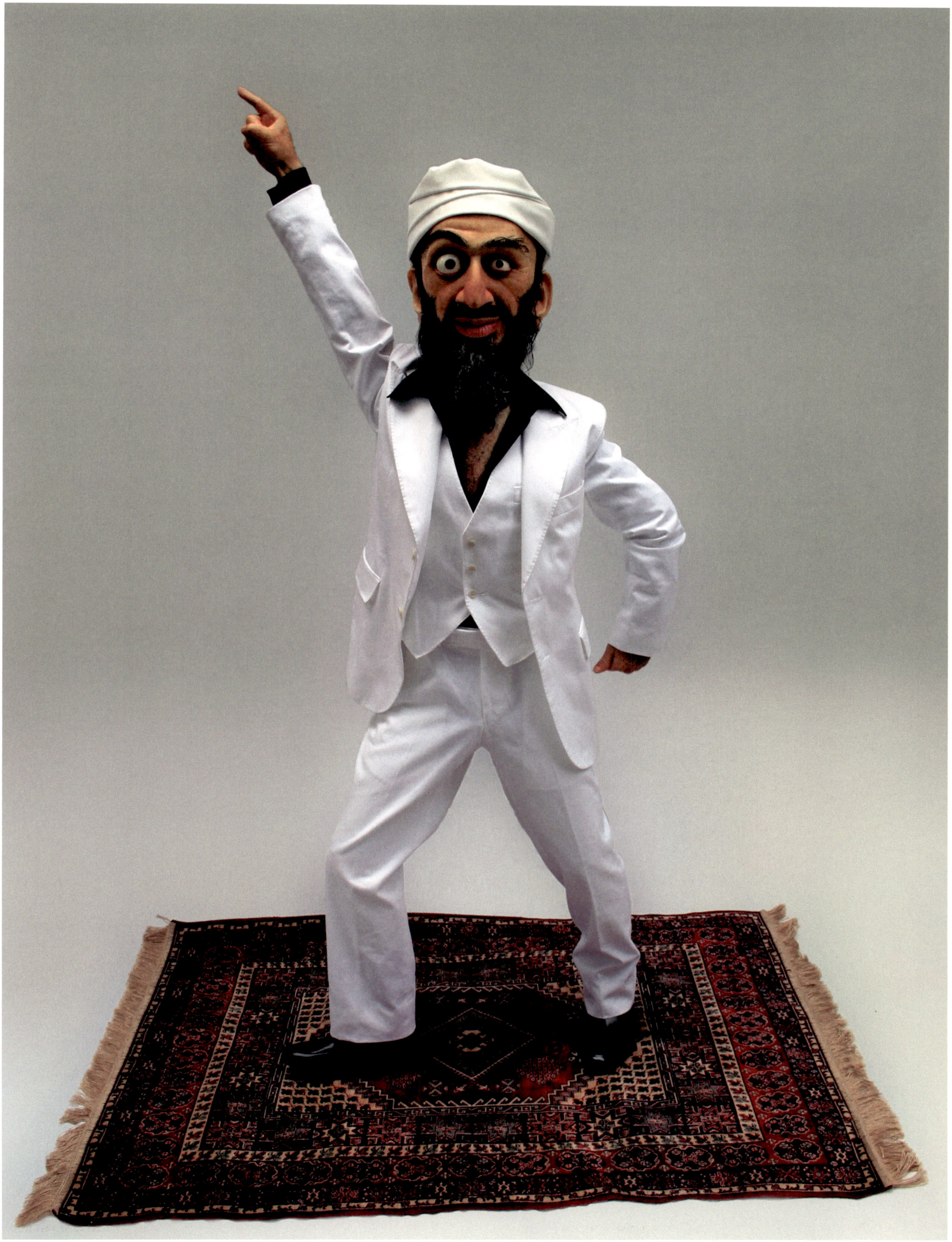

BARNABY BARFORD

"I AM NOT VILIFYING THE YOUTH OF TODAY, I'M NOT TELLING THEM OFF, BUT REFLECTING THE WAY THEY ARE PERCEIVED"

1
Does That Mean We're Not Getting Any Presents?
2009
2
Family Feast
2009
Sculpture
3
Ring-a-Ring-o-Roses
2009
4
Do It Again, I Didn't Press Record
2009
5
Cry Havoc and Let Slip the Dogs of War
2010

Porcelain, earthenware, enamel paint, painted wooden base, other media

Photos by Noah da Costa

There are no young men charming blushing, rococo ladies with bouquets of flowers amongst the porcelain figures created by artist Barnaby Barford (*1977) from London, who began to specialize in the production and design of ceramics and porcelain during his time spent studying design in Faenza and at the Royal College of Art in London. However, this kind of figure provides him with the raw materials for his own porcelain figures, which are very different in nature. The British artist finds traditional porcelain figures at flea markets, on the internet, and in antique dealers' shops. He then cuts up his acquisitions, recombines them in different configurations, and repaints them—thereby mutating what used to be sweet and harmless figures into absolute hooligans. Barford's figural arrangements are savagely ironic statements on current social phenomena. The artist intensifies the slight suggestiveness of the original figures to create appalling scenes of sex and violence. His themes—binge drinking, sex, juvenile crime, cult brands, and obsession with youth—come from contemporary culture. In one of his compositions, a child is lying on the floor, doubled up in pain. Two youths are standing over him. One has his foot raised to kick, while the other has a mobile phone in his hand and is speaking the phrase that gives the artwork its title: *Do It Again, I Didn't Press Record,* 2009.

In *The Battle of Trafalgar,* 2010—which of all his works so far is the largest and has the most figures—Barford shows us his own unique interpretation of London's historical tourist magnet. Various appalling scenes are taking place around the dirt-smeared column, amid countless pigeons; demonstrators stand around them holding signs reading "no" and "yes." There is, of course, a fine sense of black humor behind all of this and the artist is aware that some people will laugh at his work—although the realities they reflect may well cause the laughter to stick in their throats. With his savage and yet highly comical figures, the artist is examining social phenomena but without being an accuser or a guardian of morality: "I am not vilifying the youth of today, I'm not telling them off, but reflecting the way they are perceived... if you want to have a laugh and just enjoy them visually that's great, but there is also the opportunity to extract a deeper meaning."

1

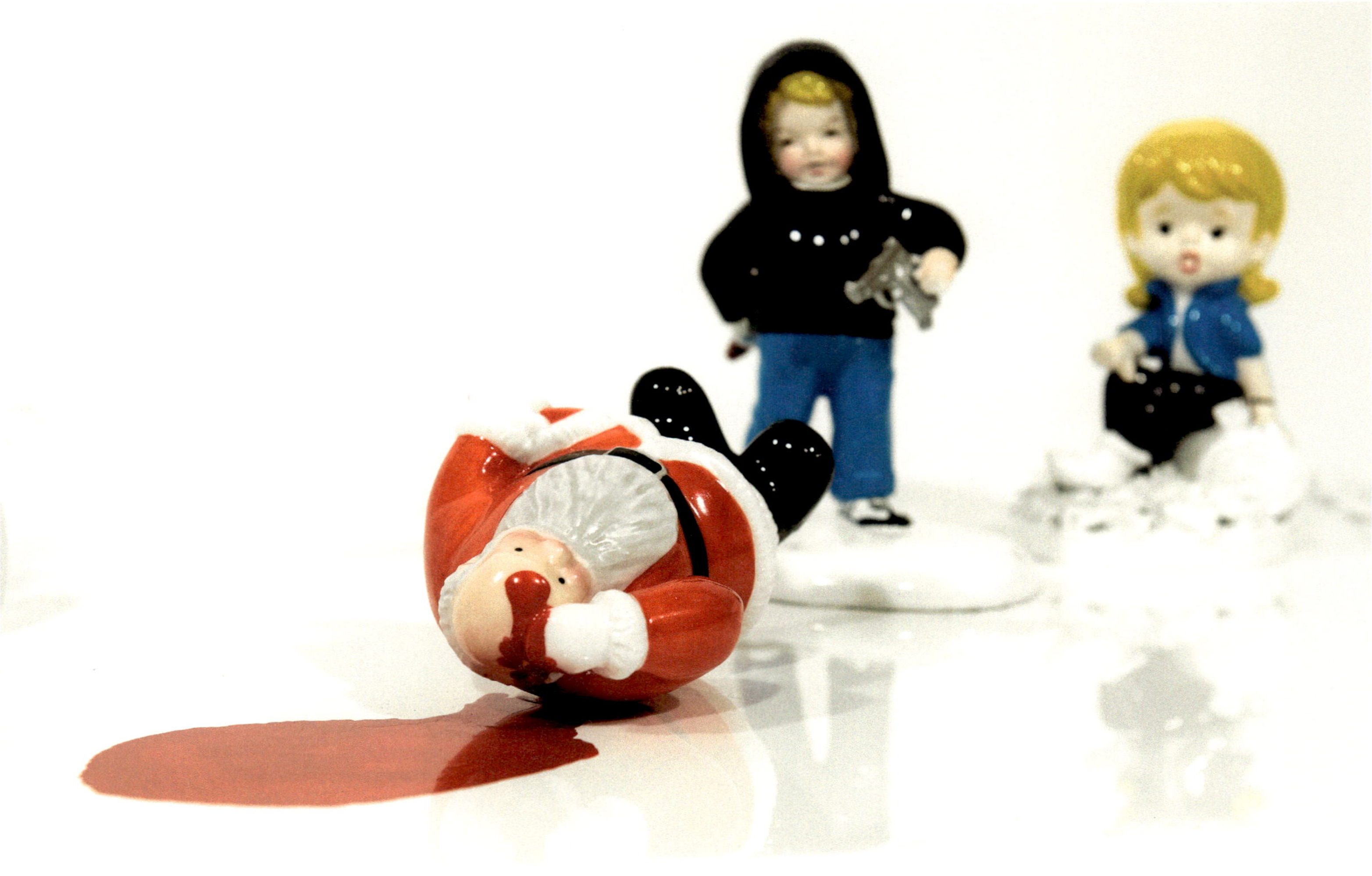

2

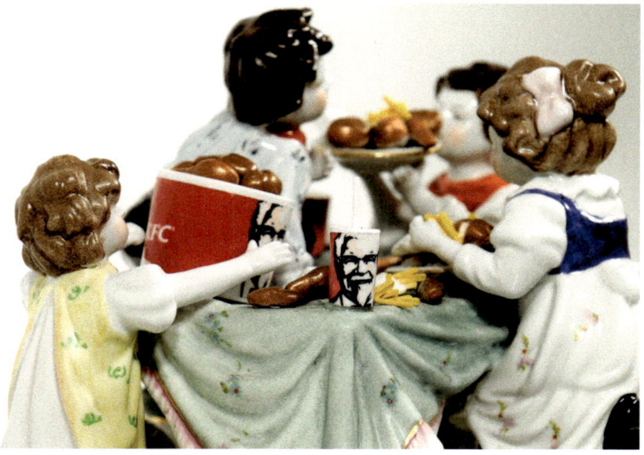

3

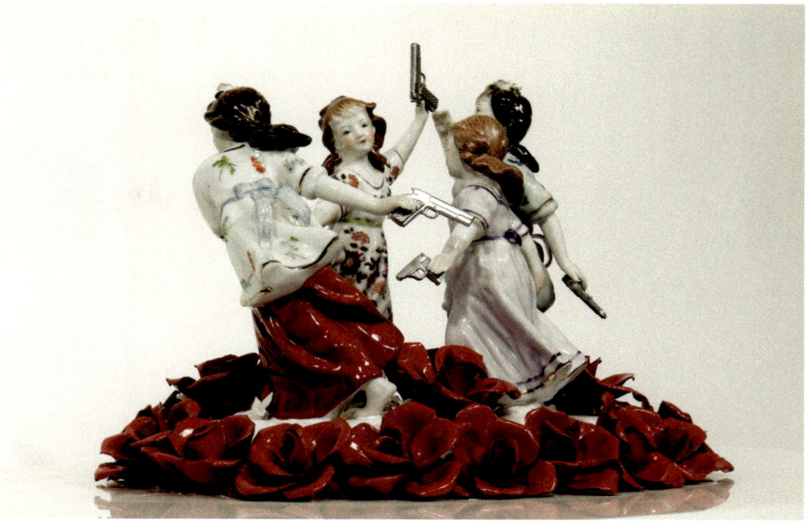

4

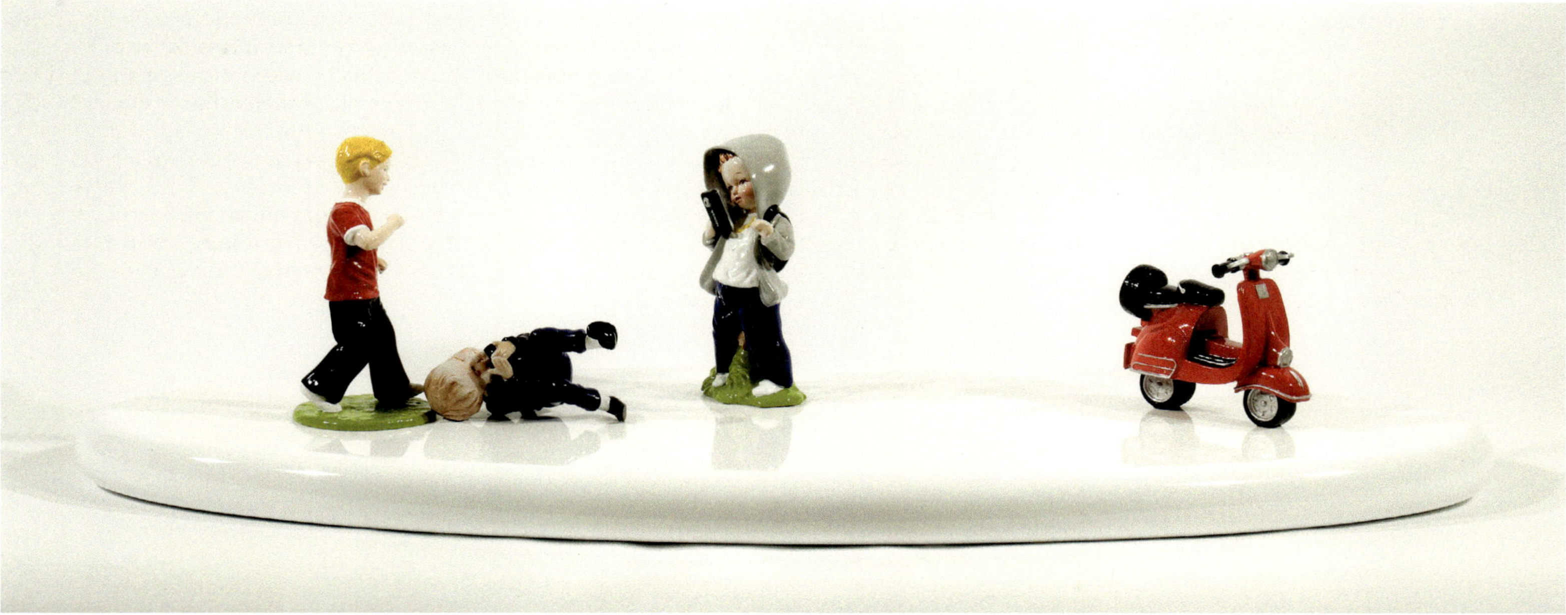

5

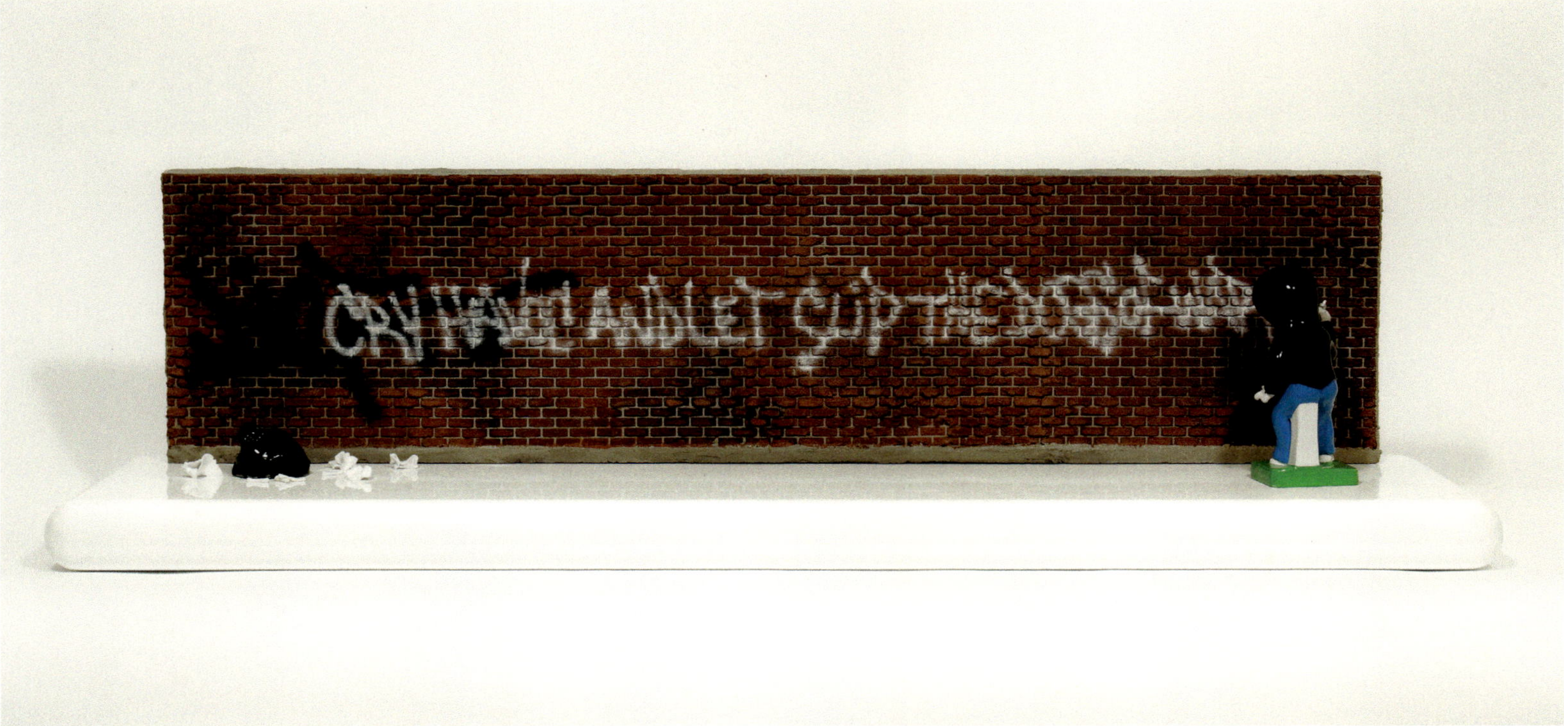

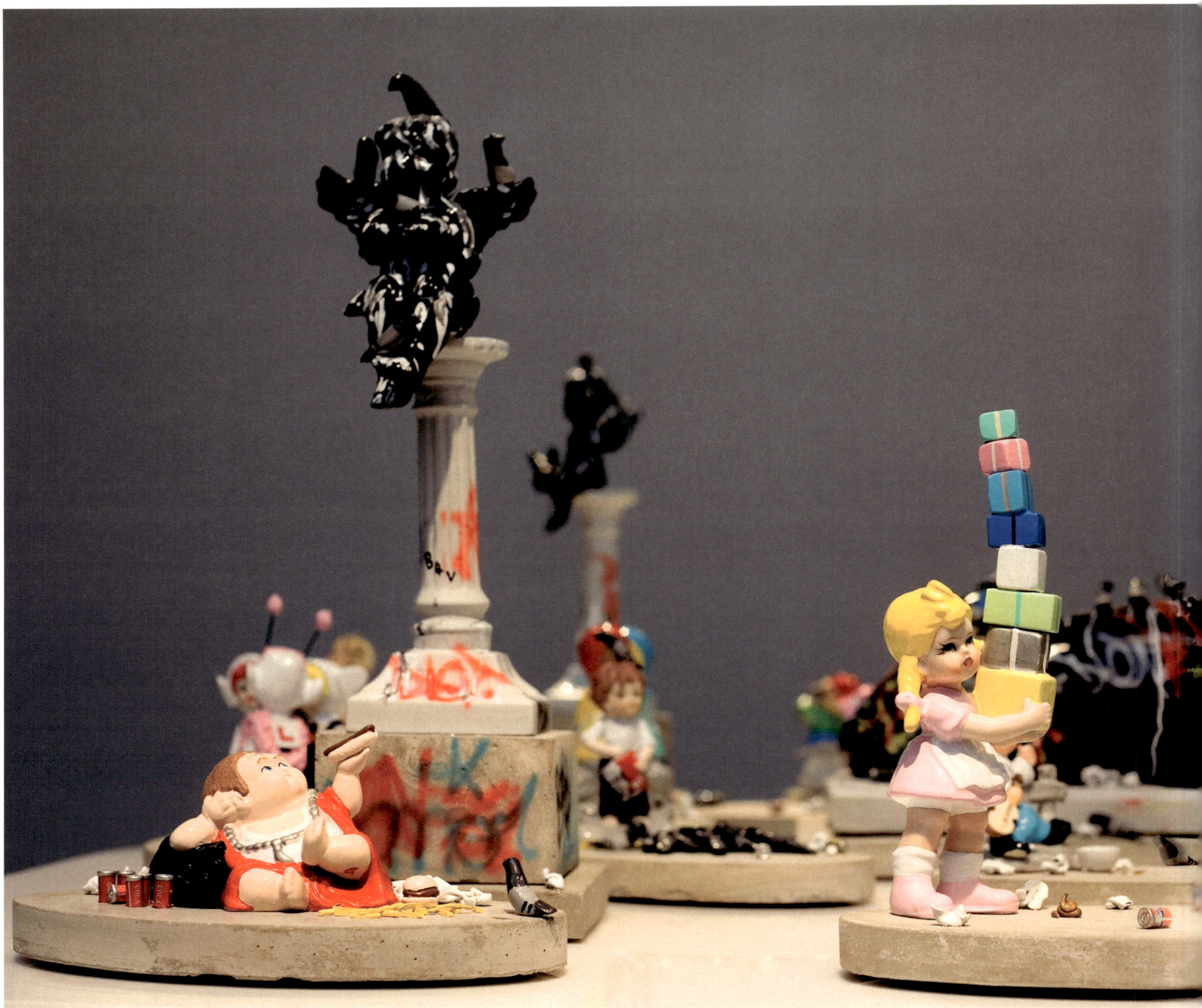

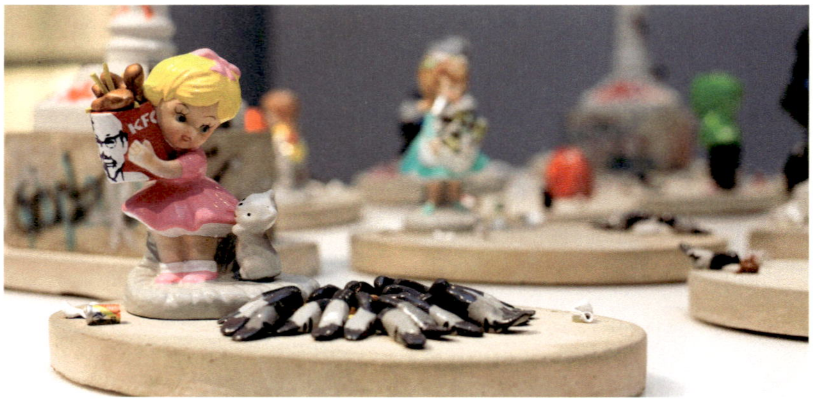
KFC

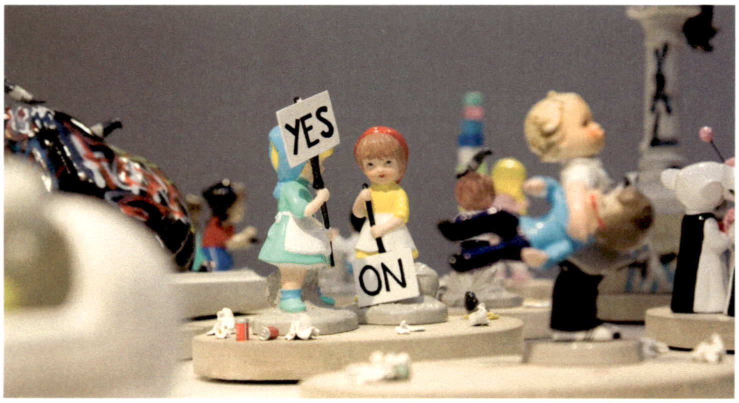
YES
ON

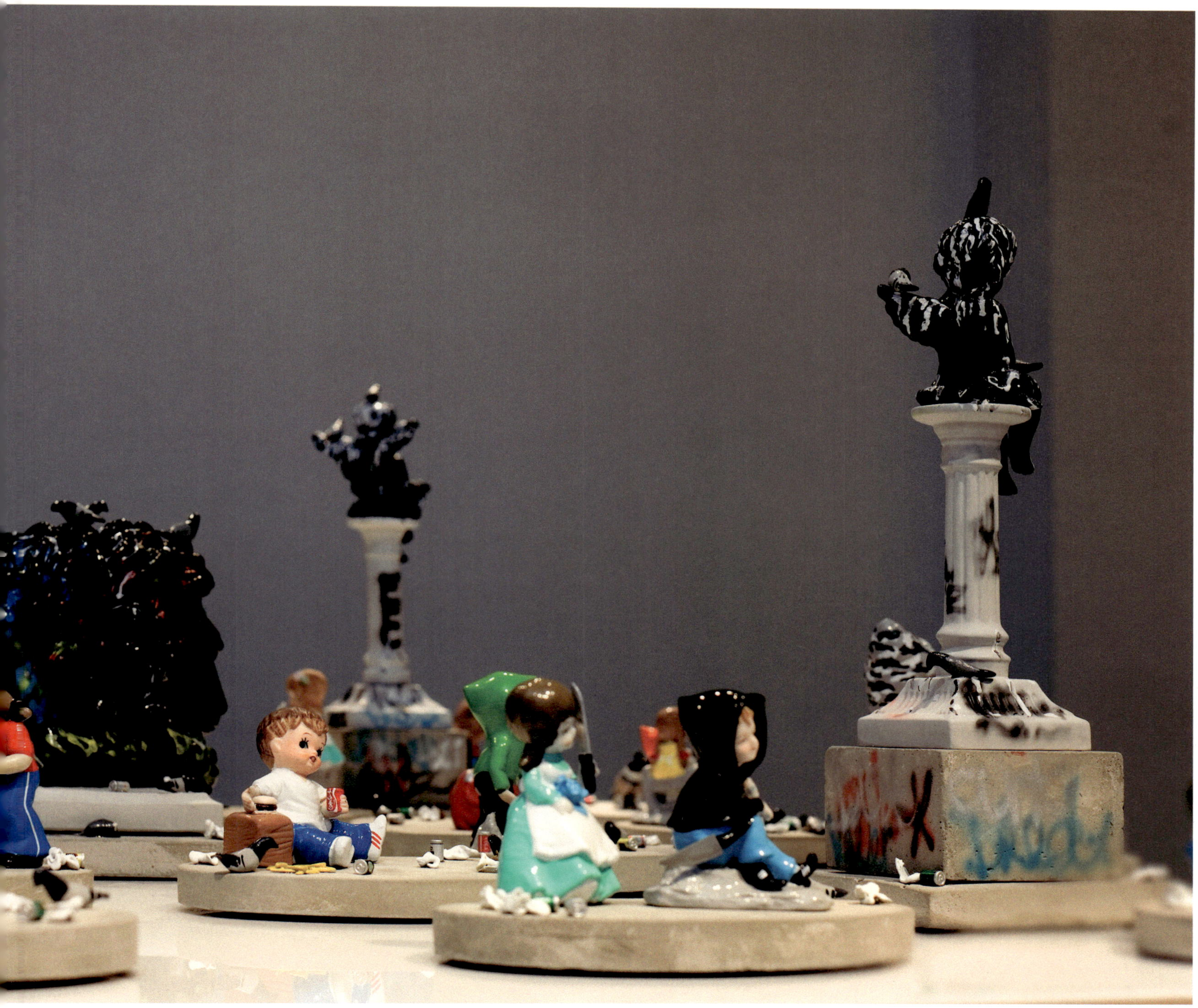

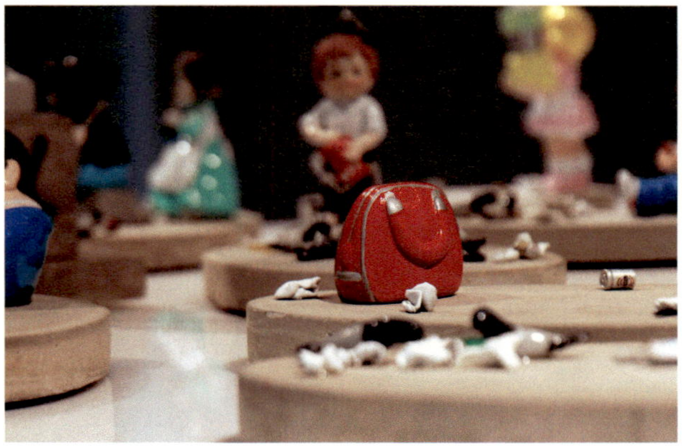

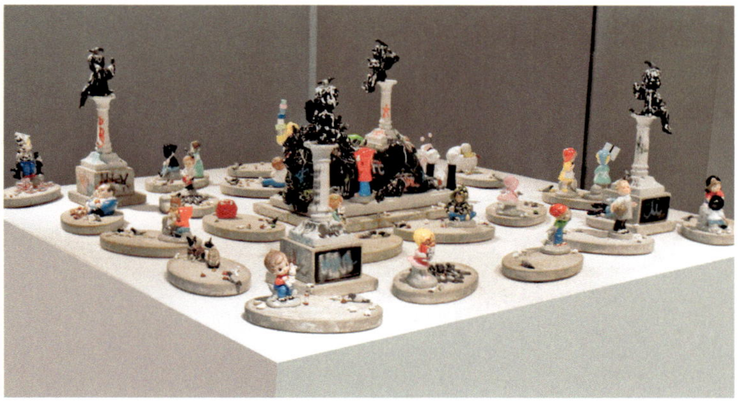

BARNABY BARFORD
The Battle of Trafalgar
2010, Images courtesy
the artist

PACKARD JENNINGS

The American artist Packard Jennings (* 1970) was born in Oakland, California, and studied art in San Francisco and in New York. He began by appropriating and modifying advertising posters. Today, "culture jamming" is still his preferred technique. In 2007, he placed an *Anarchist Action Figure,* equipped with a gas mask, a gasoline canister, a spray can, and a Molotov cocktail, and a *Mussolini Action Figure* on Wal-Mart shelves in a shop-dropping maneuver, which was intended as a criticism of the commercialization of radical ideologies. He stuck a *Pocket Survival Guide,* 2009, on supermarket products, explaining ironically in comic strip form, how one could use the packaging to survive the looming climate catastrophe—a catastrophe, caused in part by the production of this type of packaging itself. In another work, Jennings filled the return envelopes from advertising mailers with his anarchist comic pamphlet *Business Reply Pamphlet,* 2006—a practical guide to office revolt—and sent them back to the businesses that had originally sent them. To combat the Bibles found in most hotel rooms in the United States, he made stickers available online for *Bible Sticker,* 2005, which read: "This material was written by normal men almost two thousand years ago, and should be approached with an open mind and critically considered." Jennings explains his motivation by stating: "My art is born from a sense of blanket disenfranchisement; be it my feeling of powerlessness in the face of mega-corporations; my disgust with the stewardship of our country; or my broad ideological separation from American fundamentalism. (...) I make work that delves into the realm of activism, not only to connect with individuals in provocative and meaningful ways, but also to recast my role in the system. I often put my work out into the world for chance interactions with people; this involves ad hoc installations and subversive infiltration of public and semipublic spaces, where the pieces are left to their own fate. I employ humor as a device for lowering a viewer's guard to the reception of difficult content."

1
Anarchist Action Figure
2008, Videography by John Behrens and Steven Polacco

2
Bible Sticker
2005

3
Pocket Survival Guide
2009

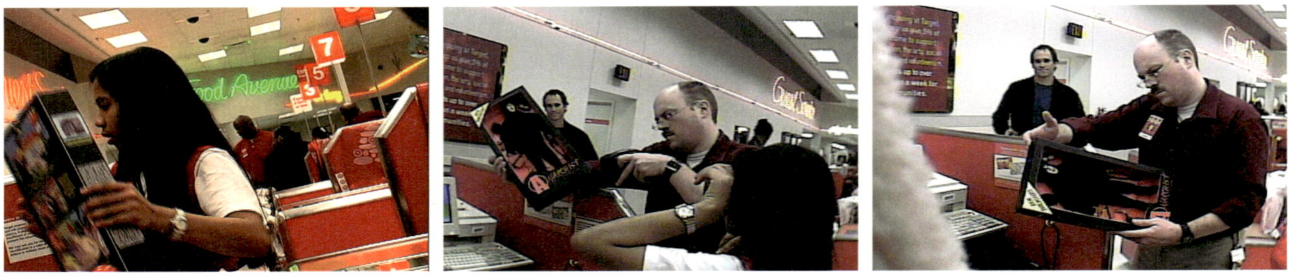

1

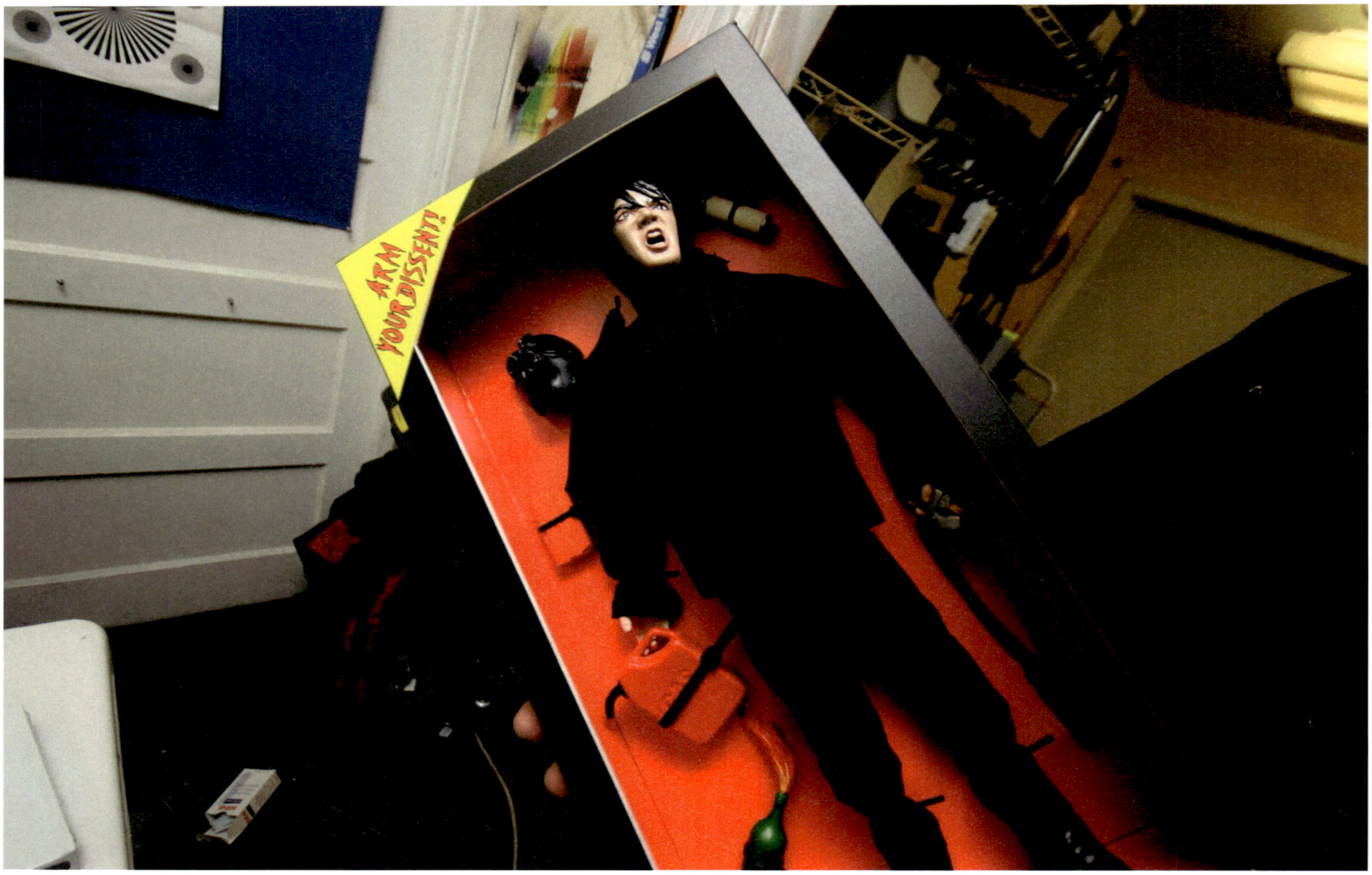

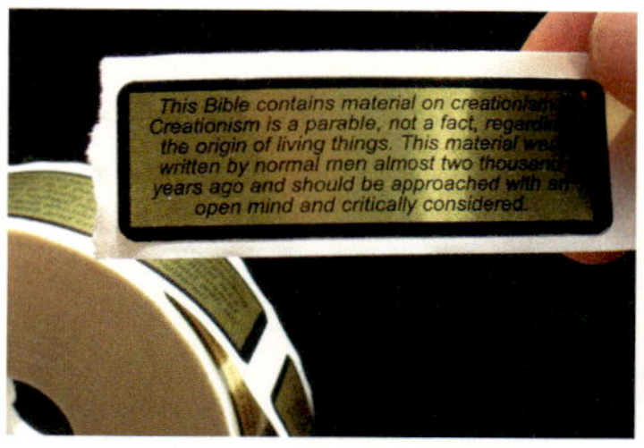

This Bible contains material on creationism.
Creationism is a parable, not a fact,
the origin of living things. This material
written by normal men almost two
years ago and should be approached with
open mind and critically considered.

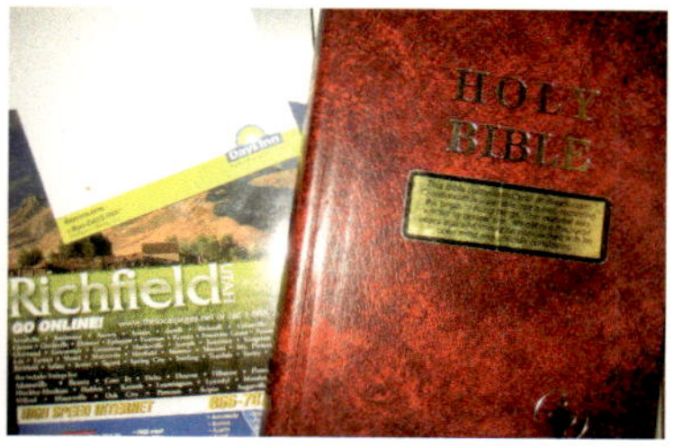

HOLY
BIBLE
Richfield

2

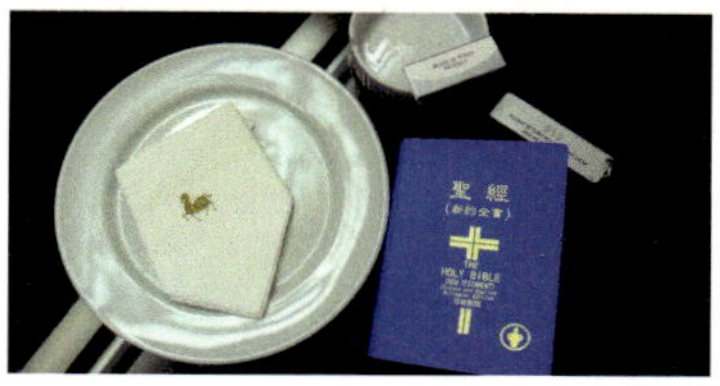

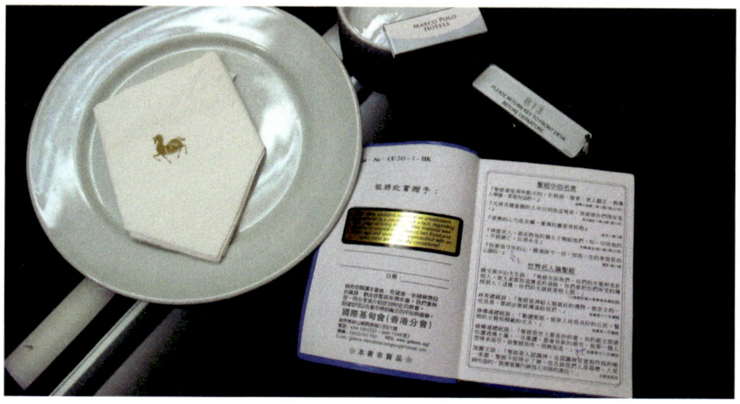

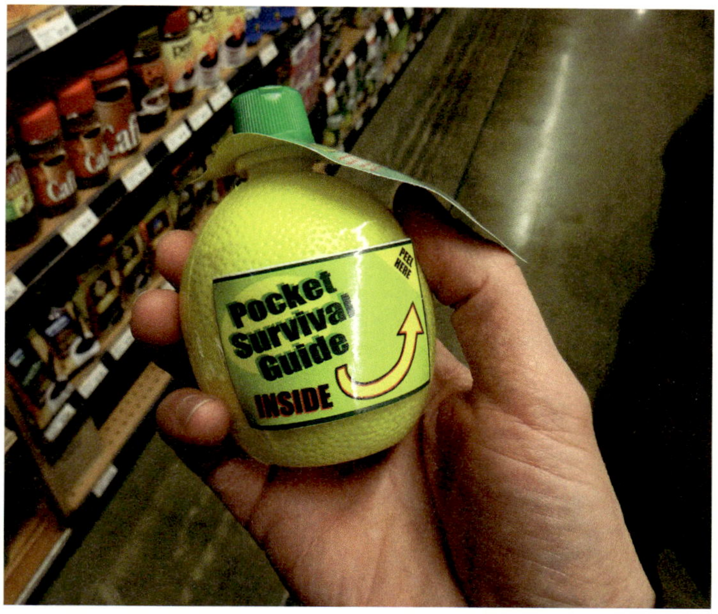

Pocket
Survival
Guide
INSIDE
PEEL HERE

3

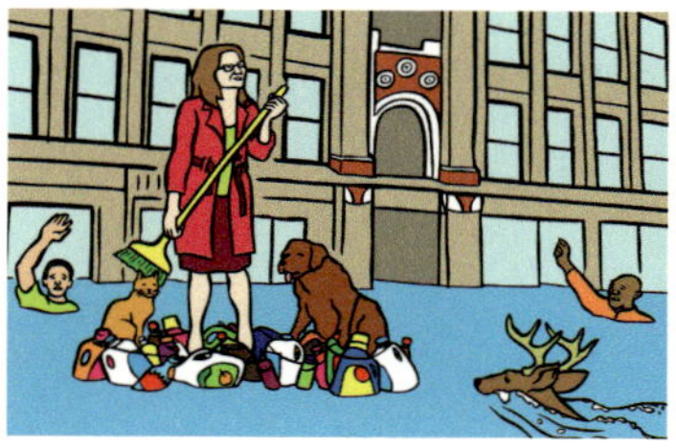

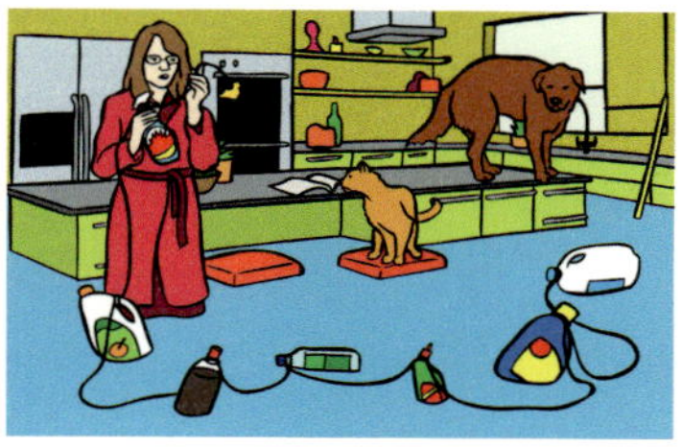

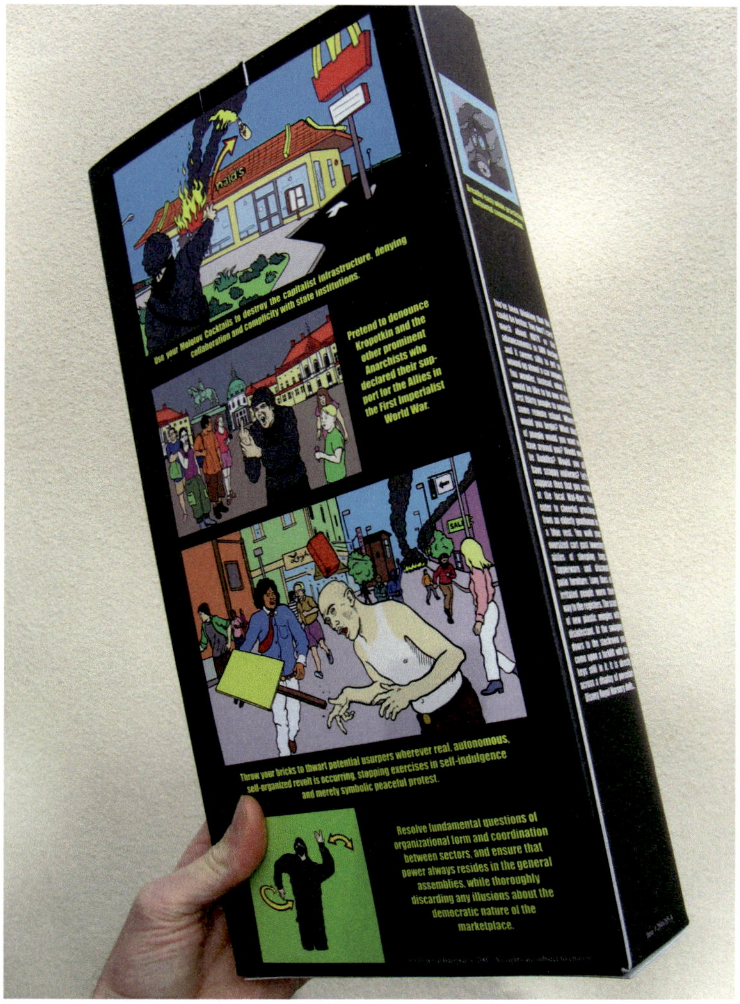

Use your Molotov Cocktails to destroy the capitalist infrastructure, denying collaboration and complicity with state institutions.
Pretend to denounce Kropotkin and the other prominent Anarchists who declared their support for the Allies in the First Imperialist World War.
Throw your bricks to thwart potential usurpers wherever real, autonomous, self-organized revolt is occurring, stopping exercises in self-indulgence and merely symbolic peaceful protest.
Resolve fundamental questions of organizational form and coordination between sectors, and ensure that power always resides in the general assemblies, while thoroughly discarding any illusions about the democratic nature of the marketplace.

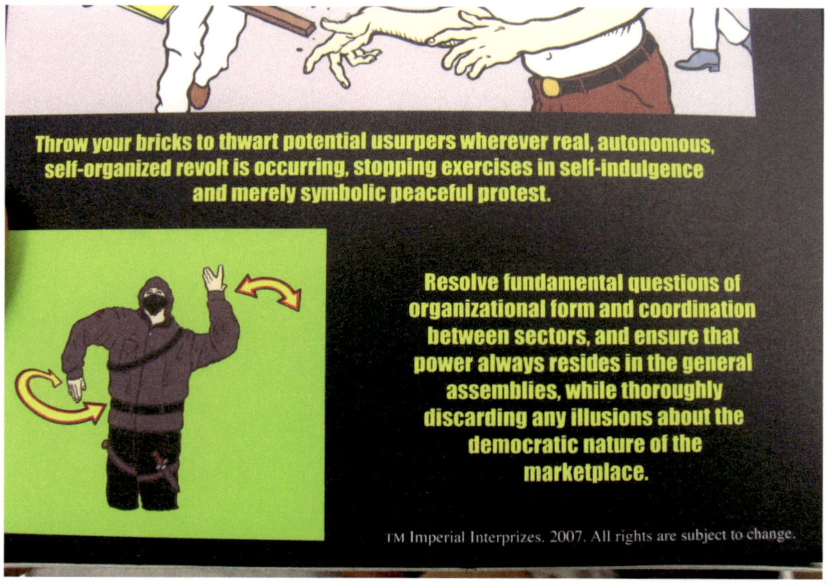

Throw your bricks to thwart potential usurpers wherever real, autonomous, self-organized revolt is occurring, stopping exercises in self-indulgence and merely symbolic peaceful protest.
Resolve fundamental questions of organizational form and coordination between sectors, and ensure that power always resides in the general assemblies, while thoroughly discarding any illusions about the democratic nature of the marketplace.
TM Imperial Interprizes. 2007. All rights are subject to change.

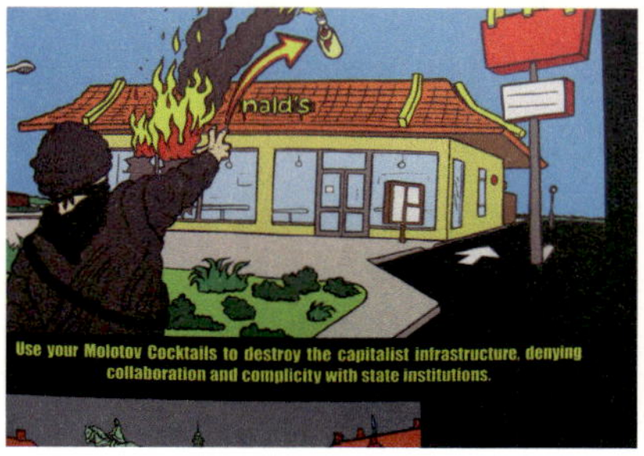

nald's
Use your Molotov Cocktails to destroy the capitalist infrastructure, denying collaboration and complicity with state institutions.

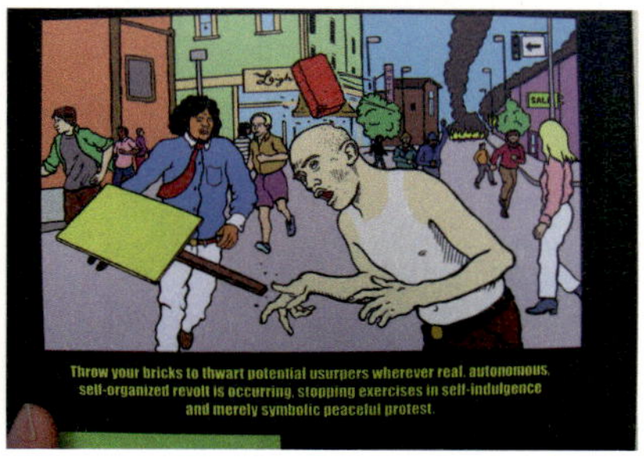

Throw your bricks to thwart potential usurpers wherever real, autonomous, self-organized revolt is occurring, stopping exercises in self-indulgence and merely symbolic peaceful protest.

RON ENGLISH

1
Jesus Returns
2006, Jersey City, USA
Illegal billboard
2
Playdate Iran
2004, Cincinnatti, USA
Illegal billboard
3
Abraham Obama
July 4, 2008, Boston, USA
Street/performance art

The American artist Ron English (* 1960) from Dallas, is considered a pioneer of subversive street art and is also a well-known exponent of American pop art. He works with popular advertising images known to almost every American and, by fusing icons of low and high art, creates new perspectives. He has been creating his trompe l'oeil-style street art since the 1980s. He works in the street space without a permit, but his art fits so seamlessly into the street scene that a casual observer would never suspect that this piece of subversive artwork was anything other than another advertising poster. It takes a second look at the supposed ad poster to reveal its often highly cutting political or satirical message. The artist does not flinch from attacking religion, as a poster from the year 2006 shows. It depicts Jesus floating towards a city in a UFO. The text advises viewers: "Jesus returns 06.06.06. Look religious."

English paints in a photo-realistic style, but for his series of the same portrait in different colors, he uses vivid comic book hues. The references to Warhol are unmistakable but they are deliberately conflated with other images—for instance, English shows Marilyn Monroe with breasts made from Mickey Mouse's face. Particularly well-known is his series *Abraham Obama,* 2008, a male portrait combining the facial features of the 16th and the 44th Presidents so perfectly that both statesmen are unmistakably visible. Both the Marilyn Monroe piece and *Abraham Obama* are available as small-format figurines in various colors. These little statues are yet another illustration of English's conscious mixing and confusing of low and high.

1
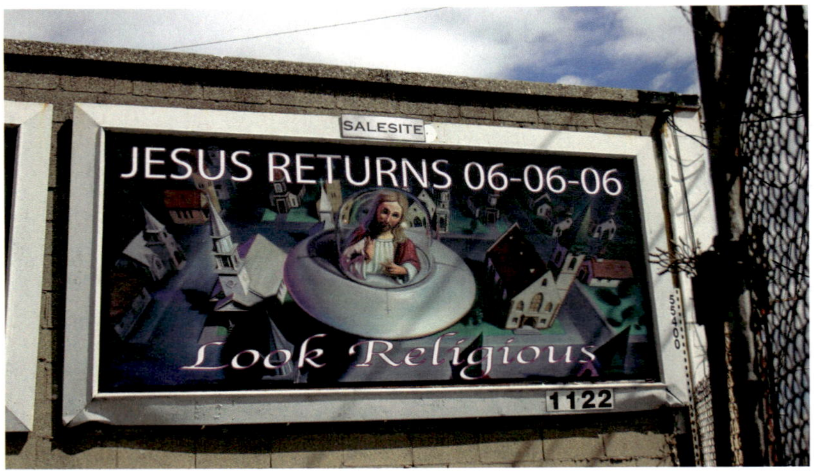

2
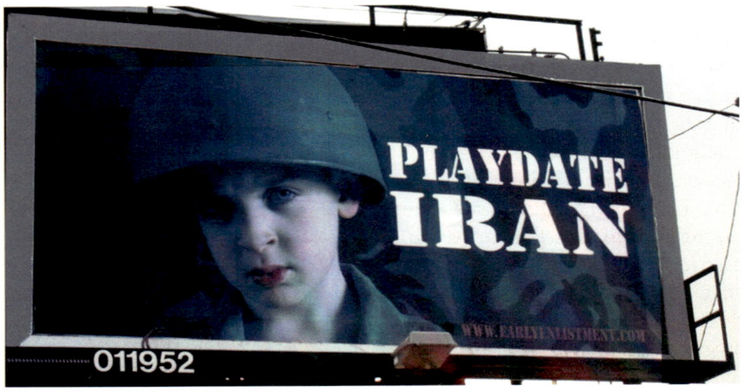

3
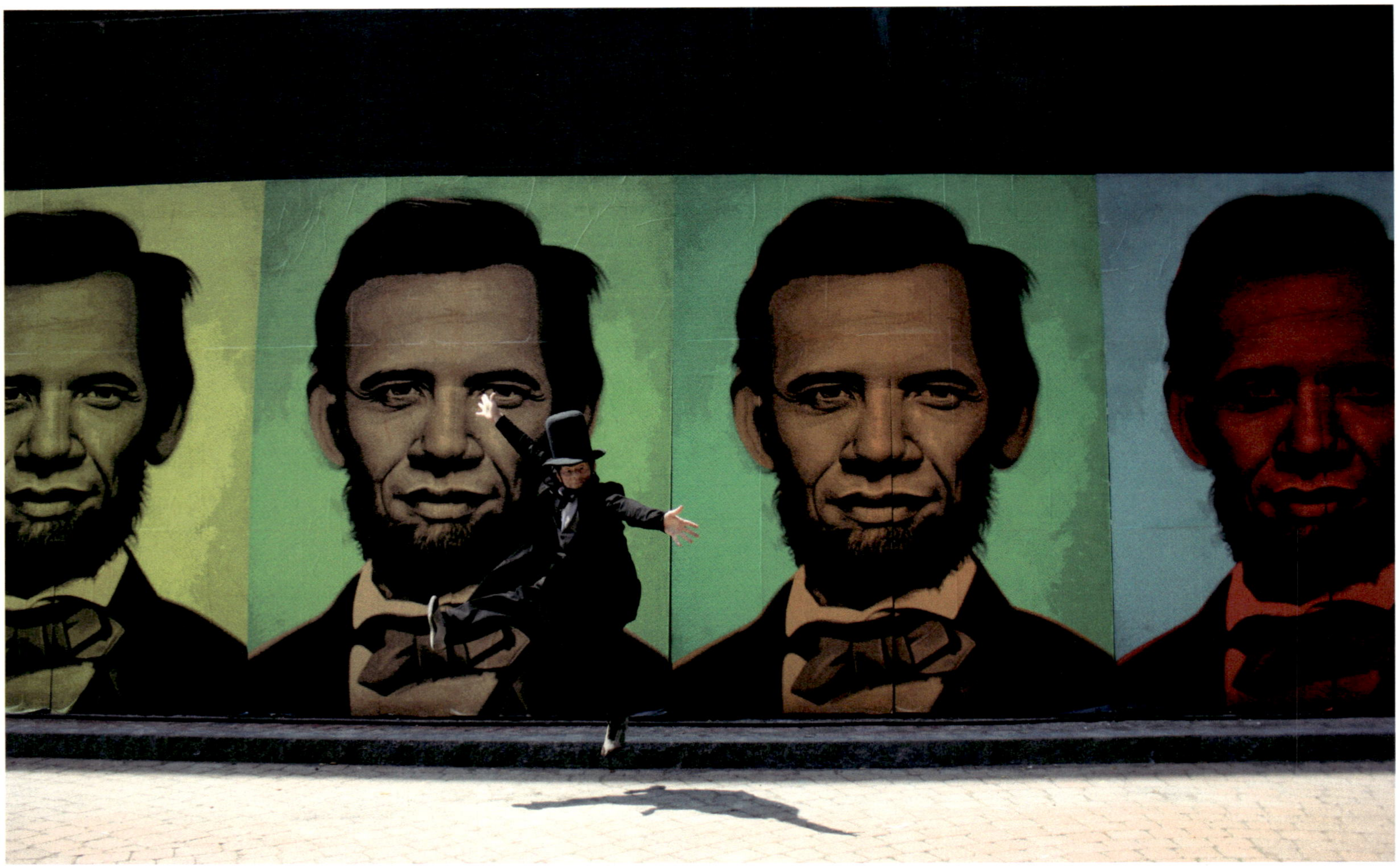

MURRAY GAYLARD

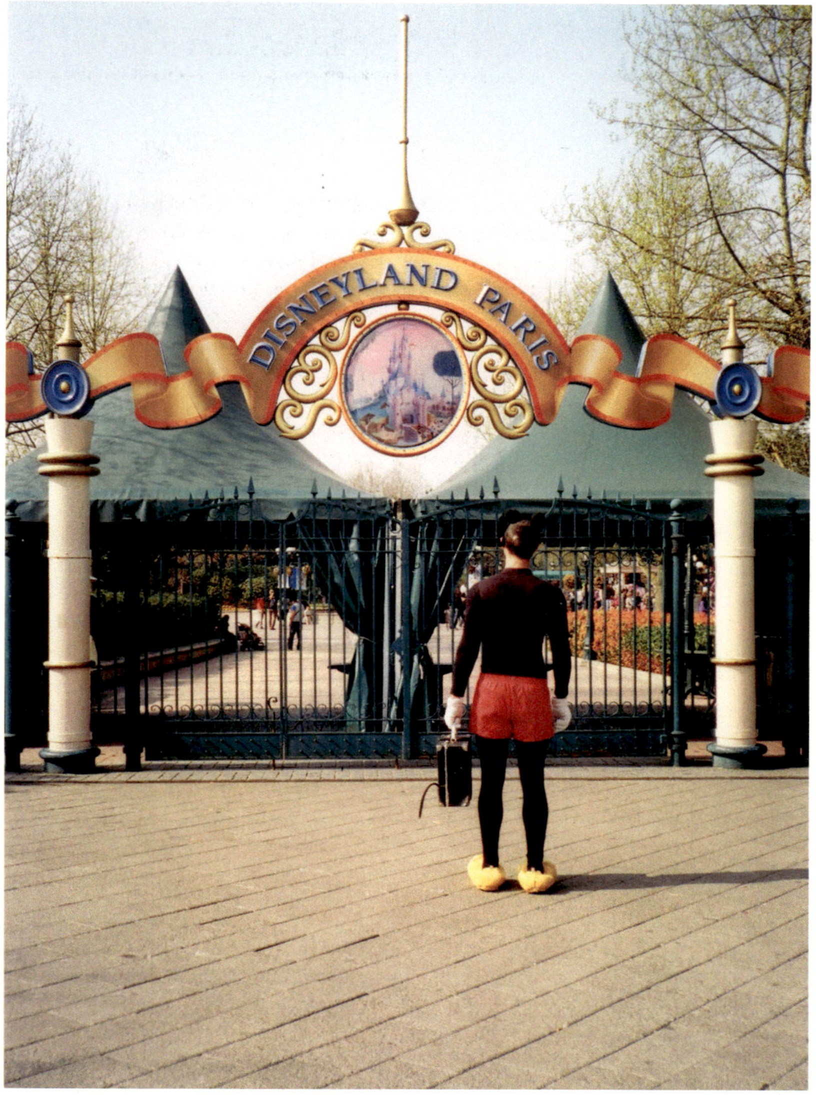

Murray Gaylard (* 1974) from Queenstown, South Africa, studied social sciences in Cape Town and at the Städelschule in Frankfurt, Germany. His work investigates what "home" really means and to what extent our identity depends on it. His performances are his way of asking: in today's world, with mobility more and more important and with countless possibilities for mobile communication, has "home" become a psychological space that we carry with us? Do we leave our dwelling places behind every time we set off—and how much of them do we carry with us all the time? When do we feel at home and when do we feel homeless? The idea of posing these questions came to him while he was living in Frankfurt. The artist himself says that: "Many people who live here feel displaced and yearn for a place where they feel more welcome, but the economy makes this an impossibility to a large extent. I think it makes it much easier that we are now able to position our 'private' in the public, with the help of cellular communication. We are able to create cocoons wherever we go." In his performance *There's No Place Like Home (Or At Least a Place That Resembles It)*, 2009, Gaylard investigates the question of whether one can develop feelings of "home" outside of one's usual surroundings and if so how—with reference to Mickey Mouse. In a homemade Mickey Mouse costume, the artist travelled from Frankfurt to Disneyland Paris (the cartoon character's "home") by hitchhiking and using public transportation. The artist chose this particular character as a metaphor "because he is a character that so clearly belongs anywhere else except on the street. Literally drawn into his surroundings, he is really very dependent on the squeaky-clean perfection of a world created by Disney, where he feels like a king and can operate within the clearly defined parameters of what he represents in this place of fantasy—like living in a cocoon of absolute safety and acceptance. Displacing Mickey Mouse is a strong metaphor for what happens when an individual is uprooted and planted in unfamiliar terrain."

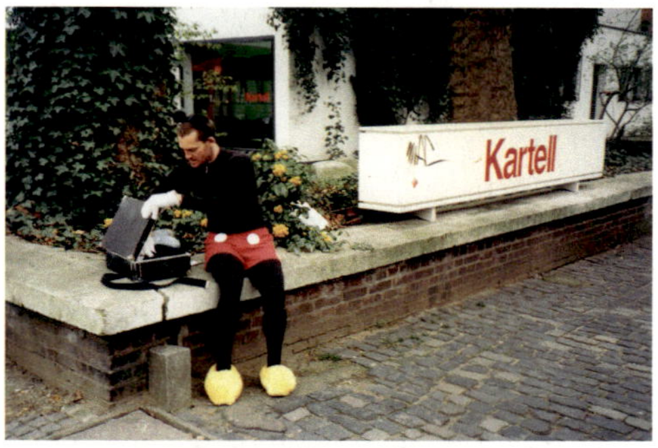

There's No Place Like Home (Or At Least a Place That Resembles It)
2009, Between Frankfurt, Germany, and Paris, France

"Thanks to Ben and to all the tourists along the way who documented my journey"

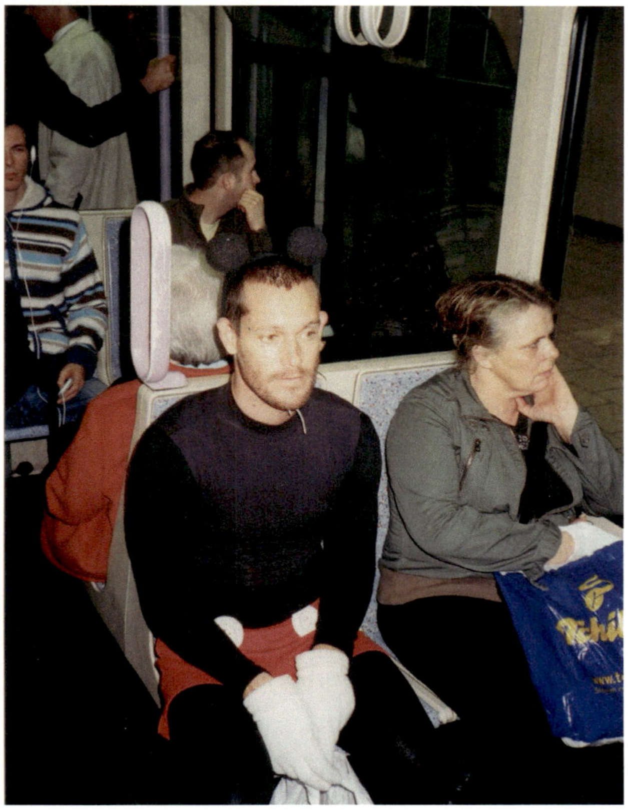

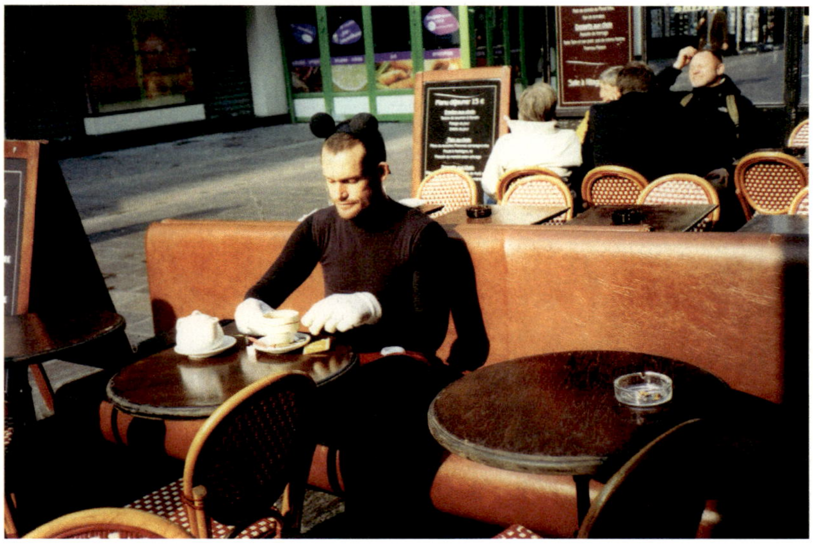

LISA ANNE AUERBACH

1
Mural for Nottingham Contemporary
2009
2
My Favorite Thing About the War on Terror is the Language of the War on Terror
3
Keep Abortion Legal
2006
4
Cunty First
2008
5
Security
6
Thank God I'm an Atheist
2009

American artist Lisa Anne Auerbach (* 1967) was born in Ann Arbor, Michigan. She originally studied photography and began knitting when she graduated and no longer had access to a darkroom for making photographs. Since then, the bicycle activist and feminist has been knitting her personal and political comments and slogans, such as "Thank God I'm an Atheist," "We are all terrorists," "Strangle the Last King with the Entrails of the Last Priest," and "Keep Abortion Legal," into woolen pullovers. She takes her inspiration from revolutionary quotations, philosophical and literary texts, pop songs, and tabloid journalism headlines. "I use humor to bring people into the work, and to temper what otherwise might be didactic, angry, or bitter sentiments," says Auerbach. "I like an uncomfortable edginess, but I also want the sweaters to have a subtlety even when they are confrontational." Auerbach says that she considers knitting messages into pullovers to be like tattooing—the text becomes an integral part of the textile. The text is less directly noticeable than slogans on T-shirts, and the pullover's material properties can serve to mollify its audience, even if one does not like the message. Auerbach's main achievement, however, is that through her sociopolitical commentaries she has given a new level of meaning to an activity generally considered old-fashioned and traditionally feminine—the knitting of sweaters—and has thereby made the creation of this new "guerrilla knitting" a feminist act.

1

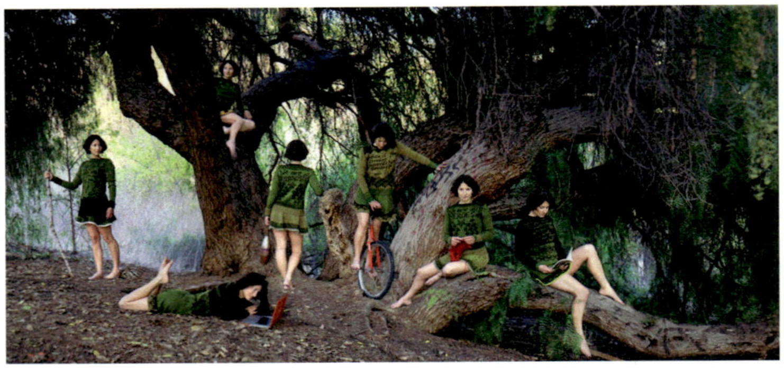

2

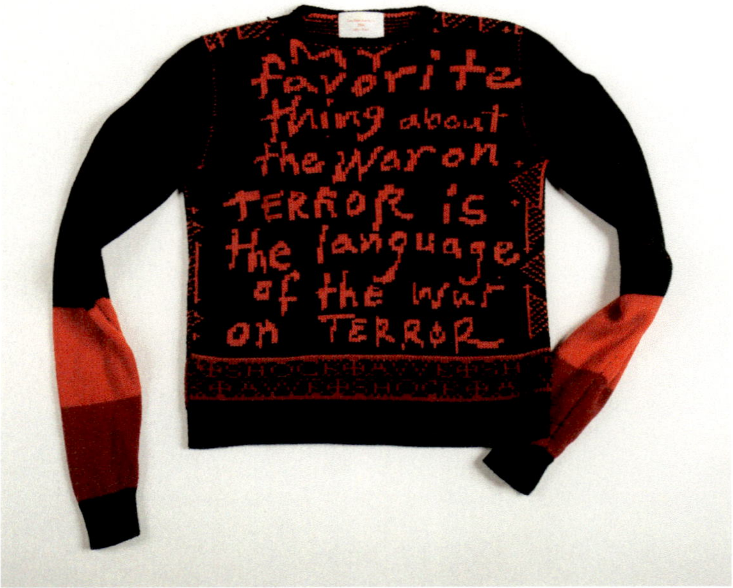

3

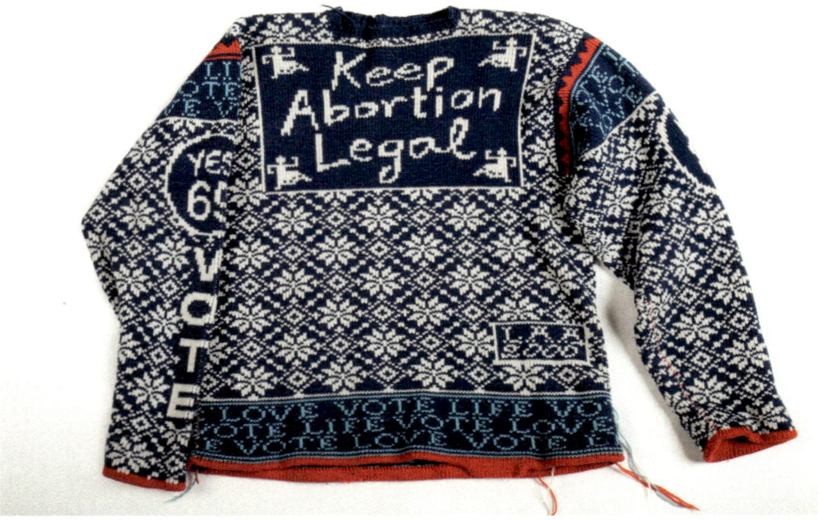

4

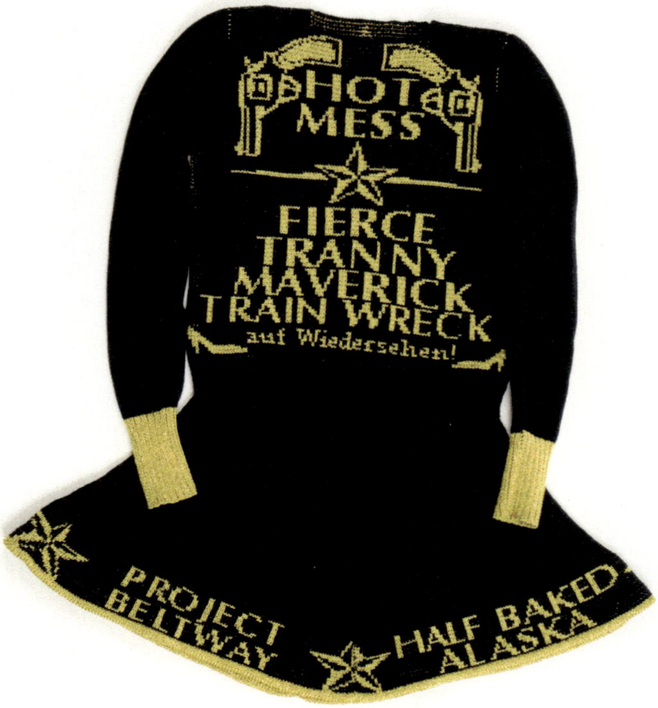

5

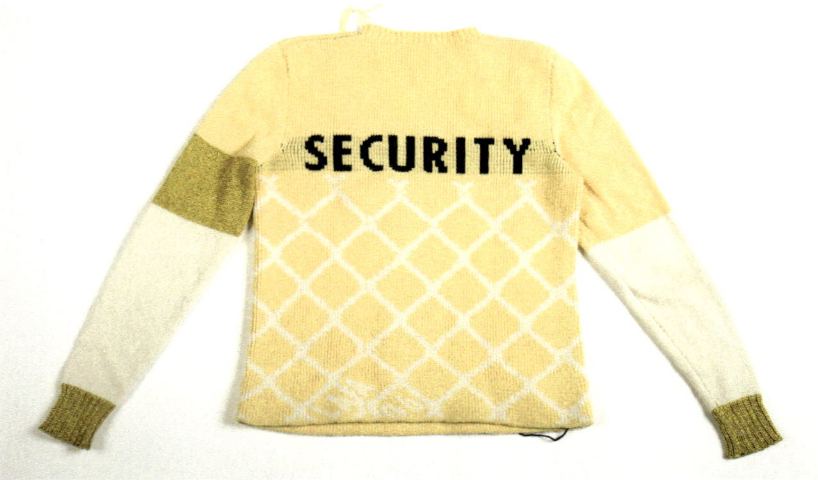

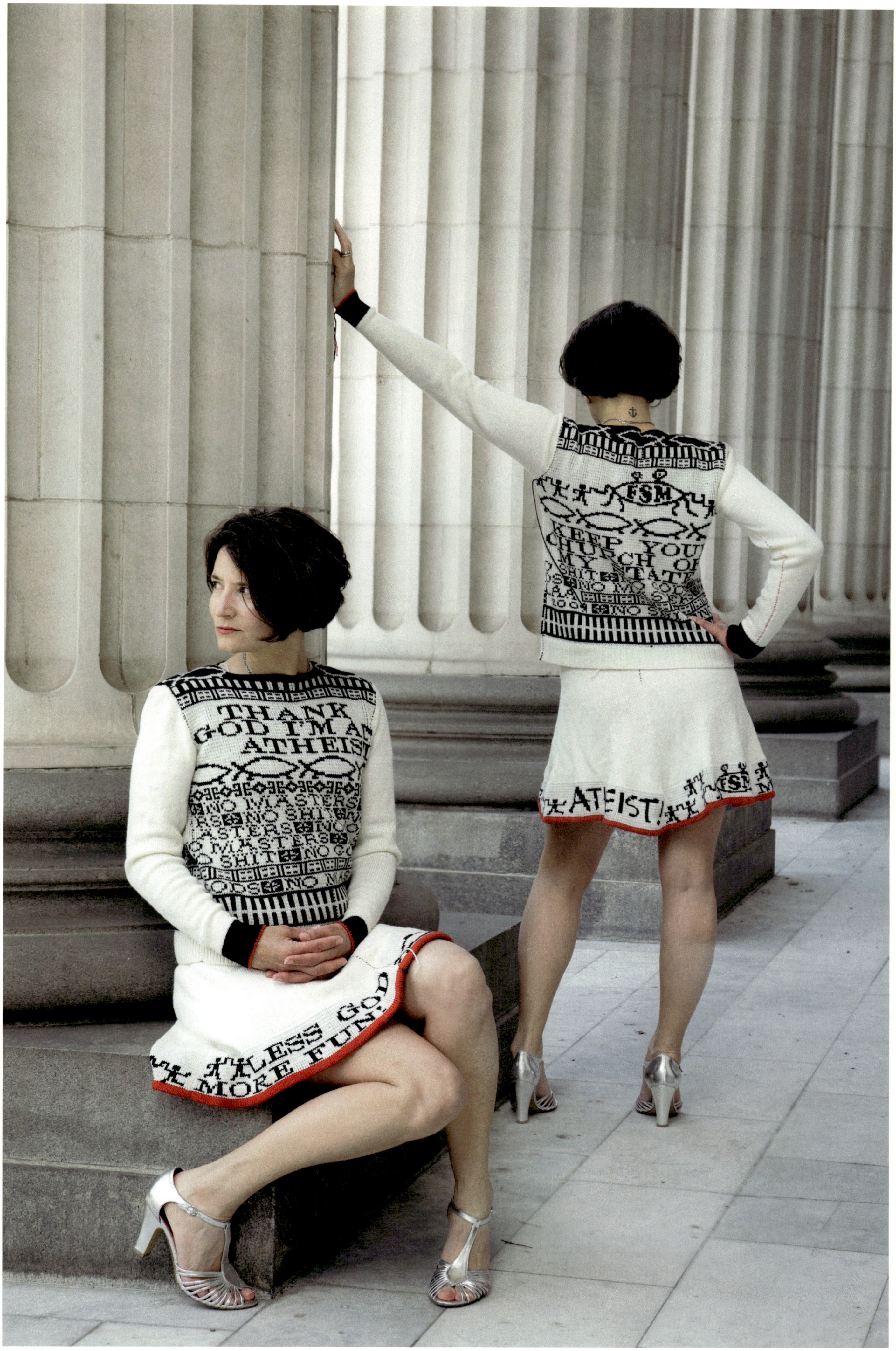
THANK
NO MASTERS
NO SHIT
FSM
ATEIST!
LESS GOD
MORE FUN

ZOË SHEEHAN SALDAÑA

The various series by New York artist Zoë Sheehan Saldaña (* 1973) from Massachusetts, are concerned with the possibilities of reproduction. The artist, who originally studied photography, analyzes "... the questions that the photographic object poses—about the contingent nature of reality ... about the way the photograph requires the viewer's imagination to play out, about the interplay between the machine-made and the handmade."

Above all, she is fascinated by the possibilities of transference from one medium to another. Over the course of the past decade, she has researched and used a whole series of media, from digital and traditional photography to computerized sewing machines and traditional craftwork. For the artist, these media all have one thing in common: "I have been interested in what shifts in the transfer and what stays the same and how the specific medium and the act of transfer heighten awareness of the image/object." Sheehan Saldaña considers her artworks to be "duplications rather than reproductions, with a fair amount of mutation built in, too ... a kind of approximation, overall. The work seems to start there and then spin its way out into different places."

For her series *Shopdropping at Wal-Mart*, 2005, for instance, she transformed machine-made, mass-produced goods into handmade originals, which in turn she converted into photographs. To start with, she purchased six assorted items of clothing from the women's department at a Wal-Mart in Hartford, Connecticut. She then did her best to buy fabrics, zippers, and buttons that matched as closely as possible those of the store-bought items—and spent many hours accurately reproducing them, sewing by hand. Finally, she sewed the Wal-Mart labels into their duplicates and attached the original price tags. She photographed the original articles (now without their labels) and her own creations full size in front of a white background, later exhibiting these "reproductions of reproductions of reproductions." This, however, was not the end of her project. Sheehan Saldaña returned to the shop with her exclusive Wal-Mart articles and found it easy to place them amongst the mass-produced articles: "I simply walked into the store, placed my items with similar stock ... and left." Presumably, six women from the Hartford area now own unique artworks by Zoë Sheehan Saldaña without being aware of it. The artist says: "I think the mystery of the whole transaction is more interesting than knowing. A conceptual piece comes alive in the thinking and talking about it."

1
No Boundaries Cotton Bikinis
2004

2
No Boundaries Sail Canvas
Tote (Orange/Yellow)
2005

3
Faded Glory Mix & Match
Reversible Hat (Red)
2005

4
Faded Glory Ruched Shoulder
Tank (China Red)
2003

1

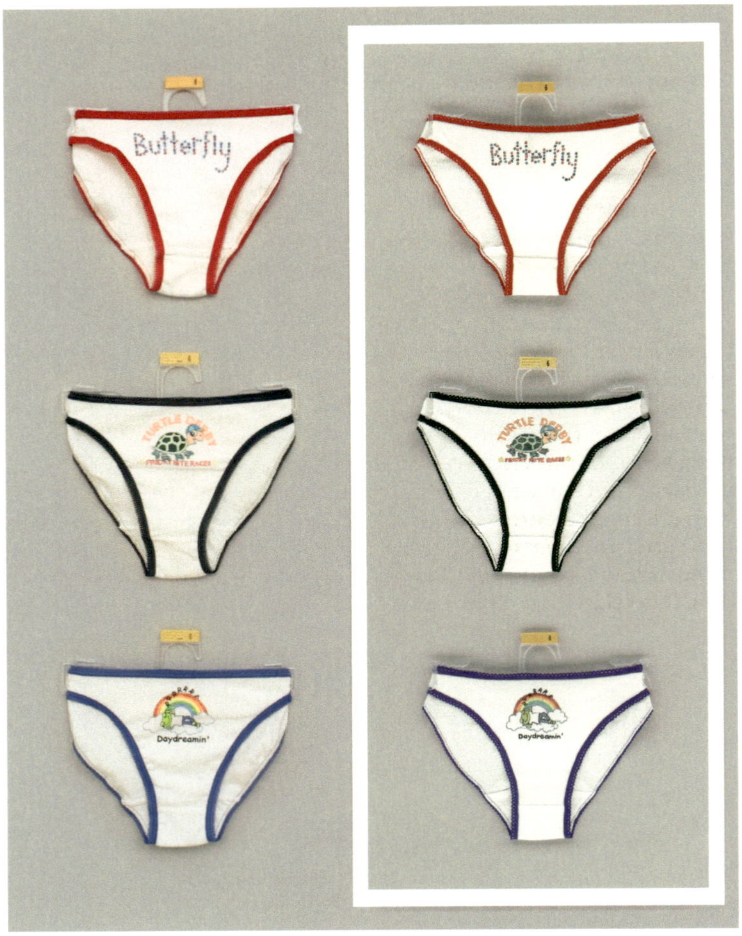

2

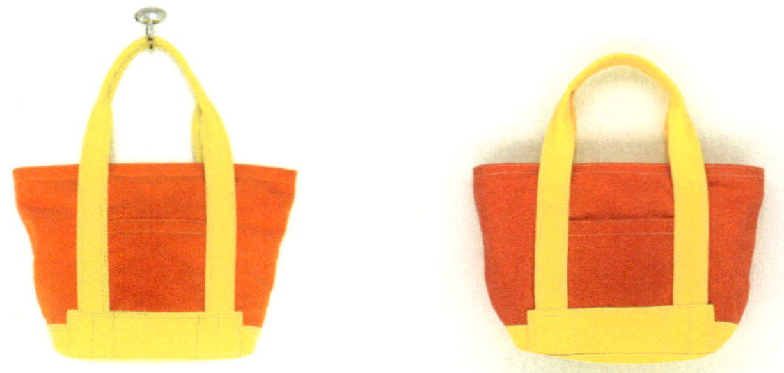

3

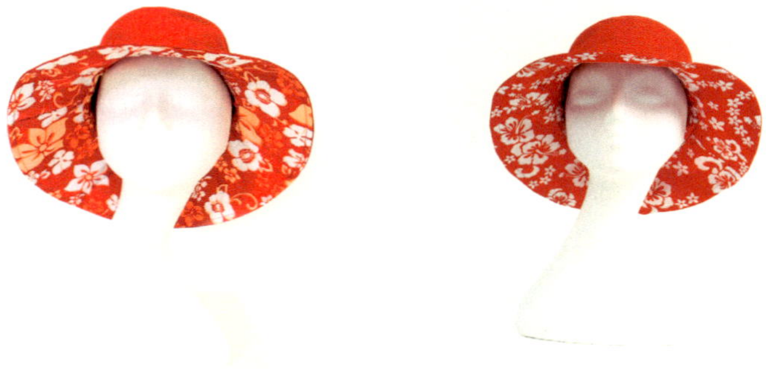

4

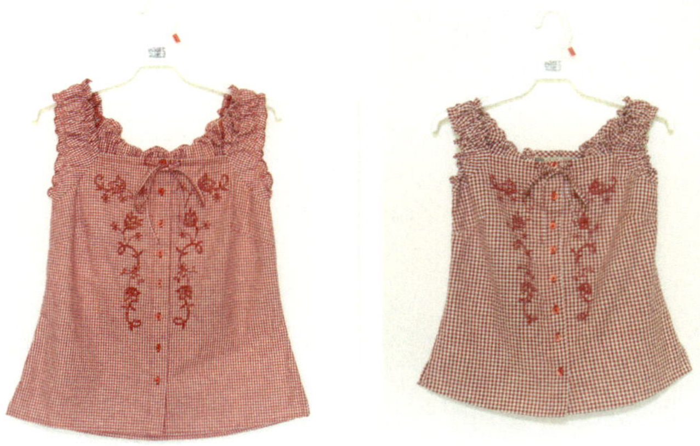

LAURA KEEBLE

London artist Laura Keeble's favorite targets include consumer culture, the rampant reign of terror of the brand names, the hyperventilating art market, and religious demagogues. She is best known for the copy of the *Diamond Skull* by Damien Hirst, which she dumped in front of Hirst's gallery together with some rubbish after the exhibition (*Forgotten something!?,* 2007). In a further spectacular intervention, she turned a cemetery into a graveyard for brands such as Chanel, Nike, and McDonalds (*Idol Worship,* 2007). "The project was based on the theory of magical thinking, looking at belief systems and idol worship, and creating an intervention that, like other work I have installed, plays with the viewer's perception—and with any luck creates a pause for thought," Keeble explains. In her new series *Idol Worship I–III,* 2010, she returns to this concept, creating colored church windows with the logos of firms such as YSL and Chanel in their centers.

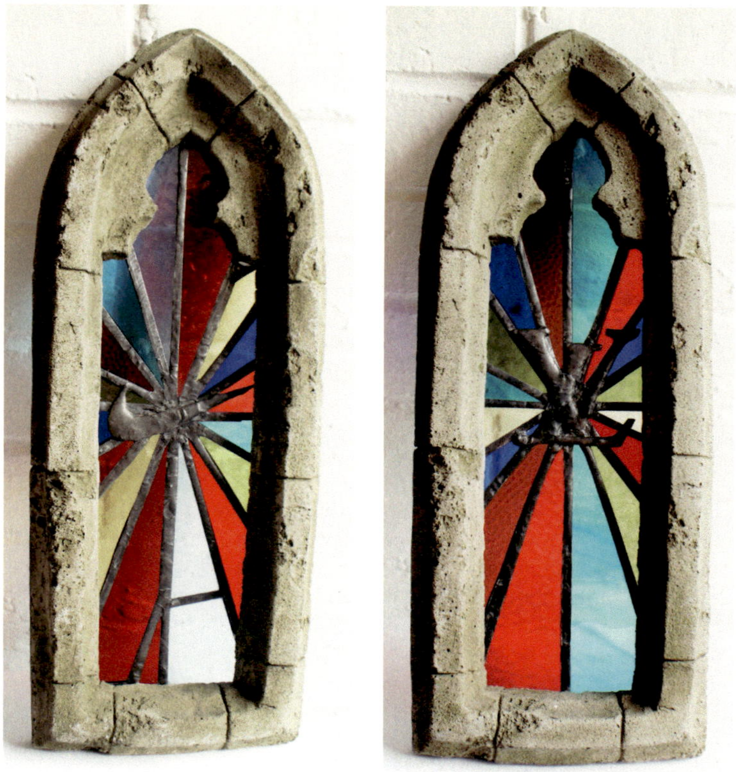
1

1
Idol Worship
2010, Stained glass, lead, Concrete
2
Idol Worship
2007

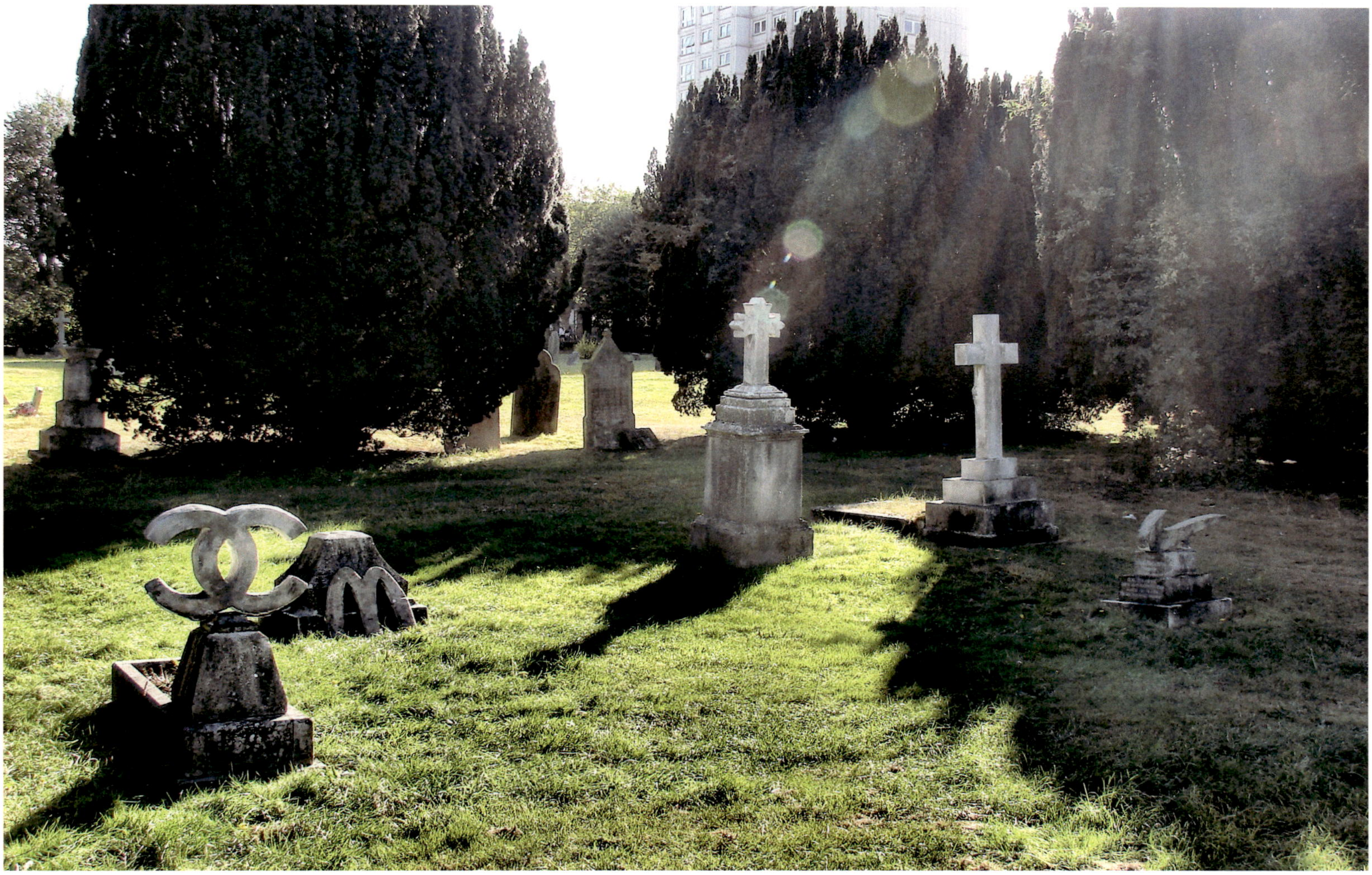
2

TOM SACHS

In his artworks, Tom Sachs, who lives in New York City, addresses the role of luxury goods in society and investigates the impact of manipulative marketing on our everyday lives. In his Allied Cultural Prosthetics workshop, he creates bricolage objects that combine luxuries with taboos. His working materials are a cordless screwdriver, glue guns, insulating tape, cheap wooden boards, cardboard, and sometimes found objects. In the 1990s, for instance, the concept artists created a series of incongruous McDonald's menus on bags and packaging materials from well-known fashion houses such as Hermès, Tiffany & Co., Prada, and Chanel. As a former shop designer for high-class New York department store Barney's, his knowledge of how our desires are played on is second to none, making his provocations savagely accurate. In 2002, he created a high-profile media scandal with an artwork entitled *Prada Deathcamp*—a model of a concentration camp made from a Prada hatbox—which he exhibited at the "Mirroring the Evil" exhibition in the Jewish Museum New York. The numerous protests at this daring juxtaposition of the horrors of history with a brand name reference gave rise to a discussion on how we deal with history within our culture: "Fascism and fashion—both involve a certain loss of individuality. I am interested in the hardware of horror and death." The functional guillotine with a Chanel logo that he built in the same year also fuelled this widespread debate. In his whole-space installation *Nutsy's*, 2003, which he exhibited at the Deutsche Guggenheim in Berlin, Sachs investigated modernist tropes such as production, consumption, and circulation. This installation encapsulated his artistic principles; it is a bricolage that presents a fusion of ghetto code, poverty, criminality, and surveillance to the viewer in a playful and highly ironic way. The artist placed modernist icons such as models of Le Corbusier's *Unité d'Habitation* and *Villa Savoye* next to a McDonald's stand, a DJ's booth with decks, and a ghetto quarter. Illusions alternated with disillusionment as one travelled along the circuit—the rise and fall of the market as humorously made visible by Sachs. However, visitors were required to take part as well as to look—in addition to the fast food and the music, they were challenged to compete for the Nutsy Cup on the enormous remote controlled car racetrack. Despite its numerous architectural and historical references, *Nutsy's* reflects our present-day world of surreptitious advertising, in a style that is part comic and part action film. As well as representing the power of mass marketing, *Nutsy's* displays the will to resistance and transgression writ large. Sachs used stolen road barriers, imitated McDonald's designs and products without a license, and integrated imitation Barcelona Chairs into the installation. Sachs's artworks shows us strategies for erecting an alternative economy while at the same time revealing how profit is made from mass consumption and its mighty brands. In doing so, the artist does not allow himself to be intimidated by the lawyers of the businesses concerned.

1
Prada Toilet
1997, Cardboard and thermal adhesive

2
Made in England
2008–2009, Mixed-media

3
Value Meal #1
1997, Paper, ink, and thermal adhesive

4
Chanel Guillotine
(Breakfast Nook)
1998, Leather, nylon, rubber, steel, synthetic polymer, and wood

Courtesy Sperone Westwater, New York

1

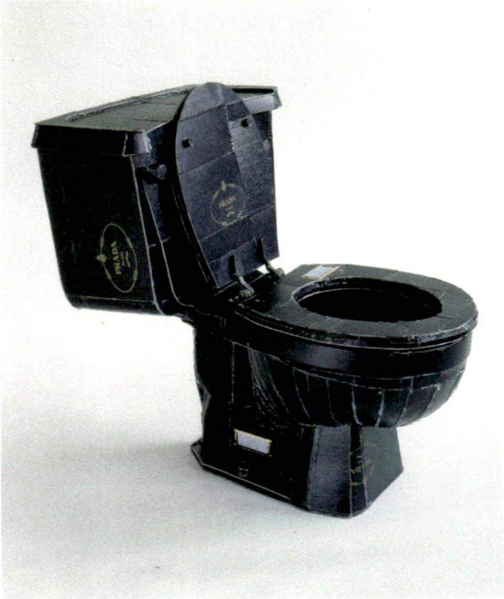

2

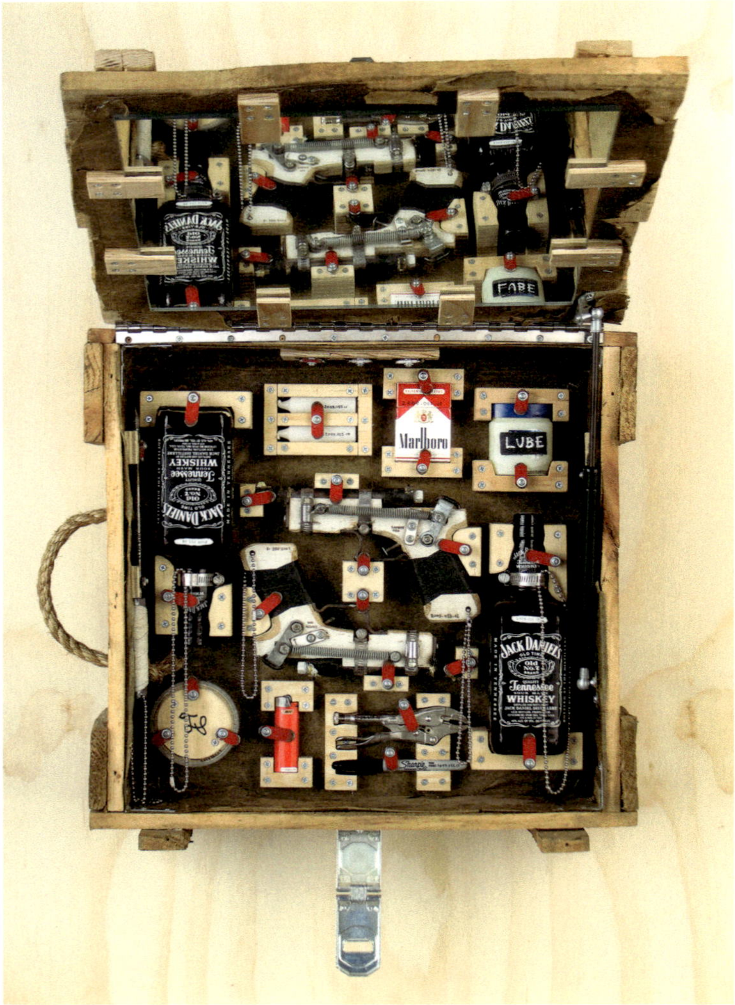

3

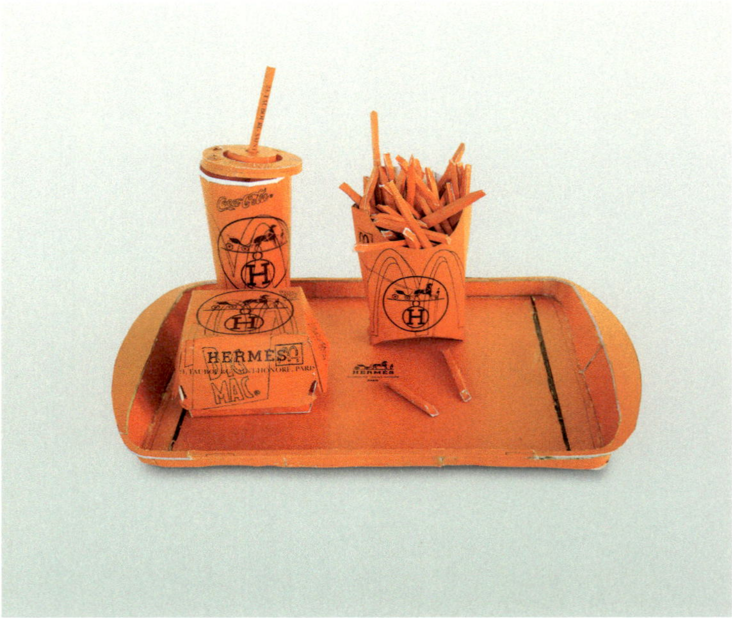

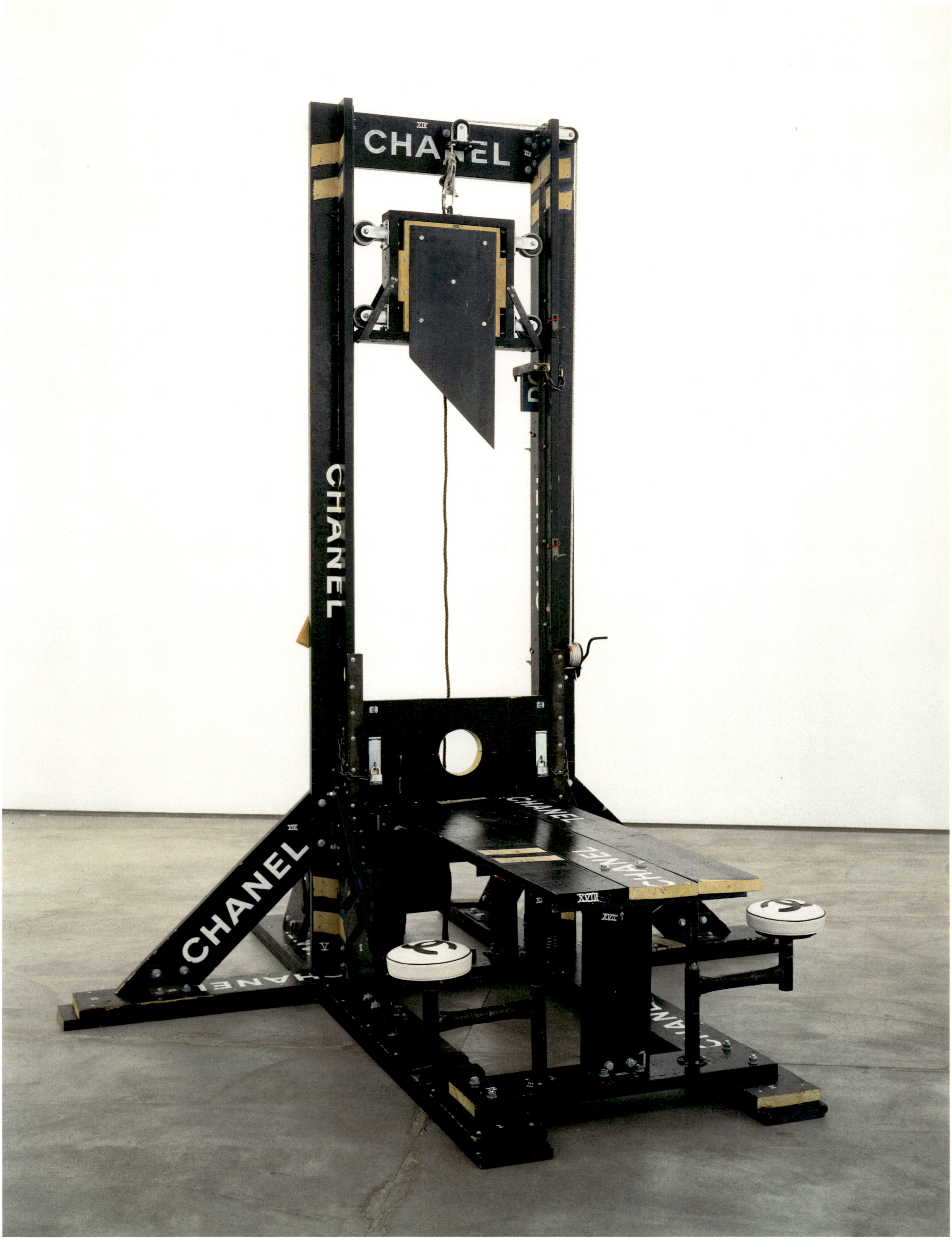
CHANEL
CHANEL
CHANEL
CHANEL
CHANEL

PSJM

1

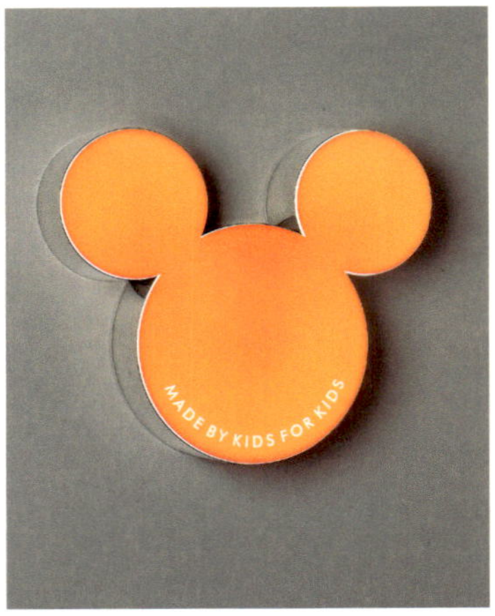

1
Made By Kids for Kids
2007, London, U.K., Light-box on stainless steel
2
Marx®
2008, La Boral, Gijón, Spain
3
American Colors:
USA Population By Race,
USA Poverty Rate By Race,
USA Prison Population By Race
Berlin, Germany, 2009

The Spanish artist Pablo San José (* 1969) started PSJ in 1998. As an artist, his interests lie in establishing a direct relationship between art and commerce. He has stated that: "The artist is the brand, the artwork is the product." San José was joined in 2003 by Cynthia Viera (* 1973), who, as a graduate of international business and marketing, brought an in-depth knowledge of commercial strategies and brand marketing to the collaboration. Thus PSJM was formed. The basis of the practice lies in substituting the sublime qualities attributed to and expected in art and the "genius" of the artist, together with brand and marketing techniques. PSJM does not question society commodifying art and culture, they rather see it as a fact and their practice revolves around this certainty. In creating work that resembles advertising or products, their message is intended to be easily read by an audience that is not well-informed about contemporary art. For PSJM, audience participation is an integral part of their work and process. PSJM has stated that: "Perhaps many people forget that without an audience, there is no art; the reader, the viewer, and the public is actively involved in the construction of the work of art, and without the act of reception/consumption, the cultural product is incomplete." PSJM often utilizes corporate logos, as well as elements from the urban environment such as graffiti, tags, stickers, slogans, signage, and advertising techniques. Their artistic ideas are critical of consumer culture, corporate greed, and global economic disparities.

In order to best-convey their ideas and the use of art as a form of language, PSJM has appropriated elements from various pertinent artistic movements. In a project titled, *The Street at Home,* the team utilizes graffiti as a form of home decoration, and stickers of tags are sold as decorative elements. In a video that decontextualizes urban underground culture, tags that are commonly found on the street are placed onto the surfaces of classic modernist residences such as Mies van der Rohe's Farnsworth House, the Barcelona Pavilion, and Philip Johnson's Glass House. The series *American Colors,* 2009, utilizes formal abstraction and minimalism as a vehicle to address issues of race and inequality, and five basic colors representing race are combined with demographic statistics. The mathematical information determines the percentage of the corresponding color or race. The title of each work provides the key to decipher the color-field code. Viewed side by side, the works, *USA Population by Race* and *USA Prison Population by Race* reveal a brutal reality of social inequality in the United States.

Brand marketing and global economics play a critical role in PSJM's practice. The artists incorporate logos to explore issues of consumers manifesting individuality and identity through the consumption of particular brands, which they then relate to the use of labor in developing countries. The series *Made for Kids by Kids,* 2007, uses light boxes of symbols for children's products, such as the Mickey Mouse ears, with the words "Made by Kids for Kids" inscribed on the surface. In another series, *Project Asia,* circular light boxes bearing the logos of the top athletic shoe companies, such as Nike, Adidas, Puma, and Reebok, are emblazoned with the text: "Made by slaves for free people." Both series question the outsourcing of manufacturing by companies in developed nations to Third World countries in Asia and Latin America, where child labor is common, and where problematic labor conditions are prevalent. In addition, these works question the hypocrisy of the intended message of freedom and individuality promoted by the brands, as well as the underlying practice of exploiting workers in the Third World.

2
The MARX® project offers a mock reflection of the paradoxes in the critique of the current capitalist system and individual identity concerns. The brand slogan "Do like us, be different" reproduces the paradoxical message seen in the media; achieve your individuality and be yourself by consuming mass-produced goods. This tension between the individual and mass production, exclusivity, and the subjective industries takes material form in MARX® products, which are unique because of their visible and differentiating series number. MARX® products use the mechanisms characteristic of the culture industry—especially commercial seduction—to create simulacra within the framework of contemporary art, which easily cross the line between fiction and reality.

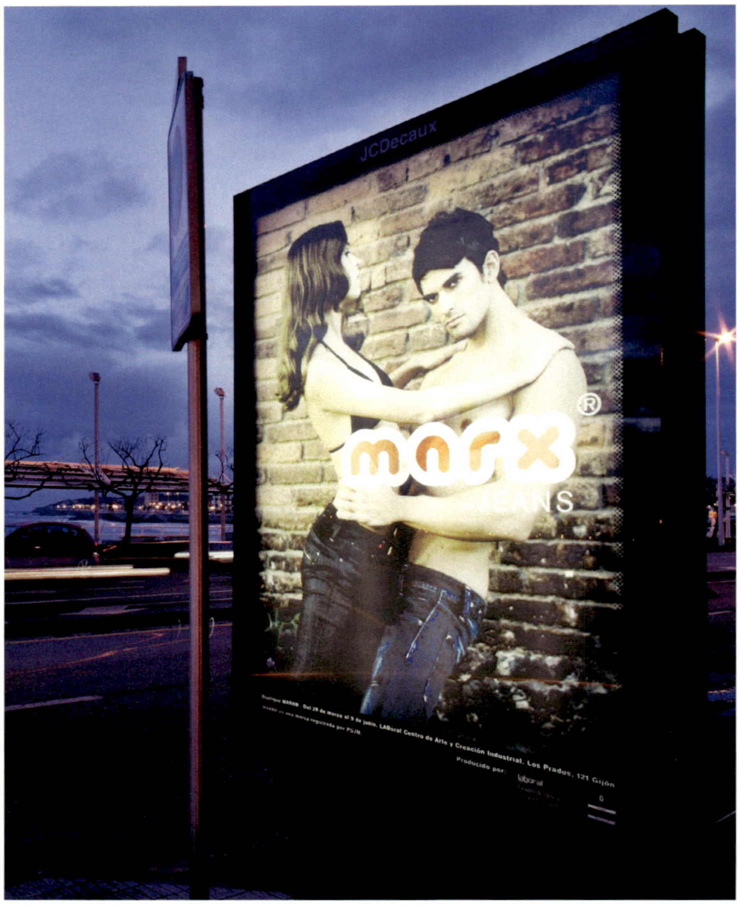

3

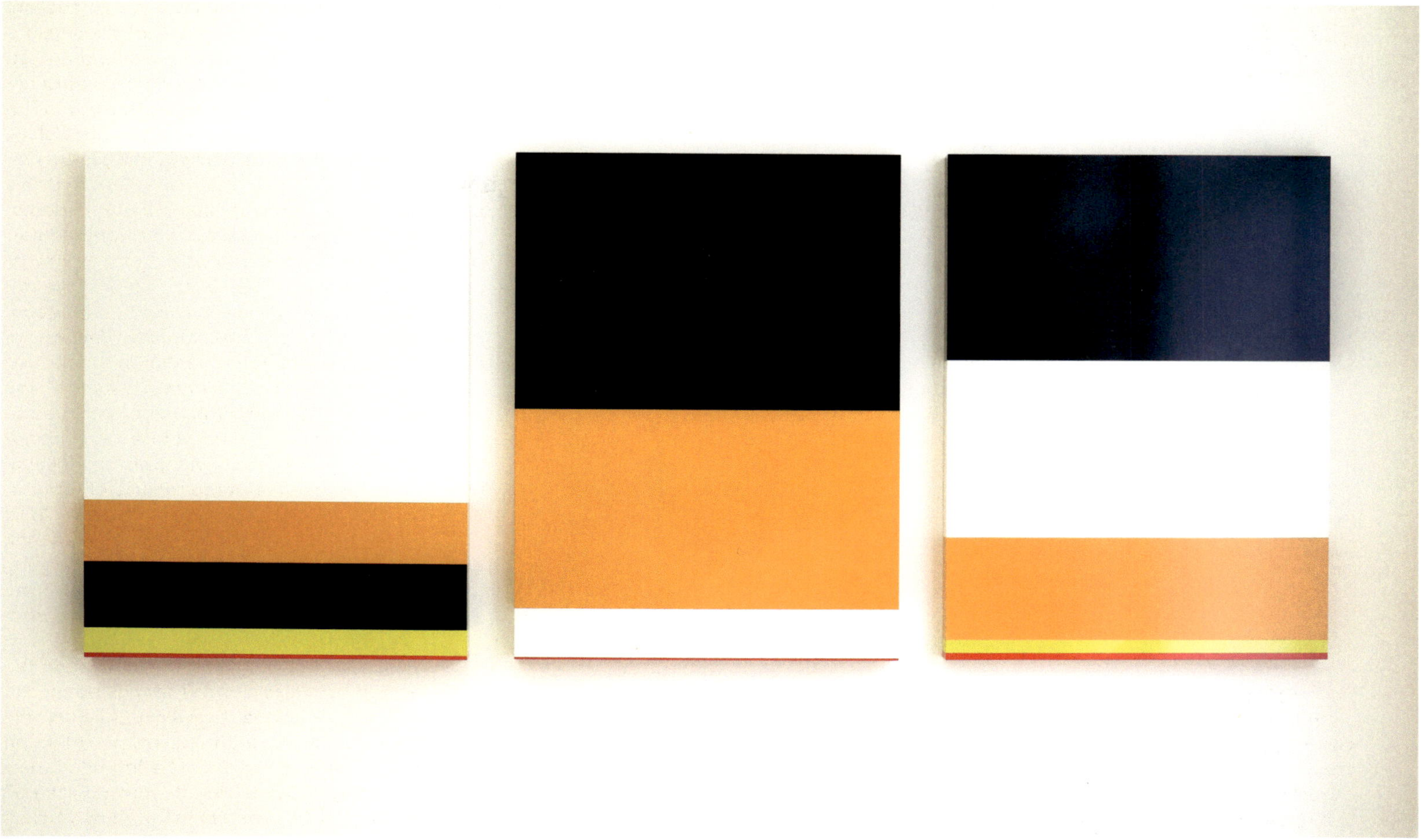

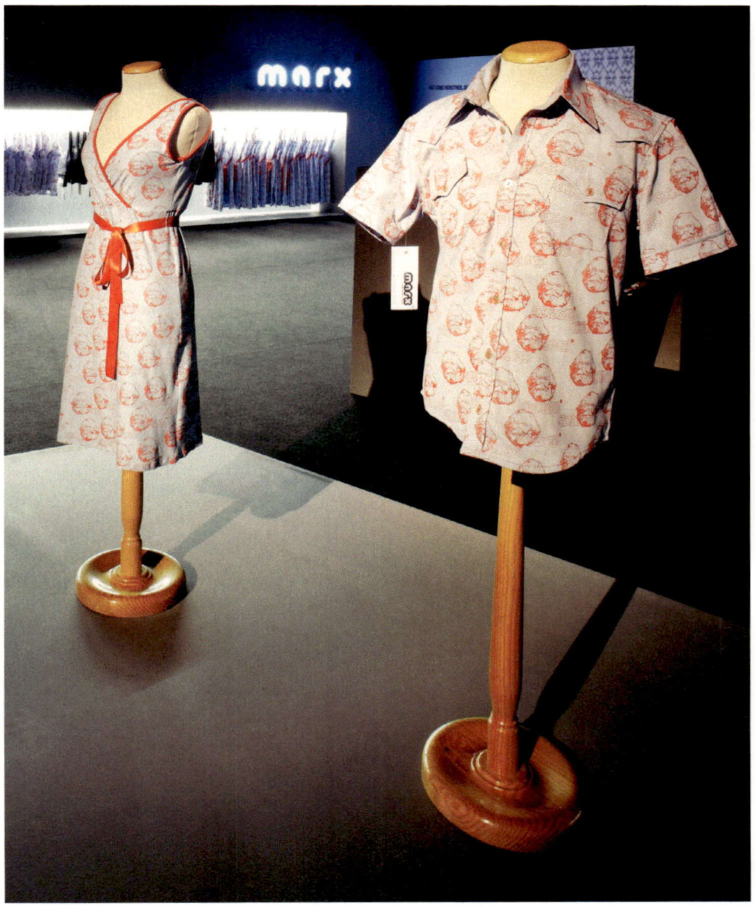

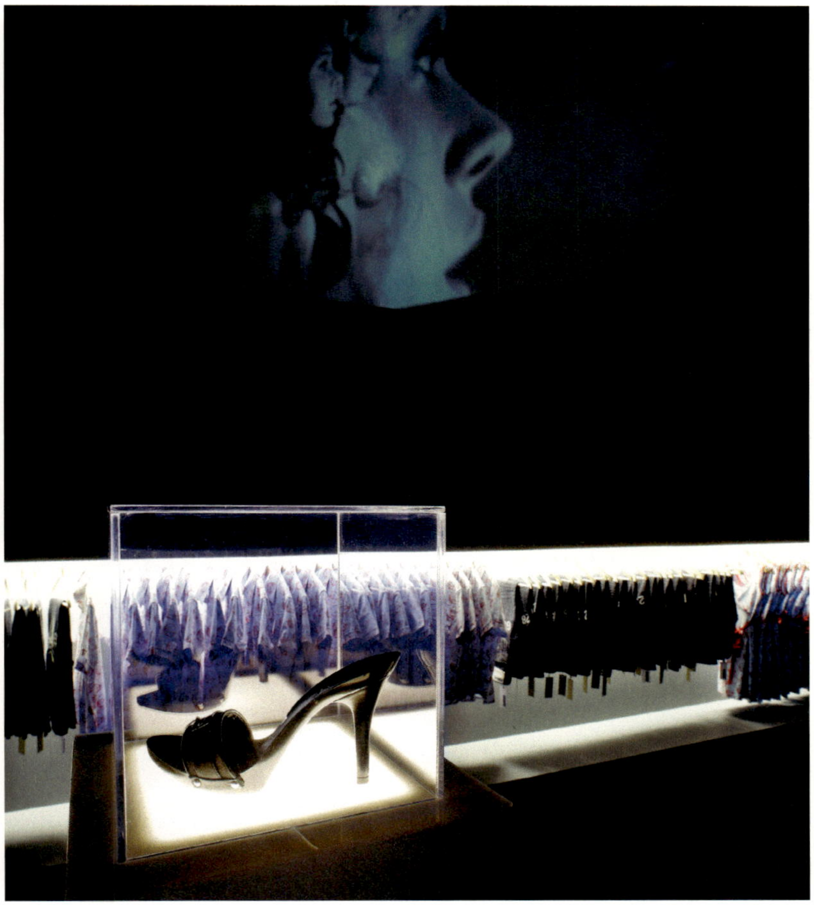

SCOTT KING

1
Roy
2008, Courtesy Herald St, London, and Bortolami, New York
2
How I'd Sink American Vogue
2006, Digital print
Courtesy Herald St, London, and Bortolami, New York
3
Al-Qaeda, Swalecliffe Court Road, Swalecliffe, Kent
2010, Screen-printed ridge tent, installation
Courtesy Herald St, London
Photo by Brendan Parker
4
Henry Kissinger
(Years of Upheaval)
2010, New York, USA,
Screenprint on primed linen
Courtesy Bortolami, New York

"Most of the stuff I've done that is deemed political is actually about the failure of a certain kind of political ideology," says Scott King (* 1969). "It's about the failure of the left, mainly. So things like *Cher Guevara,* and the *Angry Brigade Tea Towels* are really about the commoditization of once-meaningful imagery and gestures." King, who was born in the English town of Goole, started out studying graphic design, and then spent a year working as an art director for glossy magazines like *i-D* and *Sleazenation.* This has given King a consummate command of the techniques and the aesthetic vocabulary of the mass media, allowing him to subvert it in a meaningful way. His work is a combination of art, advertising, graphic design, semiotics, politics, and pop culture. King appropriates consumer culture and media symbols, turning the media themselves into bastardized icons. He repeatedly shows a relish for biting the hand that feeds him—and the more aggressively he attacks the media, the more popular his style becomes. His art zine *Prada Meinhof,* which was set up to criticize radical chic and all its fashionable and empty revolutionary gestures, became so popular that a few months after its founding, underwear with the magazine's name on the label were being sold in Berlin. King thereby succeeded in proving that when politics becomes a pose, poses become political. Later, King worked as a designer on Malcolm McLaren's—the impresario and former manager of the Sex Pistols—campaign to be elected mayor of London. He also designed record covers for bands and solo artists like Pet Shop Boys, Suicide, and Morrissey. For his works relating to British pop culture, he likes to create situationist-style sequences of images—for instance, through painting little-known and absurd quotations by both Adolf Hitler and Henry Kissinger. King also likes to fantasize about the mass media in his artworks. For *How I'd Sink American Vogue,* 2006, he designed fantasy front covers for the American edition of *Vogue* that would torpedo its image within a year. And for an exhibition, he remixed busts of political figures like Lenin and Marx with icons of British glam rock, such as Brian Eno and Roy Wood. In another dimension to his work, King also creates interventions in urban spaces in order to spread his ideas. For instance, he has erected a tent featuring Arabic characters in the English county of Kent in a work titled, *Taliban, Lucerne Drive, Whitstable, Kent,* 2010.

1
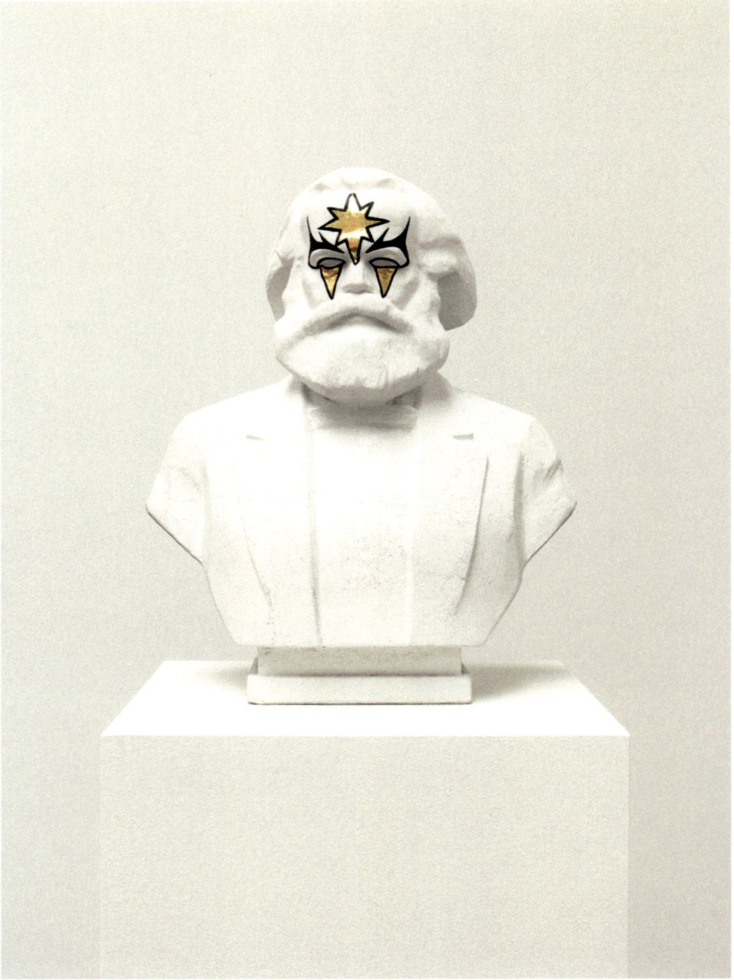

2
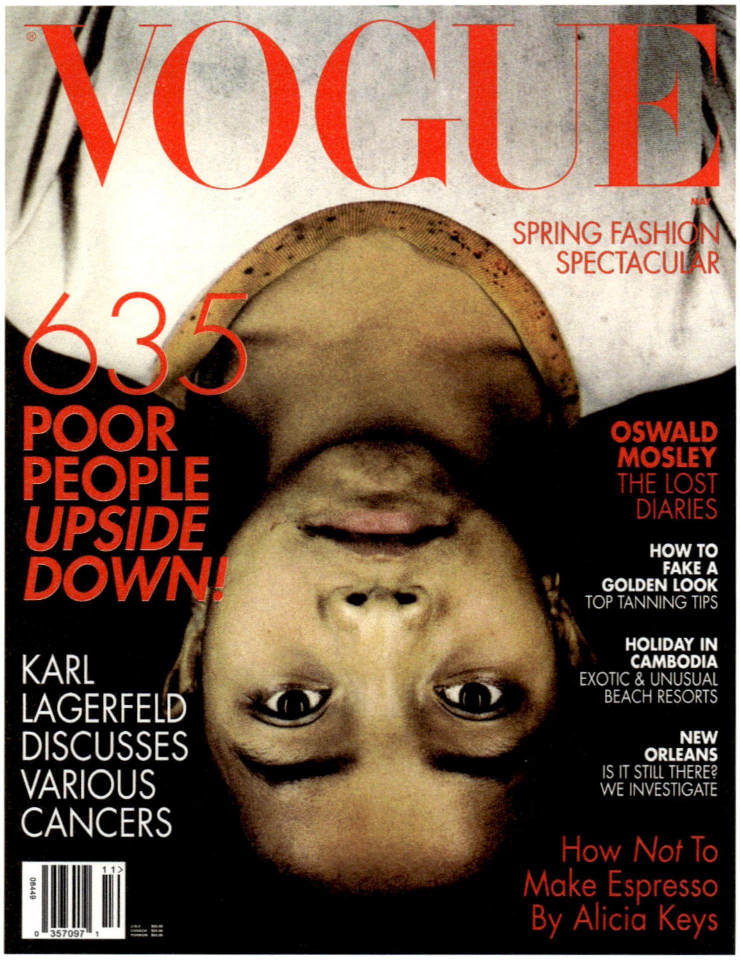

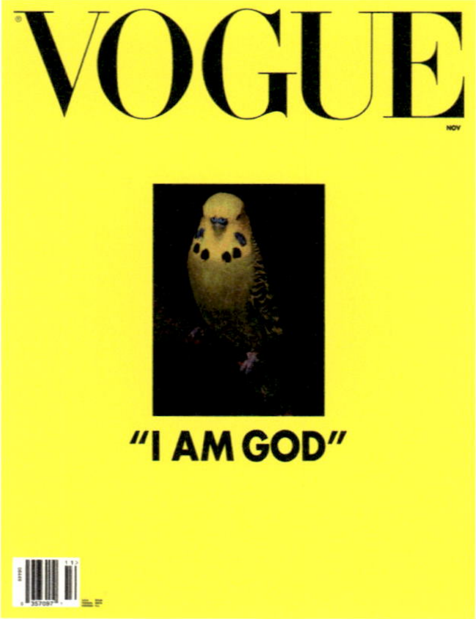

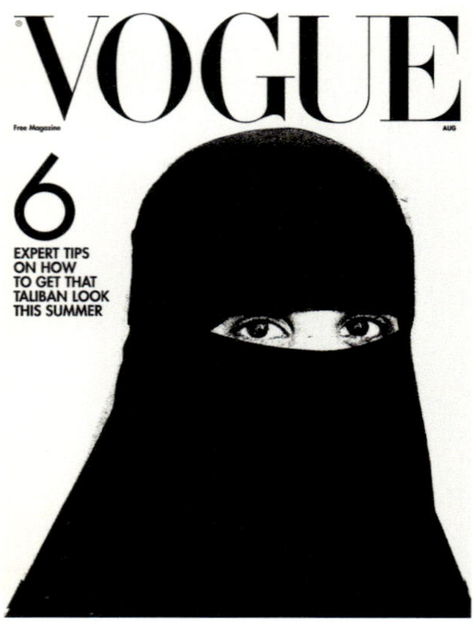

3

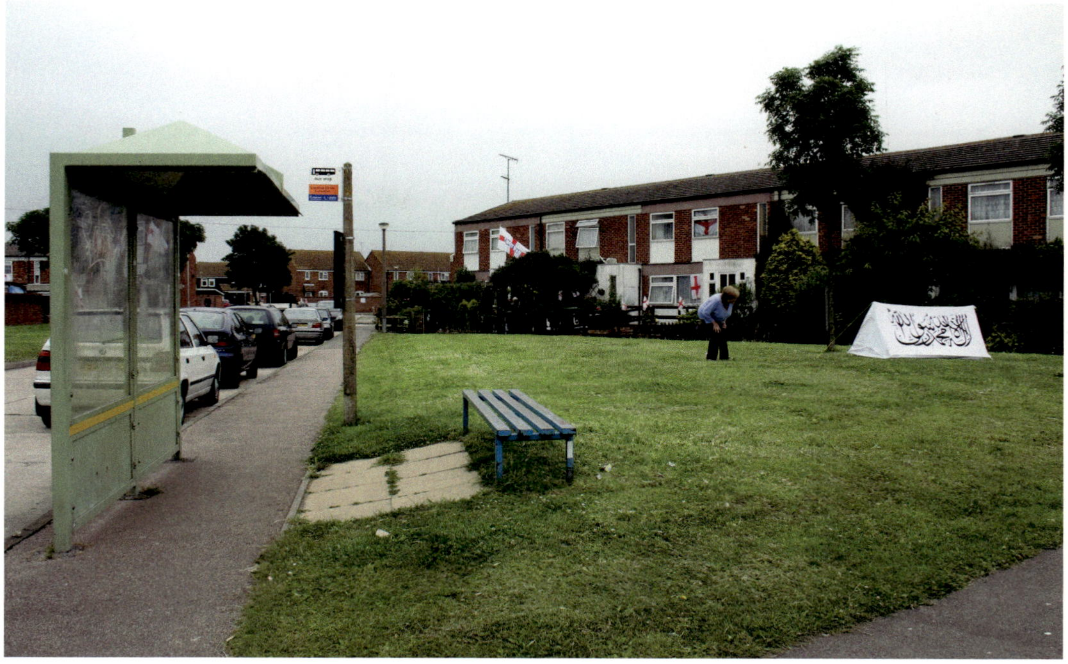

4

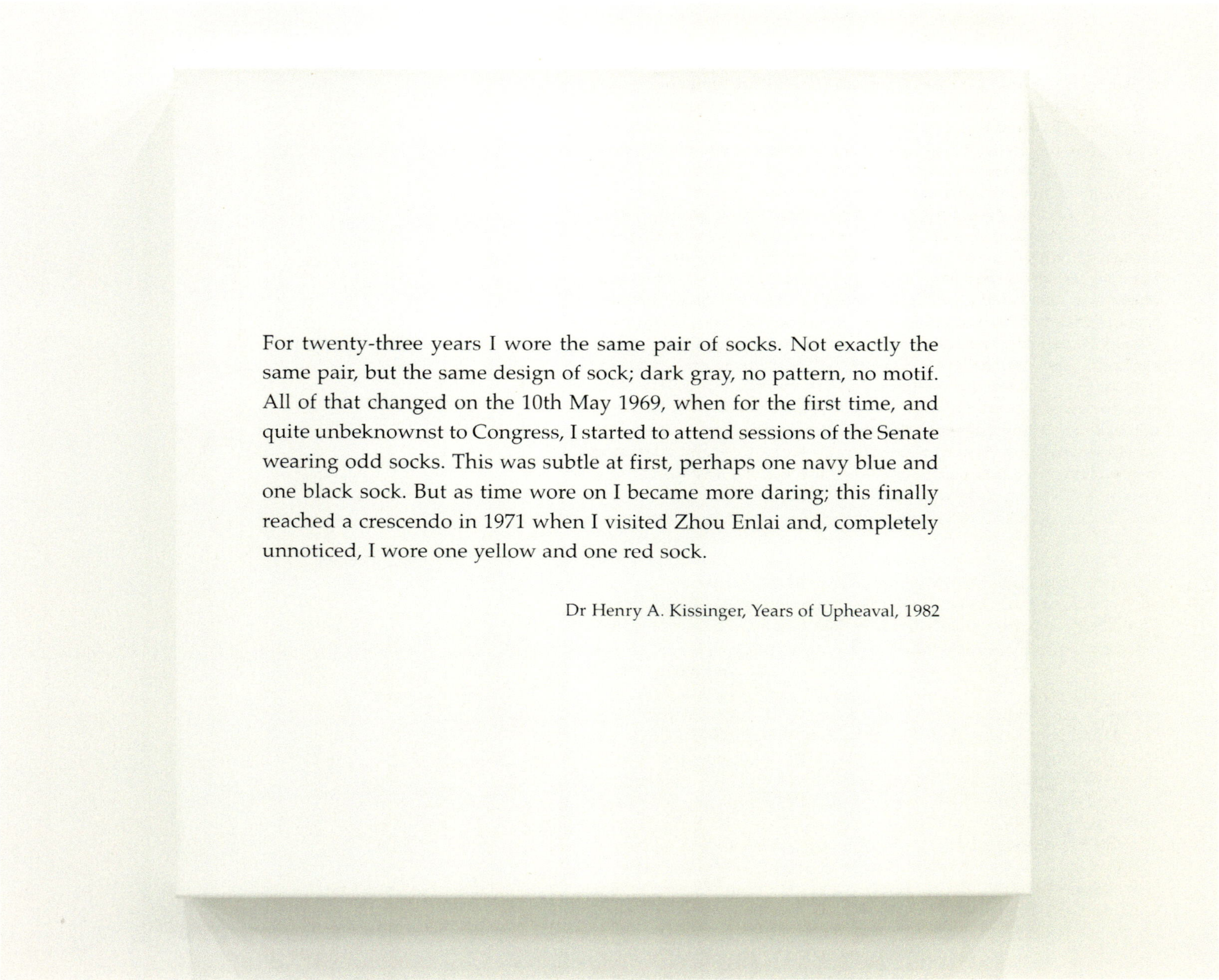
For twenty-three years I wore the same pair of socks. Not exactly the same pair, but the same design of sock; dark gray, no pattern, no motif. All of that changed on the 10th May 1969, when for the first time, and quite unbeknownst to Congress, I started to attend sessions of the Senate wearing odd socks. This was subtle at first, perhaps one navy blue and one black sock. But as time wore on I became more daring; this finally reached a crescendo in 1971 when I visited Zhou Enlai and, completely unnoticed, I wore one yellow and one red sock.
Dr Henry A. Kissinger, Years of Upheaval, 1982

EVA & FRANCO MATTES AKA 0100101110101101.ORG

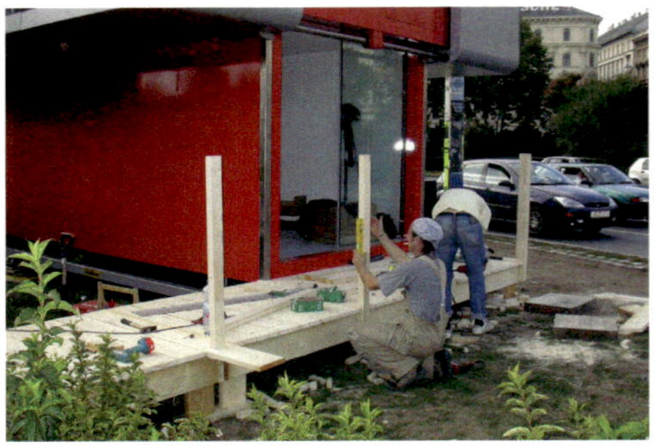

1

1
Nike Ground
2003, Karlsplatz, Vienna, Austria, Photo courtesy Public Netbase
2
Project for the Fake Nike Monument in Karlsplatz
2003, Karlsplatz, Vienna, Austria, Rendering by Eva Haas, Karin Eichberger

"Reality is overrated," is a favorite slogan of the artist duo Eva and Franco Mattes, alias 0100101110101101.ORG (both * 1976), who were born in Italy and currently live in New York. As pioneers of internet art, they are interested in reality in an age of digital falsification, the mixing of fact and fiction, and in creating connections between real experiential space and virtual space as a way to reflect the features of different societies and cultures. Their installation *Nike Ground,* 2003, has already become a classic. At the Karlsplatz in Vienna, they installed what appeared to be a Nike information booth announcing that the plaza had been bought by the trainer manufacturing company and would shortly be renamed the "Nikeplatz." The plan for the square also included building one of the biggest memorials in history: a Nike "swoosh," which was to reach up to 18 meters high. The artist duo chose Nike because the company was the ideal target for a fundamental criticism of capitalism and consumerism. The artists were also intending to draw attention to the commercialization of public spaces. Franco Mattes explains that: "We wanted to make the city a stage for a theater performance and to change the way the city is perceived by means of a hyper-real staged event." The duo also created the fictional Serbian artist Darko Maver, whose art consisted of placing brutally realistic models of victims of crimes in hotel rooms. They have also copied the Vatican's website and transferred it—with some minor alterations to the content—to the new domain vatican.org and distributed the computer virus "Biennale.psy" on the first day of the 49th Venice Biennale. For their performance *No Fun,* 2010, they confronted users of the Chatroulette platform with what appeared to be a suicide scene, and then documented the chat partners' reactions. Some participants reacted with shock; some reacted cynically; and others documented the hanging corpse by taking pictures of it with a camera. For *Stolen Pieces,* 1995–1997—an artwork that has only recently been exhibited due to the statute of limitations—the pair visited a number of museums and stole tiny pieces of well-known artworks by Joseph Beuys, Marcel Duchamp, Jeff Koons, and others, and then photographed themselves doing it. "Our idea was that if Marcel Duchamp said, 'The spectator makes the art,' we thought, well, then he can also change it," says Franco Mattes. "We saw *Stolen Pieces* as a natural consequence of collage and appropriation art, as the next step to [Robert] Rauschenberg's *Erased De Kooning Drawing,* and we thought that stealing a piece of a work would bring it back to life again, back to its original destabilizing power. We wanted to let it escape from the museum, which, to us, looked like nothing but a jail."

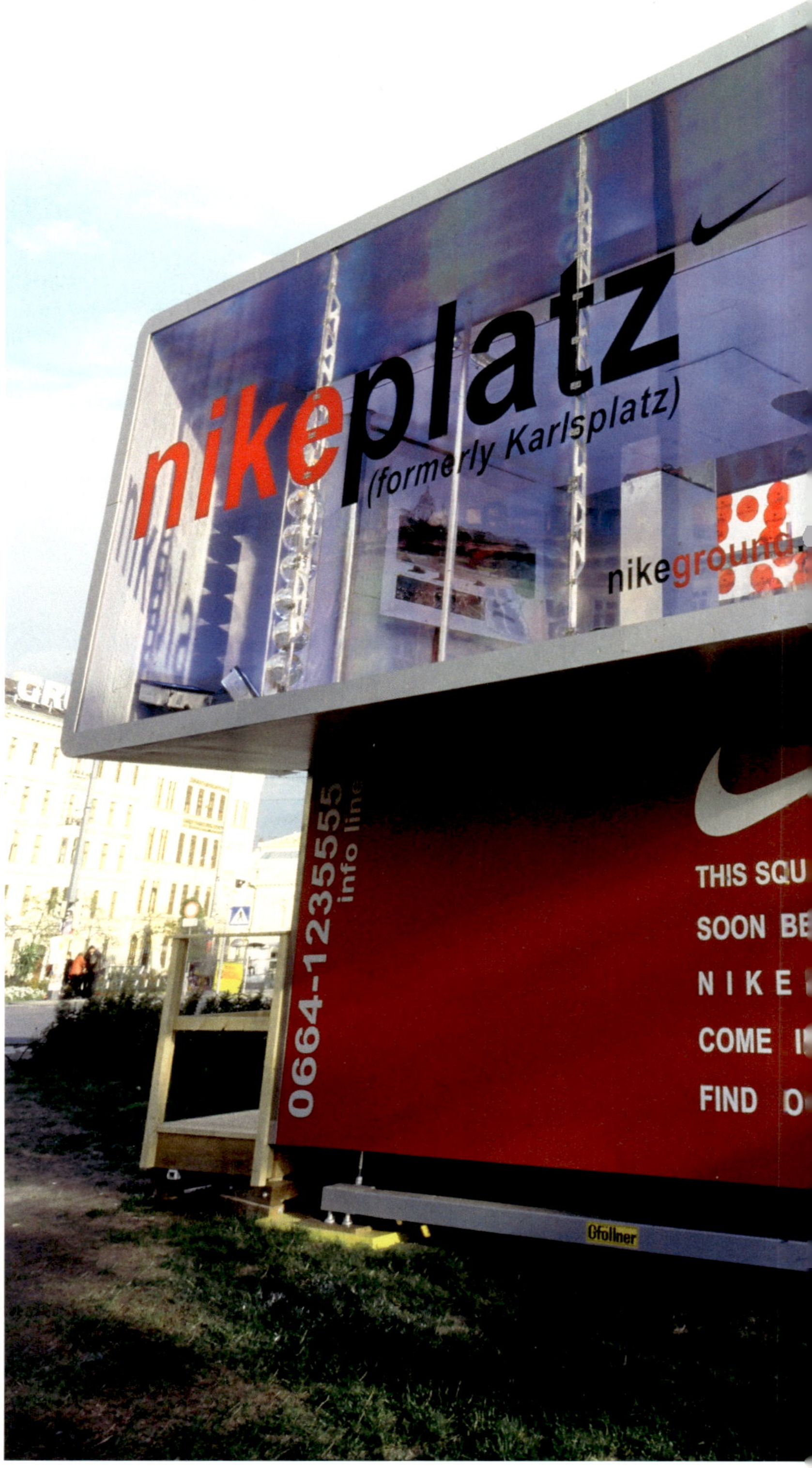

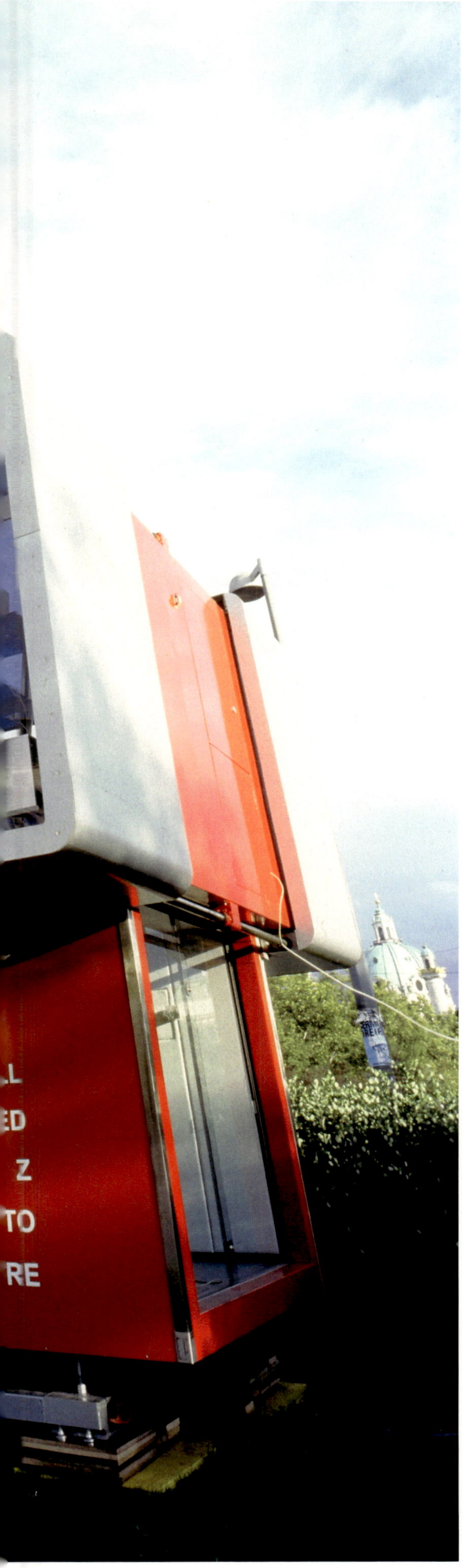

2

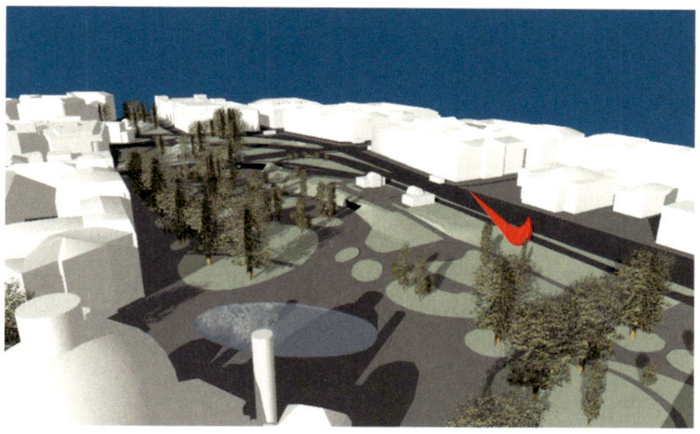

Nike Monument / Project for Nikeplatz (formerly Karlsplatz) / Vienna, Austria 2003

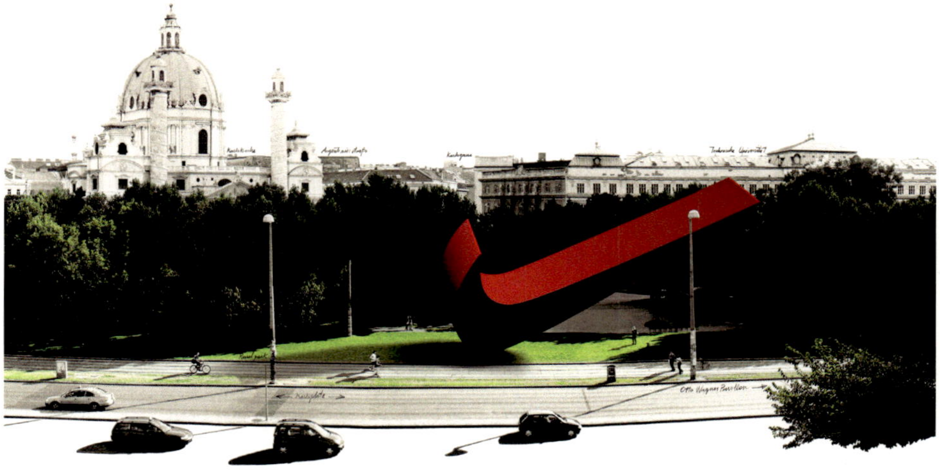

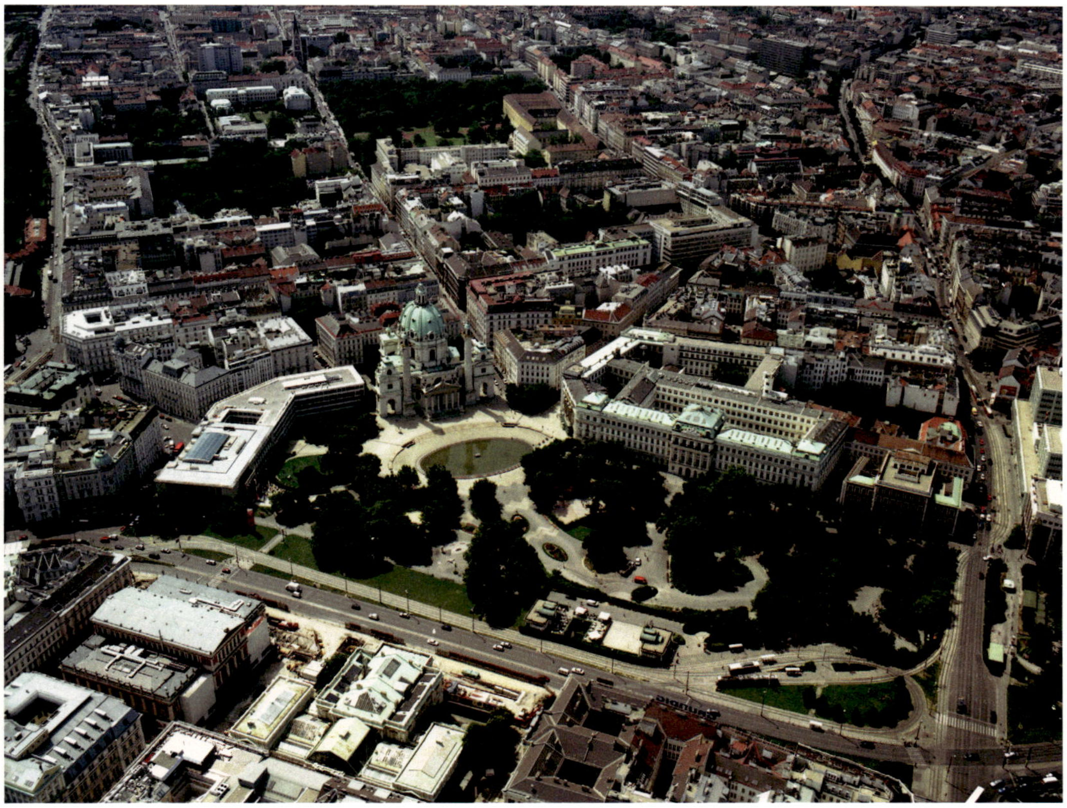

ELMGREEN & DRAGSET

The Danish/Norwegian artist duo Michael Elmgreen (*1961) from Copenhagen and Ingar Dragset (*1969) from Trondheim, have been working together since 1995. Their best-known works include *Prada Marfa,* 2005. Taking place in the middle of the Texan desert, the duo erected an exact facsimile of a Prada store—one whose doors, however, remained firmly shut. This replica, with its lighted window full of luxury, high-heeled shoes, became a monument to decay—and rapidly fell victim to vandalism by cowboys who found the installation disturbing. At the Venice Biennale, they and a number of invited artists transformed the Danish and Norwegian pavilion into two private collectors' villas, *The Collectors,* 2009, which were full of surprises—including rent boys drinking vodka and tonic in the living room, and a body in the swimming pool. This was the artists' way of addressing envy, curiosity, and voyeurism. The duo constantly surprise and astound their audience with architectonic sculptures and installations replete with theatrical overtones, such as the *Powerless Structures* series of works, in which the duo cryptically alter spaces in ways that draw attention to the cultural, social, and political functions of public spaces—for instance, a deserted gallery sunk into the ground in a park (*Powerless Structures, Fig. 45/Dug Down Gallery,* 1998) or a sex container (*Powerless Structures, Fig. 55/Cruising Pavilion,* 1998). "With a few of our projects, we knew from the start that they were likely to be best appreciated by a gay audience, but we felt that they would also be interesting to a wider audience," says Dragset. "In an expanded art-historical context, it is, perhaps, important to create something that connects with a certain definite identity, and that can create a certain increased understanding for that identity in wider social spheres." The duo forces the visitor into the claustrophobic atmosphere of a job center or a hospital, or transform art spaces into prisons or Kafkaesque waiting rooms, where one waits endlessly. A mobile home bursting out of the earth in a select Milan department store, *Short Cut,* 2003, is a symbol of mass tourism—the new colonization—and the nomadism of the artists, who travel around the world, making them campers in the name of art. For *Modern Moses,* 2006, they placed a plastic baby doll in front of a cash machine, and for the installation *When a Nation Falls in Love with Itself,* 2008, they mounted a mirror so that the Copenhagen Mermaid (a famous landmark) appeared to be looking into it—a reference to the country's narcissism. In Germany, the duo is best known for their monument to homosexual victims of National Socialist persecution. Elmgreen & Dragset use perfectly designed fictional settings to create incisive analyses—an entertaining kind of accusation that reaches a large number of people, and which fights the art establishment and its rigid laws with its own weapons.

1
Social Mobility Fig. 1
2005, "The Welfare Show," Bergen Kunsthall, Norway
2
Re-g(u)arding the Guards
2005, "The Welfare Show," Bergen Kunsthall, Norway

Courtesy Galleri Nicolai Wallner, Photos by Thor Brødreskift

3
Prada Marfa
2005, Courtesy Art Production Fund, New York, Ballroom Marfa, the artists Photo by James Evans
4
Powerless Structures, Fig. 45/ Dug Down Gallery
1998, Galleri i8, Reykjavik Art Museum, Iceland
Courtesy the artists, Photo by Borkur Arnarson
5 (next spread)
Short Cut
2003, Exhibited at Galleria Vittorio Emanuele, Milan, Italy/Museum of Contemporary Art, Chicago, USA/Art Basel, Basel, Switzerland
Courtesy Galleria Massimo de Carlo, Photo by Jens Ziehe

1

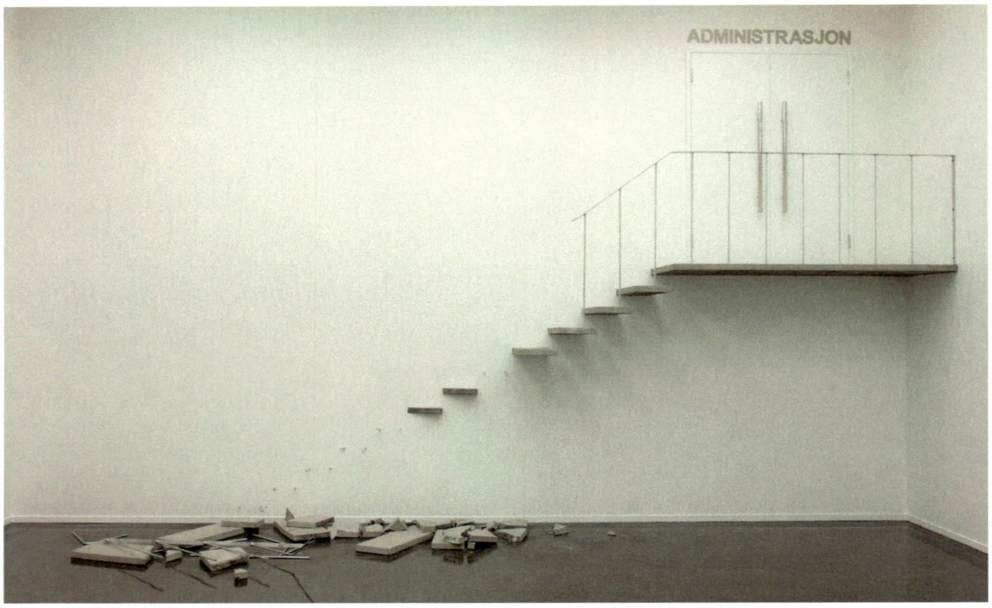

2

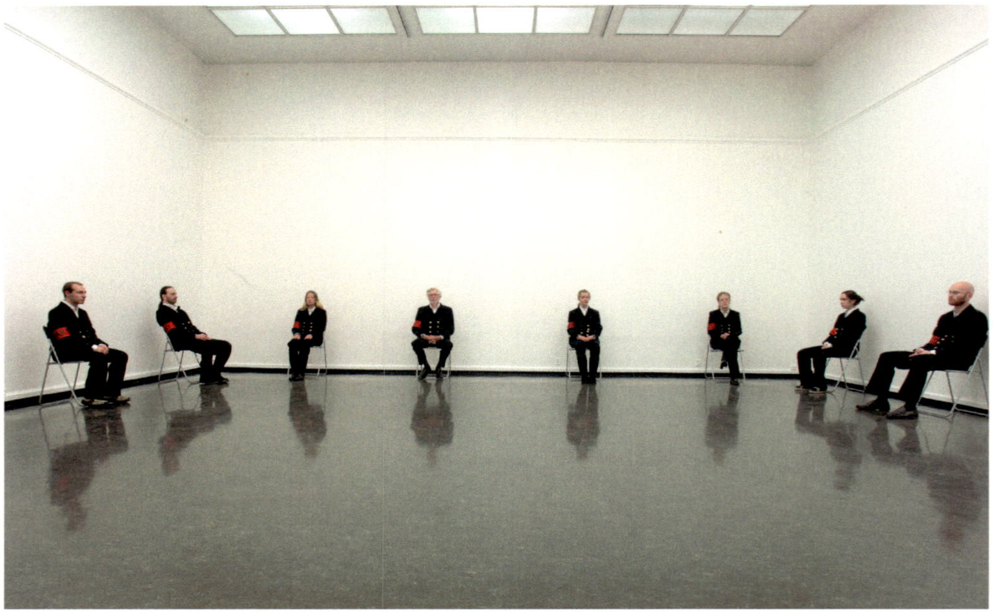

1–2
Since 1997 Michael Elmgreen and Ingar Dragset have been working on the series "Powerless Structures," which investigates the way in which prisons, social security offices, hospitals, museums, galleries, and parks act as a means of social control. "The Welfare Show" at the Serpentine Gallery extended the artists' investigation of the welfare model by inviting visitors to consider power structures such as economic disparity, health care, immigration, travel, prostitution, the police state, and the role that art plays in society. The traveling exhibition—also presented in Bergen, Vienna, and Toronto—was redesigned by the artists in response to the specific social conditions impacting each city.

3

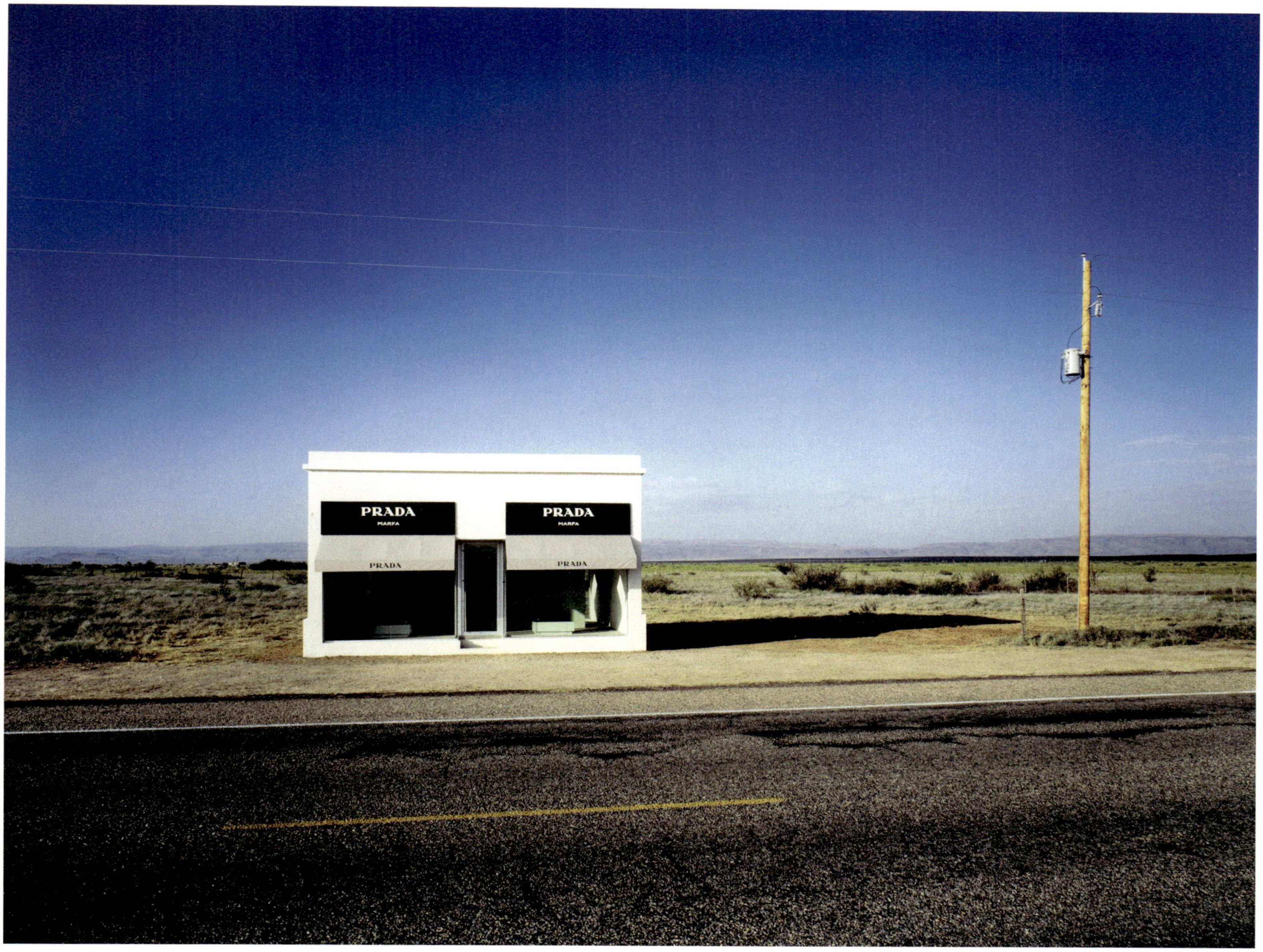

4

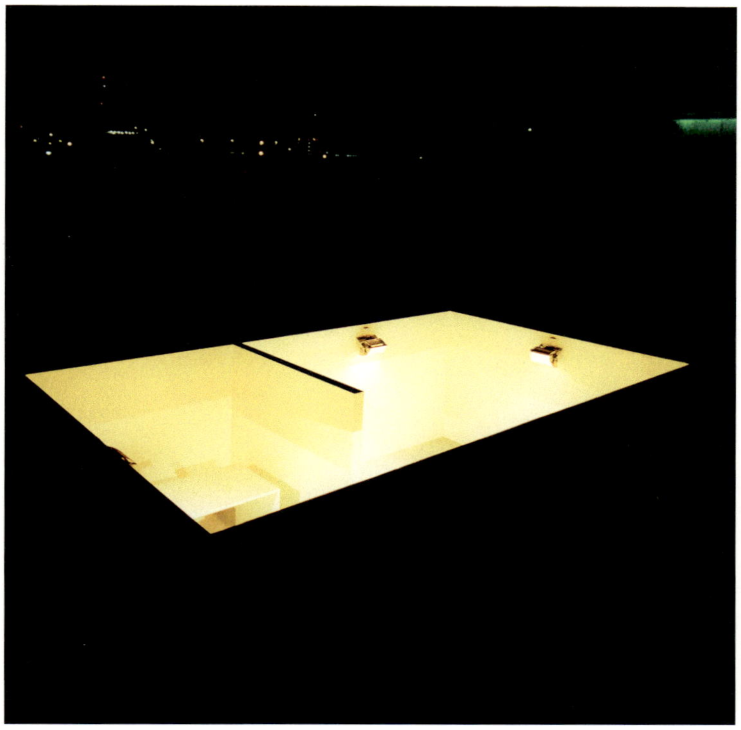

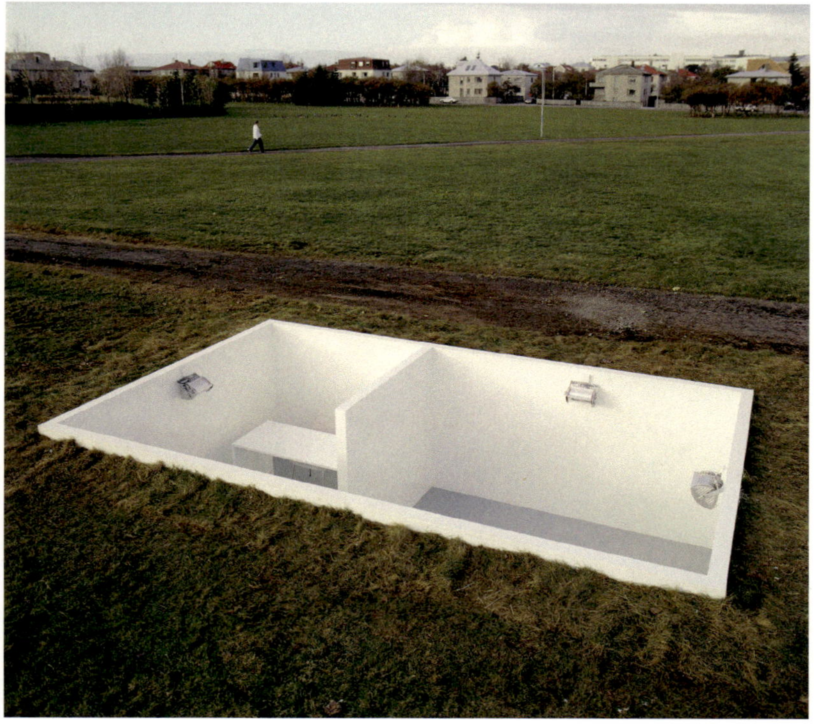

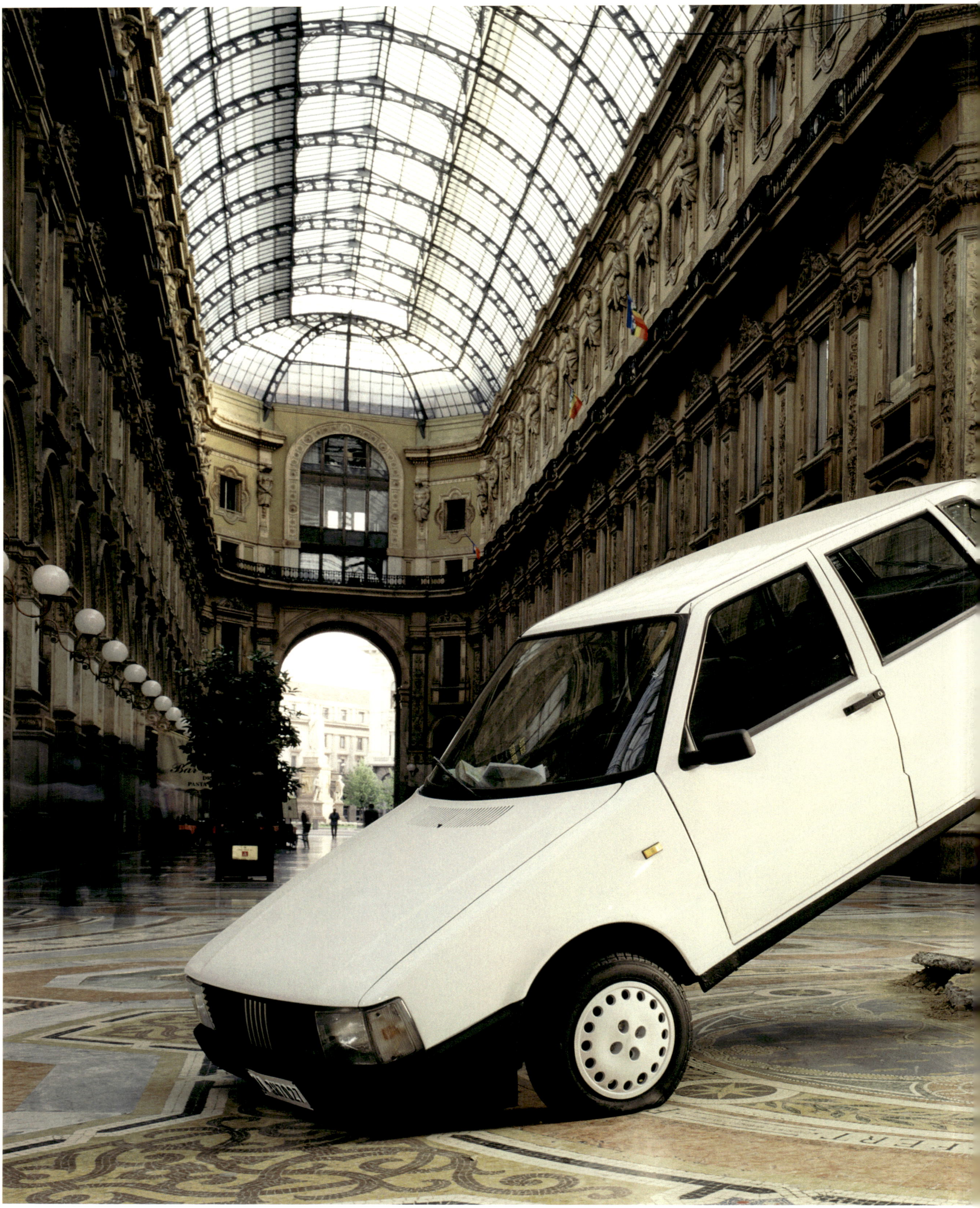

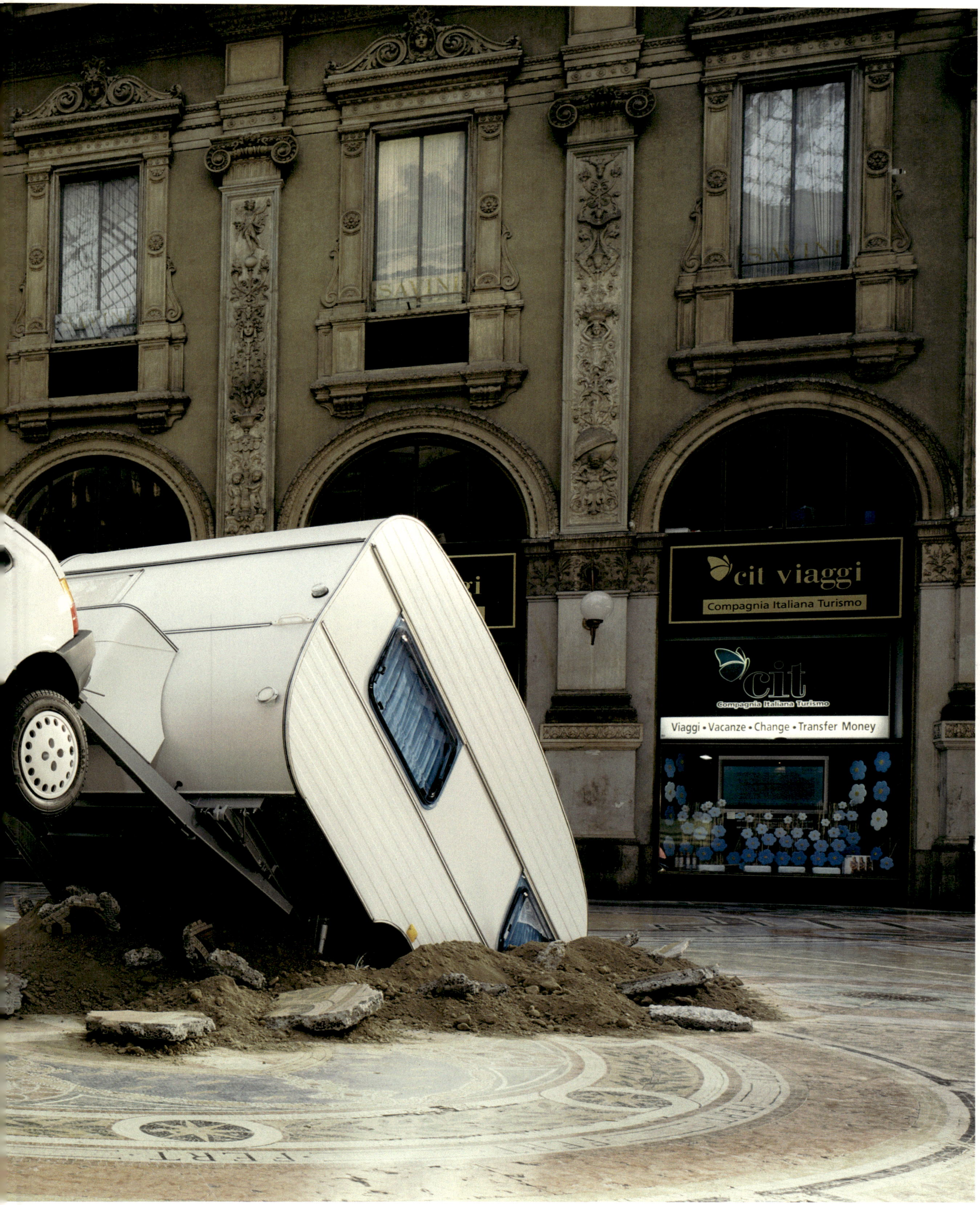
cit viaggi
Compagnia Italiana Turismo
cit
Compagnia Italiana Turismo
Viaggi • Vacanze • Change • Transfer Money

ALAIN BIEBER

I REVOLT, THEREFORE I AM

There has always been a note of rebellion in art. The genesis of modernism is a catalog of cultural radicals and militant rhetoric. In *The Futurist Manifesto,* published in 1909, Filippo Tommaso Marinetti wrote: "Set the library stacks on fire! Turn the canals in their course to flood the museum vaults! ... Oh, the joy of seeing the glorious old canvases bobbing adrift on those waters, discolored and shredded! Take up the picks and the hammers! Undermine the foundations of the venerable cities!" All the avant-garde movements emphasized destruction and revolution, believing that nothing new could be created without first clearing out the old. It took a lot of rage and time before art was able to free itself from the yoke of commissions from the church and political leaders and make itself independent of the power and influence of this or that interest group. For a long time, artists restricted themselves to imitating nature. It was not considered desirable to depict an attitude until the Enlightenment, when suddenly an artist's task was to depict reason in their work. The movements of art history—cubism, futurism, Dadaism, surrealism—became social movements whose achievements permeated and influenced the whole of our cultural lives.

ALBERT CAMUS

"ART AND REVOLT WILL DIE ONLY WITH THE LAST MAN."

But what about today? What is the meaning of art—especially political art—today? We have reached the end of art history; the end of "isms," and the end of ideologies. There are no clear enemies for artists to strive to free themselves of any more. There are also no longer any social movements that they might wish to belong to. The art scene is united by the influx of a diffuse sense of opposition. Just as the feeling of senselessness created by the First World War contributed to the birth of Dadaism, one has to first understand specific historical background to understand the artists creating politically aware art today. When Albert Camus accepted the Nobel Prize for Literature in 1957, he said: "Probably every generation sees itself as charged with remaking the world. Mine, however, knows that it will not remake the world. But its task is perhaps even greater, for it consists of keeping the world from destroying itself. Heir to a corrupt history, in which are mingled fallen revolutions, technology gone mad, dead gods, and worn out ideologies, where mediocre powers can destroy all, yet no longer know how to convince, where intelligence has debased itself to become the servant of hatred and oppression, this generation starting from its own negations has had to reestablish, both within and without, a little of that which constitutes the dignity of life and death."

We are all the children of Marx and Coca-Cola. We are also children of the anti-globalization movement, whose manifesto is Naomi Klein's *No Logo,* whose Blackspot sneakers and chic anti-logo come from Kalle Lasn's Adbusters movement. We have only just come through yet another global financial crisis, very nearly seeing the collapse of the financial markets and experiencing the negative consequences of unbridled liberalism. The post-September 11 world we live in has led to extensive universal surveillance and to a "war on terror" rhetoric that makes the fear of a nonspecific threat, stoked up ever more by politics and the mass media, omnipresent. New forms of injustice and inequality have arisen, warfare between cultures is at its height, and the power of religions and their hostility to other religions has never been so great. This is a world characterized by ecological defeatism; the threat of climate change is already endangering the just provision of social security and resources, and yet despite this the political decision-makers do not seem to concern themselves with the issue. Humanity is facing devastating natural catastrophes on a regular basis with an average of 80,000 people dying every year as a result of catastrophes such as the floods in Pakistan, earthquakes in Haiti and China, the tsunami off the coast of Thailand, and Hurricane Katrina in New Orleans. People have new opiates: desensitizing mass media, football stadiums, amusement parks, and a tourism industry that constantly promises us new adventures. The advertising industry has successfully appropriated the aesthetics of rebellion. Supposed freedom consists solely in freedom of consumer choice. Our relationship with politics has also changed. Political leaders have lost credibility all over the world and naturally this rejection of politics is in itself a political act. We have grown accustomed to politicians being either bureaucrats or celebrities, and marketing has taken control of politics. The media, once known as the fourth estate, has also lost credibility and power because severe pressure to save money has led to severe drops in quality. Investigative journalism is no longer conducted by the media, but by hackers like Julian Assange—or by artists.

In order to respond to all these shortcomings, artists take on a bewildering variety of roles. In their projects they act as journalists, urban planners, philosophers, architects, politicians, and environmental activists—as well as explainers, commentators, eyewitnesses, documentary makers, and voices of warning. In these projects, artists suggest alternatives while targeting social, political, and economic blights. They are often radical and asocial; they test the boundaries and provoke. In 1952, the situationist Asger Jorn stated that: "As for politics, I see it as a monstrous artwork, painted with blood and suffering, joys and lusts—and all this can hardly fail to inspire me." Political art is cultural resistance, a struggle against a cultural hegemony and a passionate cry. It has nothing to do with consensus and acceptance. It arises from the desire to think and act in a politically aware way; art becomes a continuation of politics by other means. A consequence of this is that there are as many different strategies among political artists as there are different motivations. In these artworks, one can see the influence of libertarian, anarchist, autonomous, ecological, feminist, communist, and humanist ideas. Many of these artists adopt guerrilla tactics: shock effects, deception strategies, disinformation, sabotage, deliberate misuses, and over-identification. They reveal certain borrowings from the philosophy of the Frankfurter Schule, the French existentialists, and the avant-garde movements of Dada, surrealism, Fluxus, the Vienna Activists, Provo, and the Situationist International. When student protests spread across most of Europe in the late 1960s, they radically changed the cultural landscape. The principal exponents of this counterculture were: Guy Debord and the Situationist International in France; the SPUR group, Joseph Beuys, and Wolf Vostell in Germany; Brion Gysin and William S. Burroughs in the United States. They fundamentally and permanently transformed the concept of art, wanting above all else to connect art with everyday life. Joseph Beuys, the artist, activist, and professor—and one of the founders of the German Green Party (Die Grünen) said: "As politics must be art, art that aspires to be politics cannot be content with depicting political issues in a directly critical way. It must provoke the higher forms of human organization." His "social sculpture" created a new, expanded vision of art, extending art to every area of life. *7000 Eichen—Stadtverwaldung statt Stadtverwaltung (7,000 Oaks—Municipal Afforestation Instead of Municipal Government),* his last large-scale installation presented at documenta 7 in 1982, involved planting oak trees in an artistic and ecological intervention that was intended to permanently transform the urban environment. Naturally, new artworks also borrow from human rights movements, subculture and pop culture, hippies, rockers, punks, the graffiti and skating scenes, and from the whole counterculture repertoire including culture jamming, agitprop, and guerrilla communication strategies. In this context, the boundaries between politically revolutionary and artistically avant-garde art are fluid. The Yes Men see p. 72 pass themselves off as representatives of international companies and carry out "identity correction" by means of preposterous declarations. The internet art duo Ubermorgen.com conducts "experiments in global communication spaces," infiltrating virtual companies and pinpointing their weaknesses. Artists like Marjetica Potrč see p. 139 and the WochenKlausur see p. 61 group come up with concrete suggestions on how to remedy sociopolitical shortcomings and attempt to implement these suggestions. They make art into an open wound in the social body.

— JOSEPH HEATH AND ANDREW POTTER —

"HERE'S A QUICK LIST OF THINGS THAT, IN THE PAST FIFTY YEARS, HAVE BEEN CONSIDERED EXTREMELY SUBVERSIVE: SMOKING, LONG HAIR FOR MEN, SHORT HAIR FOR WOMEN, BEARDS, MINISKIRTS, BIKINIS, HEROIN, JAZZ MUSIC, ROCK MUSIC, PUNK MUSIC, REGGAE MUSIC, RAP MUSIC, TATTOOS, UNDERARM HAIR, GRAFFITI, SURFING, SCOOTERS, PIERCINGS, SKINNY TIES, NOT WEARING A BRA, HOMOSEXUALITY, MARIJUANA, TORN CLOTHING, HAIR GEL, MOHICANS, AFROS, BIRTH CONTROL, POSTMODERNISM, PLAID TROUSERS, ORGANIC VEGETABLES, ARMY BOOTS, INTERRACIAL SEX. NOWADAYS, YOU CAN FIND EVERY ITEM ON THIS LIST IN A TYPICAL BRITNEY SPEARS VIDEO."

The dilemma is that what is alternative today will be mainstream tomorrow. In their book *The Rebel Sell,* Joseph Heath and Andrew Potter write: "Here's a quick list of things that, in the past fifty years, have been considered extremely subversive: smoking, long hair for men, short hair for women, beards, miniskirts, bikinis, heroin, jazz music, rock music, punk music, reggae music, rap music, tattoos, underarm hair, graffiti, surfing, scooters, piercings, skinny ties, not wearing a bra, homosexuality, marijuana, torn clothing, hair gel, mohicans, afros, birth control, postmodernism, plaid trousers, organic vegetables, army boots, interracial sex. Nowadays, you can find every item on this list in a typical Britney Spears video." Commercialization, media forces, and globalization will eventually bring alternative value systems—critical art, youth movements, or pop culture—into the cultural mainstream and incorporate them into the aesthetic of the everyday. This is how subcultures and countercultures become global pop phenomena. Their revolutionary potential is spent on creating new products, or on giving new life to the old industries. For every successful anti-attitude, there will be a business that knows how to make a profit out of it. Once art achieved freedom and autonomy, the increasingly individual and personal art that was the result led to the cult of the author and the image of the artistic genius—thereby directly contributing to the monetary valuation of art. The rebellious antiheroes were initially hailed and then eventually co-opted, exploited, converted into cash, and annihilated. In 2001, the WochenKlausur group wrote: "Even the most subversive forms of actionism and Neo-Dada were co-opted, until ultimately all that was left were objects. These relics from art happenings and photographs and sketches became rarefied fetishes to be traded. For most people of the time—and indeed this is still true today—art is about artwork. It has to be something that they can see, touch, and grasp because otherwise it cannot be sold, collected, or preserved." As ever, political art often does not go beyond self-presentation and zeitgeist phenomena but merely "the box office hits" of art history. For many young artists, art is the new rock and roll. Simply to want to be an artist and to live the life of an artist is seen as an act of rebellion against conventional society. Artists still like to style themselves as rebels, and gallerists use the "revolutionary" label to market their works because collectors also like to have a little piece of revolutionary chic to hang on their living room walls. Businesspeople are proud of possessing particularly provocative artworks that make them look both energetic and daring. The art historian Beat Wyss wrote: "We are witnesses of the conversion of the republican structures of the bourgeois state into a new absolutism of the superrich, who control art as the Medici once did. All of us, including the politicians, are obsequious toadies of an international art cartel." Because of this, the revolutionary attitude is often debased into a marketing trick; the more subversive an artist claims to be and the more he insults the art world's bourgeoisie, the more that bourgeoisie takes him to heart. Banksy and Maurizio Cattelan see p. 96 are real experts at this. This is why most art still culminates in what artist Artur Żmijewski see p. 206 describes as "an overproduction of surplus objects," or art that is primarily a luxury item for a decadent market. The Polish artist Grzegorz Kowalski is more drastic, describing the majority of art as "art pollution."

TANIA BRUGUERA

"POLITICAL ART HAS DOUBTS, NOT CERTAINTIES; IT HAS INTENTIONS, NOT PROGRAMS; IT SHARES WITH THOSE WHO FIND IT RATHER THAN IMPOSING ON THEM; IT IS DEFINED WHILE IT IS DONE; IT IS AN EXPERIENCE, NOT AN IMAGE; IT IS SOMETHING ENTERING THE FIELD OF EMOTIONS, SOMETHING THAT IS MORE COMPLEX THAN A UNIT OF THOUGHT. POLITICAL ART IS THE ART THAT IS CREATED WHEN IT IS UNFASHIONABLE AND WHEN IT IS UNCOMFORTABLE—LEGALLY UNCOMFORTABLE, CIVICALLY UNCOMFORTABLE, HUMANELY UNCOMFORTABLE."

So, what meaning does art—political art in particular—still retain? Often, simply exhibiting an opposing position is sufficient to undermine the norm. A loud laugh or a particularly asocial or absurd act is frequently enough to defy the establishment. The author Franz Xaver Kroetz said: "Bursting boundaries, not discovering boundaries, is the most interesting thing in life. Taboos are there to bring people down, to keep them small. The point is to get hold of these taboos and explode them." Some artists only probe the wound, some ask the questions that no one else is asking, and some offer concrete solutions. The difference from the political art of the past is that art increasingly refuses to produce decorative ornaments. Now art wants to infect the system like a virus, to damage it, or to change it. The intention is to *change* the infected system, to heal it; this is art setting out to change reality. However, within democratic systems the artists are behaving like parasites; they know that they cannot kill the host, but they still passionately attack the organism in order to introduce a little chaos into its orderly existence. Put another way, the artists have taken on the role of the court jester; they are free to do absolutely anything except dethrone the king. The artists have accepted that they cannot escape the capitalist system, so they operate against the system from within with irony and subversion. They are artists who are aware that they are part of the whole entertainment machinery and of the considerable entertainment value of their own art. Of course, this is not yet true for countries such as China, Russia, North Korea, Iran, or Saudi Arabia; in non-democratic societies, art is still the least dangerous avenue for free expression. But in western democracies, unambiguous political art that makes an unambiguous, partisan statements is considered naive. Artists no longer promote a political agenda. Moralizing and finger-pointing is taboo. In spite of this, the depoliticizing and fragmenting of society has led to the politicizing of artistic praxis; critical, interventionist, and investigative art has become almost a benchmark of quality for young artists. The artist Tania Bruguera has said that: "Political art has doubts, not certainties; it has intentions, not programs; it shares with those who find it rather than imposing on them; it is defined while it is done; it is an experience, not an image; it is something entering the field of emotions, something that is more complex than a unit of thought. Political art is the art that is created when it is unfashionable and when it is uncomfortable—legally uncomfortable, civically uncomfortable, humanely uncomfortable."

Uncomfortable art is unpopular—and sometimes punishable. The dividing line between such art and radical leftist terrorism is sometimes very thin, but we should not forget that a key defining characteristic of political art is that it deals only in nonviolent and symbolic "terror." As Greenpeace's successes go to show, nonviolent interventions featuring powerful images can be highly effective in getting a message across; the more bold, striking, and aggressive they are, the more likely such campaigns are to appear in the media and gain more publicity for the cause. The current global communication network and the access to media allow anyone to publicize themselves. Blogs, social networks, and photo and video-sharing sites allow powerfully symbolic campaigns—or small temporary interventions—to echo around the world and find sympathizers. This democratization and "amateurization" of information and the tools of production has robbed states, the media, and industries of power and authority. It has also allowed the formation of numerous temporary autonomous zones, very few of which really reflect the new dependencies that already loom behind the new achievements. The big businesses of the future are companies like Google, Apple, and Facebook. These businesses, who use their online services to construct closed systems, could be compared with states—complete with a population, constitution, and warfare. This also means that these companies will be the bogeymen of the future. Just as previous artists have created art to expose the exploitative practices of sweatshops, artists like Aram Bartholl, Evan Roth, and Ubermorgen.com are now criticizing the territoriality and excessive collection of data practiced by large online companies.

Then there are the two factors absolutely critical to political art: the context of the artistic method and its consequences. The politics is in the consequences that the artwork incurs. Marcel Duchamp once remarked that: "All in all, the creative act is not performed by the artist alone; the spectator brings the work in contact with the external world by deciphering and interpreting its inner qualifications and thus adds his contribution to the creative act." Political artists, then, need an excellent knowledge of the psychology of their audience and a clear sense of the specific power balance they are working within. According to Diedrich Diederichsen, the most important question for artists to ask themselves is what art should actually offer to its audience in the first place: "Which information or sensations—traumatic, boring, or agitating—are going to have consequences for my life? What event in my everyday life, with the consequences attached to it, do I want to pick out of the chain of causes and effects?" In China, Russia, or in the countries of South America, this question is easier to answer; art in these countries still has the privilege of drawing attention to social injustices without incurring the same risks as actual political action. In comparison to journalists and activists, few artists end up in prison. Their games are often even tolerated by the powerful—and perhaps even feed the system. Does this mean that the good intentions of political art only do harm? "This is art that performs functionally and obeys the ever-increasing imperative to make itself useful and useable by symbolically compensating for social shortcomings," says the artist and author Hans-Christian Dany. "This designated art fills the vacuums that have developed and stabilizes the structure. The existing power balance and smooth transaction of business are unaffected." The artist becomes merely "an actor in a democratic theater of delusion." So what can be done about this? Should artists "go on strike," as Gustav Metzger and Stewart Home have done?

Is a total refusal to produce art the only way out of this dilemma? Has art—political art in particular—lost its meaning? Nothing could be further from the truth. In spite of all doubts and impediments, artists are inspired to create politically motivated art every day because of a combination of nostalgia and yearning; nostalgia for revolutionary movements that they never experienced themselves, but which continue to be idealized by the media, as well as a yearning to take part in such movements. There is a wish to at least belong to something; it is a question of giving meaning to existence, of looking life in the face and defiantly shouting "Hurray, we're still alive!" Art gives artists something that they can be sure of; it embodies a transcendental and spiritual dimension in which they can confront the emptiness, loneliness, and boredom of the everyday. The desire for authenticity and intensity has never gone away; artists are again demanding "a higher quality of passion" (Guy Debord) and trying to make exceptional moments the new normality. Graffiti art, for instance, is inseparable from the thrill and adrenalin kick that the artist feels at three o'clock in the morning on a roof and there is the warm sense of community, which artists engaged in collective projects feel. Rejection is also a part of identity. People define themselves by exclusion: I am everything that you are not; I rebel, therefore I am. The rebellious gesture, the rejection of authority and of power structures—and of subtle domination—is also romantic. All of these artists are really romantics, but that only goes to prove that having dreams and making wishes is once again acceptable. Albert Camus said that: "In every rebellion is to be found the metaphysical demand for unity, the impossibility of capturing it, and the construction of a substitute universe. This also defines art. The demands of rebellion are really aesthetic demands." Contemporary political artists are not merely reflecting the present age; they are conceiving the future. Because those who lack the power to create real changes can still conceive such social utopias—and utopias have always been the hallmark of avant-garde art.

"IN EVERY REBELLION IS TO BE FOUND THE METAPHYSICAL DEMAND FOR UNITY, THE IMPOSSIBILITY OF CAPTURING IT, AND THE CONSTRUCTION OF A SUBSTITUTE UNIVERSE. THIS ALSO DEFINES ART. THE DEMANDS OF REBELLION ARE REALLY AESTHETIC DEMANDS."

THE HUMAN ELEMENT

TABLE OF CONTENTS

INTRODUCTION

Politically motivated art is never l'art pour l'art, art for art's sake. This is particularly true of the artists featured here. They produce works that are specifically designed to help bring about change in prevailing social, political, or cultural circumstances. Since these artists aim to tackle socio-political shortcomings, they want their art and campaigns to show how art can influence reality. They want their forward-looking projects to do more than generate interest in political issues; they want them to help people discover what exactly is involved and to encourage direct (collective) action. Artists like Germany's Hermann Josef Hack [see p. 82], who sets up his World Climate Refugee Camp in the middle of public spaces, believe that art is the only tool capable of kick-starting society's development potential, which has been crippled by economic and political interests. What sets these artists apart from activists is that their politically motivated work is rarely linked to specific party interests. The art campaigns and their messages are often mundane, which actually makes them more effective. Roland Ross [see p. 86], for example, spent a year repairing broken things that he found in public spaces. Some campaigns move people to imitate them, like Aram Bartholl's [see p. 80] *Dead Drops*, which inspired people all over the world to help build an offline data network.

Much of the artwork shown here would not have been possible without accidental participants. As with Néle Azevedo's [see p. 83] ephemeral monuments, these campaigns often specifically aim to create a shared experience among the public. Artists like Nasan Tur [see p. 68] encourage visitors to their exhibitions to do things they would never have contemplated doing otherwise. Some of the artists work in groups that change their line-up depending on the campaign, or that admit temporary members for specific projects. Guerilla art campaigns, of the kind Andy Bichlbaum from The Yes Men [see p. 72] embarked on when he impersonated a company spokesman, are also an important method of achieving specific goals. But even simple methods can accomplish a lot. The U.S. group Conflict Kitchen [see p. 58] brings Americans into contact with foreign cultures—that they are often only familiar with from the news—by serving up traditional food and entertainment from the countries the U.S. is at war with. Artists like Swoon [see p. 90] and those in the group Superflex [see p. 76] are about helping people help themselves, while also criticizing the status quo. At their heart, almost all of the works are imbued with a sense of the hope that personal commitment will inevitably make things better. That said, a project may well end up showing that some people don't actually need any help—which was exactly what the Doublethink Project [see p. 60] did. It involved a series of public campaigns that gained valuable insight into human behavior by finding that when offered things like deck chairs for free, passers-by would often refuse them.

CONFLICT KITCHEN

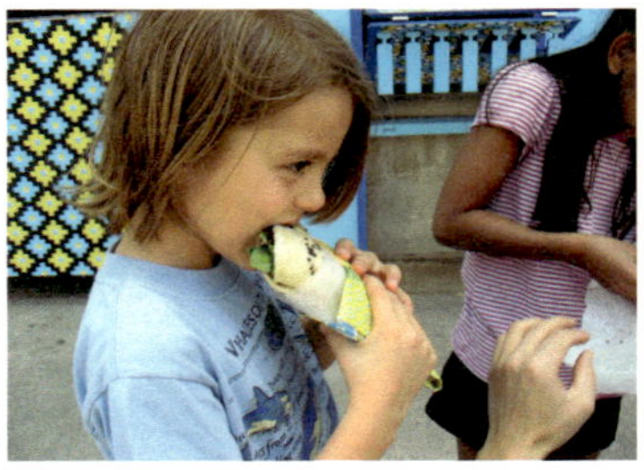

Conflict Kitchen
2010, Pittsburgh, USA

Cookery is one of humanity's oldest cultural techniques; eating connects people. In primitive societies, one's relatives were the people who one ate with daily, and even today, family life largely takes place around the dinner table. In May 2010, in the American city of Pittsburgh, the artists John Peña, Jon Rubin, and Dawn Weleski embarked on a snack bar art project, *Conflict Kitchen*—a takeout restaurant selling only foods from countries with which the U.S. government is presently at war. The project kicked off with the Kubideh—an Iranian sandwich consisting of spicy meat in a freshly baked barbari flatbread with onions, mint, and basil. The packaging was printed with texts by the Iranian community on themes ranging from poetry to politics. The artists explain that: "It is easy to forget that behind all of the government conflicts there are people and a culture. When this personal connection is lost, things become dangerous. *Conflict Kitchen* creates a public forum and space for discussions that might not normally take place, mediated by food." Alongside this snack bar, the trio also organized the showing of Iranian feature films, a talk show on Iran, and concerts of Iranian music. The existing snack bar is shortly to be followed by "Bolani Pazi"—a snack bar offering speciality Afghan foods. There is also no shortage of potential villains. A *Conflict Kitchen* devoted to North Korea and Venezuela, and discussion of related issues is already being planned.

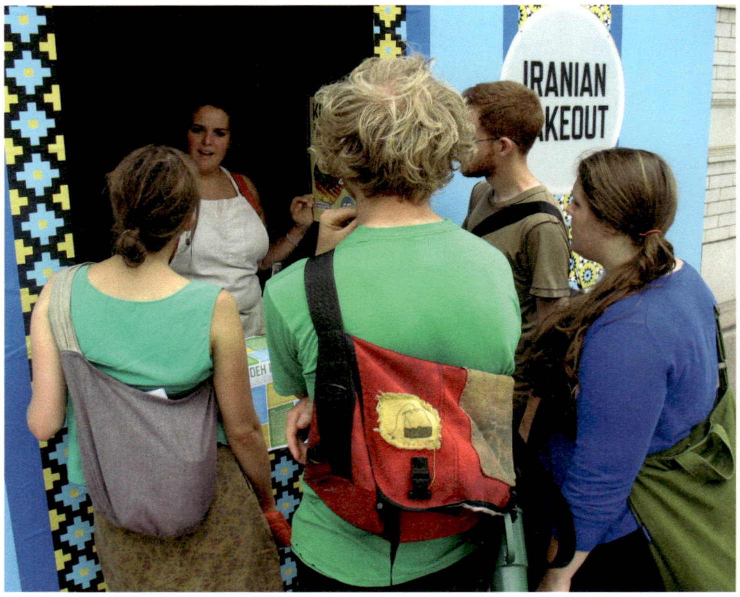

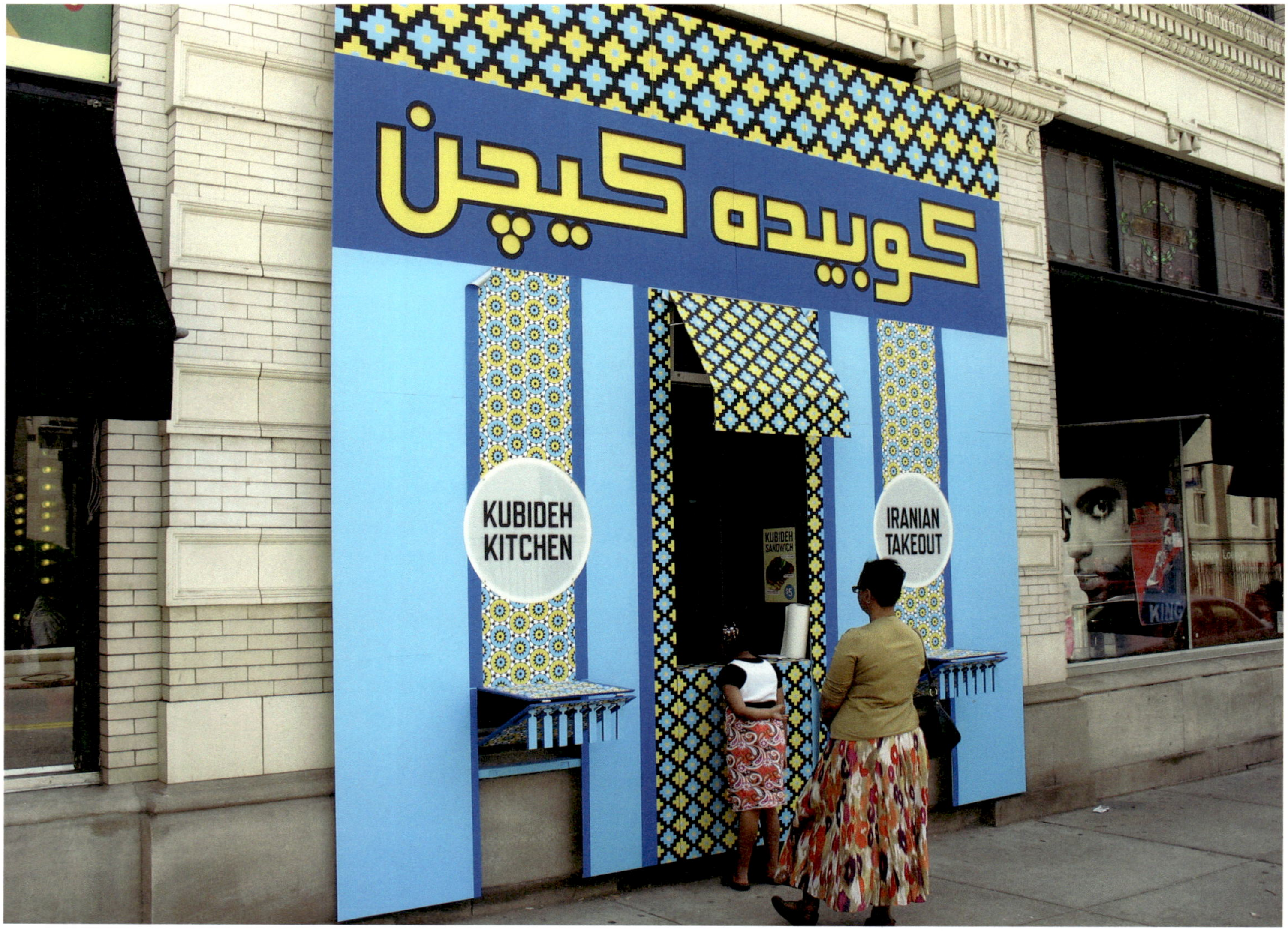

HWANG KIM

The cultural and political restrictions in North Korea are the themes of a well-known artwork by the South Korean artist and designer Hwang Kim (* 1980), who studied in Seoul at Hongik University, and in London at the Royal College of Art. *Pizzas for the People,* 2009, addresses the rigid system of cultural isolation in his homeland. In order to ensure that no western influences reach North Korea, the media is strictly controlled, shortwave radios are banned, and television receivers are encrypted. Only the three official television channels are permitted viewing for citizens. For this reason, the opening of the first original Italian pizza restaurant in North Korea received considerable attention. Two chefs were even sent specially to Rome and Naples for training, and original Italian ingredients were flown in to ensure the authenticity of the Italian dishes. According to Hwang Kim, however, this supposed milestone in the country's opening up to the western world had no impact on the vast majority of the country's terribly impoverished population. "Paradoxically, with the support of pizza-loving leader Kim Jong-il, the first-ever pizzeria was recently opened to provide an authentic Italian experience for a minority of wealthy political elite. With the aim of challenging current cultural obstacles in North Korea, I have contacted a number of Chinese smugglers in China to distribute illegal propaganda over the border to North Korea—through using the popular DVD format, as DVD players are widely found in North Korean homes." The DVDs show a video recorded in a simple kitchen. In it, the artist himself demonstrates how to make a pizza—possibly in a conscious imitation of the numerous television chefs that cover the world's screens every day, bringing dishes from all over the world into our living rooms. Step by step, the artist prepares a pizza with a shredded potato base in a pan on the stove. In North Korea, potatoes are vital to the staple diet of the population at large. The famines suffered by the population of this isolationist country during the 1990s were ended by expanding the areas under cultivation for potato growing. By using such a common ingredient of North Korean cooking as the base for the Italian national dish, the artist both emphasizes the difference between the original pizza recipe, and the kind of pizza any North Korean can prepare for themselves; in this way, it demonstrates the mixing of two different cultures. The smuggling of DVDs is a way of undermining the state, which does not permit the natural blending of cultures. Hwang Kim says that: "*Pizzas for the People* is a series of designed insertions that explore how design can contribute to and impact on a social and cultural level, subtly challenging an ideological status quo."

Pizzas for the People
North Korea, 2010

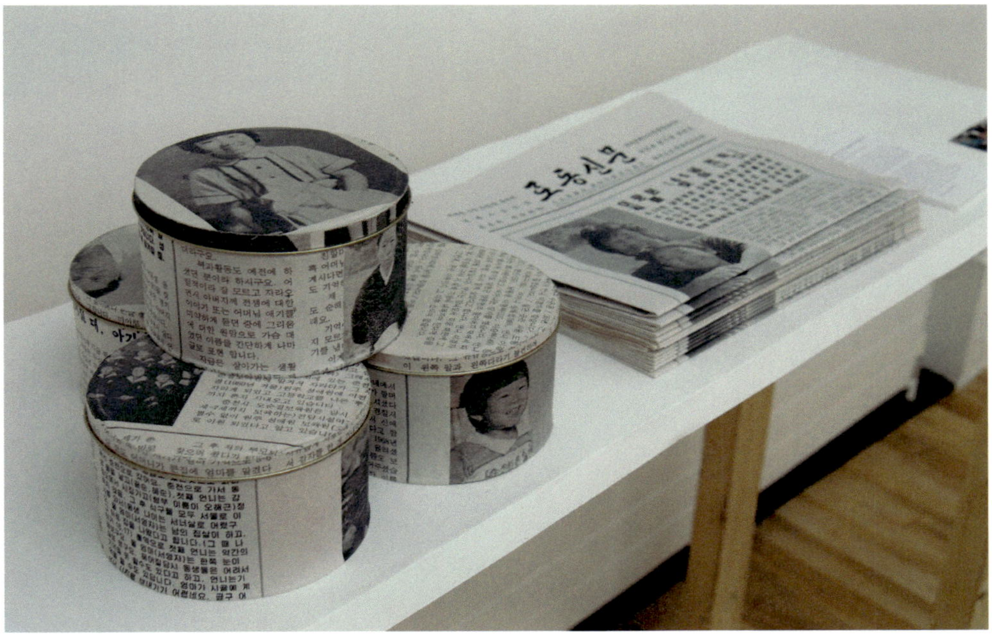

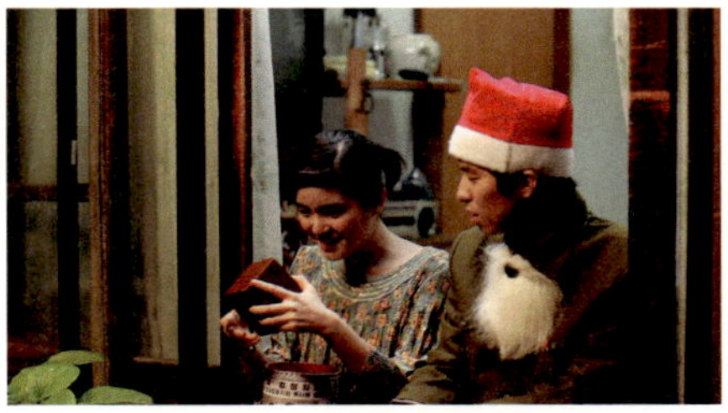

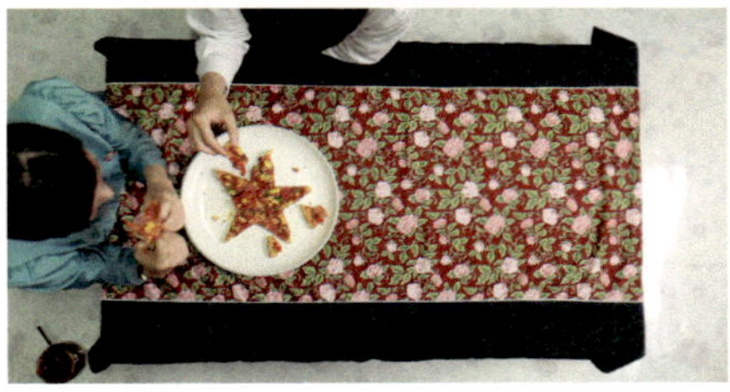

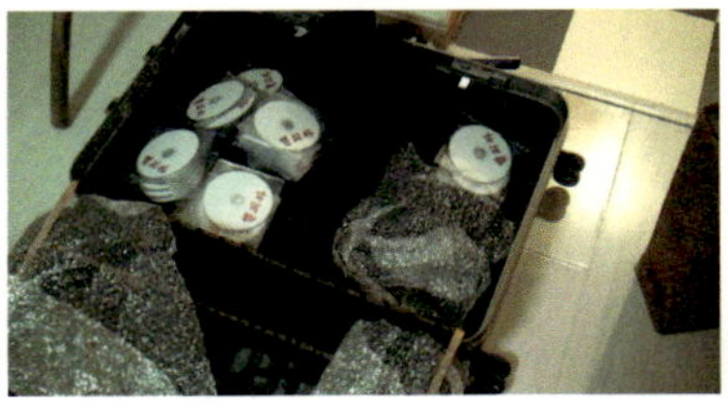

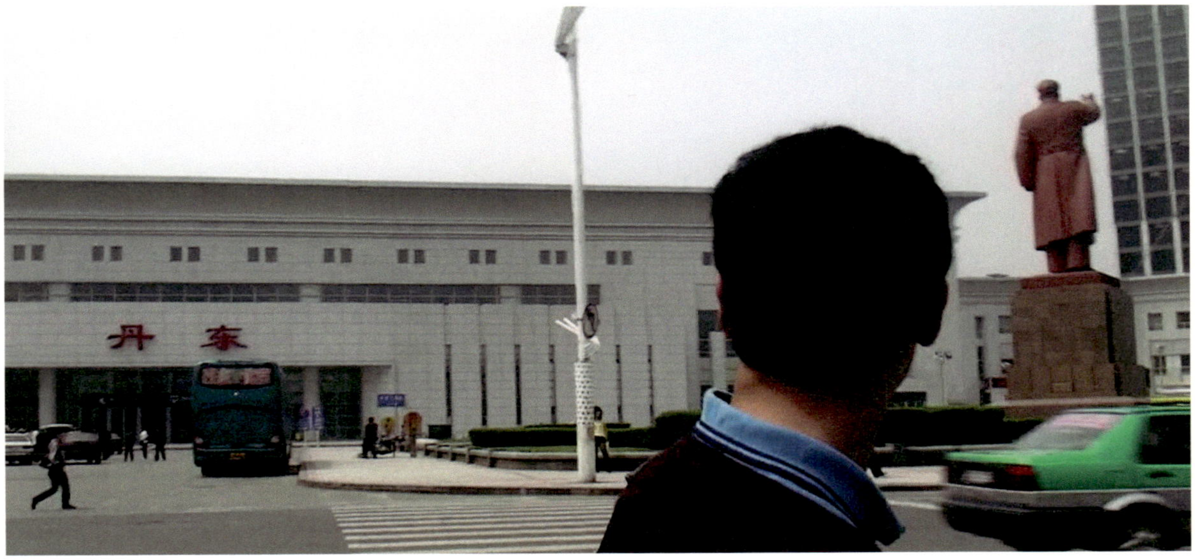

THE DOUBLETHINK PROJECT

1

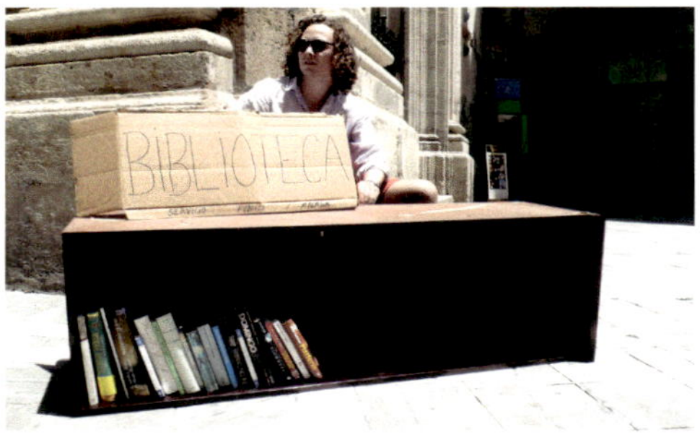

1
Library
2009, Malaga, Spain
2
Passive/Active
2009, London, U.K.
3
Hyde Park
2009, London, U.K.

London-based Christian N. Halsted and Jakob Ohrt, alias The Doublethink Project, set up experiments in public spaces. These open-ended projects examine the behavior of passersby, and are also investigations into the practicalities of art. Christian N. Halsted explains that: "Doublethink's intention is to gather different viewpoints of contemporary life within the realms of conceptual art, social science, and alternative and investigational approaches to cultural abstractions." The idea behind *Passive/ Active,* 2009, was to give back something to people walking by. The duo hung a mirror in front of a hairdresser's shop, hung a deodorant in front of a fitness center, and attached a water bottle to a tree beside a jogging track in a park. After observing people ignoring their interventions, for the second, more active part of the project, the duo read to people waiting in a queue from a book, handed out ice cream, and offered hand cream to people. "In spite of these efforts, we came to realize that neither the passive nor active interferences changed anything for passersby," was their assessment after the project. *The Library,* 2009, which offered a free public street library to people in Spain, did not last long either. "We ventured off to Malaga to start a public library and to hire one of the many unemployed people as a librarian. We quickly came to realize the actual problem in Spain wasn't a lack of job possibilities, but weather conditions that made it impossible to work. Nobody wanted to work for us (including ourselves), and nobody cared about our library. It was simply too hot." The duo have also offered free chairs in Hyde Park in London—where people are usually charged to sit in deck chairs—and provided a free information point where they were available to help passersby with all their questions and problems. "In our humble opinion, this is what modern public service is all about. We set up a free information service in one of the busiest areas of London, and tried to give people whatever they wanted." The accompanying video documentary shows that hardly anyone wanted to be helped at all.

2

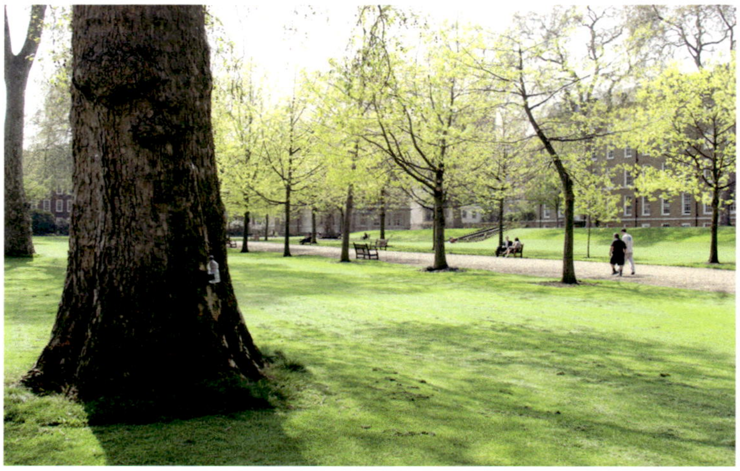

3

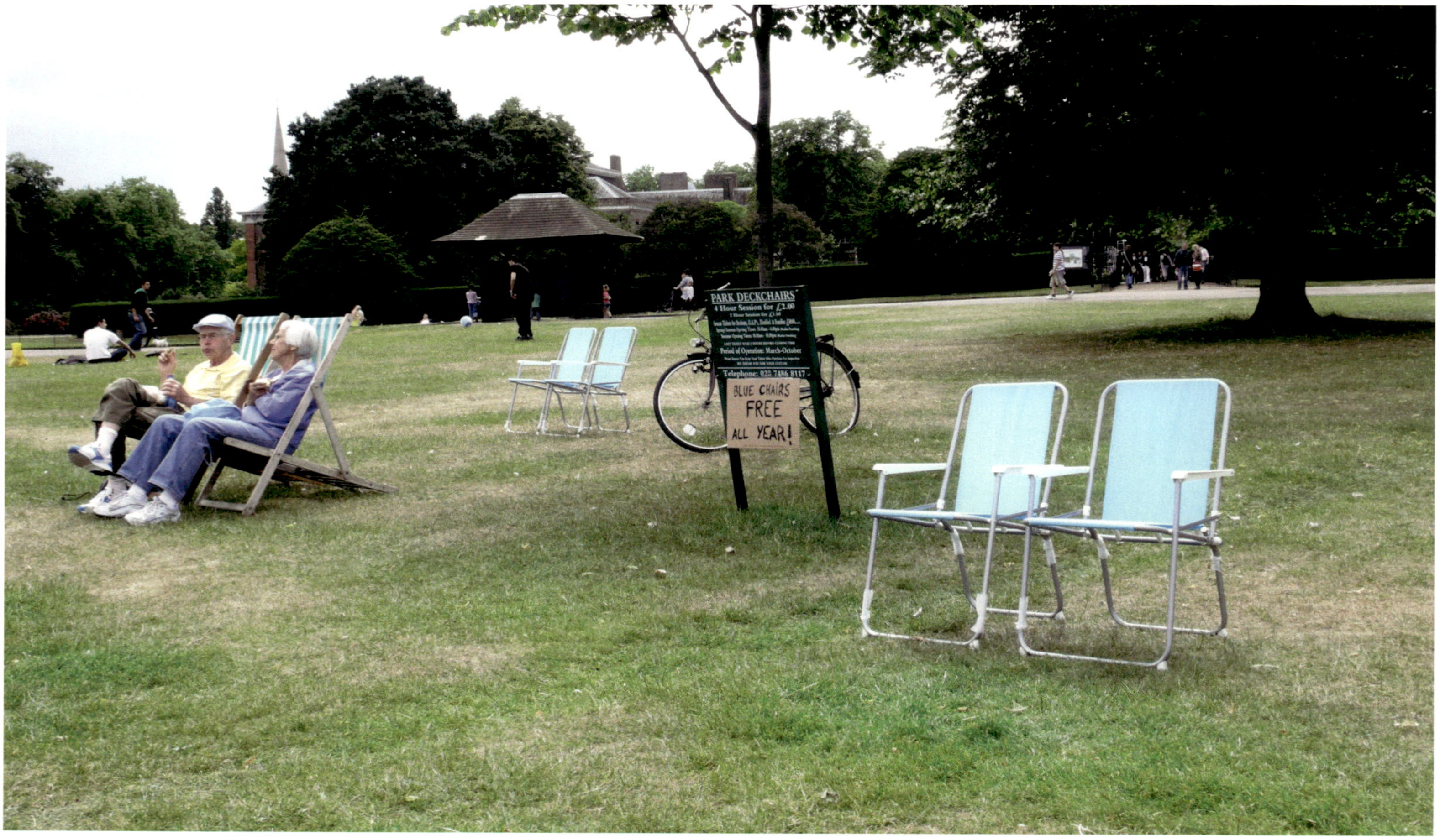

WOCHENKLAUSUR

"IF WE SUCCEED IN GAINING ACCEPTANCE FOR AN ART THAT INCLUDES OPPORTUNITIES FOR ACTION, IT WILL OVERTURN THE PRESENTLY ACCEPTED DEFINITION OF ART"

The Austrian WochenKlausur group, founded by artist and cultural scientist Wolfgang Zinggl (* 1954) who is the current Kultur-und Minderheitensprecher, or cultural and minorities spokesperson, for the Green Party, has been staging social interventions since 1993. The method is always the same: the group (often assisted in specific projects by other activists) is invited by an art institution to develop specific proposals to reverse social problems, which it then implements in collaboration with local groups. The host institution finances the project, and its exhibition rooms serve as studio and office. In this way, the group has created a medical service for the homeless, redecorated classrooms, founded a hostel for women with drug problems, helped foreign nationals to travel legally to Austria, and allowed the long-term unemployed to make decisions about their own "single euro jobs." For their experiment *Voting Systems,* 2002, the WochenKlausur group staged a fictional vote in Sweden in which the population was allowed to vote against as well as for a party. For their *Weitsichtig Wirtschaften* project in 2007 (Social Economy—a Discourse in Progress) Austrian and international economic experts were asked to contribute a text on social economies. And for *Interkulturelle Schnittmengen* (Intercultural Intersections), 2009, interest groups were brought together in a residential district of Vienna—independent of gender, heritage, religion, or age—to work on a new project, such as planting for public spaces. What at first glance looks like a mobile task force of social workers is actually an oblique artistic endeavor. WochenKlausur states that: "WochenKlausur's intentions are political in more ways than one. On the one hand, every project makes a small concrete contribution to changing society. On the other hand, all these projects prove that it is possible for art to take a role in real events. If we succeed in gaining acceptance for an art that includes opportunities for action, it will overturn the presently accepted definition of art." WochenKlausur does not criticize, provoke, or moralize. It gets to work and takes direct action—turning art into a creative asset to meet problems that cannot be solved by conventional means.

1
City Development
2010, Sligo, Ireland

2
Intercultural Intersection
2009, Vienna, Austria

1

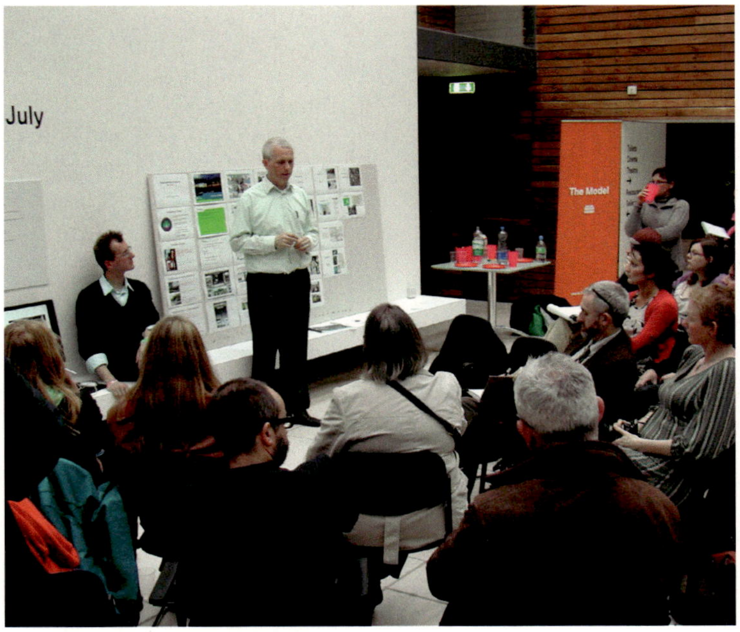

2

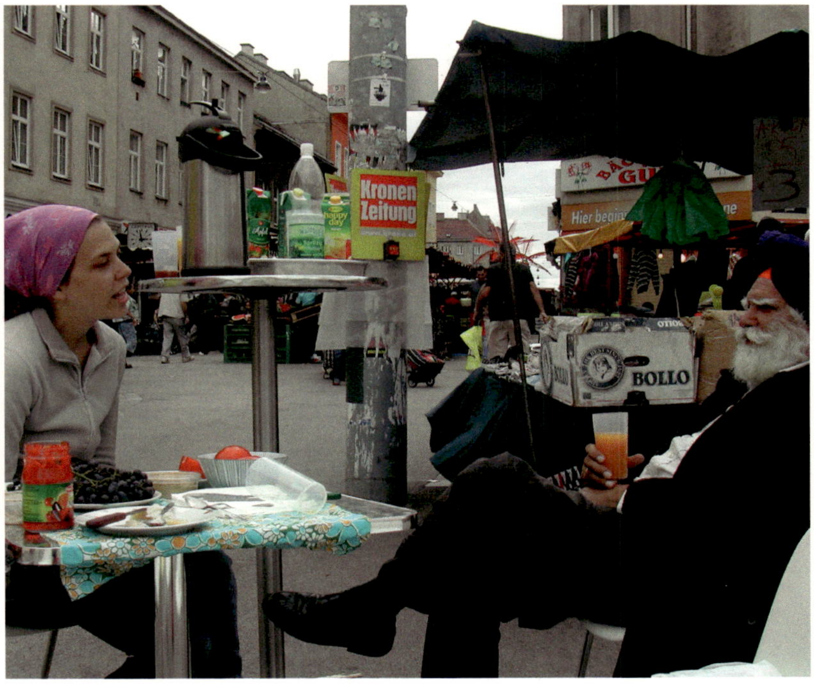

FROM THE OBJECT TO THE CONCRETE INTERVENTION

The understanding of art changes very slowly. The material character of art was already being questioned one hundred years ago, and since then artists have attempted to perform functions within art that go far beyond the production of objects. The demand for change has been coming up again and again for a long time now: that art should no longer be venerated in specially designated spaces, or form a parallel quasi-world. Art should not act as if it could exist of itself and for itself. It should deal with reality, grapple with political circumstances, and work out proposals for improving human coexistence. Unconventional ideas, an innovative spirit, and energy, which for centuries were wrapped up in formal "glass bead games," could, in some way, contribute to the solution of real problems.

SITUATIONIST MANIFESTO

"FIRST OF ALL, WE THINK THE WORLD MUST BE CHANGED"

Now, at the beginning of the twenty-first century, the demands are slowly starting to take effect. The formal aesthetic discussion has run its course, the self-referential somersaults have become inflationary, and the worship of virtuosi has given way to other qualities. In the process, a fundamental discussion of the functions of art has arisen: Who does what in art, and why?

Art can perform many functions. For pages and pages, the various functions could be listed like a catalog of stylistic -isms: Art can represent its commissioners and producers; it can be a definer and caretaker of identity; it can affect snobby allures and satiate the bourgeois hunger for knowledge and possession. Art can fatten up the leisure time of the bored masses; it can serve as an object of financial speculation; it can transmit feelings, and cause one's heart to vibrate. Furthermore, its many functions are also enmeshed in one another. For example, abstract expressionism served Cold War America as a political instrument of culturalization, just as much as it served the spiritual need for expression of the young painters who created it.

One of the functions of art has always been the transformation of living conditions. Since the advent of modernism, with its rejection of religiously founded authority, art has been an especially fertile domain for querying irrational taboos and inherited value standards, and for correcting social imbalances. This function was first put into practice by the Russian constructivists. At the same time as the 1917 change of regime in Russia, an art was introduced, which for the first time, sought to directly influence the people's consciousness and living conditions through agitation and activism. Thus a new chapter was opened in the history of art.

In Germany, the Bauhaus cultivated these developments. Science, architecture, technology, and the visual arts were all working toward one another so as to shape as many aspects of life as possible. Books and posters, vehicles, landscapes, and clothing took on new forms corresponding to function and ideology, in order to establish the new philosophies of life. Every formal renewal of the world—so thought the artists of that time—would also have to bring about a corresponding change of attitude.

For many decades it seemed that society actually could be manipulated through the alteration of visual surroundings and habits of seeing and hearing. This view still had its supporters as recently as the sixties, and the question of whether that era's youth revolt was influenced, or even triggered by rock and pop music (or if conversely the music was merely a part of the release of long-accumulated dissatisfaction) is a source of material for sociology seminars up to the present day. Looking back, the idea of "altering social relationships by altering form" appears a little naive. Of course attitudes, habits, thinking patterns, and value standards can be marginally influenced through forms. The whole of the advertising field is sustained by this thesis. But people's ideological principles, their world-views and values cannot really be changed through colors, sounds, and forms. Clothes, one could say, only make the man in romantic novels.

Following the Second World War, socially engaged art experienced several high points. "First of all, we think the world must be changed," stands at the beginning of the Situationist manifesto, written in the late fifties. Similar proclamations of and demands for change in politics, sexuality, the economy, and culture are to be found in numerous initiatives and organizations. In heated discussions with like-minded individuals, the Lettrists and activists discussed the most basic method of destroying every aspect of tradition, and were constantly on the lookout against their own institutionalization. What came after the destruction was of lesser importance. The path was the goal, and the goal was the conflict with high culture, whose forms of expression were suspected of having been co-opted by the economic ruling class for its own ends. "Artists who withdraw into the reserve of their own areas of specialization are just as much functionaries of an ossified society as skilled workers and file clerks," wrote Subversive Action. These activists, who classified themselves as "para-elites," wanted to achieve something that others did not even dare to think about. And yet, when seen from a certain historical distance, they left behind little more than manifestos, and their resolutions remained at the level of auspicious declarations of intention and maxims. However, it is also evident that the methods which were established of "constructing situations" have found successors to this day.

Simultaneously with the Situationists and Lettrists came the development of conceptual art; an art where the idea behind the object counted. Aside from early forerunners like the Austrian poet H.C. Artmann in the fifties, the first important phase of conceptual art coincided with the Vietnam War, and the assassinations of both Martin Luther King and Malcolm X. It was the time of the student revolts, the continuing struggle for civil rights, and the growth of feminism. In addition to giving rise to all sorts of playful escapades and self-referential "art industry analyses," the general questioning of value standards and authority primarily led to a marked interest in the political. Starting from the "classical" position, the postconceptualists thus developed their forms of dealing with issues like race, class, nation, and gender. They, too, remained within the traditional context of art in that they transmitted their cause using conventional forms of exhibition and presentation, which were merely placating a specialized art public, whose majority shared their views anyway. Diligently staged and photographed statements on racism, feminism, and homosexuality always reached the same few people, who nonetheless enjoyed an opportunity to prove their correctness to one another. Still, this conception of art must be understood as an important precursor of today's political activism.

THE MUSEUMS, THE ART JOURNALS, THE GALLERIES, AND THE ART ACADEMIES HAD NO PROBLEM WHATSOEVER INTEGRATING THE MYRIAD FORMS OF SO-CALLED "ANTIART." EVEN THE MOST SUBVERSIVE FORMS OF ACTIONISM AND NEO-DADA WERE CO-OPTED INTO COLLECTIONS, AND ULTIMATELY, OBJECTS WERE STILL ALL THAT REMAINED.

In the seventies, the demand for sociopolitical relevance in art was finally put into concrete action in a variety of ways. Ulrike Rosenbach's alternative television program was to emancipate the people from the media czars' monopolies; video technology was used by Richard Kriesche in the rehabilitation of disabled children (long before medicine came upon the idea); Barbara Steveni and John Latham of the Artist Placement Group presented suggestions for improving educational policy to the British government. Joseph Beuys redefined the position of art in society with the concept of the social plastic sculpture; Hans Haacke showed how political processes can be influenced through intervention; Klaus Staeck's agitprop posters elucidated the relationships between business and power; and groups like the Art Workers' Coalition declared war on the conventional art establishment and its rigid admission criteria. Filled with a euphoria not lacking a measure of hubris (with the artist portrayed as seer, shaman, healer, and revolutionary guru), these artists—and here avant-garde circles were in agreement—wanted to make contributions for improving coexistence: in psychology and sociology, with healing methods, or through incarceration. The avant-garde wanted to choose living places and communities for their creation, to stop working for eternity, and to address a public that was more than just the educated classes.

However, in the end it did not work without the old institutions. The museums, the art journals, the galleries, and the art academies had no problem whatsoever integrating the myriad forms of so-called "antiart." Even the most subversive forms of actionism and Neo-Dada were co-opted into collections, and ultimately, objects were still all that remained. Relics of actions, photographs, and sketches became fetishes for veneration, and for sale. For most people at that time—and this still applies today—art had to do with artworks. It must be something that can be seen, touched, and packed away. Everything else cannot be sold, cannot be collected, and cannot be preserved.

Qualities other than those that are immediately sensorially perceivable, which nonetheless are always tied to objects, took on increasing significance, but only at a slow pace. The seventies did show how art could develop after abandoning mimesis, after abandoning the need for expression, after abandoning the variants of abstraction, and after abandoning the question of form. Happenings, Fluxus, performances, actions, ironic variants of readymades, as well as conceptual art, led to a profound doubt of the notion that art can only be fixed in the object. The concept and idea, which were discussed as the actual artistic achievement behind every material realization—even in painting—gained ground against a conception of art that only manifests itself in material. The entire complexity of the conditions of production was, of course, called into question as well.

Action art also made a significant contribution to the developments leading to activism. Originally conceived as a cathartic satisfaction of the individual's unfulfilled drives, and a liberation of the subject from the bonds of convention, actionism soon changed its thinking, and recognized the cause of many individual and psychological problems in social injustices. The desire for catharsis could often not be fulfilled because those involved soon became aware of the senselessness of every primal scream—regardless of the depths from which it may emerge—when social conditions leave no room for an improvement in subjective well-being.

In the eighties it seemed like it was all over. All of the successes and efforts of sociopolitically committed art were pushed to the side. Repeatedly, and with growing success, these aspirations were confronted by an art fully devoid of purpose. Contemplation again came to the forefront, and with it the objects that were to evoke it: the art shrines. The reversal did not really come so much from the artists' ranks, where there continued to be an interest in utopia; it also did not come from criticism. Instead it came from the powerful scene around art—those who viewed art as a commodity—because it was earning a living from this sort of art. It was mainly the huge swarm of speculators and collectors who drove this reversal, when they saw their precious canvases being replaced by forms of art that they could not sell, and which they could not collect. Altered conceptions of art, which challenged the status quo, were not what they wanted to follow. They preferred one hundred more variations for repeating already-been-there, and they preferred to keep packing and unpacking their wares, all the while extolling them for all they were worth. Art that had nothing more in mind than using its potential to improve odious conditions was not suitable for making a profit. It could not delight the aesthetically seducible eye, or awaken any lofty sentiments.

In Poland these times were different. An actionist group, dressed in orange, went out on the streets in 1988. Speaking through megaphones they proclaimed the governing General Jaruzelski king. This was not callow anticommunism, but rather a refined strategy that these artists were using to assail the regime's hypocrisy. They also proclaimed an International Day of the Spy, on which they appeared by the hundreds with dark glasses and turned up collars, stopping passersby and halting the secret police to check their papers. On another occasion, they sang pathetic hymns in praise of the Red Army, and read out the orange manifesto of socialist surrealism. In this manifesto, the police officer was declared a work of art, as an individual, or better still, deployed en masse to charge against the activists: the wilder the charge, the better the art.

In the West, the phase of self-satisfied, market-oriented art production did not last for ever. With the nineties came a change of thinking and, in fact, a renewal of reflection on the social responsibility of art. Postmodernism's celebrated autonomy revealed itself to be an apparition to which countless palaces and new museums had been erected. These galleries brought dealers dizzying profits at first, but soon enough inflation and losses followed. Political reality was outside of this art's field of interest. The effects of a conservative economic policy, creeping social cutbacks, increasing immigration conflicts, and a general insecurity following the dissolution of the East-West power balance first became determining factors in the production of art after the collapse of the market, and the demystification of art. Since then visual art has developed in two directions: into an art that is defined by economic interests and bottom-line thinking, that lures the masses with spectacle and lots of horn-blowing. And conversely into an art that acts—independently of profit and populism—in possibilities that seek to examine and improve the conditions of coexistence. The latter direction sounds somewhat altruistic and missionary; perhaps a little too altruistic for an art that just wants to hang free and easy beyond the daily grind. However, more and more artists are finding that the decision is not so difficult, when in view of the numerous functions of art, their choice leads past the satisfaction of leisure-time needs and toward the cooperative shaping of life in society.

In contrast to the thinking of the seventies, today's art activists are no longer concerned with changing the world in its entirety. It is no longer a matter of mercilessly implementing an ideological line, as it was with Joseph Beuys's idea of transforming a whole society into a social sculpture, or as it was in the thinking of the Russian constructivists, the futurists, and many other manifesto writers of the modern. At the end of the twentieth century, activist art no longer overestimates its capabilities; but it does not underestimate them, either—it makes more modest contributions. It would be wrong, in a society in which every discussion of basic principles has been lost, to expect that something like art can make significant, decisive changes. Folksongs do not rescue whales; "Stop AIDS" posters do not stop the spread of the disease; and Klaus Staeck's agitprop posters have hardly hindered speculation in the housing market.

And yet, in certain circumstances art can change more than is assumed. Art must devote itself to developing very concrete strategies for effecting change. Wishing patients in hospitals a quick recovery by putting artistic decoration on the walls, reading Austrian literature aloud to asylum seekers, or having Mother Courage appear on stage dressed in a costume as a Kosovo Albanian, are nothing more than easy absolutions for a guilty conscience. There is "Rock Music with Lyrics on Housing Shortage," in which "tenant's need" rhymes with "speculator's greed," and then there is a designer, the New York artist Krzysztof Wodiczko, who was inventing vehicles for New York's winos and homeless people. Wodiczko constructed utopian-looking, all-purpose vehicles that were built on supermarket cart chassis that could be pushed around, with storage space for returnable cans and bottles and were designed so that the whole device could be converted into a cot for the night. Wodiczko's approach—he looks for solutions within the realm of existing possibilities, even if they do seem a little utopian—is certainly worthy of mentioning here. Still, it should also be noted that his carts are only presented in museums, which could even give rise to the suspicion that he is utilizing social destitution for the purpose of creating valuable works of art to be shown in exhibition venues. It is unimaginable that they would ever actually be employed by their intended users, as even the most banal problems, like storage, would instantly arise.

WISHING PATIENTS IN HOSPITALS A QUICK RECOVERY BY PUTTING ARTISTIC DECORATION ON THE WALLS, READING AUSTRIAN LITERATURE ALOUD TO ASYLUM SEEKERS, OR HAVING MOTHER COURAGE APPEAR ON STAGE DRESSED IN A COSTUME AS A KOSOVO ALBANIAN, ARE NOTHING MORE THAN EASY ABSOLUTIONS FOR A GUILTY CONSCIENCE.

Social renewal is a function of art that arose after art that deals only with the surface. This particular type of art's big chance lies in its ability to offer the community something that also has an effect on its surroundings. The motives behind an art that seeks a concrete intervention should not be confused with an excess of moralistic fervor. As a potential basis for action, art has enough political capital at its disposal, which should not be underestimated. The use of this potential to manipulate social circumstances is a practice of art that is just as valid as the manipulation of traditional materials. The group WochenKlausur takes this function of art and its historic precursors as its point of departure. WochenKlausur sets precise tasks for itself and, in intensive actions that are time-limited, attempts to work out solutions to the problems it has recognized. Widespread interest in the theoretical foundations and practical working methods, as well as the concrete results of WochenKlausur's projects, have encouraged the artists collective to continue working in this direction.

CHRISTOPH BÜCHEL

Christoph Büchel's primary goal is to reveal the connection between art and society, and to stimulate discourse on the role and importance of art. The Swiss artist (*1966), who was born in Basel, has been making a name for himself in the international art world with his complex and meticulously planned space installations and projects since 1990. His conceptual art works often show a critical attitude towards institutions. At the same time, the artist uses his artworks as a means of breaking up the rigid closed systems that cling to many venerable cultural institutions and which they perpetuate. In 2002, he auctioned his invitation and participation rights as an exhibiting artist to Manifesta 4 on eBay. In the same year, he kept the Helmhaus exhibition rooms in Zürich empty for his show "Capital Affair" (which was a collaboration with artist Gianni Motti), and promised the whole exhibition budget to the visitor who could find a check that had been hidden there (with a notary present to act as witness). Büchel's artworks challenge the viewer to actively take part. Sometimes visitors have to work hard to forge a path for themselves, but Büchel's provocation always practically forces them to think about the artwork and its effect and to form their own opinion. The artist's construction of reality is accurate in every detail, and he thereby propels the visitor into a game of substitution and confusion in which it is almost impossible to tell reality from fiction. In 2005, Büchel transformed the Oberlichtsaal of the Kunsthalle Basel into an installation that filled the whole space, which was entitled *Hole*—this beautiful, historic part of the building, which had been painstakingly renovated a short time before, was barely recognizable. The artist had transformed it into an industrial-looking sorting depot and a workshop. The installation could only be reached by the elevator from the lobby, as the grand stairwell had been closed. The Oberlichtsaal was used to house a "Shrink Room" with a waiting room, a psychotherapist's practice, and a large tent. Inside, the wreckage of an exploded bus—many parts of which were unrecognizable—was laid out on tables and put on shelves. The place looked like a multipurpose crisis centre set up by police investigating an accident. This painstaking search for the cause—for a logical and scientific explanation—is one of the strategies we collectively deploy in order to come to terms with our fate. The obsessive investigation of details also expresses an endeavor to gain total control over incomprehensible catastrophes, and reflects the degree of paranoia within our society. If the accompanying Shrink Room is dedicated to overcoming psychological damage by analyzing what is hidden in the psyche, *Hole*, then, is a vivid representation of the human desire to maintain social order in times of increasing fear. In the exhibition "Deutsche Grammatik" in the Kassel Fridericianum in 2008, Büchel thematized recent German history, and the country's current political and social structures. The first volume of the *Deutsche Grammatik* (German Grammar) was written by Jacob Grimm, the then-librarian of the Kasseler Fridericianum, in 1818. In his exhibition on current German culture, Büchel used its title as a metaphor. The 2,000 square meters of exhibition space were made available on a temporary basis to be utilized in a variety of ways—the operations that were moved into the art hall included a branch of discount store Mäc-Geiz, a gaming venue, a tanning studio, a fitness center, and a guesthouse whose interior fittings looked as though they came from the 1970s, complete with a bowling alley and a function hall. A tiered rotating Christmas tree was installed in the Fridericianum's rotunda, and the ruins of a destroyed exhibition space could be seen on the first floor, along with an apartment divided in two by a wall. A whole wing was used to stage a kind of fair, while another wing was the venue for reconstructing the shredded files of the Ministerium für Staatssicherheit (Ministry for State Security) of the former German Democratic Republic. The Friedrichsplatz, which lies in front of the exhibition building, was transformed into plowed farmland, to which a "newly discovered" bomb was added.

For his two-day "politica," which the artist described as "the first political party fair in Germany," Büchel invited all parties admitted by the Bundeswahlleiter (Germany's federal election supervisor) to present their standpoints through the medium of an exhibition stand and by giving speeches. The participation of the extreme right-wing National Democratic Party was calculated to cause a scandal. After initially agreeing to attend, the Christian Democratic Union, the Social Democratic Party, the Green Party, the Free Democratic Party, and Die Linke (The Left) all withdrew from the event—leaving it to others to confront the right-wing extremists.

1
Deutsche Grammatik
2008, Installation view at Kunsthalle Fridericianum, Kassel, Germany, Photos by A. Burger and Nils Klinger

2
Hole
2005, Installation view at Kunsthalle Basel, Basel, Switzerland, Photo by Christoph Büchel

Courtesy the artist and Hauser & Wirth

1

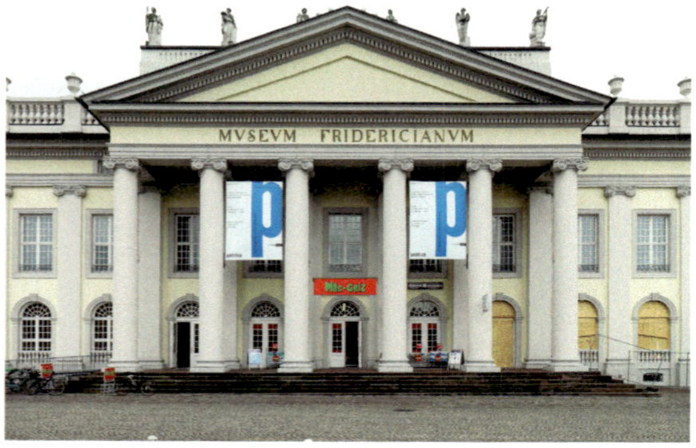

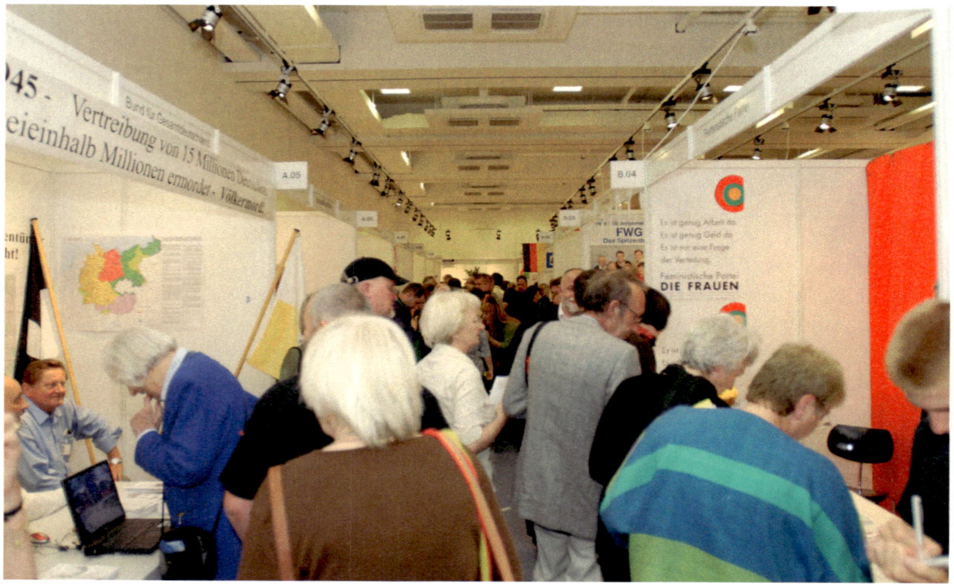

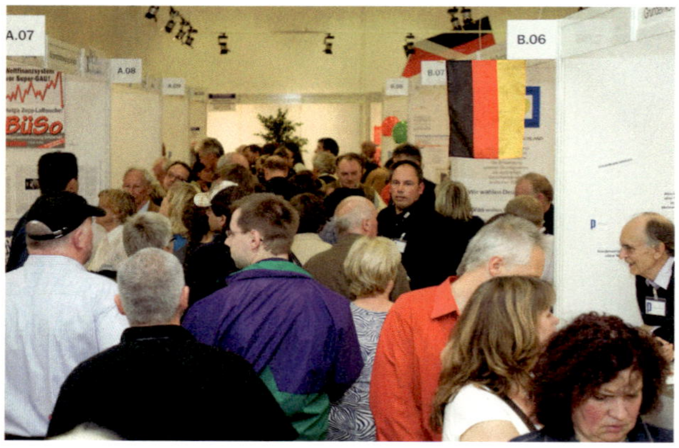

2

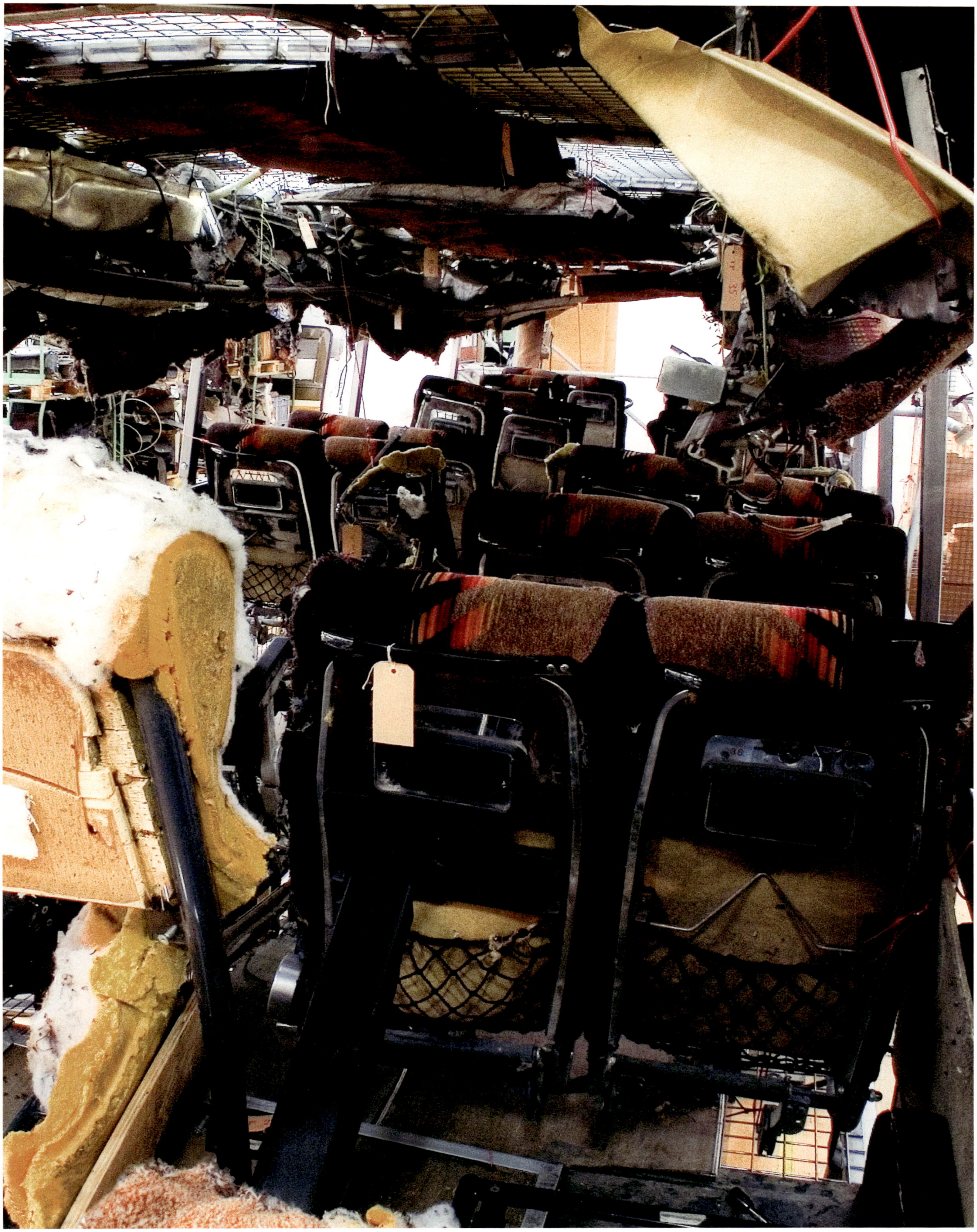

NASAN TUR

Nasan Tur (* 1974) is a German artist with Turkish ancestry, who was born in Offenbach, Germany. His installations, performances, and interventions interfere subversively with the everyday in a way that brings viewers up short, and forces them to rethink their reality. For his video artwork *Somersaulting Man,* 2001–2004, he turned somersaults in the center of crowded locations, such as airports and tourist attractions in Istanbul, Tokyo, Paris, and Frankfurt, often without attracting any attention from passersby. In this video, Tur reflects on the relationship between the viewer and artwork in a public space in a wonderfully ironic way. In other artwork series, he invites viewers to participate directly. The installation *Was Ich Euch Schon Immer Sagen Wollte* (What I Always Wanted to Say to You), 2006, for instance, allows the viewer to pick up a microphone and transmit his or her words through a sound system that points toward the street—that is, toward the public. By imposing an inescapable decision on viewers, the artist intrudes into their private sphere and makes them engage with the artwork. For *Backpacks,* 2006, Tur brought together five backpacks, each of which contained different objects. One contained a speaker's platform, complete with microphone and amplifier; another contained a gas cooker, with pots and seasonings; and yet another contained heavy tools and a black mask. The final two backpacks contained a drum, an air horn, a white flag and paint, a megaphone, and a blank transparency. After presenting personal identification and signing an agreement, exhibition visitors could borrow a rucksack of their choice for a day, and use it as they wished. They were able to choose where to demonstrate and against what, what to sabotage, what to cook, what to be a fan of, or which subject to speak about. Tur's sole condition is that the user must have him or herself photographed, or videoed during these activities. Most commonly, the cooking backpack is chosen, because cooking in the open air rapidly leads to social exchanges between strangers. Encouraging people to communicate is also the motivation behind many other artworks by the artist. The equipment in the backpacks also led exhibition visitors to commit subversive acts, as the videos prove. For instance, a woman traveled alone through Belgrade at night proclaiming her belief in the unity of all Balkan ethnicities; in another example, a masked man committed sabotage using a drill. In these artworks, Tur relinquishes his role as the creator of the work beyond a certain point, and becomes a viewer. For instance, those wishing to stage a spontaneous protest can obtain the basic requirements they might need from the *Demo Kit* (Demonstration Kit Machine.) Tur's artworks pose the question: What is the difference between art and agitation? He goes a step further by spraying the orthographically incorrect slogan "Time for Revollusion" on the wall of a museum as graffiti, or by hanging the (equally incorrect) words "KOMUNISMUS," "SOZIALLISMUS," and "KAPIETALISMUS," one above the other in high-quality illuminated letters to mark the start of an exhibition. These key words seem to have long since sunk beneath the homogeneity of advertising language. With the sense of irony that runs through all his artwork, Tur duly confines them to the museum, revealing political art as a relic of the past.

1
KOMUNISMUS SOZIALLISMUS
KAPIETALISMUS
2009, Tanas, Berlin, Germany

2
Demo Kits
2010

3
Backpacks:
Speaker-Backpack,
Cooking-Backpack,
Demonstration-Backpack,
Sabotage-Backpack,
Fan-Backpack
2006, October Salon, Belgrade, Serbia, Mixed-media, usable sculptures

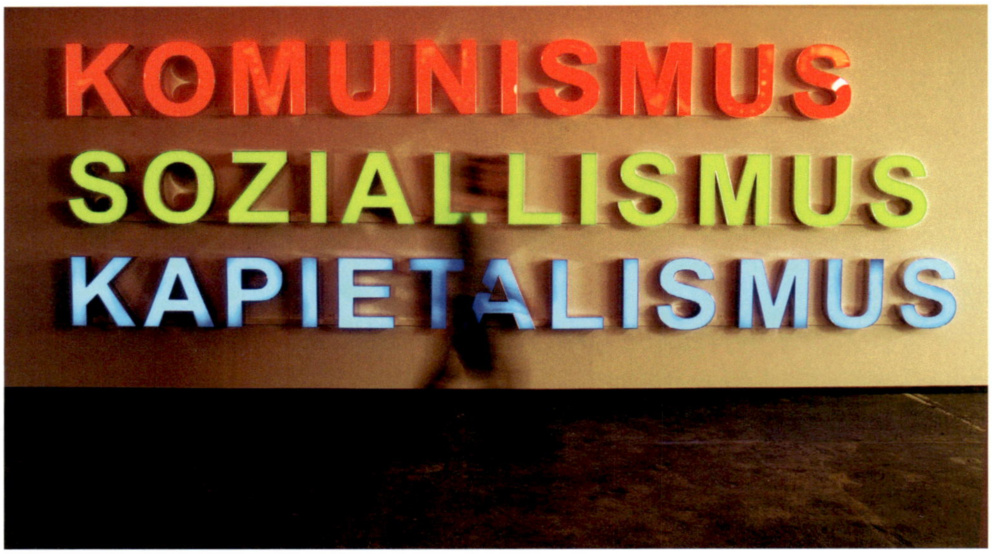

1

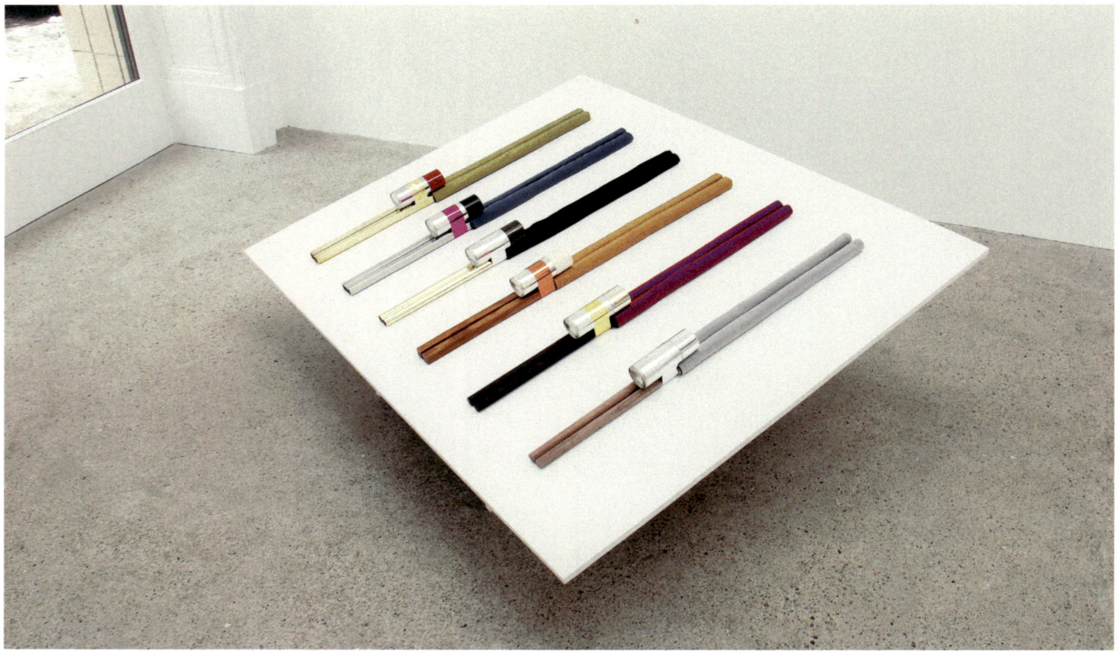
2

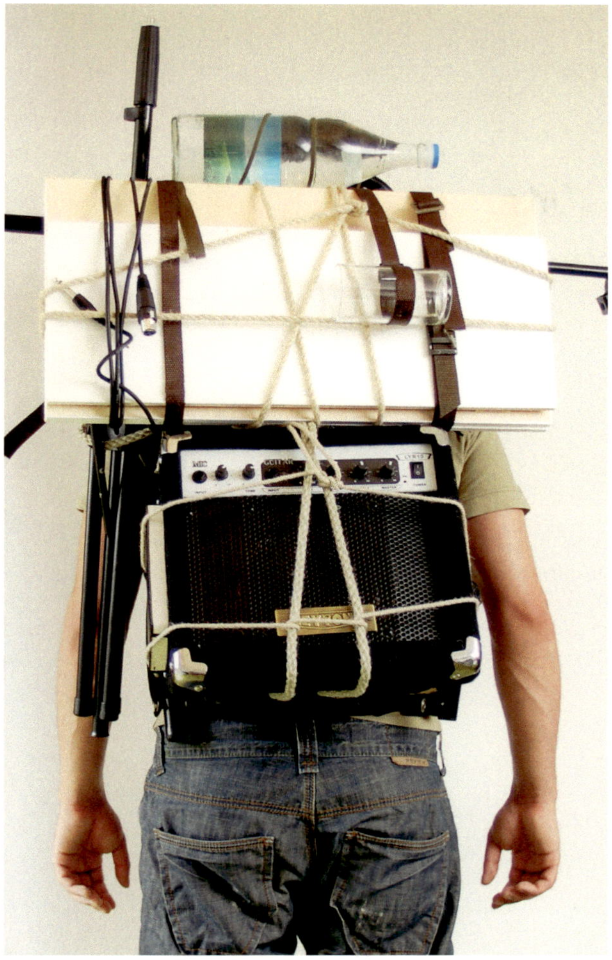

3

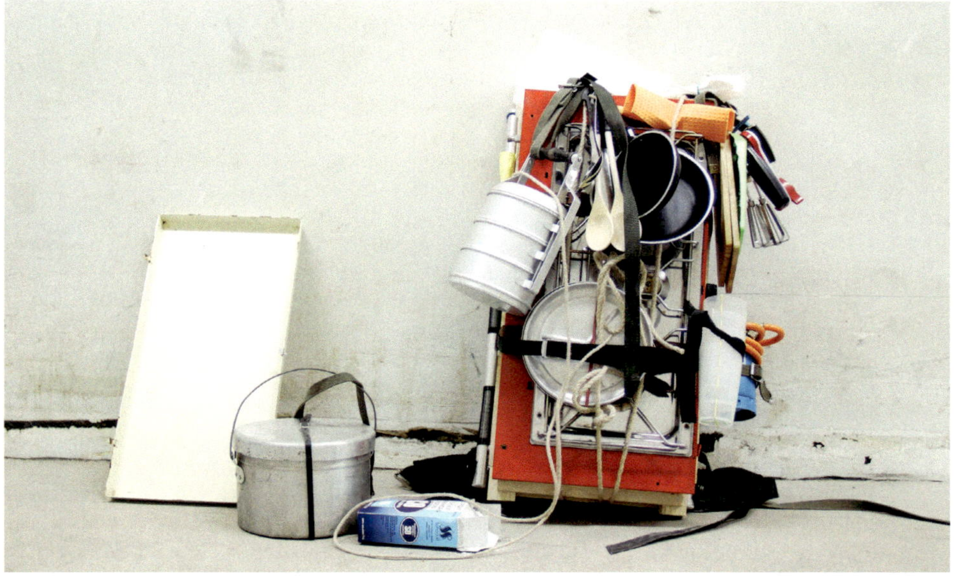

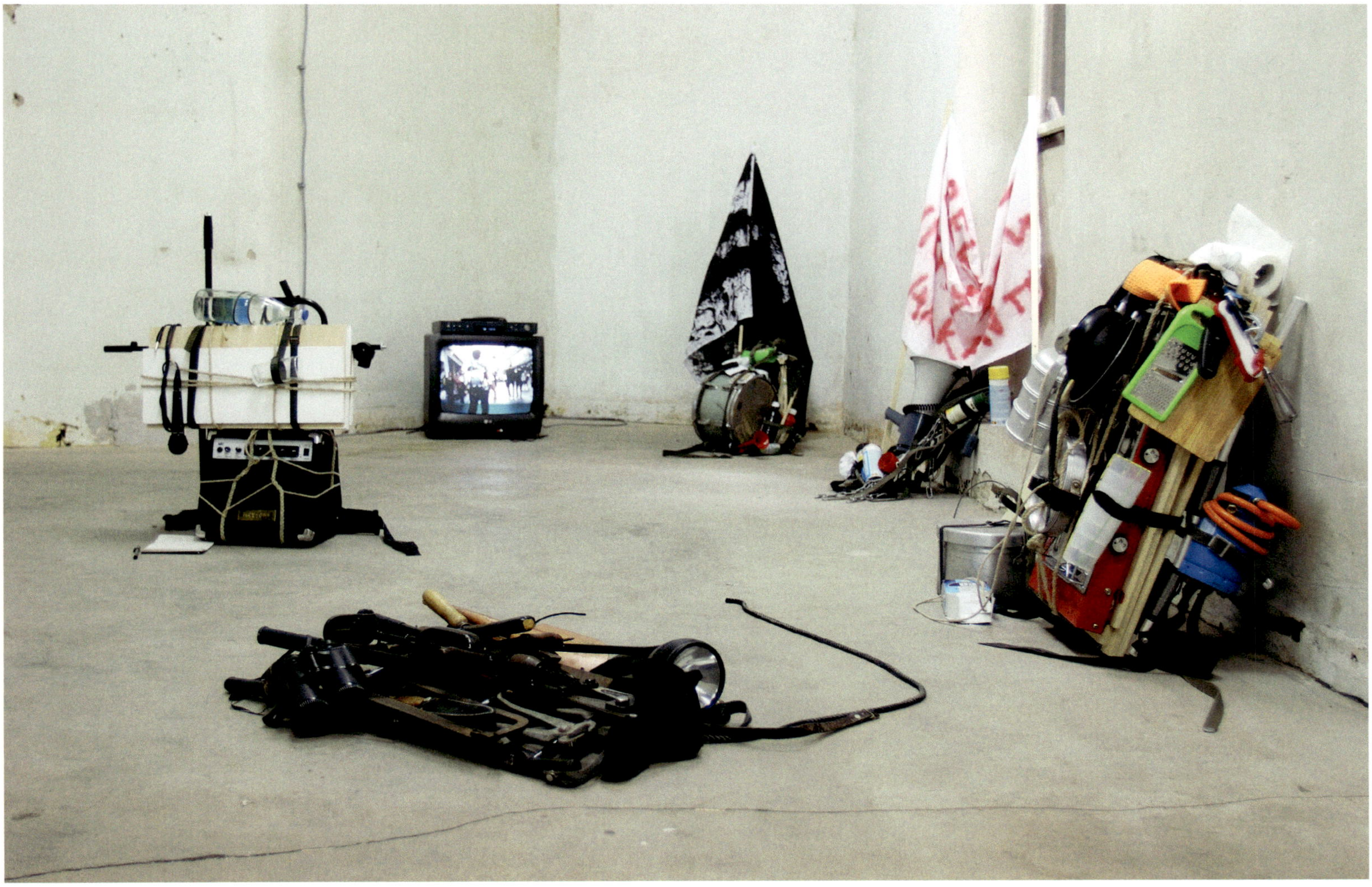

HARMEN DE HOOP

The Dutch artist Harmen de Hoop (* 1959), created his first illegal artworks in public spaces in the year 1985—when nobody had heard of the street art phenomenon. "I didn't want to be Julian Schnabel or Jeff Koons," says the artist, who studied as an architect. "I found these big art world egos awful. That's why I have always worked anonymously, and [have] never told anyone where my artworks are." His interventions are symbolic attacks on the functionality and order of the city. "All my artworks transmit political, social, and philosophical ideas—but I'm not interested in overtly political artworks. The artists who create them are generally naive. What I am interested in is the authentic moment—my artworks are an unpretentious, personal dialogue with passersby." He installs sculptures that he has bought in a flea market as art in a public space; liberates plastic plants and replants them in parks; transforms a traffic island into a children's play area; and, in a desperate act of revolt, once got demonstrators to distribute large numbers of flyers for an action titled: *Protest (Useless Action)*. In another intervention into public space, his anti-car flyers were thrown directly off a freeway flyover. "I don't think art should be just illustrating: for example, illustrating some aspect of youth culture, and then thinking [that] it actually says something about youth culture," says de Hoop. "That isn't enough for me, and that is the same for me as political art that has an agenda. Just showing that there is racism in the world, is, in my opinion, not enough, you have to reflect on the complexity of human existence."

1
No More Violence
(Useless Action #13)
2010, Rotterdam, Netherlands

2
Protest (Useless Action #7)
2010, Cologne, Germany

1

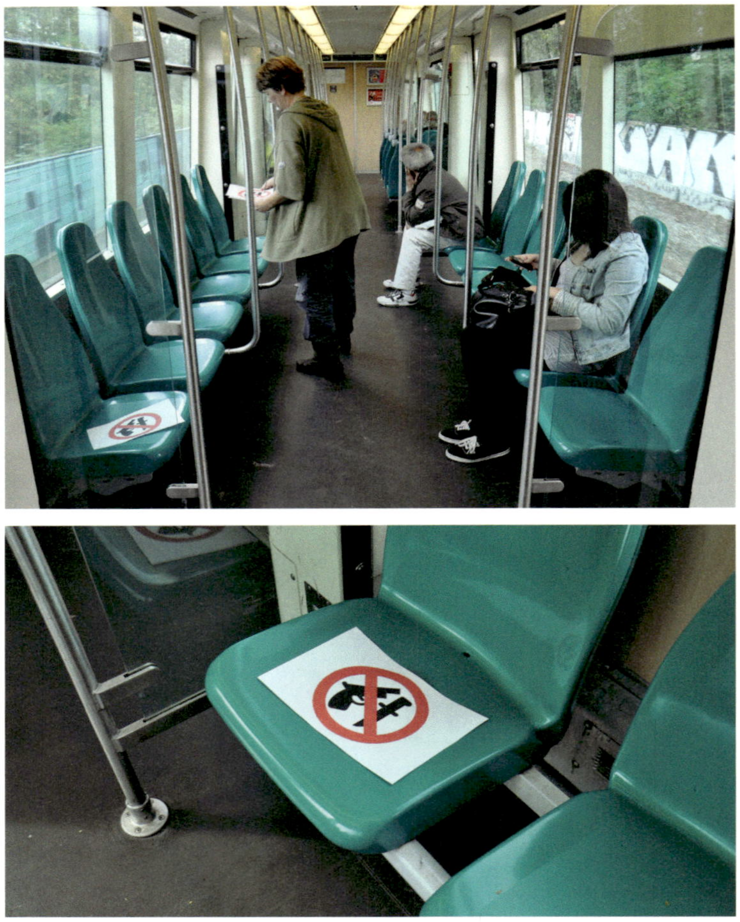

2

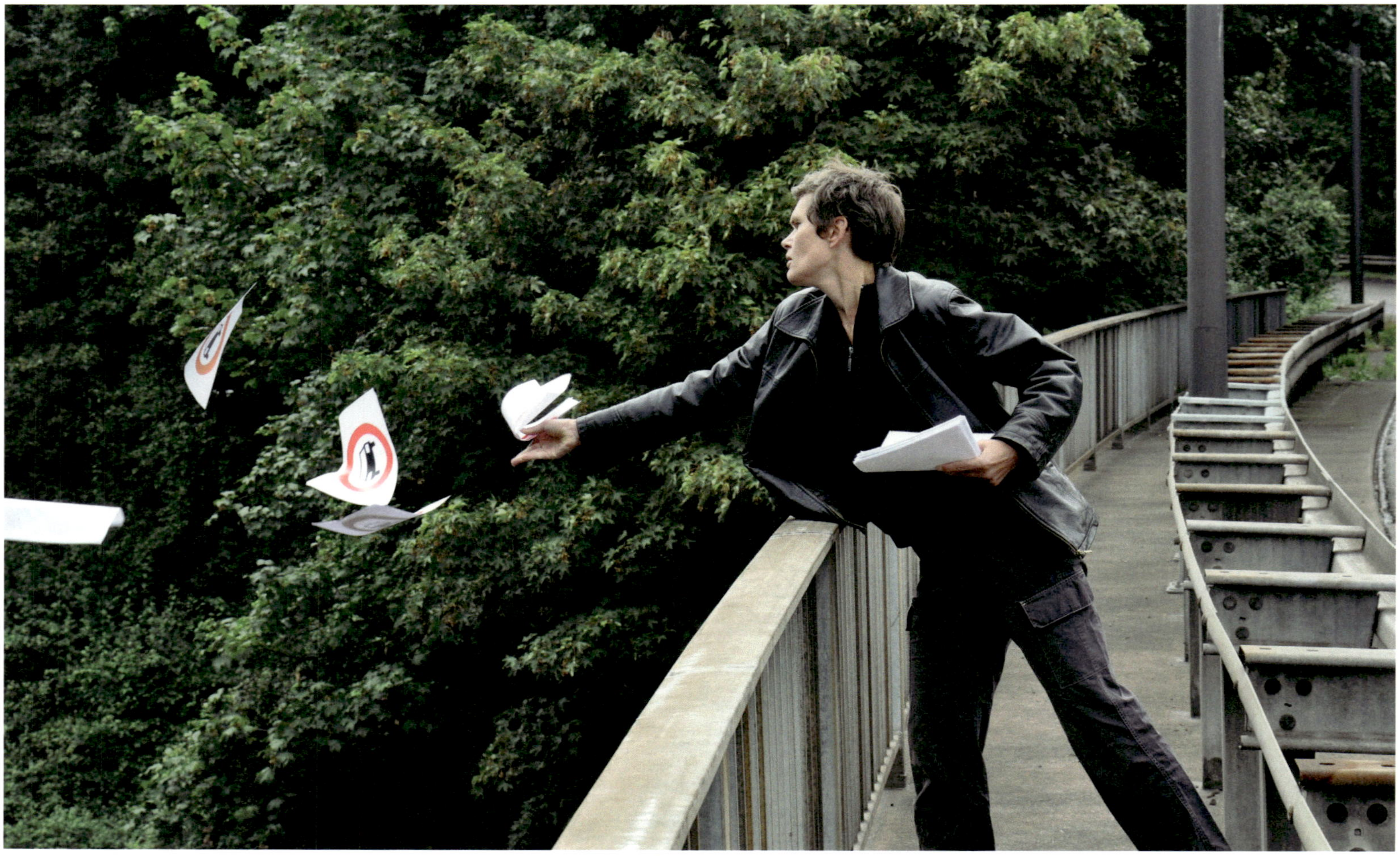

NAVID TSCHOPP-SADROSSADAT

1
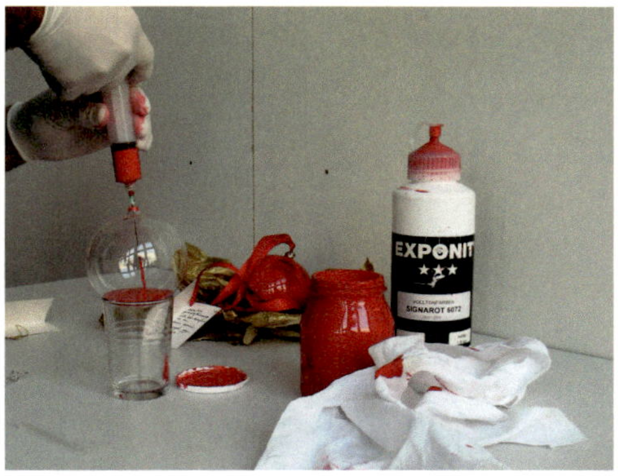

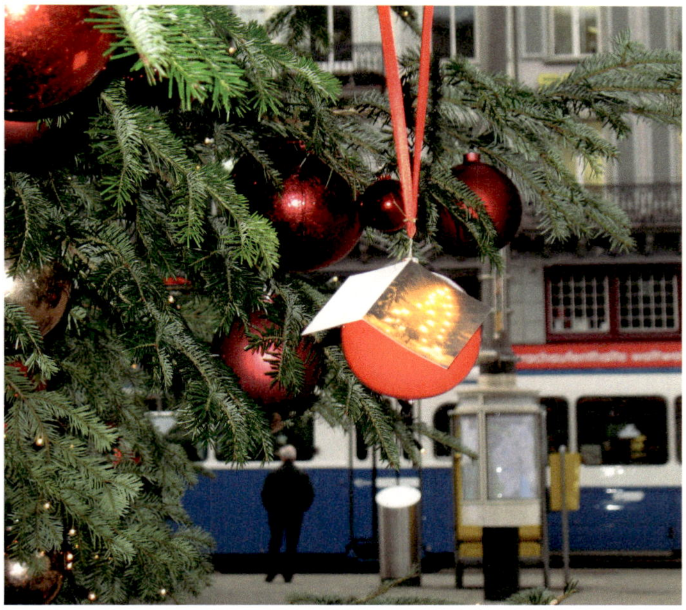

1
Weihnachtsaktion
zur Finanzkrise
December 18, 2008–January 6, 2009, Zurich Paradeplatz, Switzerland, Christmas tree balls filled with red paint in front of the UBS and Credit Suisse headquarters
2
Public Lounge
2007, Zurich, Switzerland

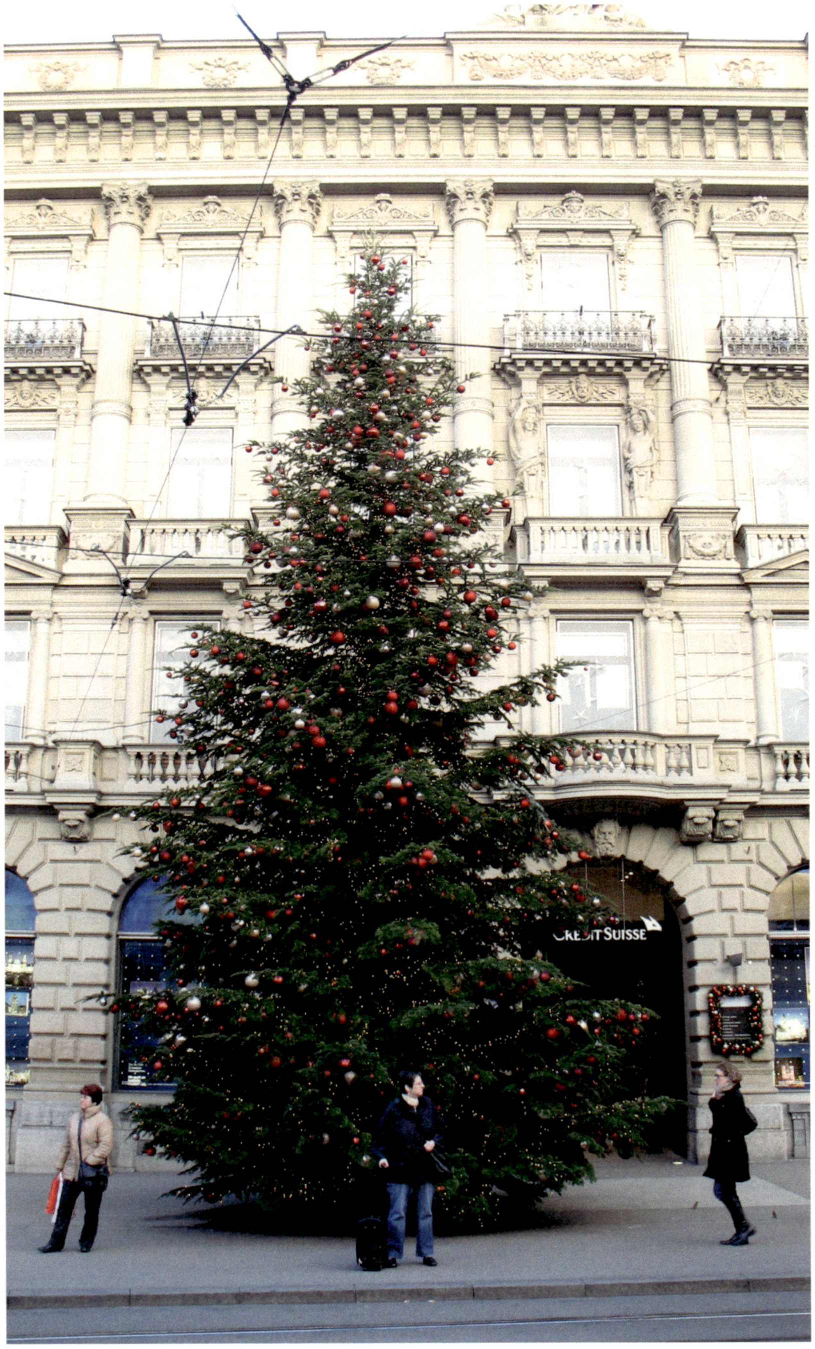

Navid Tschopp-Sadrossadat (* 1978) was born in Mashhad, Iran, and lives and works in Switzerland, where he creates temporary public space interventions that often directly involve the public. For his sculpture *Schneeauto* (Snow Car), 2006, he built a full-size car from snow, and blocked a parking space with it for ten days. For *Sammeltage* (Collection Days), 2007, he created alternative spaces with materials found on the street—for instance, the *Public Lounge*, where he placed a corner sofa on a pedestrian route made from bundles of old paper. And for his *Weihnachtsaktion zur Finanzkrise* (Christmas Financial Crisis Action), 2010, he hung balls filled with red paint on a Christmas tree in Zurich in front of a bank. These paintballs, disguised as Christmas tree decorations, could be removed and used as passersby saw fit. His graduation piece *Topologische Agenda—Der Weg zum Master* (Topological Agenda—the Way to the Master), 2010, consisted of 1,001 white magnets that Tschopp-Sadrossadat threw onto the steel façade of a refuse incineration facility in Zurich. For two years, he passed this façade on his way to his college studio, and on each occasion he threw a magnet onto it, creating a constantly changing texture. This unsolicited "building art" project climaxed with Tschopp-Sadrossadat solemnly presenting the facility's owners with a deed of gift.

2
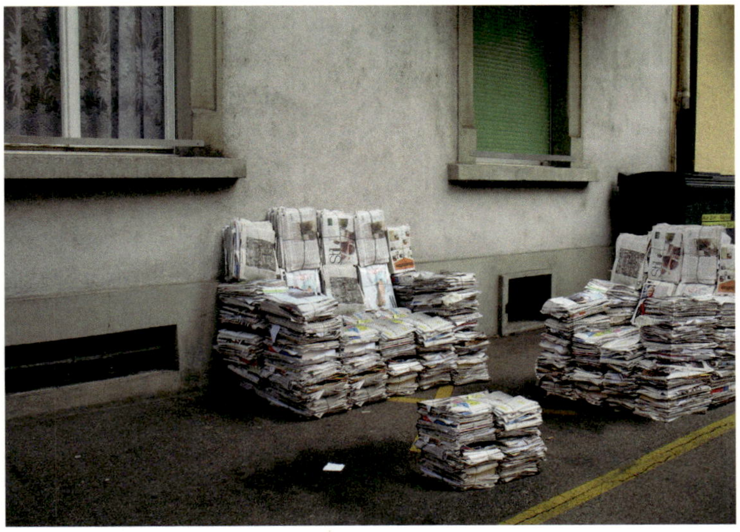

THE YES MEN

A guerrilla communication operation in pinstripes, The Yes Men have been posing as representatives of global companies and governments, and carrying out so-called "identity corrections" by means of exaggerated declarations and absurd campaigns for years now. The group cooperates with a number of international activists, but is essentially a duo: Jacques Servin (alias Andy Bichlbaum) and Igor Vamos (alias Mike Bonanno), both of whom are also lecturers at New York universities. On December 3, 2004, which was the twentieth anniversary of the chemical catastrophe in Bhopal in India, Bichlbaum appeared on the BBC World channel posing as a representative of Dow Chemical, apologizing for the accident and announcing that the victims would finally receive compensation. The company's share price immediately fell dramatically—and, after years of obscurity, an accident that left up to 25,000 people dead and 500,000 people injured was finally brought to renewed public attention. In 2006, The Yes Men posed as representatives of the military supplier Halliburton, presenting the *SurvivaBall*, a huge, round protective suit that they claimed would protect managers from climate change. In 2007 they posed as representatives of ExxonMobil at a gas and oil industry trade fair, presenting the product *Vivoleum*—oil extracted from corpses. To quote: "With more fossil fuels comes a greater chance of disaster, but that means more feedstock for Vivoleum." In 2008, they achieved their greatest coup so far by putting out around 1.2 million copies of a counterfeit *New York Times* newspaper that not only announced the end of the Iraq war, but also the indictment of George Bush for high treason.

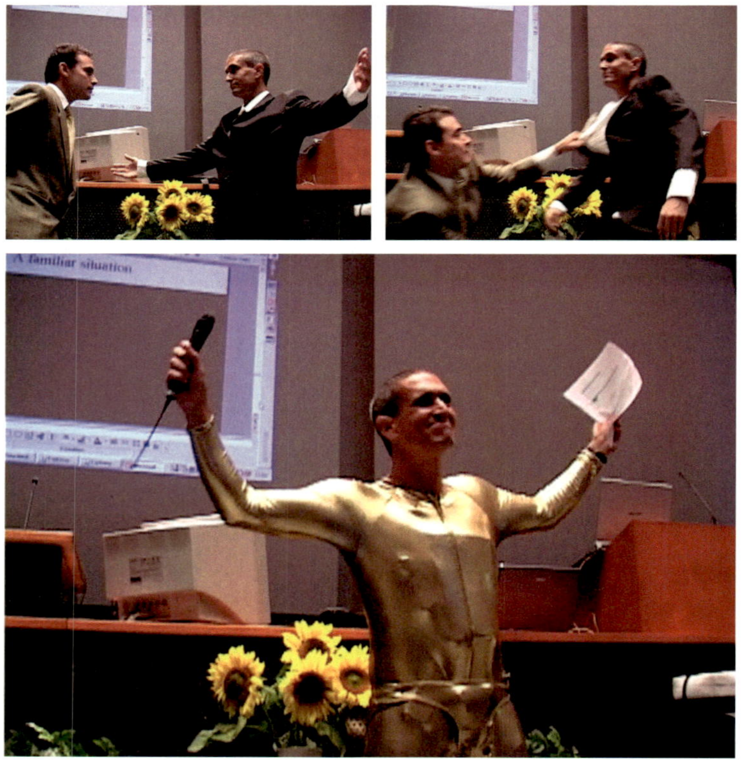

Beyond the Golden Parachute
2001, Tampere, Sweden
In 2001, Andy and Mike presented a short history of textiles at a conference in Finland, describing how the U.S. Civil War was a waste of money because slavery was replaced by remote sweatshop labor, such as we have today. The only problem now is the efficiency of the sweatshops and a lack of control over workers. Their answer was the management solution of the future: a shimmering golden leotard, whose crotch sports a three-foot-long golden phallus, or the Employee Visualization Appendage. The audience gave a round of applause, but asked no questions—only a few people admitted to being mystified, but no one was bothered by the content of the speech. If the conference attendees could so blithely follow The Yes Men down such paths, real business leaders could convince these "experts" of anything.

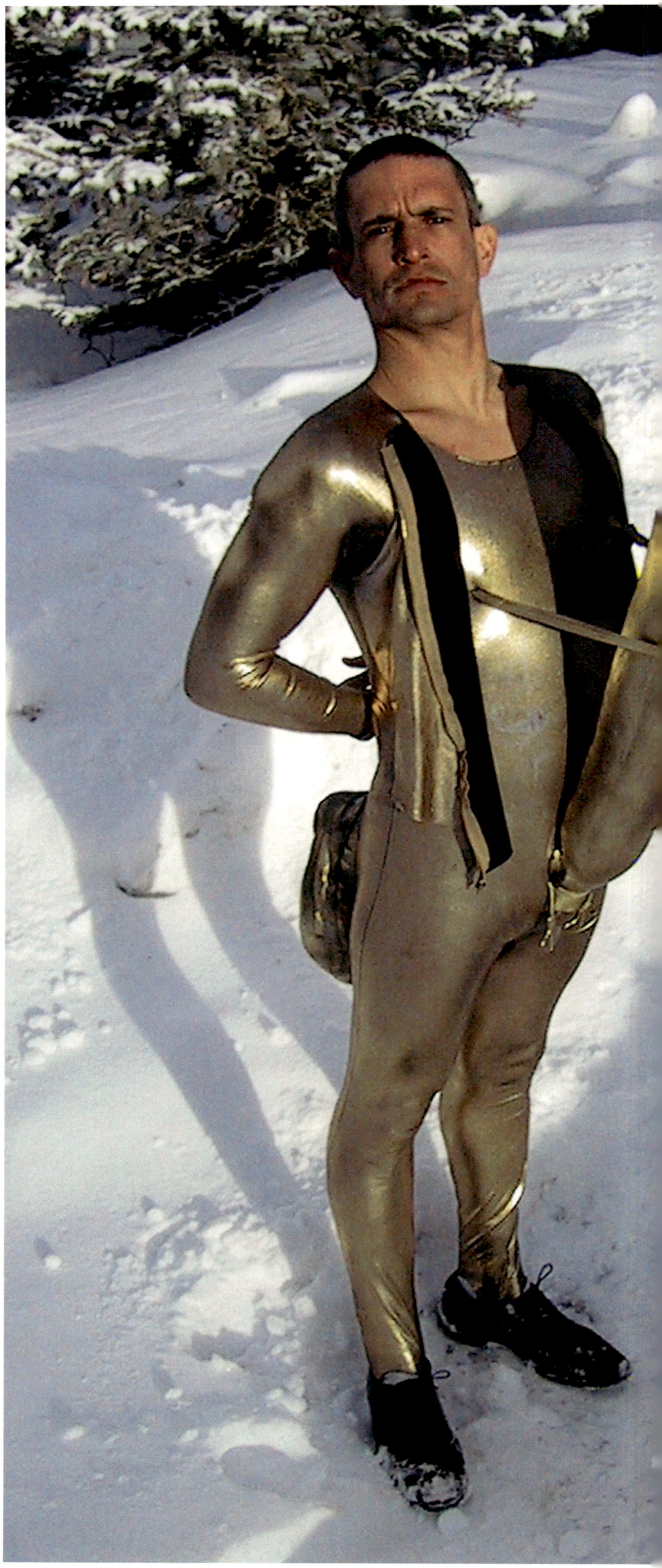

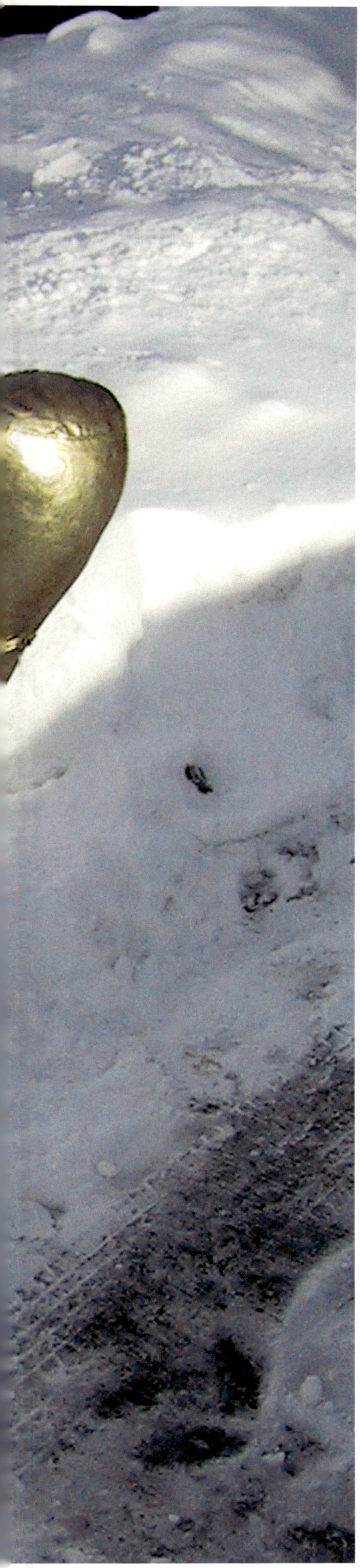

“AT ONE POINT WE CALLED IT IDENTITY CORRECTION. WHERE CRIMINALS USE IDENTITY THEFT TO PREY ON THE POWERLESS AND MAKE MONEY, WE PREY ON THE POWERFUL AND USE THEIR IDENTITIES AND POSITION TO GET THE WORD OUT ABOUT SOMETHING THAT NEEDS TO BE FIXED.”

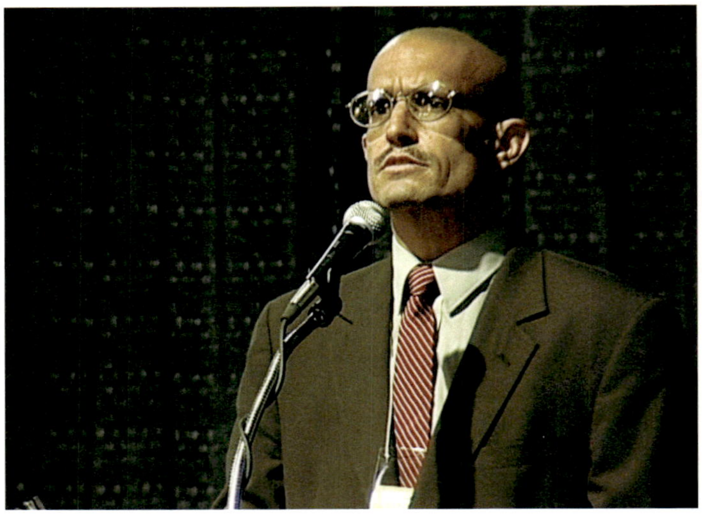

2

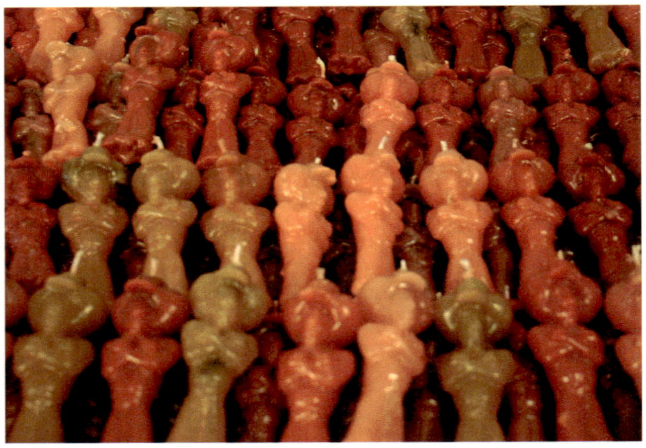

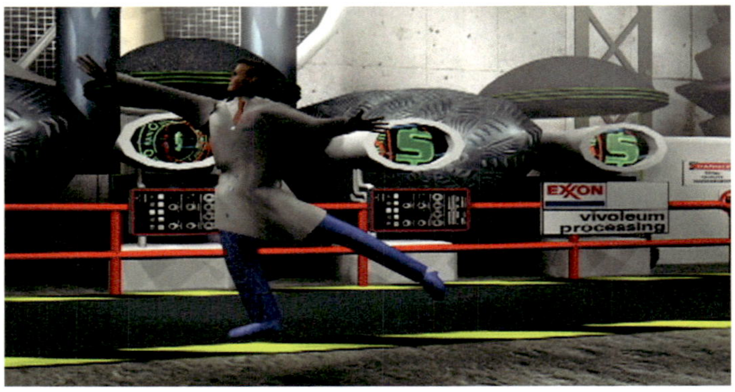

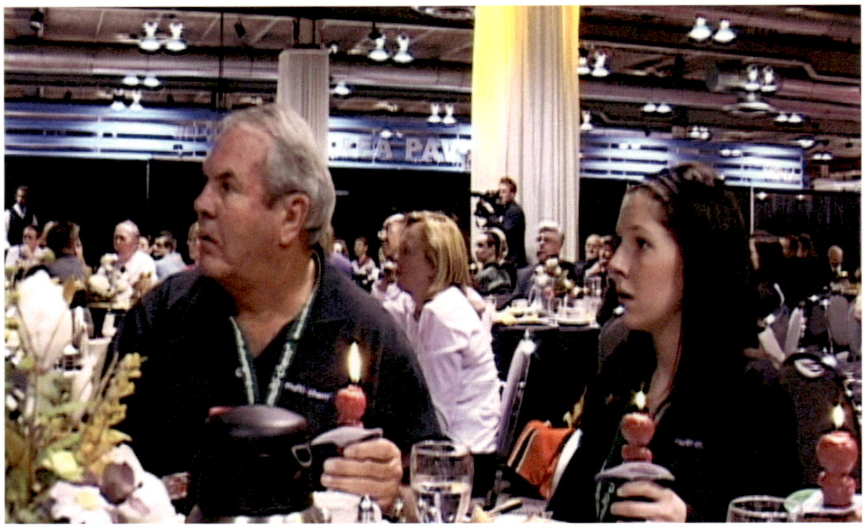

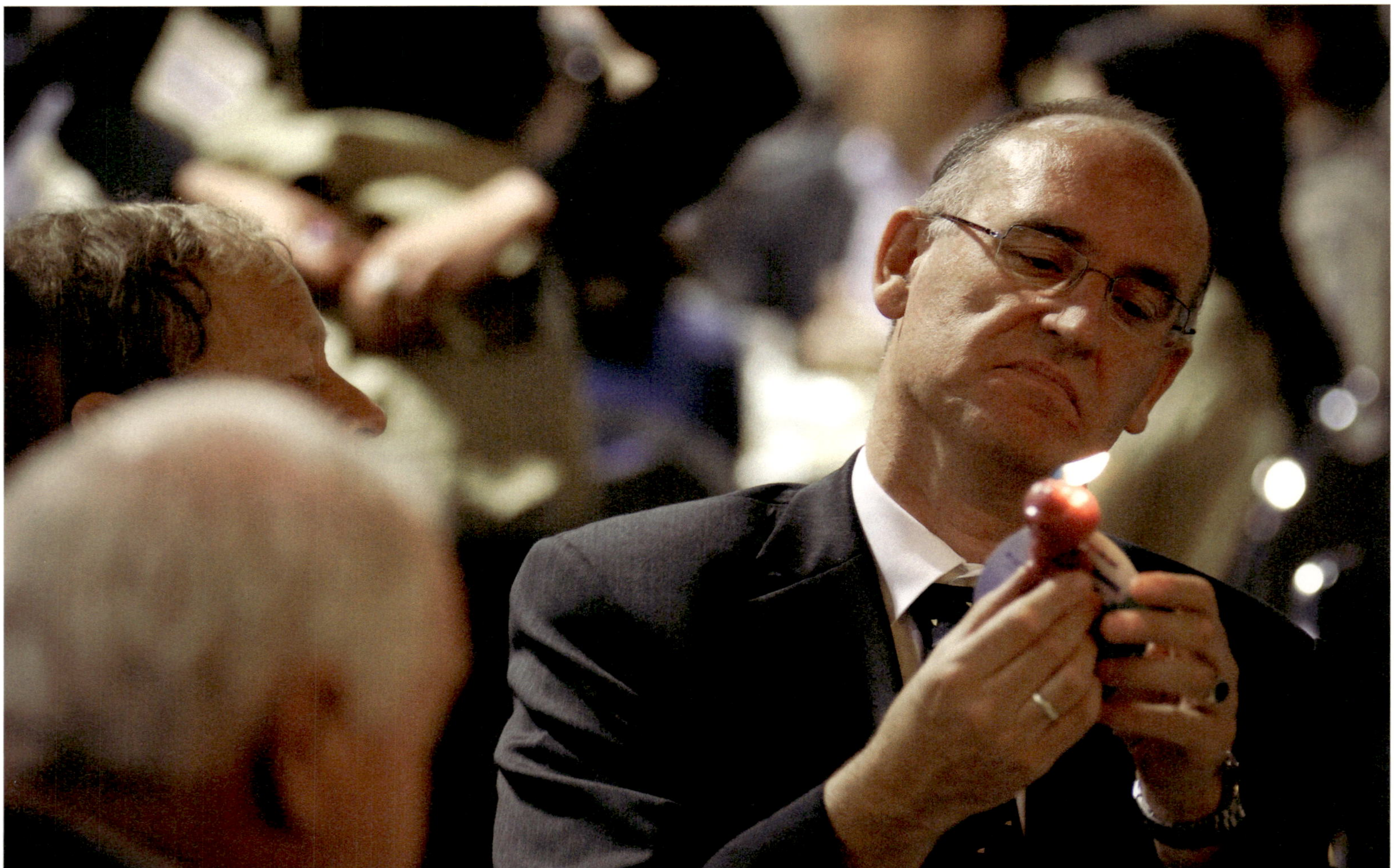

THE YES MEN

2
Exxon's Climate-Victim Candles
2007, Calgary, Canada

3
Halliburton Solves
Global Warming!
2006

3
Dow Does the Right Thing
2004, Worldwide

3

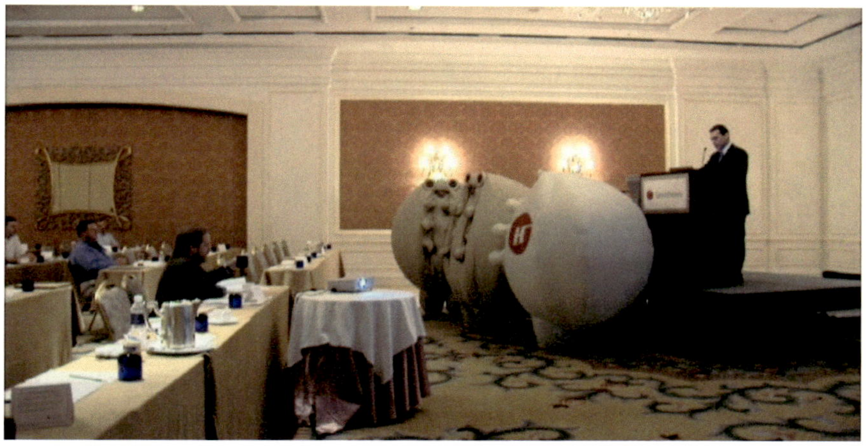

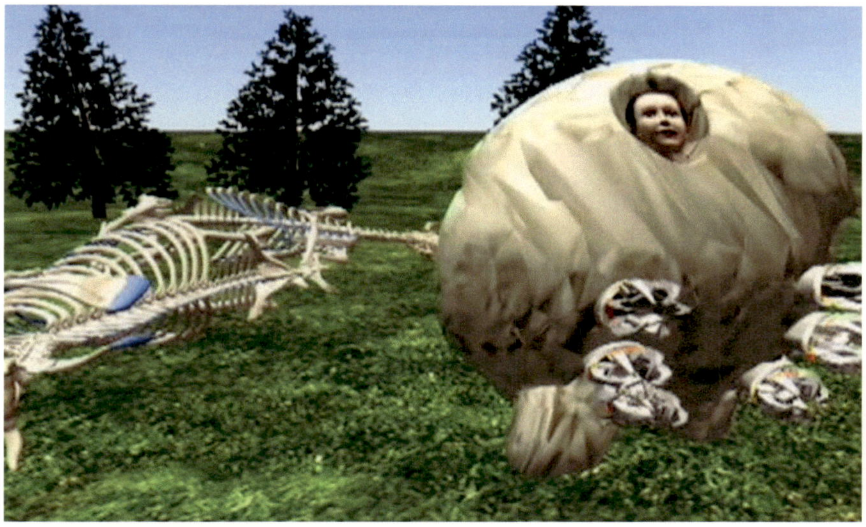

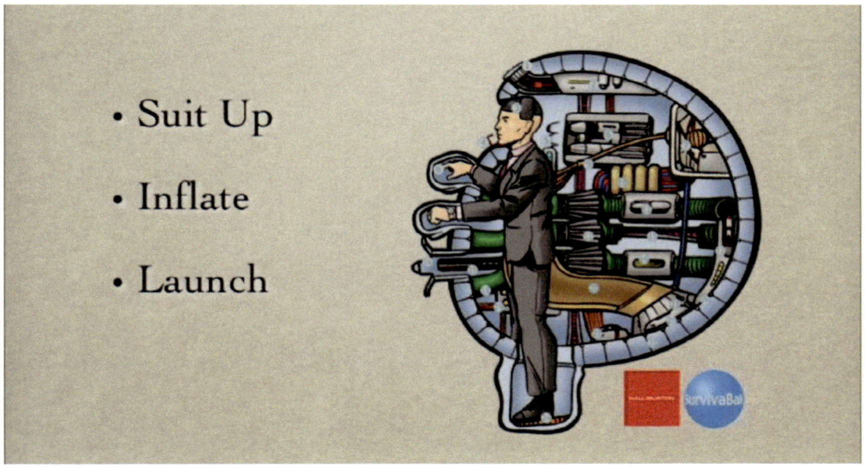

4

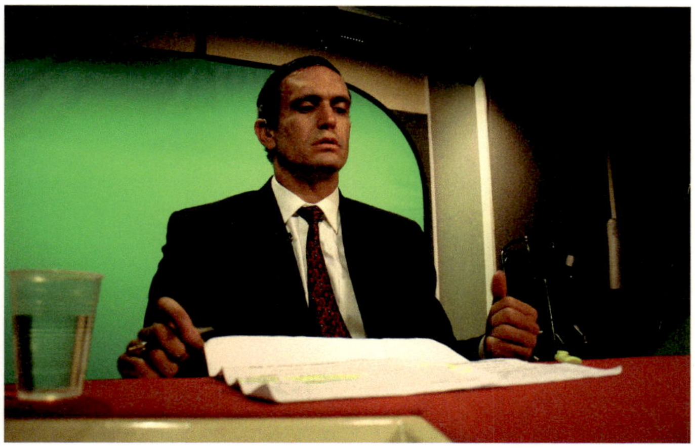

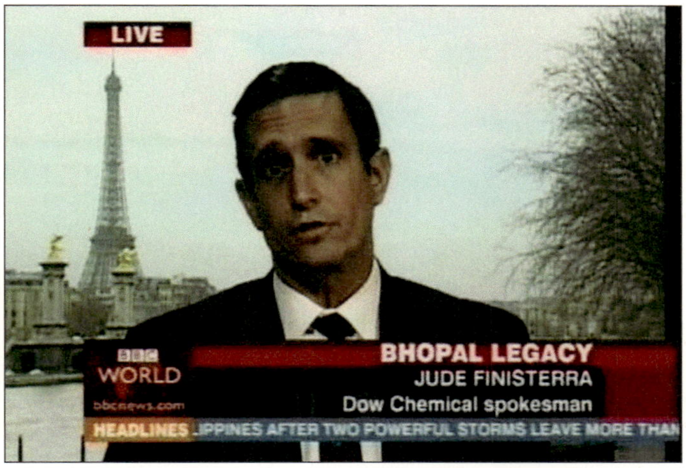

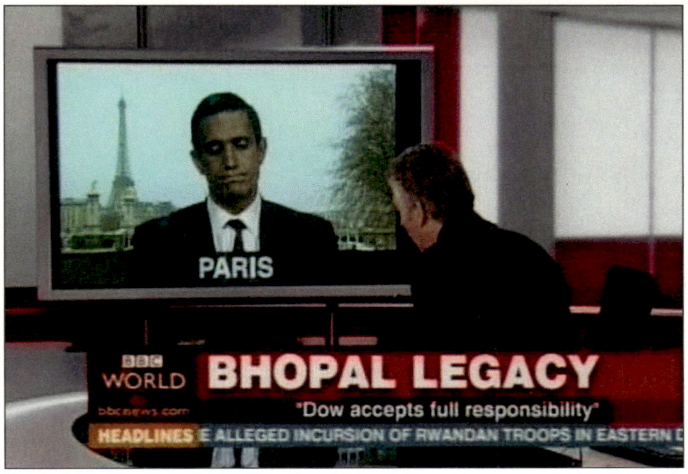

SUPERFLEX

Since 1993, the Danish artist group SUPERFLEX, which consists of Rasmus Nielsen, Jakob Fenger, and Bjørnstjerne Christiansen, has been working on a worldwide series of projects concerned with economic power relationships, democratic production, and self-organisation. In 1997, for instance, the artists collaborated with Danish and African engineers to create the East African *Supergas* project: a simple mobile biogas unit run on organic materials that provides enough energy to supply a single household's needs. An African family could buy this biogas system for a small sum, thereby gaining a degree of economic independence and self-sufficiency. One of their best-known projects was *Guaraná Power*, 2003, a collaboration between SUPERFLEX and the Brazilian farmers who cultivate guaraná, a plant whose berries contain caffeine. Together with the artists, the farmers developed a beverage with its own logo and unique brand philosophy to counteract guaraná berry price dumping by large firms who have a monopoly on the plant and on the Guaraná brand. The development of *Guaraná Power* was based on the idea of using global brands and their strategies as raw material for an alternative economic and social model—today, production and marketing of *Guaraná Power* has been taken over by an independent association. This shows that encouraging people to think can provide a route to self-help; the group pressures its viewers to think critically rather than just accepting the apparent facts. For instance, many artworks by SUPERFLEX focus on the financial crisis. In the film *The Financial Crisis (Session I-IV)*, 2009, a hypnotist takes the viewers through its four phases. At the Cork Midsummer Festival in Ireland, the artist managed to implement an exceptional art project; all citizens of the town were urged not to use the word "recession" for a day. At the instigation of the lord mayor, Councillor Dara Murphy, the town council decided to ban the use of the word for the duration of June 17, 2010. For an artwork meaningfully entitled *Power Toilets*, 2010, the group installed a copy of the toilets from the UN Security Council's New York headquarters—a symbol of unity following the Second World War—in the Park van Luna in Heerhugowaard for public use. The group is also ready to ironically investigate its own subversive power, as its 2002 poster campaign shows. In numerous foreign cities in which they exhibited, SUPERFLEX posted bright orange posters with "FOREIGNERS, PLEASE DON'T LEAVE US ALONE WITH THE DANES!" written on them.

1
Today We Do Not Use
the Word Recession

2
Burning Car
2008, HD with sound, PAL
16:9, 9:30 minutes

3
Foreigners, Please Don't Leave
Us Alone with the Danes!
2002, Wall painting

4
The Financial Crisis
(Session I–IV)
2009

5
Power Toilets
2010

6
Superdanish
2004, wall painting, 13 × 3.5 m,
Shown at the Powerplant

All photos by SUPERFLEX

1
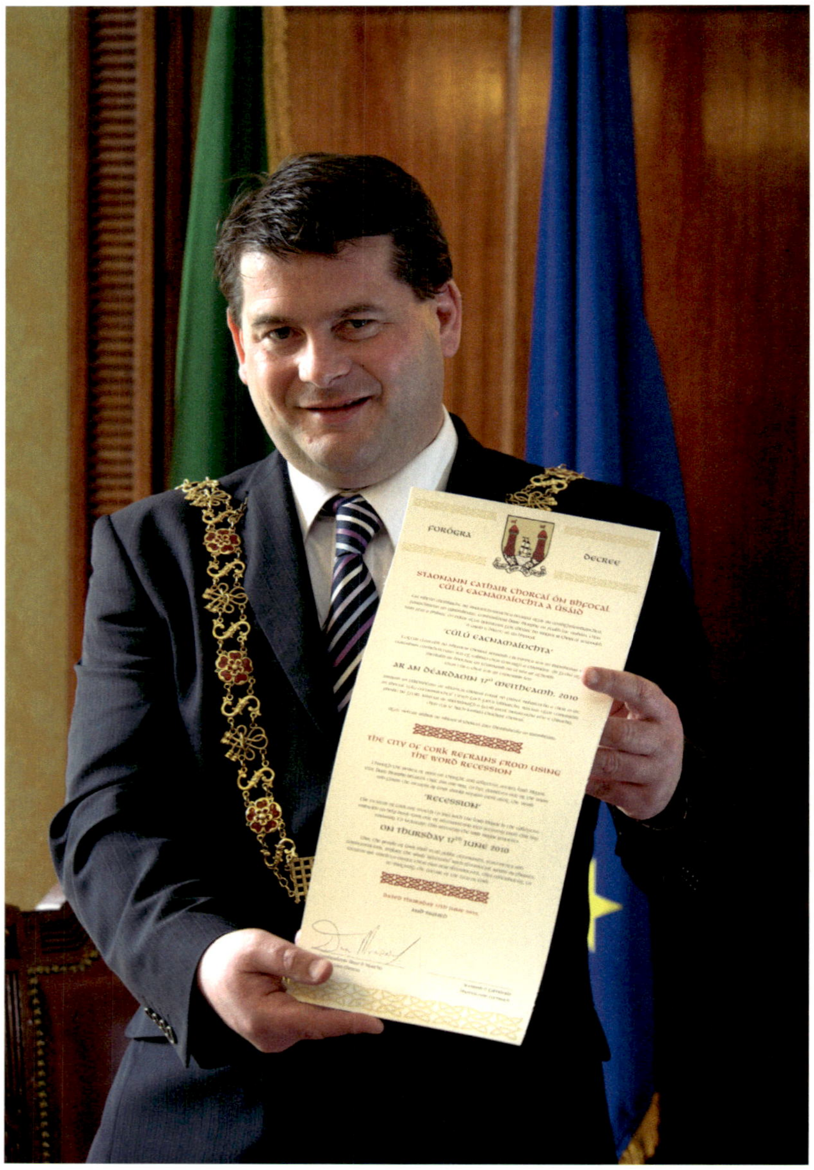

2
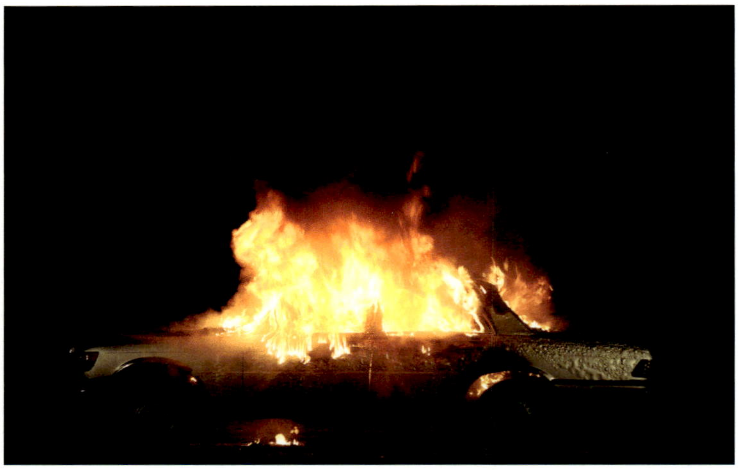

3
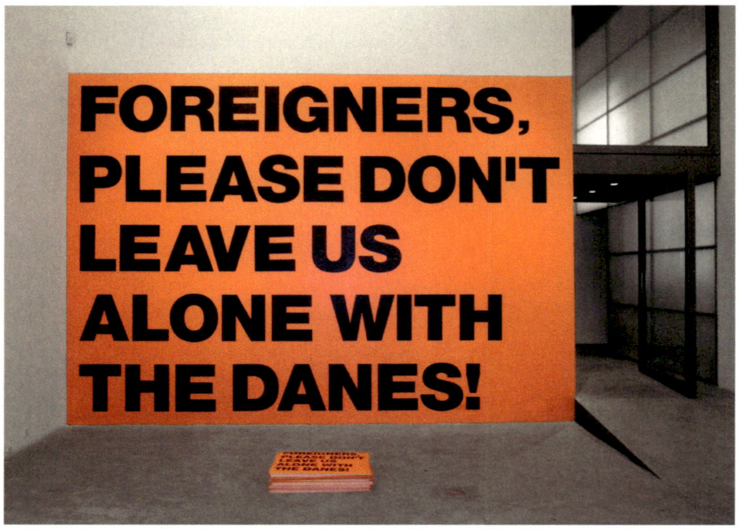

4

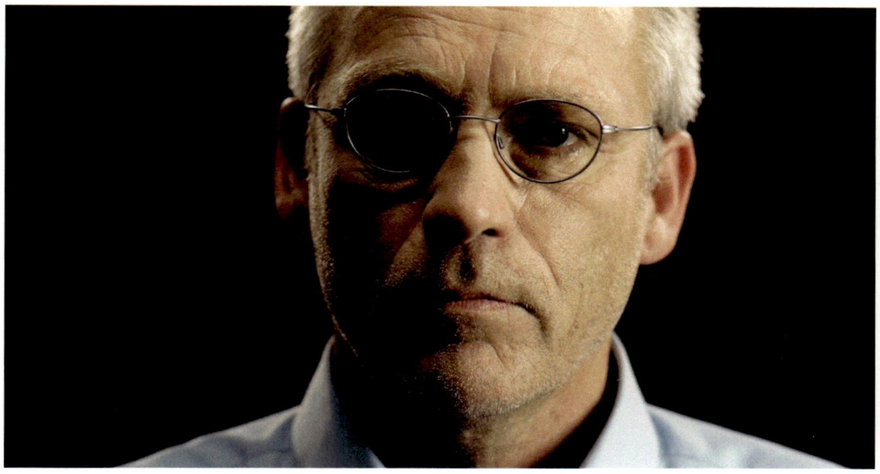

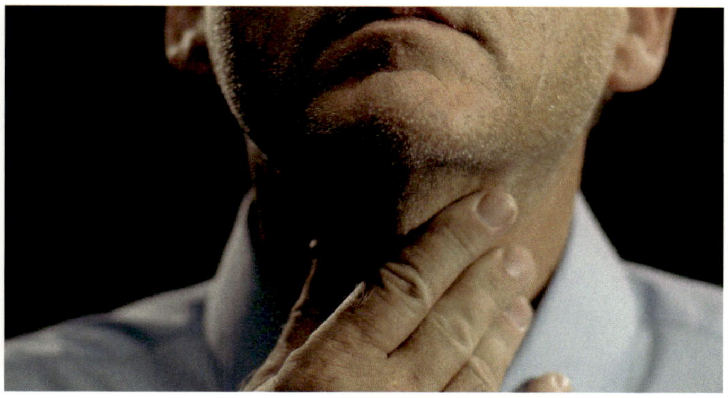

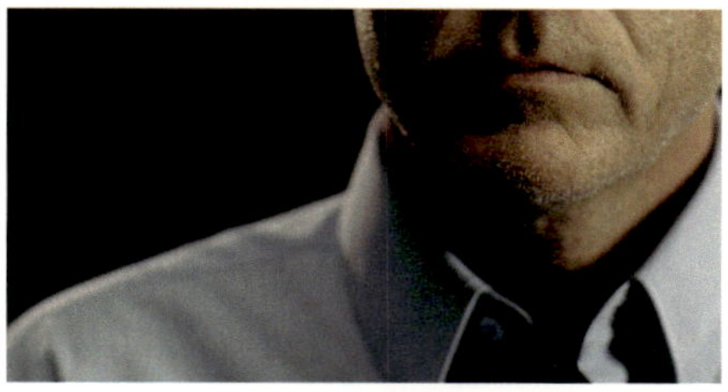

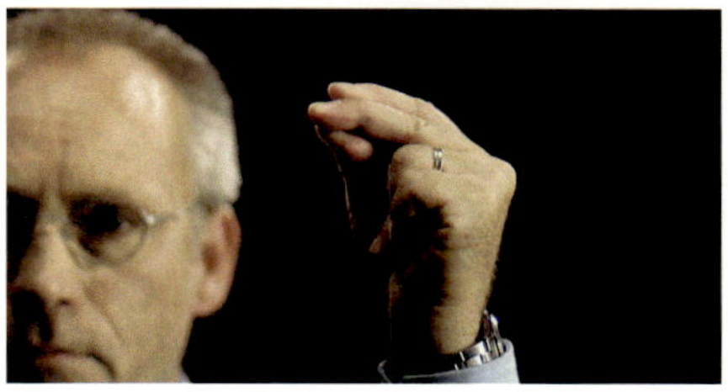

5

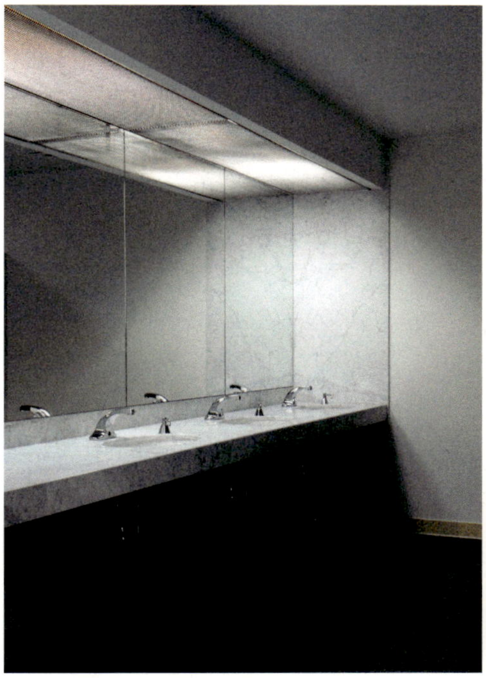

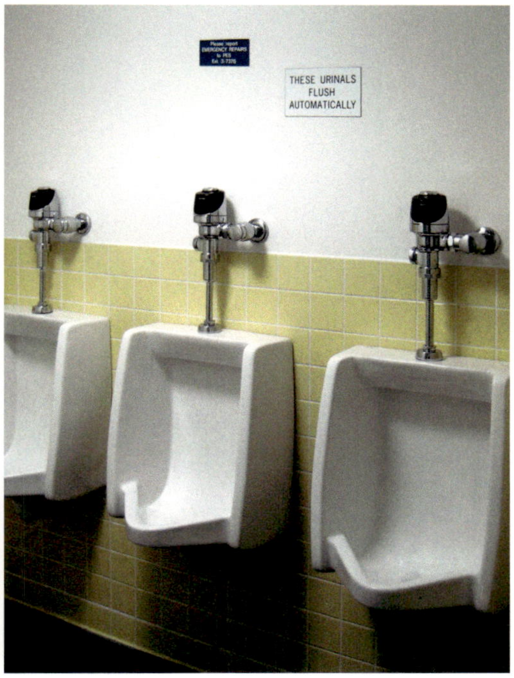

6

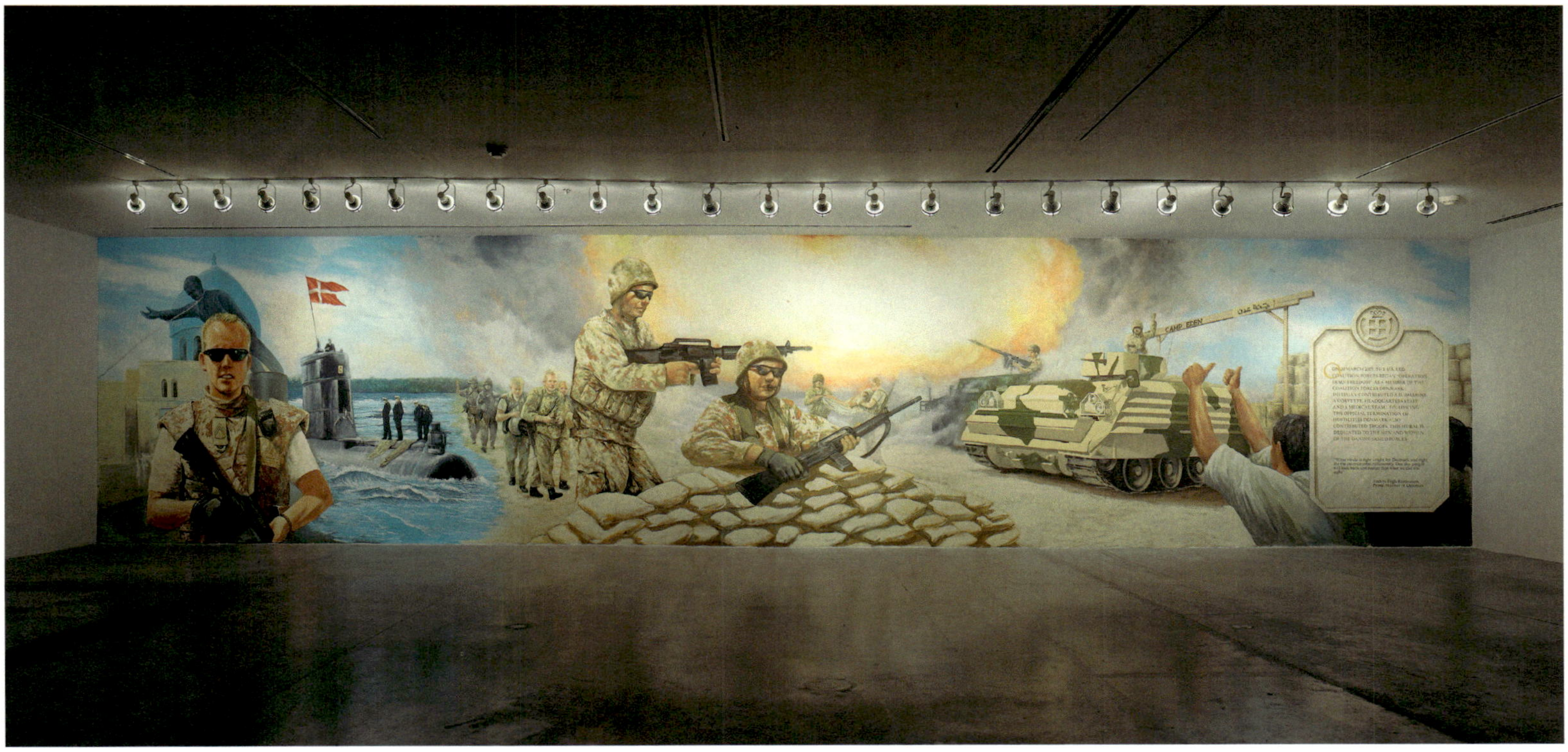

EVAN ROTH

1

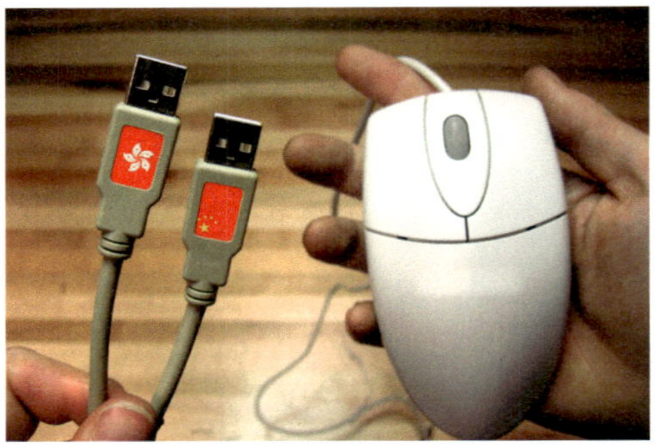

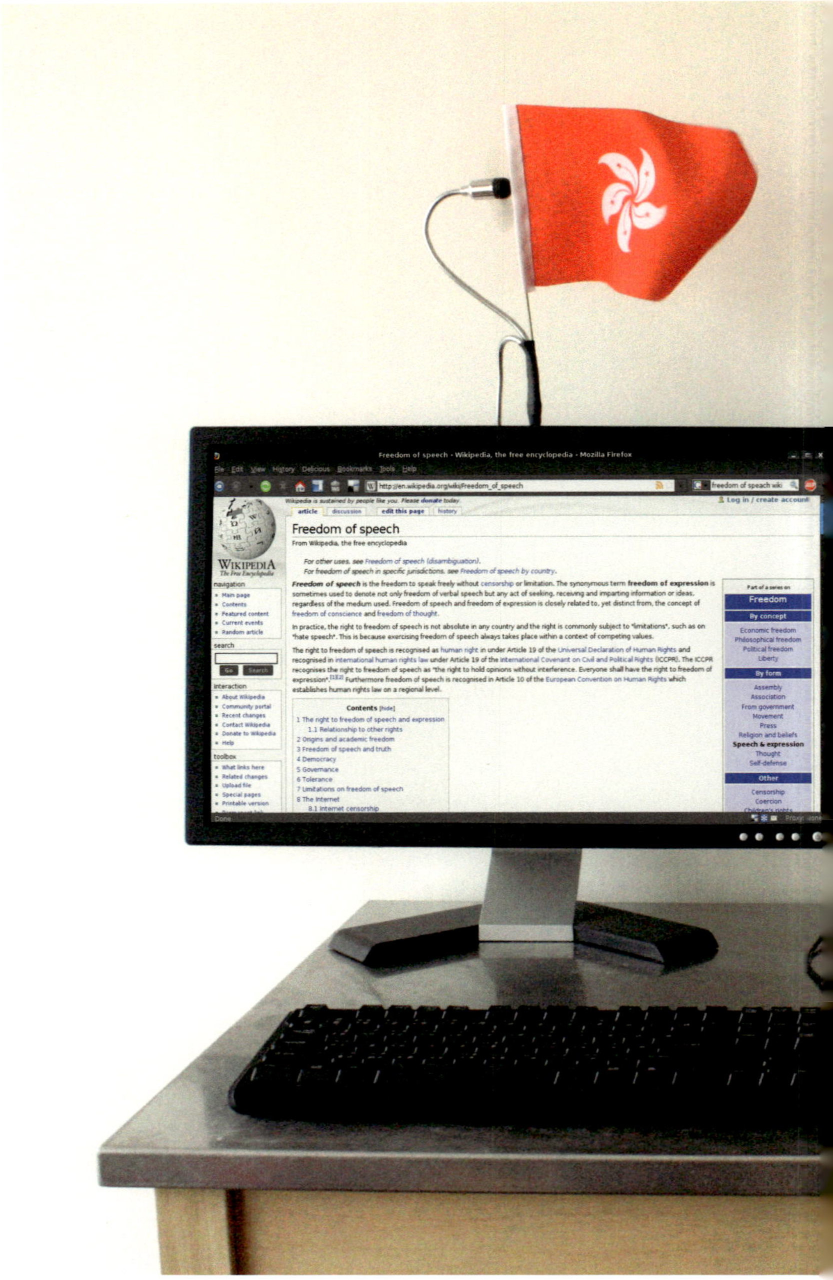

1
China Channel
(with Aram Bartholl & Tobias Leingruber)
A Firefox add-on which offers internet user outside China to surf the web as if they were in China.
2
Available Online For Free
3
TSA Communication
4
IP Donor

Evan Roth (* 1978) is a graffiti geek and media artist, whose projects feature open source material and popular culture. In 2005, he founded the Graffiti Research Lab, which has since evolved into a kind of technical support system for the graffiti scene. Through the lab, Roth provides artists and activists with open source tools for their projects, including *LED throwies*—light emitting diodes that can be temporarily secured to objects using a magnet—and laser tagging, which involves tagging the whole wall of a house by means of a projector and a laser pointer. This collective was a stepping stone on the road to the founding of the Free Art and Technology Lab in 2007, a network of artists, scientists, lawyers, musicians, and engineers from all over the world, who work together to research and develop new creative techniques and media, and who also combat copyright protection patent law. Roth takes pleasure in small-scale subversive attacks that highlight weaknesses. One of these involved putting stickers on software, music CDs, and DVDs in stores which read: "Available Online For Free." In his *Public Domain Donor,* 2008, campaign—based on the familiar organ donor card—Roth endeavored to spread the message that in case of death people should leave all their intellectual property to the general public. His project *TSA Communication,* 2008, allowed people to communicate with airport security staff. It involved a metal plate inserted in a pocket or rucksack which concealed the contents from x-ray scanners—instead, a short message along the lines of, "Mind your own business" and "Nothing to see here" could be seen on the computer screen. Roth operates like a hacker—he launches targeted attacks to sabotage existing systems, employing the language of pop culture. He states that: "There are two principal things that characterize the Free Art & Technology Lab. On one side, there is the open source culture and advertisement-free culture, but also the idea that all this should be fun. Art and political activism doesn't have to be boring; the interface of it can be accessible to more people. We try to push this candy coding, get those audiences who are using YouTube videos, that is our primary audience."

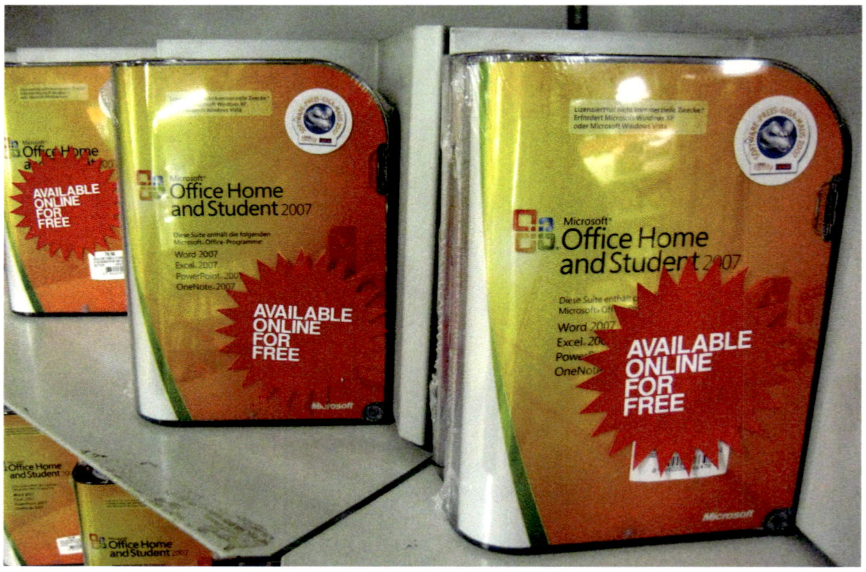

2

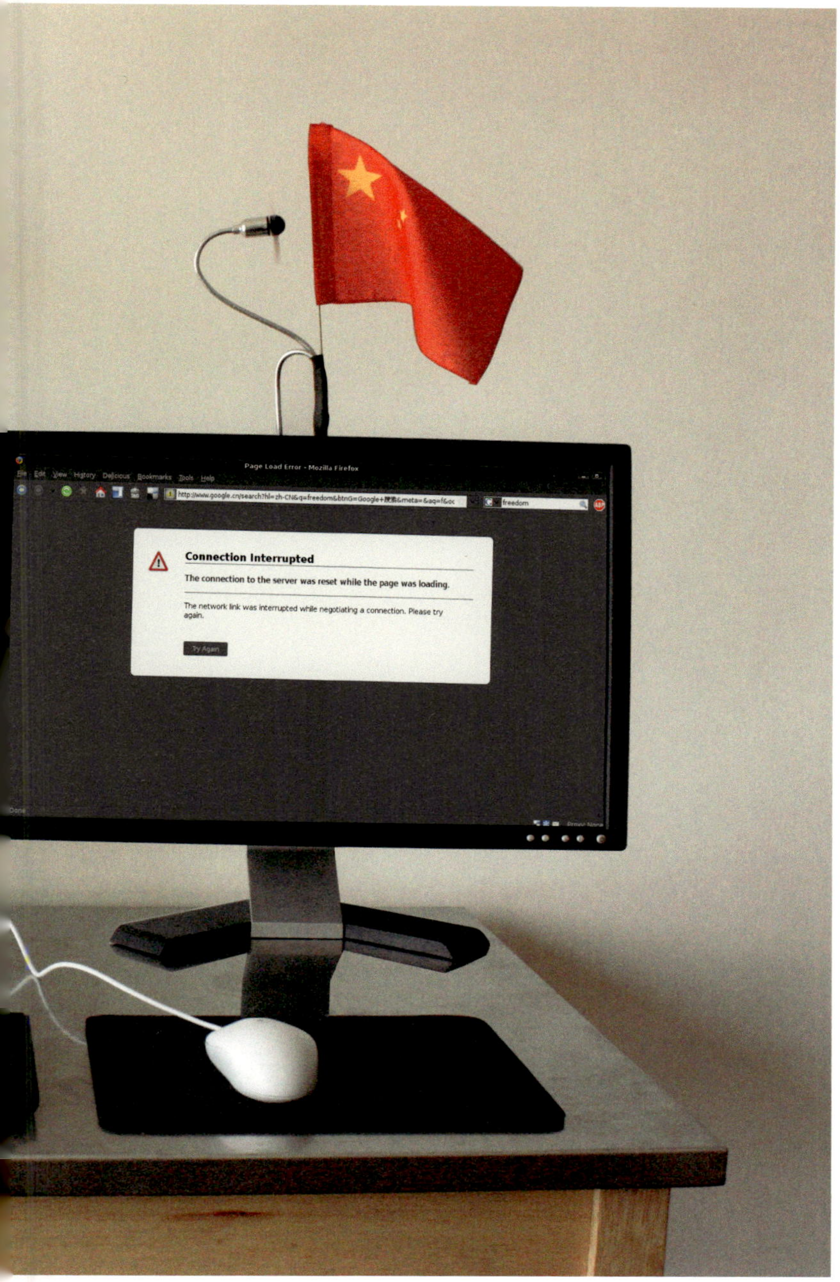
Page Load Error - Mozilla Firefox
Connection Interrupted
The connection to the server was reset while the page was loading.
The network link was interrupted while negotiating a connection. Please try again.

3

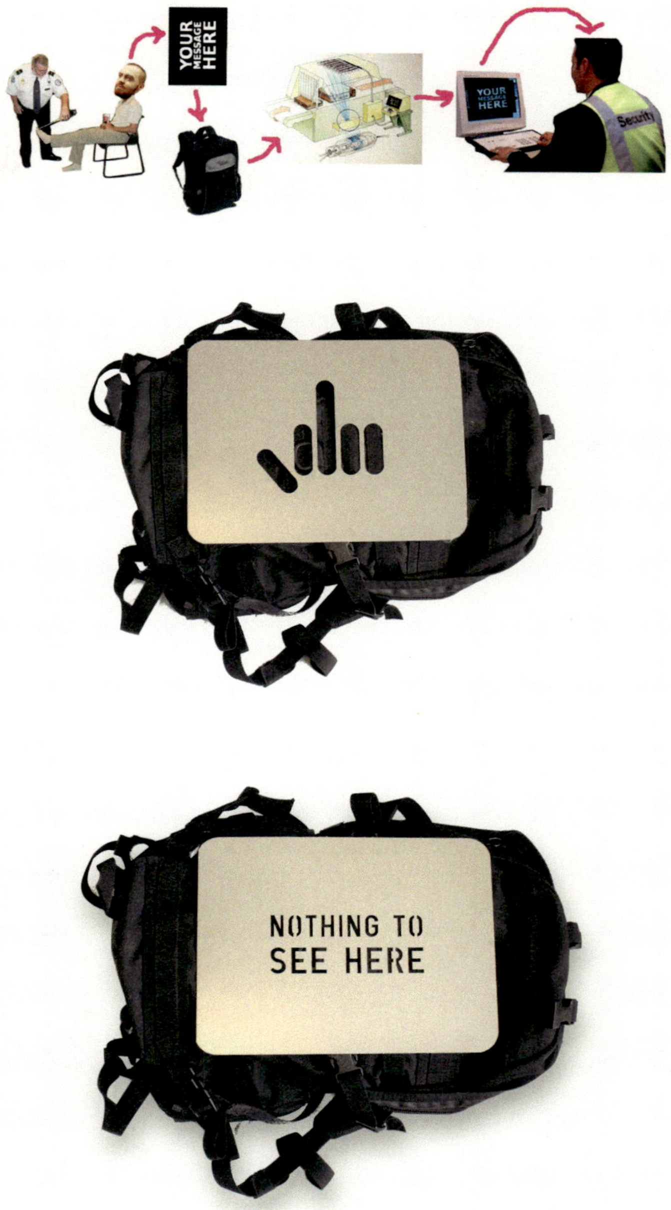
YOUR MESSAGE HERE
YOUR MESSAGE HERE
Security
NOTHING TO SEE HERE

4

E: (NONE)
R: (NONE)
ENTER ADDRESS CHANGE:
You must notify DMV within 10 days.
In event of death please donate all intellectual property to the public domain.
Donor Signature E.Roth
Date 02/26/08
Intellectual Property Donor

ARAM BARTHOLL

1

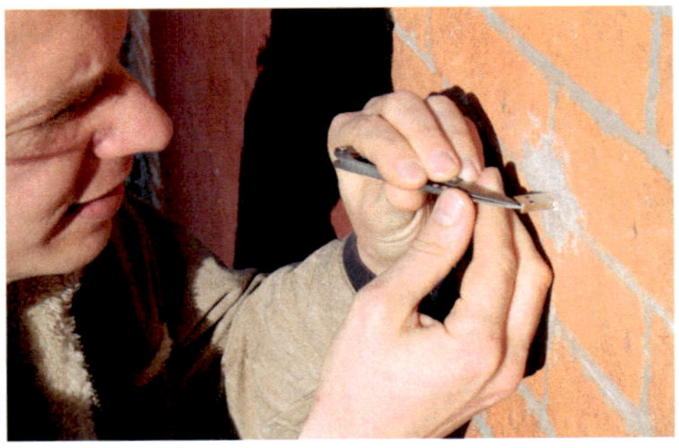

Aram Bartholl (* 1972) was creating art dealing with online "geo services" long before Google Street View became controversial in Germany. The Berlin-based media artist created his *Map* installation, 2006–2010, by setting up oversized versions of the kind of marker pins seen as icons in Google Maps in locations in Germany, Poland, and Taiwan. Bartholl's artworks frequently transfer symbols from the internet into real space, creating a link with the virtual world, and thereby highlighting new dangers and power relationships. "On the screen, the pin is just a little icon," Bartholl explains, "but the influence this kind of service has on how we perceive our cities is enormous." The Google operation's omnipresence has made it Bartholl's favourite target. For example, he has collaborated with the Free Art & Technology Lab to build a Google Street View car, *How to Build a Fake Google Street View Car,* 2010, which he then drove through Berlin, evoking reactions from passersby with his absurd behavior. For his *Google Portrait Series,* 2007–2009, he painted QR barcodes representing the different Google searches on his name in China, England, and Germany. These are contemporary portraits based on the Google algorithm; they are intimate in a very real way and show just how fundamental Google has become to our identities. For his recent work *Dead Drops,* 2010, he mortared USB sticks into walls, inspiring many people to follow his example, and thereby creating offline file-sharing networks all over the world.

1
Dead Drops
2010, New York, USA
2
How to Build a Fake Google Street View Car
2010, with Free Art & Technology Lab
3
Map
2010, Taipei, Taiwan

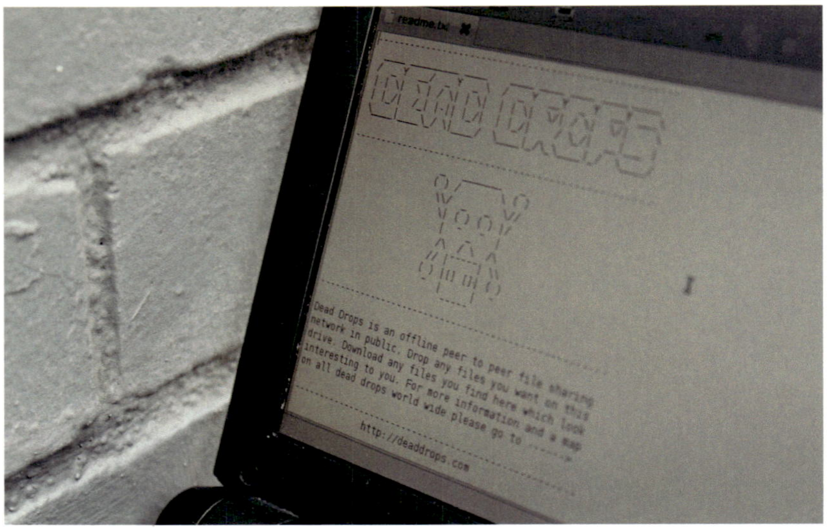

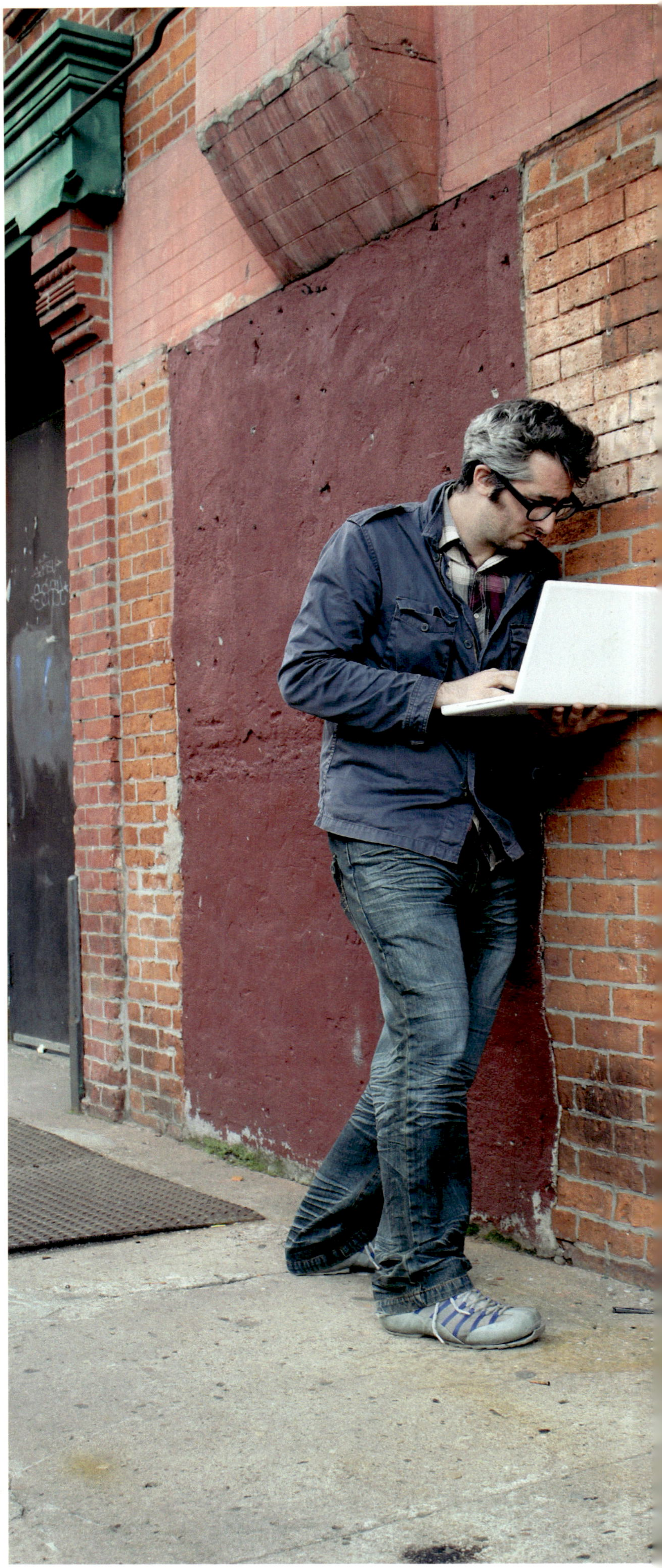

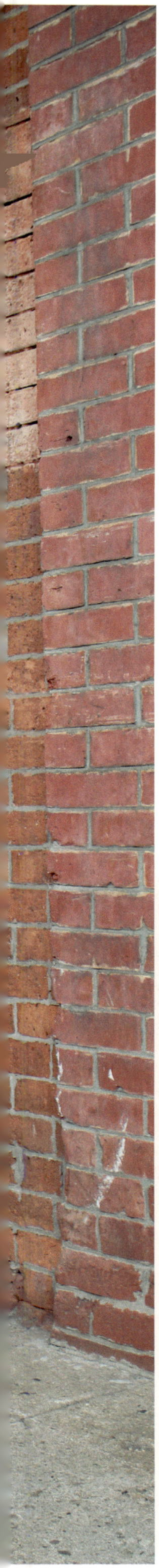

2

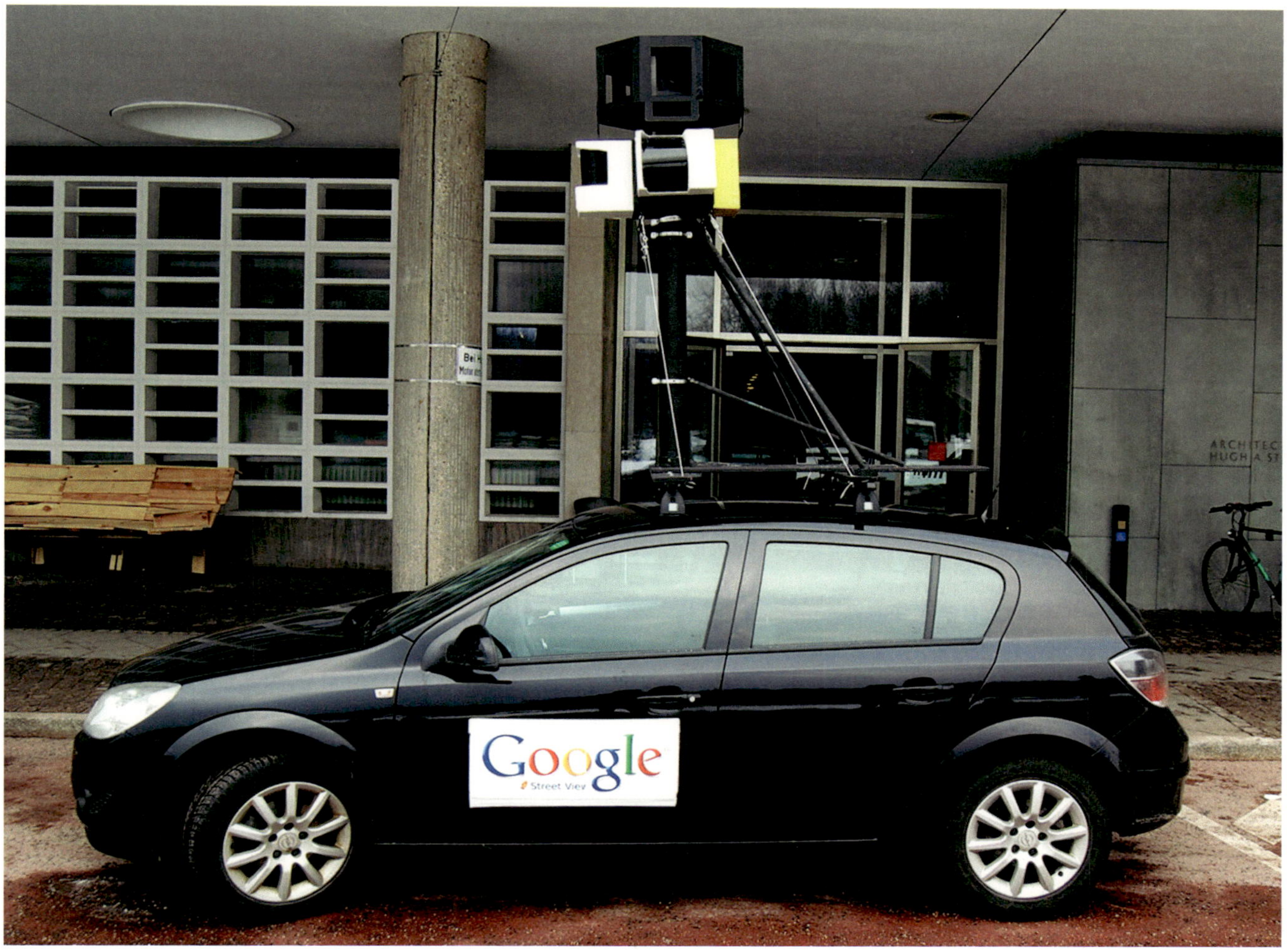

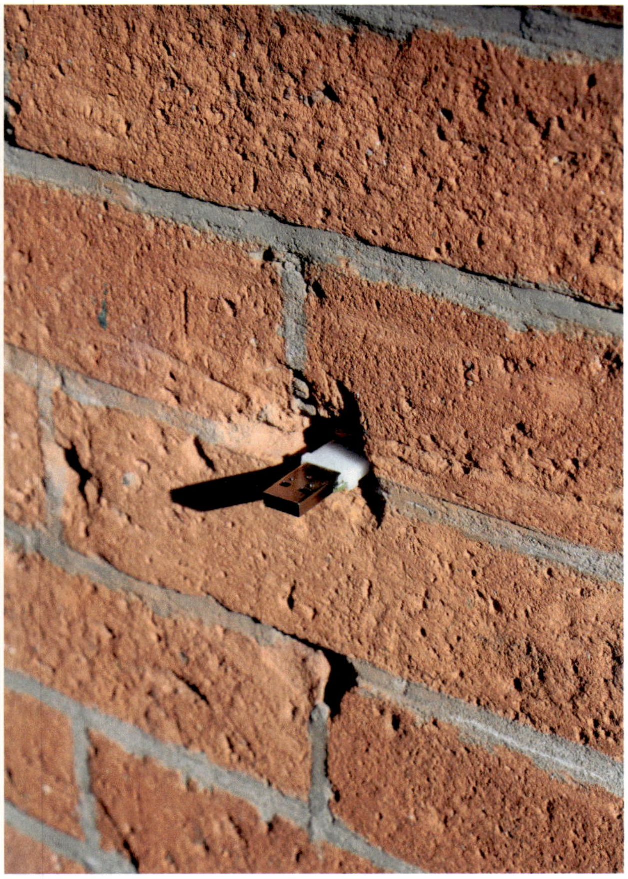

3

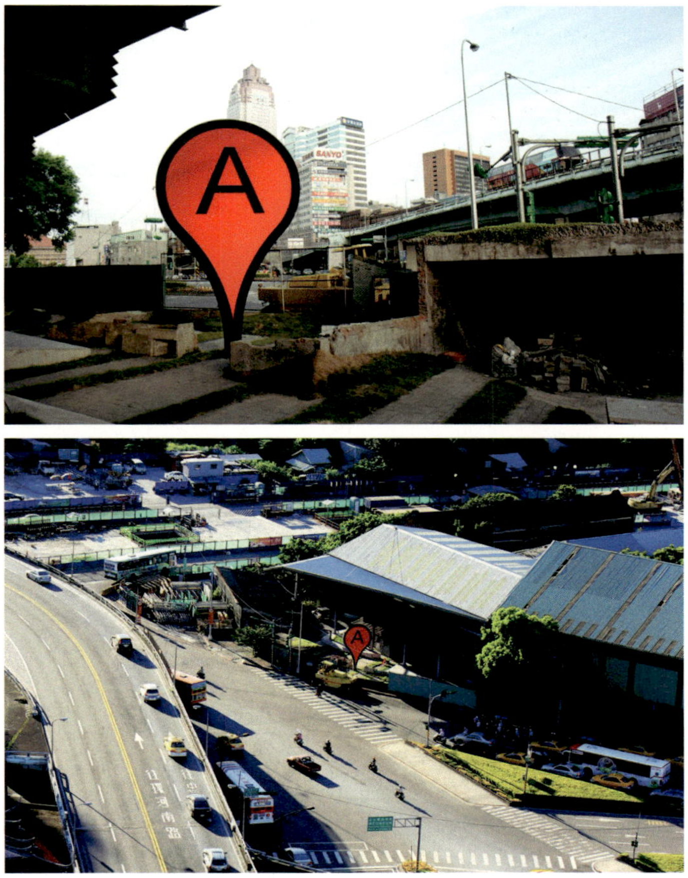

HERMANN JOSEF HACK

Düsseldorf artist Hermann Josef Hack (* 1956) believes that: "In an age when politicians make policies for politicians, the established arts scene produces art about art for art historians and art collectors." This is the reason why he places his *World Climate Refugee Camps* in the street space itself. His miniature tents have already been placed under the Brandenburg Gate in Berlin, in Frankfurt's airport, and in Leipzig's Marktplatz. Sometimes Hack paints direction signs on tent flysheets, a reference to fictional destinations such as the climate refugee camp, or an "Ambulant Embassy of the Climate Refugee Republic." He firmly believes that only art can stop climate change. "My work is about getting people interested in political issues so that they can find out for themselves what it is all about. Only art is able to restore the developmental potential of our society, which has been retarded by economic and political forces." Hack's mission is to warn people about the threat posed by climate change, but he does not consider himself to be an activist. "For activists, art is only a means to an end, a vehicle for their messages. Good political art, however, transcends partisan interests, and overcomes traditional formats in our society that will no longer be relevant in the future. Good art gives rise to new insights, and, ideally, to concrete action."

1
Urban Exhibition
2010, Hamburg, Germany

2
World Climate Refugee Camp
2009, Brandenburg Gate, Berlin, Germany

1

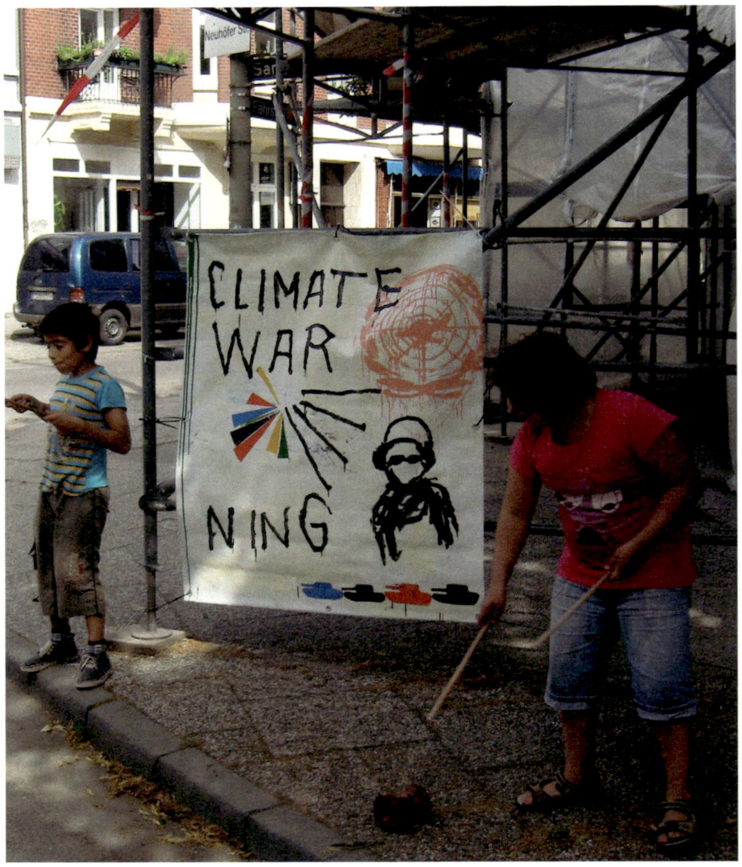

2

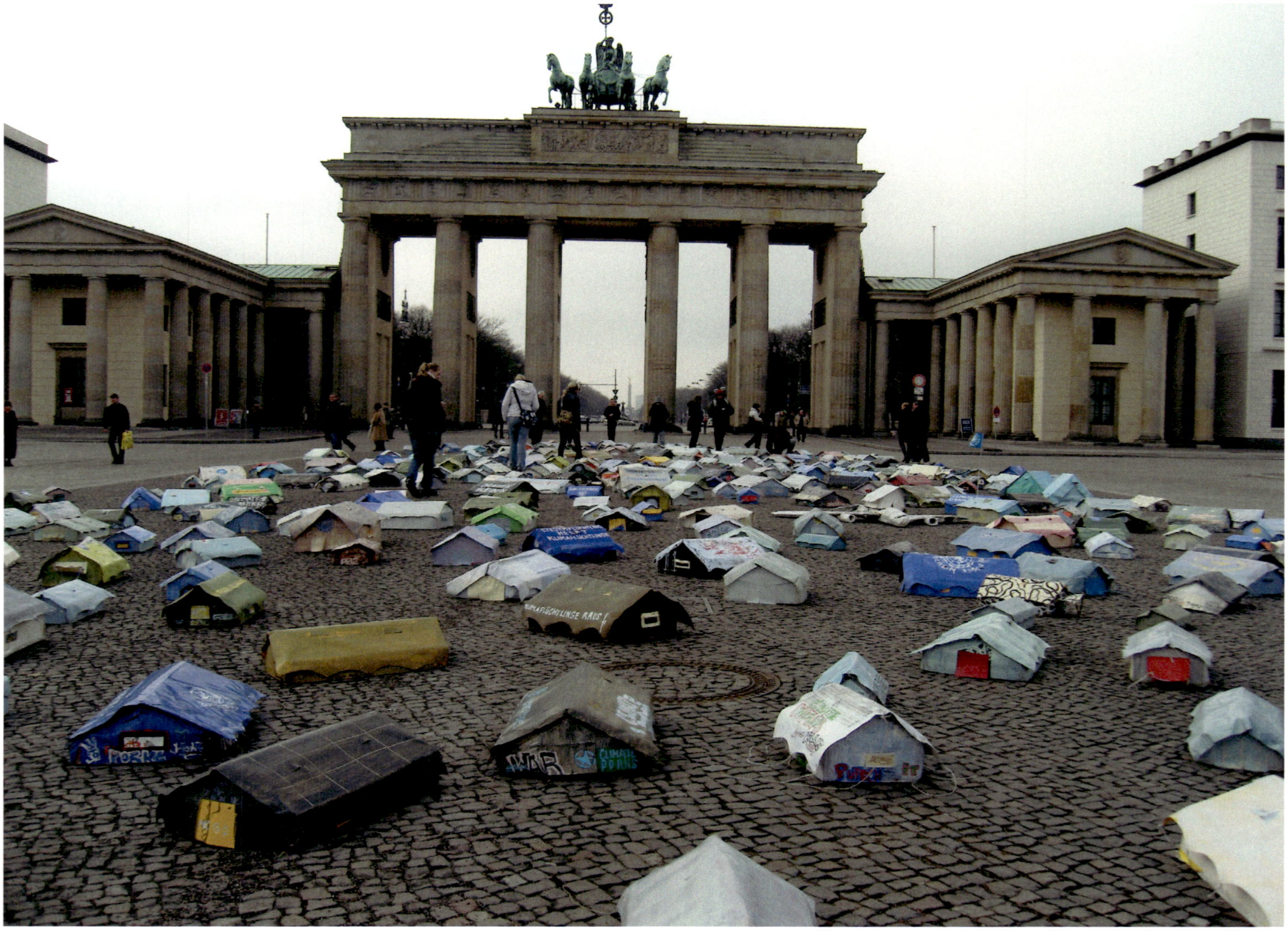

NÉLE AZEVEDO

The ephemeral miniature memorials of Brazilian artist Néle Azevedo from Santos Dumont, make us look at cities' monumental heroic memorials in a different way. Over the course of her numerous art projects, she has created her own special type of anti-memorial. In the summer, she placed hundreds of little ice sculptures (20 cm in height)—seated, faceless, identical men—in crowded plazas in major international cities such as Brazil, Havana, Tokyo, Paris, Florence, and Berlin. The artist gets passersby to help with her projects, which often last only a few minutes, and this shared act of creation is an integral part of the way she works. It is only thanks to the artist's many helpers that these memorials made of ice can be erected before the ice melts away completely. And yet, due to the continual melting process, the artwork will never reach the completed stage—it will simply vanish as if it had never existed. The only part of this memorial that endures are the photographs. However, because the meltwater flows into the ground, the artist is "giving" the artwork to the city, and those who took part in setting up the memorial will remember this unique experience. In Azevedo's artworks, the memorial is no longer reserved for individual heroes—it becomes a collective experience for everyone.

1
Minimum Monument
2009, Berlin, Germany
2
Minimum Monument
2003, Brasilia, Brazil

Photos by Néle Azevedo

1
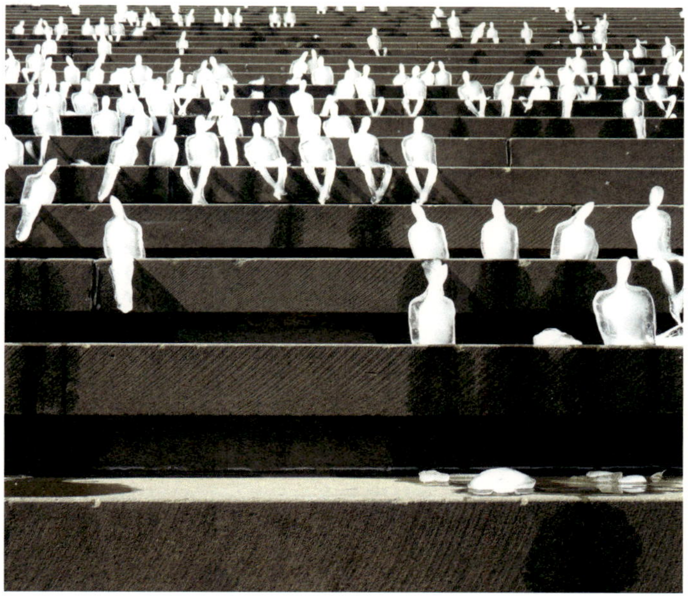

2
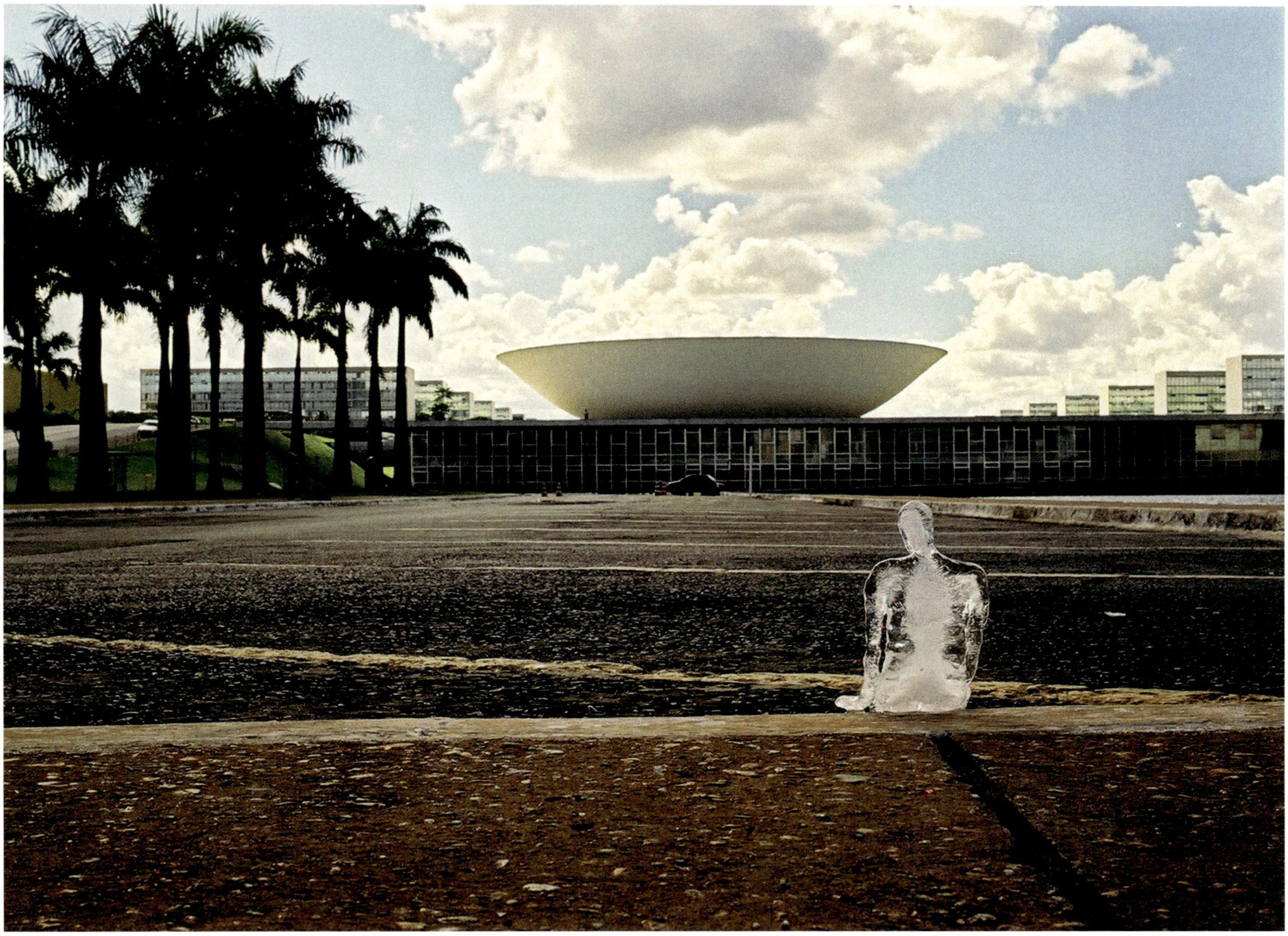

OLIVER GOODHALL

Designer and architect Oliver Goodhall (* 1983) from Harrow, has set himself some ambitious goals: "My projects are designed to expand engagement between policy-making and creative practice in the public realm. My intent is to be logically utopian and playfully analytical. My project outcomes may be informative, revealing, outlandish—or hopefully all of these." The implementation of his largest project to date, *Nuclear Is Good. What Will It Take to Convince You?,* 2010, was certainly ambitious.

In 2009, the British government announced that it was building nuclear power stations in 11 locations in England to help to reduce CO_2 emissions. In his project, Goodhall tried to come up with convincing arguments in favor of nuclear energy. He wanted to open up a debate on energy politics in general and nuclear energy in particular. With this aim in mind, he created a video and held a round of tours and discussions and a special "nuclear weapons free" picnic on the site of a future nuclear power station in Sussex. His guests—nuclear engineers, environmentalists, and designers—ate mushrooms and poisonous-looking ice cream. Goodhall also offered some concrete suggestions, including a protective cloud floating over the power station to allay citizens' fears of a catastrophe and to disperse the radiation into the atmosphere, incentives for citizens who disposed of their own nuclear waste, and an evacuation team constantly on call in case of a problem in the power station. Goodhall explains that: "My proposals came from nine months of research and investigation and were heavily influenced by conversations I had with professionals from the fields of ethics, political science, materials chemistry, and the government's Department of Energy and Climate Change. Reactions were varied, but these other professional fields are engaging with the topics I was interested in: affecting policy choices and contributing to decision making."

Nuclear Is Good. What Will It Take to Convince You?
2010, U.K.

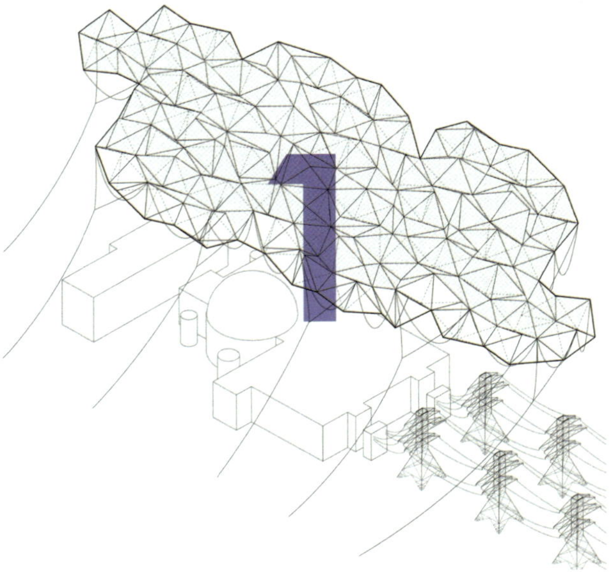

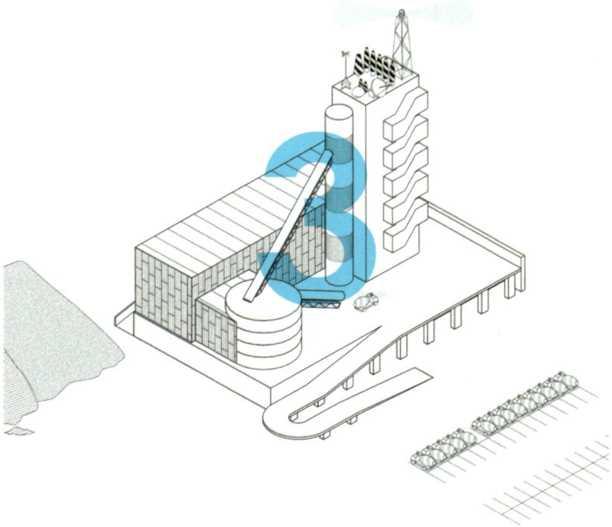

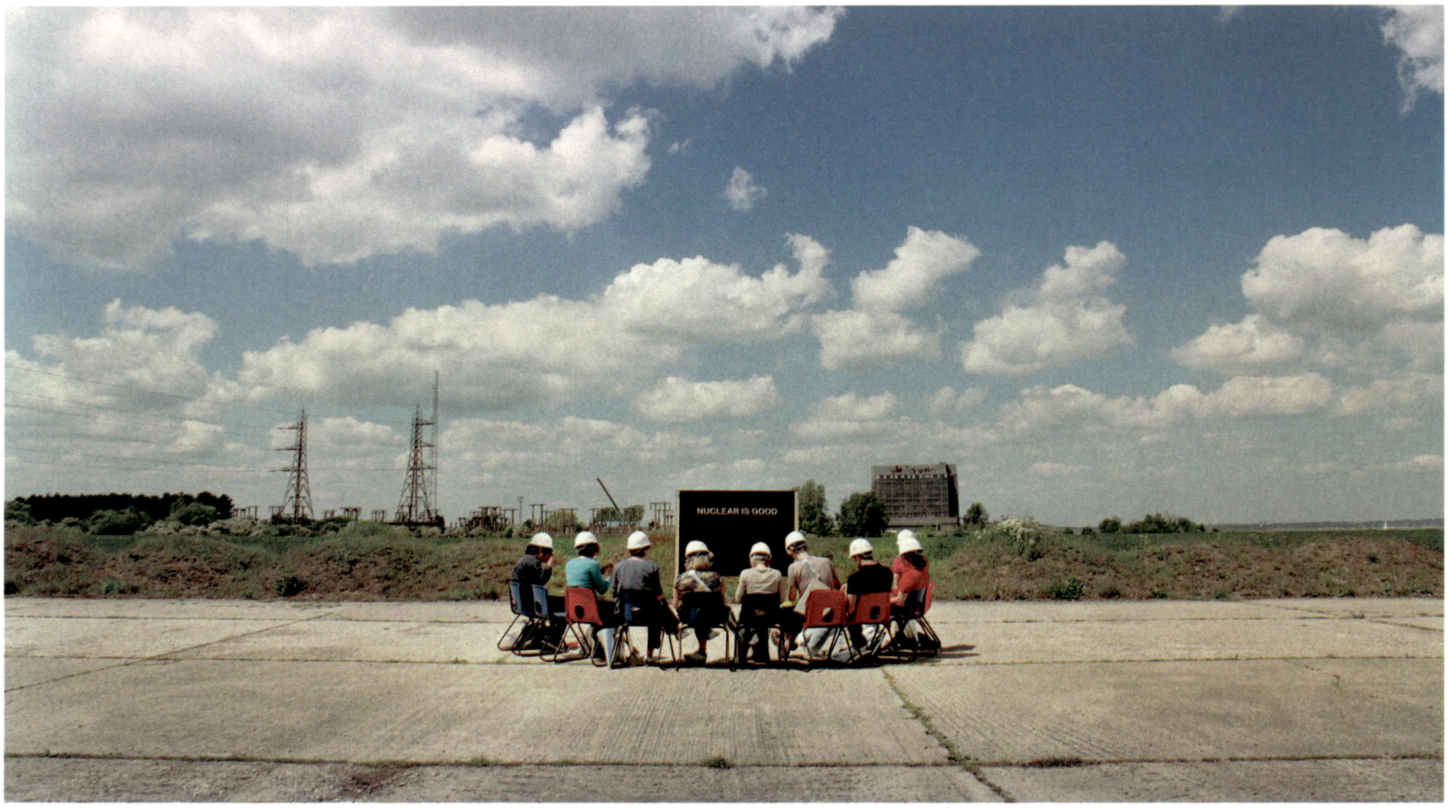

FOLKE KÖBBERLING/ MARTIN KALTWASSER

1

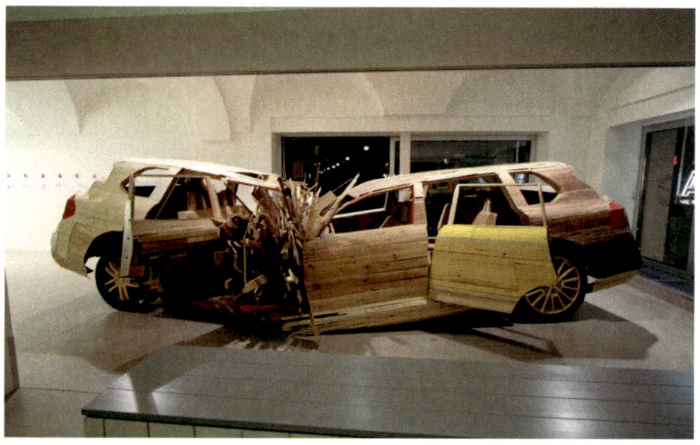

1
Crushed Cayenne
2
White Trash
3
Cars Into Bicycles
Photo by Gliese

Artist duo Folke Köbberling (* 1969) and Martin Kaltwasser (* 1965)—who live and work in Los Angeles and Berlin—create artworks that are about the way that public spaces constantly change. They want to set something up in opposition to the rise in car traffic, the increased surveillance culture, and the pressure to consume. They work with discarded materials, and with trash—in particular with things that have been replaced with something new. The two artists painstakingly track down these scraps in order to create something totally original with them. In 2008, they built a replica of a sport utility vehicle (SUV) from scraps of wood, and for this project they deliberately chose a conspicuous make of car. On an SUV, the jeep-like bodywork is higher and broader than that of a conventional car, and is equipped with military-looking bumpers known as "cow catchers." The motor is very powerful with correspondingly high emissions, and yet the SUV's popularity goes from strength to strength. It has become an accessory for nouveau riche individuals who wish to demonstrate their social status and power in public—in fact, because of the way the vehicle is built, occupants actually look down out of the car's elevated inner space on to the rest of the traffic, through windows that are generally darkened. The artist duo's SUV replica has no refinements at all—it is stripped of its glamour and reduced to a vehicle with the unadorned aesthetic of a tank. And, above all, the wooden duplicate is robbed of the vehicle's primary function—that of moving quickly, it has been turned into a symbol of *decelera*tion. In the same year, Köbberling/Kaltwasser exhibited two 1:1 Porsche Cayenne models that were also made meticulously from scraps of wood, depicted at the moment of collision (the vehicles were first shown in Berlin and then in Munich). The crash is impressive and one can really hear the splitting wood—while, at the same time, the wooden object has its own compelling aesthetic. Unlike the "tank" version, visitors can enter *Crushed Cayenne* and sit in the seats. *Crushed Cayenne* is a criticism of asocial, self-centered behavior on the road. The artists heighten the irony by depicting a crash between two cars of the same type, thereby negating the principle of "power to the stronger."

2

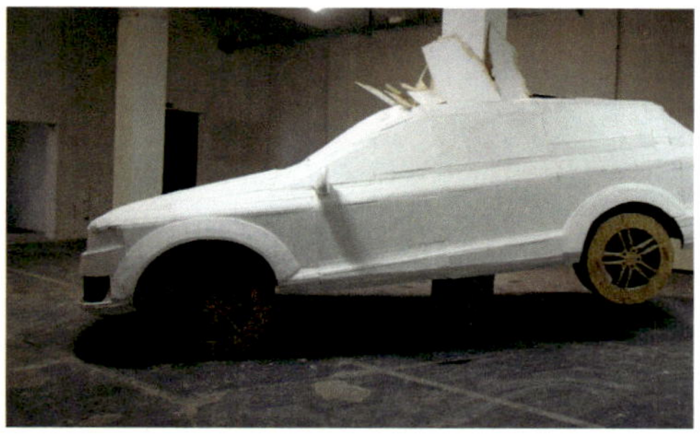

3

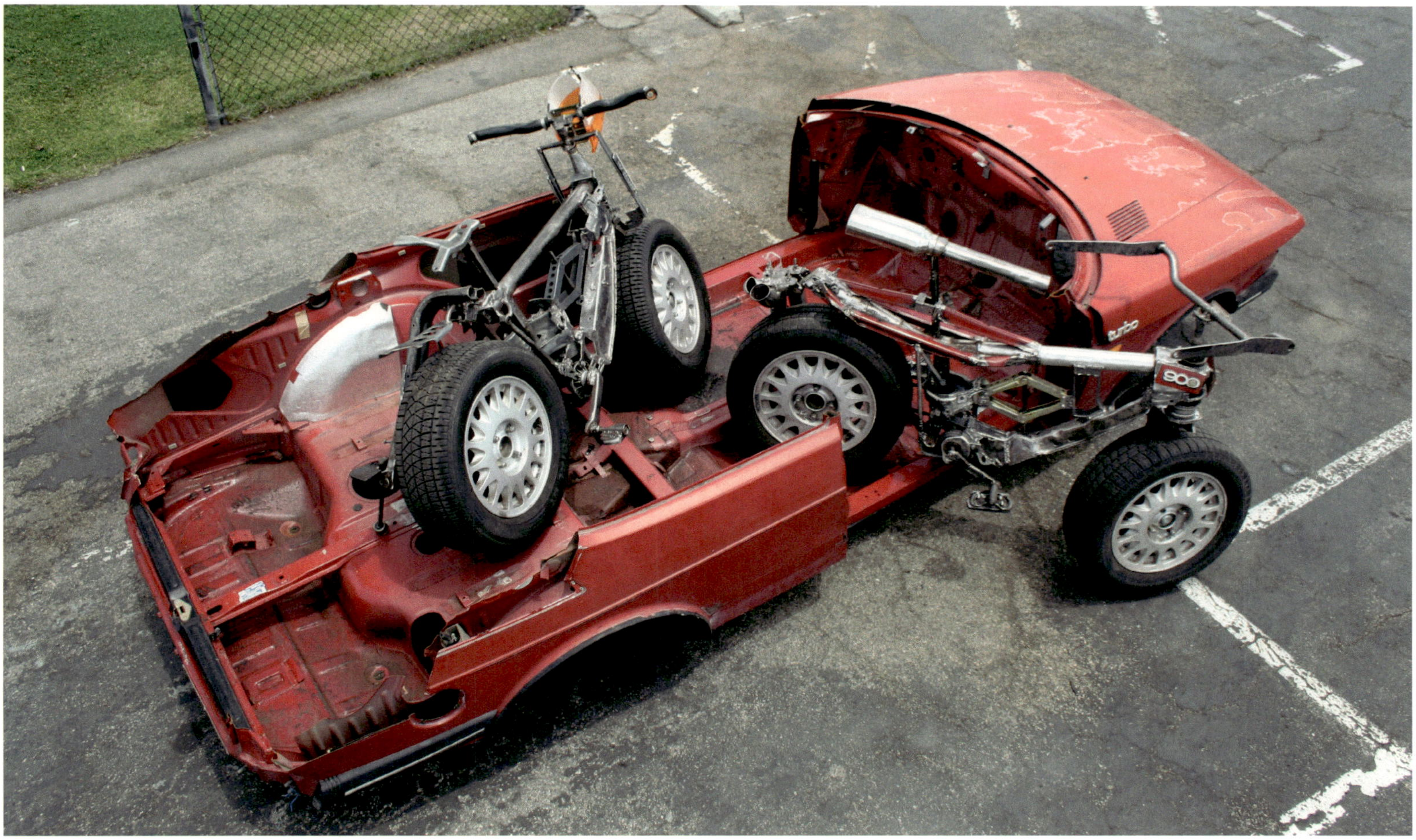

ROLAND ROOS

1–10
Free Repair
1–2
2009, Zurich, Switzerland
3
2010, Vienna, Austria
4–7
2008–2009, Zurich, Switzerland
8
2010, Vienna, Austria
9
2009, Bern, Switzerland
10–11
2010, Warsaw, Poland
12–14
2008, Bratislava, Slovakia
15
2010, London, U.K.
16
2009, Auressio, Switzerland
17
2008, Kolin, Czech Republic
18
2010, Brussels, Belgium
18
2010, Torun, Poland

In his two-year project, *Free Repair*, 2008–2010, Roland Roos (* 1974) from Lucerne, conducted an intervention in an urban space that, for an artist, was rather unusual because the fundamental artistic concept behind this intervention meant that it was not at all conspicuous. His idea was beguiling in its simplicity: he repaired, removed, and replaced damaged objects in public spaces. The artist repainted faded street signs and repaired (amongst other things) a jetty for boats, various children's swings, toilet paper holders, lights in public buildings, advertising billboards, and even car tires; i. e. anything broken that he found in a public place.

Roos was not employed, had no permit, and did not present anyone with a bill. He would record the preexisting situation with a photograph—making the photograph a one-off artwork—and would then photograph the same items after his intervention. He then put the resulting pair of pictures on sale for 320 Swiss francs. This sum equalled the average price of the materials and the effort involved in making the repair.

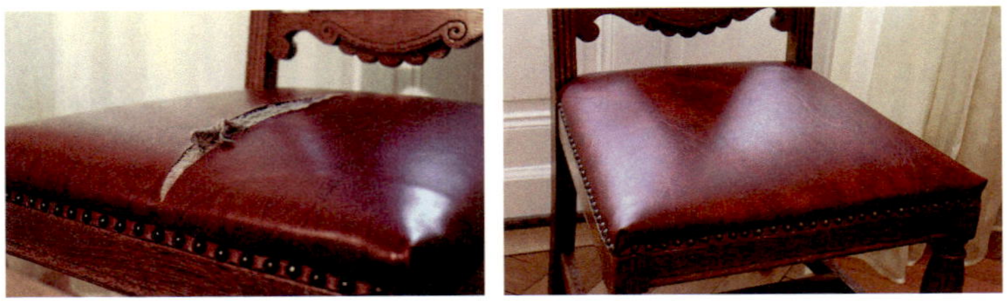
1

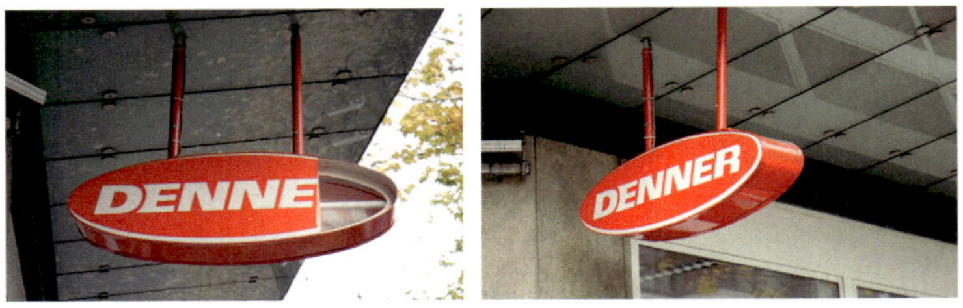

2

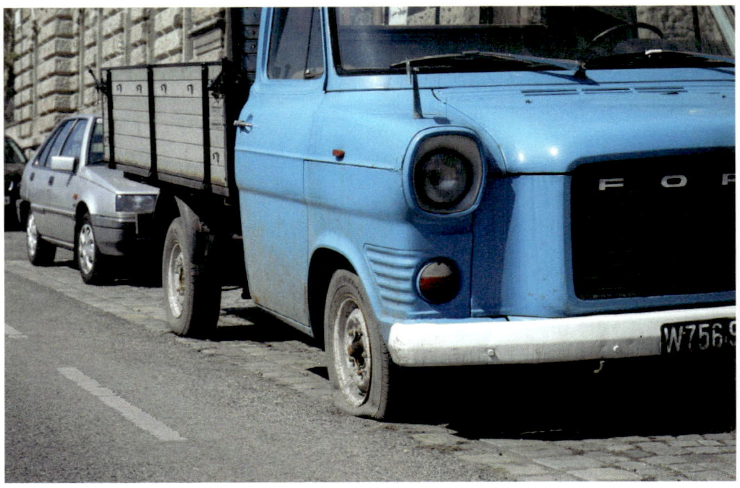
3

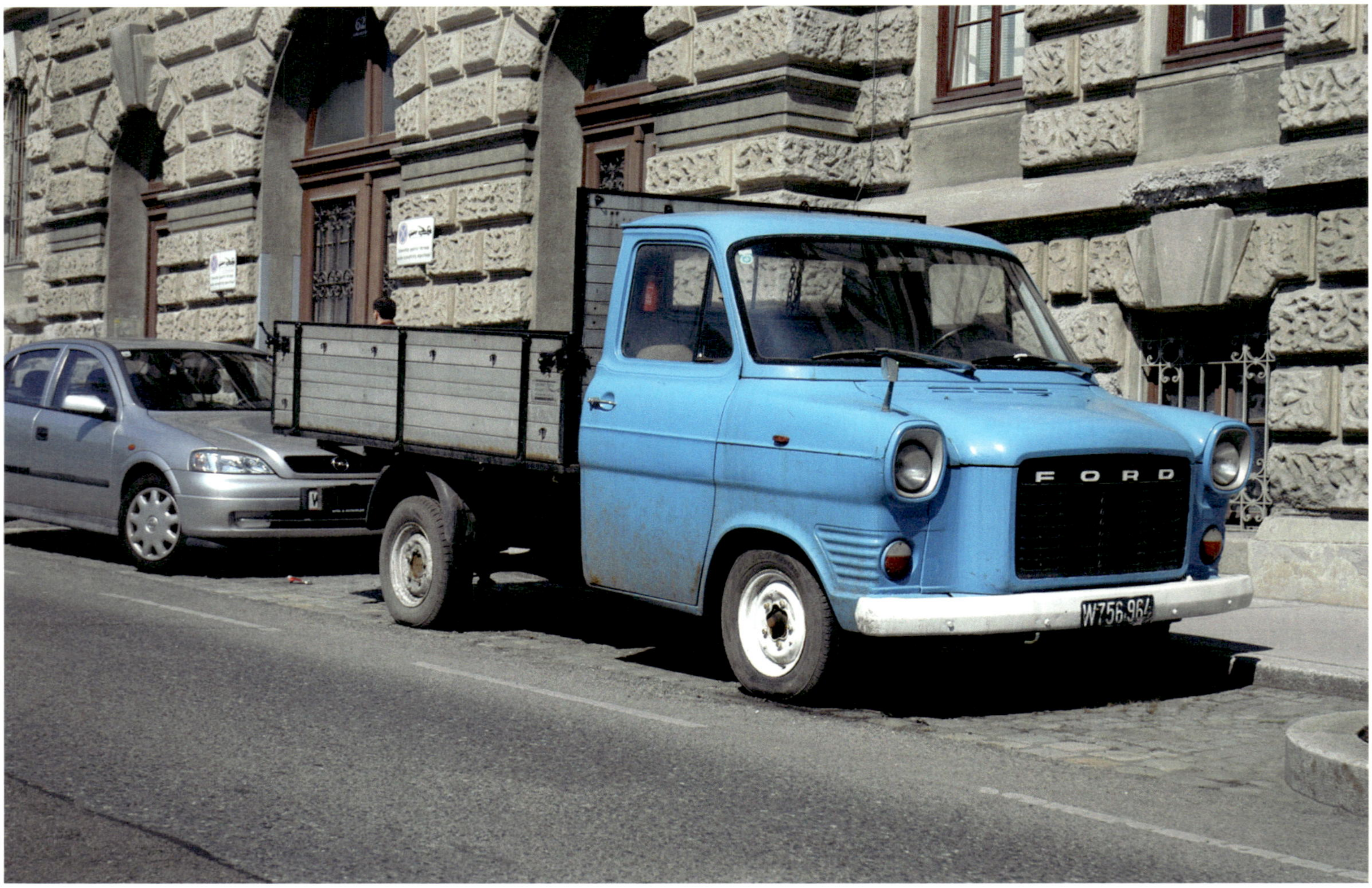

4
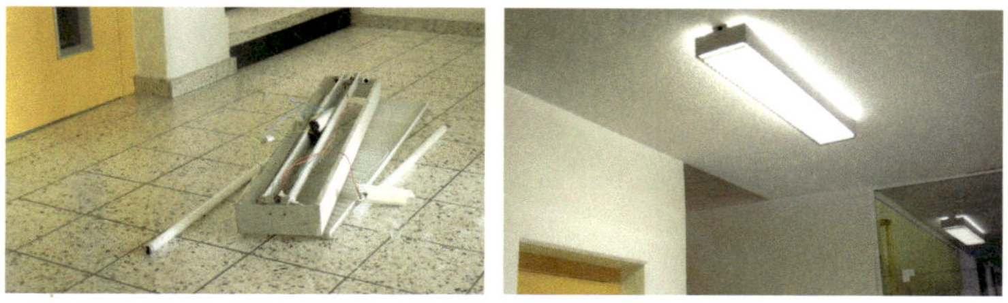

5
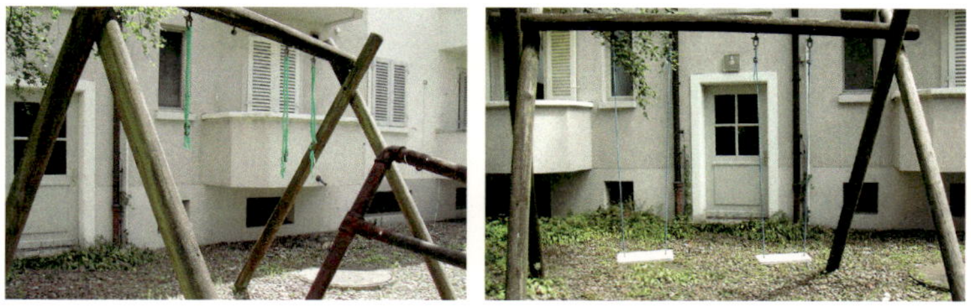

6
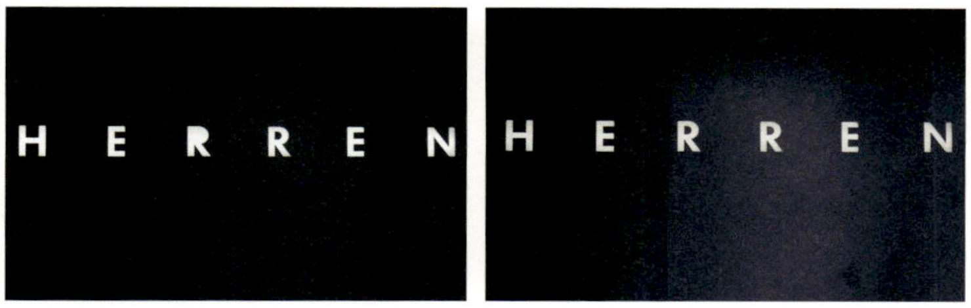

7
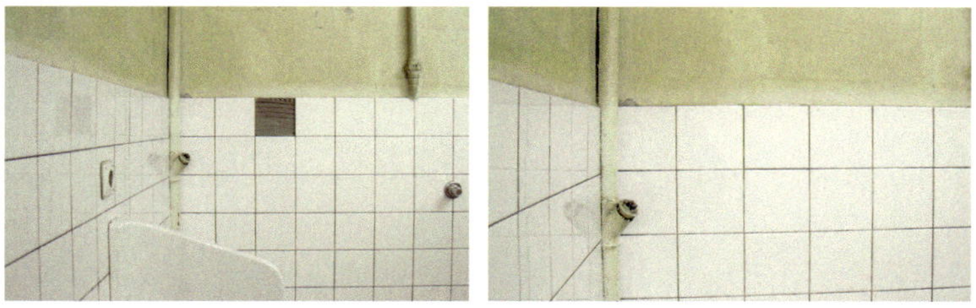

8
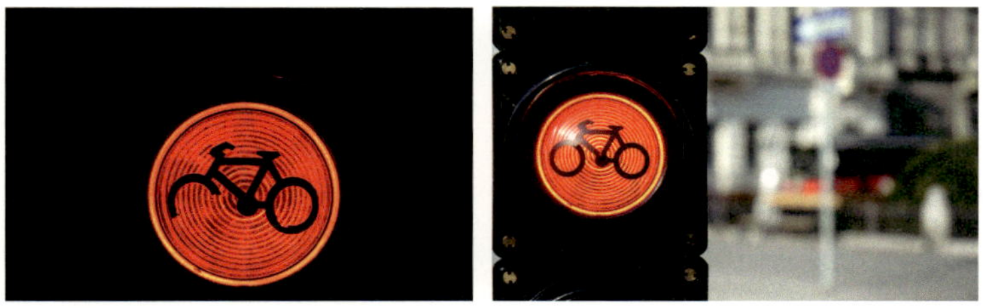

9
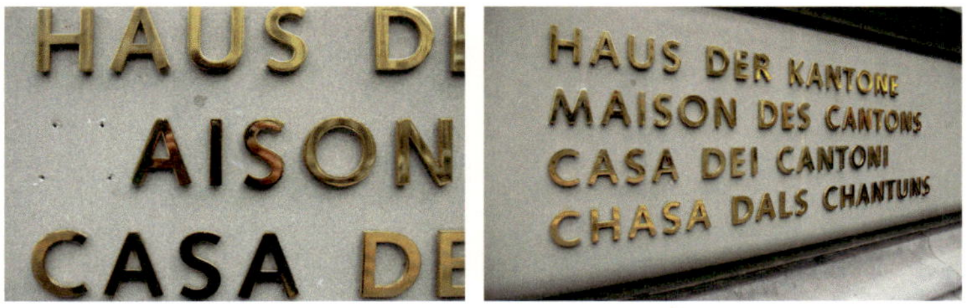

10
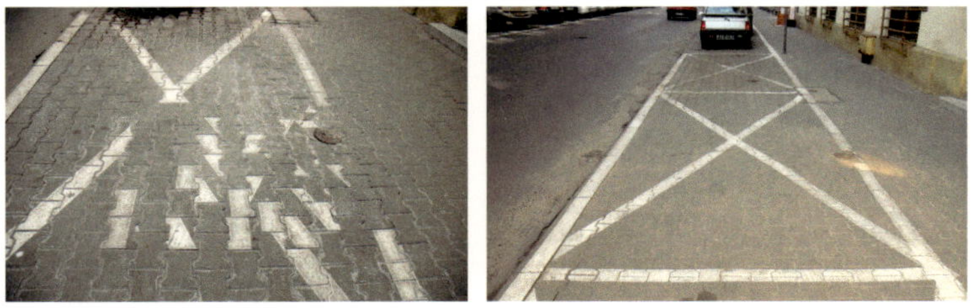

11
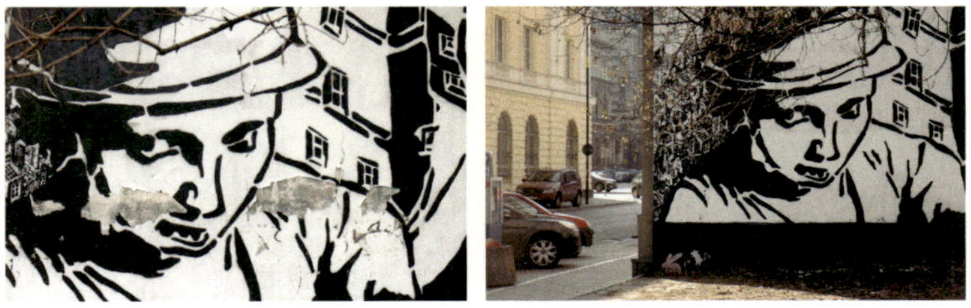

12
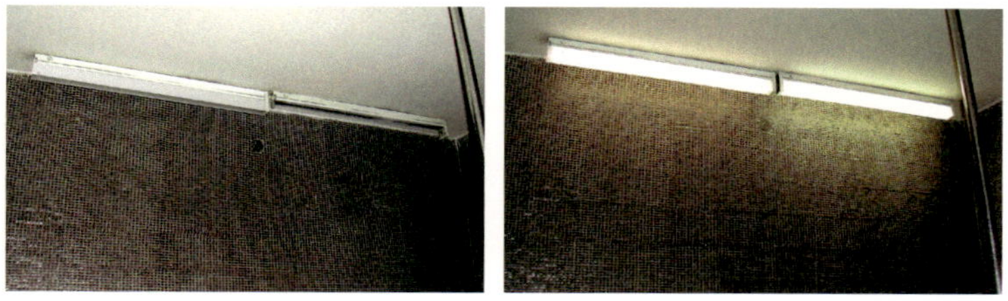

13
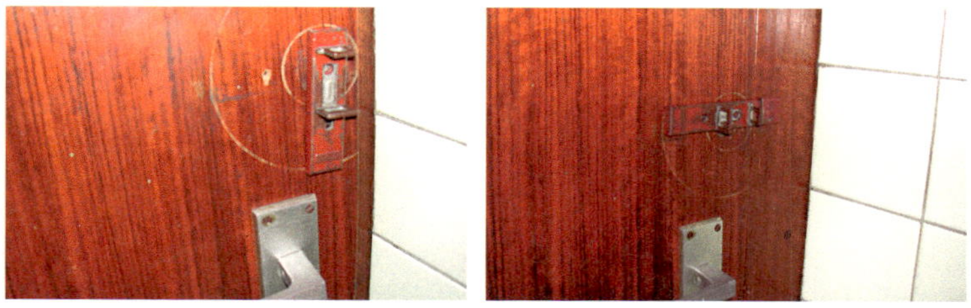

14
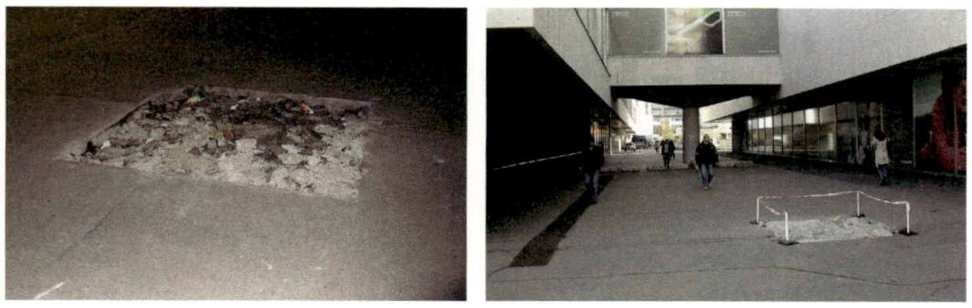

15
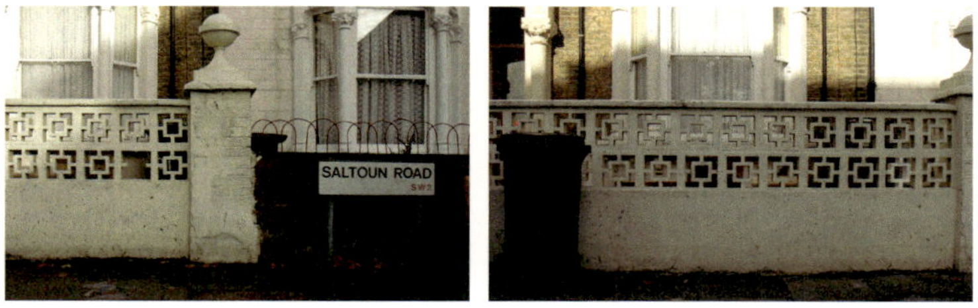

16
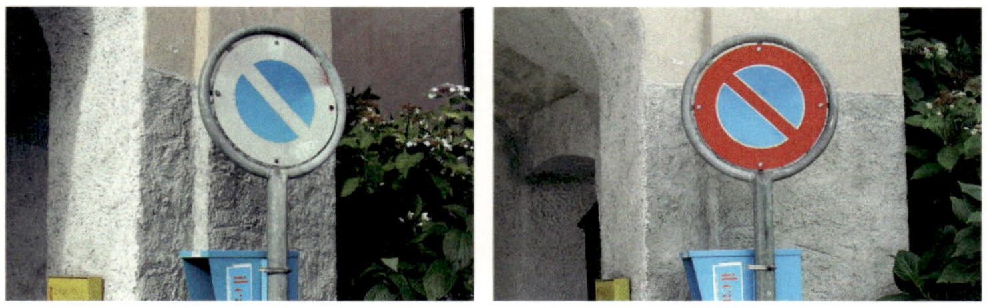

17
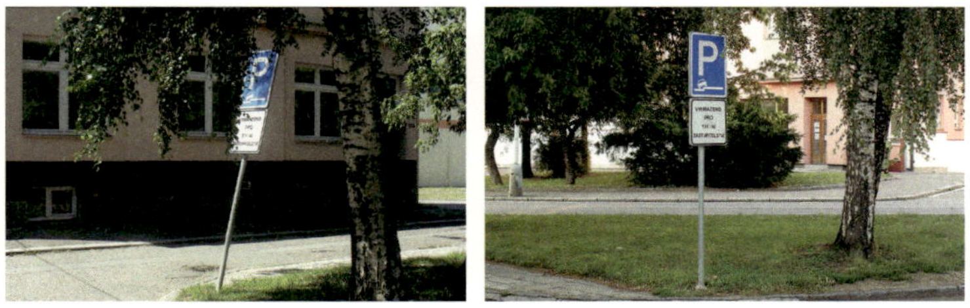

18
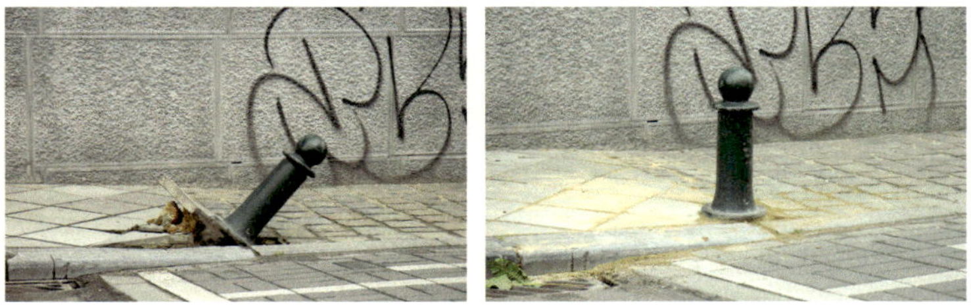

19
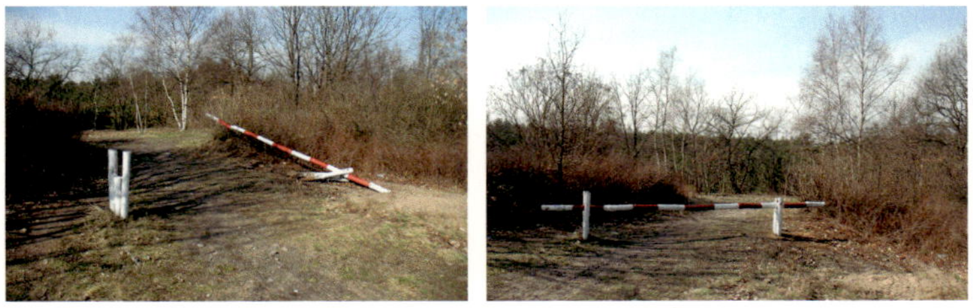

LENKA CLAYTON

“I TOOK THE TRUTH AND TRIED TO ESTABLISH ITS HISTORY”

The British artist Lenka Clayton (* 1977) from Derbyshire, lives and works in the United States. She juxtaposes the destructive realities of war with a utopian recreation of what can never be recreated. For her series *Repairing Lebanon,* Clayton commissioned a photographer working in Lebanon to create five photographs of buildings that were bombed during the Lebanon War of 2006. The artist wanted to create a portrait of the war that would make us think rather than provide answers or explanations. She believes that because there are so many different opinions on this war, war pictures are interpreted differently, depending on which side you are on. With her artwork, she wanted to create a political rather than a polemical message.

Repairing Lebanon
2007, Digitally manipulated photograph

Clayton created her “reconstructed building” series according to strict rules: she must not know what the building originally looked like, she must rely exclusively on the information contained in the photographs provided to her, and she must not add anything that she could not conclusively deduce from what remained. The artist painstakingly studied the photographs and tried to establish what the building might originally have looked like: “I asked for no information about the original buildings and had no idea how they had looked. The repairs were carried out using the ruins of the architecture as the only guide to the structure of the repaired building. All tones and textures were limited to the information available within the original image.” Working six to seven hours a day, it took her approximately three weeks to “repair” one of these buildings on her computer. Not personally meeting the photographers she was working with was another part of her working strategy: “I liked the idea of working with someone—in this case a photographer—without ever meeting them. It also fascinated me that for the photographers, the pictures represented the absolute truth. A photographer’s job is to make pictures like this every day. For me, however, they were just the starting point; I wanted to repair the buildings and knew that the results of my work would have nothing to do with the reality that existed for the person who took the photograph. I took the truth and tried to establish its history.”

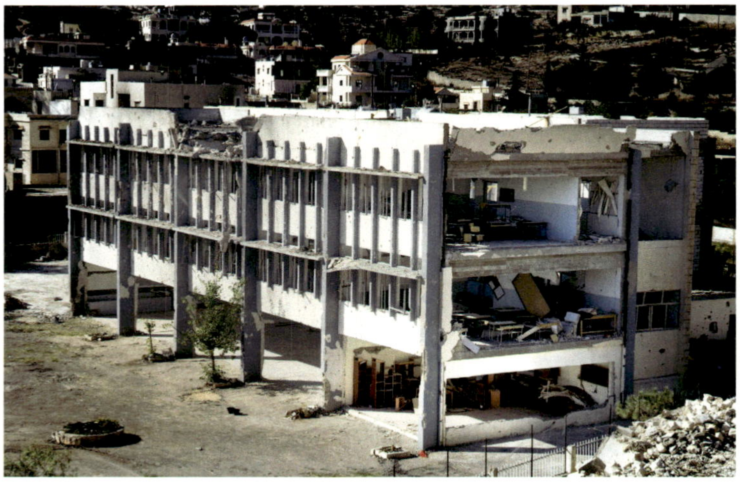

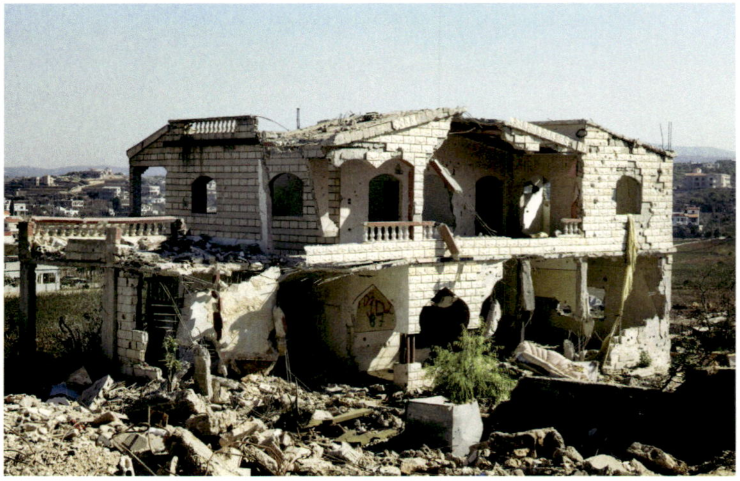

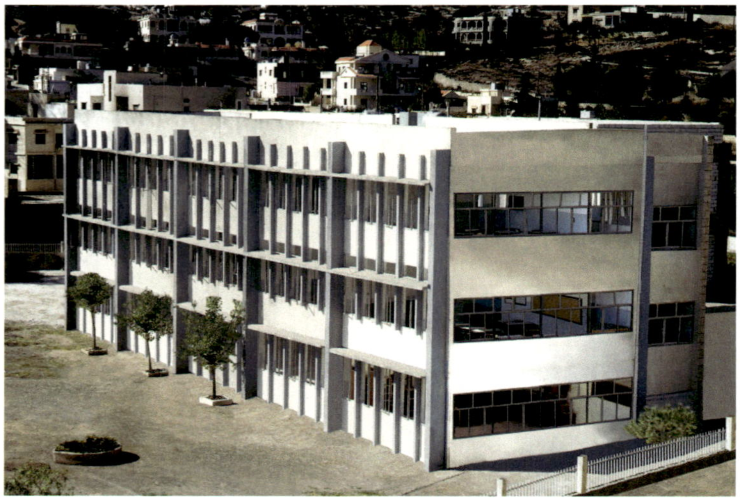

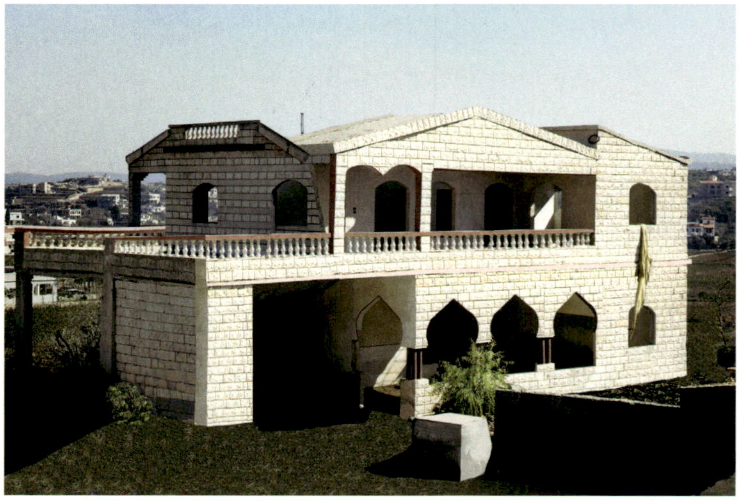

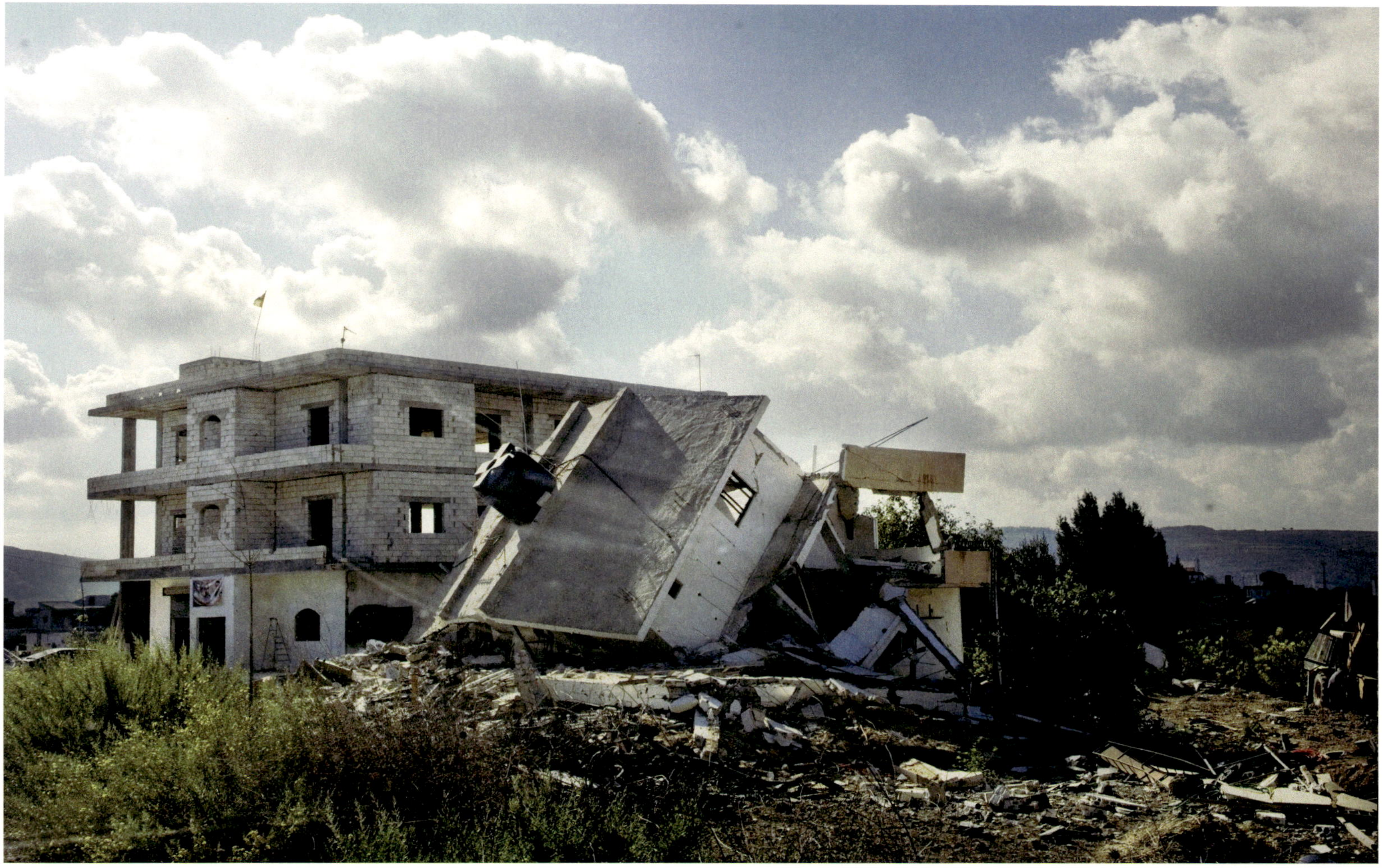

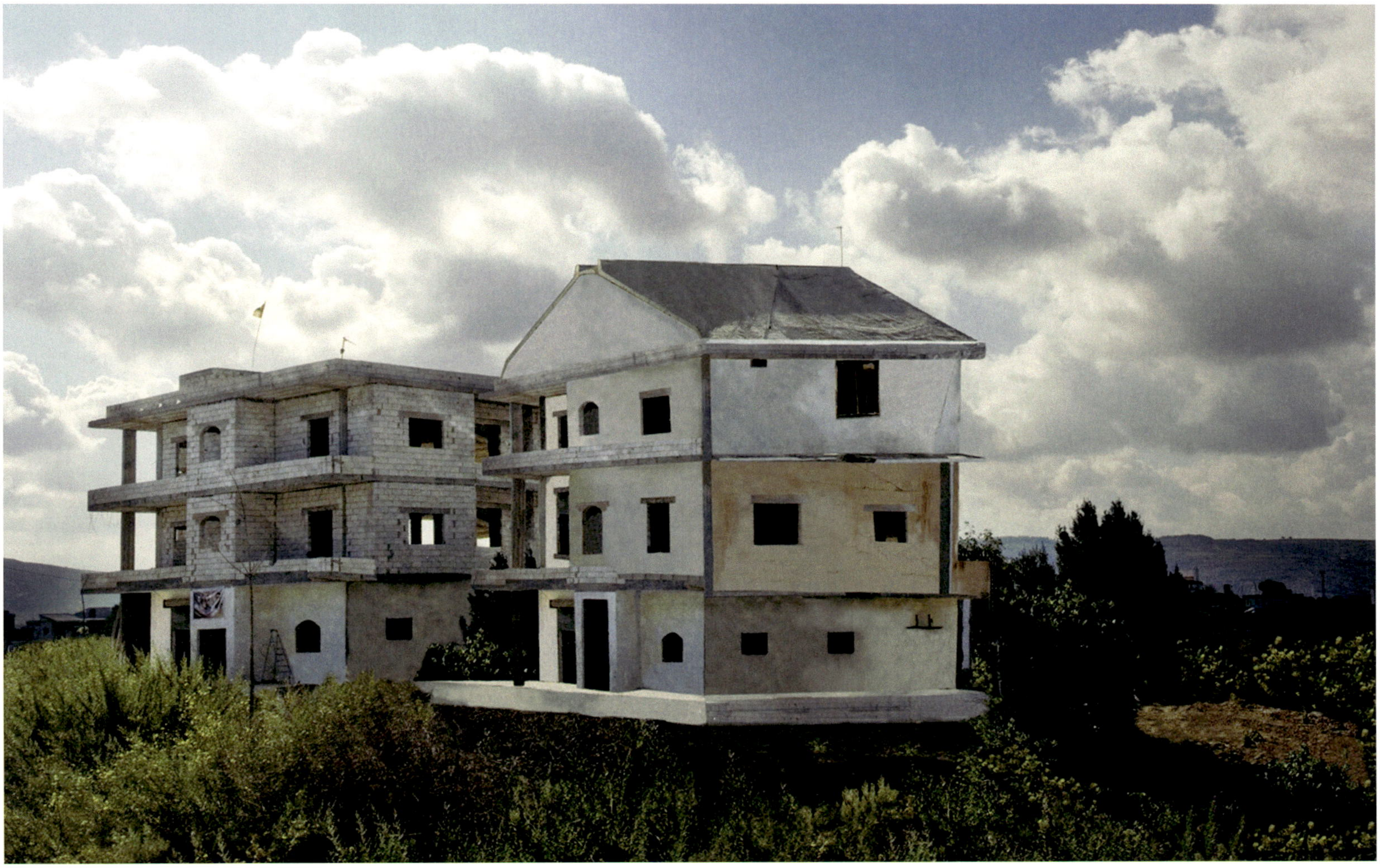

SWOON

1–2
Konbit Shelter
2010, Braddock, USA
3
Swimming Cities of
Switchback Sea
2008, Hudson River,
New York, USA
4–5 (next spread)
Swimming Cities
of Serenissima
2009, Venice, Italy

Photos by Tod Seelie

Although the Brooklyn-based artist Swoon (* 1977) is best known for wheatpasting intricately cut life-size portraits on city walls around the world, the core of her activities revolve around building community. Swoon's labor-intensive practice requires collaborations with friends, volunteers, assistants, and accomplices. Props and materials are also essential; these elements are usually reclaimed from the excess of discarded goods found in most cities. From the guy who sources thousands of meters of used rope, to the Mexican woman making tortillas portrayed in her images, Swoon works with others in order to make her art possible. Her portraits of people living in marginal communities are clearly in recognition of the other, in many cases those people left behind by globalization.

Swoon's labor-intensive practice is contrasted by the ephemeral nature of her work. The paper pasted in public space will eventually tatter, fray, or be power-washed away; in another project, the boats built to travel down the Mississippi caught fire in Missouri. The precious nature of the art object is subverted by her use of trash and recycled goods as her materials of choice. Swoon's intention is not to create valuable works of art destined for museums—although that is where some of her works are finding a home—but to create a purpose for which a community gathers, works together, and builds more than just objects or vessels, but also creates an experience. Although the act of constructing boats to travel down American rivers, or from the Slovenian coast to Venice, Italy, may appear to be madcap adventures, they are the product of painstaking planning, logistics, and negotiating with numerous bureaucratic barriers. Swoon is extremely adept at obtaining the necessary permits. As unlikely as it seems, Swoon's boats are usually permitted for travel. The crafts destined for Venice were designed to fit under the bridges that span the Grand Canal; and the U.S. Coast Guard agreed to authorize her trip down the Hudson to her opening in Long Island City. Dealing with bureaucracy and planning is an integral part of the process; the last thing the artist wants is her boat stuck in the Grand Canal or else confiscated. The boats made of junk are provocative by nature—the Venetian police would not let them travel up the Grand Canal, and so in response the crew returned late at night and went up and down the canal from 3:00 to 6:00 A.M.

In her latest endeavor, the *Konbit Shelter* project, Swoon has brought together her group of friends and collaborators to rebuild a community in Haiti devastated by the earthquake that hit in January 2010. This project challenges the traditional notions of political art, activism, and relief efforts. Free from the mandates and limitations that relief organizations are saddled with, Swoon and her collaborators developed a multi-tiered strategy that is designed to have the most impact on the community of Barriere Jeudi. A nonprofit organization was established and funds were raised through the sale of art, and through donations. The available resources determined the scale of the project as well as the size of the town. The social challenges, extreme poverty, lack of infrastructure, and building materials such as lumber, combined with the need for hurricane and earthquake resistant structures, led to the use of the superadobe technique, using earth-bag architecture. Developed by Nader Khalili, this technique is well-suited for impoverished communities in that it is easily applied without the use of building machinery or a specialized workforce, and 90 percent of the material used for construction is earth, with just 10 percent being cement. Furthermore, a local workforce was paid to build the community center, injecting much-needed cash into the local economy, creating jobs, and training a workforce. The multi-room community center will initially function as a workshop from which the rest of the homes will be built. The long-term plan is to establish a building initiative where an artist and architect will go to Barriere Jeudi and work with a family to build their home.

1

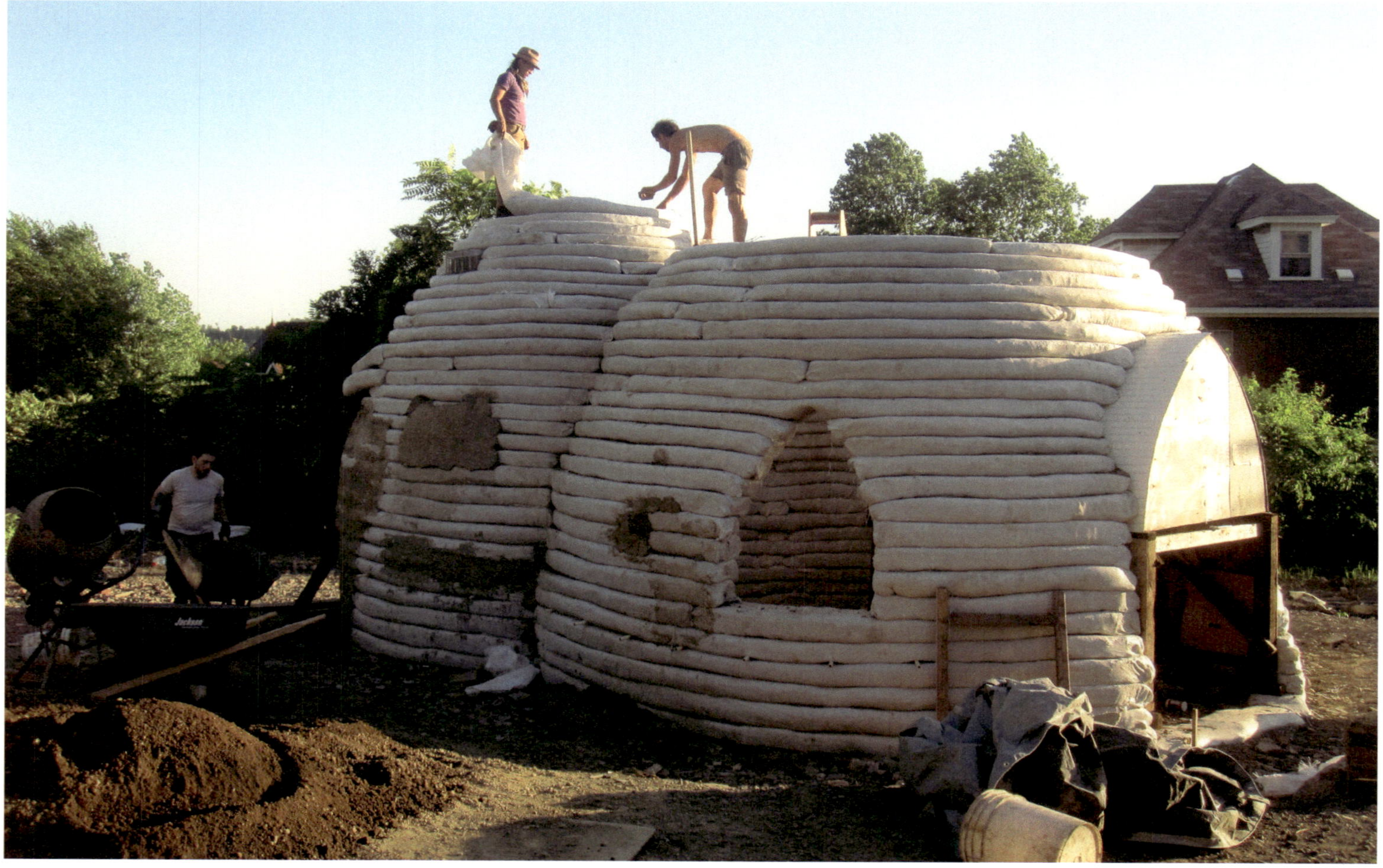

2

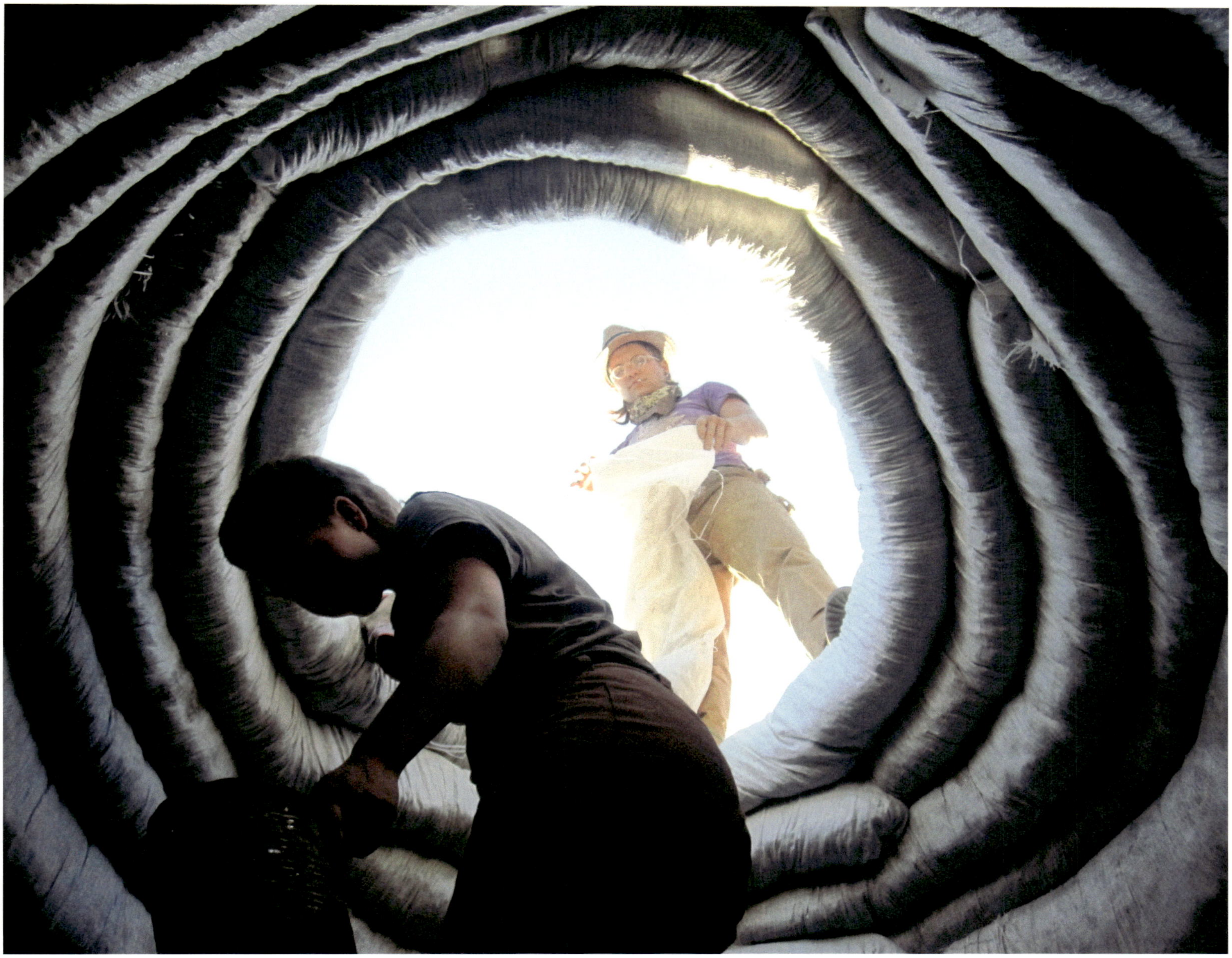

3

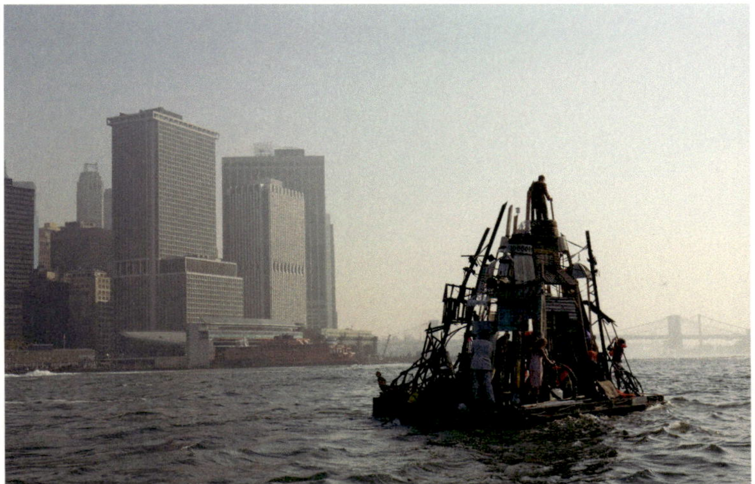

4

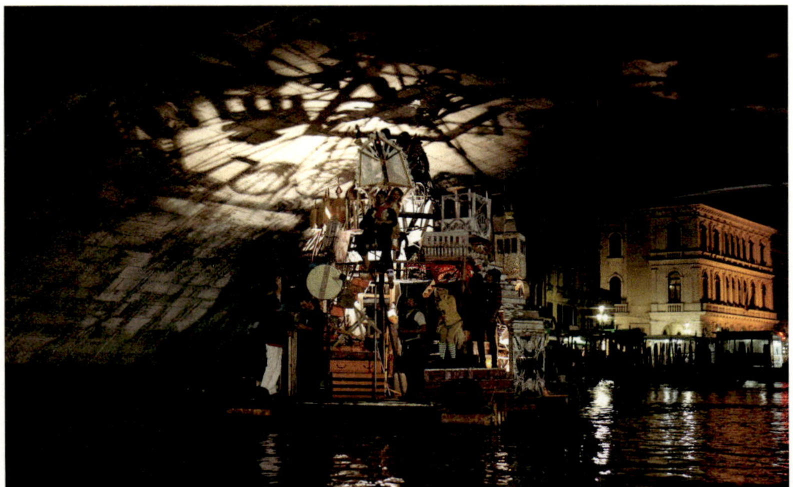

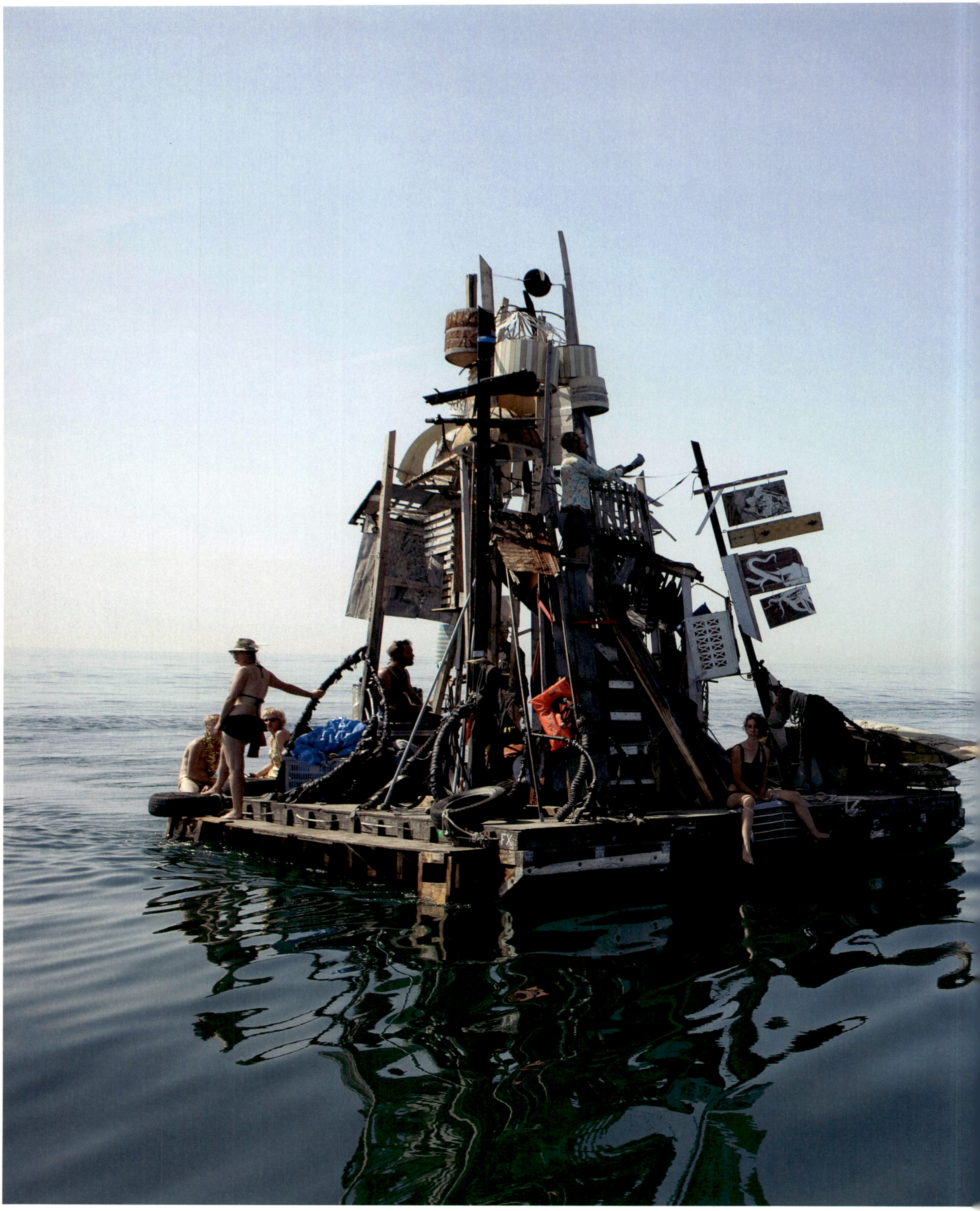
FX

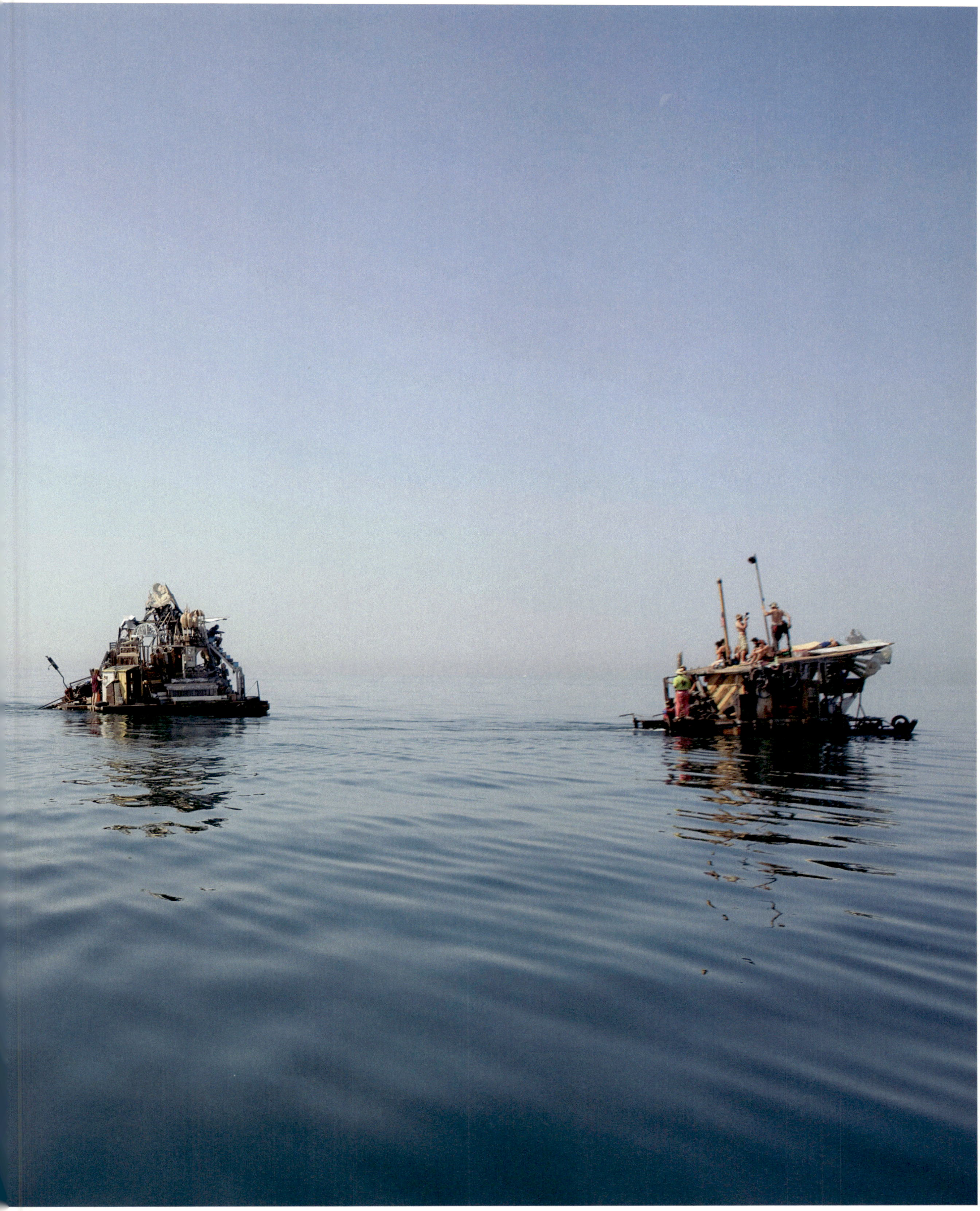

SANCTU-
ARY

TABLE OF CONTENTS

INTRODUCTION

The word "sanctuary" has many definitions. It can mean refuge, asylum, or holy place—all themes that the artists featured here explore in their work. They use unfamiliar situations to call familiar spaces into question. The artists fight their way into the familiar, abruptly turning individuals into recipients of art and forcing them to confront a moment of unexpectedness and to reflect on and reorganize their own environments and question their own morals. Artists Maurizio Cattelan [see p. 96] and Mark Jenkins [see p. 98] use lifelike dolls and place them in strange and often threatening situations. Their works, like many other works presented here, are not intended for a museum. Whereas appearing in that context would make them immediately recognizable as art, seeing them in public spaces is disconcerting. Security in public spaces is also a popular subject among the artists here. They explore issues surrounding security systems and totalitarian surveillance. Some campaigns involve artists stepping into illegal territory, like the Czech artist collective Ztohoven [see p. 112] did when it forged passports to highlight ways that data can be misused. The artists also deliberately overstep moral boundaries to provoke reactions. For his macabre but eye-opening campaign, well-known artist Santiago Sierra [see p. 122] transformed a Cologne synagogue into a gas chamber in an effort to counteract the trivialization of the memory of the Holocaust. For many years Sierra has also been exploring what people are worth by staging campaigns where he gets people to perform absurd tasks for miserable pay. Artist duo Wiebke Grösch and Frank Metzger [see p. 120] also use absurdity to refer to injustices in urban spaces. One of their projects involved having foreign newspaper sellers in Frankfurt sell papers from their home countries instead of the *Frankfurter Allgemeine Zeitung* as usual. Some of the artists see cities as urban playgrounds and use hefty doses of irony and cynicism to lift the lid on the social problems lurking there. Brad Downey [see p. 130] focuses on shaking up the urban order with campaigns that include ripping up the sidewalk and building a castle with the sand underneath.

Artists like Julien Berthier [see p. 134], Marjetica Potrc [see p. 139] and Gregor Schneider [see p. 140] use architectural designs to spell out social differences. Schneider's black, Mecca-inspired cube—which he was unable to exhibit—also ignited countless debates about whether it was acceptable for an artwork to quote a religious shrine so directly. Other artists also operate in the area of religion. They are fully aware of the scandal they could provoke, since the scandal itself is the aim of their work. British artist Sarah Maple [see p. 110], for example, uses her paintings and photographs to subtly undermine religious moral ideals.

MAURIZIO CATTELAN

"THE WORST POSSIBLE THING IS WHEN IDEOLOGICAL ART BECOMES DIDACTIC"

The Italian artist Maurizio Cattelan (*1960) from Padua, is a mixture of Don Camillo, Pinocchio, and court jester; he regularly uses a great deal of black humor to dismantle everything that is sacred to other people. He became known for his extremely lifelike figures such as the sculpture *La Nona Ora* (The Ninth Hour), 1999, which depicts Pope John Paul II lying on the ground having been struck by a meteorite, or *Him*, 2001, which shows a miniature version of Adolf Hitler, kneeling innocently. "Why would you want to be a party wrecker? It's more fun to try to hijack the party than to spoil it. And I found out very early in life that people tend to prefer the class clown to the class nerd," says Cattelan, who has conquered the art world as a self-taught artist. He previously worked as a cook, a gardener, and in a morgue before starting to make furniture. Since then, the art world has come to be one of his favorite targets—and the more he boycotts it, the more passionately it loves him. The Italian curator Massimiliano Gioni appeared as Cattelan's double for years, with the intention of undermining the concepts of originality and authorship, by delivering university lectures and giving interviews in his name. Later the two of them, working with curator Ali Subotnick, also founded the smallest gallery in the world: The Wrong Gallery. It covered an area of one square meter and its door was always locked, but despite this, 40 of the most influential contemporary artists exhibited in it. In the early years of his artistic practice, Cattelan set up the Oblomov Foundation, which was to award an artist a grant if he or she produced no art for a full year in return. And in 1999 he intensively promoted the Sixth Caribbean Biennale on the island of St. Kitts—however, there was never a biennale there, and no artworks were shown there, either. The budget simply ran to the participants' holidays on the island—including artists such as Olafur Eliasson, Douglas Gordon, and Wolfgang Tillmans. Even the critics, who had made a special journey to St. Kitts, ultimately celebrated this action as a successful criticism of the proliferating biennale industry. "What I realized was that there are three different kinds of revolutionaries: those who want to change things; those who are into the fight but couldn't care less if things change or not; and those who work following their instinct, by responding to a situation in a personal way, which can end up having collective results—and which can affect the world a lot more," says Cattelan. "That last model is possibly the one I'm interested in most." And when Cattelan shows a crucified horse lying on the ground, with an improvised wooden sign in its belly inscribed with "INRI"—the initials for the Latin version of "Jesus of Nazareth, King of the Jews"—this is seen as either blasphemous or visionary. And certainly in his *Untitled*, 2009, inspired by the English expression "flogging a dead horse," Cattelan has once more created a provocative and cynically caustic comment on the church and superstition, while at the same time producing an object worth millions that art collectors will be fighting over. "The worst possible thing is when ideological art becomes didactic," says Cattelan. "What you get as a result is little more than propaganda—and then it doesn't matter which side of the barricade you're on."

1
We
2010, Wood, fiberglass, polyurethane rubber, fabric
Photo by Zeno Zotti
Courtesy the artist and Galerie Perrotin, Paris

2
All
2007, Group of nine sculptures in White Carrara Marble, Installation view, Kunsthaus Bregenz , Austria
Photo by Markus Tretter/KUB Bregenz
Courtesy the artist and Galerie Perrotin, Paris

3
Untitled
2004
Photo by Attilio Maranzano
Courtesy Fondazione Nicola Trussardi

1

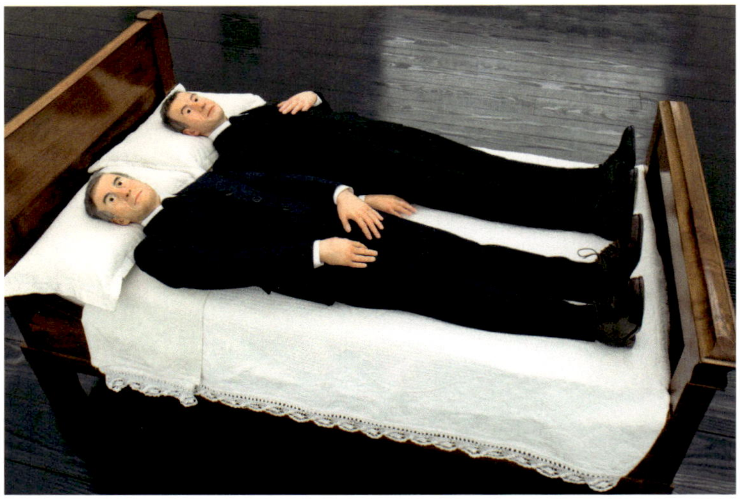

2

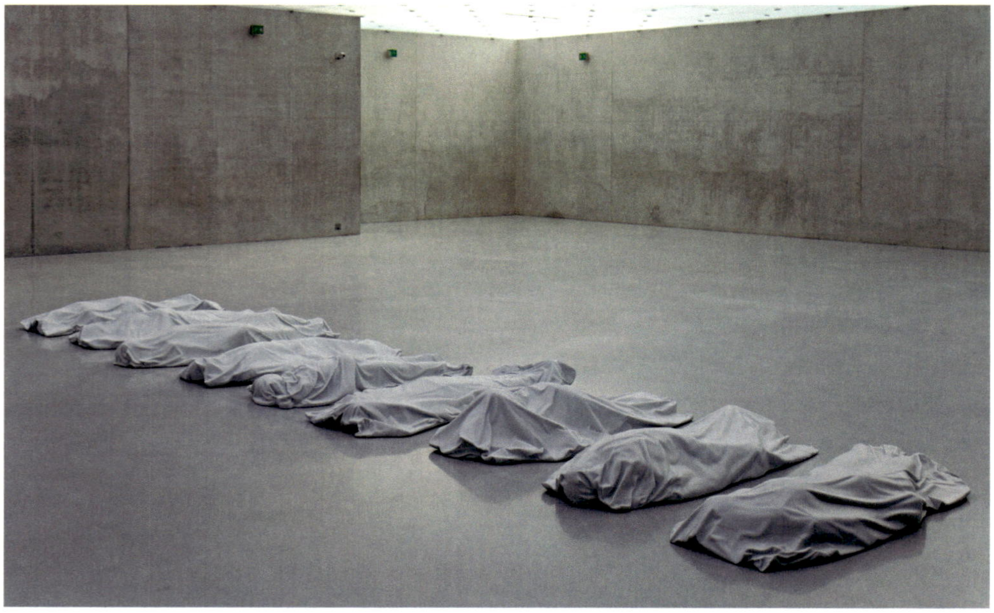

3

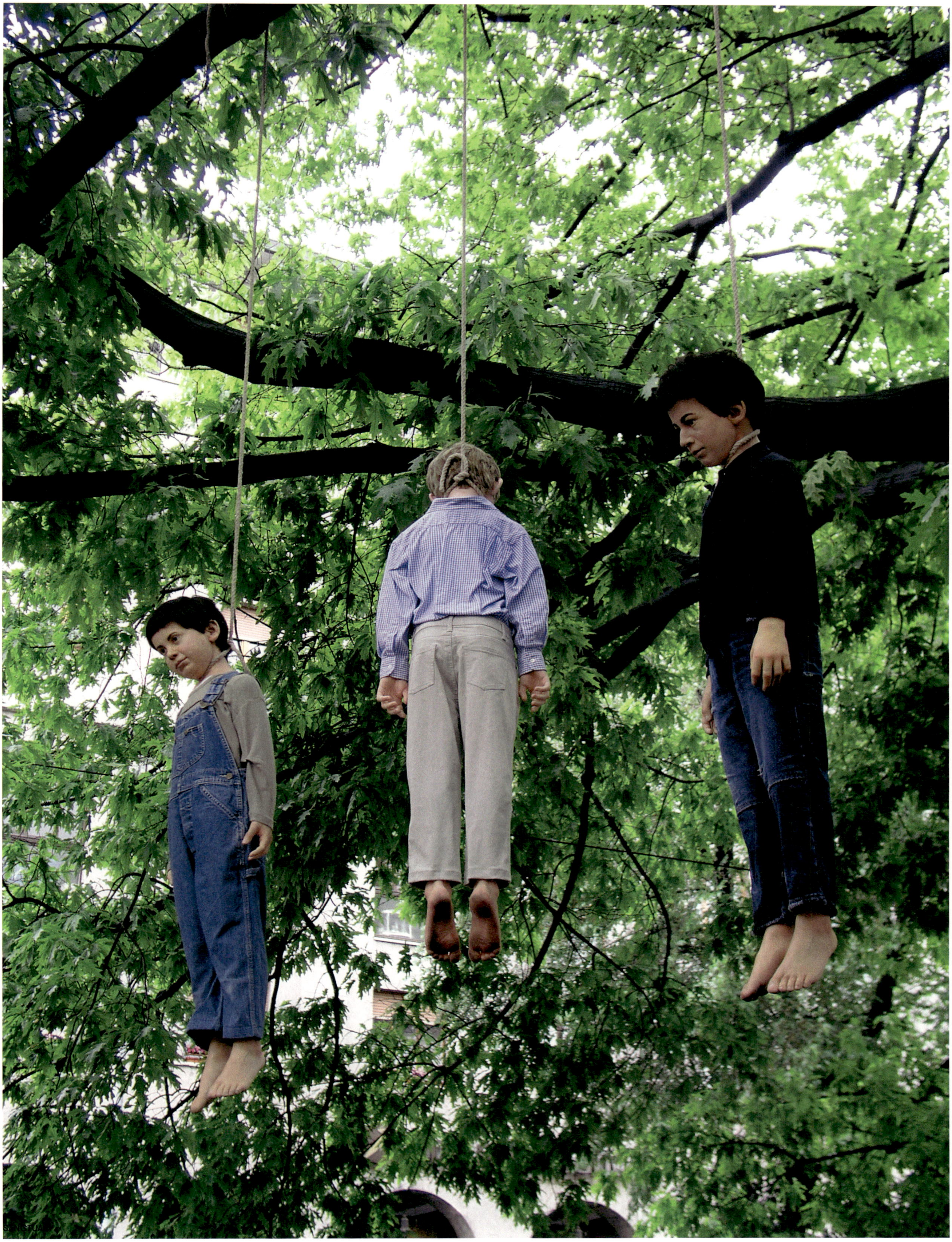

MARK JENKINS

1
All You Can Eat
2007, São Paulo, Brazil,
Indoor installation at SESC
Pinheiros
2
Trashers
2007, London, U.K., Non-commissioned street installation
3
U.S. Diplomats
2007, São Paulo, Brazil,
Indoor installation at SESC
Pinheiros
4
Embed Series
2006, Washington, DC, USA,
Non-commissioned street
installation

The American artist Mark Jenkins (* 1970) from Fairfax, Virginia, provokes passersby with life-size figures made of parcel tape, who are depicted begging in the streets, or floating in the river as corpses. When he set up his polar bear sculptures in Washington as a public relations campaign for Greenpeace, a bear sculpture—which was attached to a refuse bin—caused such a panic that it even triggered a bomb disposal squad callout. "Most people are afraid when they see my sculptures. But usually this first second of fear quickly turns into a laugh," says Jenkins. Many of his tape sculptures look like Maurizio Cattelan's lifelike figures, or Duane Hanson's hyperrealistic polyester resin people. One of his works is like a beggar: the figure is cowering cross-legged on the concrete, has pulled its hoodie right down over its face, and is letting its head loll. In another installation, what you are first aware of are four tightly packed rubbish bags in a heap—only on a second glance do you notice that there are human legs sticking out of all the sacks.

"My sculptures don't work in a museum," says Jenkins. "It would be like putting a firework in water and telling it to explode. My art would work best if no one knew my work. If I did not have a website and didn't give any interviews. In a museum we are lions in the zoo." In fact, Jenkins presents sociocritical experiments in public spaces, as he is concerned with making people look at things rather than look away, and his sculptures are intended to wrest people out of their lethargy in order to make them act.

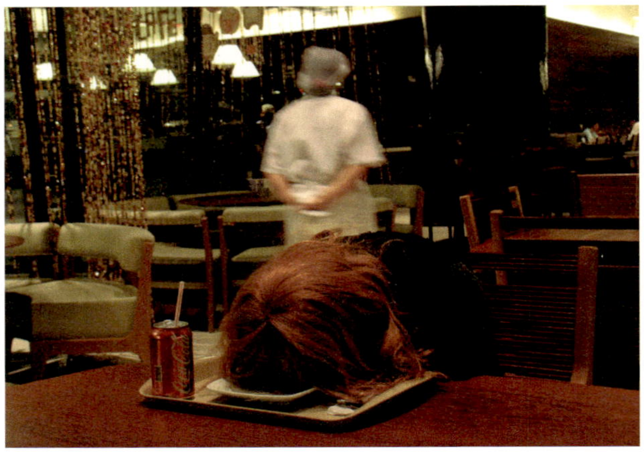
1

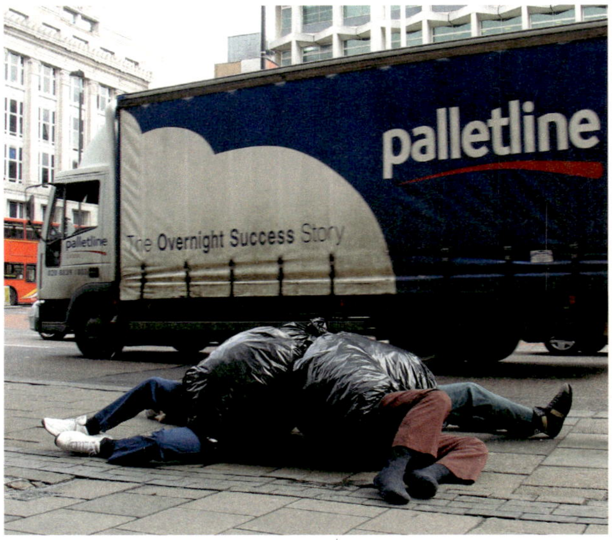

2

3
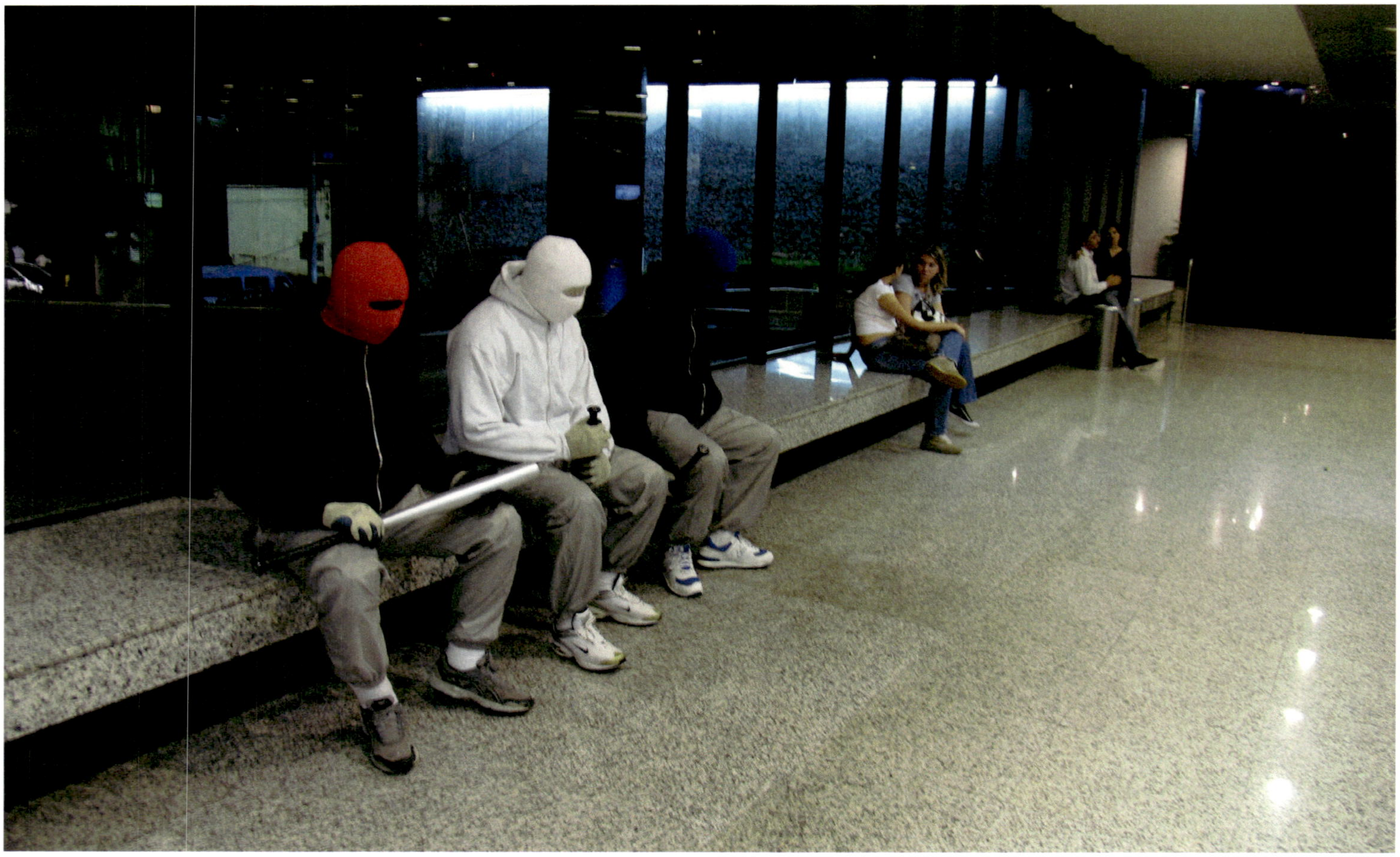

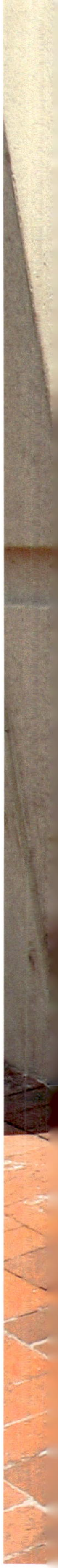

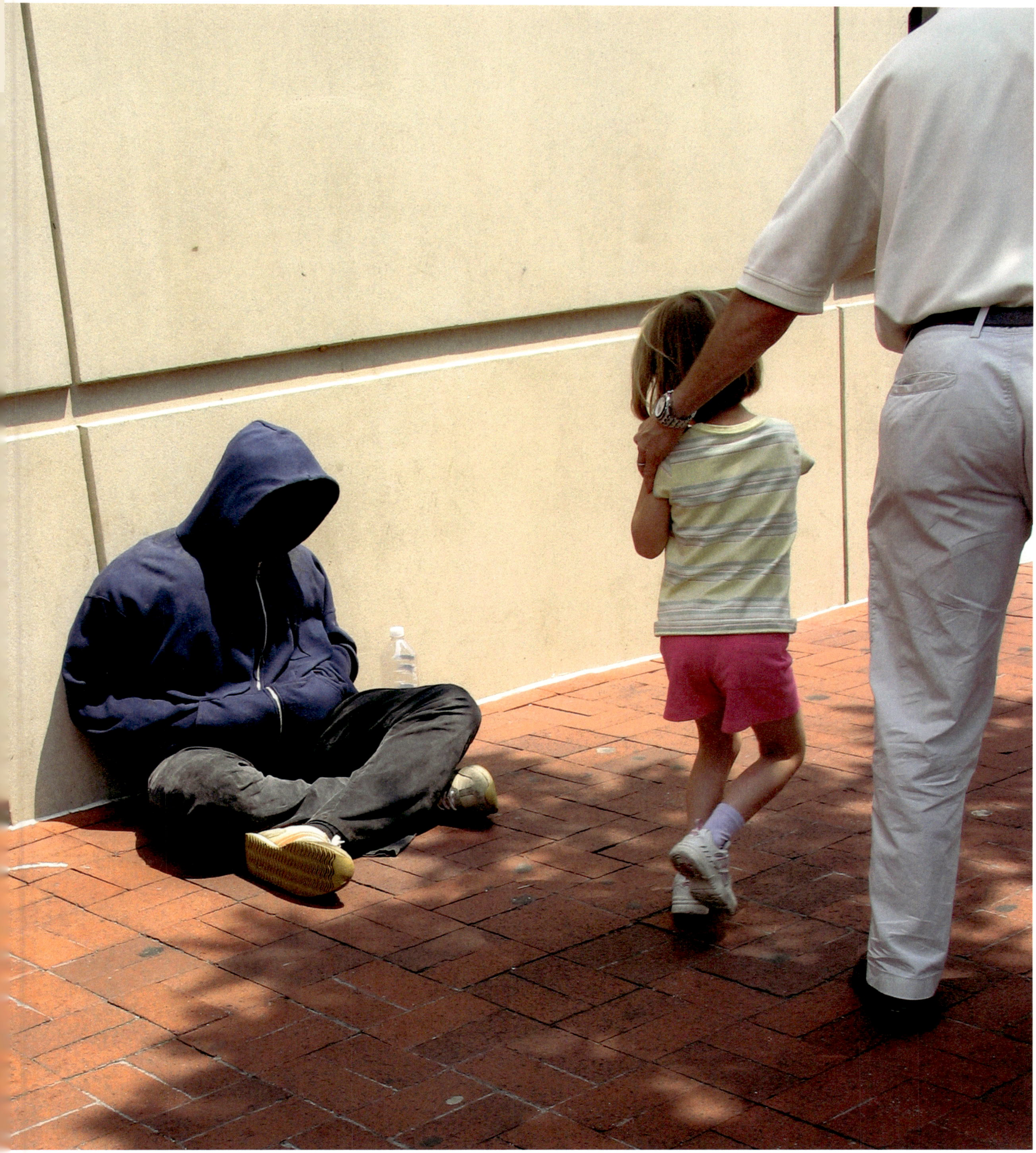

4

PAUL CHAN

"I THINK THAT ART CAN BE MANY THINGS AT ONCE, AND THEY CAN ALL BE CONTRADICTORY"

1
Waiting for Godot in New Orleans
2007, Creative Time and the Classical Theatre of Harlem, Courtesy the artist and Greene Naftali Gallery, New York
2
Now Promise Now Threat
2005, Single-channel video
3
Baghdad in No Particular Order
2003, Single-channel video

American artist Paul Chan (* 1973) wants to liberate established concepts and notions from what they are into what they can become. He does not limit himself to the traditions of prescribed interpretations of culture, theories, and ideas, and has incorporated into his practice the strategy of juxtaposing opposing forces. Not so much yin and yang—the Chinese representation of cosmic duality—opposing forces that balance each other out, but the contradictions that dwell in ideological extremes. Chan brings these forces together in an effort to break the paradigm and reveal new possibilities. Through his work as an artist and avowed social activist, he explores the contradictions and complexities inherent in existence, as well as in the social, religious, and political systems humanity has developed. His work reminds us that contradictions, however frustrating or unfair, are part of life. Chan's work takes the form of several mediums; among them are his signature rudimentary style of video, drawing, and live performances of Samuel Beckett's *Waiting for Godot* in post-Katrina New Orleans.

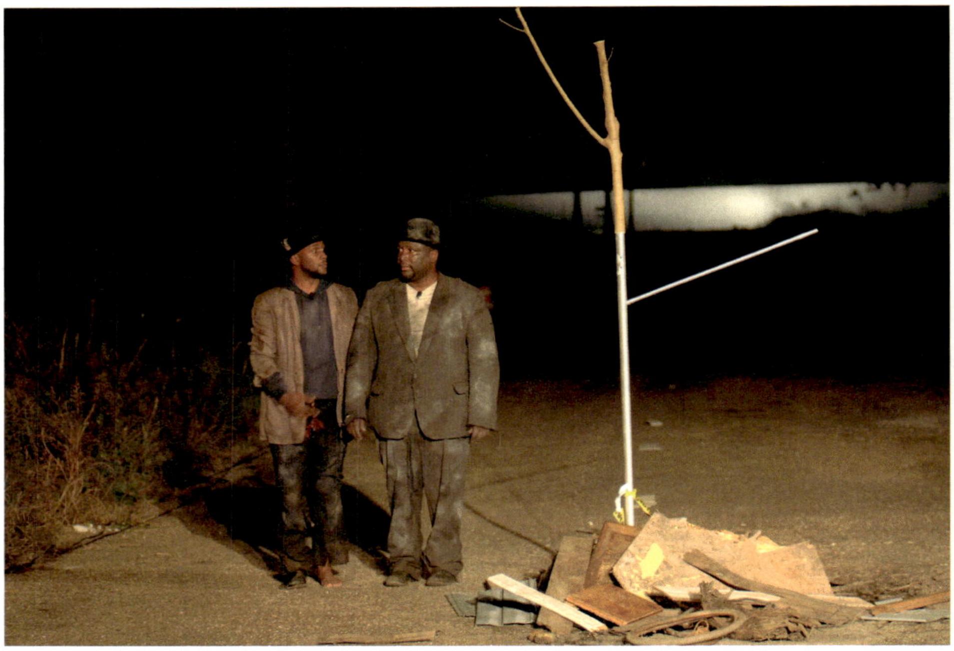

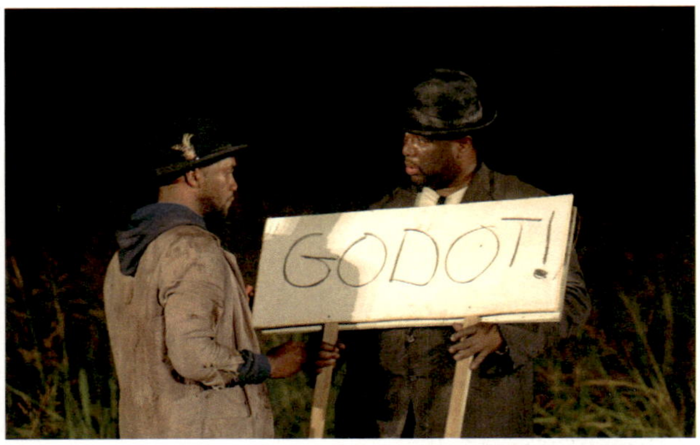

1

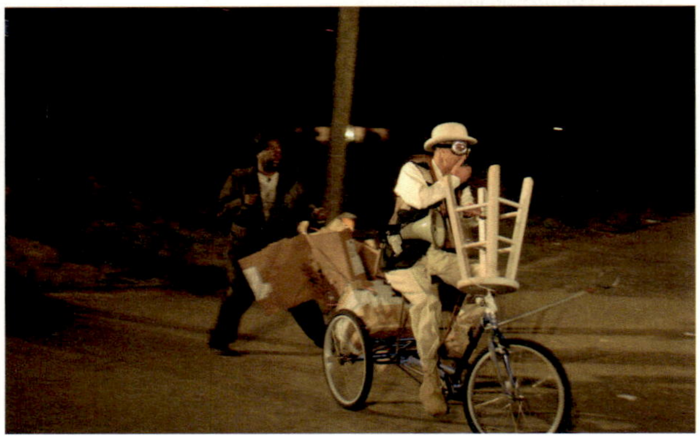

Chan's work is riddled with opposites: hi-tech video technology is used to produce what appear to be low-tech animations; hi-brow literary references are mixed with popular culture, the Bible, and the Marquis de Sade. Chan has even drawn an unorthodox correlation between the fantasy world created by the American outsider artist Henry Darger, and the nineteenth-century utopian philosopher Charles Fourier. In the video, *My Birds ... Trash ... the Future,* 2004, the naked figures of Pier Paolo Pasolini and Biggie Smalls struggle for survival in a hostile wasteland, which resembles the setting of Beckett's *Waiting for Godot.*

Chan makes a clear distinction between his work as an artist and his work as a social activist. He will not mix one with the other. This position underscores the complexity of political art and activism, illustrating the tension between the inherent compromises in politics and group dynamics needed to move the machine, and the individualistic, uncompromising position of an artist and their practice. Although his work is not overtly political, it does respond to political situations. In 2005, after the reelection of George Bush, Chan went home to Omaha, Nebraska, to make a video about the "red states," which had handed Bush his victory. The single-channel video, *Now Promise Now Threat,* is described by the artist as, "part documentary, part visually something else." The video mixes interviews shot by the artist with local footage, execution videos, and screens of color. It uses Omaha as the "red state" site to explore the inherent contradictions that appear when religion and politics mix. For instance, a woman who is opposed to abortion criticizes the hypocrisy of an anti-abortion movement whose members are pro-war.

2

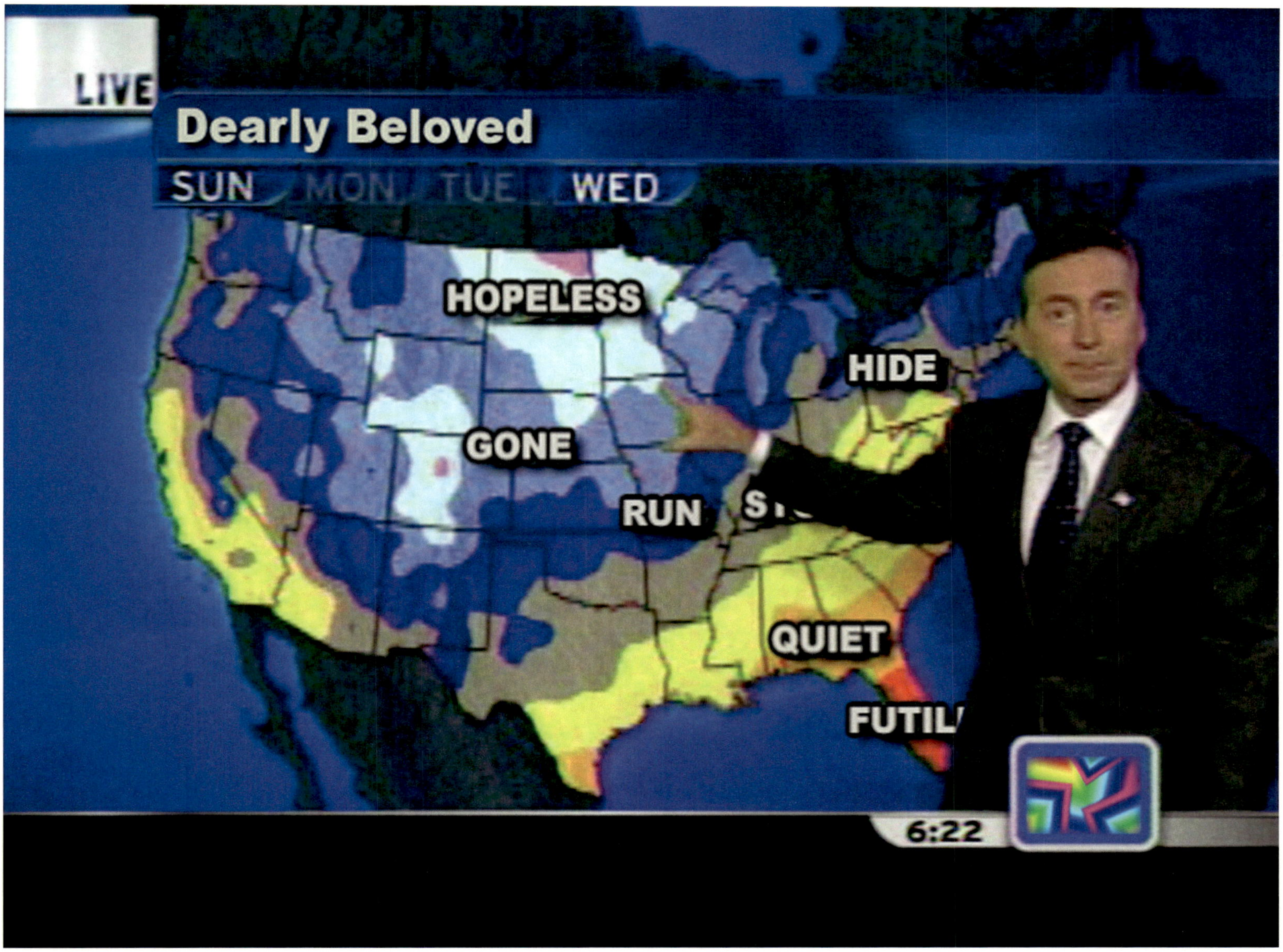
LIVE
Dearly Beloved
SUN MON TUE WED
HOPELESS
HIDE
GONE
RUN
QUIET
6:22

3

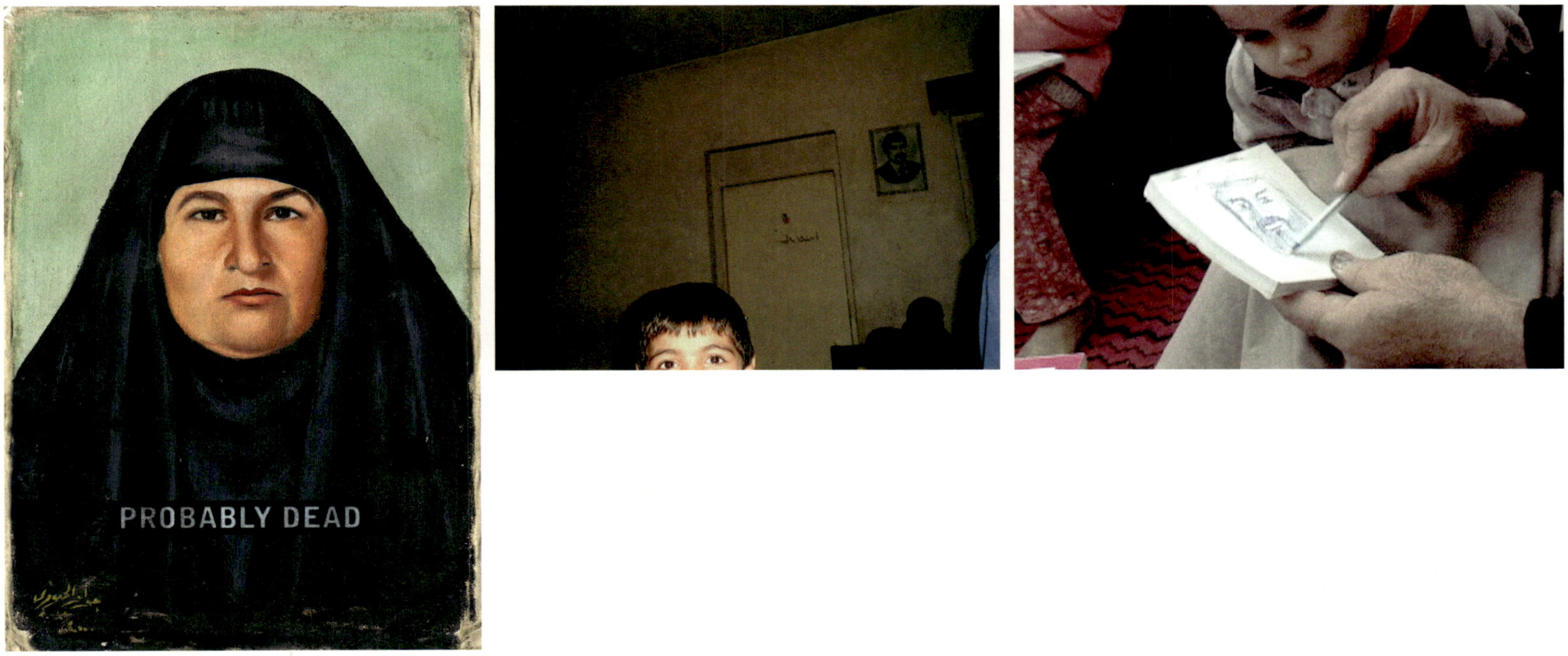
PROBABLY DEAD

AERNOUT MIK

1

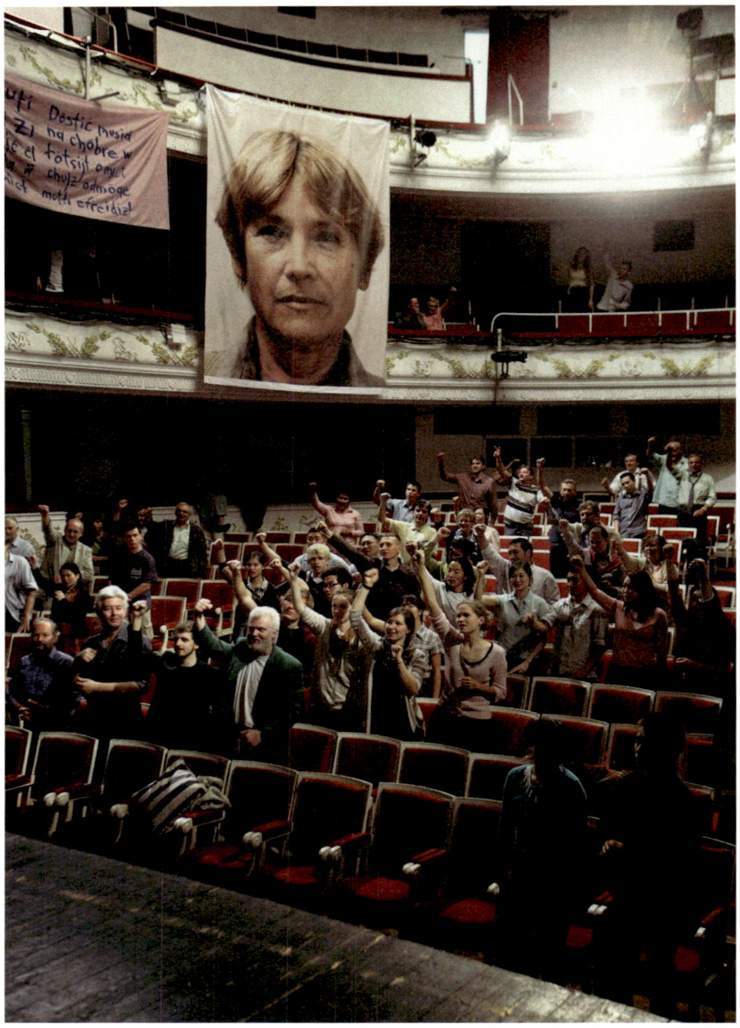

1
Communitas
2010, Produced by Teatr Dramatyczny, Warsaw, Poland, Biennale de São Paulo, Brazil, and supported by the Fonds BKVB, Netherlands
Photos by Florian Braun
Courtesy carlier | gebauer, Berlin

Dutch artist Aernout Mik (* 1962) studied at the Academie Minerva in Groningen, and is today regarded as one of the foremost video artists of his generation. Mik's films are staged exercises in group dynamics—his experiments feature amateur actors, and analyze human conditioning. The action takes place in an artificial setting, but one that is reminiscent of familiar places such as offices, banking halls, or car repair workshops. The principle of cause and effect is negated, and the protagonists move through time and space in a seemingly aimless way. The scenes in his videos defy any narration—they are loops without any development, climax, or conclusion. Situations often escalate, so that an emotional situation is apparently being documented, but what is actually happening is always unclear. This makes the films alienating and threatening, like disquieting, mad dreams.

"As an artist, can you generate space for political discussion with and through your work? How can you use images to create an opening for thinking? People are afraid that politicizing immediately turns art into an instrument. That fear is understandable, but it is no reason to avoid the connection to theory and politics. I want to put art back into society," explains Mik. Their filmic virtuosity and lack of a narrative makes his films a puzzle, leaving plenty of space for interpretation, and for turning them into projection surfaces for our own fears. In *Middlemen,* 2001, exhausted protagonists sit on the floor of a bank, which is strewn with papers, staring into nothingness. In *Training Ground,* 2006, police officers are apparently carrying out checks on migrants, and in *Communitas,* 2010, Mik brings together Polish citizens and Vietnamese migrants, who express political outrage in every way possible: they debate, dispute, and shout. There is a mood of revolutionary upheaval in the air—and an apparent fear of an unknown threat coming from the outside. Many of these disastrous scenes have tragicomic undertones, and they often contain references to topical political debates. Mik's films are concerned with the relationship of the individual and the crowd with power; the manipulation of the mass media, and the crisis and collapse of social order; and with violence propagated by group dynamics. "The force of the mass has a tremendous influence; people are first and foremost social creatures. Ritual is an artificial form, a mutual contract that gives free rein to the power of the group. As soon as you bring several people together, there is a power relationship. It is unavoidable," says Mik. "I let these power relationships evolve, but I also let them get derailed, like a subversive act. Spinning out of orbit like this is a way of creating space. You see everything fall apart, but at the same time you feel increasing opportunities for change. New possibilities are created."

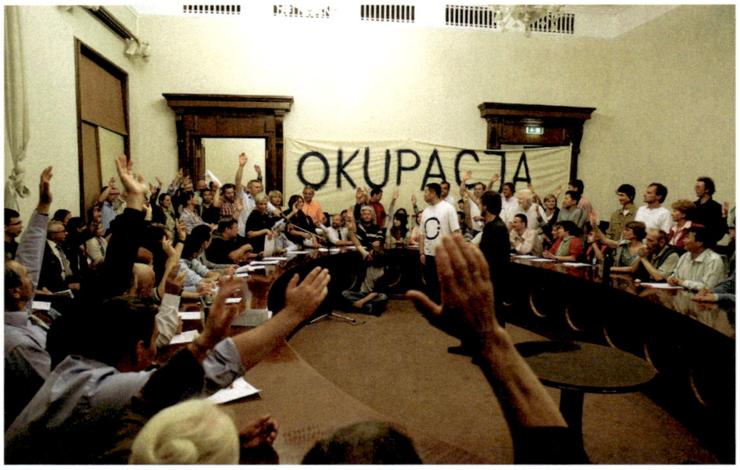

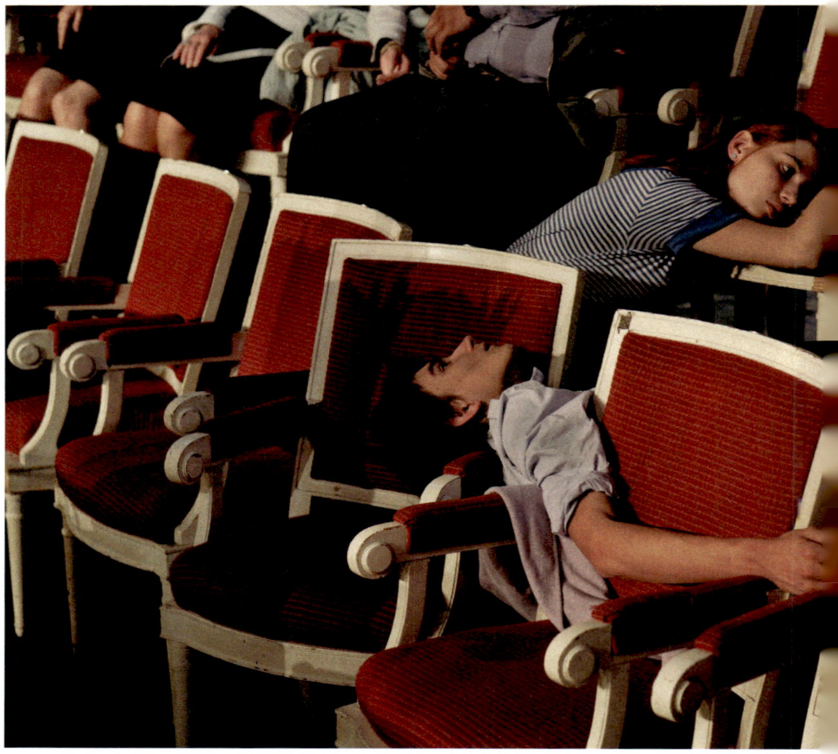

1

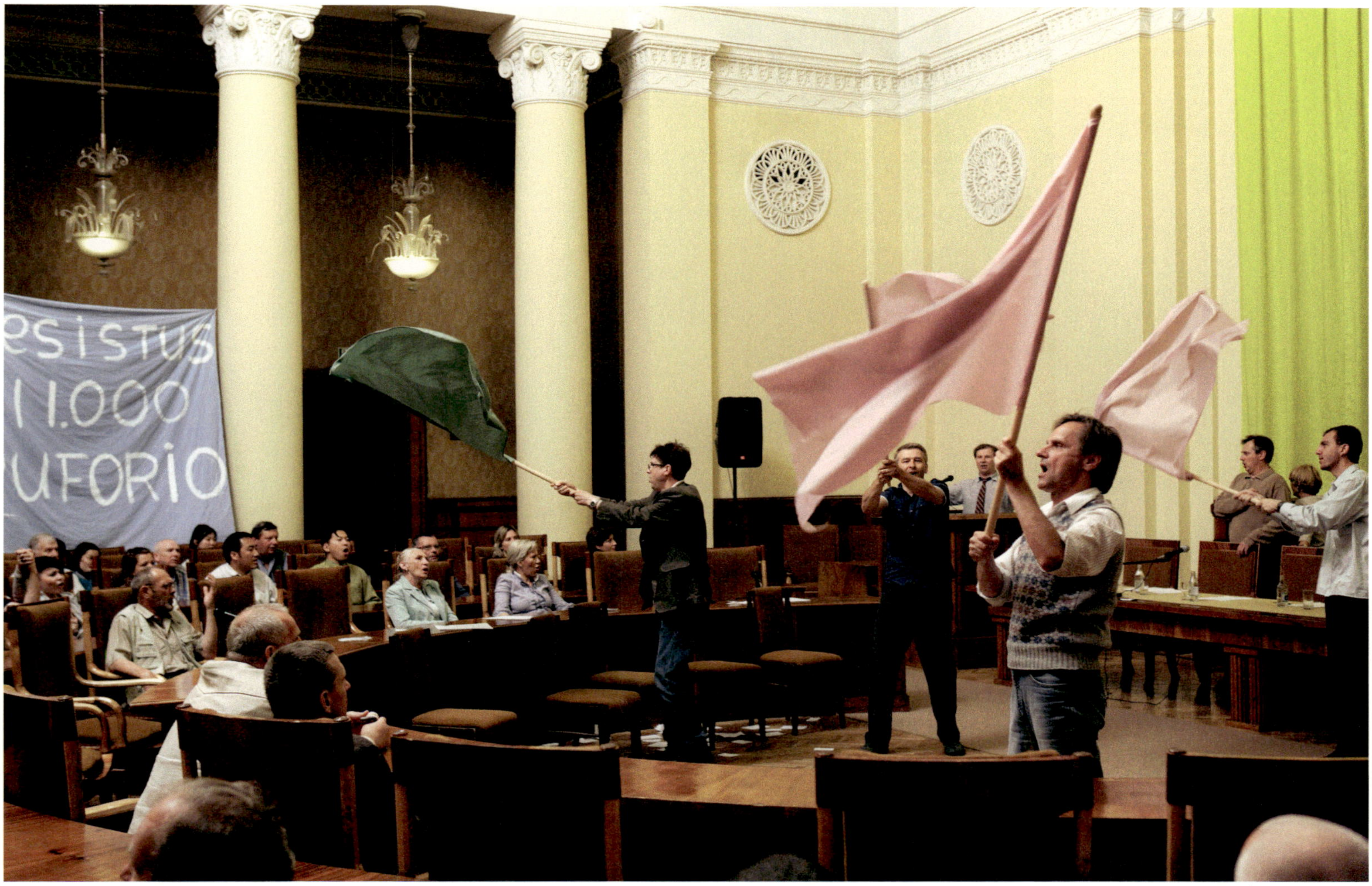

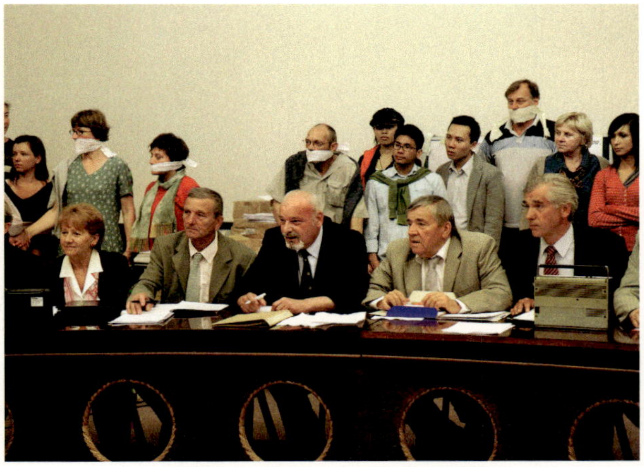

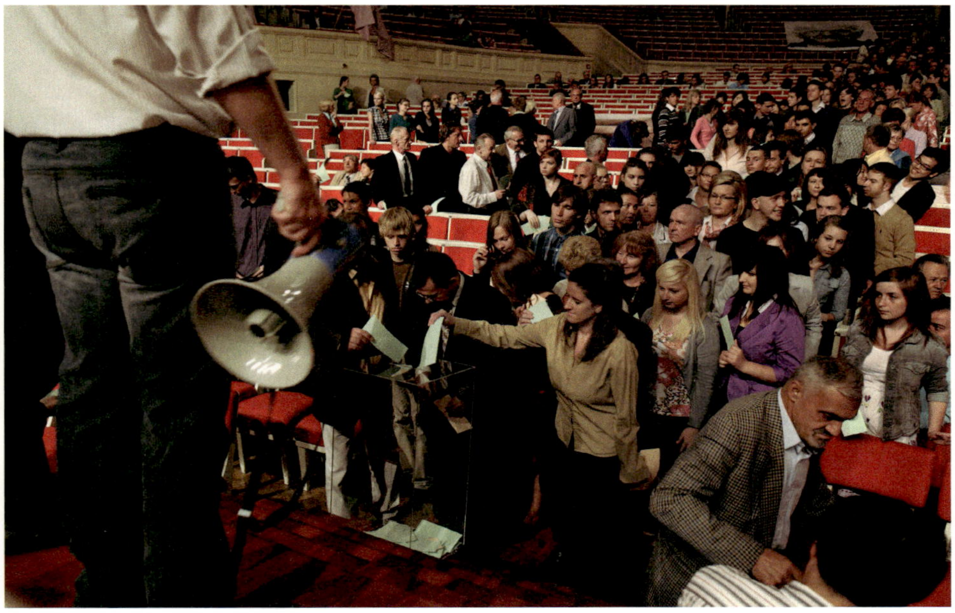

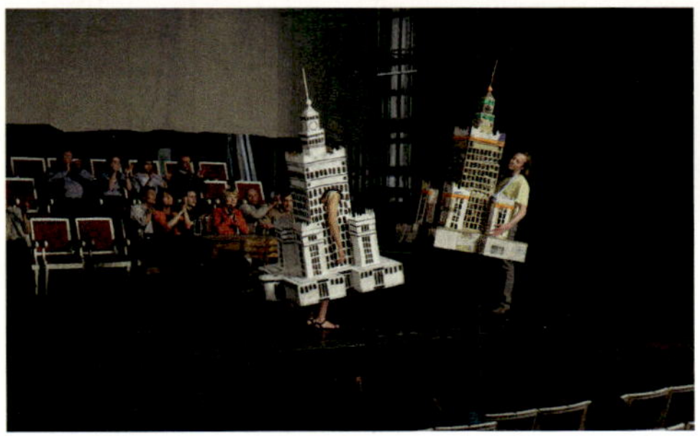

AERNOUT MIK
2
Middlemen
2001, Video installation
3
Training Ground
2006, Two-screen video installation
4
Schoolyard
2009

Photos by Florian Braun
Courtesy carlier | gebauer, Berlin

2

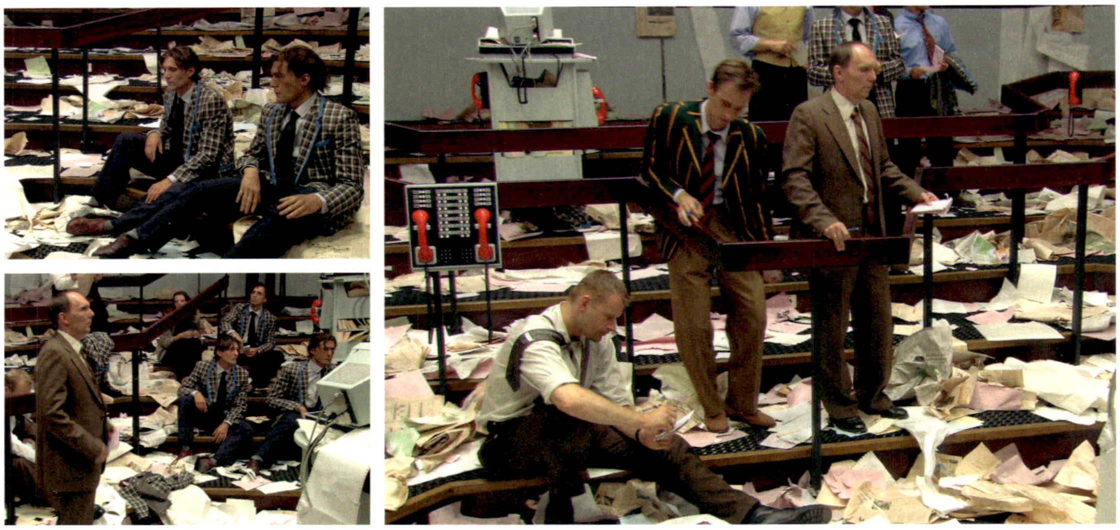

3

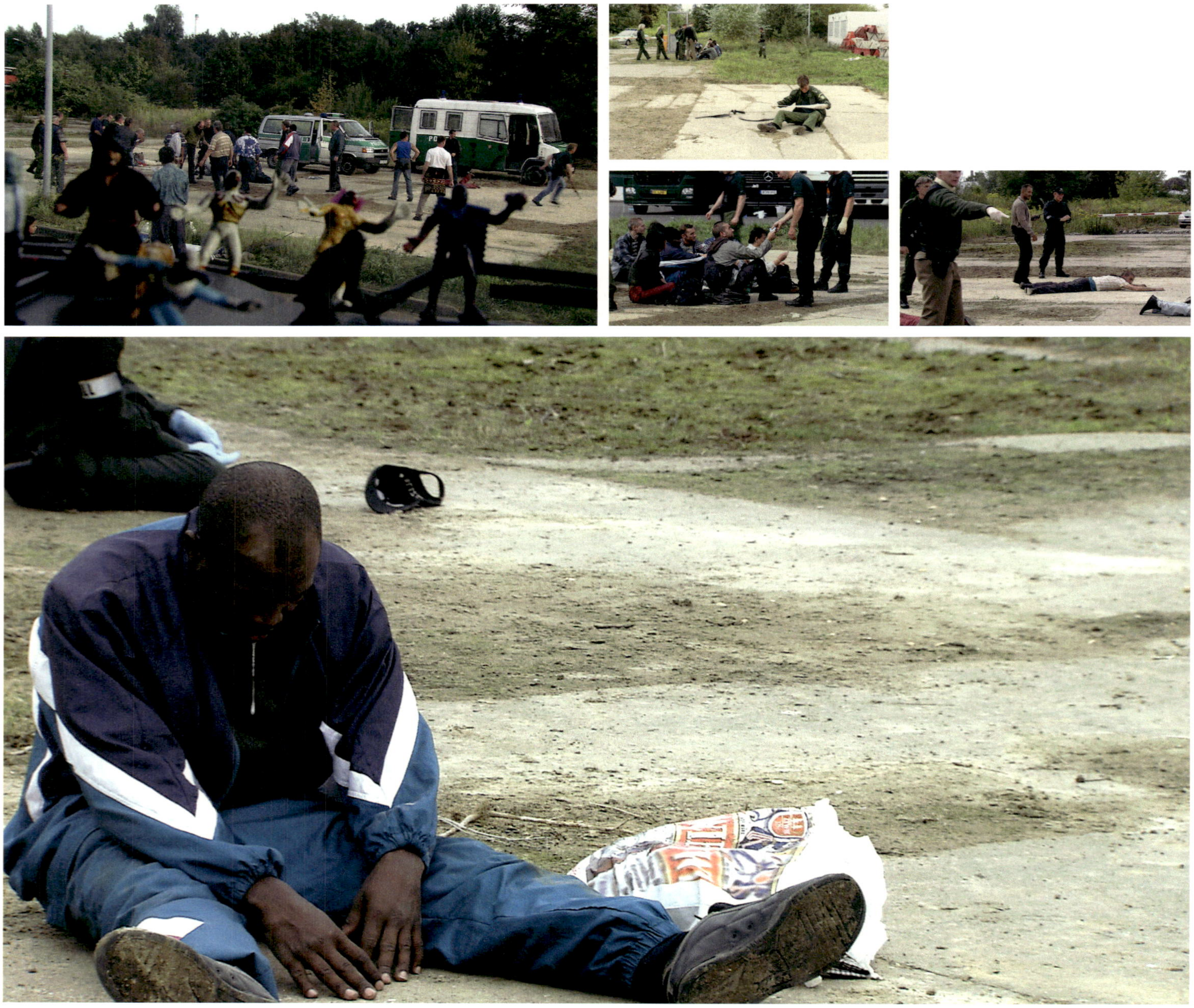

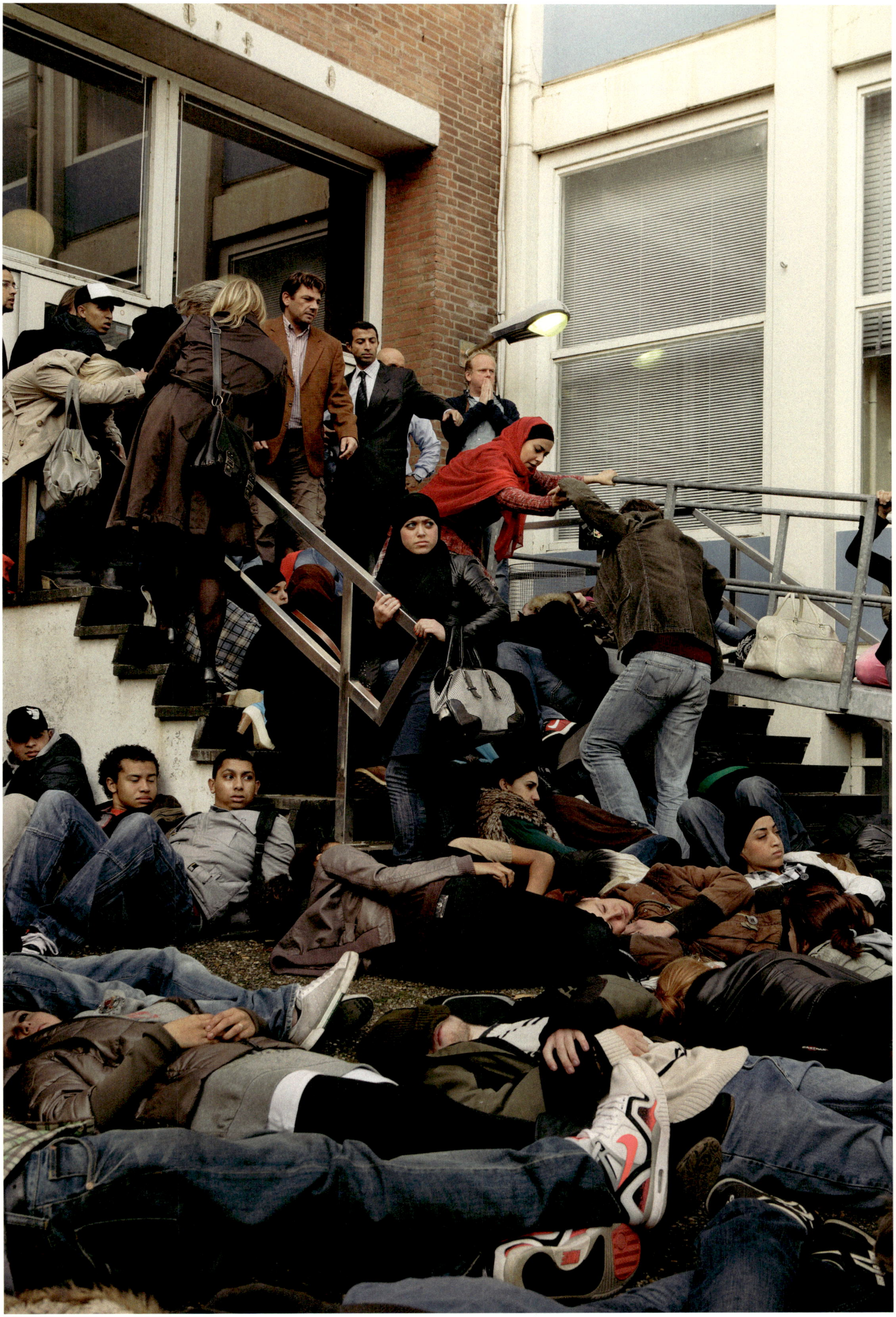

JÉRÔME LEUBA

Swiss artist Jérôme Leuba (* 1970) studied art in Geneva. In his *Battlefield* series of works, he probes open wounds. His performances, photographs, videos, and art objects are little individual pinpricks, and his themes are conflict zones and current areas of tension. Leuba provokes reactions, and uses staged situations to disquiet and irritate. In this way, he undermines social structures, and the images and symbols of the collective consciousness, making us think about how we view them. For his *Battlefield #47* project in 2009, Leuba sat on a balcony for two months, six days a week, from 12:00 A.M. to 6:00 P.M., watching the passing crowd, with a replica Swiss army firearm lying next to him. This really rather unspectacular performance nonetheless attracted a lot of attention because of its disquieting resemblance to massacres and suicide attacks. Leuba's *Battlefield #19/If You See Something, Say Something* project in 2008 also raised fears. He left a number of items of luggage in a museum: plastic bags, suitcases, and backpacks. This led to repeatedly alarmed visitors alerting surveillance staff about the left-behind items. Since 9/11, we have become so conditioned to potential terrorist threats, that when we see a piece of luggage lying around, our first thought is not that someone has lost something, but that it could be a bomb. This is another example of Leuba examining the reflexes that media images trigger in us. He constantly plays with clichés, norms, and group dynamics, by confusing and disquieting the viewer. For instance, in *Battlefield #49/Bystander,* three bodies lay apart, motionless on the ground for three days in a popular park in Geneva. In another work, when several families in the United States built themselves father-figures from cardboard, Leuba created the video artwork *Battlefield #46/Flat Daddy,* 2009. It shows a Berlin family involving their portable cardboard father in the most absurd situations. Its contextual displacement makes this video singularly fascinating. In his *Battlefields,* Leuba conducts elegant guerrilla warfare; his weapon is subtle subversion and his interventions are political in a refined way by revealing their full force in the viewer's imagination. Leuba himself says that: "I love to see things that you don't see at first glance."

1
Battlefield #47
2009, "Utopics", 11th Swiss Public Art Exhibition, Biel, Switzerland

2
Battlefield #49/Bystander
2008, Points d'impact, Performance Festival, Geneva, Switzerland

3
Battlefield #19/If You See Something, Say Something
2008, "Shifting Identities" at Kunsthaus Zurich, Switzerland

1
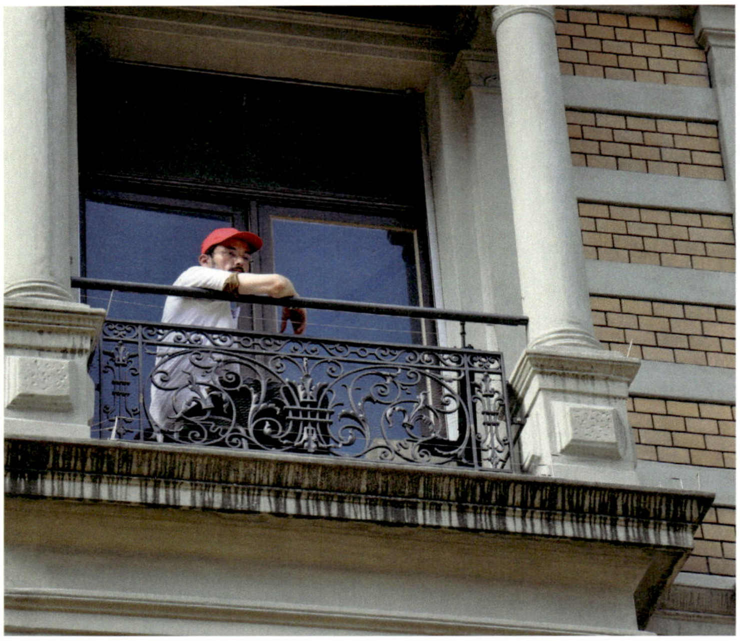

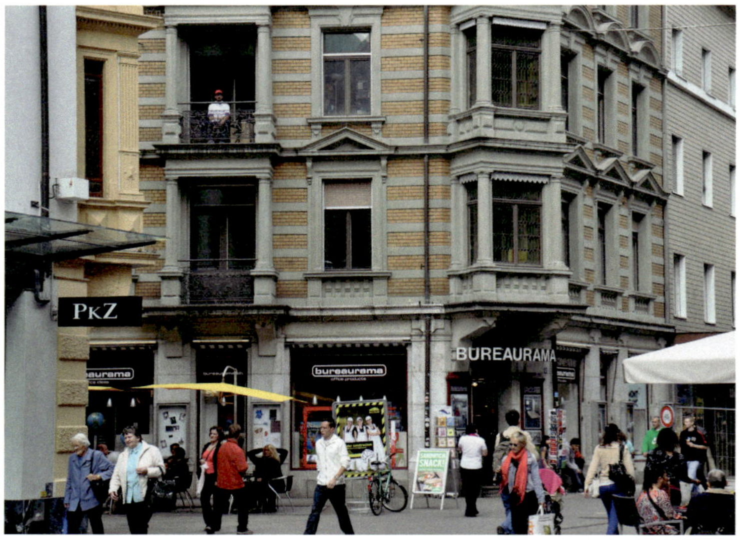

3
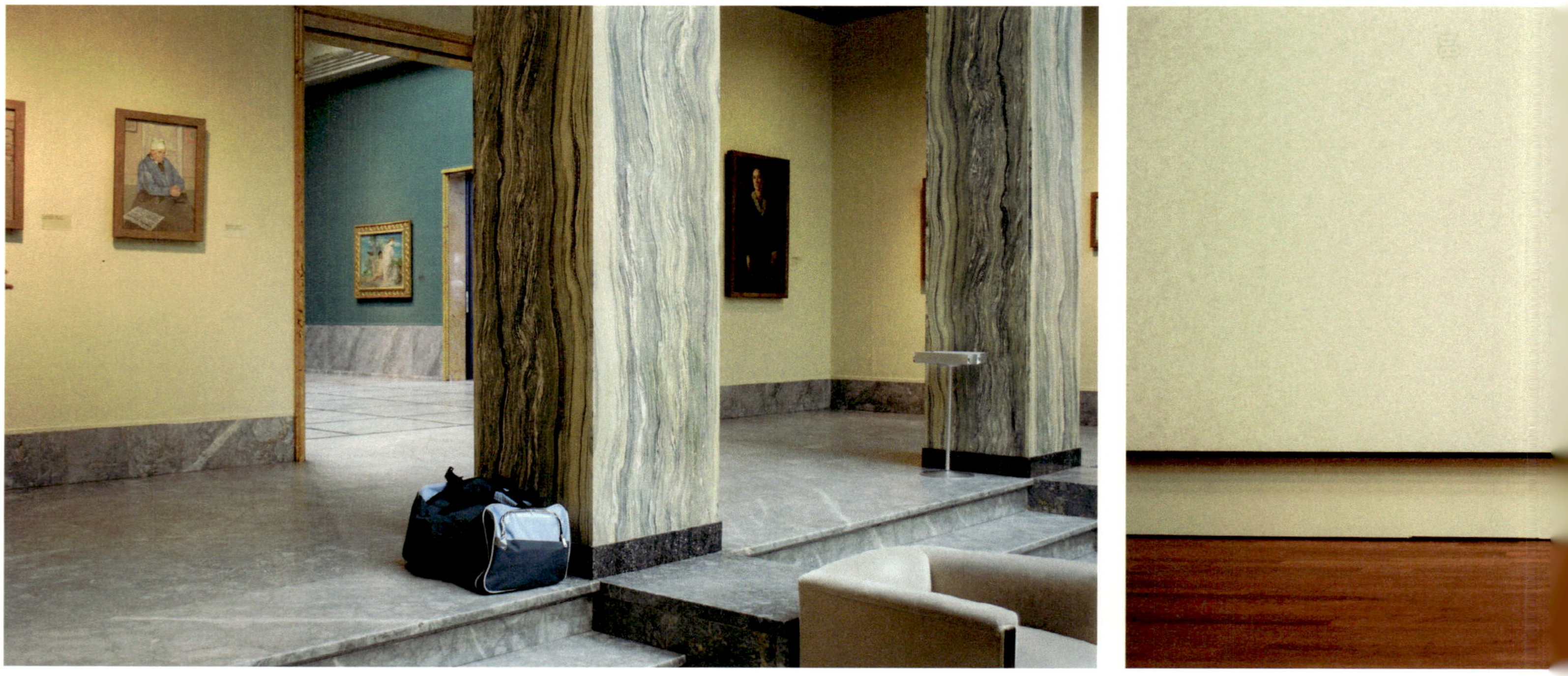

2

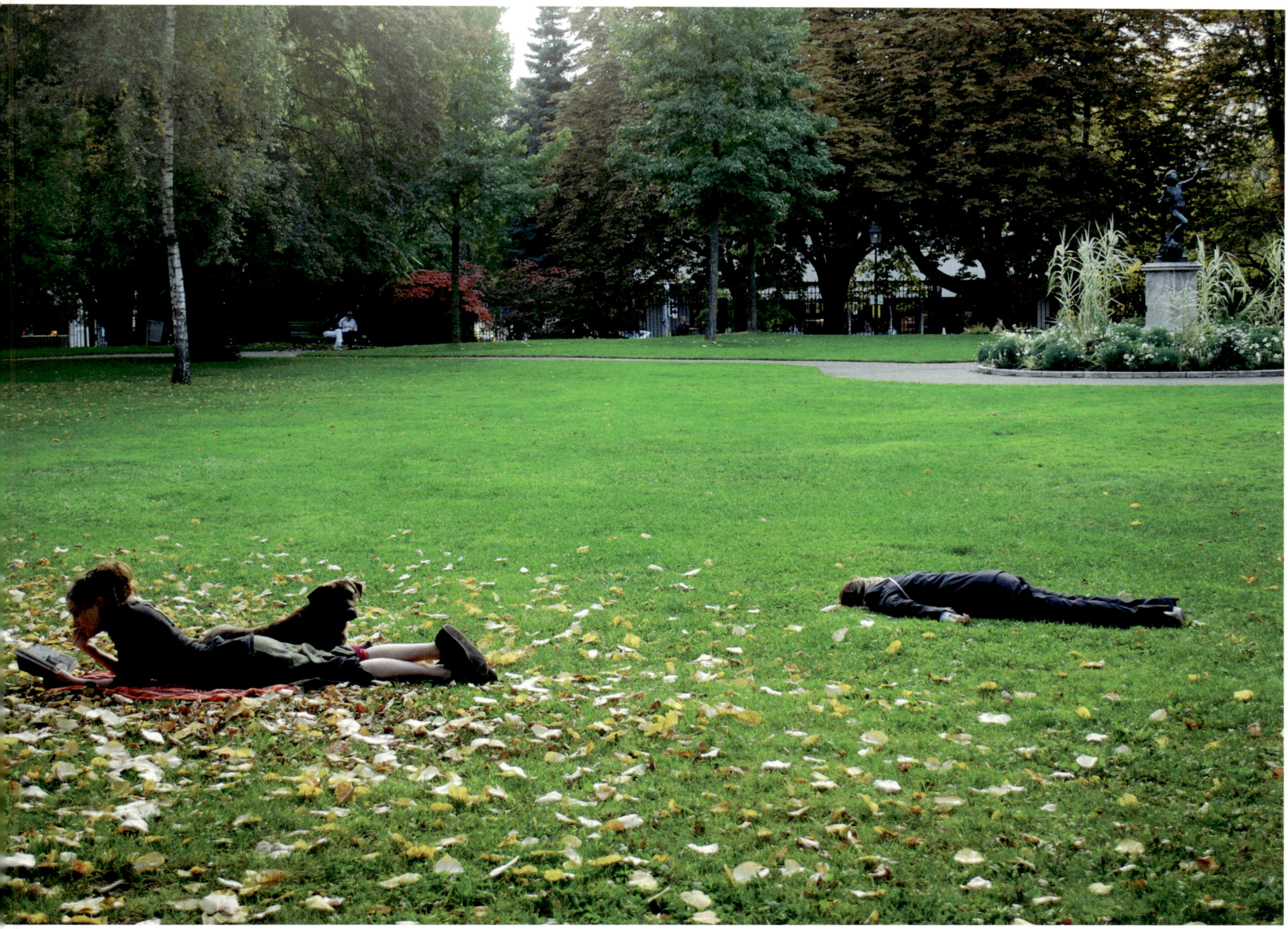

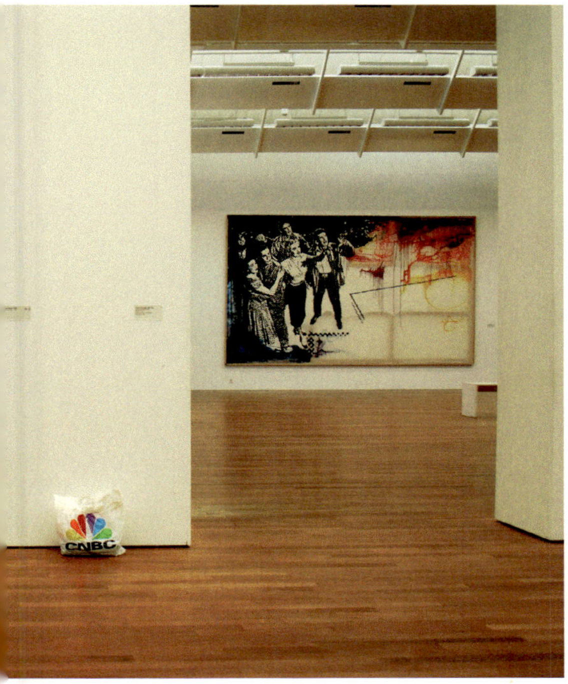

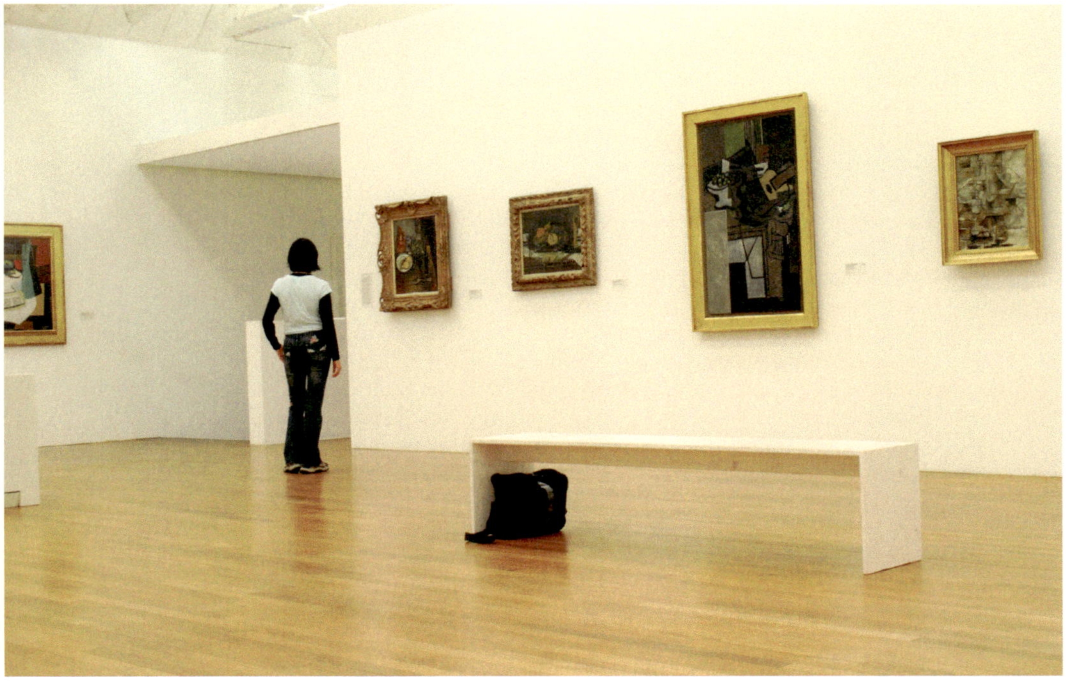

KENDELL GEERS

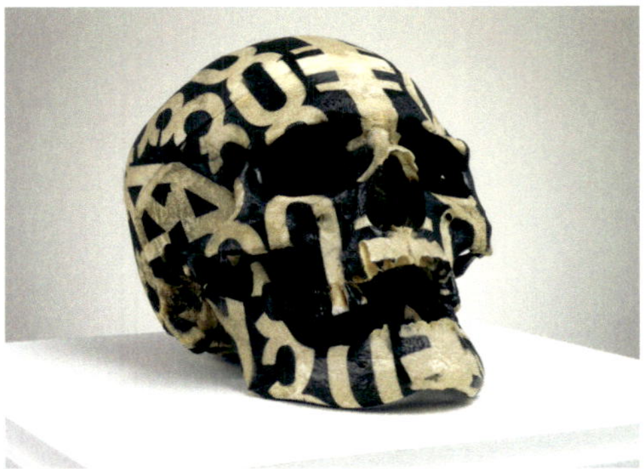
1

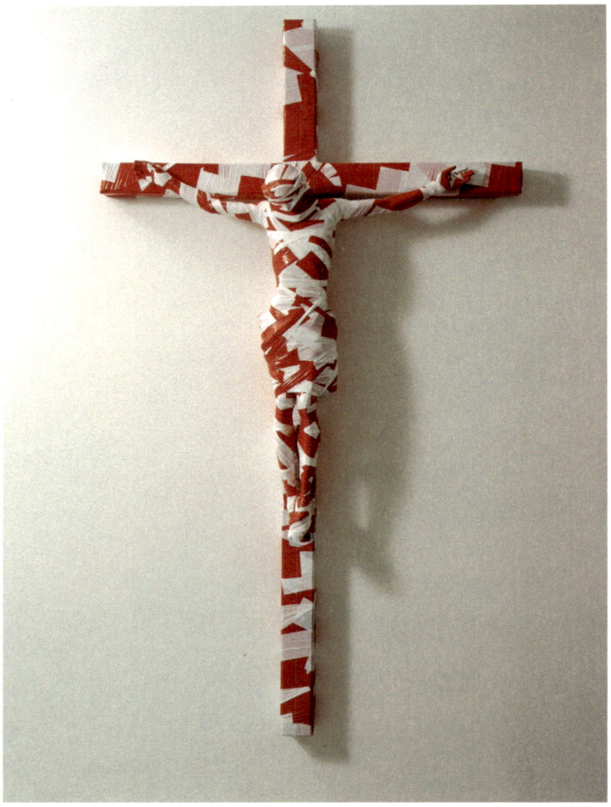
2

1
Fuckface
2005, Spray paint on human skull
2
I.N.R.I.
1993, Edition of three
3
Garden of Earthly Delights
2004, Photos by Lydie Nesvadba
4
Jesusfuckingchrist
2006, Wood and spray paint

Courtesy the artist and Stephen Friedman Gallery, London

The complexities and contradictions of growing up in apartheid-era South Africa shaped the highly critical worldview of artist Kendell Geers (*1968). The outrage and frustration experienced as a citizen of an oppressive state are clearly expressed throughout his body of work. Geers uses objects and a conceptual artistic strategy, as a vehicle to engage audiences with his politically charged messages. Geers has the ability to transform everyday objects, images, and even documents into provocative works of art. His main role as an artist is to challenge us to deal with unspoken truths. His work and ideas confront all of us with a harsh reality; effectively articulating issues of identity, imposition of culture, racism, xenophobia, injustice, and the abuse of power. Geers likes to reveal what society has swept under the carpet.

Having been denied basic freedoms that citizens of most democratic nations take for granted, Geers is hypersensitive to the correlation between the entrenchment of power and diminishing civil rights. In several works, Geers utilizes tactical gear, and tools used by the police to address the use of force to impose order—as well as the abuses that have taken place not just in his native South Africa, but around the world. In *The Time of the Harvest,* 2005, the artist uses a simple metal shelving system to display the helmets worn by the Belgian gendarmes who beat protestors during the student riots in the late 1960s. *Cry Wolf,* 1999, incorporates an unruly pileup of red police sirens, cables, and power cords that depict the chaos of a riot. In another series of works, black police batons are arranged to form shapes such as stars and circles. The tools of the trade used by law enforcement carry with them a sense of power and order; Geers employs these elements to reminds us of the difference between a *police force* and a *police state.* He is suggesting that if this remains unchecked, those who are meant to protect society will eventually dominate it.

Through abstraction, distortion, and repetition, Geers inoculates symbols of extreme violence, profanity, and pornography. Several series of work use the word "fuck" as a sort of pattern that can be replicated on wallpaper, mirrored glass, wrapped around objects, and is also painted on his face. In *Mouthing Off,* 1993, pornographic videos are manipulated into abstract forms as if seen through the lens of a kaleidoscope. The monumental installation, *Akropolis Now (The Director's Cut),* 2004, uses razor wire to create a formalist structure. The wire is manipulated into bundles and forms that highlight the repetitive nature of the material resembling the modular qualities of minimalist sculpture. The repetition and mirroring of the word "fuck," the visual distortion of pornographic images, and the presentation of barbed wire as a form of minimalist sculpture, reflect and defy a modernist bias toward formal abstraction and conceptual art. In Geers's case, his life experience is too strong to be erased by the formal language of art and shines right through the formalist construct.

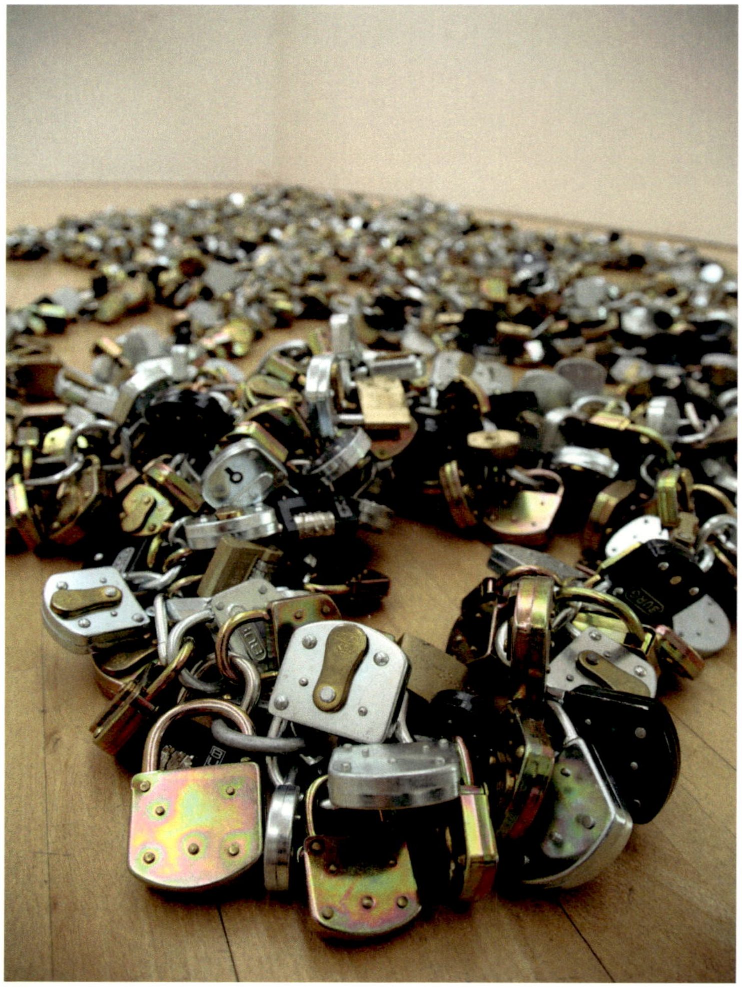
3

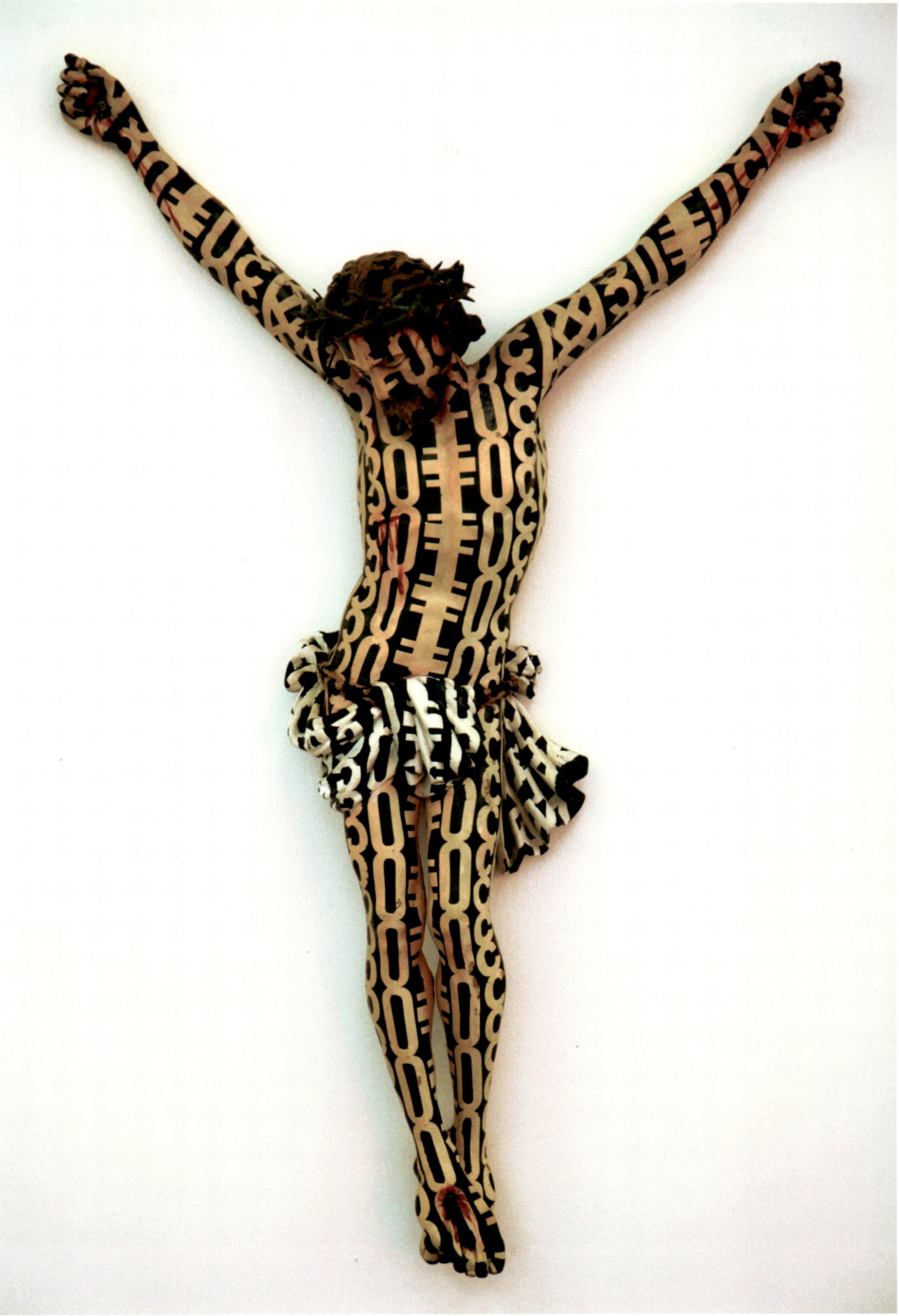

1

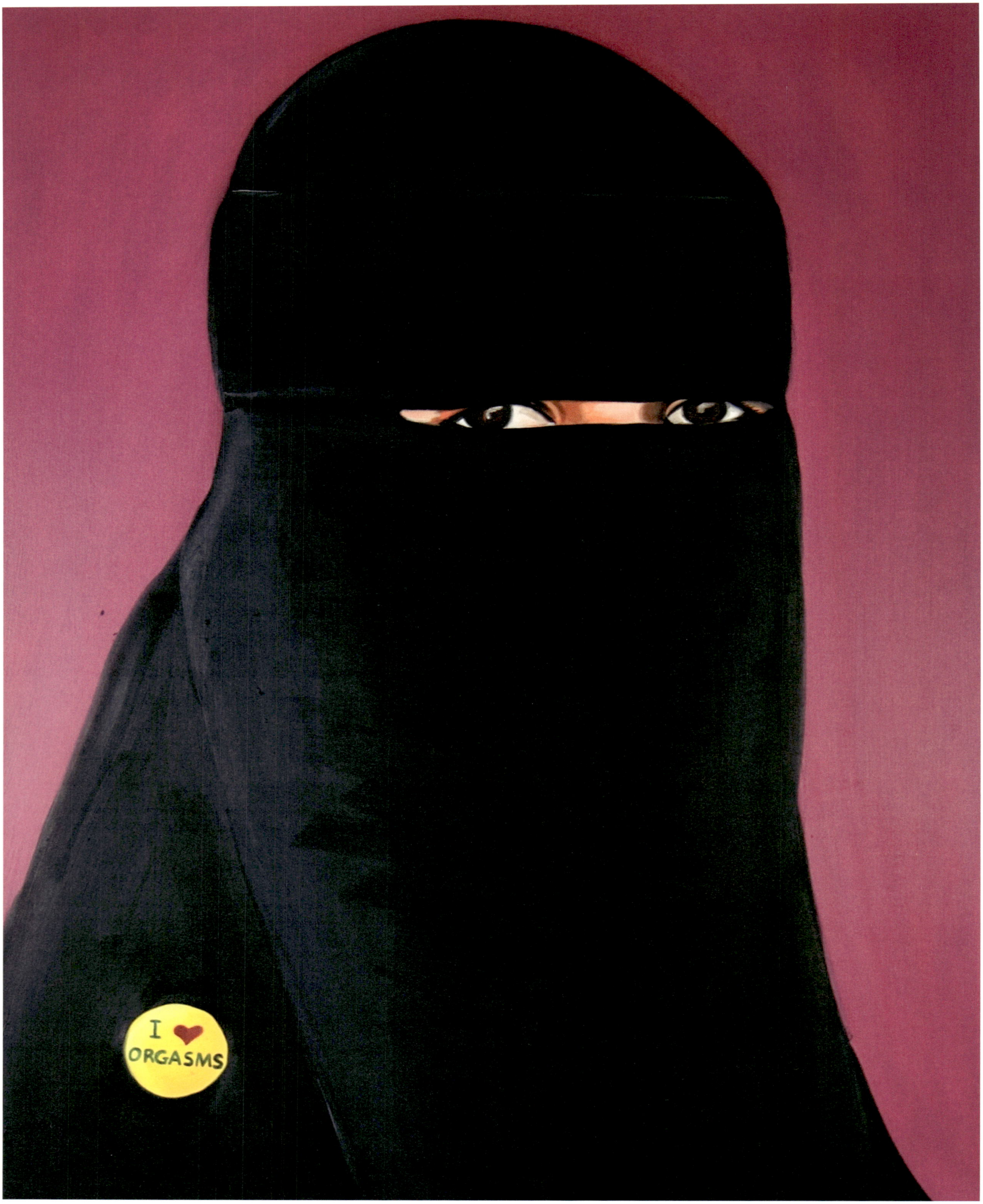

SARAH MAPLE

1
I Heart Orgasms
2008, Oil on board
2
Bananarama
2007, Oil on board
3
Signs
2007, Digital print

The British artist Sarah Maple (* 1985) has a Muslim mother and a Christian father. She studied art at Kingston University in London. Her paintings and photographs deal largely with themes such as feminism, religion, sex, and identity. Our modern pop culture cosmos and the mediascape provide inspiration for her humorous works. "The aim is to give my audience food for thought," says Maple. "I believe comedy is a great tool to achieve this, which is why I choose to portray my conceptual ideas through a light-hearted and tongue-in-cheek approach." For her painted self-portrait *Bananarama,* Maple depicted herself dressed in her mother's headscarf and biting into a banana—a picture that was likely to cause trouble. Despite her mixed cultural background—and although she describes herself as a "western Muslim woman"—Maple faces constant criticism from the Islamic community. But this is part of what she is trying to achieve: the scandal surrounding the picture shows the extent of the taboo surrounding the sexuality of Islamic women. Her portrait of a woman in a burka with a little sticker reading, "I Heart Orgasms," subtly sabotages religious-based concepts of morality. "The work comes from quite a personal place, because it's me trying to combine these two things," Maple explains. Of course, she is also self-consciously making use of her role as the sexy enfant terrible. Even so, it is a long time since anyone has addressed classic feminist themes in such a charming, fresh, and uninhibited way.

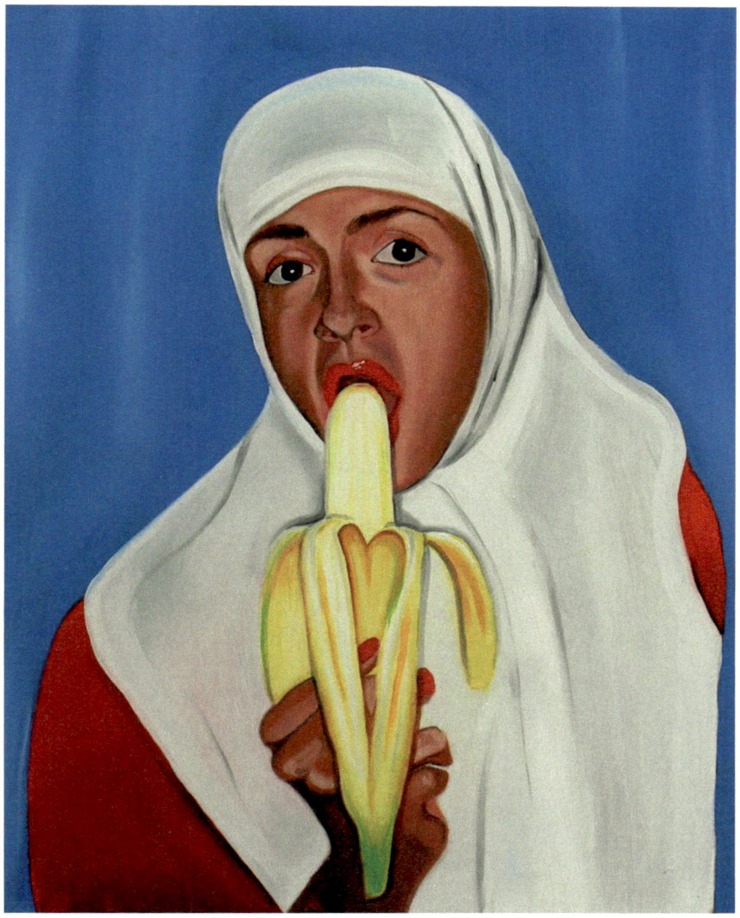

2

3

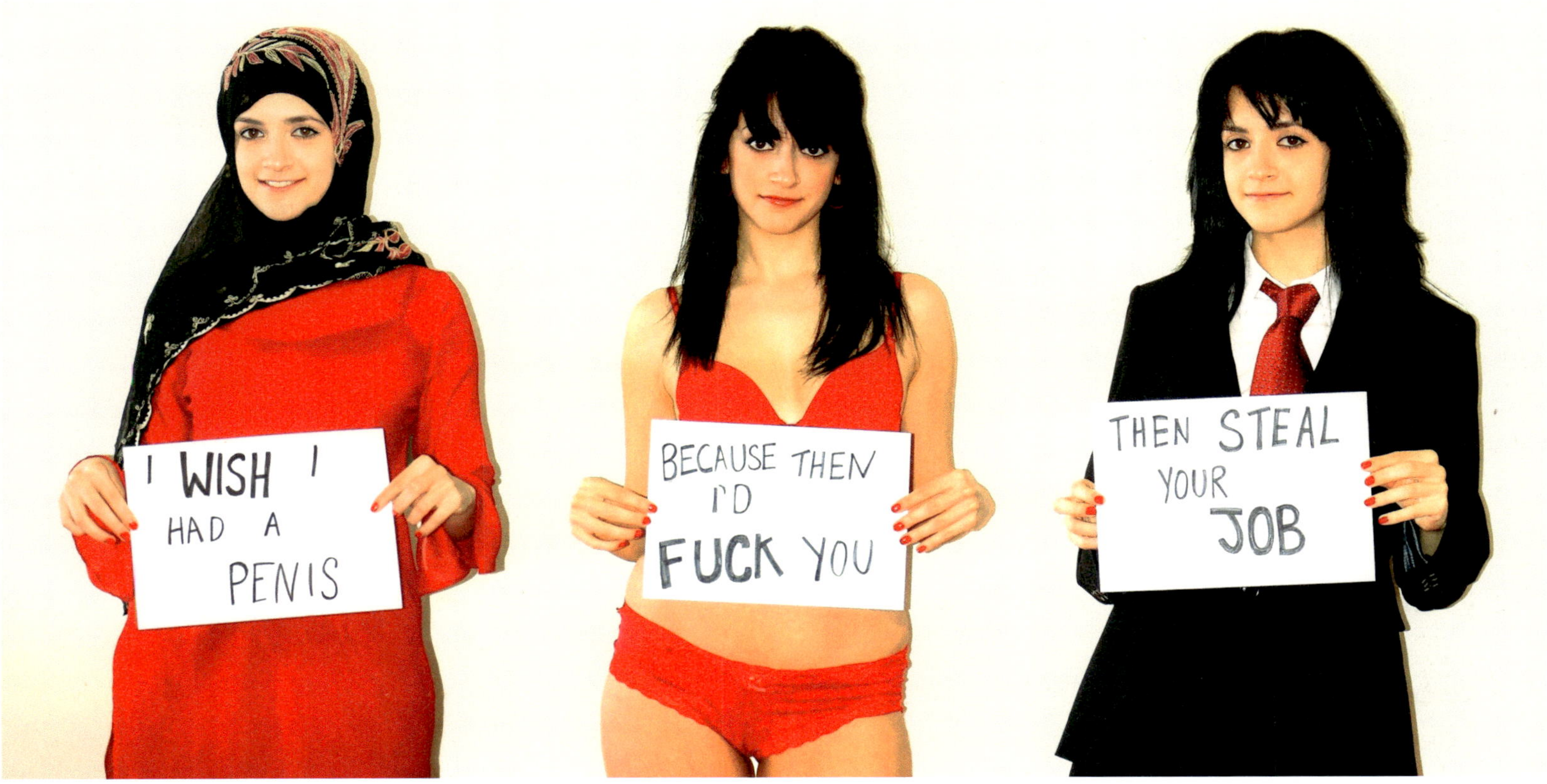

ZTOHOVEN

1

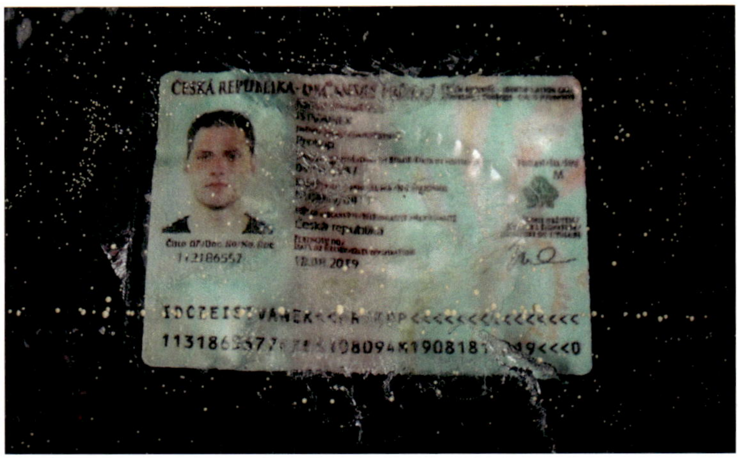

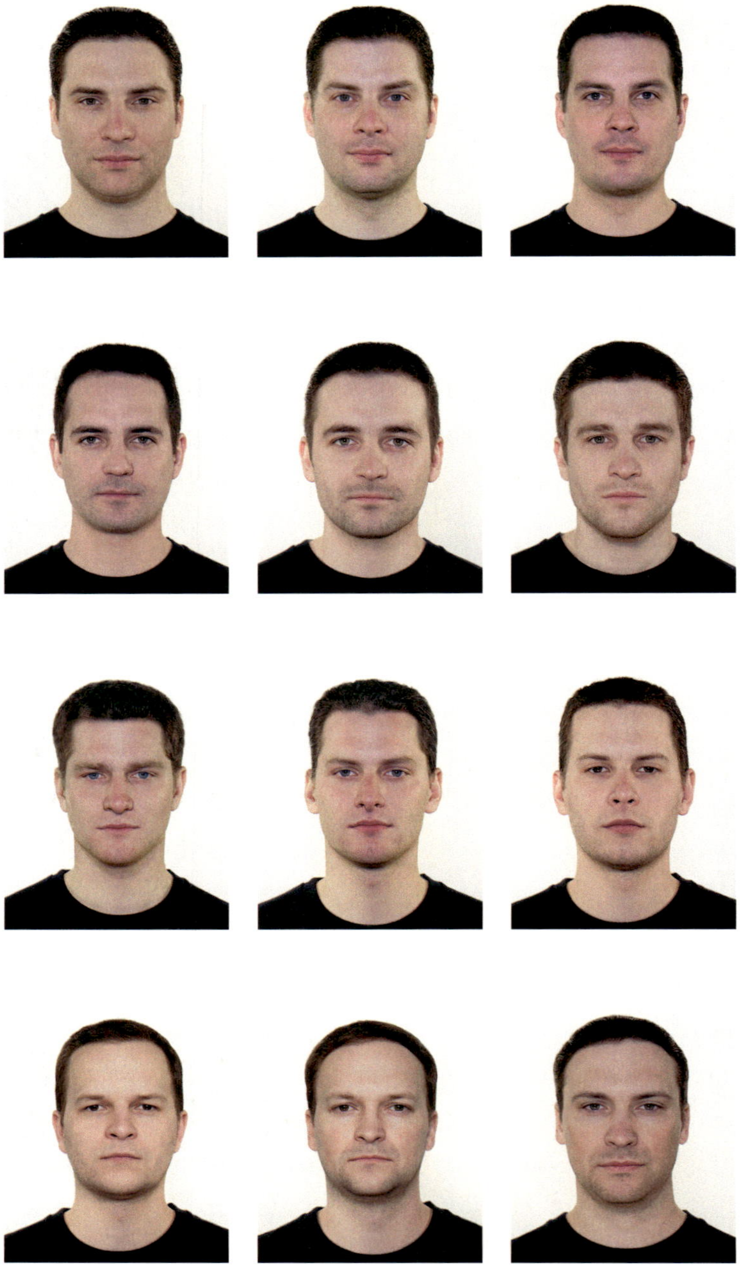

1
Citizen K.
2009–2010
2 (next spread)
Media Reality
2007, Czech Republic

Ztohoven's first success involved an atom bomb on morning television. On the June 17, 2007, the Czech collective Ztohoven (in English "get out of here" [z toho ven] or "100 pieces of shit" [sto hoven]) hacked into a TV weather program that shows webcam pictures from Czech beauty spots with the current temperature readings, accompanied by elevator music. That day, the image of the Krkonoše Mountains was embellished with a mushroom cloud. The sequel to this coup—*Media Reality*—was played out in the law courts, with the Ztohoven collective threatened with up to three years in prison. As it turned out, however, Ztohoven won the Prague National Gallery newcomers' prize, the NG33. They became famous, and were acquitted shortly afterward. The intention behind their action was to draw attention to the distorted view of reality in the media. The founder of the group, David Brudnak, alias Roman Tyc (* 1975) from Chanov, Czech Republic, had already undertaken an action in which he doctored over 50 Prague pedestrian crossing traffic lights, replacing the little figures on the traffic lights with figures drinking beer and urinating standing up. And on the 20th anniversary of the Velvet Revolution, when the Czech Republic became democratic, he doctored a historic memorial plaque. The plaque had a victory sign in bronze standing for the year 1989—Tyc added hands raised in a Hitler salute for the year 1939 and hands with a raised middle finger to represent the year 2009. Ztohoven's new project is equally spectacular and will incur further legal consequences. For *Citizen K,* 2009–2010, members of the group lived under false identities for six months. For each person, Ztohoven used image-morphing tools to superimpose one passport photograph onto another—creating a portrait that combines the facial features of two different people. The two artists would then each apply for identity papers through official channels under the other's name. They used this documentation to travel, vote, and even to get married. This performance was intended as a critique of the misuse of personal data and of constant surveillance. It points to a loss of identity; in our mechanized time, individuals have been reduced to numbers. The issue is the protection of our identities and of the private sphere. The project manifesto states that: "We are all society, we all create the system, and we watch one another. We are not numbers, we are not biometric data, so let us not be mere pawns in the hands of the big players on the game board of these times. If we do not wish to fear our own face, we must save it!"

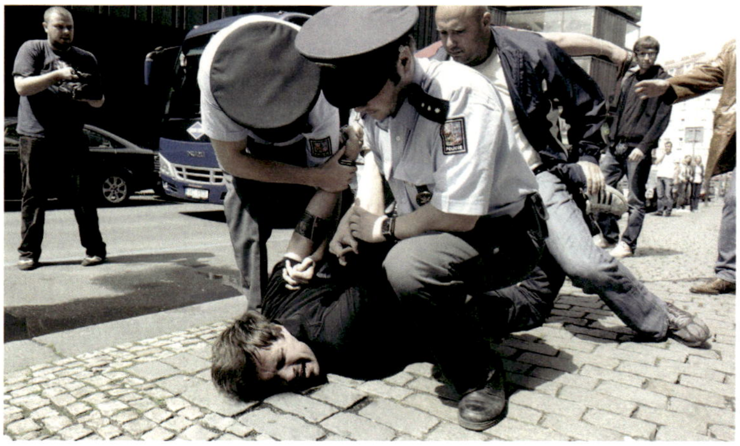

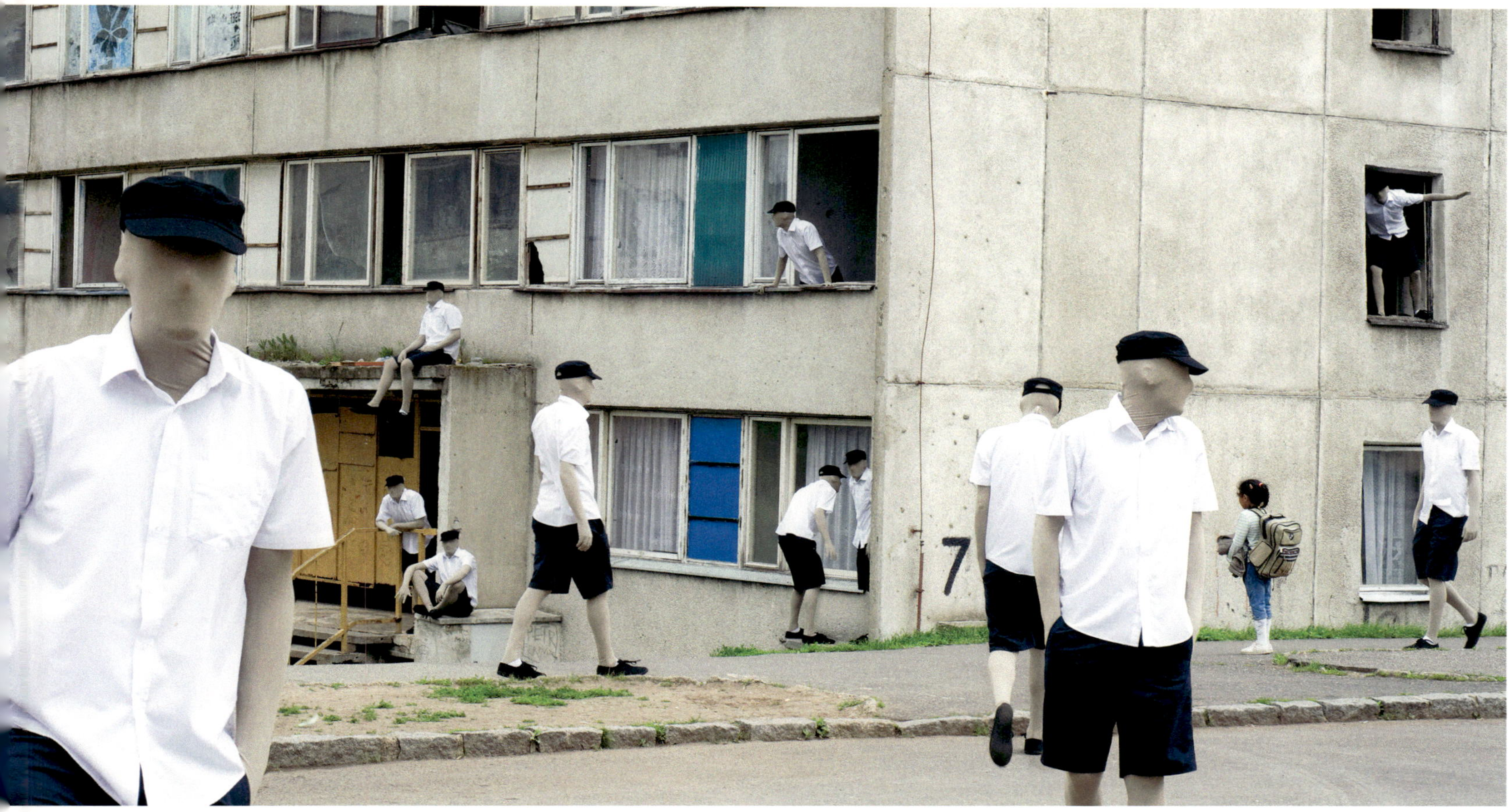

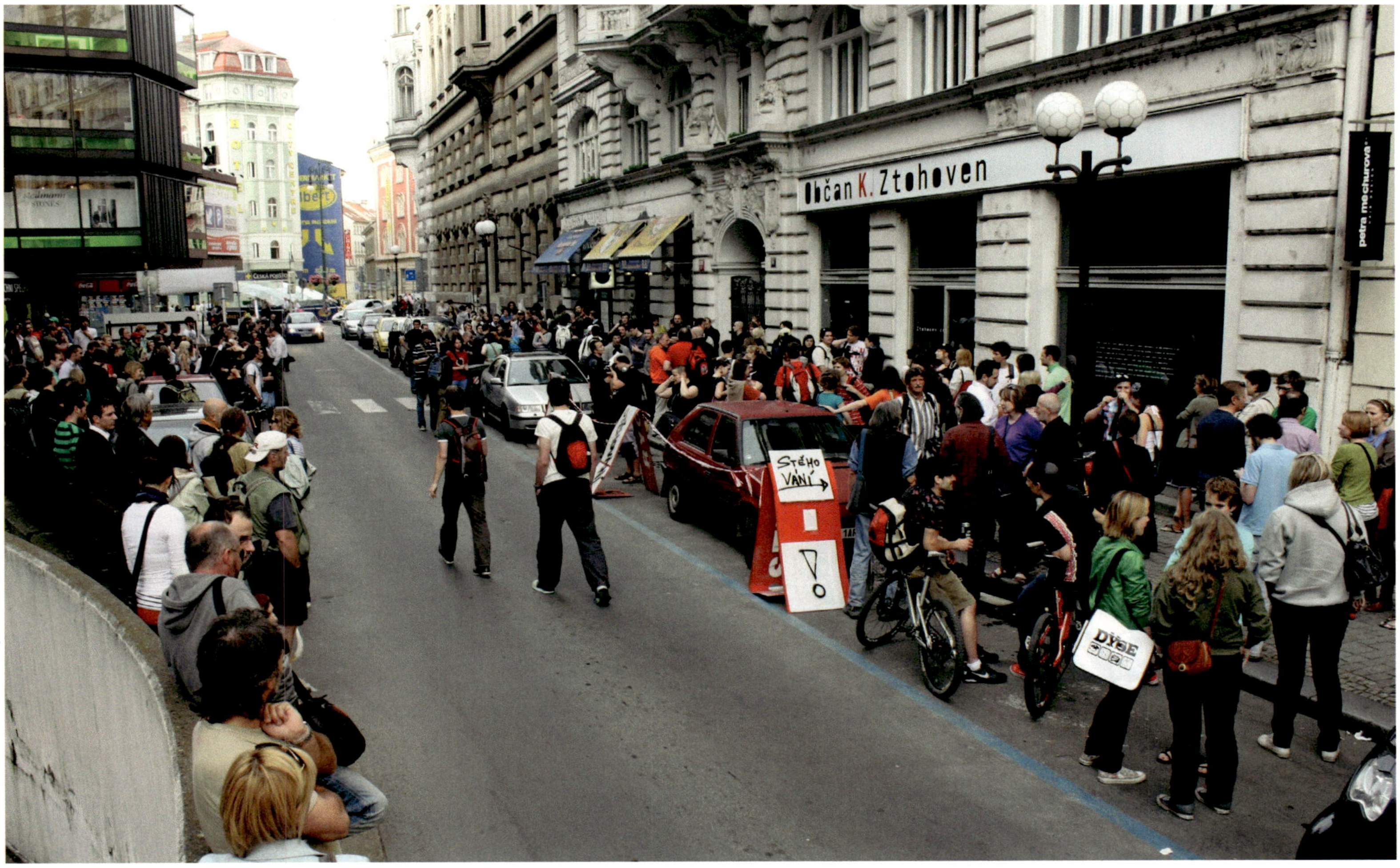
Občan K. Ztohoven

2

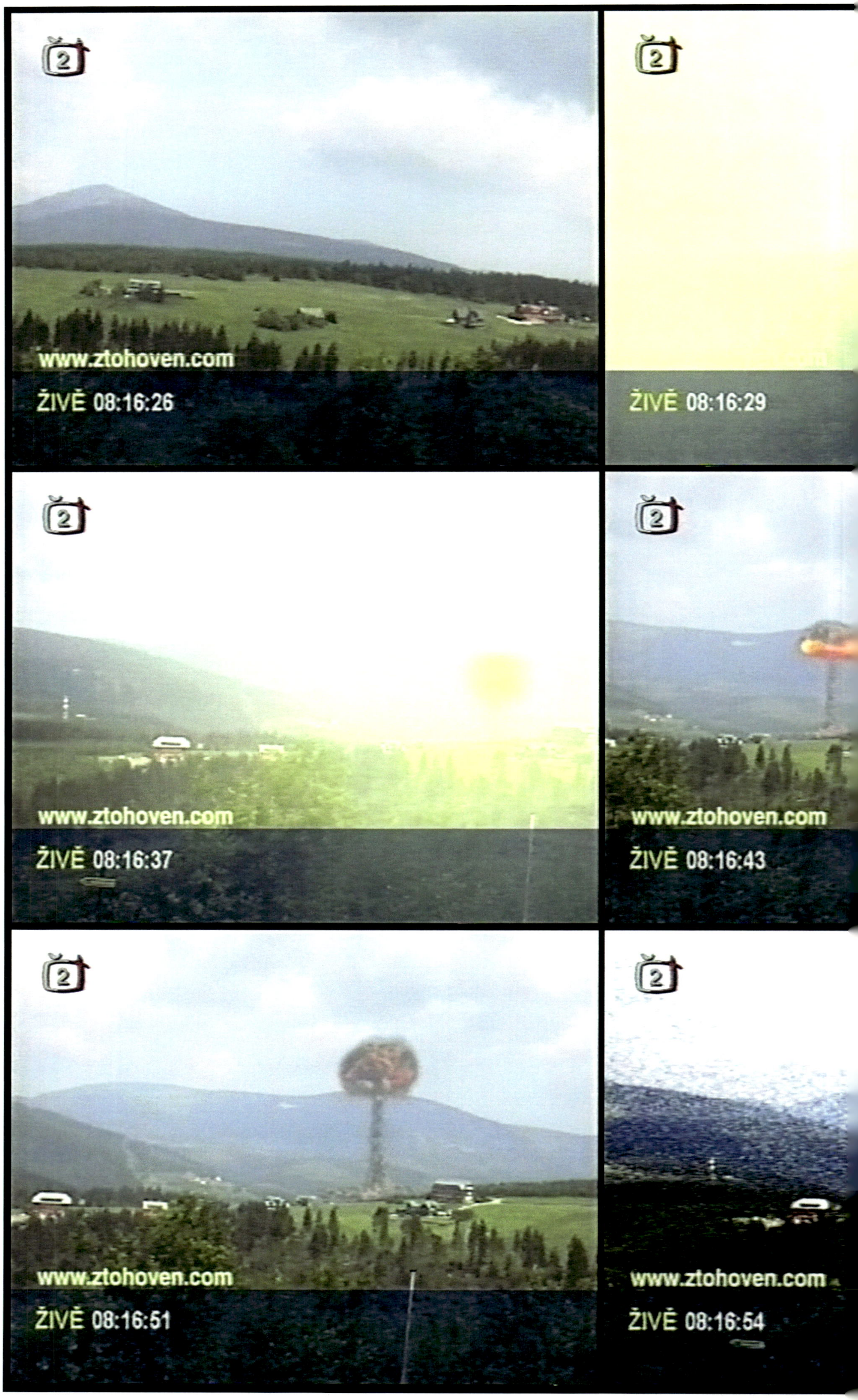
www.ztohoven.com
ŽIVĚ 08:16:26
ŽIVĚ 08:16:29
www.ztohoven.com
ŽIVĚ 08:16:37
www.ztohoven.com
ŽIVĚ 08:16:43
www.ztohoven.com
ŽIVĚ 08:16:51
www.ztohoven.com
ŽIVĚ 08:16:54

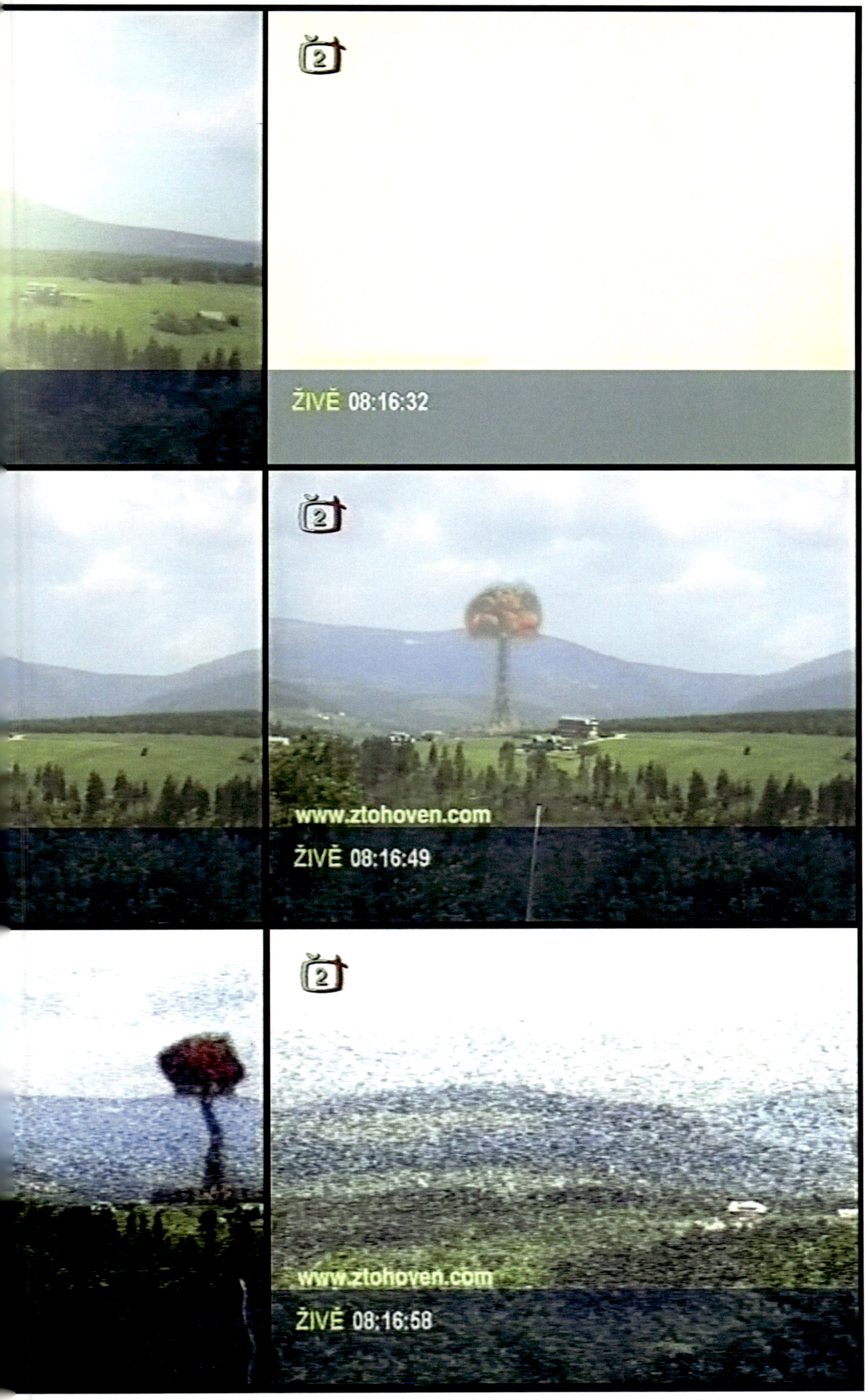
ŽIVĚ 08:16:32
www.ztohoven.com
ŽIVĚ 08:16:49
www.ztohoven.com
ŽIVĚ 08:16:58

CHRISTOPH FAULHABER

Christoph Faulhaber (* 1972) was born in Osnabrück, Germany, and studied both art and architecture. Within his practice, his artworks investigate public spaces. "Specifically, my art is about the themes of image and public space: image, reproduction, representation, and social codes," Faulhaber explains. "When is the camera read as a weapon, and the image read as terrorism? From 2004 to 2007, Lukasz Chrobok and I worked on the project *Mister Security*—a fictional security service, which involved us "monitoring" U.S. embassies and consulates in Germany." Equipped with bomber jackets and cameras, they photographed the public spaces in front of the embassies. They were usually arrested, questioned, and searched a few minutes after arriving, and their cameras would be confiscated. When Faulhaber was invited to travel to the United States on an art scholarship, he was visited a few days after his arrival by FBI officials who interrogated him; this led to him losing the scholarship, and having to travel home to Germany. "The resulting contact with Homeland Security, the FBI, and the State Department shows both how thin the barrier between art and reality is and that it is only a small step from this list into another reality," says Faulhaber. Despite this, he does not consider himself to be a political artist.

1
Mister Security
(with Lukasz Chrobok)
2005, Warsaw, Poland
© Lukasz Chrobok
and Christoph Faulhaber

2
6 Portraits
(from the Palau-Triptych)
2010, Palau and Dafen, China

3
Guantánamo
Allocation Center
2009, HafenCity, Hamburg, Germany

© VG Bild-Kunst, Bonn 2011

"I am more concerned with what art is doing today—what materials are available to an artist," he says. "In an age when we read everything we encounter as a picture or a symbol and have to make an interpretation of every situation to work out what it is all about, art endeavors to appropriate this new concept of the image. Pictures begin to take on a life of their own, to reproduce—but is there a life outside of pictures?" In his project *Guantánamo Auffanglager* (Guantánamo Reception Camp), 2009, he once again brought an abstract political debate back to real life. On a wasteland site in Hamburg's HafenCity, Faulhaber erected a construction project placard on which, amid a number of official logos, an English text stated that the city of Hamburg intended to erect a reception camp for former detainees from the Guantánamo US military prison. At the time, Faulhaber said that: "Naturally the project belongs within the art sphere, and makes no secret of the fact. But it also threatens to become real." As it turned out, his art had anticipated reality again: six months later, the city of Hamburg declared its willingness to take in a Guantánamo detainee.

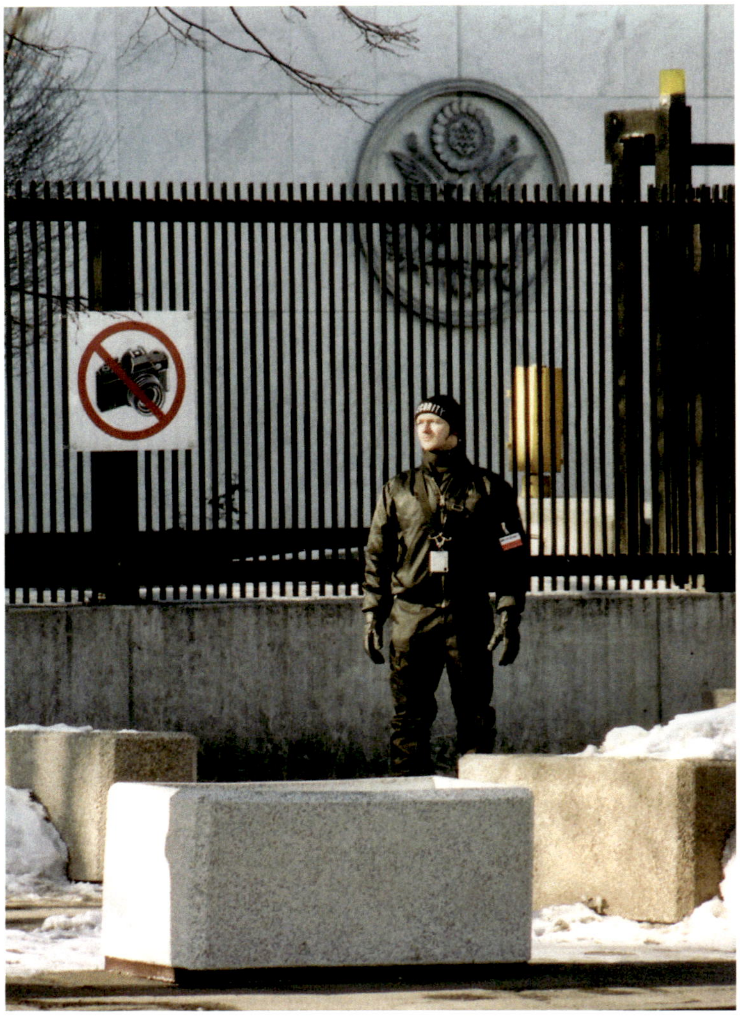

1

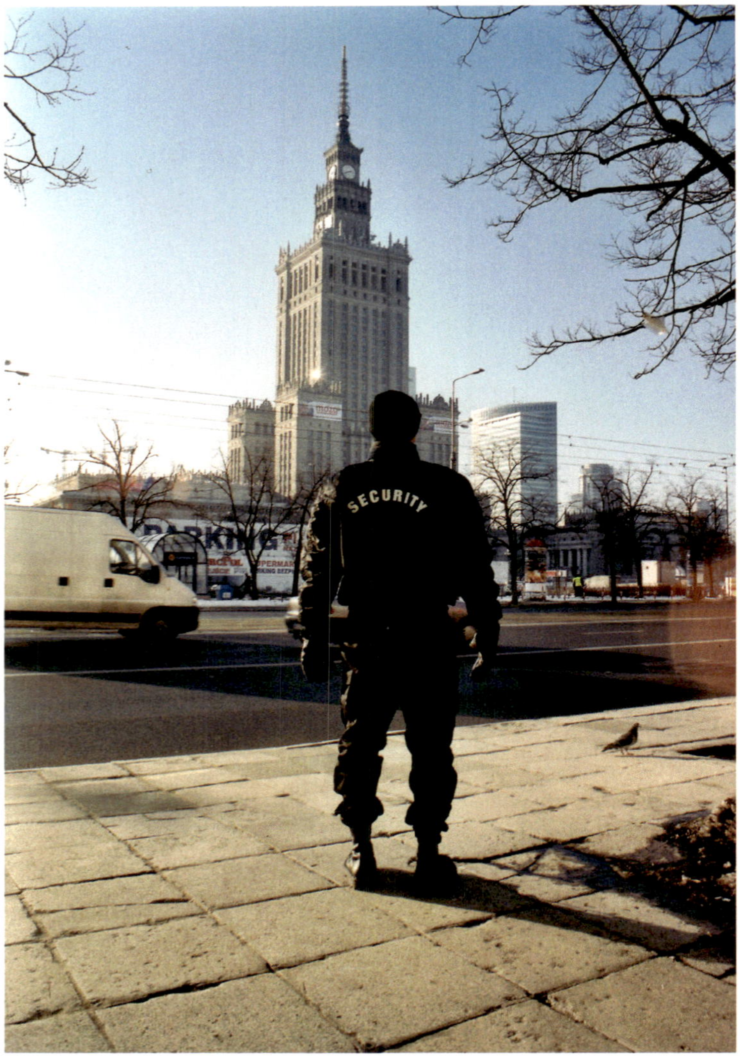

3

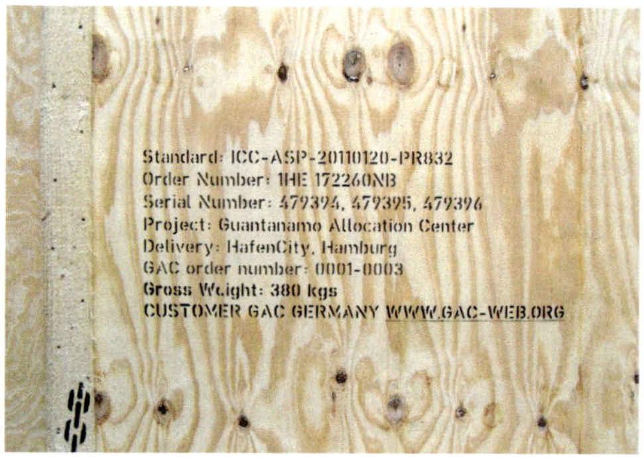

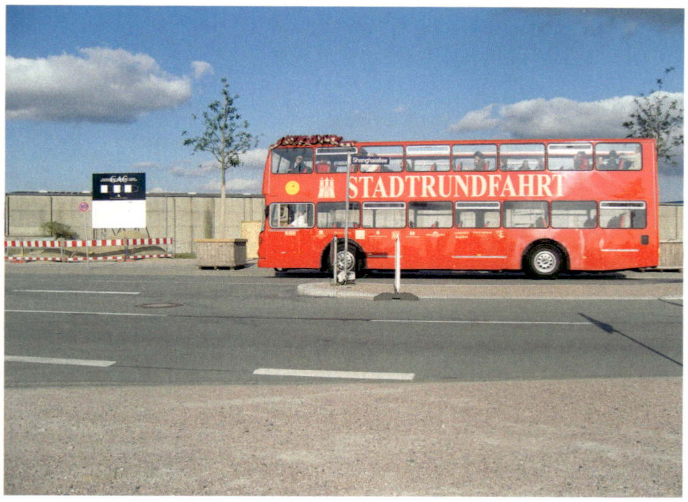

2

In November 2009, six Guantánamo Bay detainees were released to the island of Palau in the South Pacific. Faulhaber traveled to this tiny island nation to visit them and interview their interpreter and his Excellency, the President of Palau. Next Faulhaber went to Shenzhen, China, to visit the Oil Painting Village in Dafen, the world's largest colony for reproducing and copying artworks. He worked with local artists to produce oil paintings from photographs of the men. This series of work focuses on questions surrounding the ideological and philosophical notion of the contemporary picture.

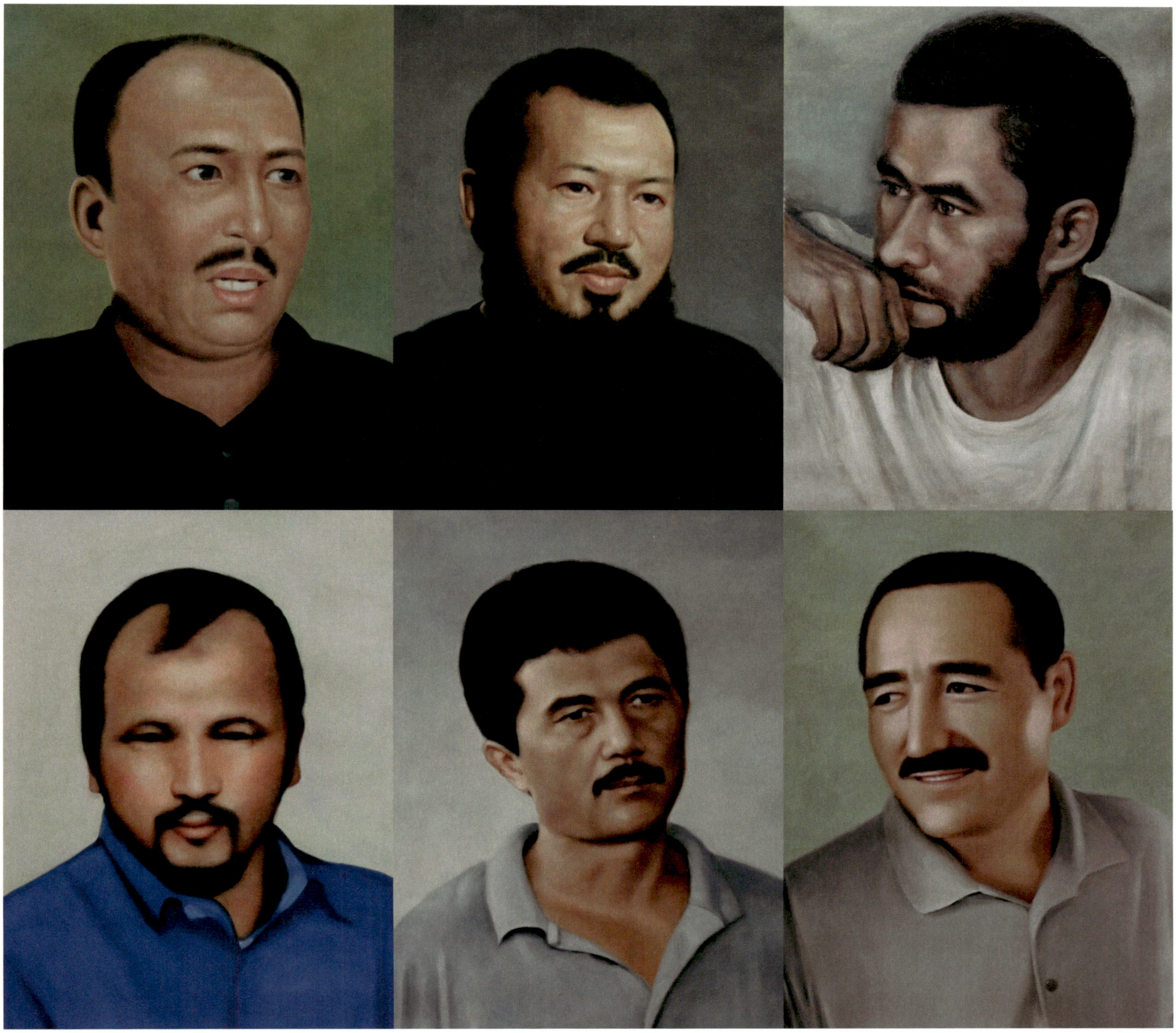

ONDREJ BRODY & KRISTOFER PAETAU

Ondrej Brody & Kristofer Paetau (Brody * 1980; Paetau * 1972) are conceptual provocateurs with a sense of humor. This Czech/Finnish artist duo create artworks that impressively deconstruct the aesthetic factors of authority; disrupt the rules of cultural grammar, probe social sensitivities, deconstruct traditional concepts of morality, draw attention to social problems, and carry the whole "art circus" to absurd extremes. "There is something unpredictable about all good art," says Paetau, who was born in Borgå in Finland. During the Art Forum Berlin art fair, Paetau suffered an attack of nausea that caused him to vomit for several minutes in one of the booths (*Art Forum Accident,* 2005). A short video artwork by Brody, who was born in Prague—*A Visit to a Mosque,* 2004, which depicts a visit to a Berlin mosque—is rather more elegant and subtle. It shows an antechamber with shelves attached to the walls, where worshipers can place their shoes. Slowly, the camera moves down the line of shoes pair by pair, while we hear the sound of the Imam praying—and then the camera comes to rest on a pair of American cowboy boots, which are standing in front of the shelf because they are too big to fit onto it. The video cleverly plays with red herrings, stereotypes, and personal clichés. For their homage to Édouard Manet's painting of the same name, *Le Déjeuner sur l'Herbe,* 2006, the artists recruited four Czech pornographic film actors to recreate the lunchtime scene. They eat Camembert cheese and chocolate mousse, while articulating statements in stuttering French, such as: "These artists, they simply have no imagination." For the project *Painting China Now,* 2007, the duo paid a Chinese fine art painter a small amount of money to create 30 oil paintings of individuals tortured by the Chinese authorities. In this artwork, Brody and Paetau have redefined the concept of realism in art: the technically perfect figurative paintings produce a strange hot-and-cold mix of emotions. The pictures are kitsch and shocking, as well as cruel and beguiling. Capitalism and political suppression are united in spirit and on a small canvas. However, one of the duo's most radical artworks is *Dog Carpets,* 2007. As a way of revealing and illustrating the contradictory and false sense of morality with regard to house pets and hunting trophies, Brody and Paetau simply stuffed three dogs and a cat, and turned them into bedside rugs. This is, in the true sense of the word, wonderfully cynical which in the original Greek, literally means "like a snapping dog." Brody & Paetau's artworks question the legitimacy of power, open up potential spaces for utopias, transform closed discourses into open situations, and cause us to question the seemingly self-evident by creating moments of confusion. The viewer feels as if he or she is in a fight with Nelson Muntz, the school bully in the cartoon series *The Simpsons*: one is constantly being tripped up to the sound of a jeering "Ha ha!" and forever being duped and falling for it—ending up feeling trapped and provoked. If you can get up and laugh alongside, then these absurd and grotesque art installations can be a lot of fun.

1
Dog Carpets
2007, Prague, Czech Republic

2
Wang Bin Torture
in Commercial Quality, High Quality, and Museum Quality
2010, China

3
Painting China Now
2007, China

1

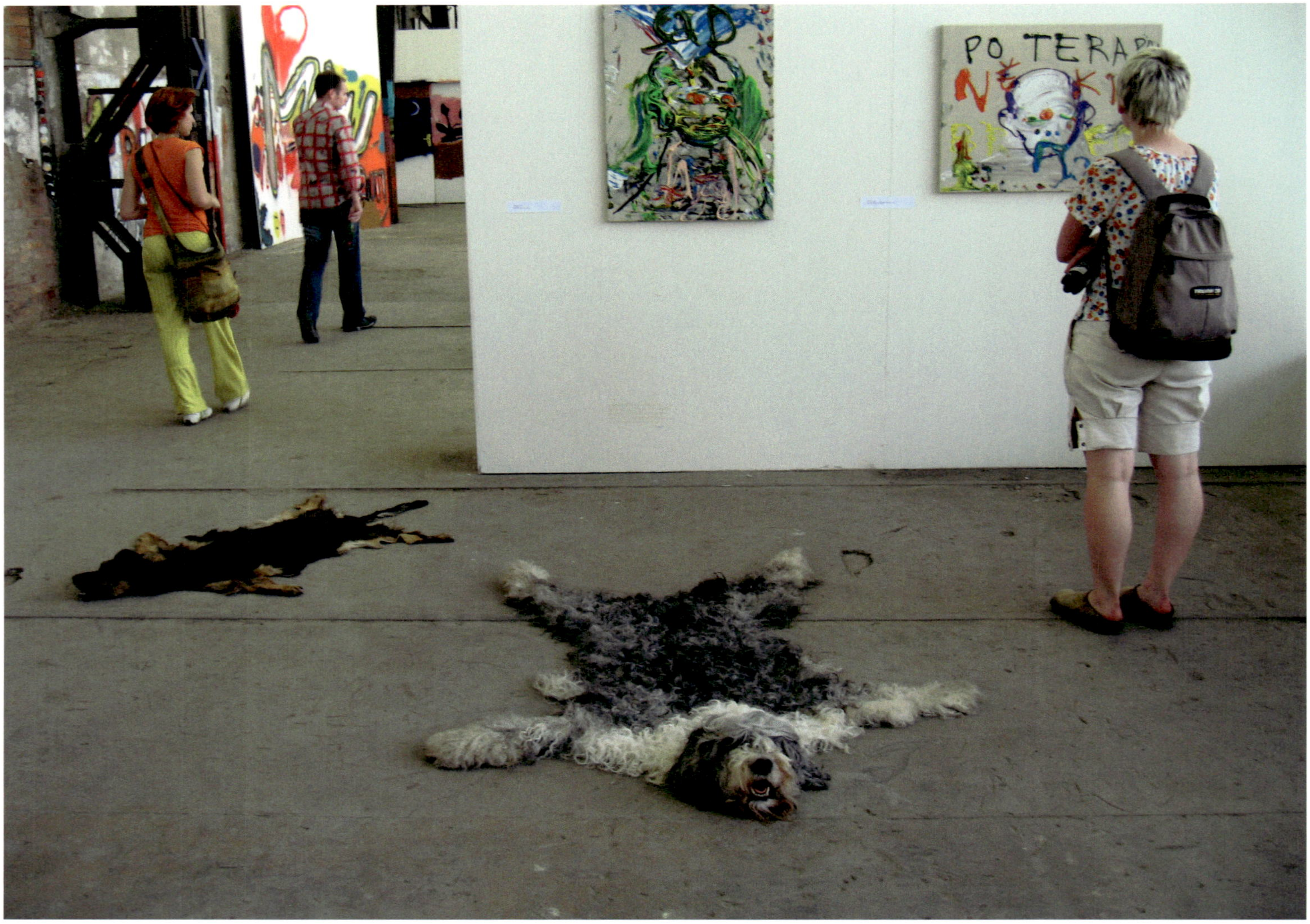

2

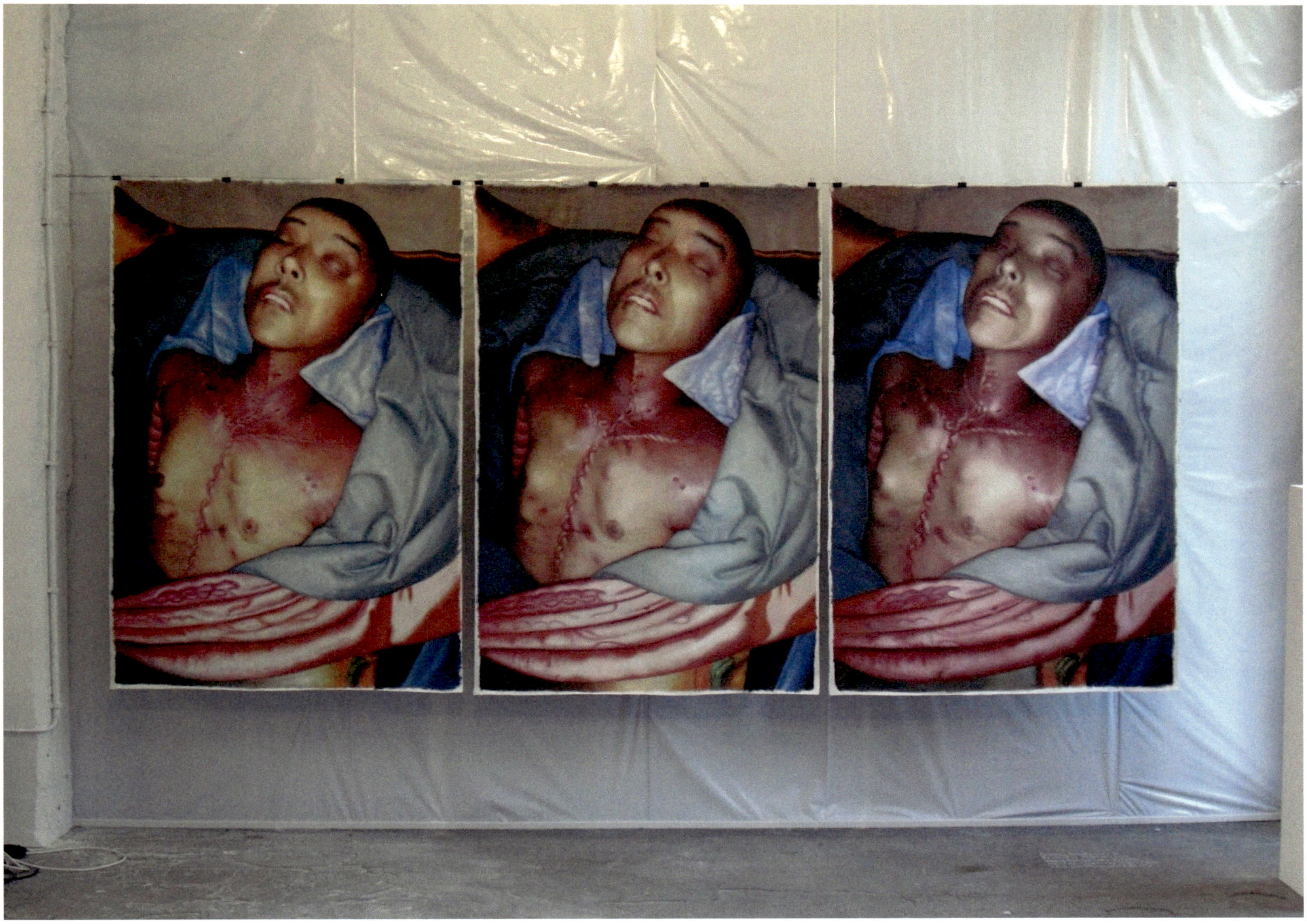

3

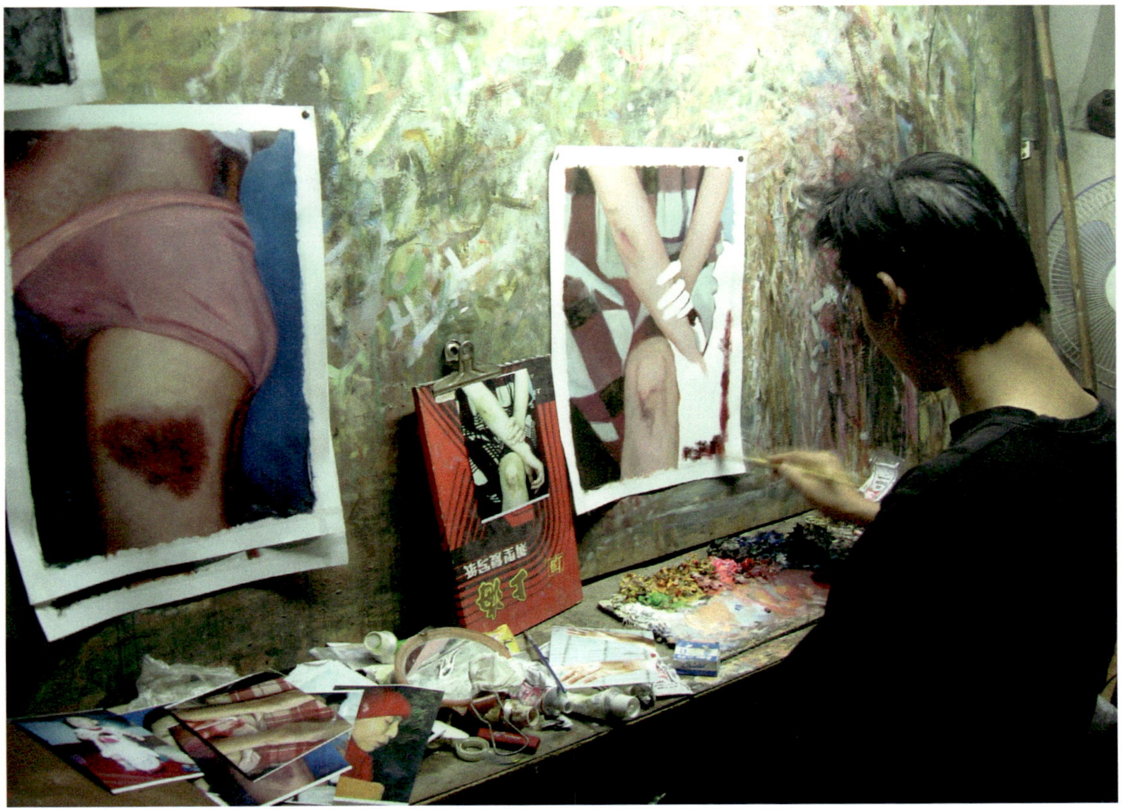

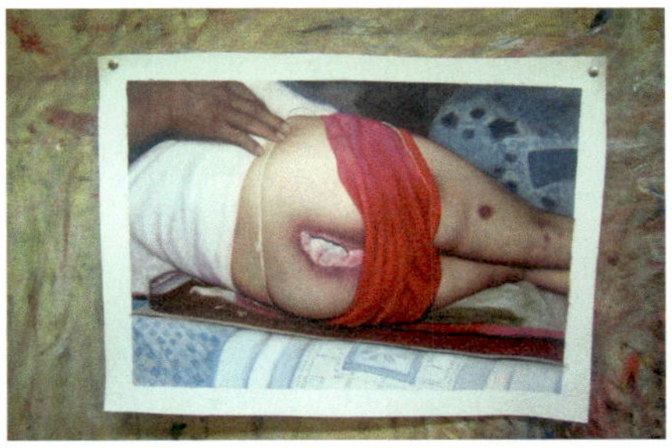

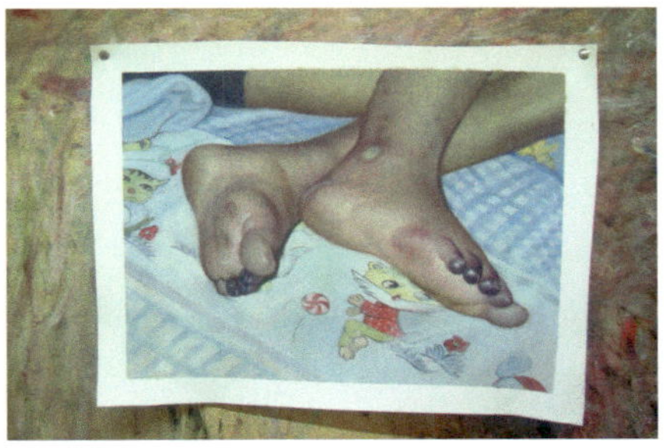

WIEBKE GRÖSCH/ FRANK METZGER

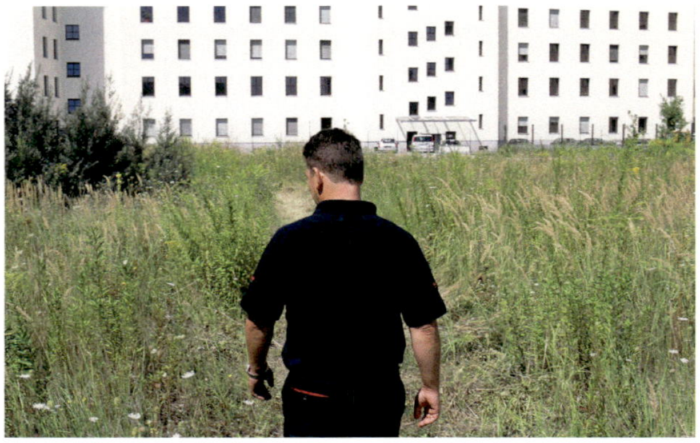

1

1
News from Home
2009, Frankfurt/Main, Germany, Courtesy Schirn Kunsthalle, Frankfurt and the artists, Photos by Wiebke Grösch/ Frank Metzger

2
Neue Grenzen
2007, Berlin, Germany

Frankfurt artist duo Wiebke Grösch (* 1970) and Frank Metzger (* 1969) focus on sociocultural and urban issues. The sale of daily papers in Frankfurt is largely the province of migrants from Sri Lanka, Bangladesh, and Ethiopia. For their performance *News From Home,* 2009, the artists arranged for the migrants to sell a paper from their homeland. "We wanted to work with the specific image of the newspaper seller and to adapt it, to thematize their precarious working conditions, and to subtly make the job still more senseless: someone is standing there with a newspaper that I cannot read," Grösch explains. Other projects by the duo, which are always based on extensive research, thematize the representation mechanisms of architecture and urban spaces. Their artworks center on the linked themes of surveillance, privatization, urban utopias, and also draws attention to historical and social transformations.

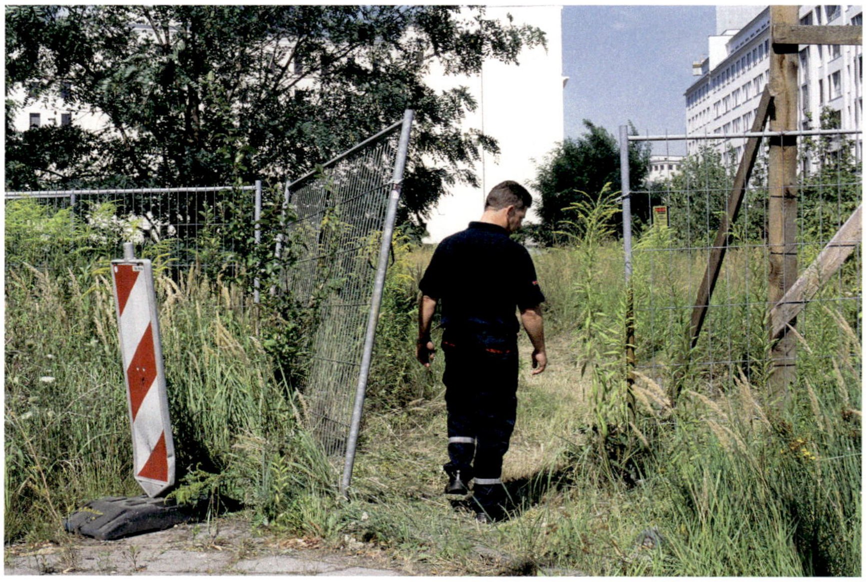

2

A private security guard was hired in August 2007 to patrol the grounds of the Skulpturenpark Berlin_Zentrum (a sculpture park). Every day at the same time, he walked along the path where the Berlin wall once stood, referring to the history of the place and the increasing privatization of public spaces. After the Wall vanished, new borders and barriers were created by property and real estate owners because what is not fenced off shows traces of use; kids, office workers, and dog owners take over the grounds. Around them are sidewalks, rows of trees, and parking spots that represent public order. The security service, which is usually found on company premises, pedestrian areas, shopping malls, and train stations, is now patrolling a space where there appears to be nothing to protect. The security man thus becomes an actor of a recurring performative action—but in reality is only controlling himself.

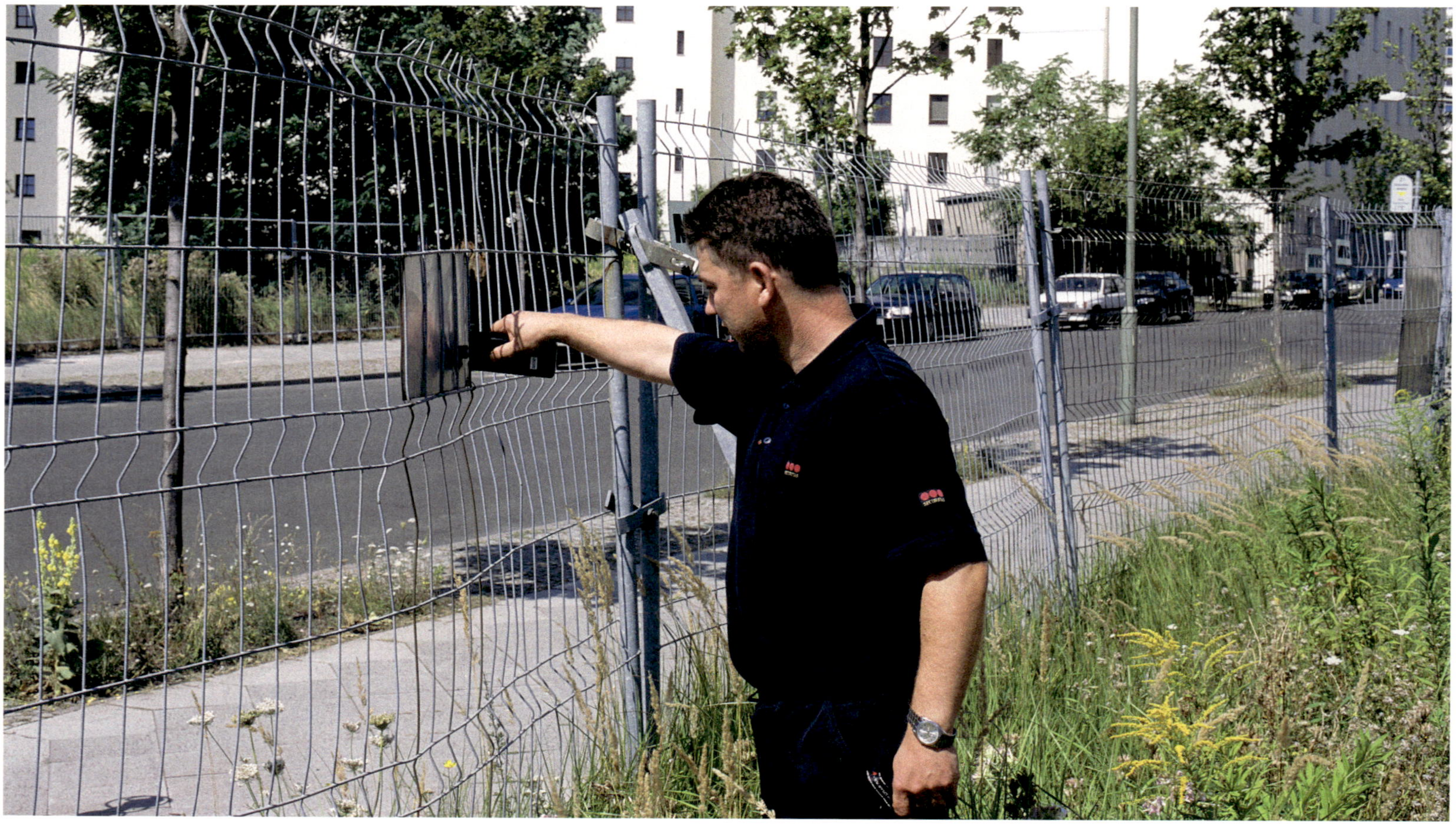

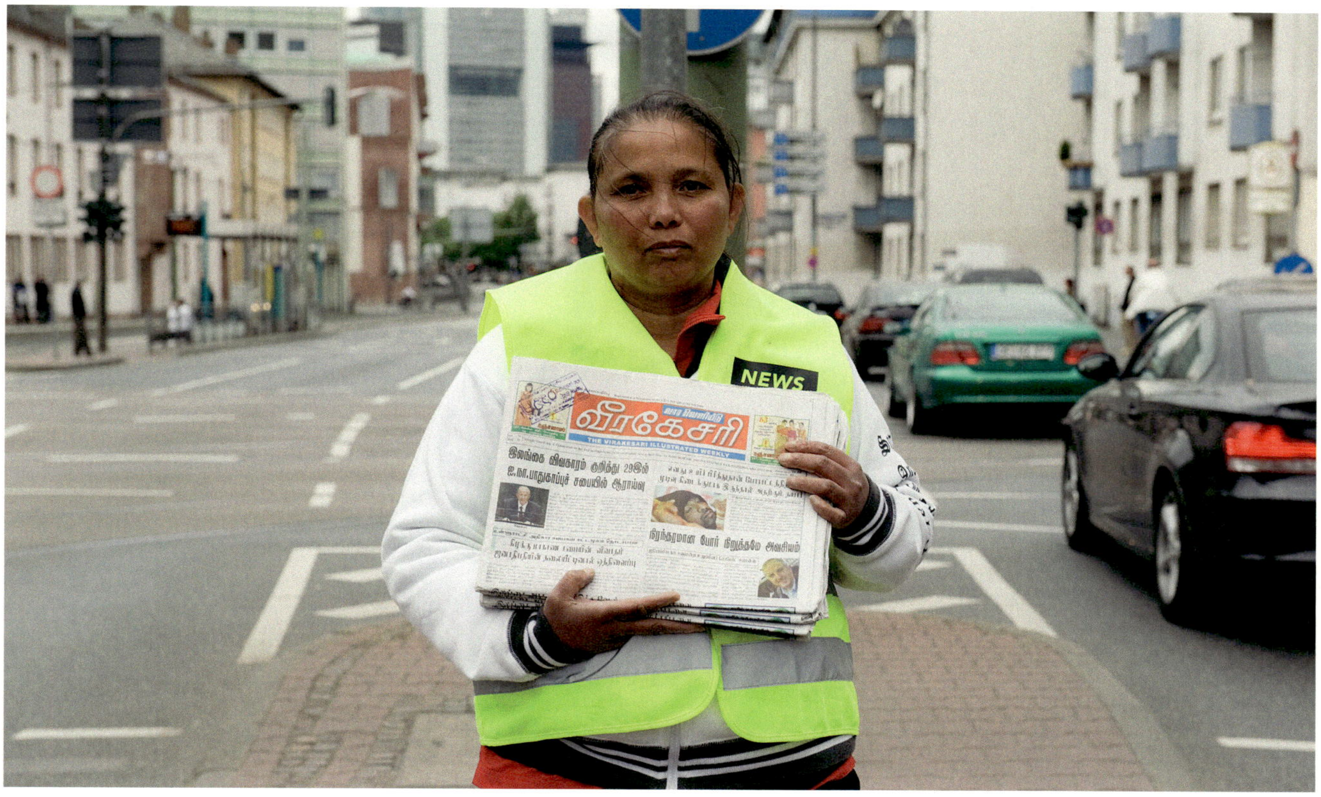
NEWS
வீரகேசரி
THE VIRAKESARI ILLUSTRATED WEEKLY

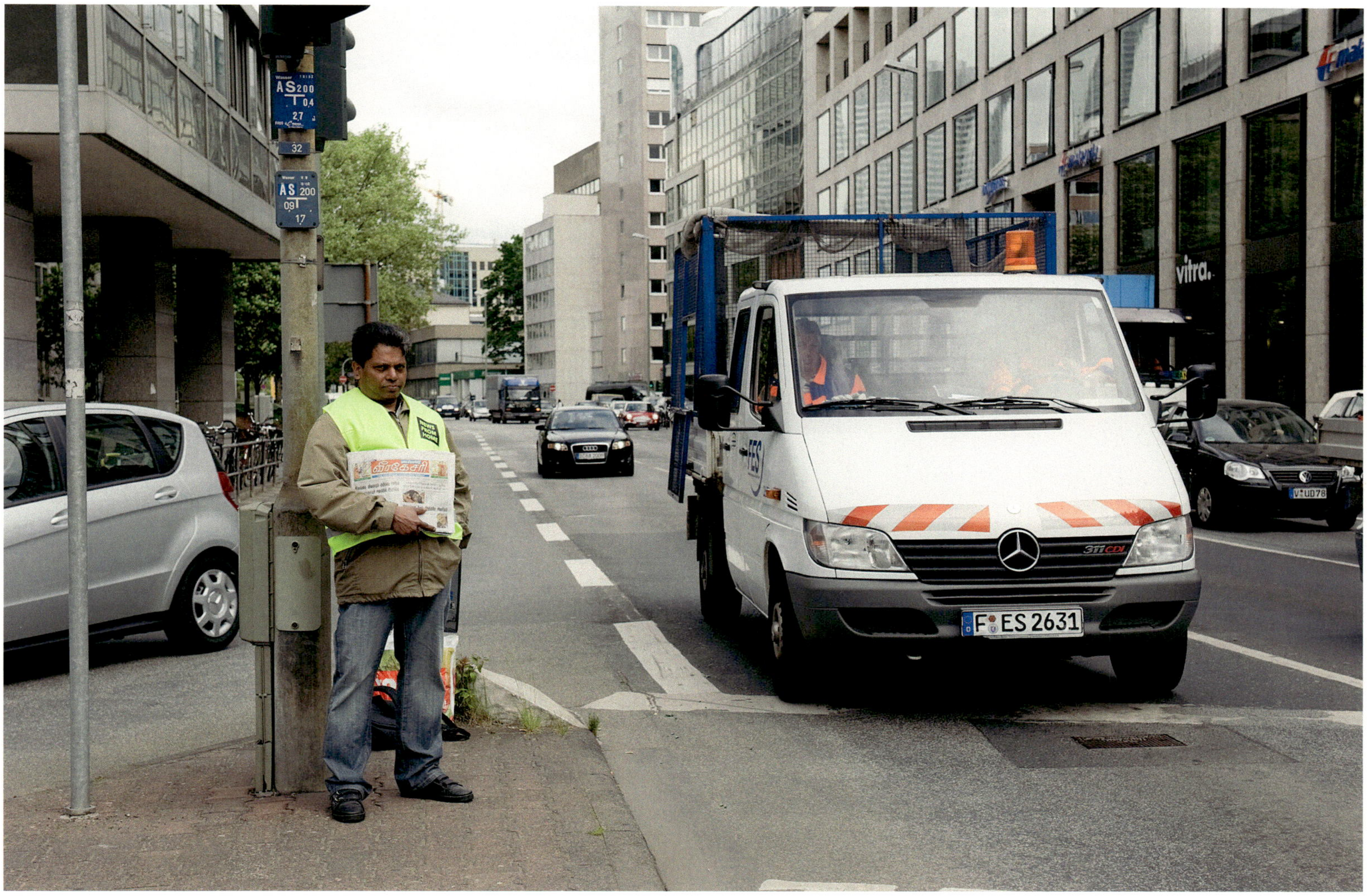
vitra.
F ES 2631

SANTIAGO SIERRA

As the singer Liza Minnelli sang in the film *Cabaret*, "money makes the world go round." *Wer das Geld hat, hat die Macht, bis es unterm Auto kracht* (Whoever has the money has the power—until a bomb goes off under their car), as Red Army Faction supporters used to declare. Then, as now, you could say that money equals power. Money can buy you everything: power and murderers, prostitutes and politicians, children and chocolate bars. The Spanish artist Santiago Sierra (* 1966), who was born in Madrid and currently lives in Mexico City, presents us with this bitter reality in his disturbing performances, which have been creating scandals for decades. One such scandal surrounded his German artwork *245 m³*, 2006, which was located in

1
La Trampa/The Trap
2007, Matucana 100, Santiago de Chile, Chile

2
3 Cubos de 100 cm de Lado Cada Uno, Movidos 700 cm/
3 Cubes of 100 cm on Each Side Moved 700 cm
2002, Kunsthalle St. Gallen, St. Gallen, Switzerland

3
245 m³
2006

tent's cap made from jute, and was paid 100 euros." This work brought into view the question most commonly posed by Sierra in his artworks: What does a human being cost? Sierra once reproduced the exploitation of the globalized economy in an art context by paying beggars, who were a familiar sight in the city, to present themselves in a gallery. As soon as visitors arrived, the beggars asked for money and complained; their "complaining chorus" was amplified within the space by microphones and speakers. In Havana, he paid ten young people 20 euros each to masturbate in front of a camera. In 2001, at the Venice Biennale, he induced non-Europeans to dye their hair blond. For another project, he took exhibition visitors to one of the poorest neighborhoods in Guatemala City in a completely sealed bus. In an Italian city, Sierra paid prostitutes to make a polyurethane cast of their genitals, later placing these casts on display. On another occasion, he paid migrants to move a massive stone block from one corner of a gallery to the other. Sierra's "working materials" are almost always homeless people, drug addicts, asylum seekers, or prostitutes—people who live on the edges of society;

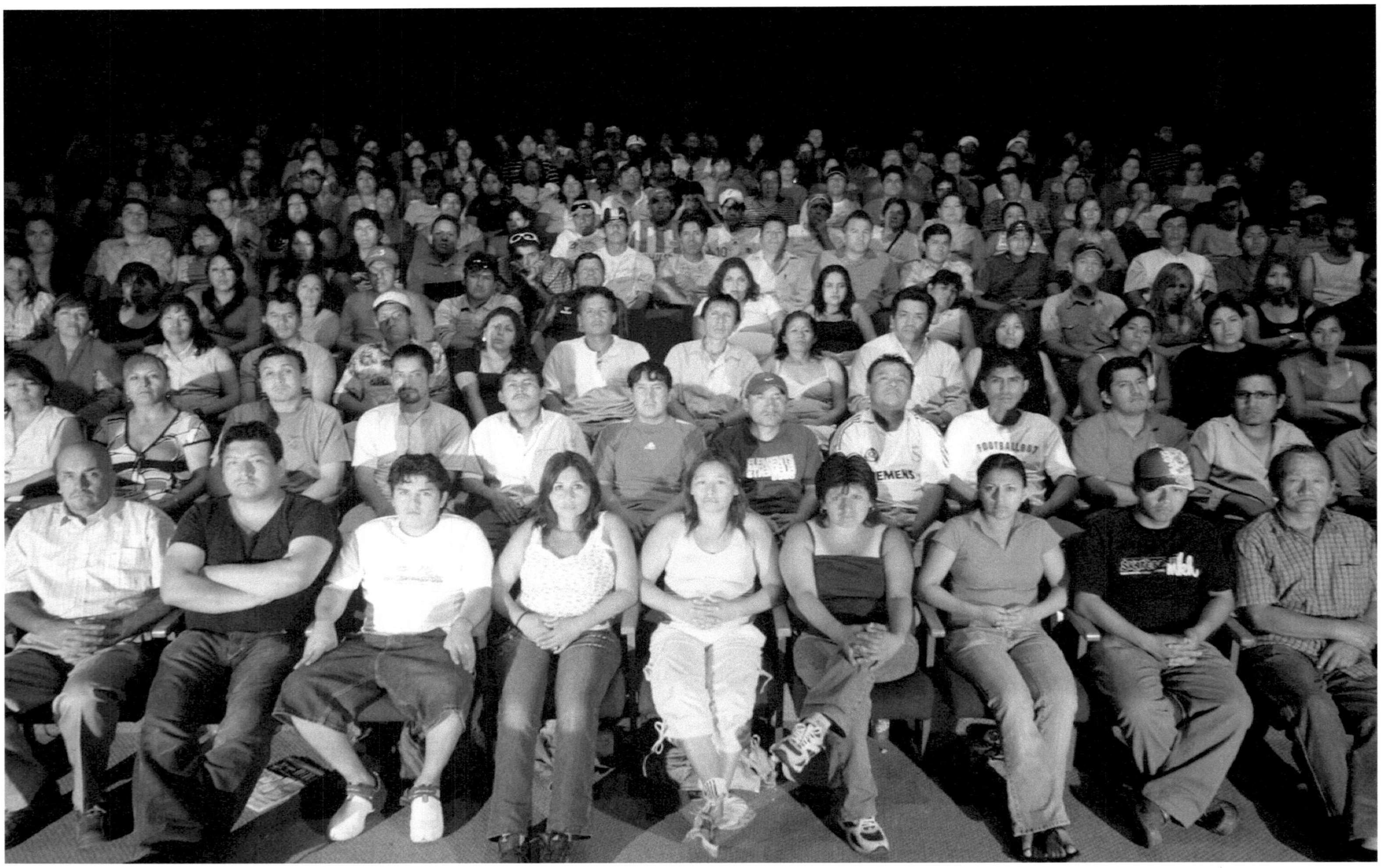

1
This work was made specifically for 13 people—a combination of politicians, art critics, journalists, curators, and artists. Each participant was invited to enter a long wooden corridor that was under construction, eventually finding themselves in the middle of a theater with 186 severe-looking Peruvian workers. Unable to exit at that point, they were forced to retrace their footsteps. Once outside, an invigilator gave them the keys to their cars and thanked them for their presence.

Pulheim-Stommeln, near Cologne. To create this installation, Sierra collected the exhaust fumes of six cars and released the fumes inside a former synagogue. Visitors could enter the synagogue individually for a few minutes at a time, wearing a gas mask and being accompanied by a firefighter. Inside the room, there was enough carbon monoxide to kill a person in half an hour. This art happening ended prematurely due to protests. One Christmas Eve, Sierra staged a project called *The Anarchists* in Rome. The artist created black-and-white pictures, a video, and an objective description of the project to document his artwork: "At circa 00:00 hours, on the 25th of December, a group of eight militant anarchists were persuaded to attend a Mass celebrated by the Pope. Each of them wore a pointed, black peni-

the expelled, forgotten, used, and discarded. "If I thought about how to give real visibility to these people, I wouldn't have chosen the art world as a platform to do it, but rather a determined a political activism—but I don't trust that either," says Sierra. "Let's say that I do things because I think they should be included in the art world, but I don't have grandiose dreams that I'll actually achieve anyone's redemption, because that's absurd."

2

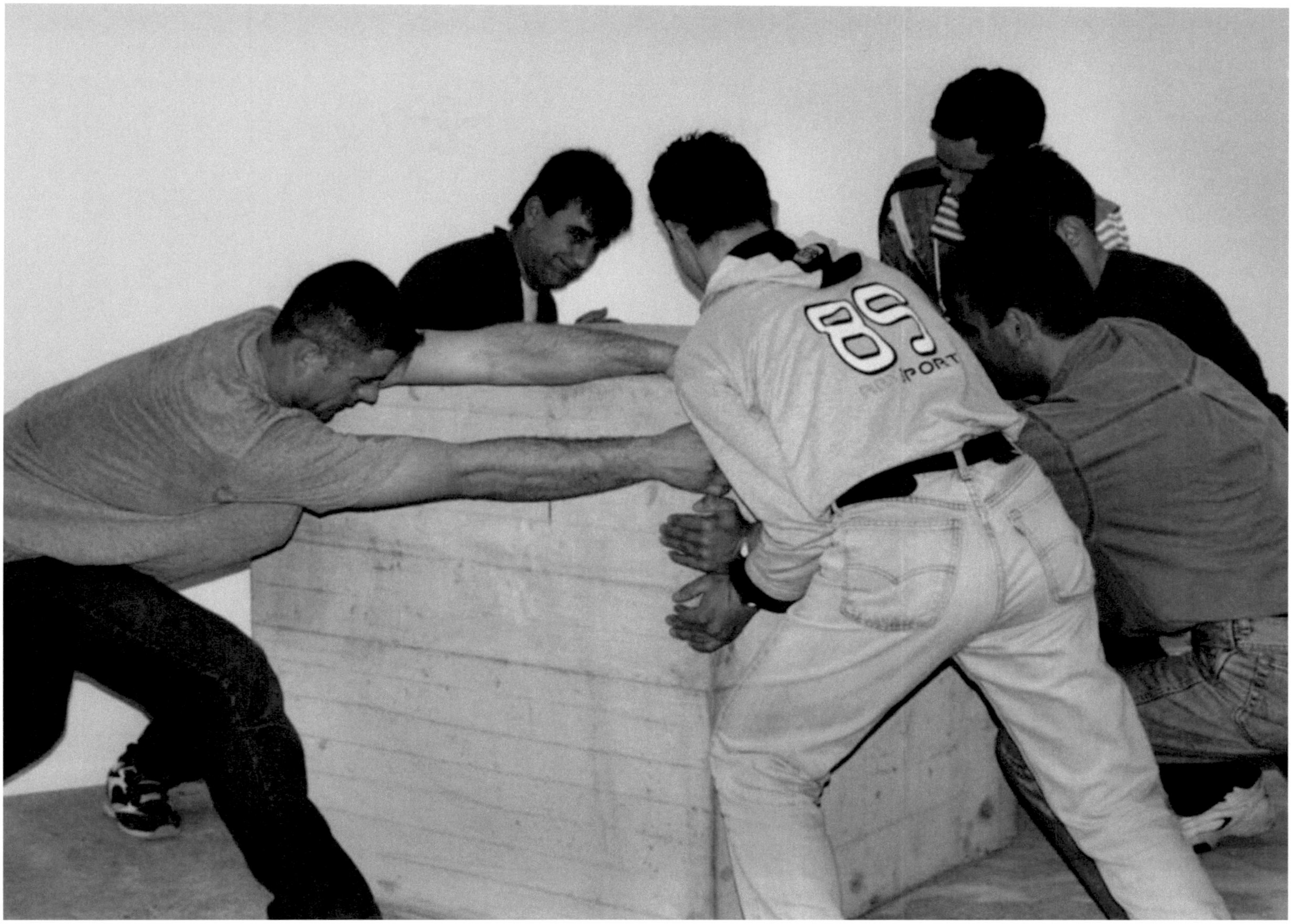

3

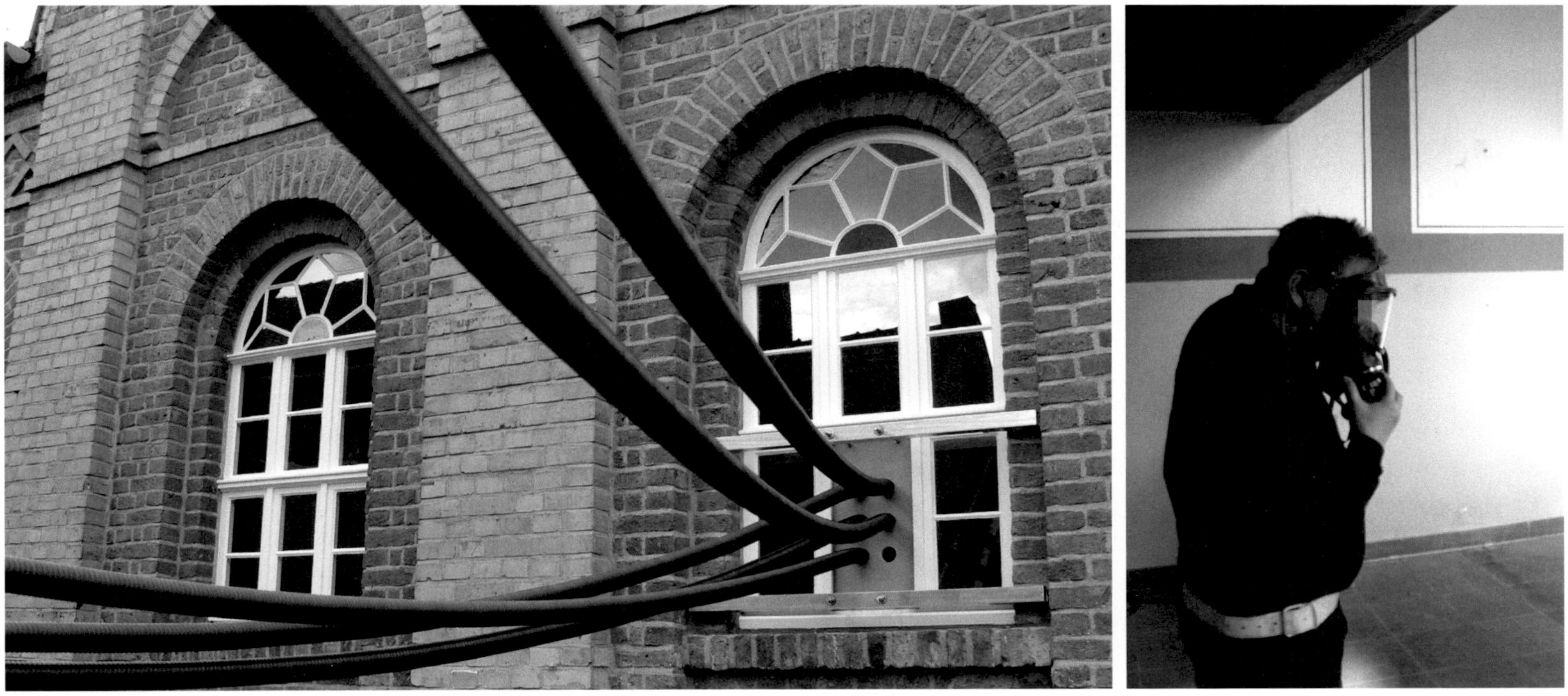

4

The skin on the backs of ten people who declared they had zero dollars was photographed. A medium tone in a grey-scale was assigned to that value. The skin on the backs of ten people who declared to have a thousand dollars was photographed. A different medium tone in a greyscale was assigned to that value. Finally, the skin on the backs of ten people who declared to have a million dollars was photographed and again a different tone was assigned to that value. Once tones of grey had been assigned to a dollar amount, the value of black and white was calculated in dollars. The value of black turned out to be -2.106 dollars and the value of white 11.548415 dollars.

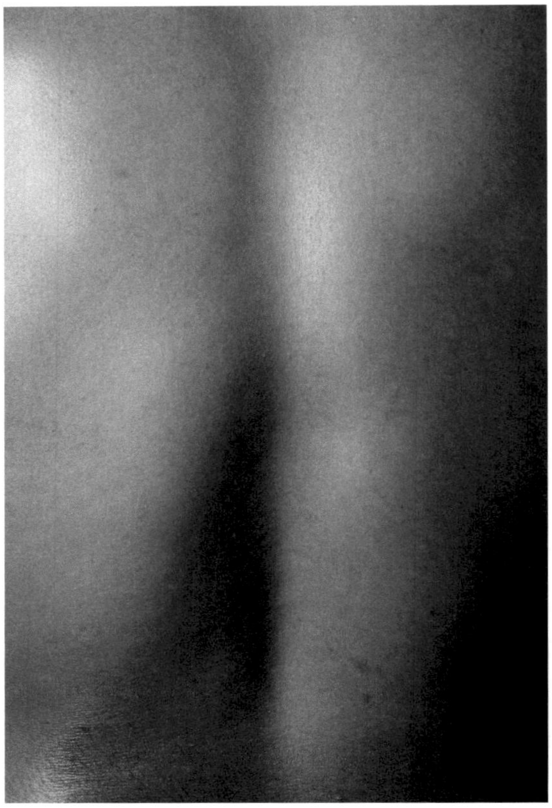

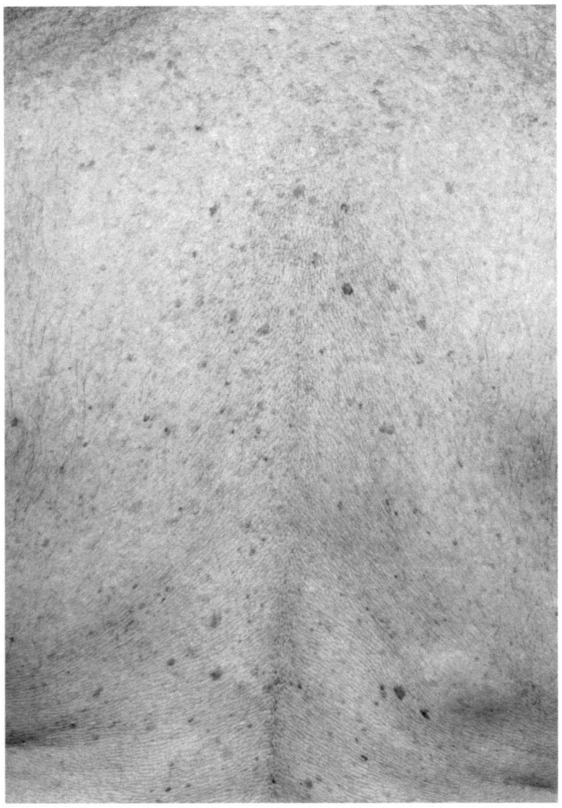

5

The Kunsthalle Wien contacted 30 workers, seeking people with skin colors ranging from very light to very dark. Their skin color was deduced on the telephone by asking where they came from. They were then called together. The first 27 people to arrive were arranged in their underwear, facing the wall. Those who had the appropriate mixture of white and color turned up when the action had already ended, which is illustrated in the result: the in-between shades are missing.

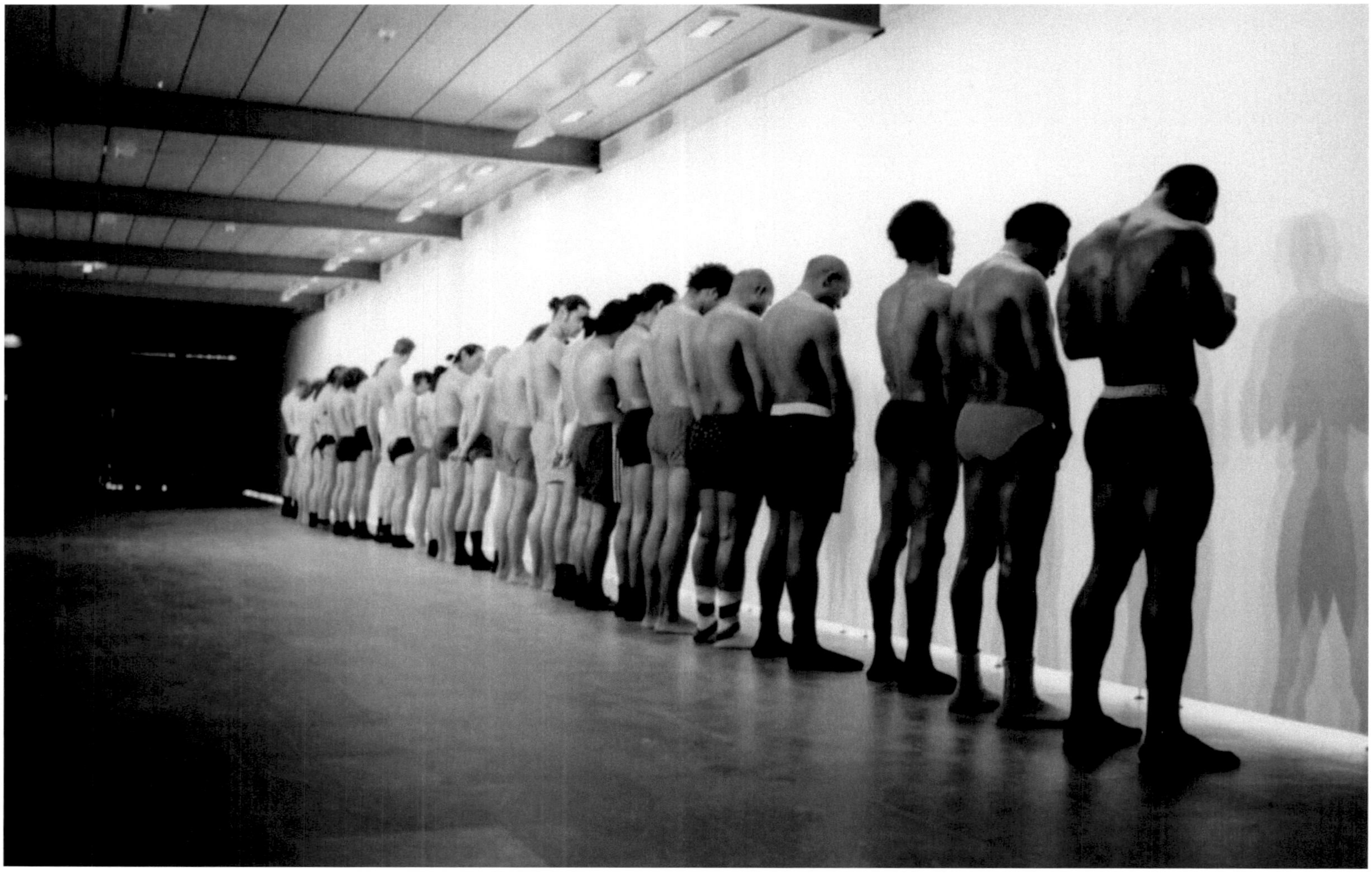

6

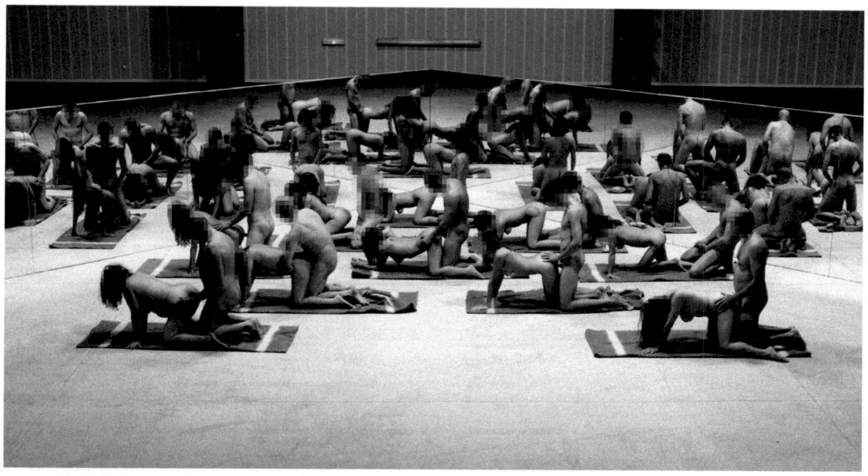

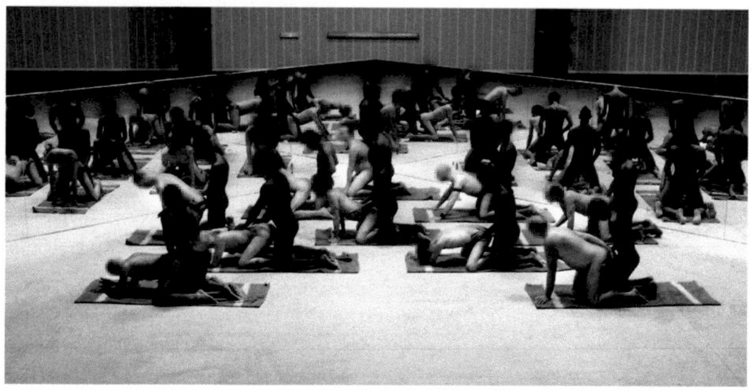

SANTIAGO SIERRA

4

Estudio Económico de la Piel de los Caraqueños/Economical Study on the Skin of Caracans
2006, Caracas, Venezuela

5

Contratación y Ordenación de 30 Trabajadores Conforme a Su Color de Piel/Hiring and Arrangement of 30 Workers in Relation to Their Skin Color
2002, Project Space, Kunsthalle Wien, Vienna, Austria

6

Los Penetrados/The Penetrated
El Torax, Terrassa, Spain
2008, First act: Ten white race men penetrated ten white race women, Last act: Ten black race men penetrated ten white race men

7

Línea de 160 cm Tatuada Sobre 4 Personas/160 cm Line Tattooed on 4 People
2000, El Gallo Arte Contemporáneo, Salamanca, Spain

7

Four prostitutes addicted to heroin were hired to give their consent to be tattooed for the price of a shot of heroin. Normally they charge 3,000 pesetas (17 dollars) for fellatio; the price of a shot of heroin is 12,000 pesetas, or 67 dollars.

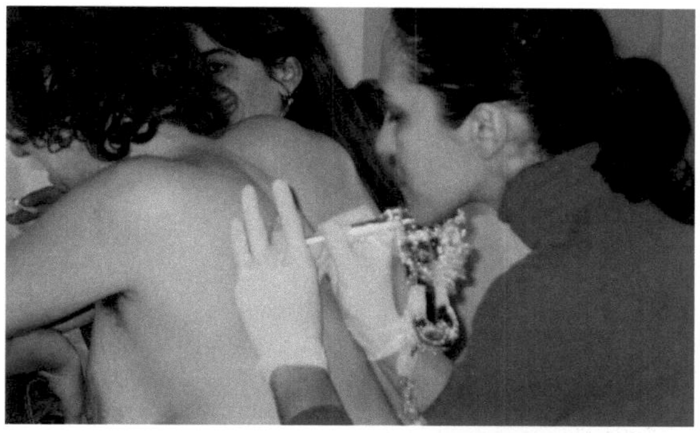

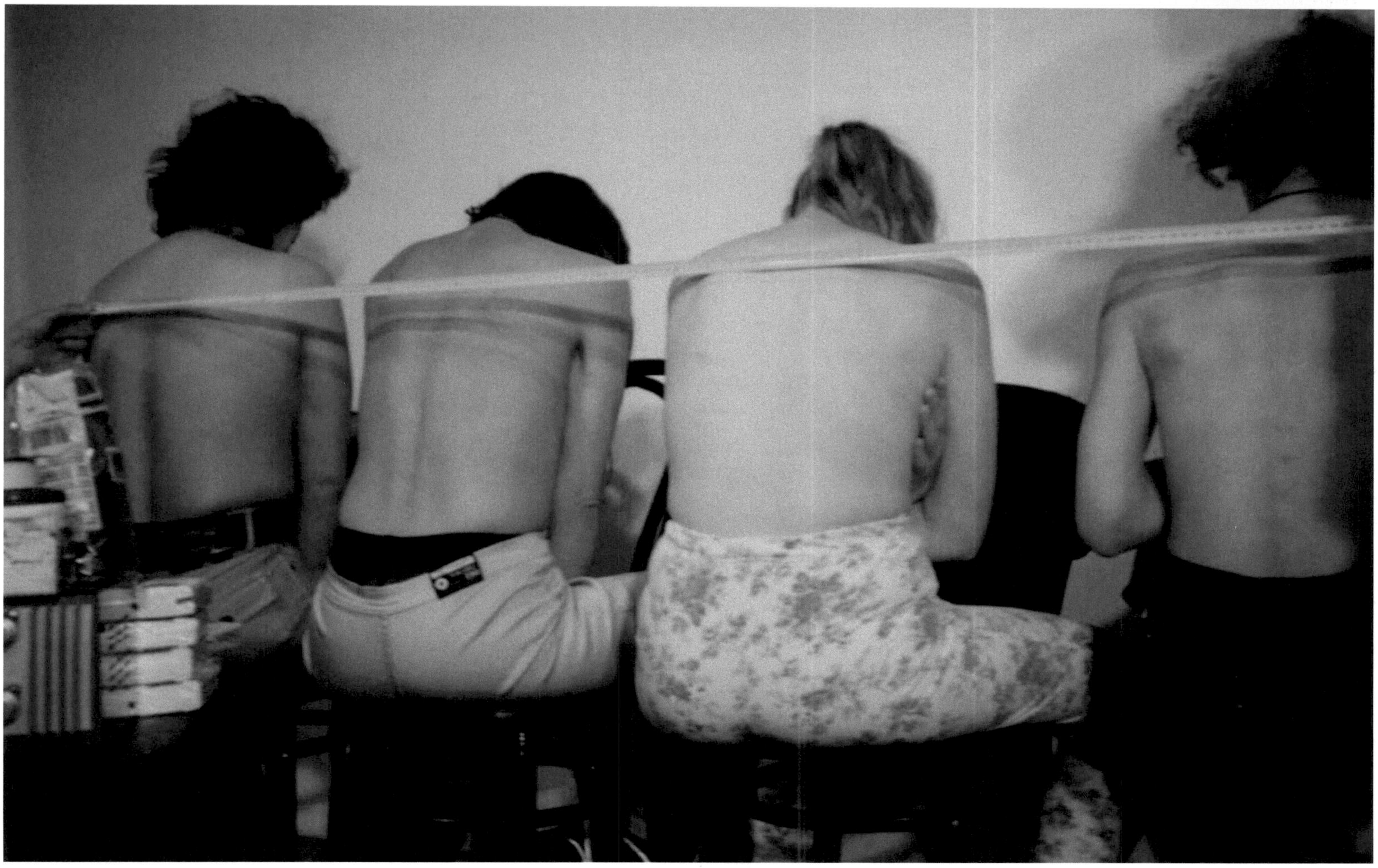

HELMUT SMITS

"I THOUGHT IT WOULD BE INTERESTING TO GO INTO IKEA AS IF I WAS A PRIMITIVE HUMAN BEING AND MAKE FIRE USING PRODUCTS FOUND THERE"

The Dutch artist Helmut Smits (* 1974) uses sculptures, videos, and urban interventions to attack his targets—primarily global companies and icons of consumerist culture. He displayed a fattened McDonalds logo (*Fat M,* 2010) in a stadium, and composed a fake obituary for mascot Ronald McDonald (*Obituary,* 2009), who had supposedly died at the age of 46 due to "poor nutrition and the depressing surroundings he lived in every day." For his installation *Territories,* 2005, he liberated the animal logos of Puma, Lacoste, and the bank ING, returning them to the wild as oversized stand-up displays. For his performance, *FLAMMA (A Basic Need)/Making Fire with IKEA Products,* 2008, he managed to make a fire using standard IKEA products. Smits explains his idea by stating: "I thought it would be interesting to go into IKEA as if I was a primitive human being and make fire using products found there... The project also fits the back-to-basics image of IKEA, and the Swedish lifestyle. IKEA does not, however, sell lighters or matches." In his audiovisual war memorial, *The End,* 2009, Smits gives death a face by showing all the soldiers who have died in Afghanistan in alphabetical order like the credits of a film, accompanied by the song *The Letter* by the Box Tops, which is a reference to the antiwar film *Good Morning, Vietnam.* The artwork *0.26 Gallon of Oil,* 2007, looks banal at first glance, but is actually extremely complex. Smits created this piece of object art by filling a Coca-Cola bottle with oil—and strangely, one cannot tell the difference. Smits: "I liked the fact that oil looks the same as Coca-Cola. One (Coca-Cola) is the product that America dominates the world with, the other (oil) is the product that America consumes the most worldwide."

1
Parking for White Cars Only
2006

2
Photo Tip
2004, Wood, print, sandbags, chair

3
FLAMMA (A Basic Need)
Making Fire with IKEA Products
2008, Photo by Leo Veger

1

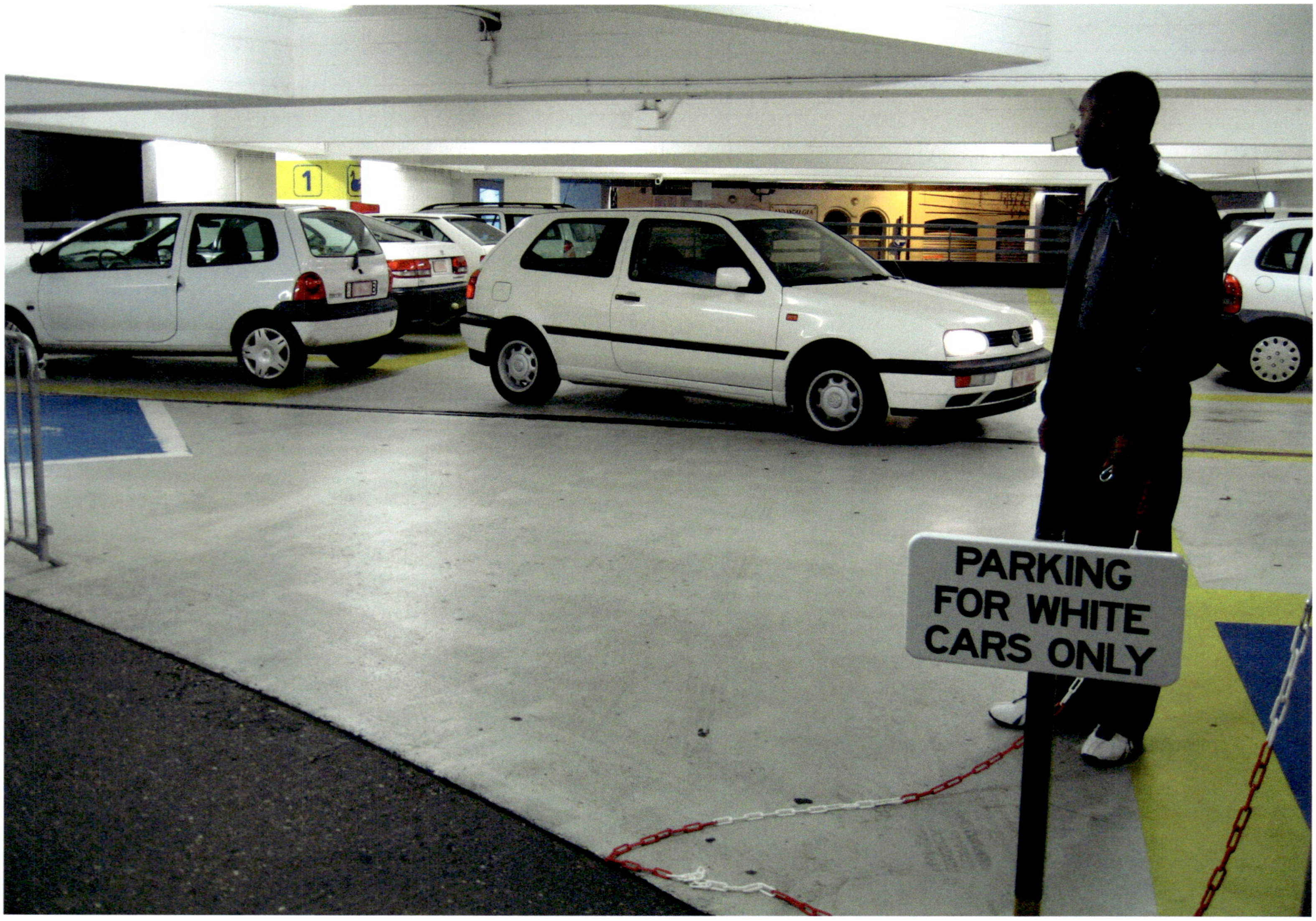

2

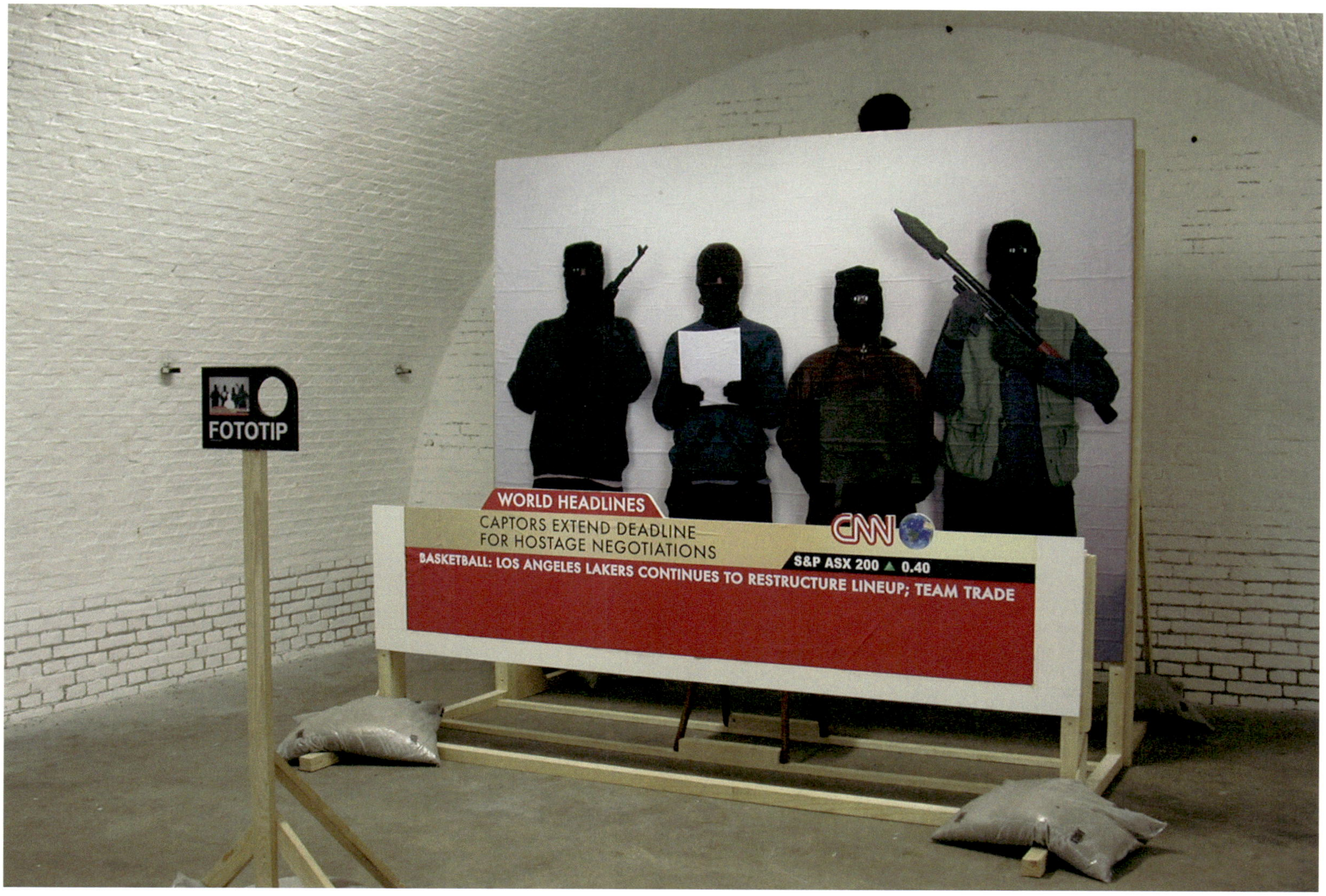
FOTOTIP
WORLD HEADLINES
CAPTORS EXTEND DEADLINE
FOR HOSTAGE NEGOTIATIONS
CNN
S&P ASX 200 ▲ 0.40
BASKETBALL: LOS ANGELES LAKERS CONTINUES TO RESTRUCTURE LINEUP; TEAM TRADE

3

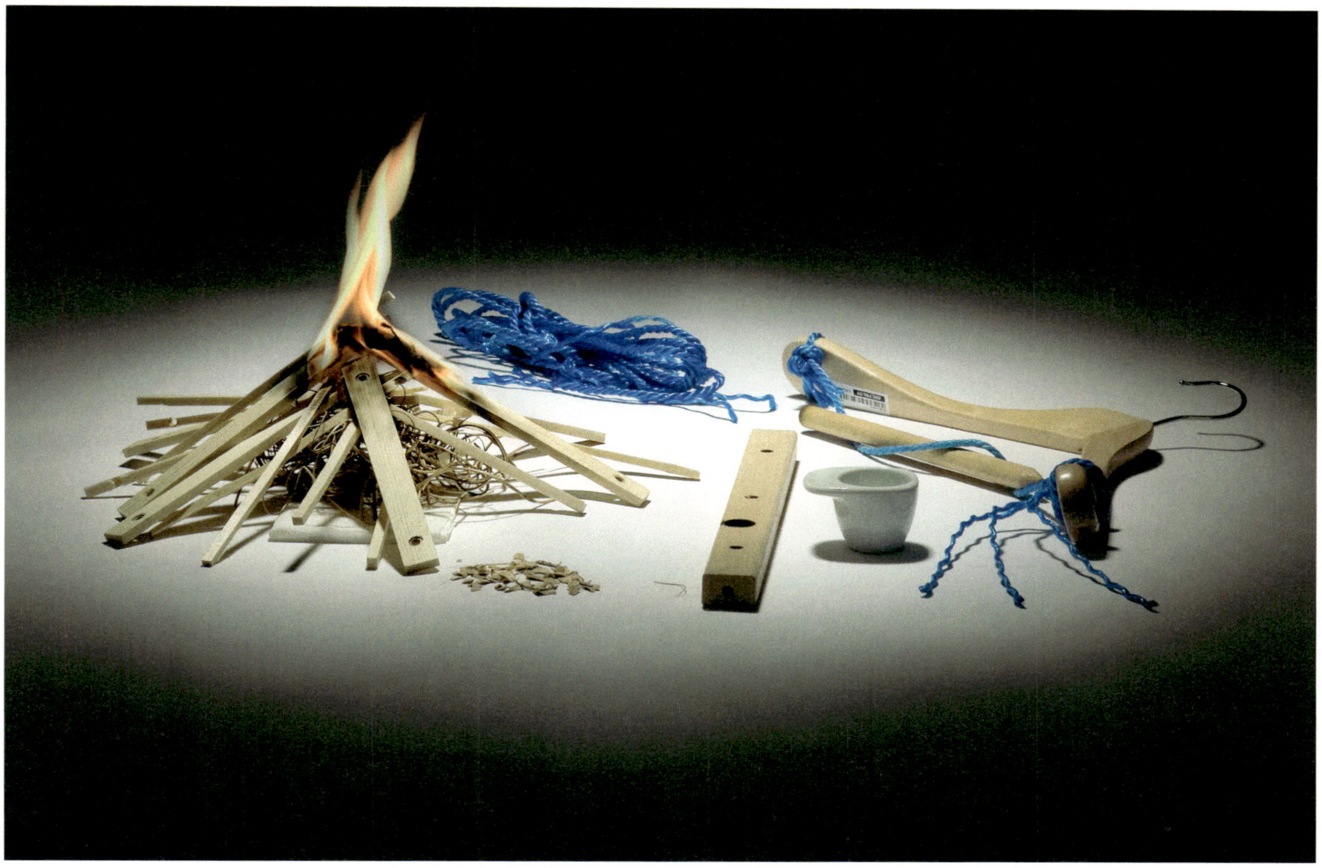

MARCO EVARISTTI

"WE ALL HAVE A NEED TO DECORATE MOTHER NATURE BECAUSE SHE BELONGS TO ALL OF US"

1
Helena
2000
2
Pink Toilet at Mont Rouge
2007
3
The Ice Cube Project
2004
4
The Last Fashion
2008

Courtesy ME Contemporary, Copenhagen

The artwork of Marco Evaristti (*1963), who was born in Santiago, Chile, and lives in Denmark, constantly addresses controversial topical social issues. In a fearlessly provocative, and sometimes almost naive way, he investigates the limits of political power, the safeguarding of human rights, the exercising of territorial power, and the mechanisms of media reporting. His technique is characterized by extreme real experiences, using macabre means to challenge the viewers and make them question their own sense of morality. In the installation *Helena*, which brought Evaristti to international attention in 2000, the audience becomes an active agent. The artist exhibited liquidizers filled with water that had goldfish swimming in them; leaving it up to the visitor whether to switch on the liquidizer and kill the fish, or simply to look at the artwork. While the killing of animals for food is generally uncritically accepted, this particular confrontational piece created considerable outrage and had significant consequences. On one occasion, the installation was actually destroyed and animal rights activists took Evaristti to court, although he was ultimately acquitted. What the artist is trying to achieve with this kind of artwork is to illustrate the concept of democracy. In this seemingly naive way, he addresses moral issues that affect us all. For the Copenhagen Fashion Week 2008, he designed a fashion collection for prisoners on death row in the United States entitled *The Last Fashion*. The catalogue text reads: "If we are to kill these people, then let us do it in style." Some of these elaborate garments are clearly dysfunctional in some respects; for instance, there are trousers with pockets that are only open at the bottom. Like most haute couture articles, the clothes are such complex creations that the wearer needs help to put them on, or to take them off. The clothes are bitter reminders of the fate of the intended wearers—condemned individuals will never have to undress themselves again, and they will not need to carry anything in their pockets for their final journey. In this way, visitors to the show were asked to consider whether the artist really believed that he was combatting the death penalty with a fashion show. Gossip magazines were filled with talk about a shocking scandal; once again Evaristti had succeeded in bringing his theme to public attention. His most major project to date is the founding of the *Pink State*, a concept that explores the nature of territorial claims. The aim of the artist's *Red Faction* trilogy of expeditions was to occupy certain territories; from 2004 to 2008, he used 3,000 liters of red paint to color an iceberg off Greenland, which is officially sovereign Danish territory with internal autonomy. The artist declared it "his" iceberg and hoisted his state flag, which depicted a pink elephant. This was followed in 2007 by the *Mont Rouge Project*, in which the artist colored part of Mont Blanc red. For this intervention, Evaristti was briefly arrested, and his paint was confiscated; in the end, he covered the peak with 300 square meters of red cloth. Finally in 2008, Evaristti painted a desert dune and a camel red.

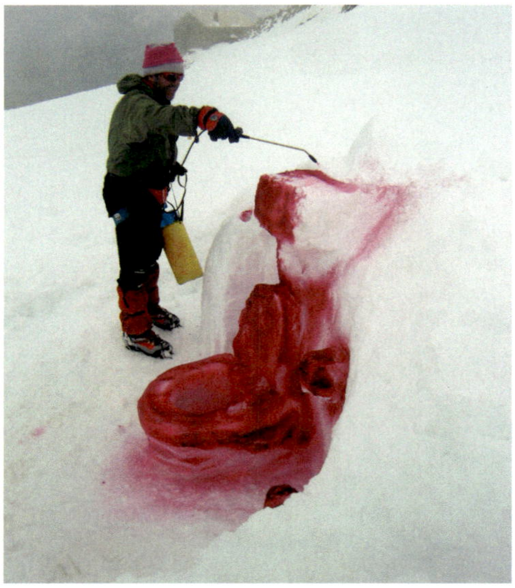

2

1

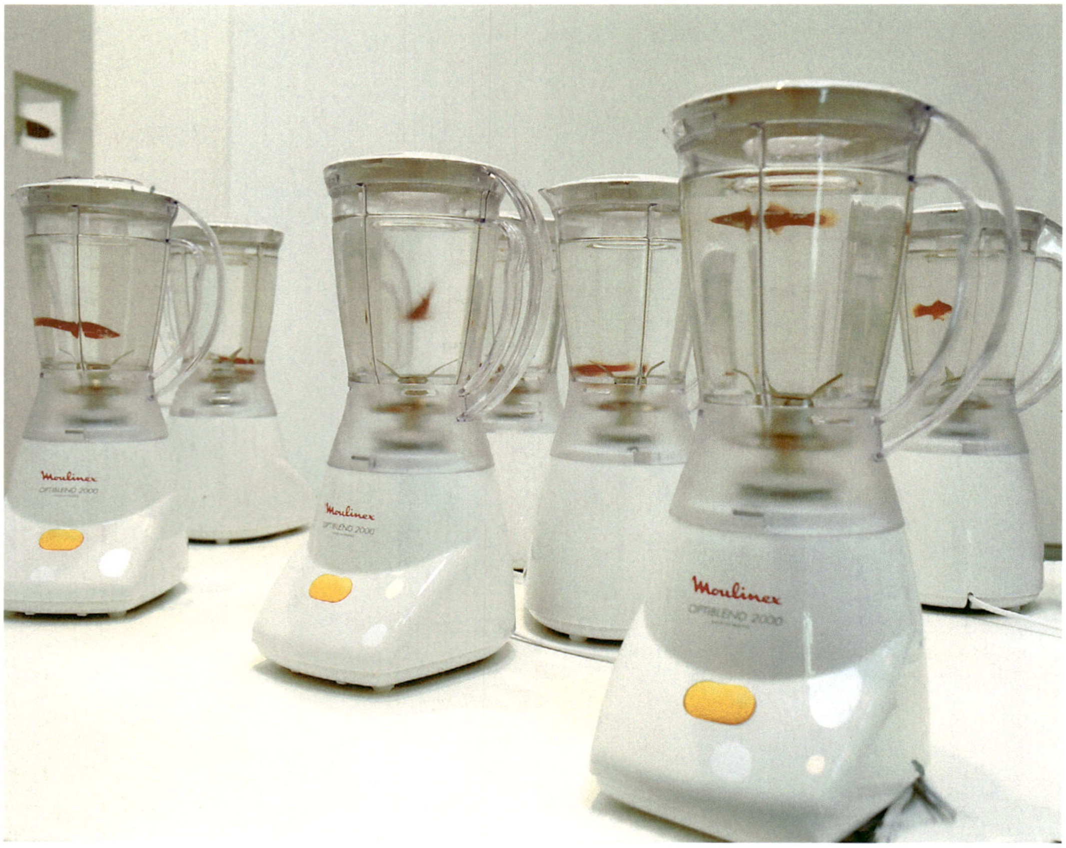

3

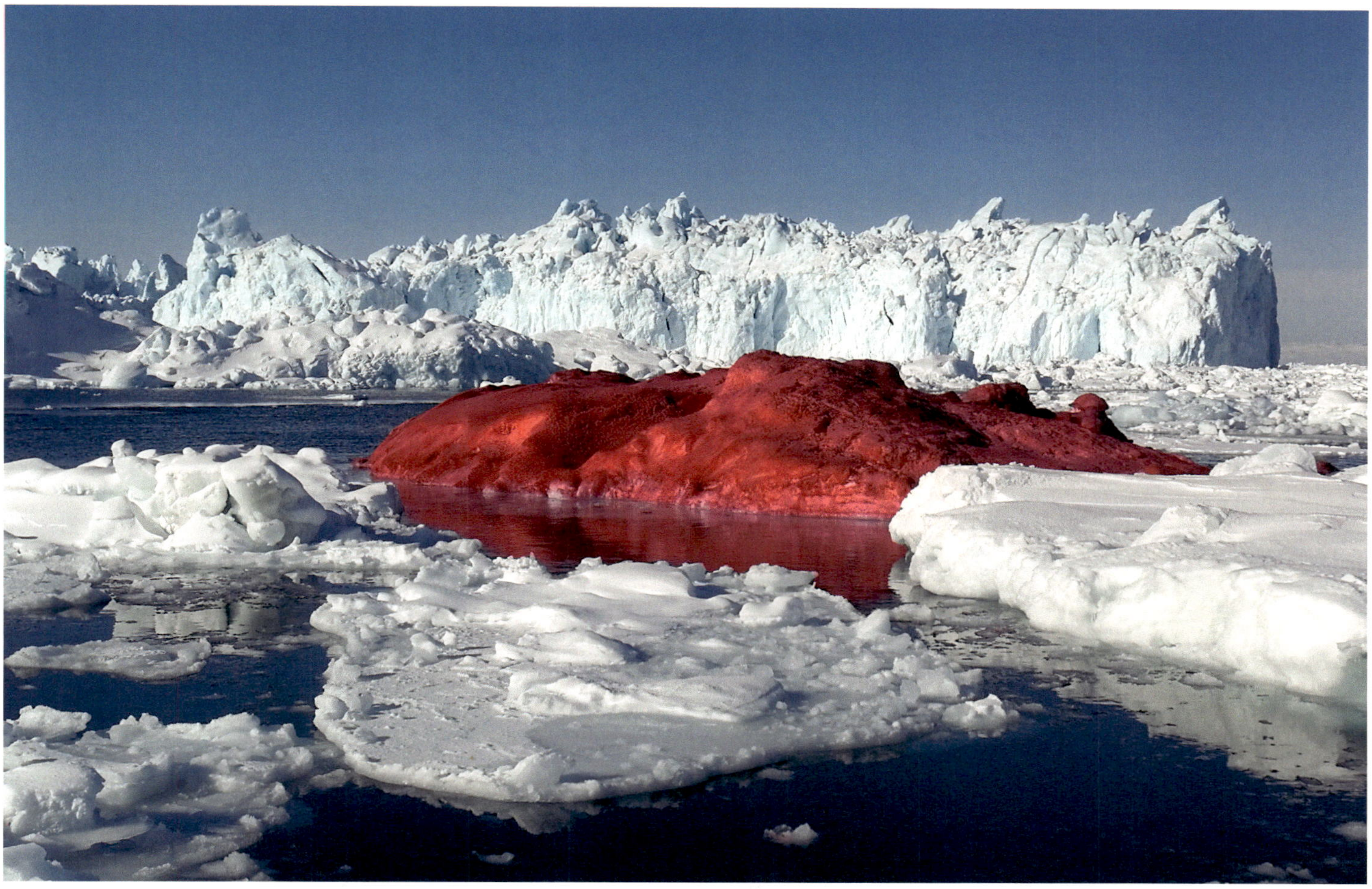

4

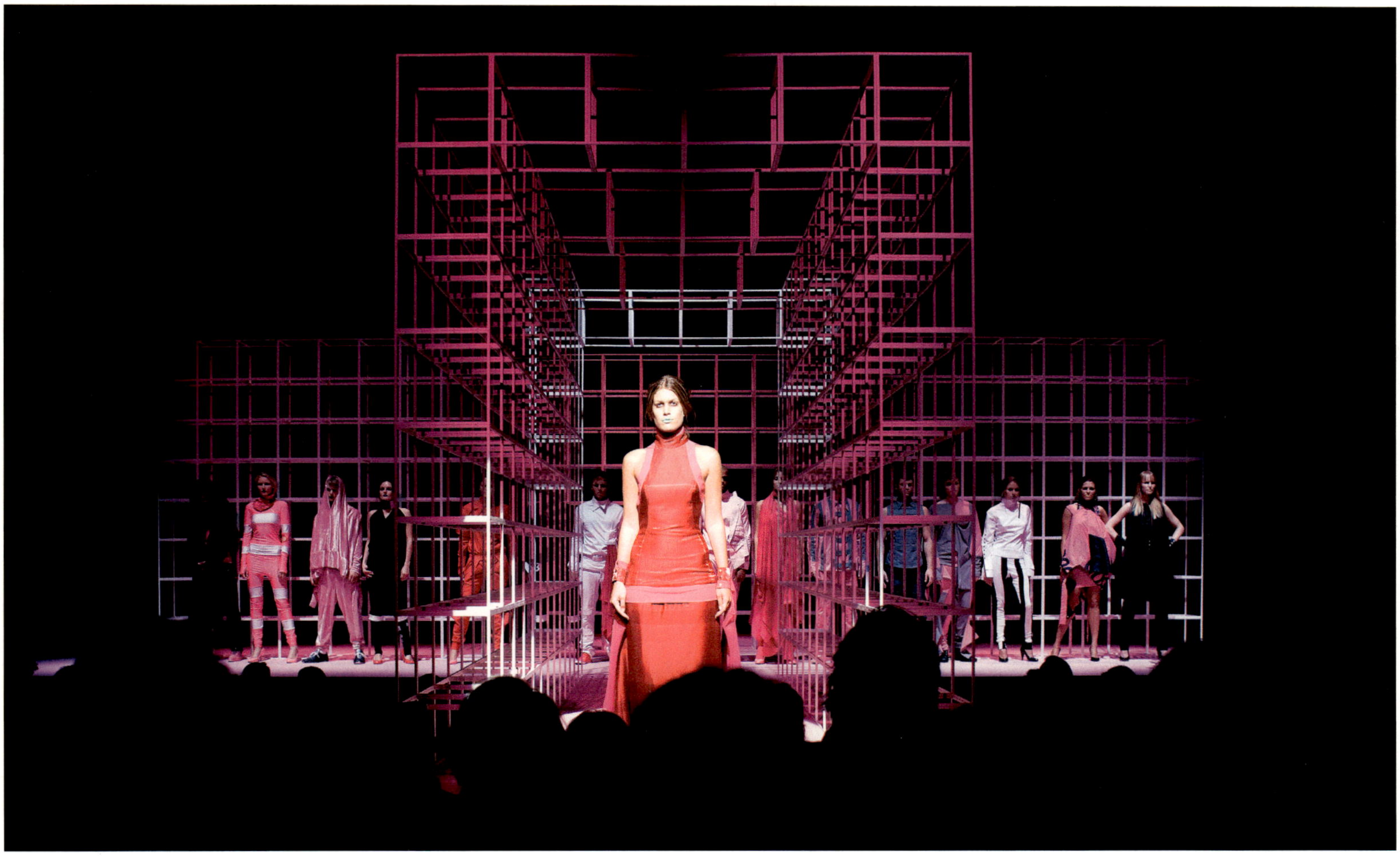

BRAD DOWNEY

1
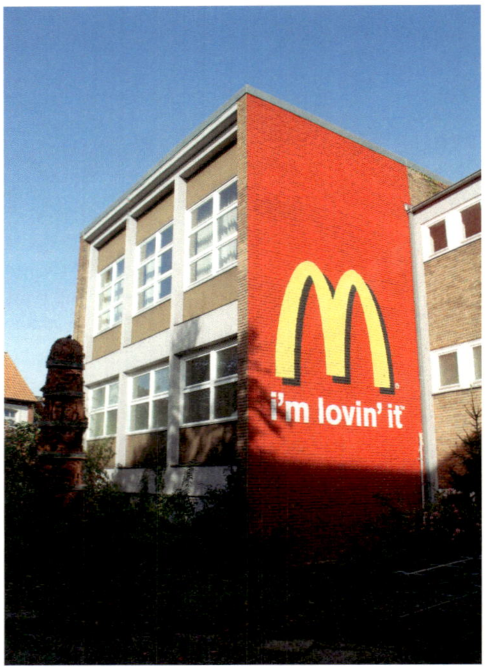

1
i'm Lovin' it
2009, Lüneburg, Germany
2
Don't Worry About
That Shit, René/In Soliloquy
with Madson Jones
2008, Berlin, Germany
Photos by Richard Schwarz
3
Broken Bike Lane
2008, Berlin, Germany
Photo by Vincent Maigler
4 (next spread)
Castles Beneath Cities
2008, Amsterdam,
Netherlands

"I would like to change the structure of the city," says the American artist Brad Downey (*1980), who lives in Berlin. "Everything is regulated, in a fixed grid. Every stone has its own appointed position. I want to change that, to break it up. I want to set the city in motion, and to accumulate real experiences in a real space." Brad Downey tears up the pavement and constructs a mountain with the sand beneath, turns cycle path markings into an abstract drawing—or paints a monumental McDonald's logo on a university building. A particularly harsh comment on the McDonaldsization of society and the commercialization of street art, the artwork *i'm lovin' it,* 2009, was created for an exhibition organized and financed by the Universität Lüneburg, art collector Rik Reinking, and even by property owners. Downey created a work that—far from contributing to the decoration of the city—was considered "remarkably ugly" by residents. Perhaps today street art has to look like advertising to really be radical and disquieting. After all, the time is long gone when street artists were considered vandals—today they are a part of the established art world. Advertising campaigns like to imitate their chaotic aesthetics, and street art has even become a kind of indication of gentrification, because today it is considered the sign of a hip district. "All the same, street art is like Baudrillard in Disneyland," says Downey. "It is not hidden away inside museums. It functions within our everyday living space. It is art for the masses, but it can also be intellectual and conceptual." Another example of this is Downey's performance *Don't Worry About That Shit, René/In Soliloquy with Madson Jones,* 2008. When French clothing brand Lacoste celebrated its 75th birthday in Berlin, it invited 11 artists to create window displays for the Kaufhaus des Westens (KaDeWe)—the largest monument to consumerism in Europe. By the time of the official exhibition preview, Downey had already presented his original artwork: he used a fire extinguisher to spray the 100-meter-long KaDeWe window with Lacoste-green paint (in another brilliant stroke, he used washable finger paint for children). The result can be best described through daily newspaper headlines. The shop window, smeared with green paint, was first reported by *Bild* as "KaDeWe turned green overnight" and the *Berliner Zeitung* followed with: "Paint attack on KaDeWe." The papers suspected radical, left-wing anti-consumerism campaigners, or pro-Tibet activists (because the clothes displayed in the window at the time were by Chinese designer Vera Wang.) First KaDeWe contacted the police, then the name of the real culprit appeared in blogs and the press picked up on the real explanation: "Was the attack on KaDeWe an artist's joke?" *(Tagesspiegel)* and "Was Lacoste behind the KaDeWe paint attack?" (*Welt*). At this point, Downey held a press conference at which he claimed responsibility for this performance (dedicating it to Till Eulenspiegel, an impudent trickster figure originating in German folklore) and declared that: "I didn't deceive anyone. This wasn't a radical act! They paid me for what I described, and that was what they got. The only thing I didn't tell them was that it was going to be done to their own building. But if they were going to pay me for vandalism, why shouldn't it be their own building?" The further consequences of this act have been widely reported: Petra Fladenhofer, the KaDeWe's spokesperson, reacted hysterically, stating that, "This is beyond our comprehension." Instead of being pleased by all the media attention—more than could ever have been achieved with the planned shop-window exhibition—Lacoste and KaDeWe excluded Downey from the exhibition. Thanks to the boomerang effect, this reaction naturally proved to be counterproductive. Shortly afterward, the *taz* daily newspaper ran an article headed: "Art performance: the crocodile bites itself: On its 75th birthday, the brand's actions risk jeopardizing its positive image. Suddenly the pink polo-neck seems to stand for Porky Pig, the pedantic, humorless, squealing, little, killjoy pig. And all this because Lacoste invited the wrong people to its birthday party."

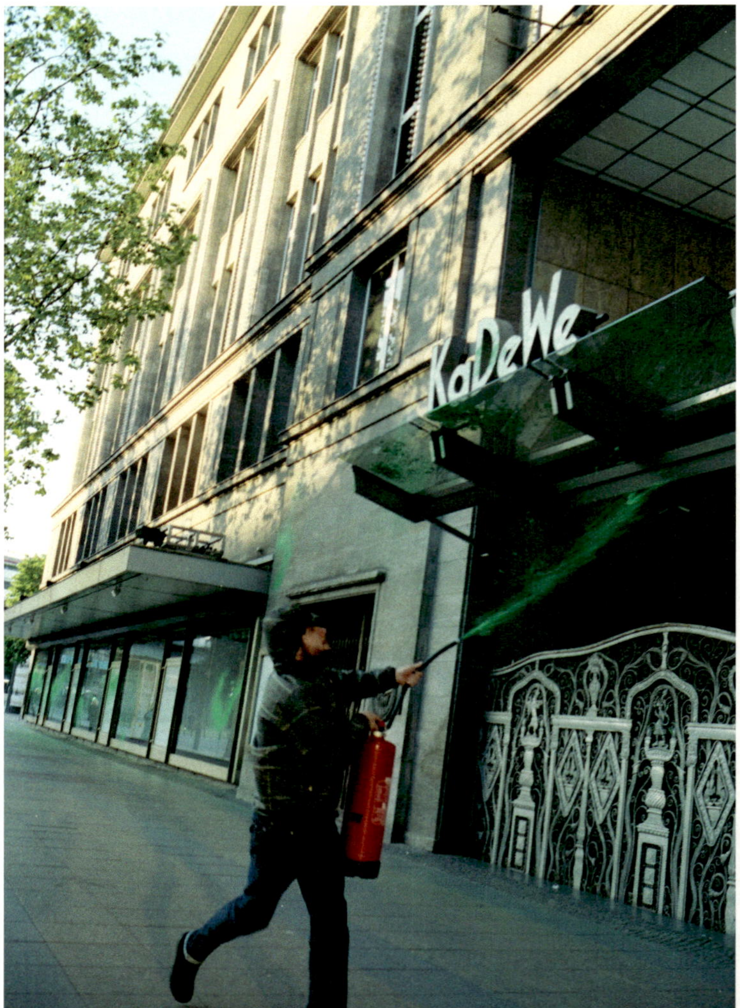

2
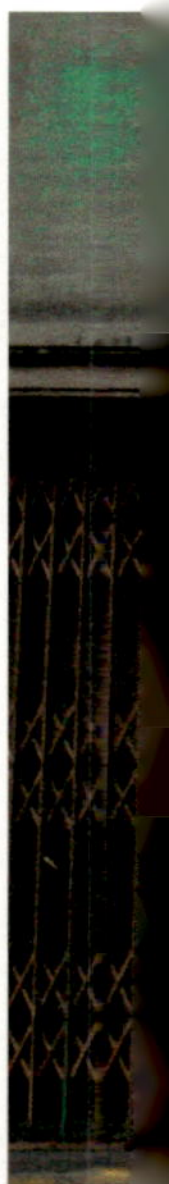

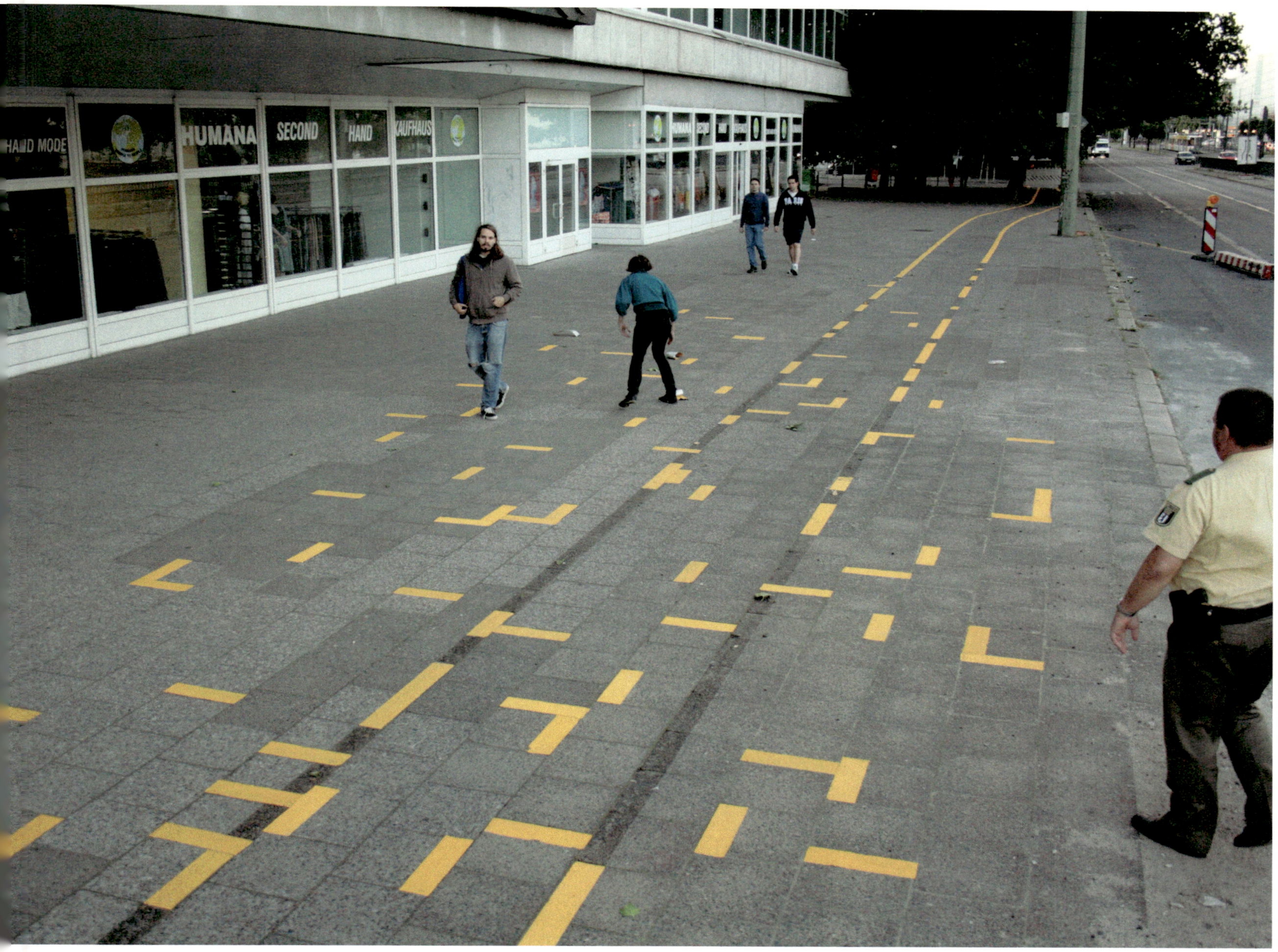

3

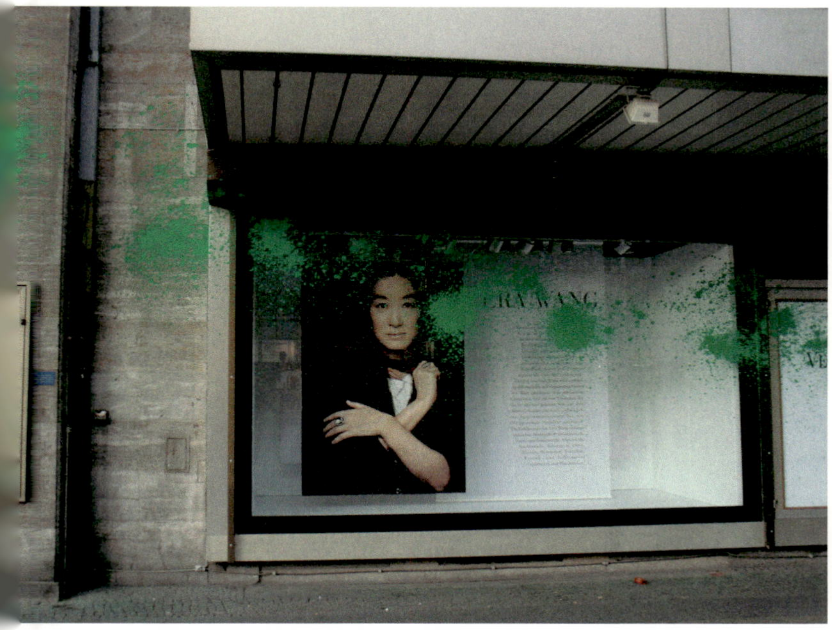

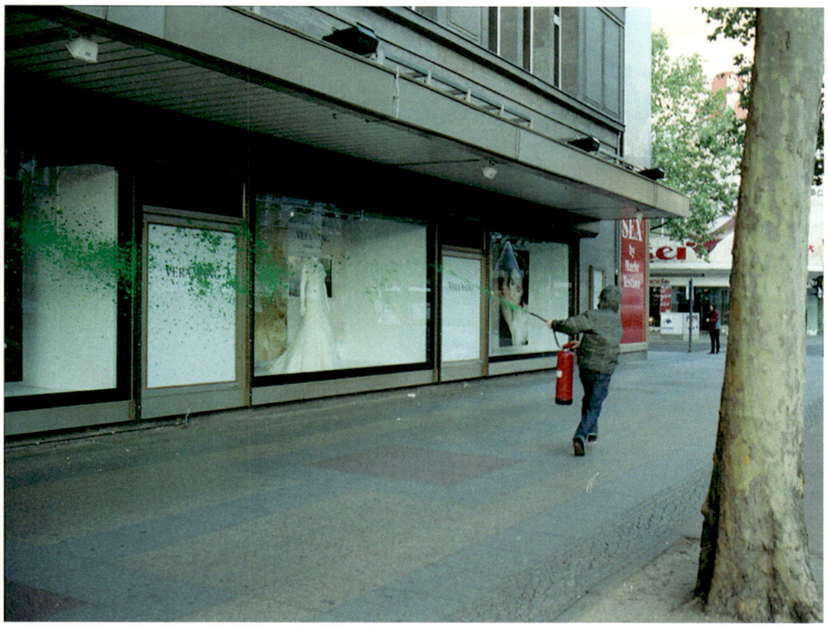

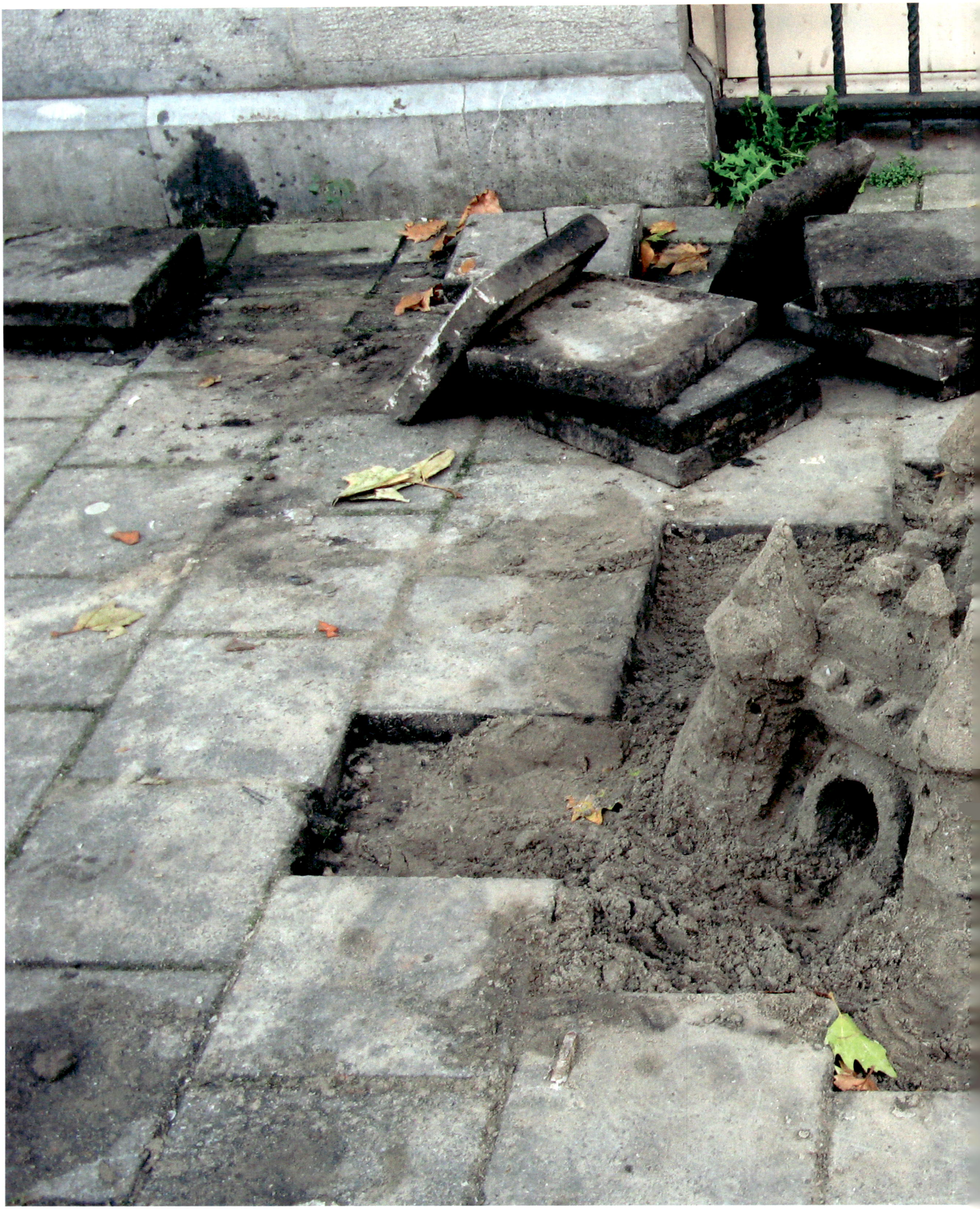

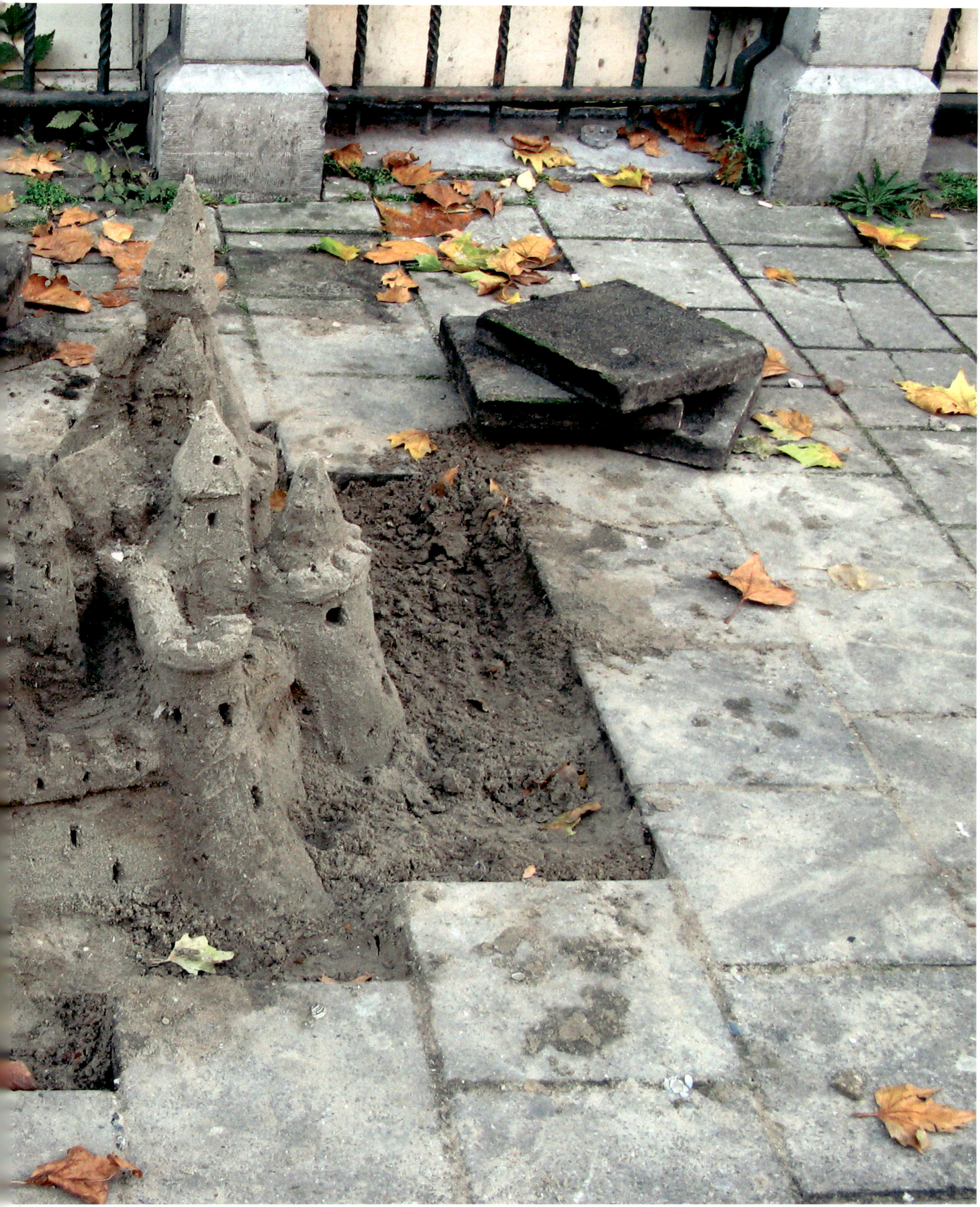

JULIEN BERTHIER

Julien Berthier (* 1975) from Besançon, France, studied at the École Nationale Supérieure des Beaux-Arts in Paris until 2000 and now lives and works in Paris. His best-known work is the sinking ship called *Love-Love,* 2007. Berthier divided a yacht into two halves for his sculpture, gave the boat a new keel and kept it in a sinking position. However, despite these adjustments, its two electric motors make it completely functional, and Berthier regularly takes it on trips to Normandy, Lake Constance, or London. "I wanted to freeze the moment just a few seconds before the boat disappears, creating an endless vision of the dramatic moment," Berthier tells us. "It's completely functional and perfectly safe, you can even steer it from the upside down seat I have installed." Berthier works with sculptures, videos, photographs, and drawings—and often sketches unrealized projects in his humorous designs. His works, which are a mixture of poetry and social criticism, seem so comic and tragic because they draw attention to problems without really being able to change anything. For example, with his *Additional Balcony,* 2008, Berthier was offering a service that made it possible for flats without balconies to have a genuine Parisian Haussmann balcony—but in this case, you needed a large crane to attach a plastic imitation to the building from the outside.

1
Additional Balcony
2008

2
Hypnos
2008, Five naturalized pigeons with polyester masks

3
Love-Love
2007

Courtesy Galerie GP&N Vallois, Paris

1

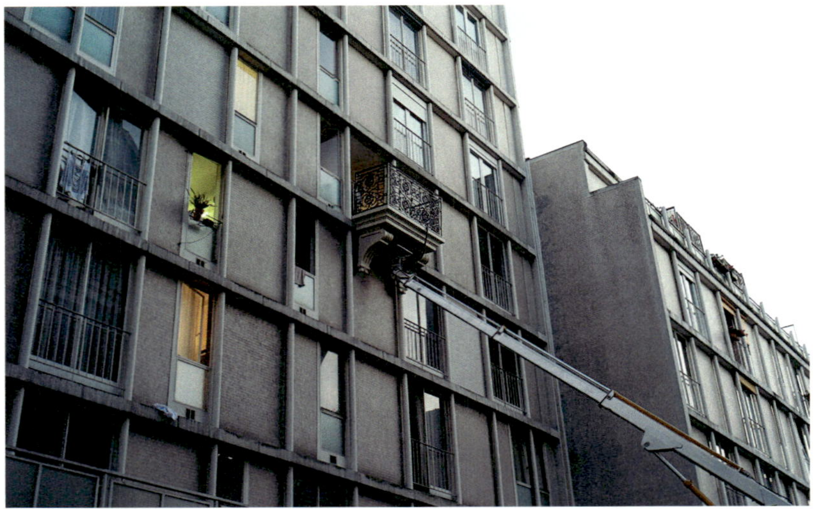

2

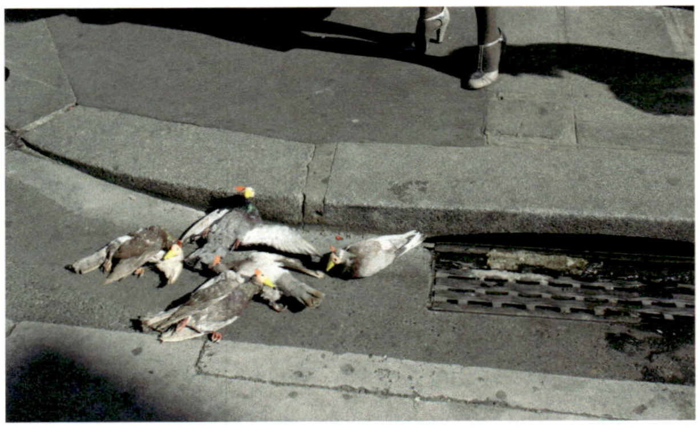

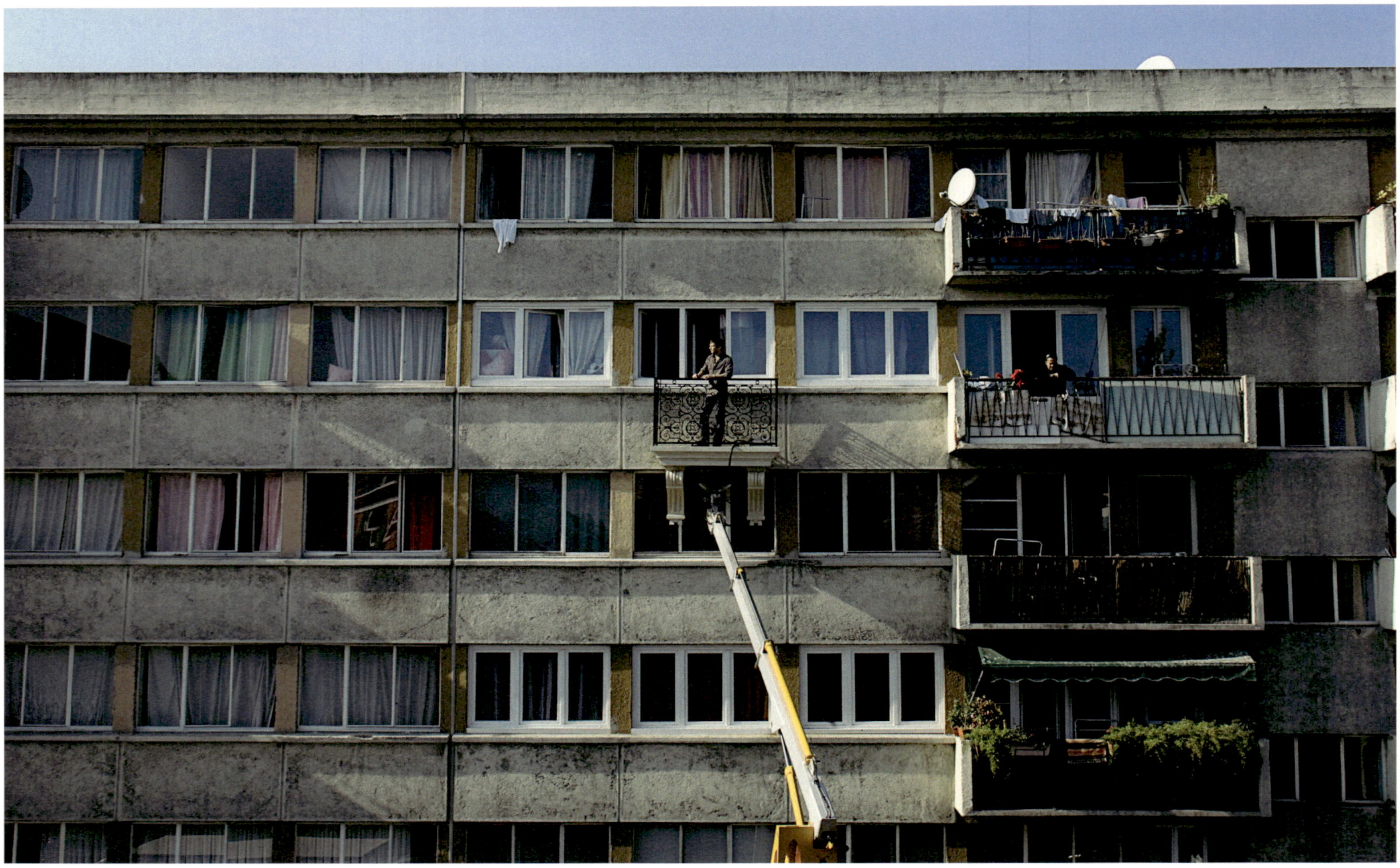

3

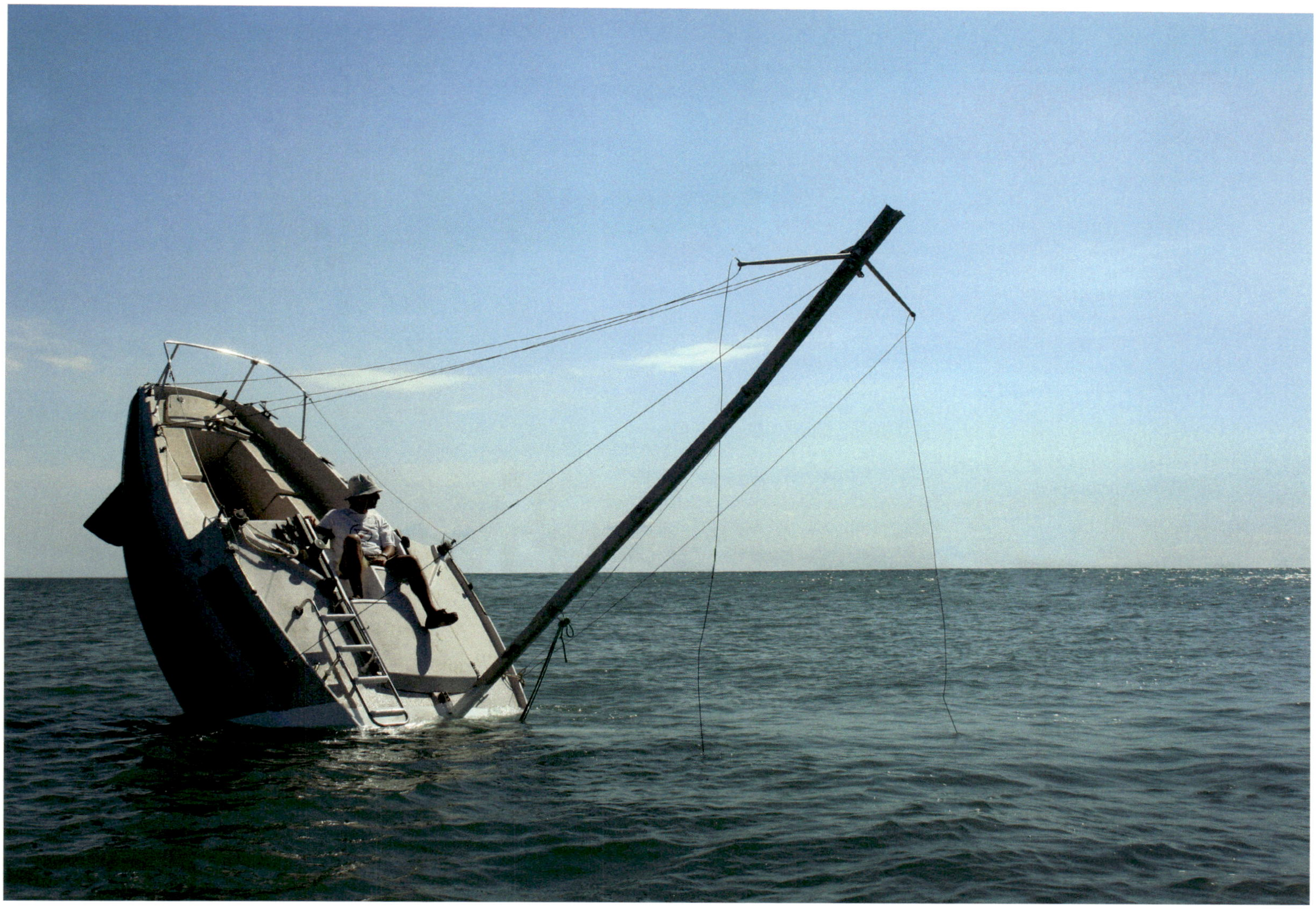

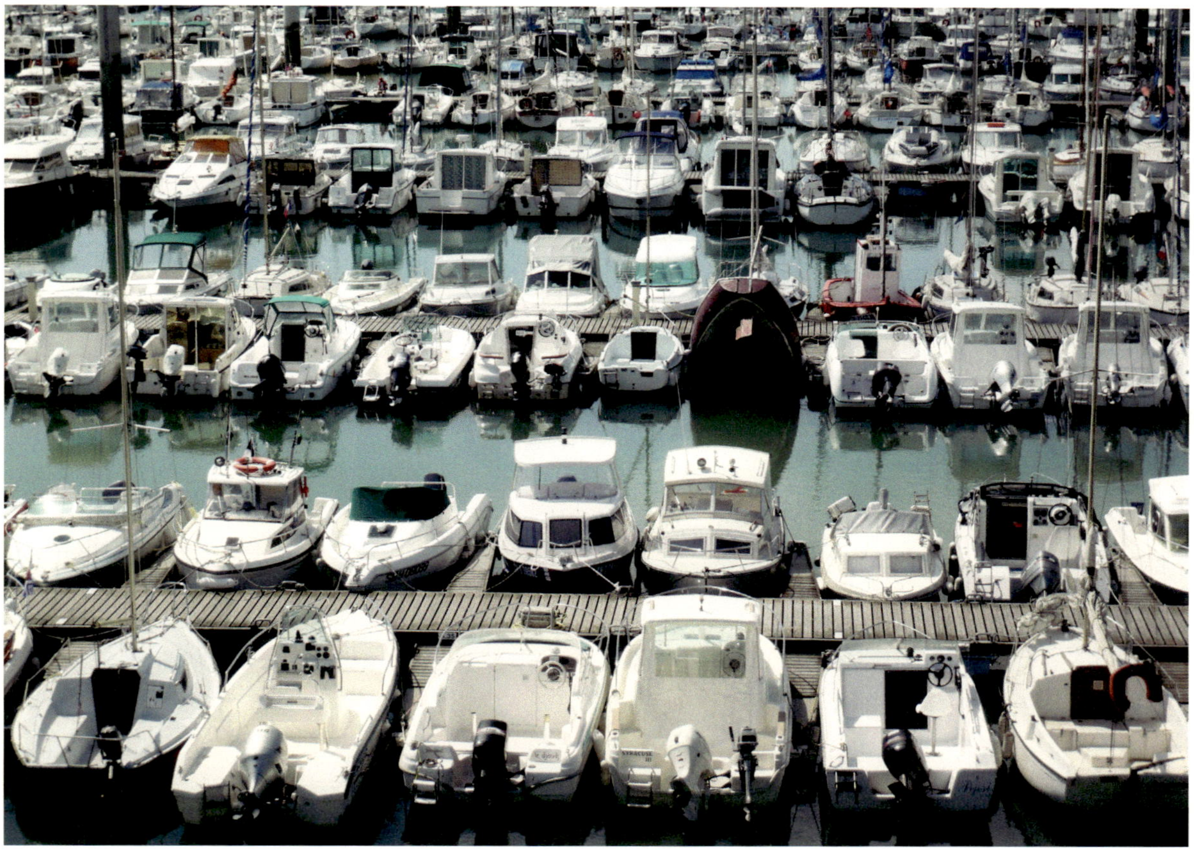

THE WA

The Wa (* 1981) is a street guerrilla artist who uses art techniques to fight for more social justice, for the ideal of an authority-free space, and at the same time fights against cultural hegemony. He studied fine art in France before moving to Berlin, where he met like-minded people, such as the street artists Brad Downey and Akim, with whom he has collaborated on several projects. His illegal interventions and sculptures are like stumbling blocks in public spaces: the CVs of jobseekers are displayed as City Light posters in Marseille; a marble likeness of Nicolas Sarkozy is placed on a bridge in Paris; or an oversized valve in Shanghai that makes the world look like a hot air balloon. The Wa's context-sensitive artworks undermine the system and playfully revolutionize the everyday world. For his art happening *Switch Tense,* 2010, he staged a demonstration in Hamburg's HafenCity with painstakingly painted protest placards that stated: "We are China," "Vote to Remove Official Voyeurs," and "No Neighborhood for Nazis." He left a trail of dirt, plastic beer bottles, and confused visitors behind him, and celebrated immediately afterwards with salmon and champagne in a meeting point for the homeless. "Some people call my art 'urban hacking' or 'artivism.' Perhaps it is just a colorful way of making people think," says The Wa. "I always have this one phrase from Pierre Bourdieu in my mind: 'Democracy is the balance between people who have power and those who fight against them.'" For The Wa, the boundaries between political/revolutionary and artistic avant-garde subversion are fluid—and he often makes barely recognizable references to European avant-garde movements, such as situationism, Dada, and fluxus. But The Wa's greatest dream is a project that would surely have delighted Marcel Duchamp: to one day build a fountain that can actually be used.

Switch Tense
2010, Hamburg HafenCity, Germany, Photos by Christian Rinke and Tim Holthöfer

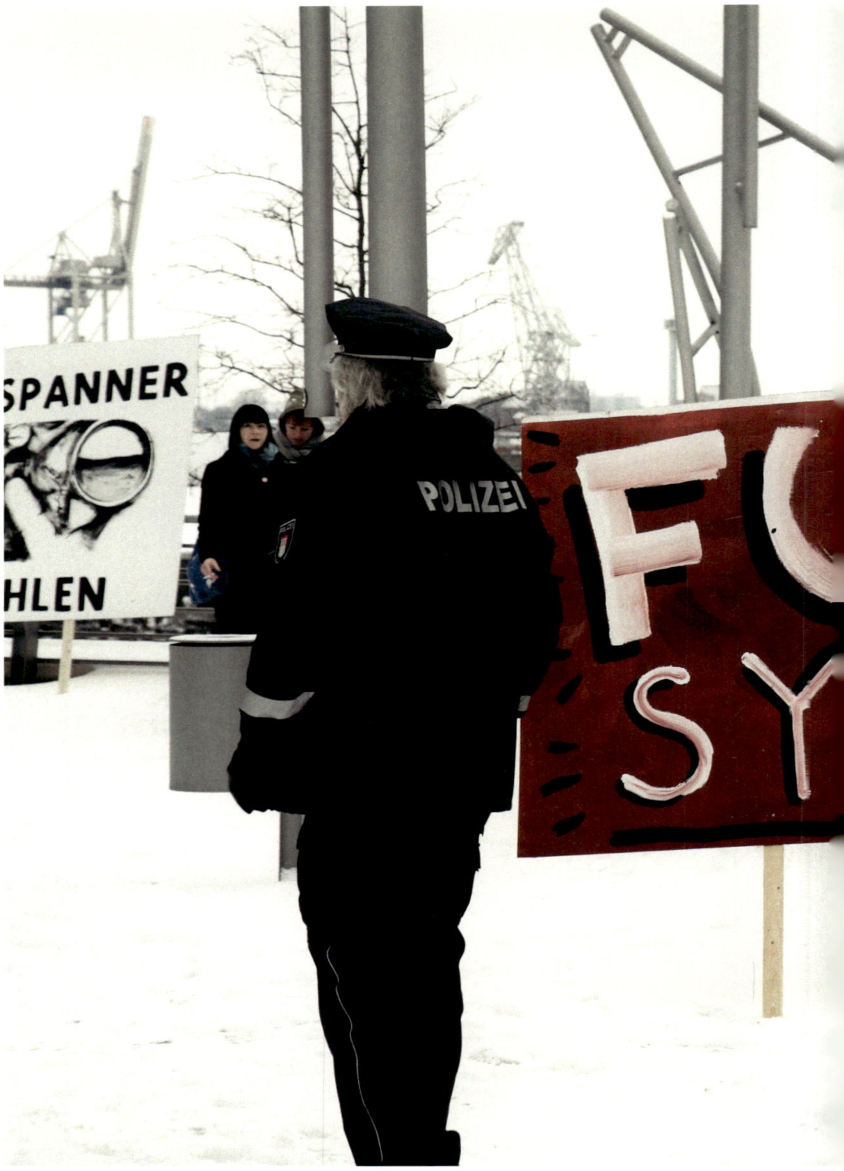

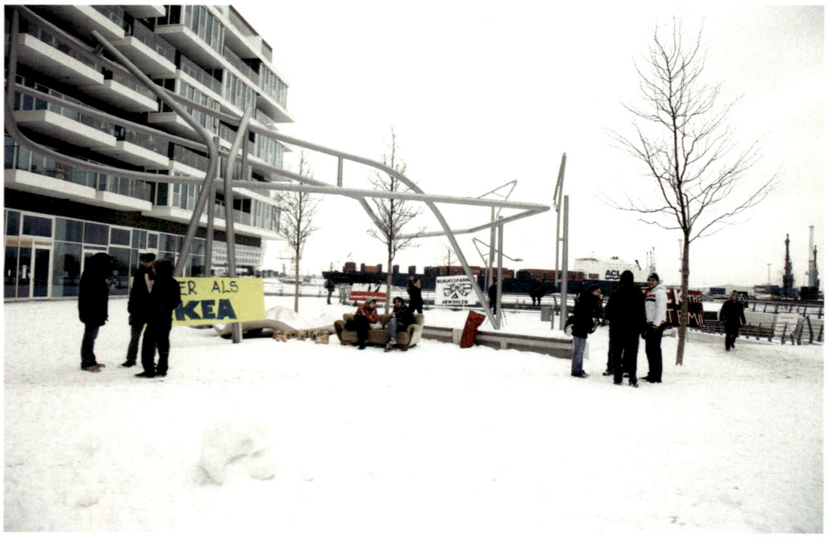

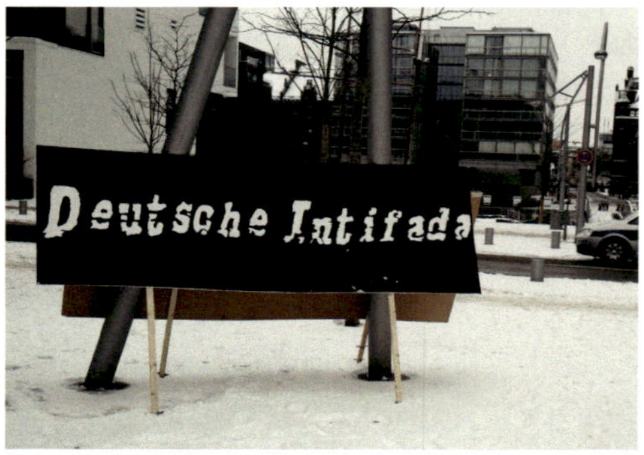

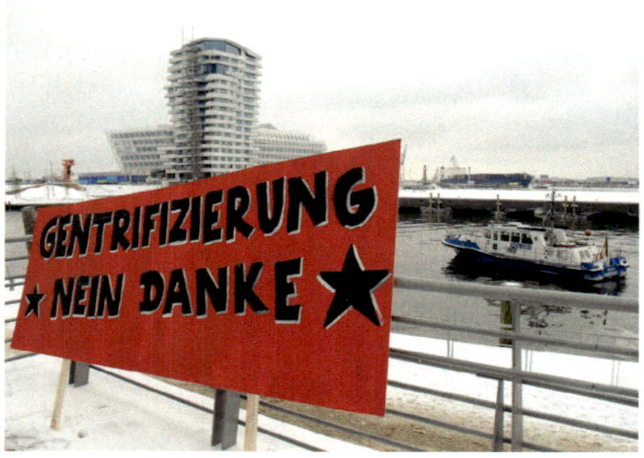

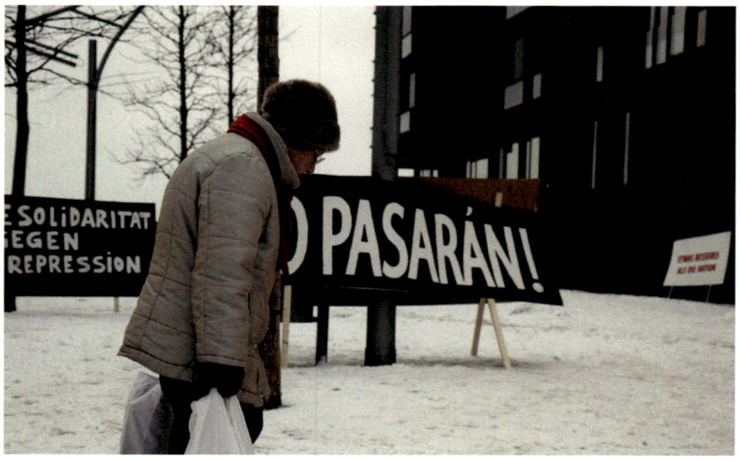

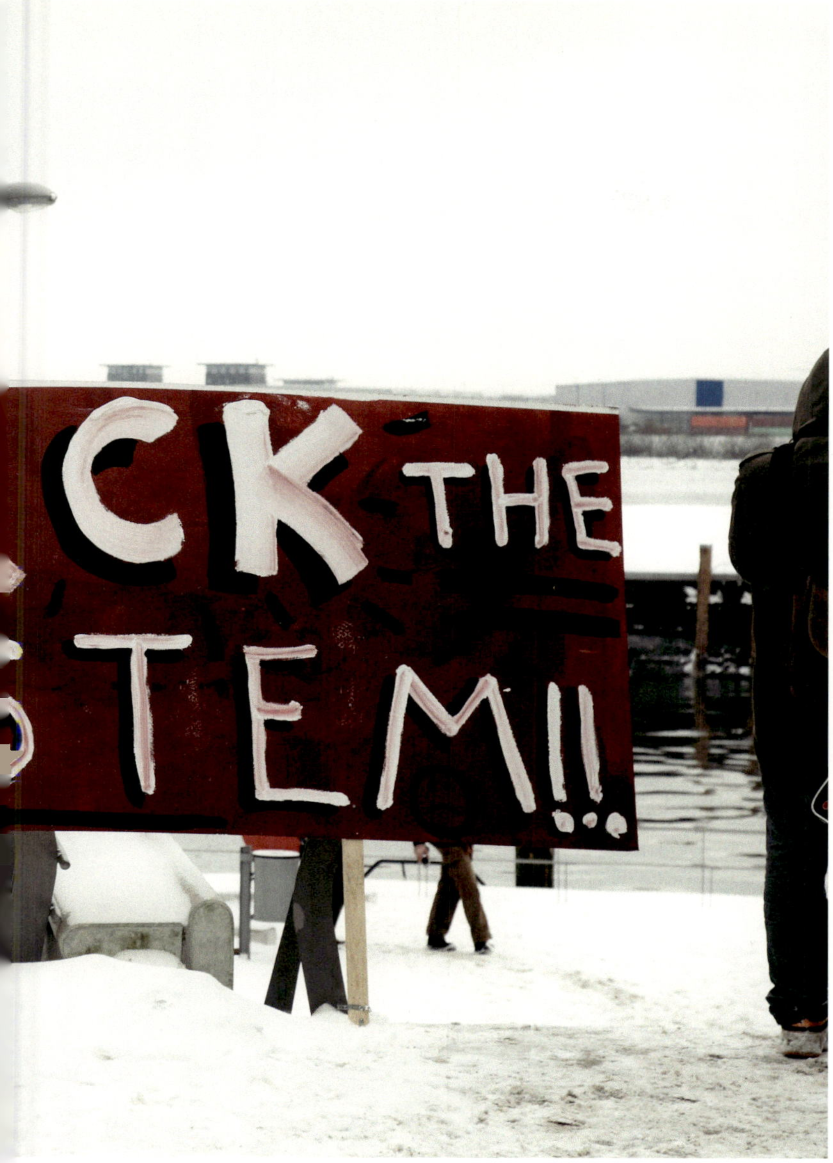
CK THE
TEM!!

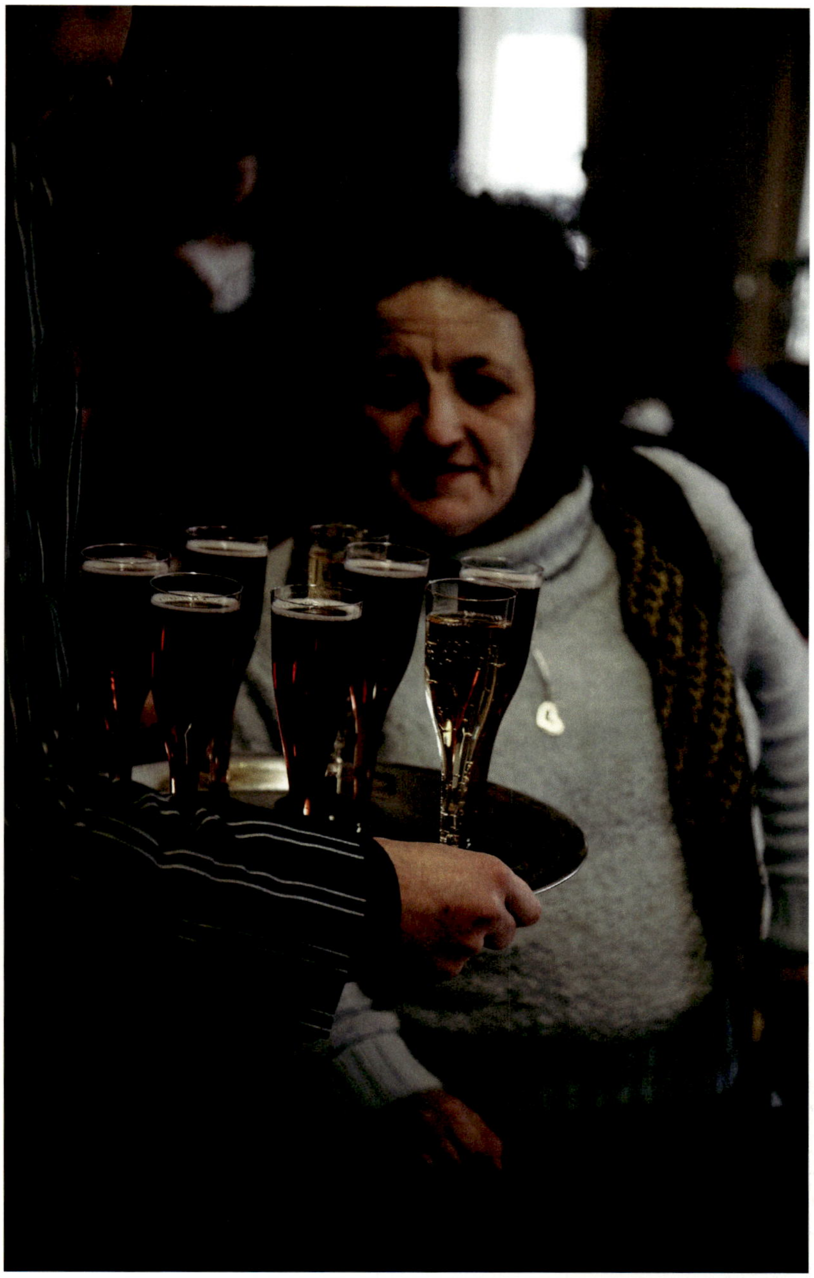

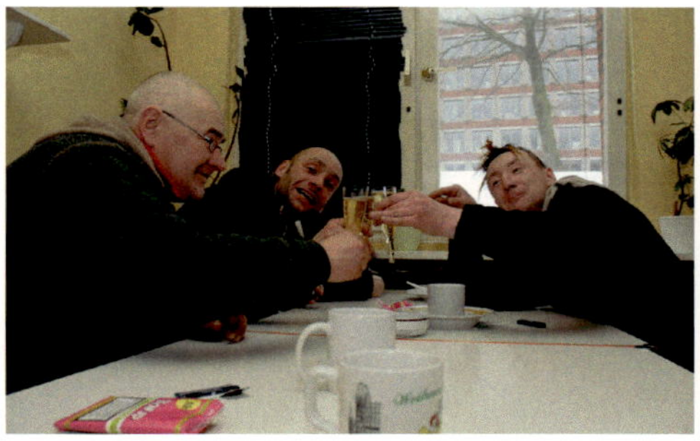

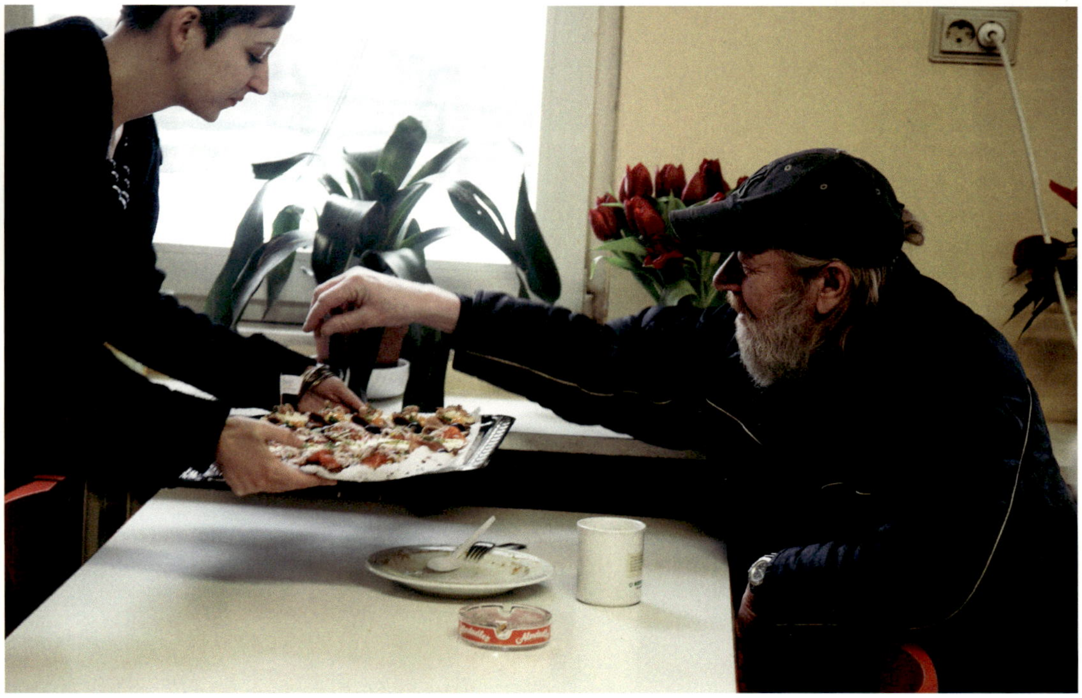

THYLACINE

Together, Fabian Hachen (* 1977) and Mischa Düblin (* 1973) are the Swiss artist duo Thylacine. Their installations and performances are dedicated to the contrast between art and life. They respond to societal situations with a delicate sense of irony and bring the audience face-to-face with subtle spatial interventions. For their project *Wile E. Coyote,* 2008, which is named after the obsessive cartoon character who vainly pursues Road Runner, the duo bricked themselves in during an exhibition opening. Over the days that followed, people could look into and crawl into their escape hole. For the performance *Pure & Clean,* 2009, the duo had the gallery cleaned by a professional team of janitors during the opening preview. Thylacine's intention was to suggest that by searching for art in the empty space, the visitors themselves became the exhibited objects. For the performance *Sale!,* 2010, Thylacine built a supermarket checkout in the Swiss Art Awards exhibition space, with an employee waiting behind the checkout and with an empty conveyor belt endlessly running. In this project, the artists were trying (among other things) to draw attention to the way they live their lives somewhere between art and paid work. The project *On the Floor,* 2010, in which visitors found aesthetically beautiful photographs of a homeless person inside the gallery, while the person depicted in the images sat on the ground outside the gallery, also thematizes social gaps by drawing attention to the artifice between them and the boundary between an art context and reality.

On the Floor
2010, Kunstverein Freiburg, Freiburg im Breisgau, Germany

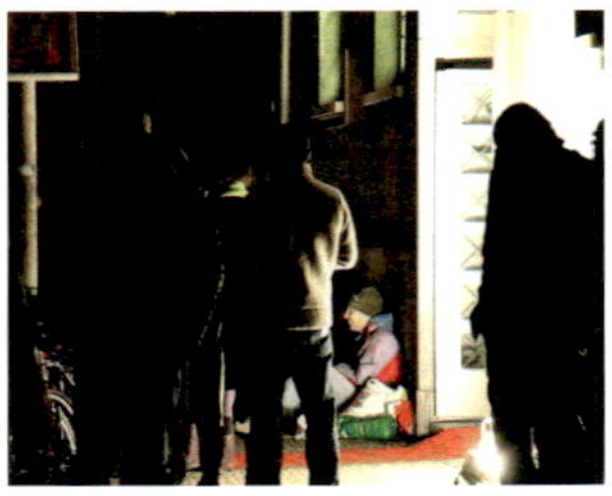

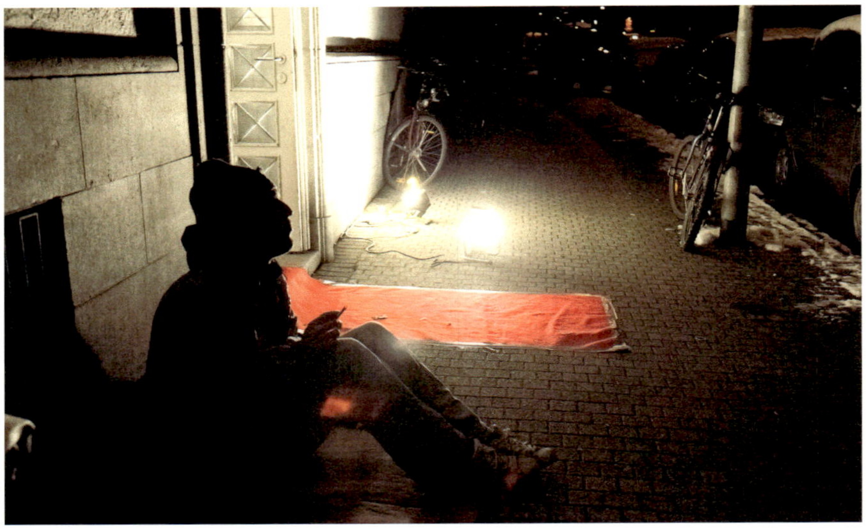

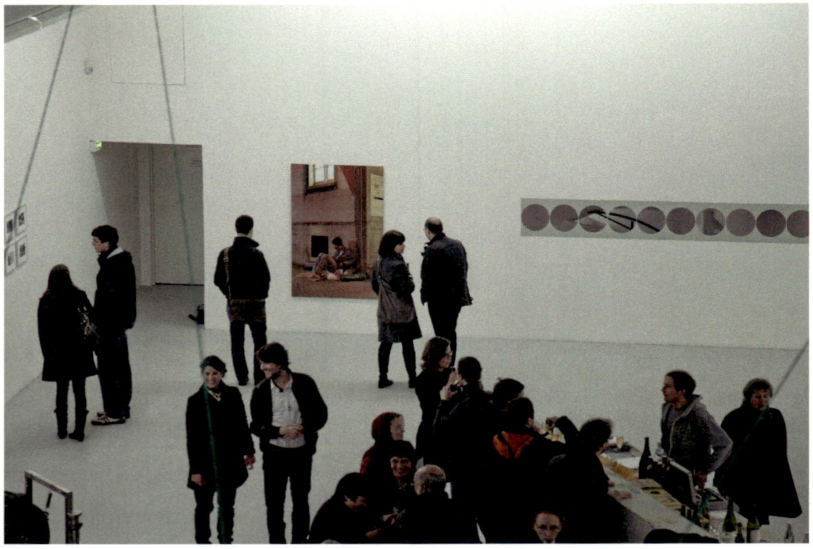

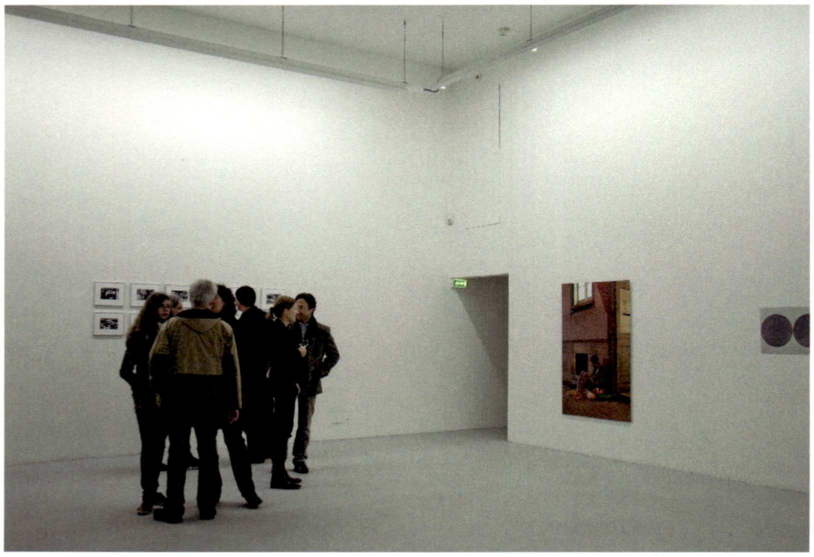

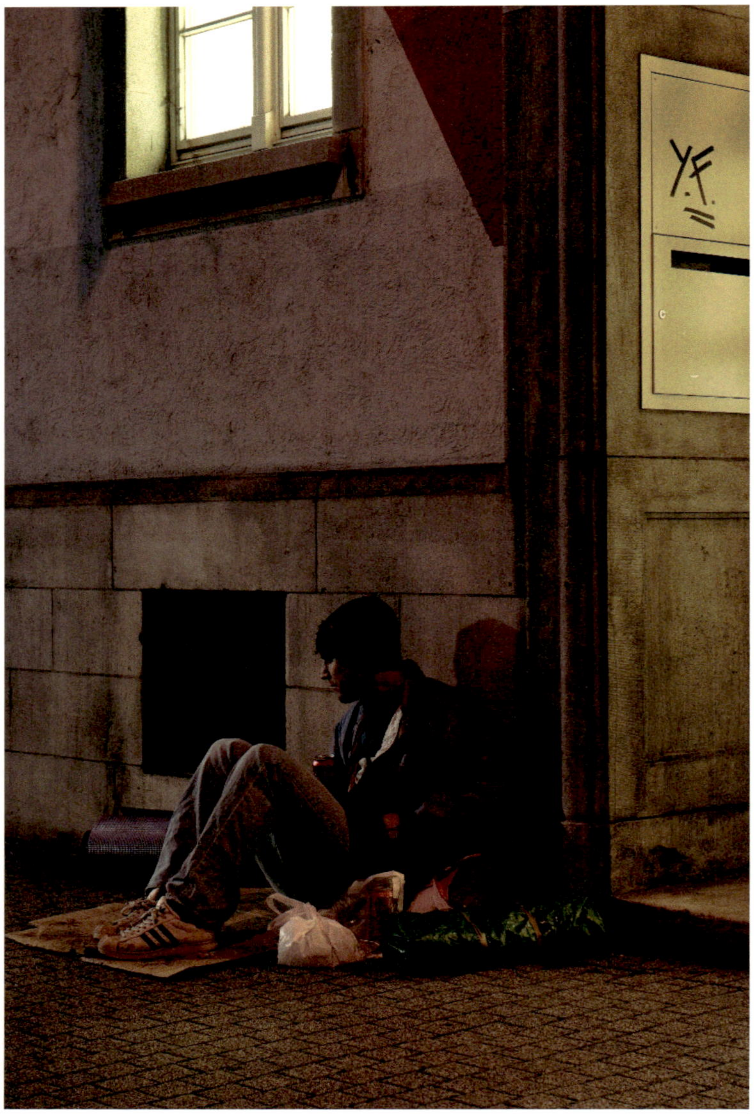

MARJETICA POTRČ

Marjetica Potrč (* 1953) is a Slovenian artist and architect, who addresses themes such as ecology and sustainability. Potrč's drawings document her urban journeys and research projects. She works with local groups to develop approaches to solving social problems, and initiates open processes. For her exhibitions, she reconstructs the architectonic structures that she has discovered on her journeys. Potrč states that: "I show core units and similar buildings in galleries and museums, so that we're able to see them. What fascinates me in life, I transplant to the gallery. These galleries are, after all, places where we think about the human condition." The inadequate water supply in a Venezuelan slum led her to collaborate with the Israeli architect Liyat Esakov to develop a toilet that worked without water, which also fulfilled hygienic requirements; the work was titled, *Dry Toilet*, 2003. In her installation *Hybrid House: Caracas, West Bank, West Palm Beach*, 2003, she brought together architectonic structures from three current international conflict areas—Caracas, Florida, and Palestine—in a single building to illustrate conflicts relating to space, security, energy supply, water, and communication technology. For *Caracas: House with Extended Territory*, 2003, she reconstructed a structure generally used to manage a comparatively large space within a slum, and built an additional façade with Greek columns in front of the main structure—like a kind of veranda—to emphasize the claim on the additional space. And for *Rural Studio: The Lucy House Tornado Shelter*, 2007, she reconstructed a building erected by the architect Samuel Mockbee and his students that deftly combined residential architecture with protective shelter architecture—as the crinkled, folded roof also concealed a tornado shelter. Potrč sees architecture as an indicator of the social status quo: "No doubt that architecture is a societal construction. Society is the city. Social ideas and cities change, though."

1

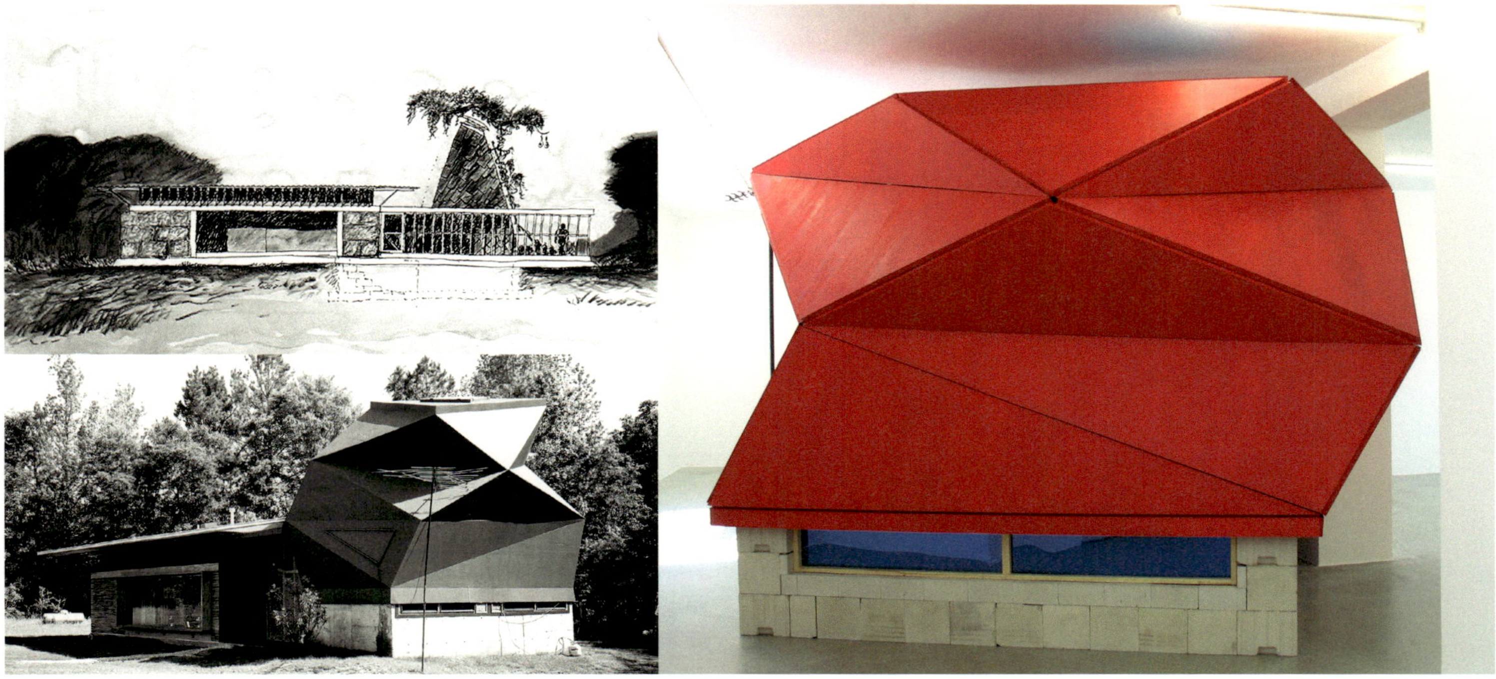

1
Rural Studio: The Lucy House Tornado Shelter
2007, Nordenhake Gallery, Berlin, Germany, Drawing by Samuel Mockbee, Black-and-white-photo by Beatrice Dallot, Photo by Marjetica Potrč, Courtesy the artist and Galerie Nordenhake, Berlin/Stockholm

2

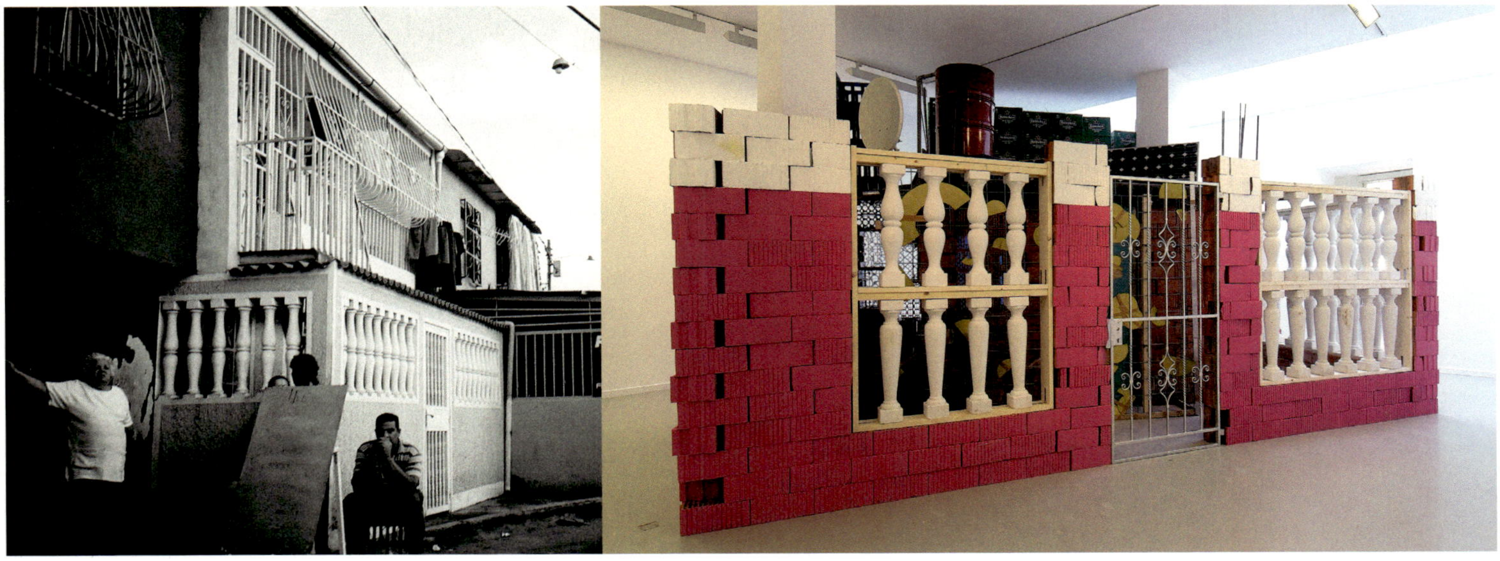

2
Caracas: House with Extended Territory
2003, Nordenhake Gallery, Berlin; 2004, De Appel, Amsterdam; 2005, MUSAC, Leon; 2006, PAC, Milano, Installation at De Appel, Amsterdam, 2004, Black-and-white-photo by Peter Cox, Photo by Marjetica Potrč
Collection of MUSAC

GREGOR SCHNEIDER

"IT IS AS IF ONE WERE WONDERING THROUGH THE LAYERINGS AND SHUTTERINGS OF ONE'S OWN BRAIN, FOLLOWING THE MECHANISMS OF PERCEPTION AND KNOWLEDGE"

1
Hamburger Bahnhof – Museum für Gegenwart
2006, Berlin, Germany, Graphic elaboration
2
Bondi Beach, 21 Beach Cells
2007, Bondi Beach, Sydney, Australia, Kaldor Public Art Projects
3
Passageway No. 1
2005–2007, Düsseldorf, Germany
WEISSE FOLTER, K20K21 Kunstsammlung Nordrhein-Westfalen
4
High Security and Isolation Cell No. 2
2005, Düsseldorf, Germany
WEISSE FOLTER, K20K21 Kunstsammlung Nordrhein-Westfalen

Gregor Schneider (* 1969) is a master of psychological horror. His artworks constantly reference death, terror, isolation, and fear. This has gained him a reputation as one of the most disquieting artists working today. Schneider describes himself as, "a builder of spaces." He recently courted controversy by suggesting that he might build a "dying room." The concept alone was scandalous: his intention was to display the death of a terminally ill person as part of an exhibition, to illustrate "the beauty of death." "The rooms that I build can be a source of fear, and the functions that I give them can cause people to panic. But once they have been created, they are ideal for overcoming fear."

Schneider rose to prominence with his *Totes Haus u r,* which won him the Grand Prize at the Venice Biennale. For this installation, he put his parents' house in Mönchengladbach-Rheydt on display. He had spent two years turning its rooms into a house of horror. Schneider created double floors and soundproofed rooms, introduced new walls and installed mirrored windows—thereby demonstrating a nightmarish sense of entrapment associated with a family home. His *Cube* installation had a similar polarizing effect. Inspired by Kazimir Malevich's painting of the black square and by the most sacred Islamic object, the Kaaba, Schneider's intention was to construct a huge, black cube in Venice. His plan, however, was frustrated by political concerns, and a fear of attack. He created the installation *Bondi Beach, 21 Beach Cells,* 2007, on the beach near Sydney in Australia: a labyrinth of 21 cells, some open, some enclosed, with the standard beach accoutrements—a sunshade, an inflatable raft, and a garbage can. However, the installation is also worryingly reminiscent of the Guantánamo Bay internment camp, and is a statement about immigration, terrorism, and asylum. *Passageway No. 1,* 2005–2007, is also a Kafkaesque and claustrophobic space—a long corridor with tiny cells. Is it a prison, a hospital, a research laboratory, or an official headquarters? Its functional architecture and sense of anonymous communality has a chilling effect on the viewer. *High Security and Isolation Cell,* 2005, is an internally accessible reconstruction of an isolation cell, which creates a similar sense of physical unease as soon as one enters it. Schneider uses his spaces as a way of showing the viewer how fear makes us helpless all over the world, and, as such, appeals to a global conscience.

1

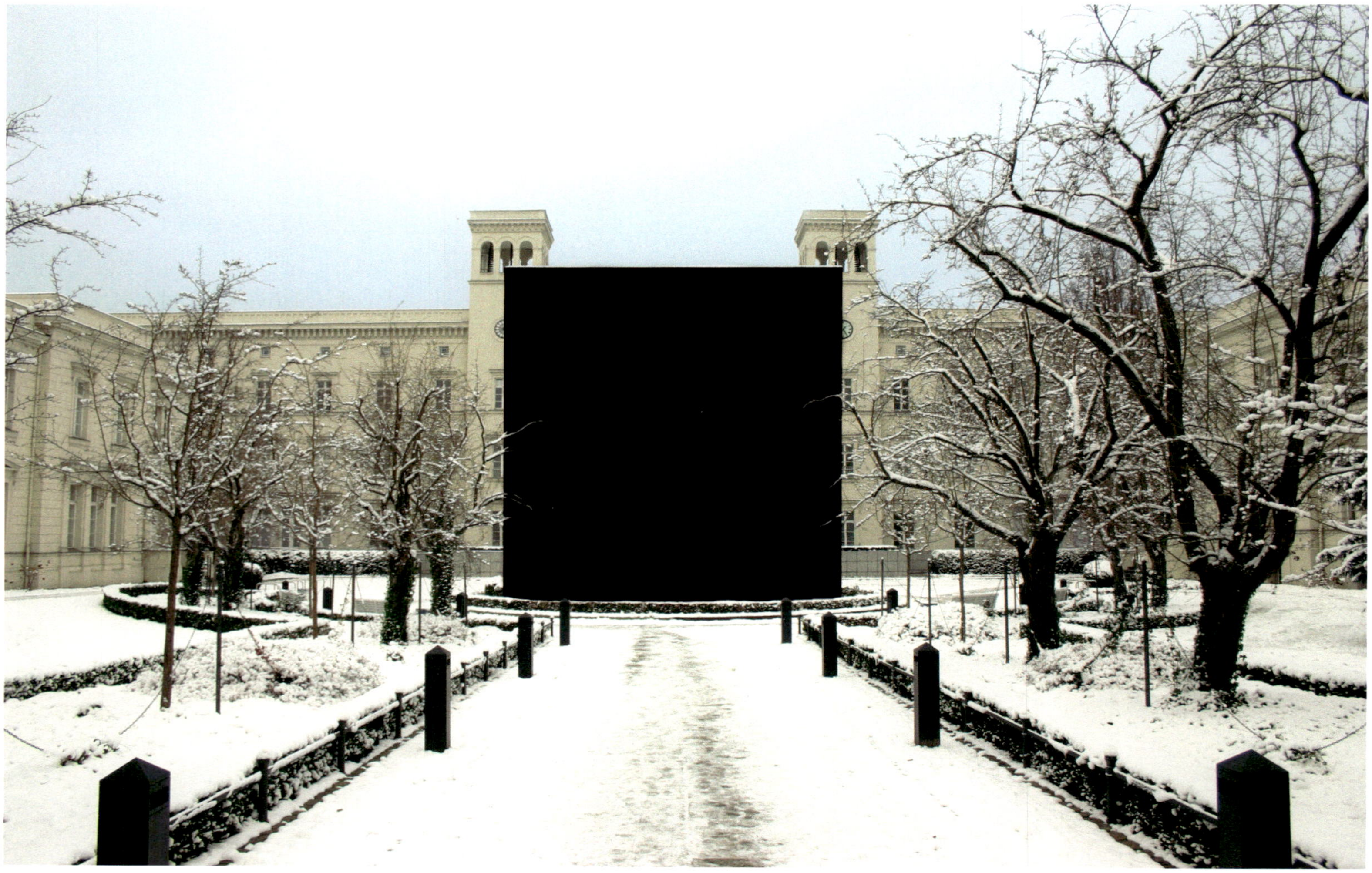

2

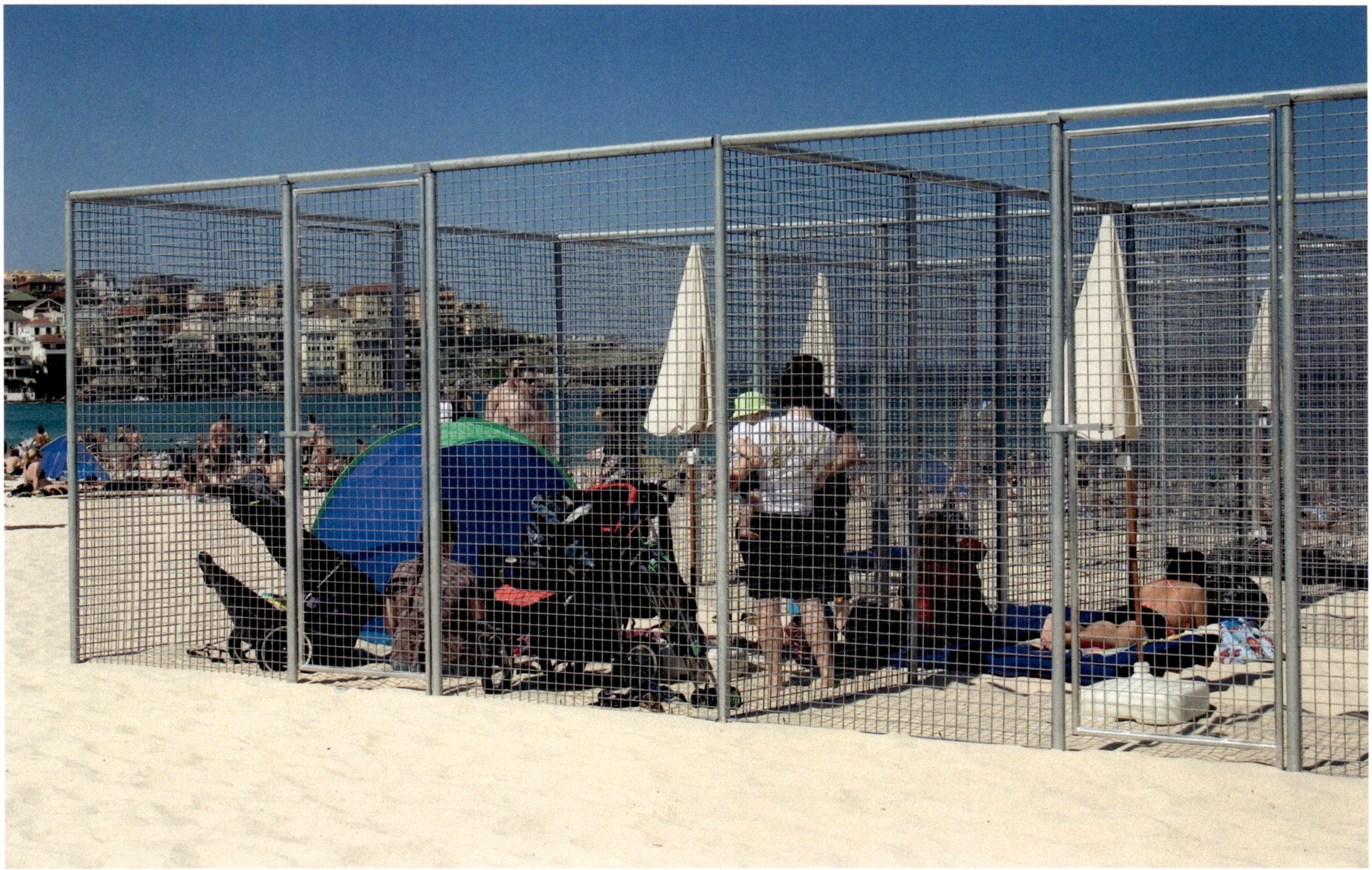

3

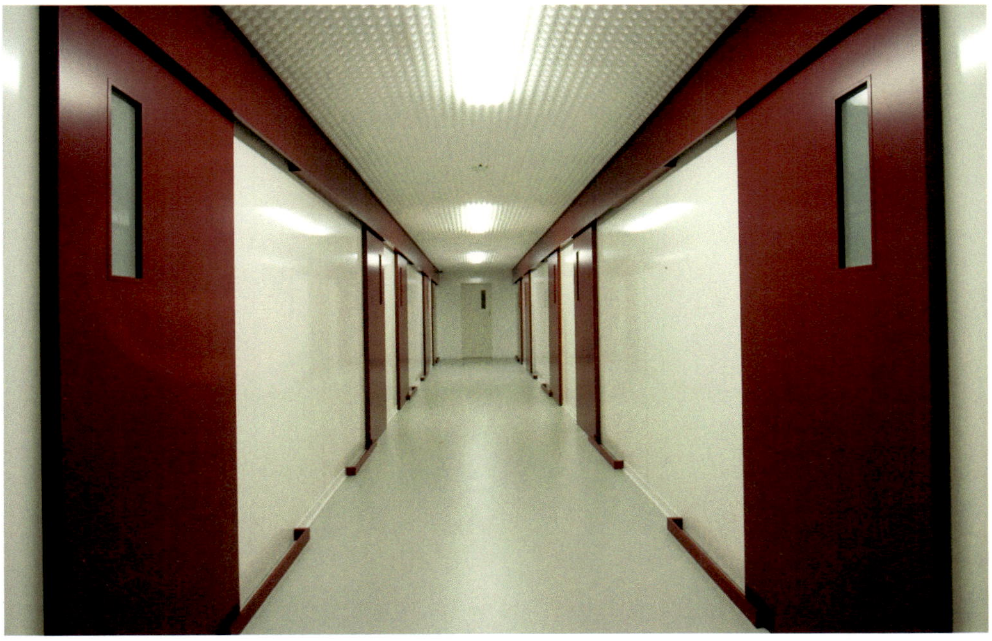

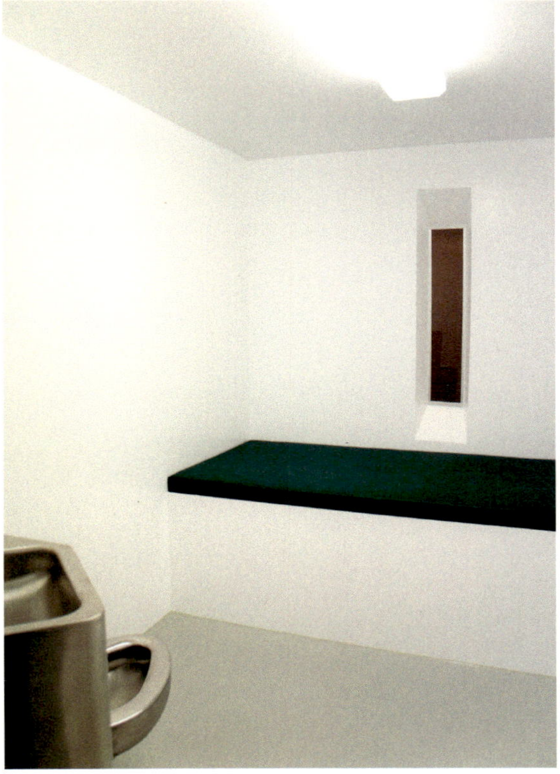

4

OSA (OFFICE FOR SUBVERSIVE ARCHITECTURE)

OSA, or the Office for Subversive Architecture, which was founded in 2002, is an architecture network whose members live and work in different European cities. The aim of OSA is to bring experimental designs that are halfway between art and architecture into urban spaces, as a means of initiating new ways of using those urban spaces. For instance, in the summer of 2008, members of the group—assisted by 25 students and school pupils—erected a mini golf course in a plaza in front of a theater in Darmstadt, Germany. The architect Oliver Langbein—one of the founding members—said: "Our project was a targeted way of making young people aware of which public places they use [and] in what ways." Britta Eiermann of OSA explained that: "The idea was to get something out of seemingly deserted and dismal places," and to suggest that it just takes a closer look to reveal potential uses for certain spaces. In fact, the Georg-Büchner-Platz in Darmstadt—with its empty pools and old drainage pipes (which proved highly suitable for playing a short round of golf)—was plainly ideal. However, the group is also concerned with revealing flaws, such as situations that make it impossible to put a space to any sensible use even if the site is provided with the necessary equipment.

For instance, the *Sitios de Seguridad para Niños* project has its roots in the Mexican drug war, which as of mid-2010 has cost tens of thousands of lives and has made security in public spaces in Mexico an increasingly hot topic. The government reacted in ways that are familiar to anyone living in Europe or the United States: the security forces presence was increased and video surveillance was implemented. Ultimately, however, these measures do no more than create an appearance of security, and the measures that supposedly ensure that security is maintained place heavy restrictions on freedom in public spaces. The majority of the public welcomes such measures, in the belief that they make them safe. OSA's project was an attempt to make people think critically about this issue. In the Parque de la Revolución in the center of Guadalajara, they built a large cage in the middle of a children's play area—deliberately putting the structure in an "unfavorable" position that made it impossible to use the children's play equipment. Bars were placed to run exactly through the mobile part of the seesaw so that it cannot go up and down. The cage also prevents the basketball hoop from being used. The group's original plan was to come back the next day and painstakingly paint the cage golden, without addressing the issue of the nonfunctional play equipment. In the event, a number of children came along and volunteered to help paint and decorate the cage. The group allowed the residents' response to develop its own dynamic, recognizing that the focus of the participating local population was now on beautifying the golden cage rather than on the security issue.

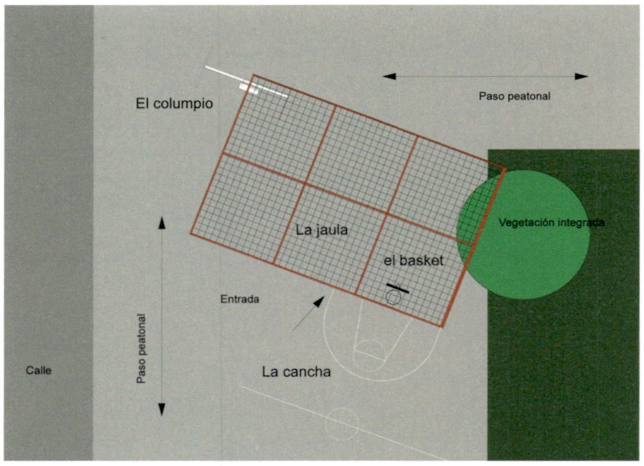

Sitios de Seguridad para Niños
2008, Parque de la Revolución, Guadalajara, Mexico
Drawing by Bernhard Rehn
Photos by Rodrigo Cortés and Oliver Langbein

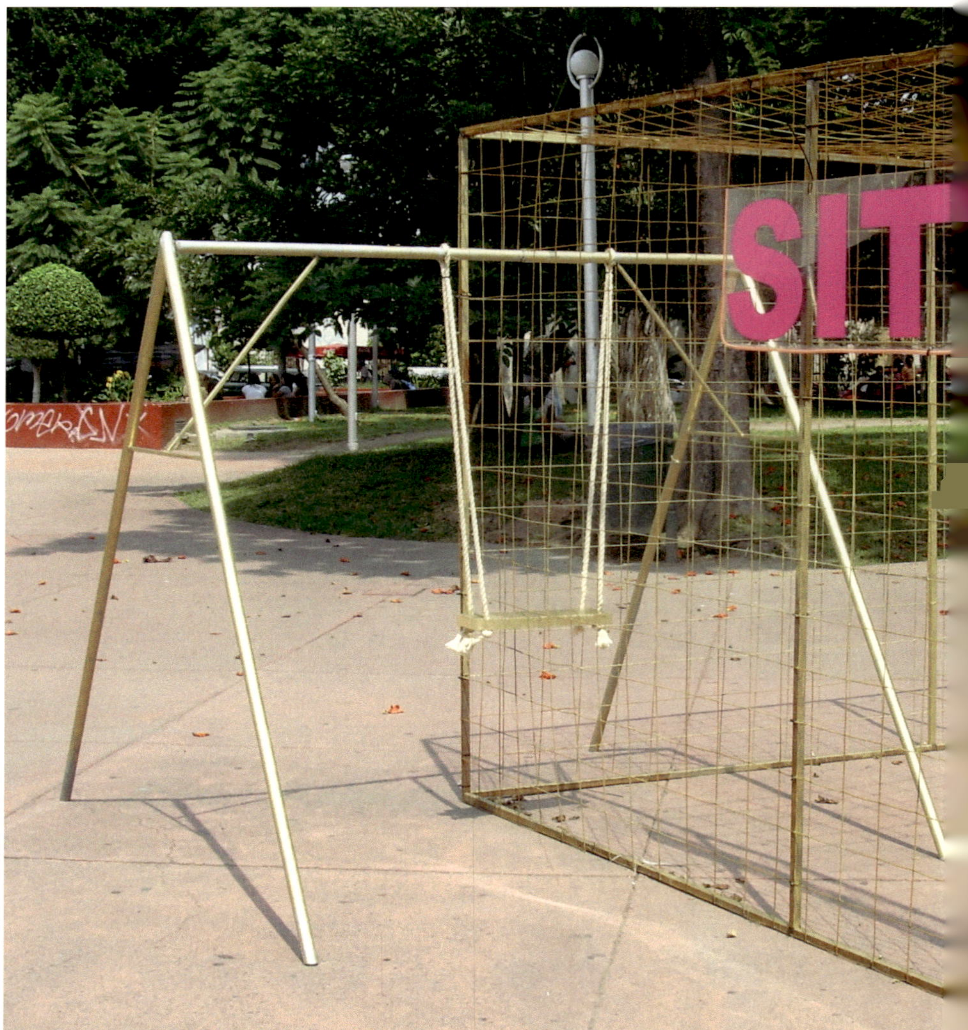

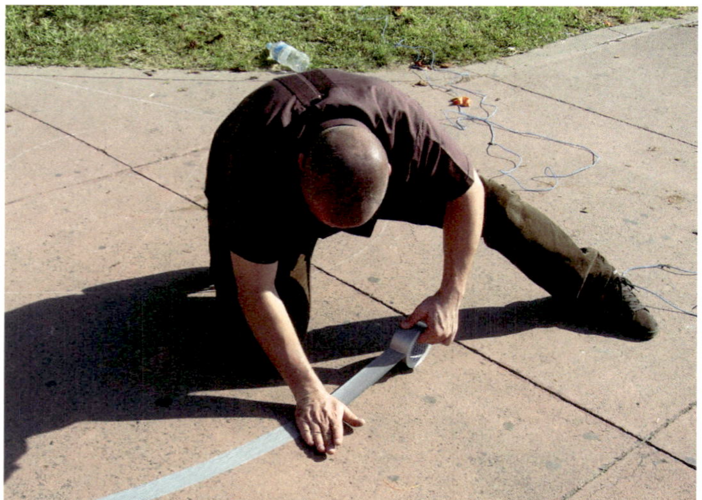

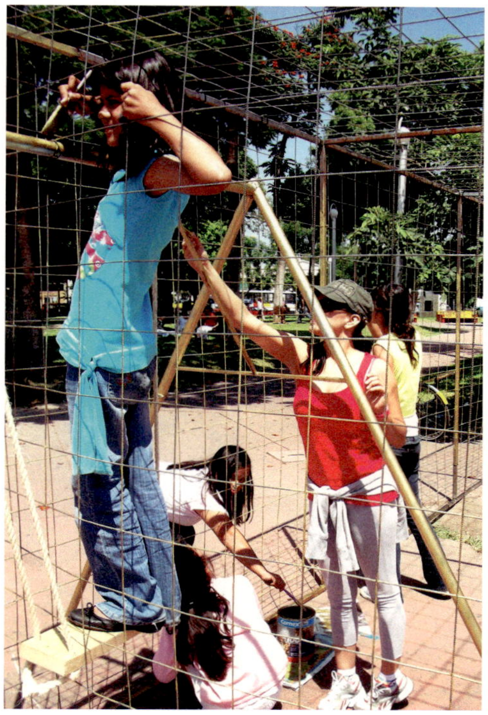

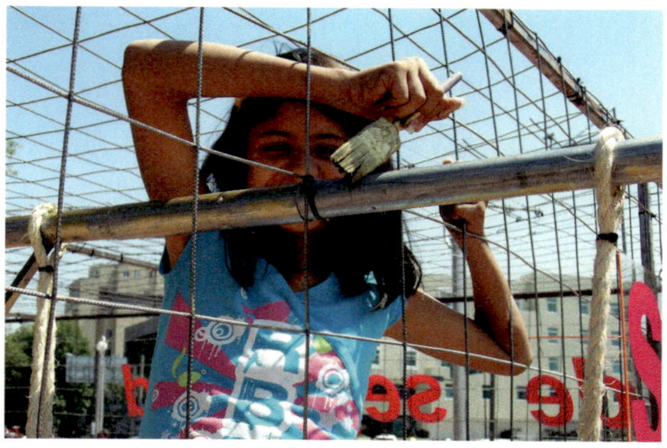

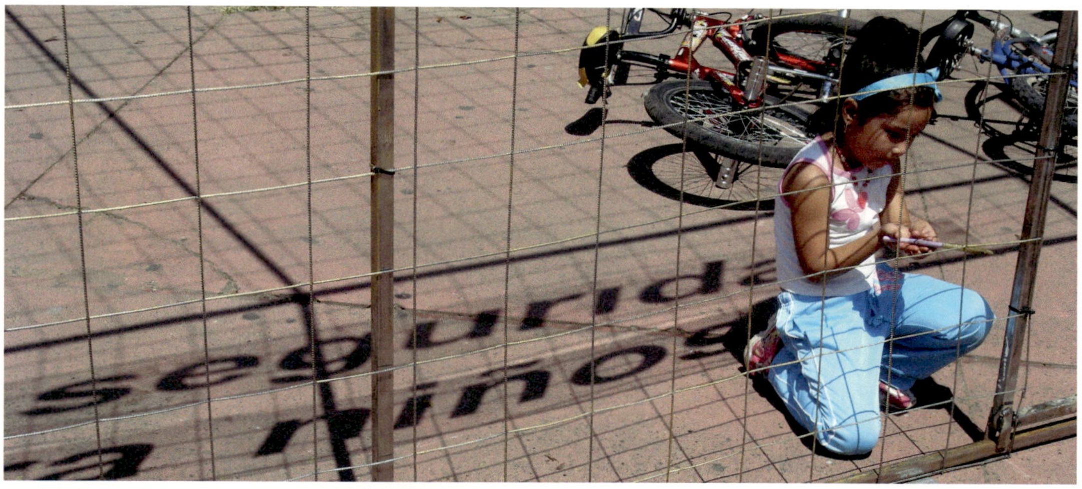

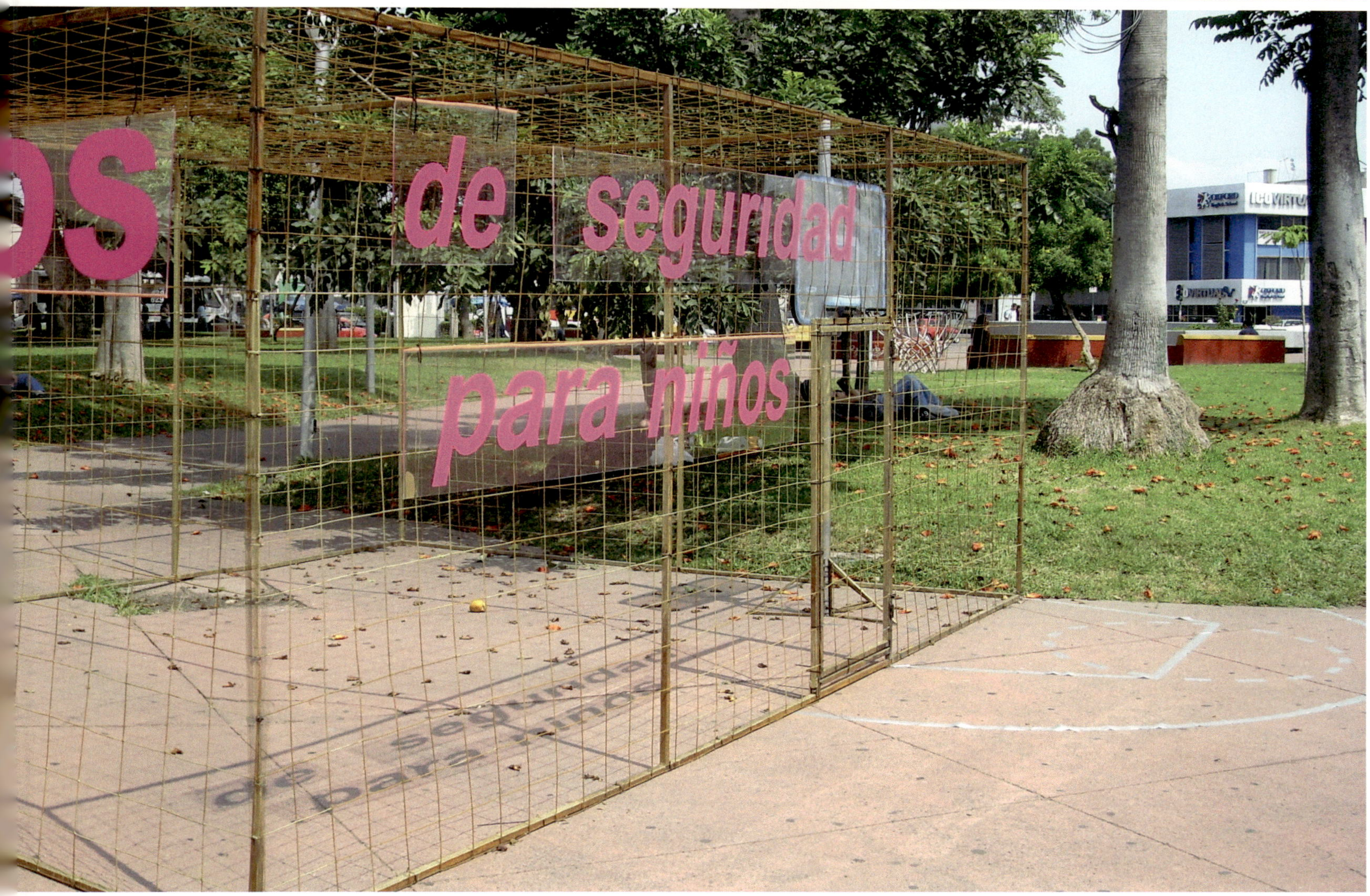
os
de
seguridad
para niños

THINK GLOBAL, ACT LOCAL

TABLE OF CONTENTS

INTRODUCTION

Political art is increasingly appearing in countries and regions plagued by injustice and/or ruled by totalitarian regimes. The artists here reflect these issues in their work. The Russian group Voina [see p. 146], for example, has found its own way of fighting the battle by staging radical and absurd campaigns to attack Russian politics and society. Many of the works presented here, along with their individual statements, can only be understood if viewers possess the relevant background knowledge. However, the artworks, and the contexts that the artists hope they will convey, often attract a wide audience thanks to the internet, where art websites and blogs feature and explain the works. Some of the artists included here, such as Ai Weiwei [see p. 160] and Mona Hatoum [see p. 202], have also become world-renowned by participating in major exhibitions like the documenta in Kassel. Although they appear regularly in international exhibitions, many of them have never taken part in a large exhibition in their home country. This is because strict government censorship in some countries places severe limitations on art. The result is that artists living in those countries frequently have to find their own ways of showing their work. Many of the artists mentioned here have had to struggle with sanctions and curtailment of their artistic freedom. Some of the works have been banned from exhibitions, mostly at the demand of the regime that they targeted. All the artists here have a common desire to use their art to highlight problems that either directly or indirectly affect them. At times they take drastic steps to make themselves and others feel. Serbian artist Milica Tomić [see p. 204] uses wounds on her own body to depict the problems of collective identities, while Regina José Galindo [see p. 198] tells the horrific history of Guatemala in her painful physical performances.

The history of a country is often the artist's own history. The father of the Gao Brothers [see p. 174] was a victim of the Cultural Revolution, and for over 14 years the brothers themselves were not allowed to leave China. Nonetheless, they organized performances worldwide via the internet. Artists like Susan Hefuna [see p. 200] and Mona Hatoum [see p. 202] address the experience of living in several cultures—foreignness in the country where they live and foreignness in their own culture. Others, like Yang Yi [see p. 168] and Jiang Pengyi [see p. 164] illustrate the loss or transformation of their homeland. Street artists JR [see p. 178] and Vhils [see p. 182] use city walls as a canvas for works that are directly linked to the surrounding neighborhood and its history. Moris [see p. 192] uses his diverse work to explore life on the fringes of Mexico City—a life that he lives and experiences himself. All the works here express this insider's perspective and take modern communication far beyond the borders of their home countries.

VOINA GROUP

"Voina" is Russian for "war," and here it is used literally. Oleg Vorotnikov, Natalia Sokol, Alexei Plutser-Sarno, and Leonid Nikolayev form the core of the Voina group, which was founded in 2007. Alexei Plutser-Sarno explains that the campaigns by this collective of artists are "carefully staged military operations." "The Voina activists are romantic heroes of a new epoch, they are new Robin Hoods, who defeat the evil powers. We want a world revolution, carried out by artistic means and without any victim," says Plutser-Sarno. Voina operates aggressively and decisively, but with a keen sense of the absurd, attacking Russian politics and society. The group are opposed to an authoritarian Russia, to corruption, to cronyism, and to a dominant Orthodox church. The group receives no support from any gallery, curator, or private patron—and in the winter of 2008, according to their biography, they were living in an unheated garage in a Moscow suburb. "Instead of boredom and dust, we bring fun into art spaces in the best traditions of carnival medieval art. We revive the lively, expressive, sincere art that makes people have a deep emotional experience. The monumentality and scale harmonize with the rich content—in contrast to the overblown form lacking of content," Plutser-Sarno explains. The group's actions naturally bring them into conflict with the law—two activists are currently remanded in custody. After an action involving a charge of "throwing stray cats around in fast food restaurants," both Voina activists and cats had to spend time in a police station. But the senior police officer refused to use the cats as material evidence of a crime. The intention behind this performance was "to break up the drudgery of (workers') routine workday." In their claim of responsibility, Voina stated that: "Barricades of hamburgers divide the nation, though on both sides of these barricades are people lacking free life and normal food! Besides, cats fly amazingly beautiful, rule with their tails in the flight, land cool, and eat up hamburgers very fast!" Voina favors a mix of anarchy, art, and the absurd. For the event *Cop In A Priest's Cassock,* 2008, Oleg Vorotnikov stole 5 big packs of deli meals from a supermarket—dressed in an Orthodox priest's robe and a policeman's cap. One day before the presidential election, the group held a mass sex orgy in the Timiryazev State Museum of Biology entitled *Fuck for the Heir Medvedev's Little Bear!,* 2008—a reference to the surname of current head of the Kremlin, Dmitri Medvedev ("bear"). They turned several police cars upside down just opposite the entrance of the Russian Museum and called them an art installation (*The Palace Revolution,* 2010). Because of this action, Vorotnikov and Nikolayev have been held in police custody since November 15, 2010; Sokol and Plutser-Sarno are wanted. In a St. Petersburg supermarket, one of their activists stole a chicken by concealing it in her vagina (*Why kill and steal the Chicken? The tale about how the cunt fed Voina!,* 2010). On Che Guevara's birthday, they painted a phallus 65-meter-tall and 27-meter-wide on the Liteiny bascule bridge in Saint Petersburg. The raising of the bridge resulted in an erection pointing directly at the KGB building (*Dick Captured by KGB,* 2010). "Art should be honest, noble and unselfish. And I think that an honest artist just can't paint pussy cats, fishes, and pots with flowers when it's Holocaust at its height. He can't be silent about the horrible crimes that are committed around him," says Plutser-Sarno.

1
Dick Captured by KGB, or
Voina's 65-Metres-High Cock
2010, St. Petersburg, Russia

2
Cock in the Ass,
or Punk Concert in
the Courtroom
2009, Moscow, Russia

2
On May 29, 2009, the Voina Group held an action in federal court during the hearing of the prominent Russian curator, Andrei Yerofeyev, who was being prosecuted for his art exhibitions. The Voina activists secretly carried guitars, microphones, and amplifiers into the courtroom and plugged them into sockets behind the back row of benches. Just after the judge had declared the session open, the activists presented themselves as the punk band Cock in the Ass. They turned the stage equipment up to full volume, jumped onto the benches, and performed their main hit "All Cops are Bastards—You Ought to Remember That!" from the album Fuck the Police Those Motherfucking Bosses.

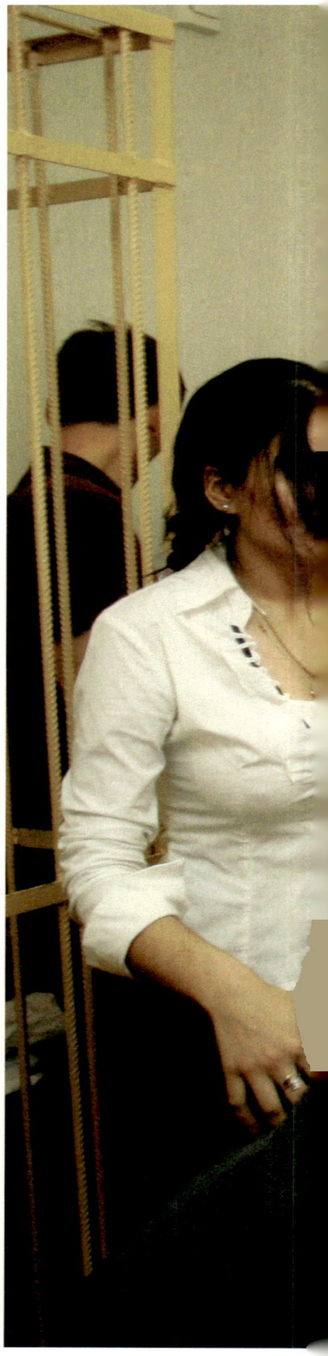

1

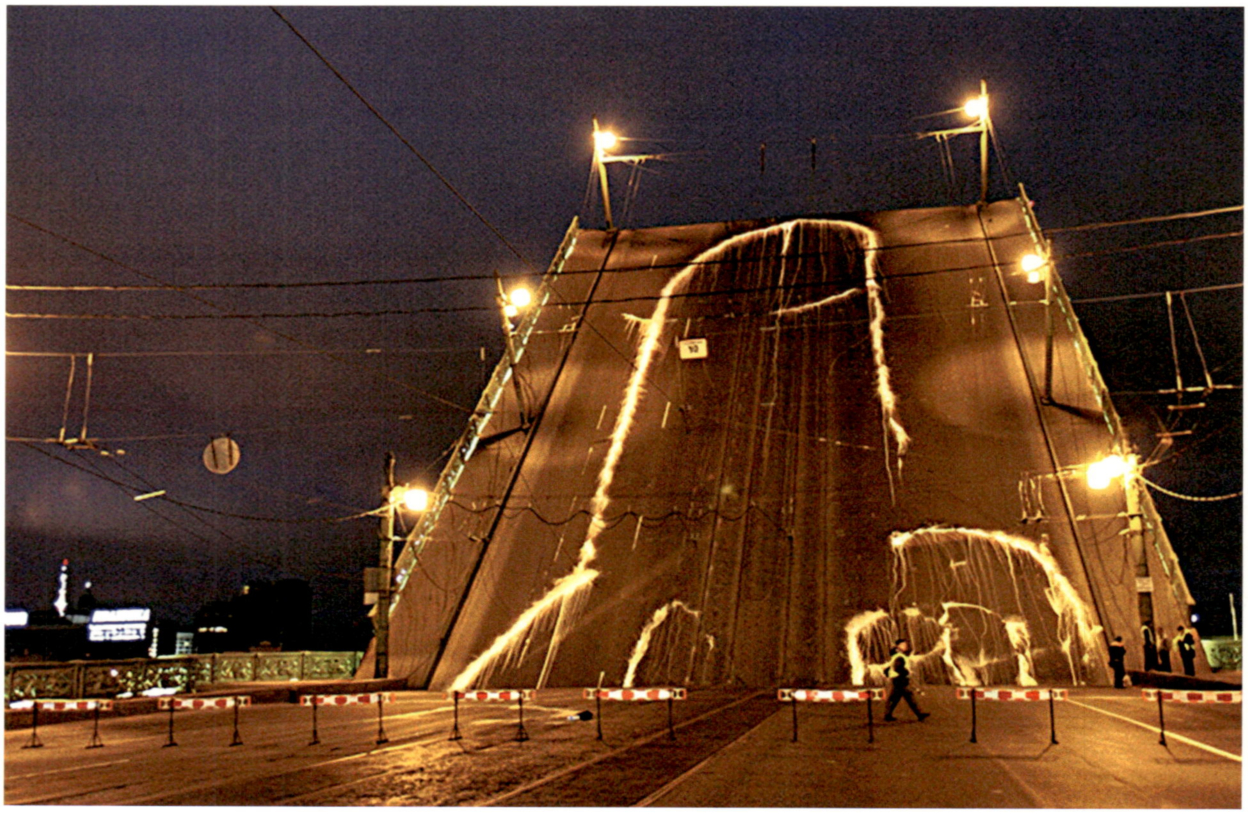

“BARRICADES OF HAMBURGERS DIVIDE THE NATION, THOUGH ON BOTH SIDES OF THESE BARRICADES ARE PEOPLE LACKING FREE LIFE AND NORMAL FOOD! BESIDES, CATS FLY AMAZINGLY BEAUTIFUL, RULE WITH THEIR TAILS IN THE FLIGHT, LAND COOL, AND EAT UP HAMBURGERS VERY FAST!”

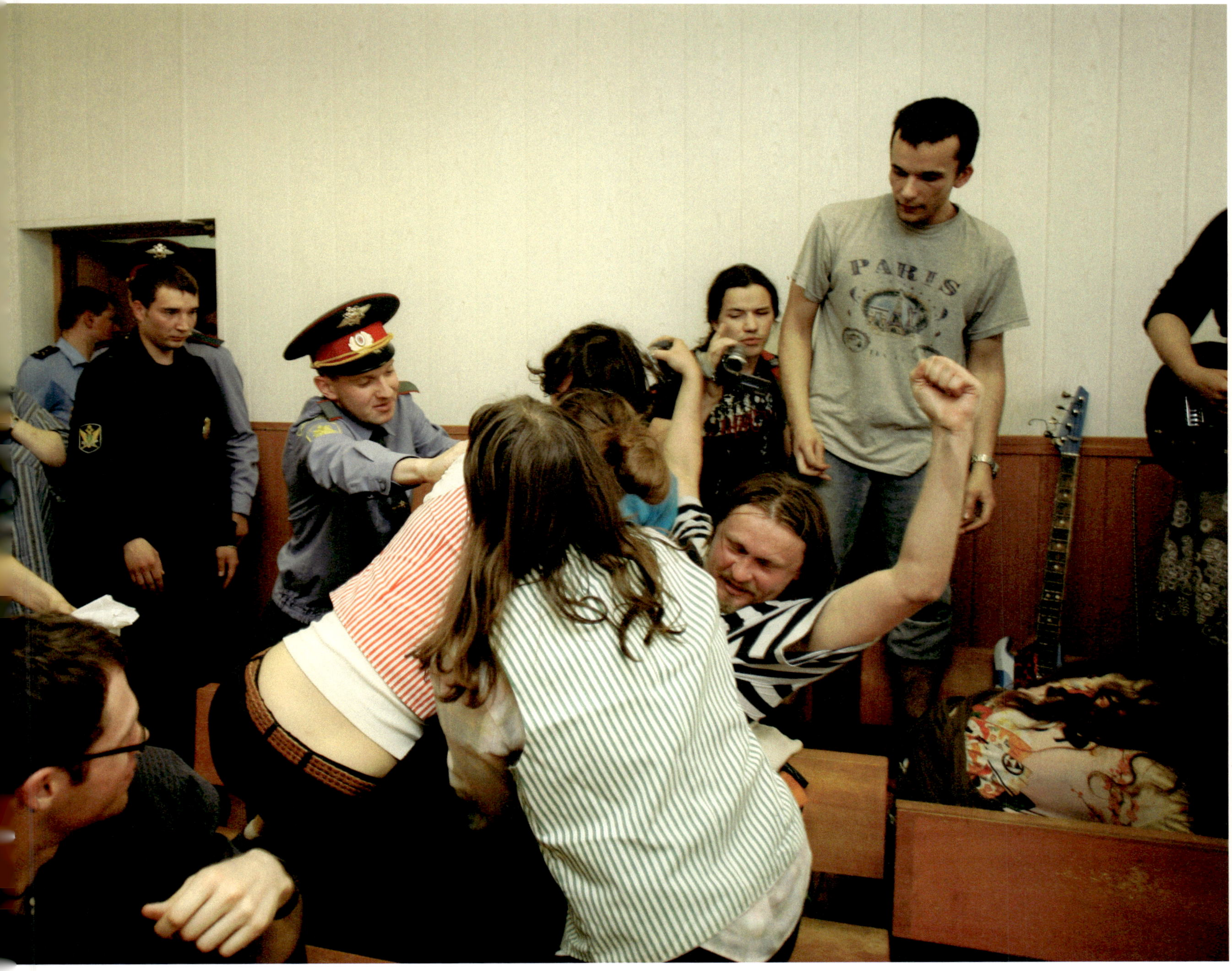

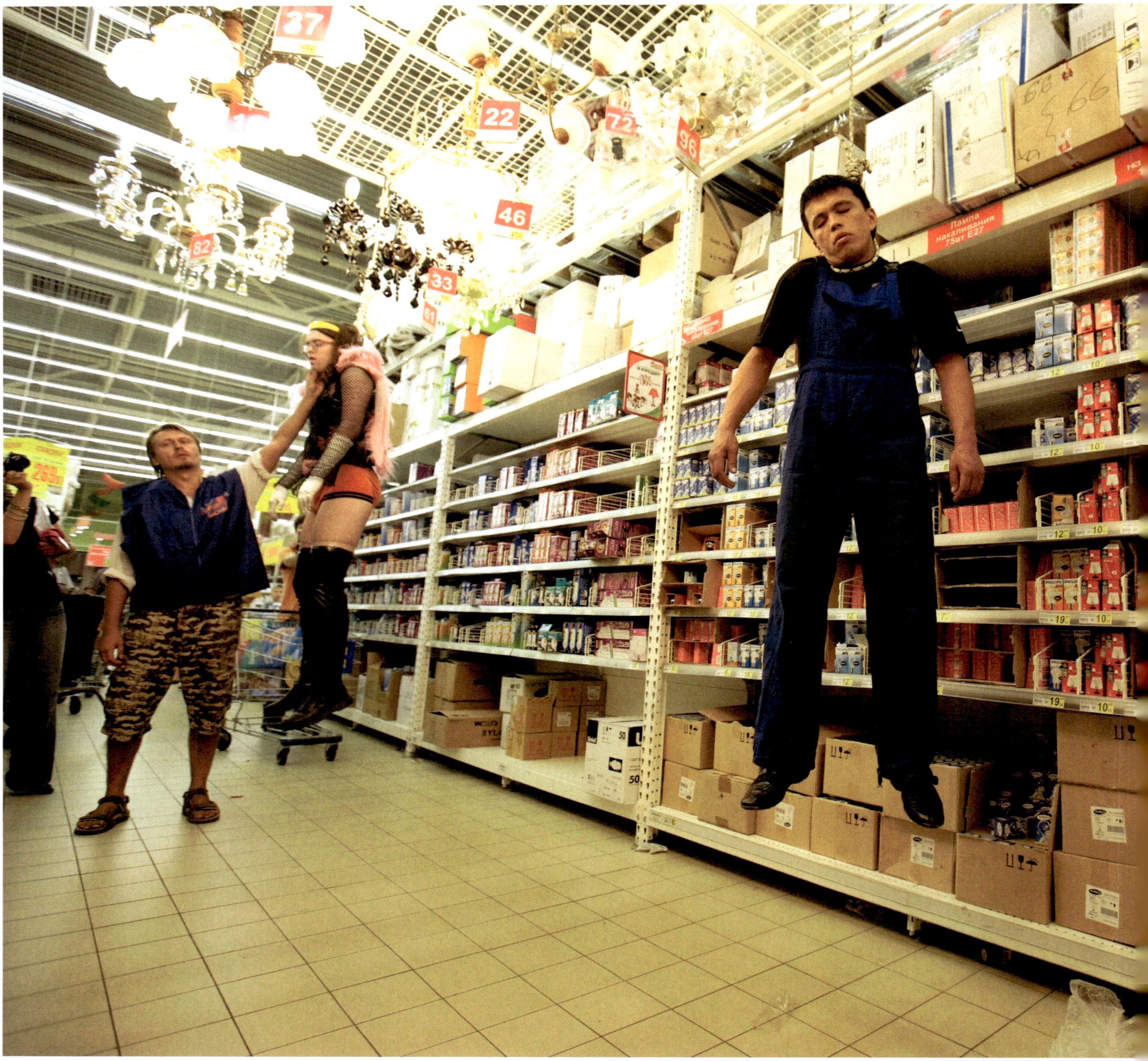

3

On September 7th, 2008—Moscow City Day—the Voina Group went to the "Light" department in the city's biggest supermarket and staged a mock execution by hanging three illegal Central Asian migrant workers and two homosexuals (one of whom was a Jew) in the aisles of the store. The action was aimed at corrupt Russian authorities who incite homophobia, misanthropy, and anti-Semitism. The action, which took place under the slogan "No one gives a fuck about Pestel!", was done as a reminder of five Decembrists--Russian revolutionists, who were hanged in 1826. One of them was the outstanding nobleman Pavel Pestel, who wanted to free the enslaved peasants in Russia. The group wanted to make Russians remember the libertarian ideals of the country's first revolutionists.

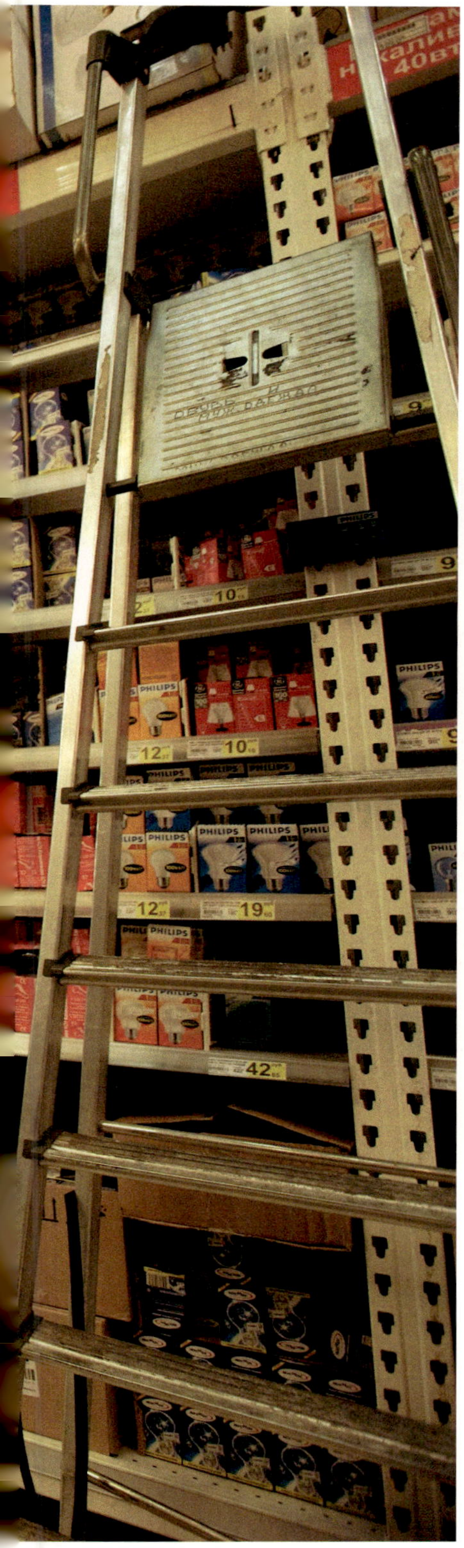

VOINA GROUP

3
Decembrists Commemoration, or Public Execution in the Supermarket
2008, Moscow, Russia

4
FEAST, or Wake in the Metro
2007, Moscow, Russia

5
Palace Revolution, or Beg for mercy, cop!
2010, St. Petersburg, Russia

6 (next spread)
Fuck for the Heir Medvedev's Little Bear!, or Pre-Electoral Bang in the State Museum
2008, Moscow, Russia

5

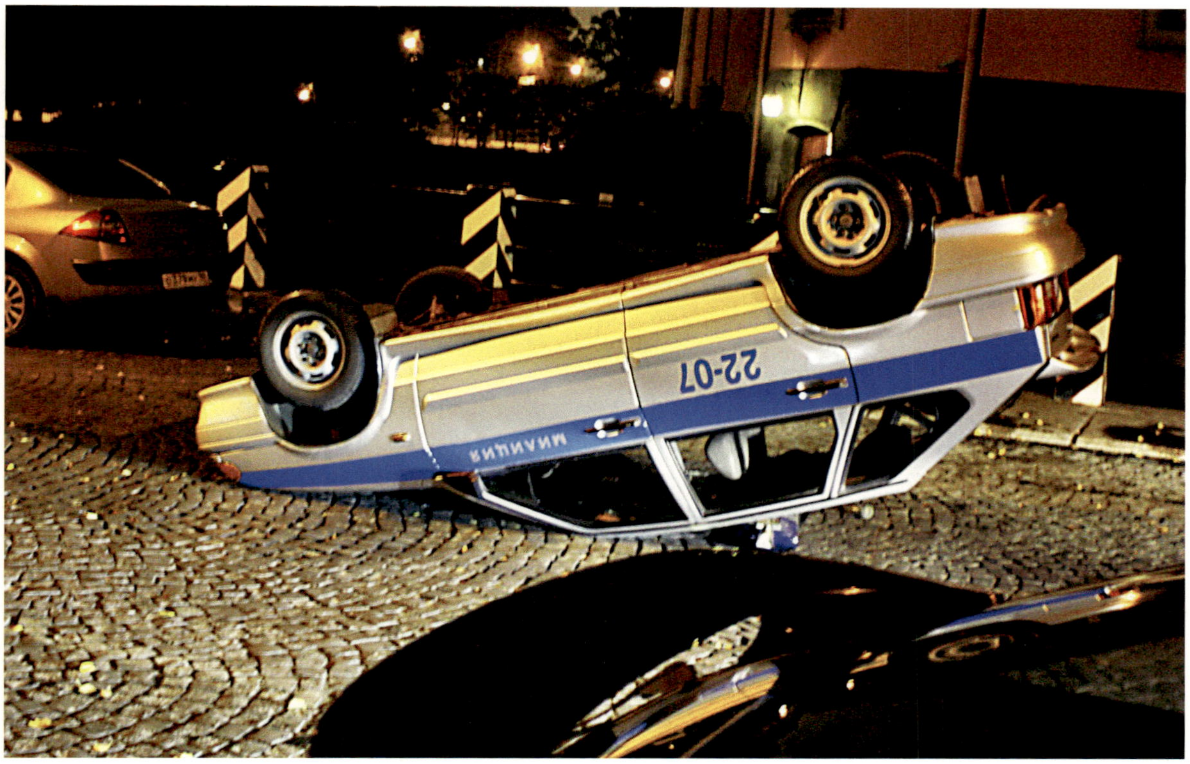

4
On August 24, 2007, on the Circular Line of the Moscow Metro, the Voina Group held a wake for the artist and activist Dmitri Prigov. The event lasted 40 minutes, even though the Circular Line is patrolled by more than 100 armed police officers. At midnight, 50 Voina activists set up a commemorative feast on a long table with vodka, food, plates, and glasses, making a complete round in their friend's memory. The action was repeated in Kiev, where the wake was held on all three lines of the city's subway system, resulting in the Voina activists being arrested on one of the lines. The Kiev City Hall banned the resulting action video from being shown at the local exhibition.

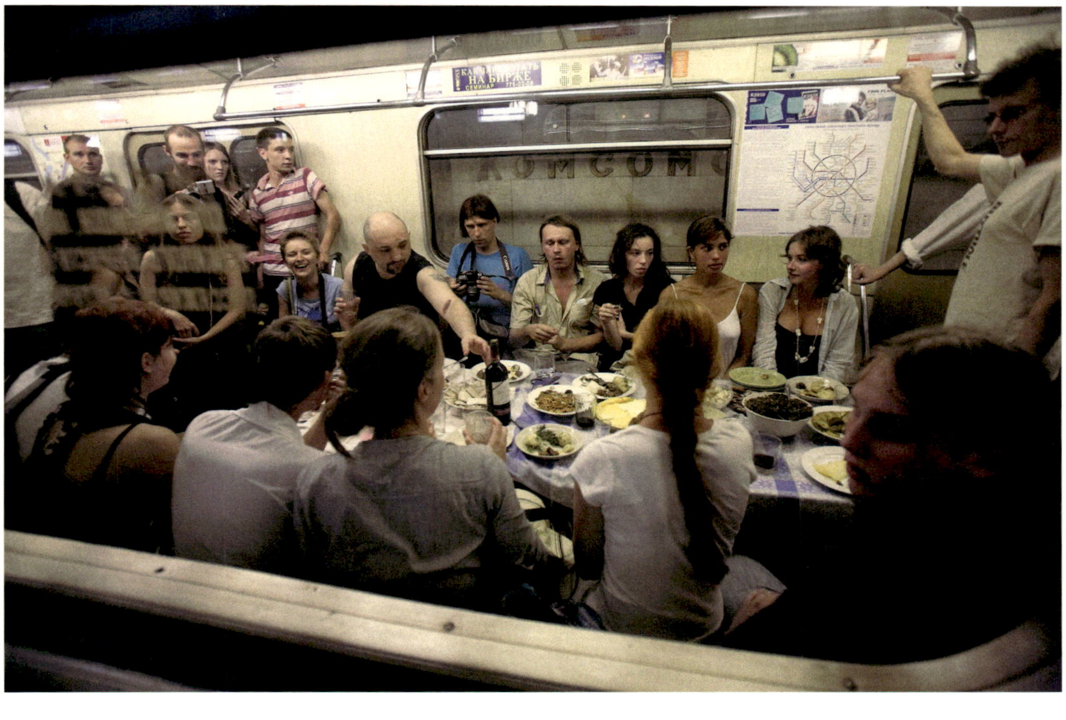

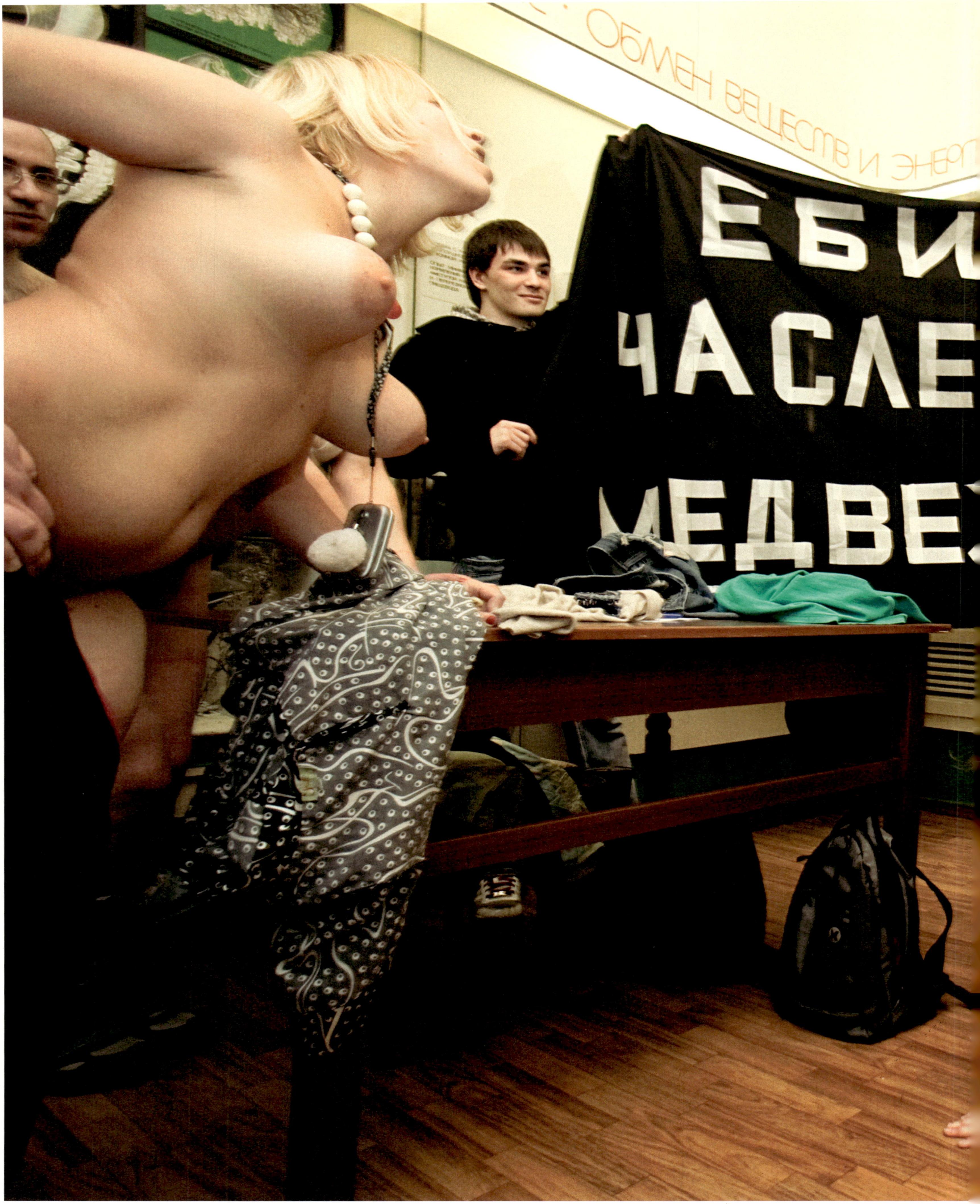
ОБМЕН ВЕЩЕСТВ И
ЕБИ
ЧАСЛЕ
МЕДВЕ

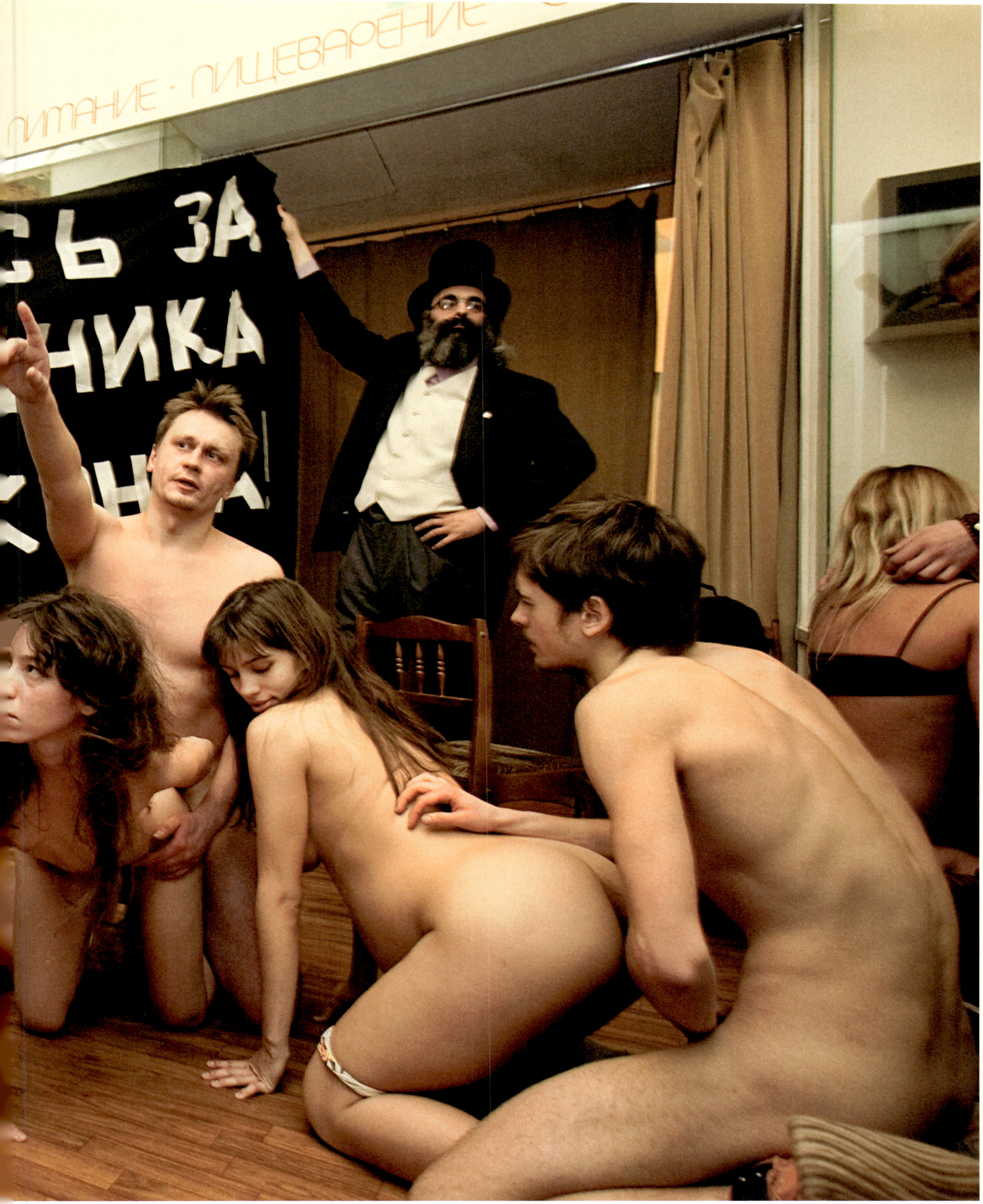
ПИТАНИЕ · ПИЩЕВАРЕНИЕ
СЬ ЗА
НИКА

BLUE NOSES GROUP

The Russian Ministry of Culture stopped the Blue Noses Group's photograph *The Era of Mercy,* 2005, which showed two policemen kissing in the snow, from being exhibited in a Paris exhibition, alleging that it was "pornographic," and "a disgrace to Russia." And, naturally, the duo's collage *Mask Show: Naked Truth,* 2000, which depicted Bush, Bin Laden, and Putin nestling together half-naked on a sofa, also met with protests. Viacheslav Mizin (* 1962), who was born in Novosibirsk, and Alexander Shaburov (* 1965), who was born in Beryozovsky, are the key members of the Blue Noses Group. The name is a reference to the artists' Siberian heritage, and refers to frozen noses. Since forming in 1999, they have been satirically targeting the condition of the Russian soul with "snotty" criticism of the government, through their disrespectful photographs and videos. No one is safe from their blend of adolescent humor and political provocation: they have parodied the Russian mafia, the Orthodox church, politicians, film stars, the mass media, the propaganda of those that are in power, and even classic Russian works of art in their clownish projects. In *Che Guevara 30 Years After (The Revolution Goes On),* 2005, they turned Che Guevara, the revolutionary icon, into an aging, increasingly flabby alcoholic. The duo also took a suprematist composition by the foremost Russian artist, Kazimir Malevich and turned it into *Kitchen Suprematism,* 2005–2006, a composition consisting of black bread and sausages, which were placed on a kitchen table. The pair describe their low-tech art with a predilection for the trash esthetic as, "hooligan improvisation." You can tell that the duo grew up with Marx—but with Groucho rather than Karl. "We try to make fun of things," Mizin explains. "We are destroying dogmas!"

1
NATO Welcome!
2007

2
Che Guevara 30 Years After
(The Revolution Goes On)
2005

3
The Era of Mercy
2005

4
Mask Show: Naked Truth
2000 and 2007

Courtesy Guelman Gallery, Moscow and Galerie Volker Diehl, Berlin

1

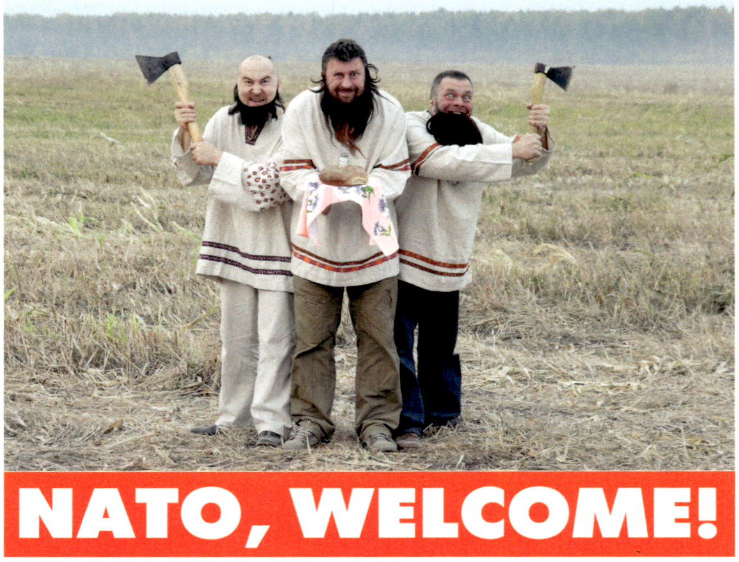

2

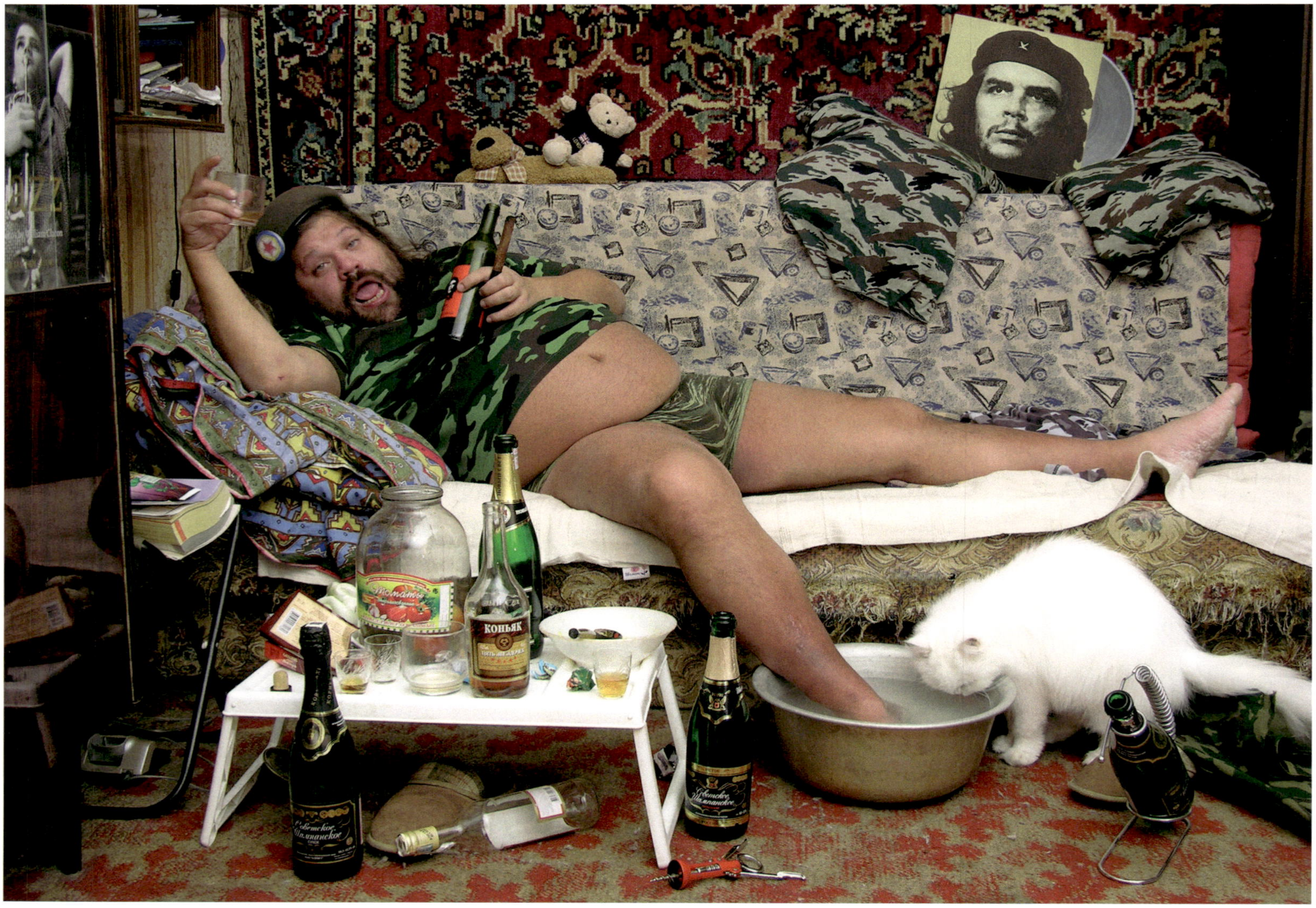

3

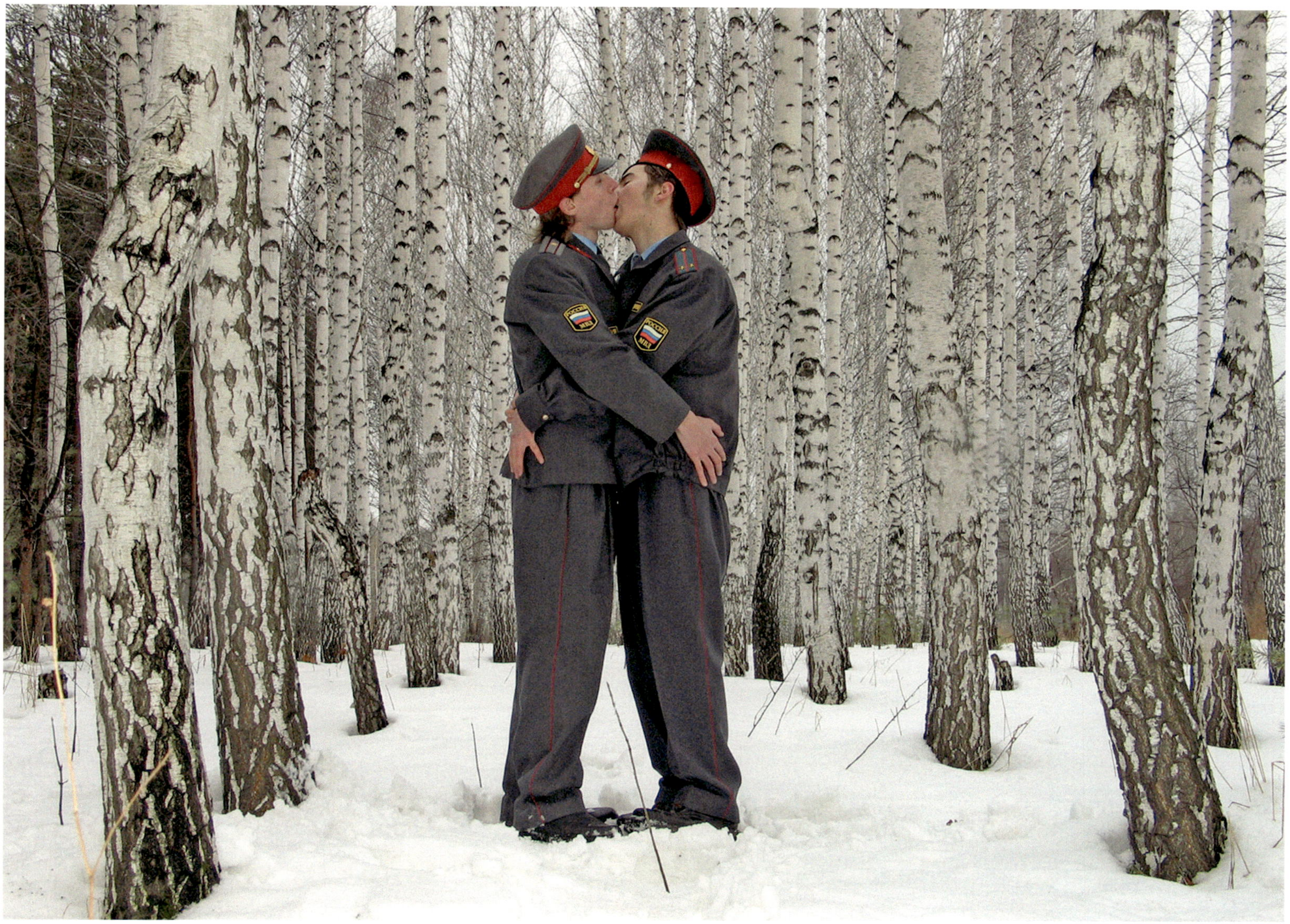

4

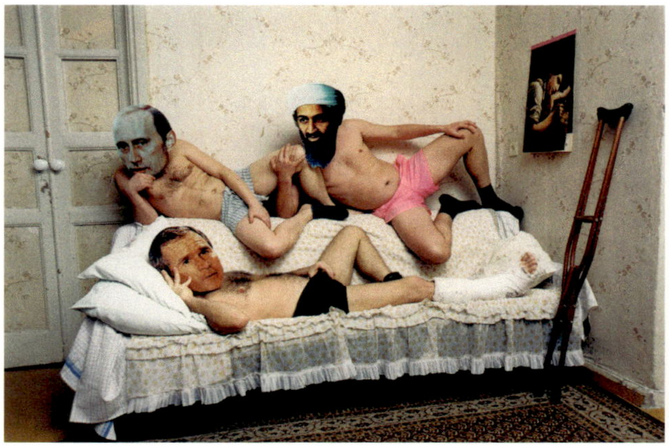

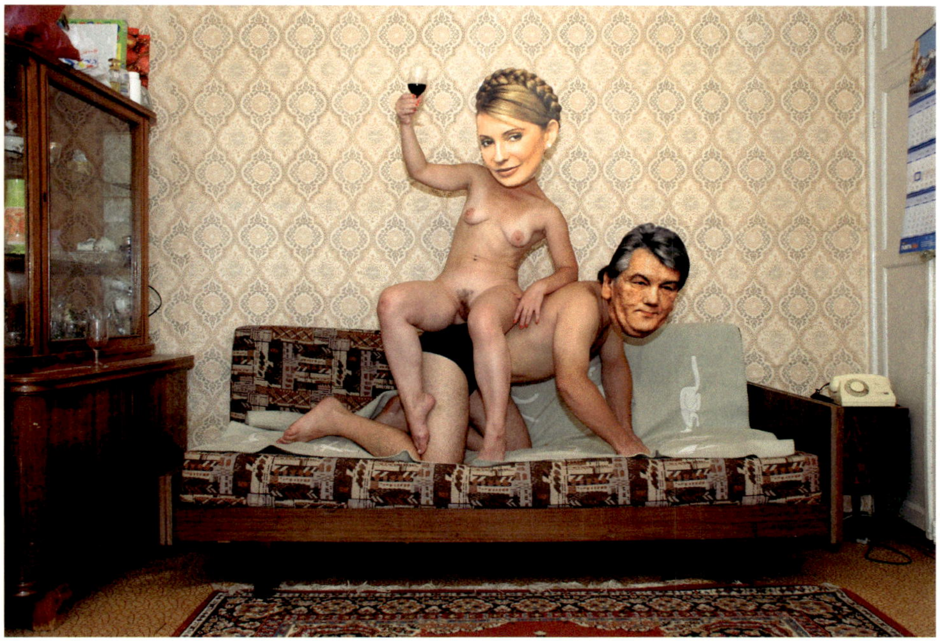

HAN BING

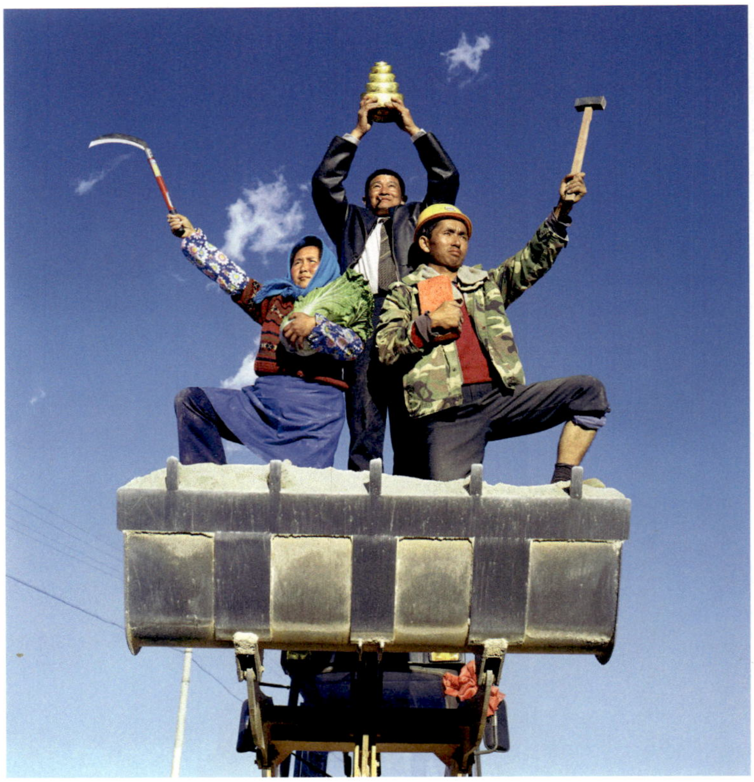

1

In his photographs, videos, performances, and installations, Han Bing (* 1974), who was born in Jiangsu, China, thematizes conflicts in today's China. "I want to make art that engages with the world, that takes a look at how our world is being made, and how it's making us. Specifically, processes of social development and so-called 'modernization' have influenced my work a great deal," says Han. "I am interested in the formations of people's dreams, individually and collectively, in the lies we're told, as well as the lies we tell ourselves." Born in a poor, rural region, and going on to become an art student in Peking, Han Bing has experienced his nation's contradictions, problems, and its furious modernization, globalization, and urbanization for himself. He likes to use a cabbage as a metaphor for a lapdog: since 2000, he has been taking a cabbage for a walk as part of his *Walking the Cabbage* performance. The cabbage—a multigenerational symbol of identity in China—used to be the rural population's staple diet and was essential for surviving long winters. People with a large supply of cabbages were considered well-off. Having a dog and having time to take it for walks, to play with it, and feed it is the new status symbol in China today. Rather than making fun of the cabbage, Han is creating a homage to it. "The objects—shovels, cabbages, bricks, and the like—that I imbue with love in my work are not usually seen as glamorous, sexy, or precious things. But they sustain the lives of so many people worldwide." In his project *New Culture Movement,* 2006, families, workers, and children stand in front of half-finished houses, proudly holding a red brick in their hands. The brick has replaced Mao's book, and is used to suggest that the communist dream has given way to a capitalist dream. For Han, the brick is the new manifesto of the current age. Building a home of one's own represents the desire for a new beginning, for a place where one belongs, and for more material wealth. In *Age of Big Construction,* 2006, and *Theater of Modernization,* 2007, the artist uses bulldozers and construction vehicles to create a presentation, in which destruction collides with construction. In the jaws of the bulldozer, opposite ends of society come together; peasants, workers, intellectuals, soldiers, and the nouveau riche are united, looking as if they are trying to stage a comic revolutionary opera. "Because the question I'm investigating revolves around the struggles, desires, and predicaments of ordinary people in what I call 'the theater of Chinese modernization,' in this series, I use a 'dialectic of opposites' to try to create a conceptual and visual space for overcoming," he explains. "Seducing machines of demolition and urban construction, I use the warmth and fragility of my flesh to neutralize the frigid machine of China's frenzied campaign of 'modernization,' I use fluffy cloud-like clumps of cotton to hold up tons of steel, and I use love to heal the violence of 'modernization.'"

1
Theater of Modernization/
The Nouveau Riche Leads
the People 1 & 2
2007, China

2
The Walking
the Cabbage Movement
2008, Manchester, U.K.
Performance/video

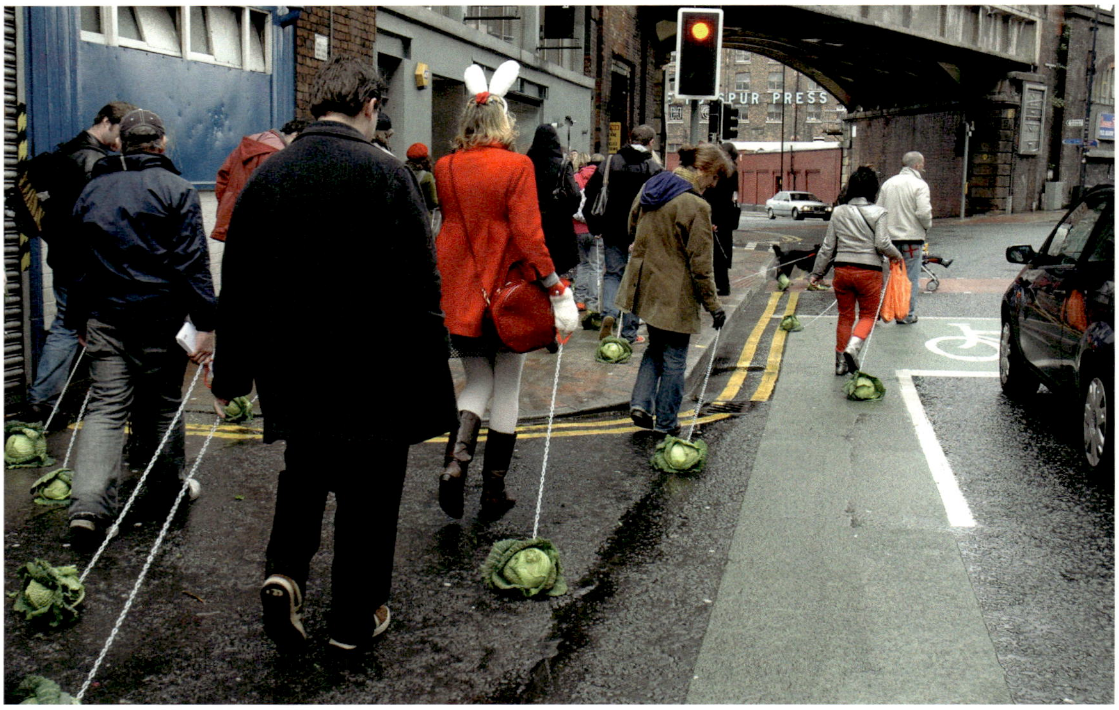

2

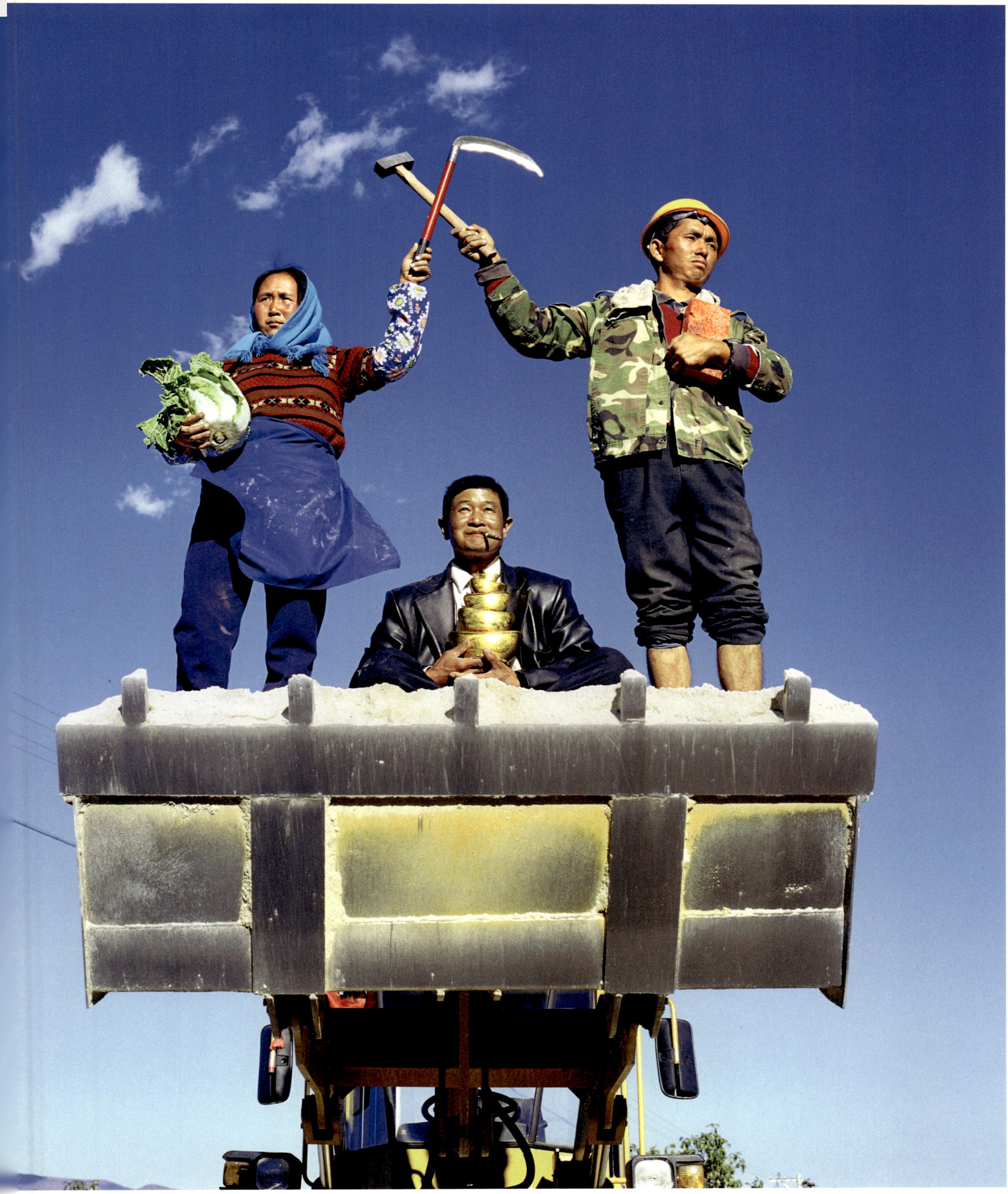

3

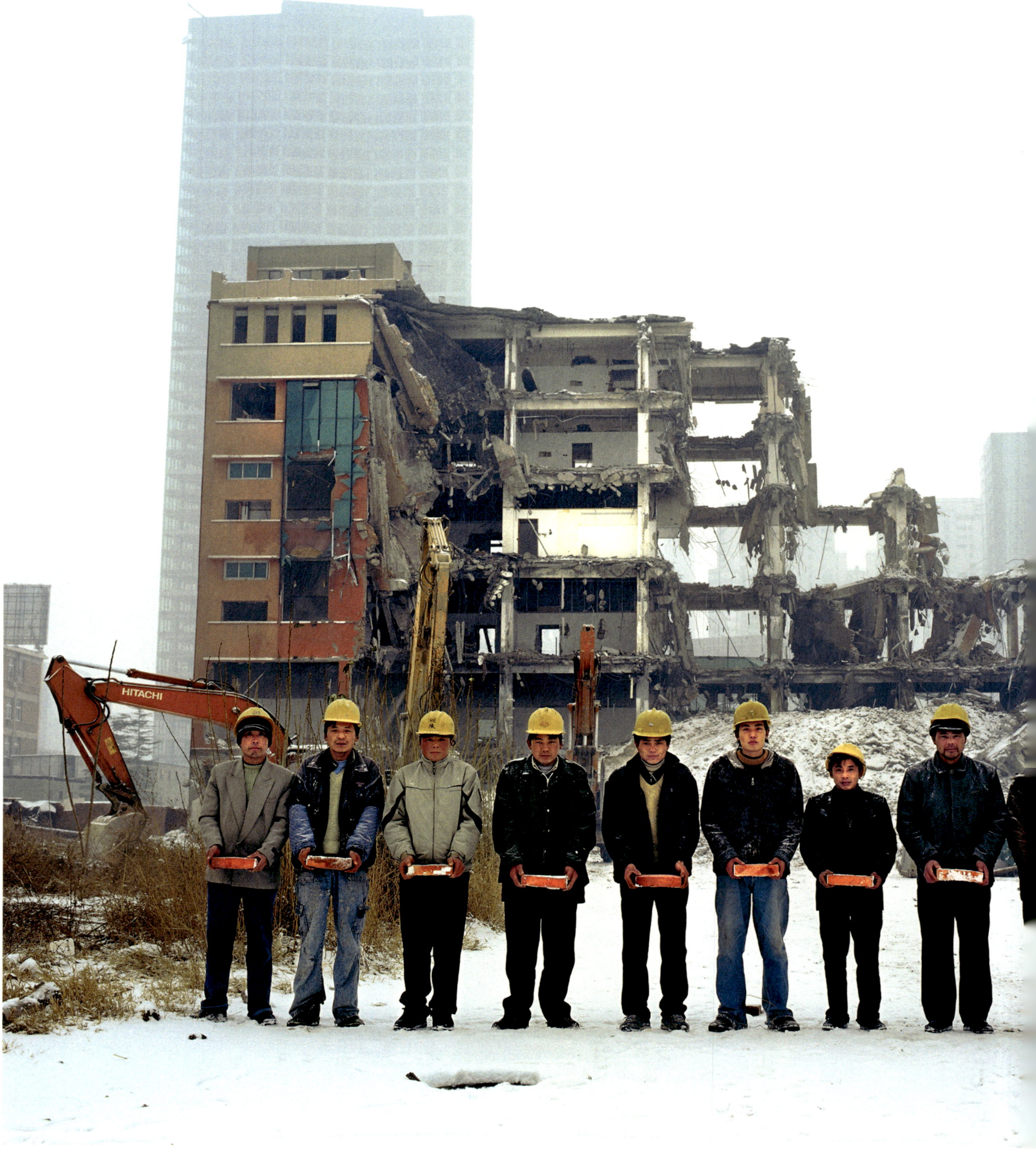

"I WANT PEOPLE TO QUESTION THE DEFINITION OF 'NORMAL PRACTICE' AND TO REFLECT ON HOW MUCH OF OUR DAILY LIVES ARE ROUTINES WE'VE BLINDLY ABSORBED"

3
Superfluous Remnants of an Already Backward Modernity
Everyday Precious, No. 2
2004, China

4
New Culture Movement
2006, China

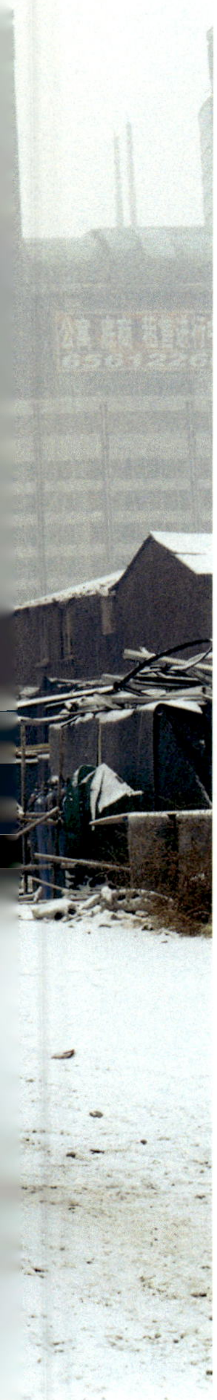

4

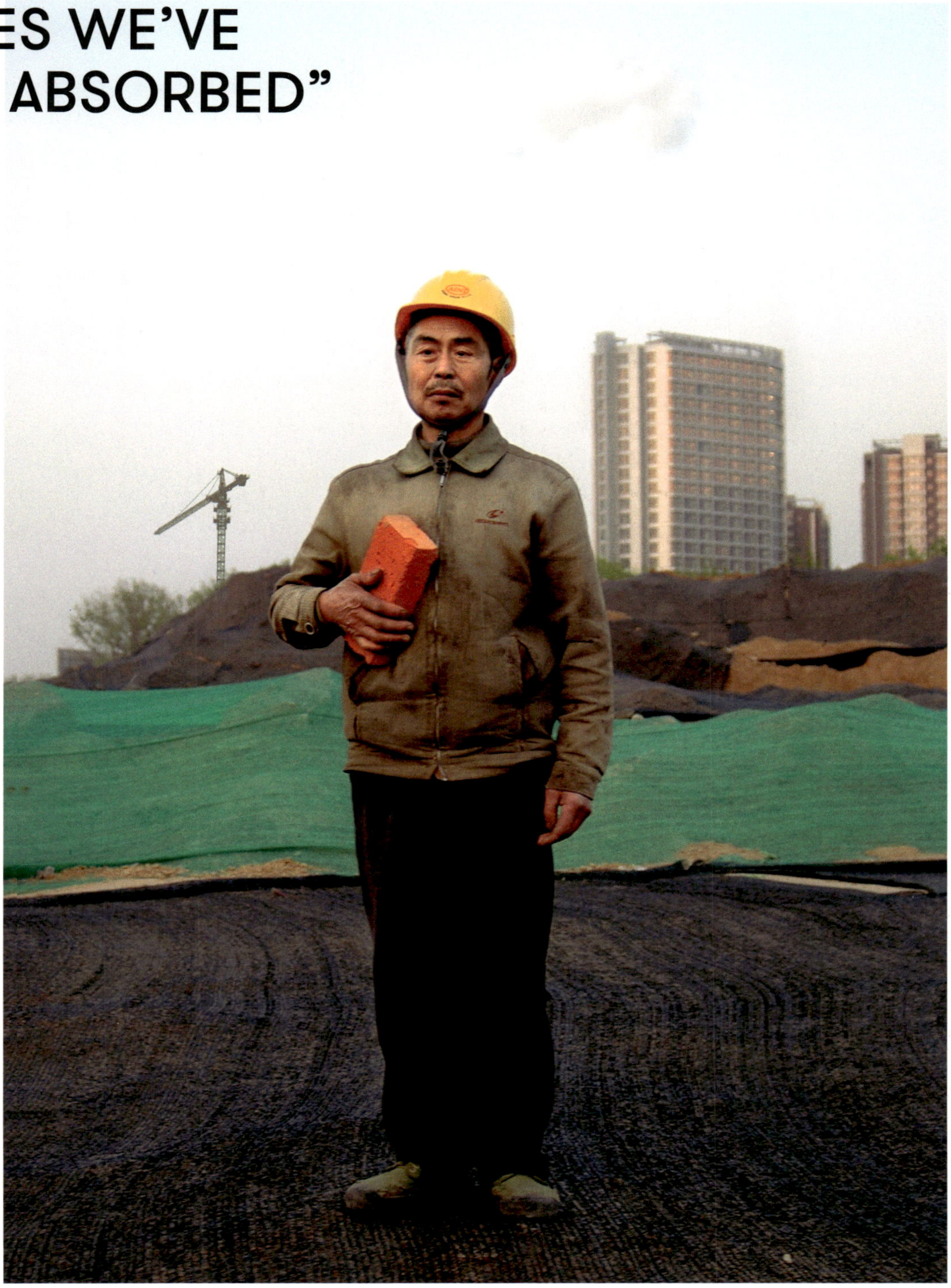

LI WEI

Sometimes the Bejing-based performance artist Li Wei (* 1970), who was born in Hubei, China, plunges headfirst into asphalt and sometimes he seems to plunge from a dizzying height. His photographs, which are not without a certain comical touch and make no attempt to hide their borrowings from comic books, are also political statements by an artist who gave up studying painting to live and work in Bejing's famous and notorious East Village artist colony in the mid-1990s. In his extreme, metaphorically charged presentations, the artist is trying to reveal the situation that humanity—the Chinese people in particular—find themselves in today due to the reason-defying processes of change that are a consequence of globalization. One of his earliest pieces, *Green Guy • Flag,* 1999, shows the artist painted green from head to toe against the background of a red flag. Li Wei explains that: "The key thing is the amount of effort needed to reach the flag. This is the force we need to defend our personal scope of freedom. The work is an homage to human resolve, which is what the color red is about here. It has nothing to do with the Chinese national color."

One of his most successful performance series is *Falls,* which he embarked on in 2002. Photographs show the artist with his head and upper body stuck into a road, an expanse of ice, and the roof of a ruined house. His legs are pointing straight up at the sky. These are not pictures created on a computer; an enormous amount of physical effort was required, although the artist did make use of a support construction. He considers it vital to achieve this physical attitude through his own physical effort and to thereby have a direct physical experience of the absurdity of the situation. "If you picture someone falling to earth from another planet, there would really be no soft landing, whether the landing were in China or in another part of the world. This feeling of having fallen headfirst into the unknown and of having nothing firm under one's feet is familiar to everyone. One doesn't have to actually fall from another planet to feel that way."

1
Flag. Venezia
2005, Venice, Italy

2
Green Guy • Flag
1999, Bejing, China

3
25 Levels of Freedom
2004, Bejing, China

4
Pain of the World 1
2006, Madrid, Spain

1

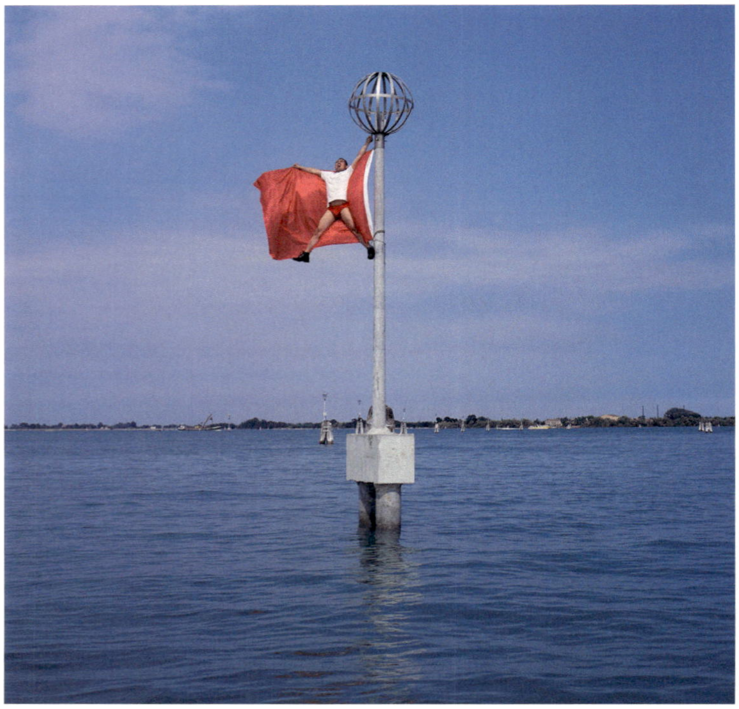

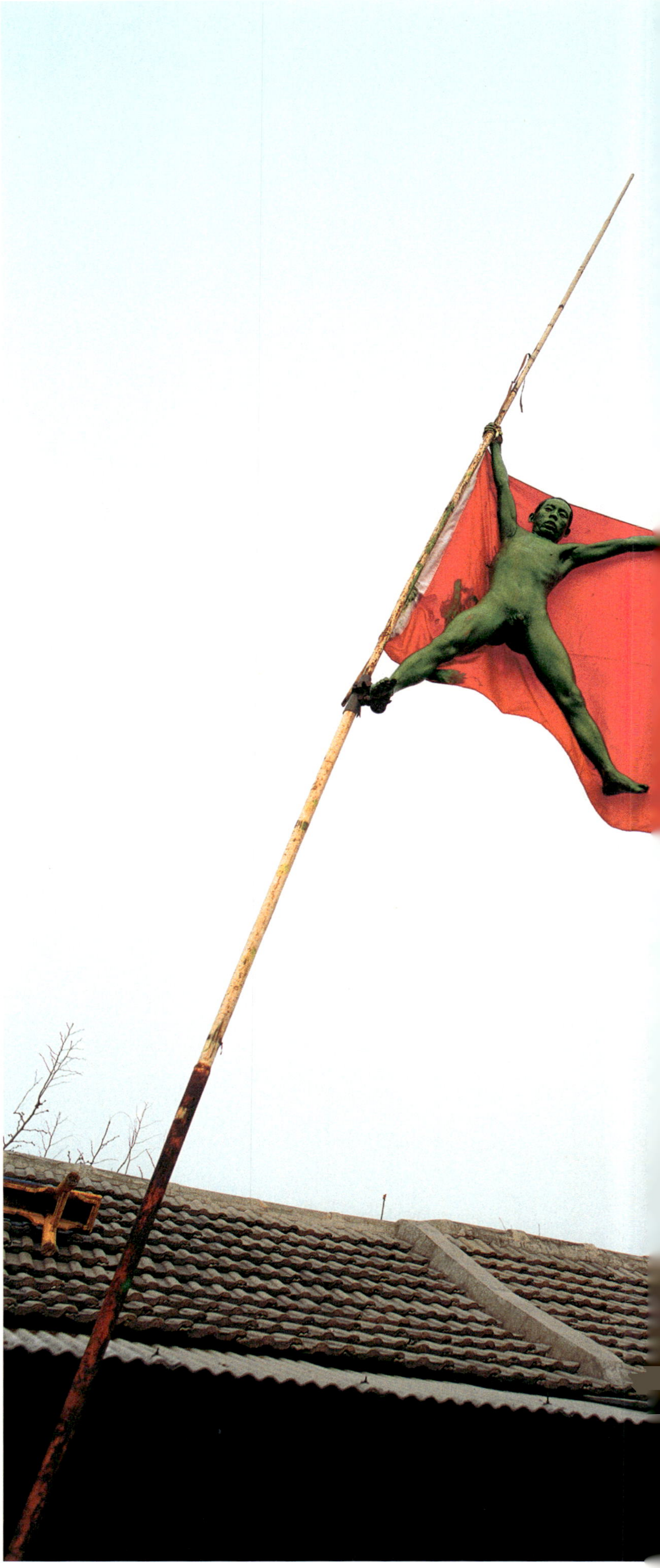

2

3

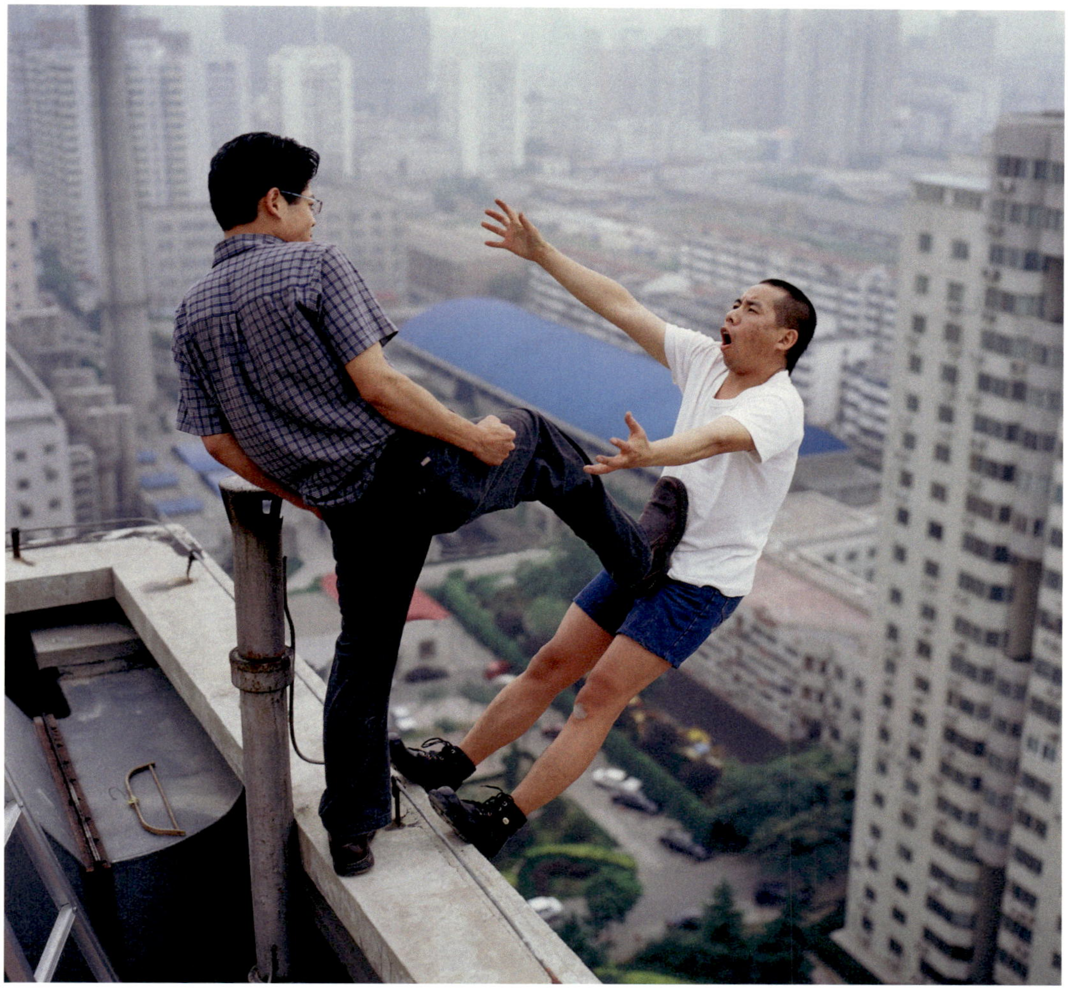

4

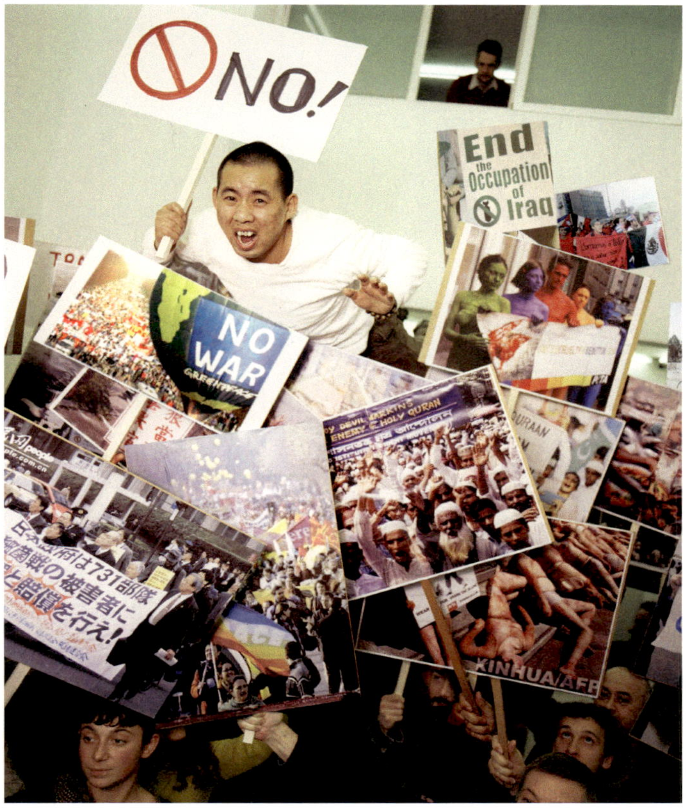

AI WEIWEI

1
Cao Ni Ma
2009
2
Ai Weiwei with rockstar Zuoxiao Zuzhou in the elevator when taken in custody by the police, Sichuan, China, August 2009
3
Fairytale
2007, Kassel, Germany
4
Remembering
2009, Backpacks and metal structure approximately 920 × 10.605 cm

Conceptual artist Ai Weiwei (* 1957) has been aware of the hazards of Chinese politics since he was a small boy. When he was ten years old, his father, the Chinese poet and government critic Ai Qing, was exiled, and as punishment had to clean public toilets. From 1981 to 1993, Ai lived in the United States, mainly in New York. He graduated from the Parsons School of Design and, after learning that his father was seriously ill, returned to China. Since then, he has been vocal in calling for a democratic and free China. He uses art to campaign for freedom of speech, and for free access to information, criticizing human rights violations, economic exploitation, and environmental pollution. "From a very young age I started to sense that an individual has to set an example in society," says Ai. "Your own acts and behavior tell the world who you are and at the same time what kind of society you think it should be." When the artist tried to investigate the disastrous Sichuan earthquake of 2008—whose 80,000 casualties included a large number of schoolchildren whose deaths were probably due to the corrupt and substandard construction of school buildings—he was attacked by police and suffered a cerebral hemorrhage. He used this issue as the basis for his exhibition in the Haus der Kunst in Munich, placing children's backpacks against the building's outer façade to form the sentence: "She lived seven happy years on this earth." The phrase is taken from an e-mail that Ai received from the mother of a girl who died when a school collapsed. His current installation *Sunflower Seeds,* 2010–2011, in London's Tate Modern gallery involves 100 million hand-painted sunflower seeds made from porcelain. This poetic installation is heavily symbolic. In Communist Party propaganda, the sun was the emblem of Mao Zedong, with the people of China as the seeds. At the same time, sunflower seeds were also the most important staple food in China. In the famine of the late 1950s alone, more than 30 million Chinese people died. Ai's sunflower seeds are a metaphor for China's social and political problems; they are a treatment of history. This is conceptual art as an act of remembrance.

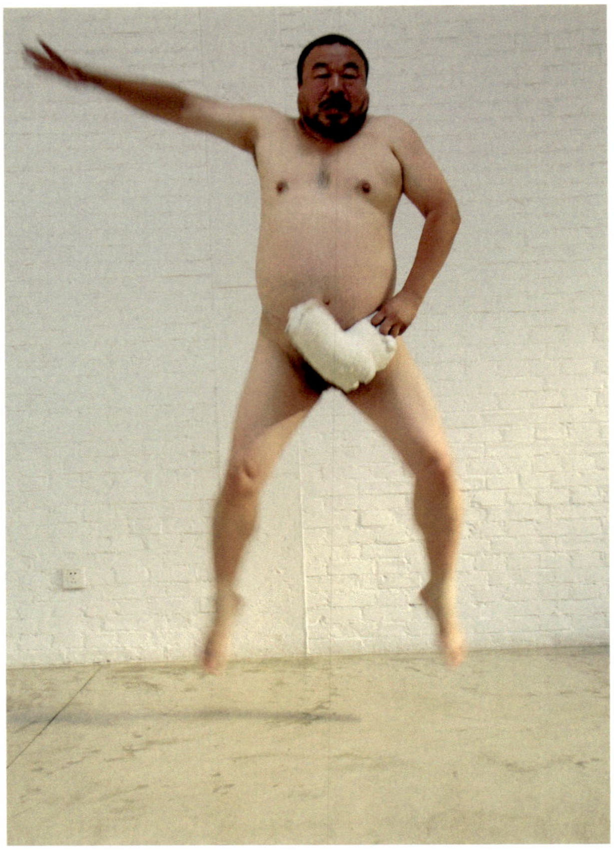

1
Ai's naked jump is a double mockery of the internet censors in China, who use porn identification software, which bloggers realized did not recognize many nude images—but on the other hand would single out images of swimmers or Garfield comics. The stuffed animal serving as Ai's maple leaf is itself an icon of the Chinese blogger rebellion. Although it looks like a cute pony, it is a fictitious creature named Cao Ni Ma, which literally translates to "grass mud-horse." When it is pronounced, however, it sounds like a swear word promoting having sex with one's own mother.

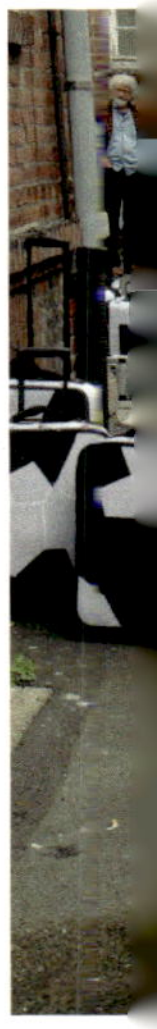

4

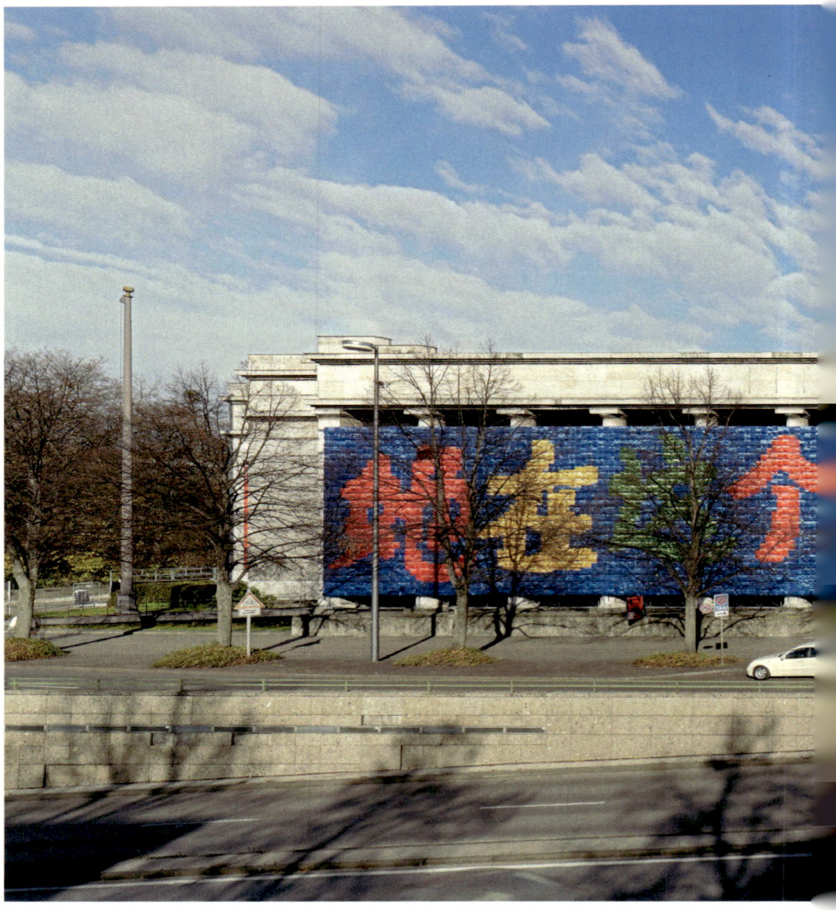

2

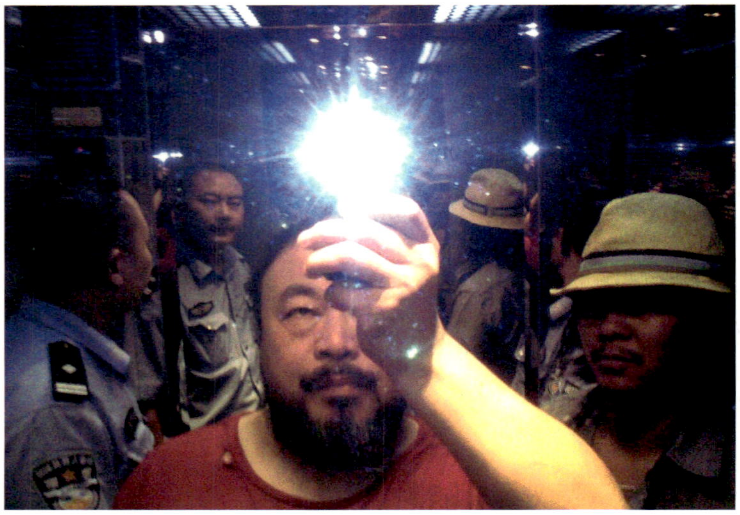

3

1,001 Chinese people were the focal point of *Fairytale*. They traveled to Kassel for the documenta 12, viewed the exhibition, and became part of a euro 3.1 million piece with social, political, and cultural components. Candidates who would normally not be able to travel overseas because of financial reasons were chosen for the project.

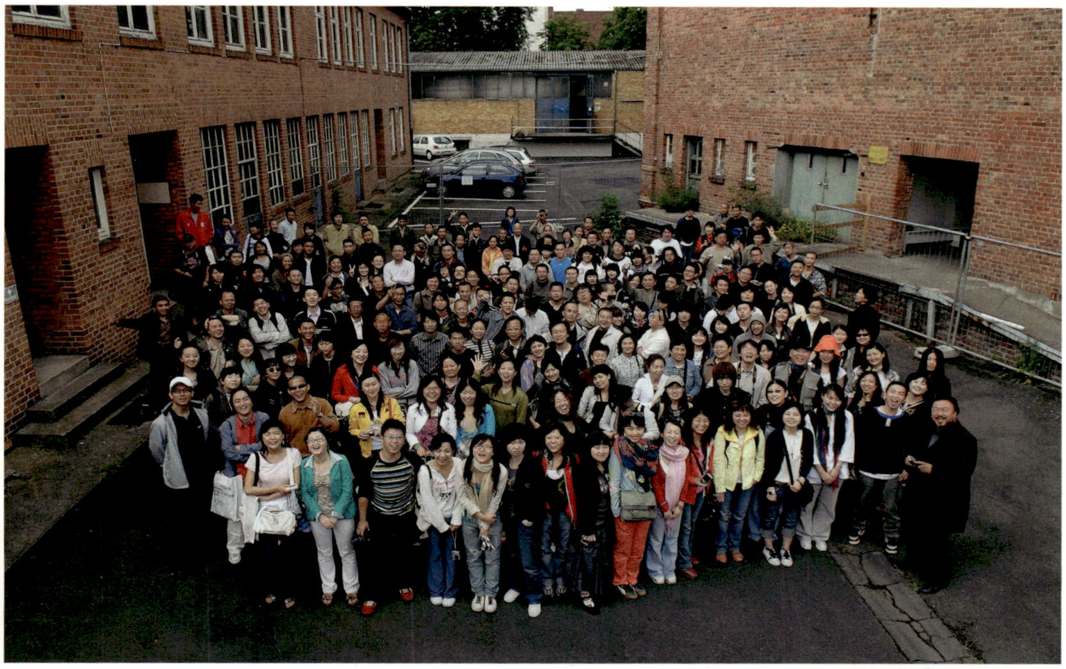

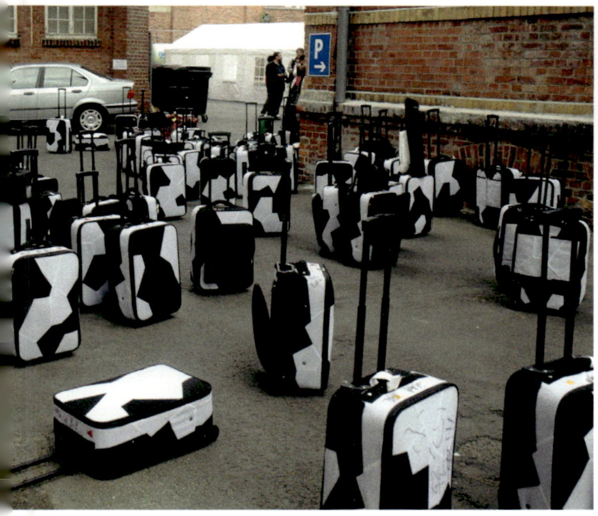

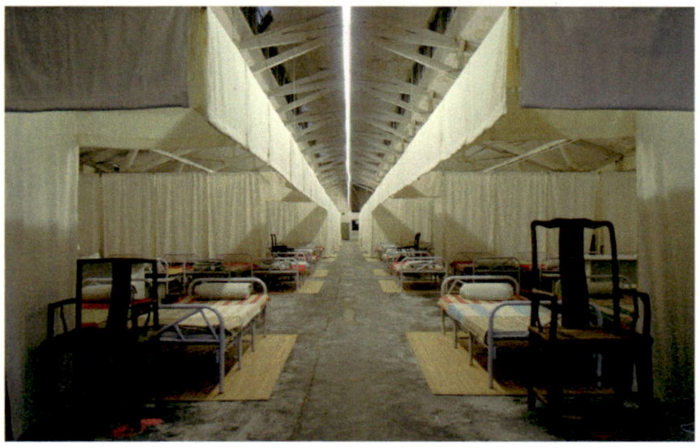

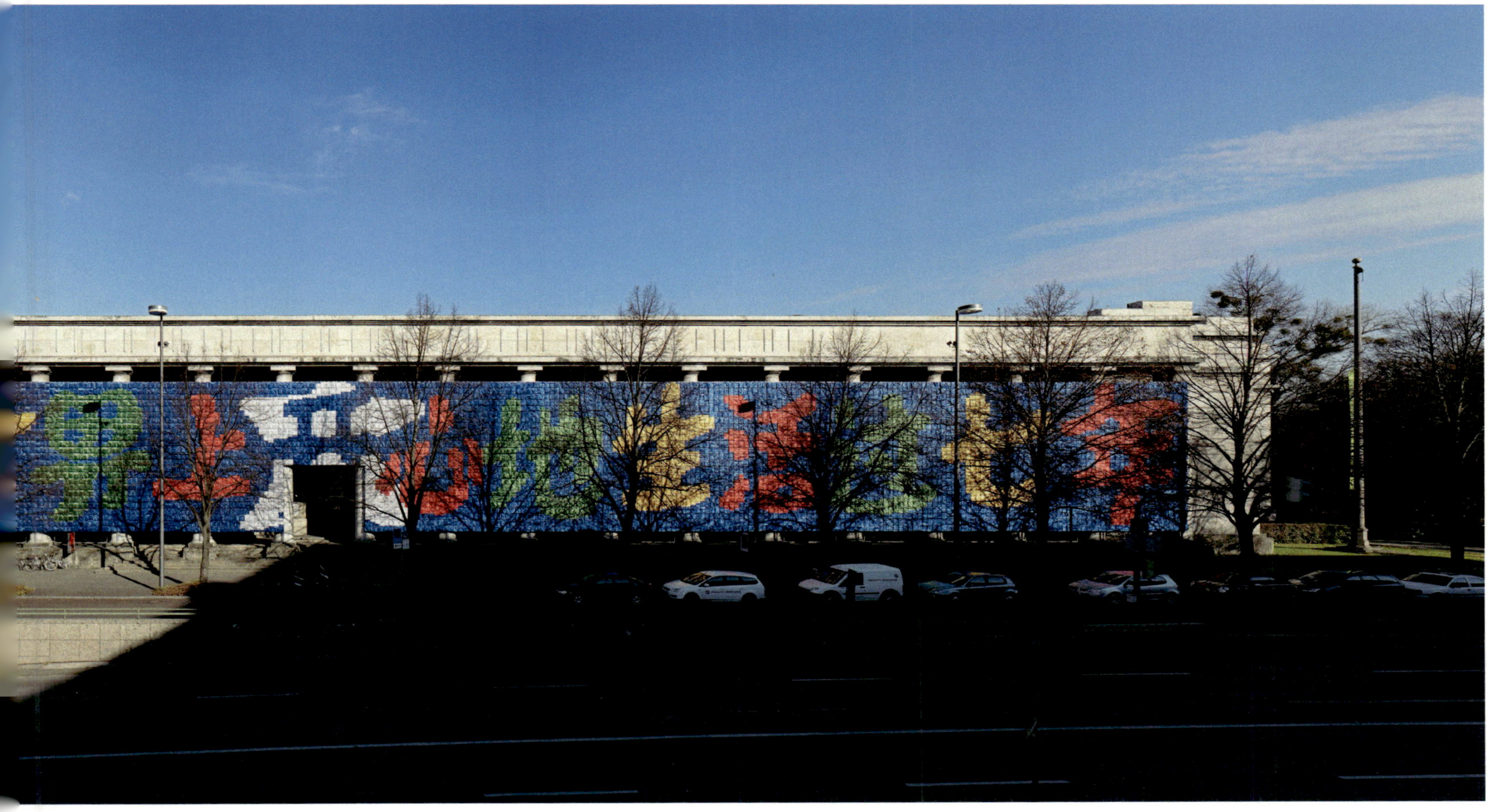

AI WEIWEI

5
Sunflower Seeds
2010, London, U.K.
147 tons of sunflower seeds
Porcelain, Photo by Tate
Photography

6
Kui Hua Zi
2009, 1.000 kg Porcelain

7
Teahouse
2009, Mori Art Museum,
Tokyo, Compressed tea,
180 × 120 × 180 cm
(378 cubes 20 × 20 × 20 cm,
54 triangle shaped)
Photo by Mori Art Museum

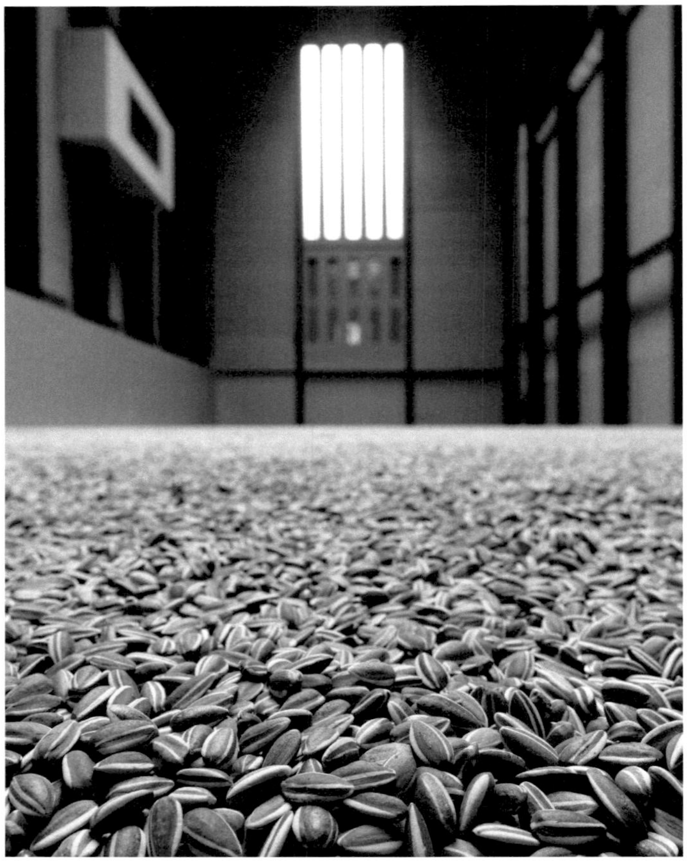

5

"YOUR OWN ACTS AND BEHAVIOR TELL THE WORLD WHO YOU ARE AND AT THE SAME TIME WHAT KIND OF SOCIETY YOU THINK IT SHOULD BE"

6

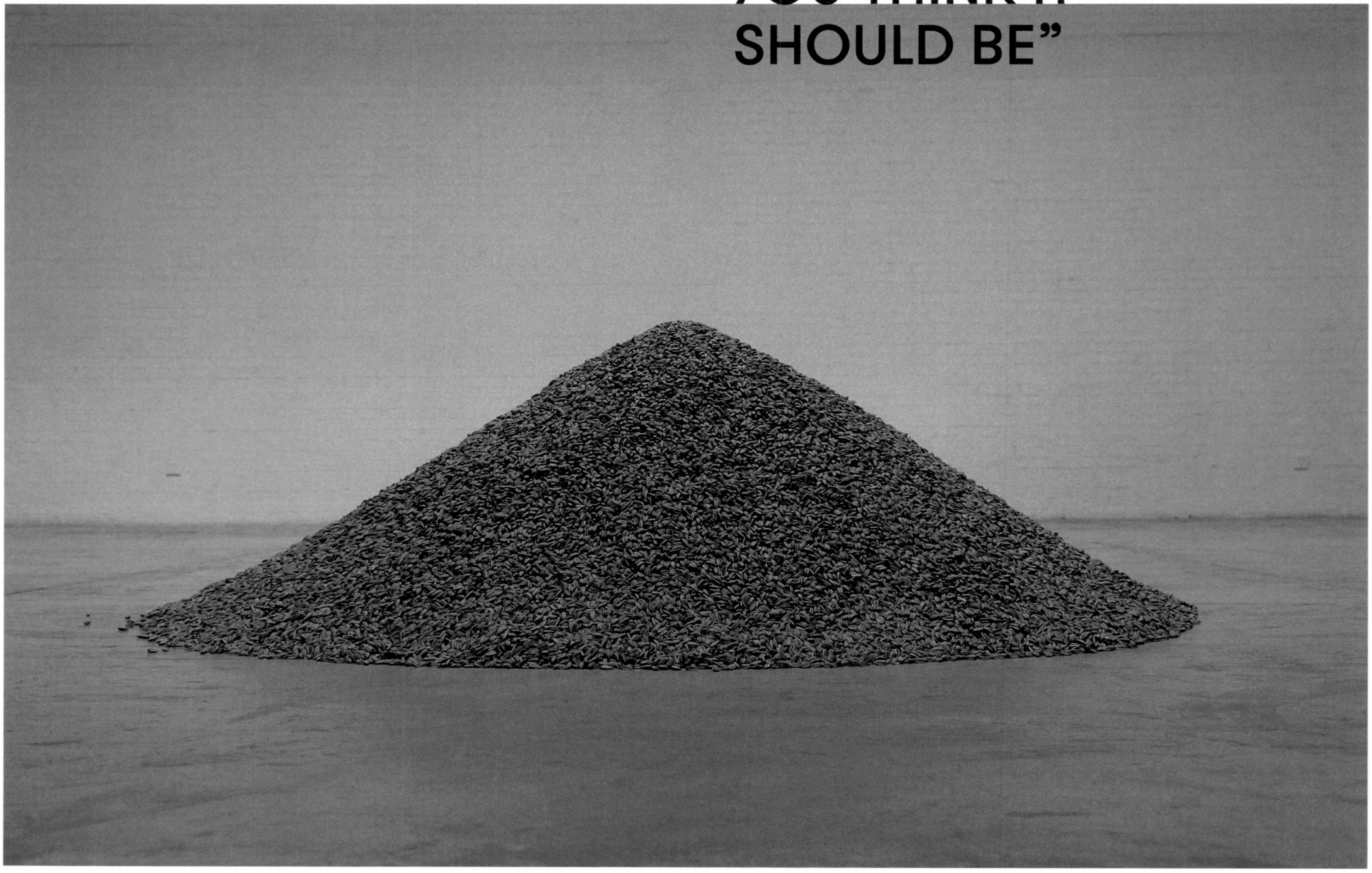

7

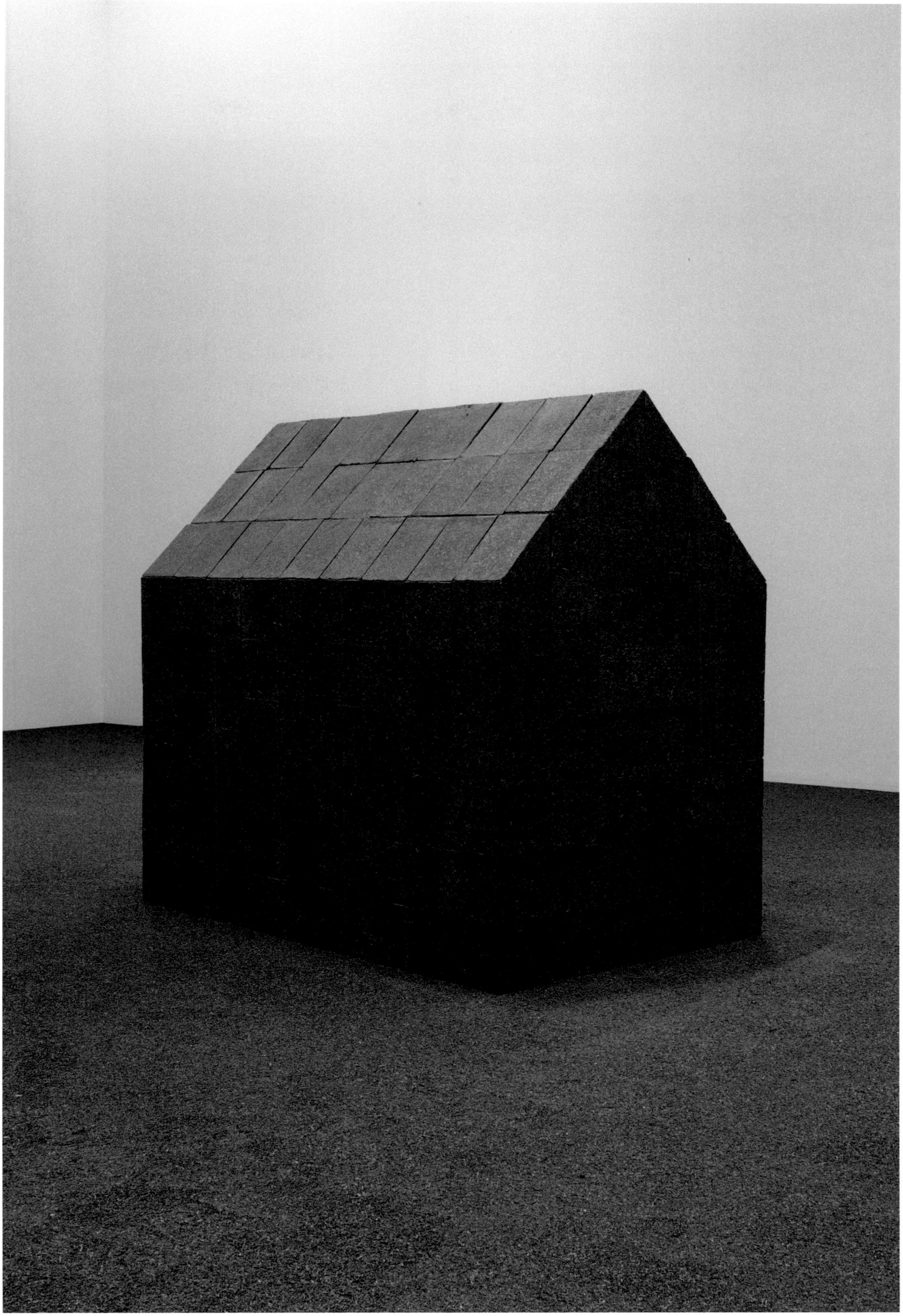

JIANG PENGYI

The Chinese artist Jiang Pengyi's (* 1977) photographs deal with how the rapid growth of modern architecture crowds out and destroys all older architectural elements and with it the traces of a lost past. Jiang left his birthplace of Yuanjiang in Hunan province as a teenager, and his first experience of the big city was a culture shock. As a professional photographer capturing the cityscapes of Peking, Chinese urbanism, with its innumerable futuristic skyscrapers, is a major theme of his artwork. "The city is a place where buildings furiously propagate. In China, it is almost like a carnival. All kinds of unthinkable new buildings gather from all over the world to compensate the desires of a newly rising powerful country, and to satisfy a thirst for marvelous spectacles. The marvelous spectacle of these buildings is a holy miracle, and what these offices require is the unconditional acceptance of the spectators, and to acquire people's obeisance through sighs and admiration." In his early artwork, *All Back to Dust,* 2006–2007, he transformed modernism's monstrous architectural edifices into miniatures, which he would generally place somewhere in the landscape and cover up with junk and trash, to give the impression that they had just been discarded. Jiang uses digital manipulation to create magical worlds that, instead of denying the reality, make us aware of the real world's inadequacies and its struggle to become something entirely new and different. "I've combined these buildings from various places with other forms, dragging them out from their aesthetics, so that they lose their perfect, grand, spectacular, and exciting attraction, which they use to seduce and to hypnotize. They seem a lot smaller, and are paid a lot less attention. It is a lot more enjoyable to look at them like this. What I want to say is a lot like the view of sacred Buddhist texts: the grand objects outside are composed of countless microscopic particles. In fact, they are all just piles of dust." In the series *Unregistered City,* 2008–2010, the artist goes a step further. Instead of being buried in rubbish tips, his miniature buildings stand erect in abandoned old-fashioned houses. The photographer makes the skyscrapers look tiny—they are no match for the masonry of the old world. It looks almost as if he wishes to reverse the trend of urbanization; and yet at the same time, Jiang is drawing attention to the nature of continuous progress: what looks modern today will one day only be a relic of the distant past. His series, *The Private Goods Belonged to Somebody,* 2008, is also concerned with the past. Here, the artist presents abandoned household items in such a way that they look as if they've been left behind, and have the effect of evoking memories of bygone days. *A Maze Recovered by Memory,* for instance, references a game from Jiang's childhood. For him, items such as a broken birdcage, a toy airplane, and balls of yarn evoke feelings of yearning and allow one to open a door to buried memories.

1

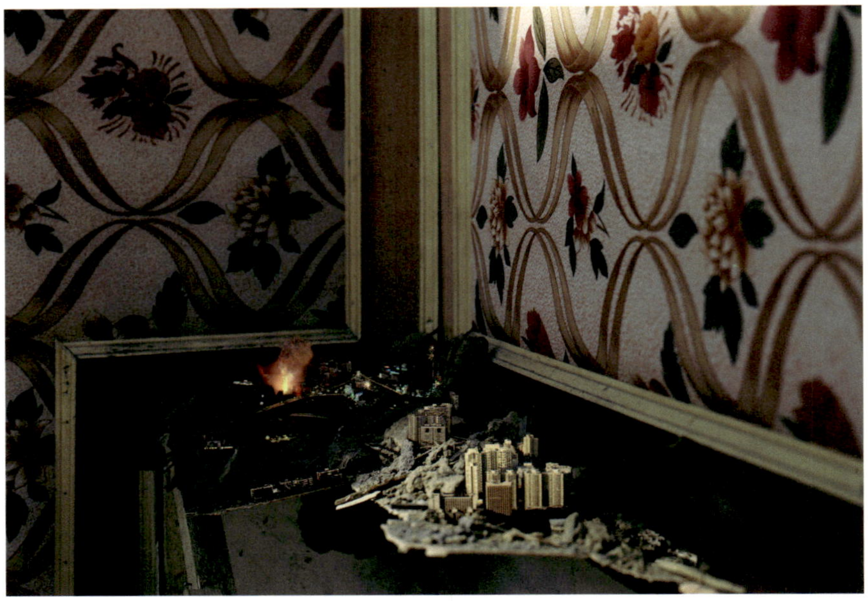

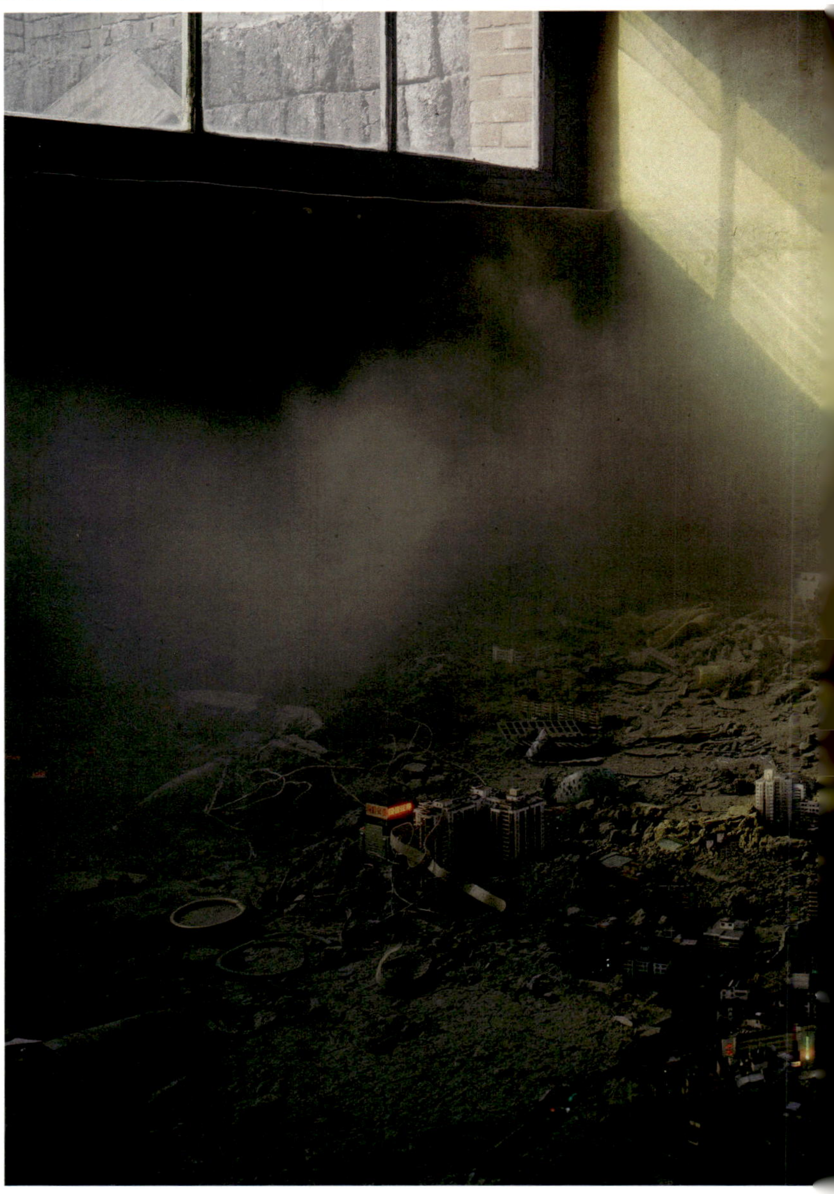

1
Unregistered City, No. 1 & No. 3
2008–2010, China

2
The Private Goods Belonged to Somebody: The Portable Woman
2008, China

3
All Back to Dust, No. 1 & No. 2
2006–2007, China

4 (next spread)
Unregistered City, No. 2
2008–2010, China

“THE GRAND OBJECTS OUTSIDE ARE COMPOSED OF COUNTLESS MICROSCOPIC PARTICLES. IN FACT, THEY ARE ALL JUST PILES OF DUST”

2

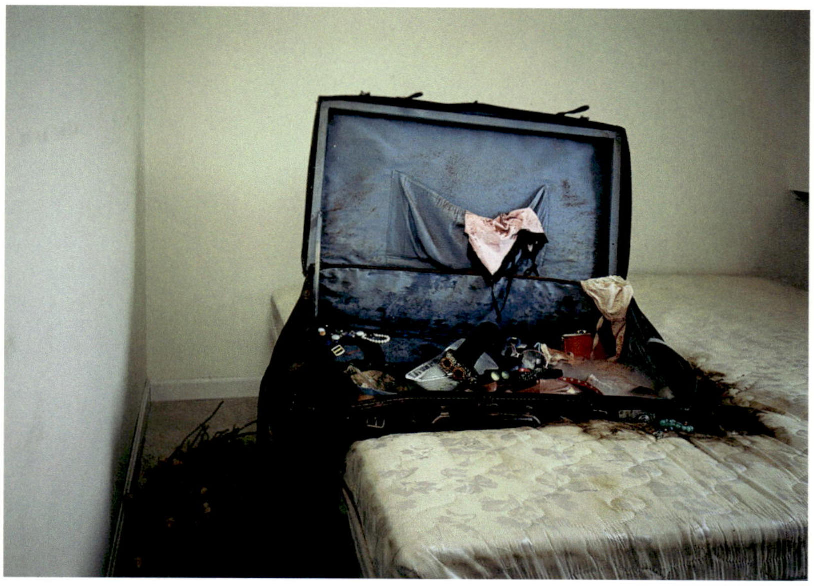

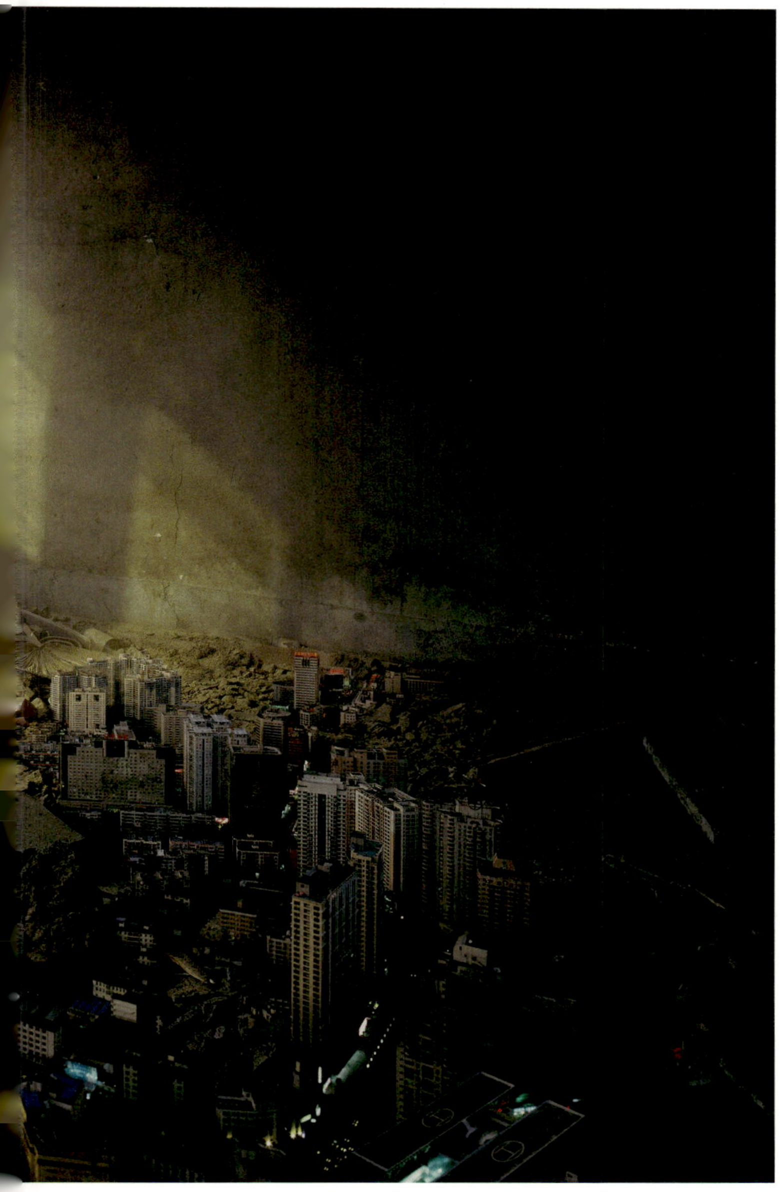

3

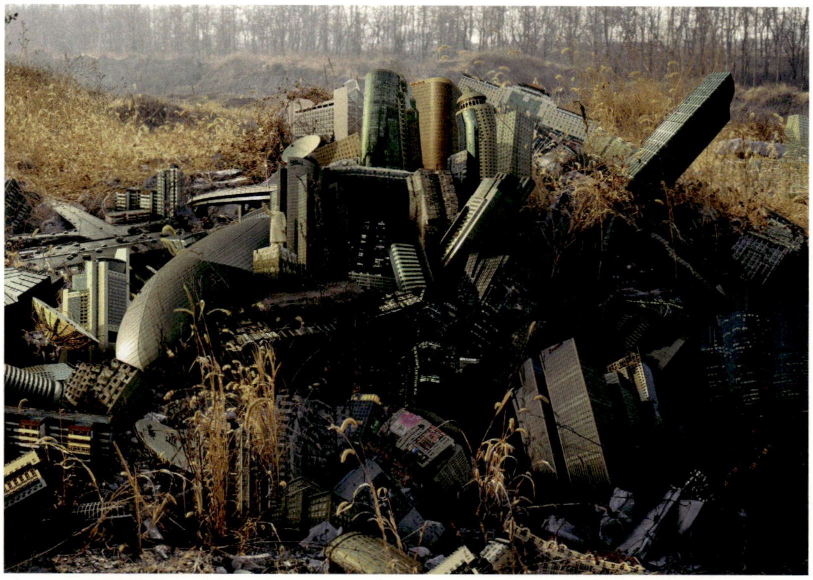

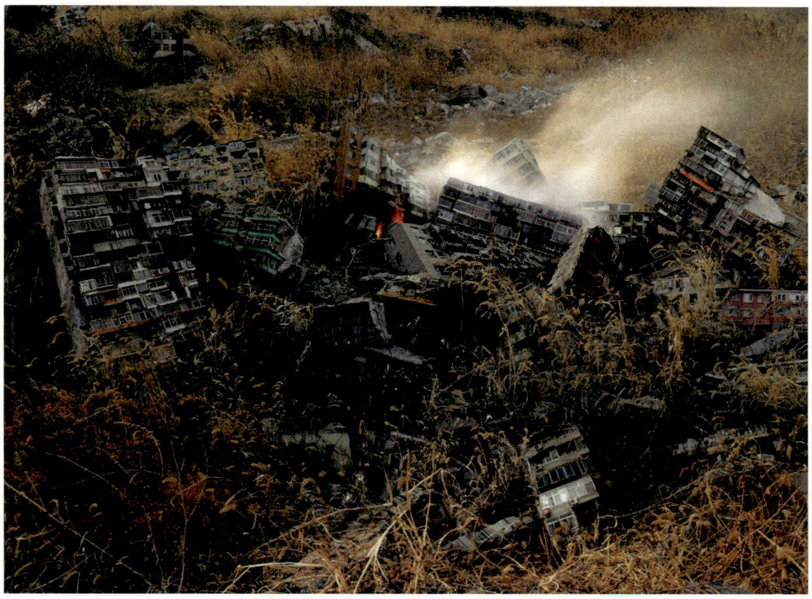

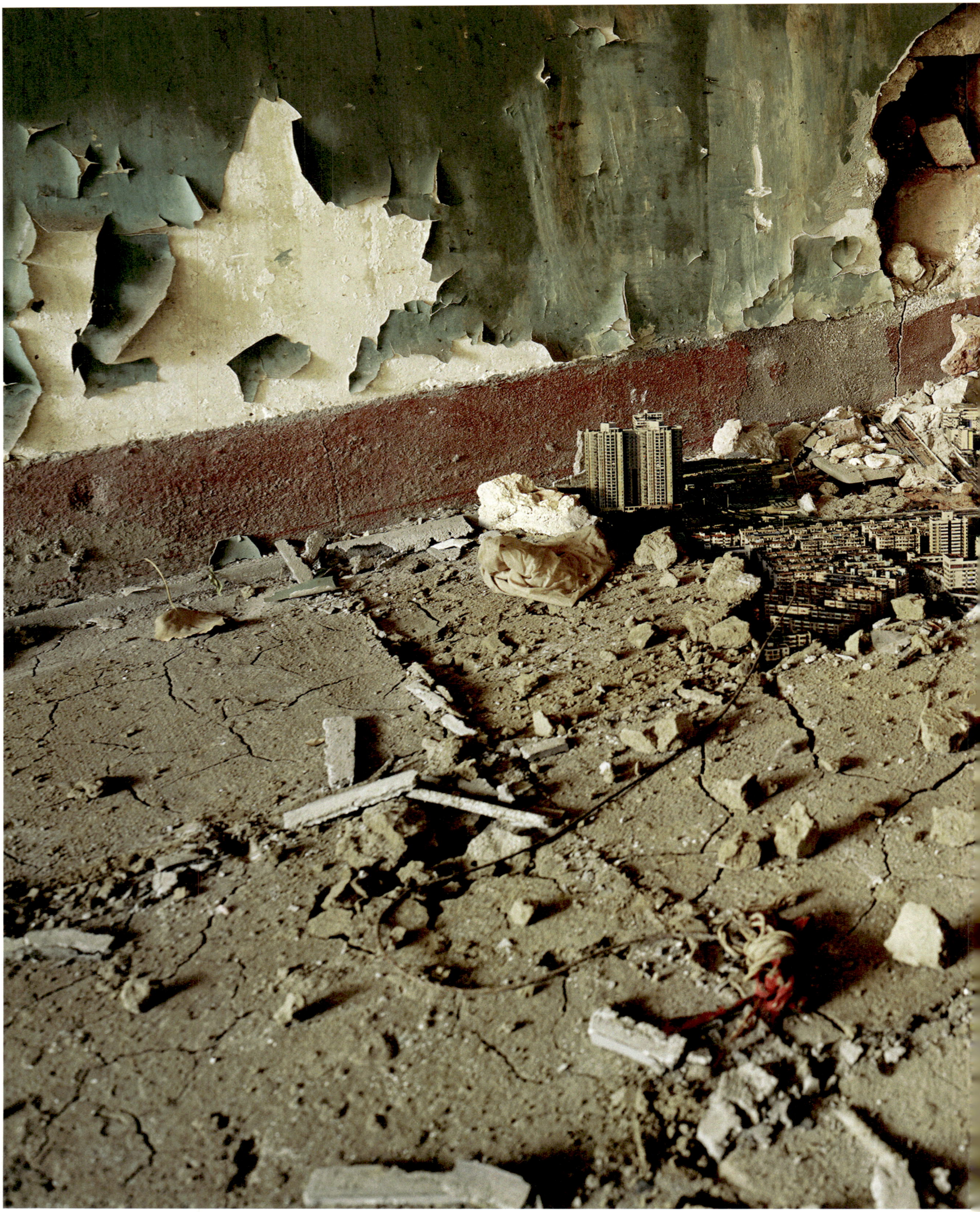

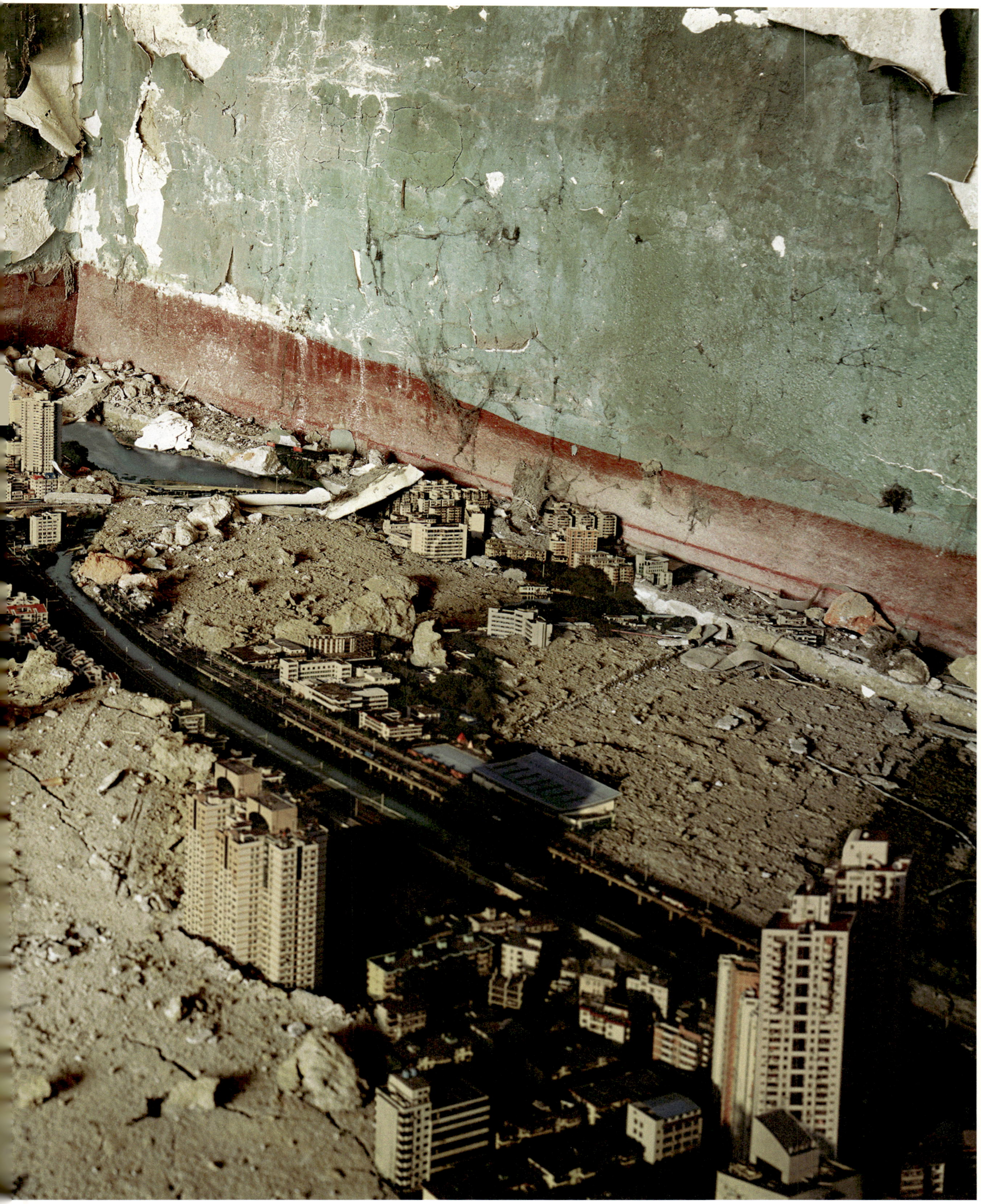

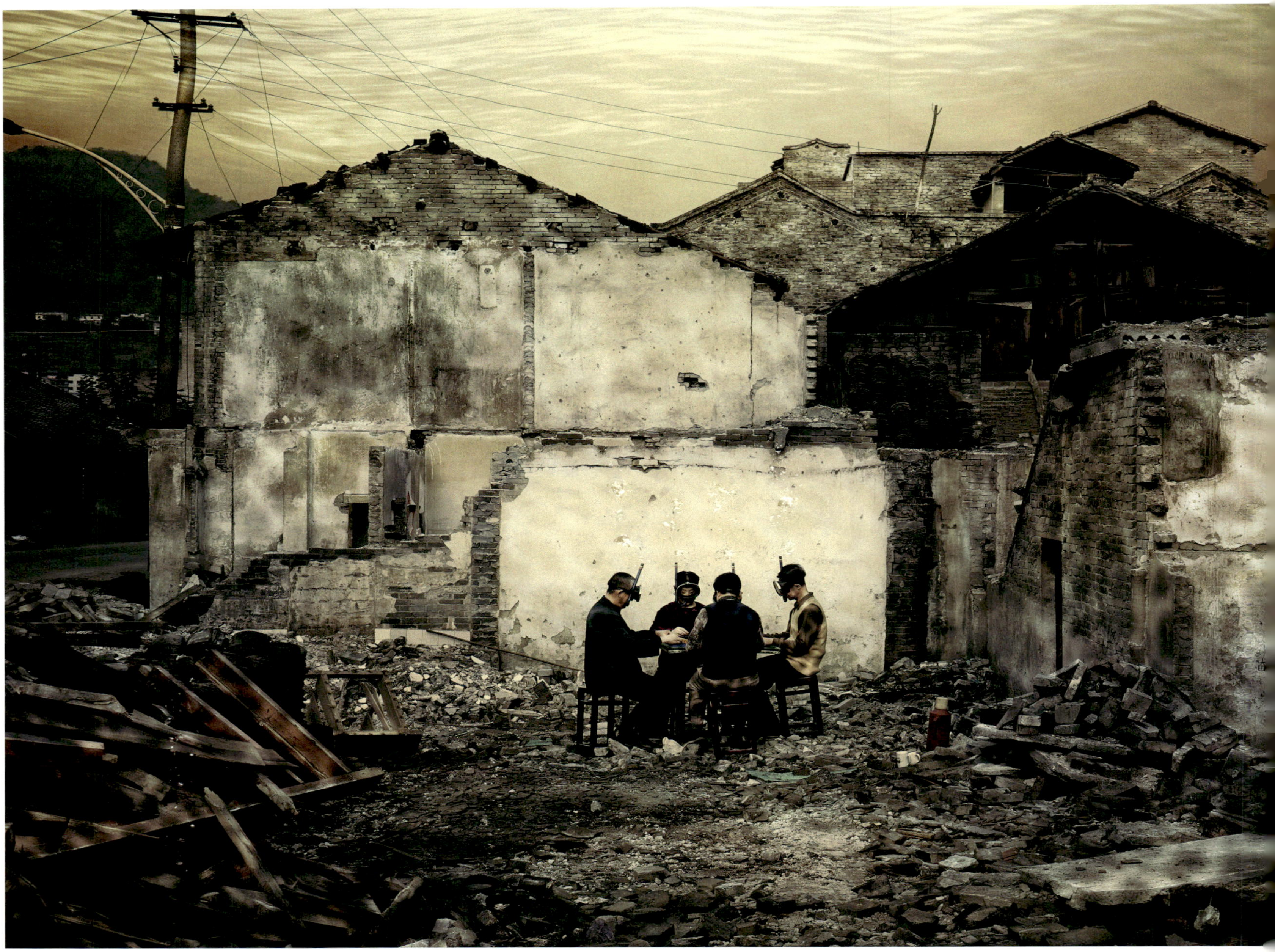

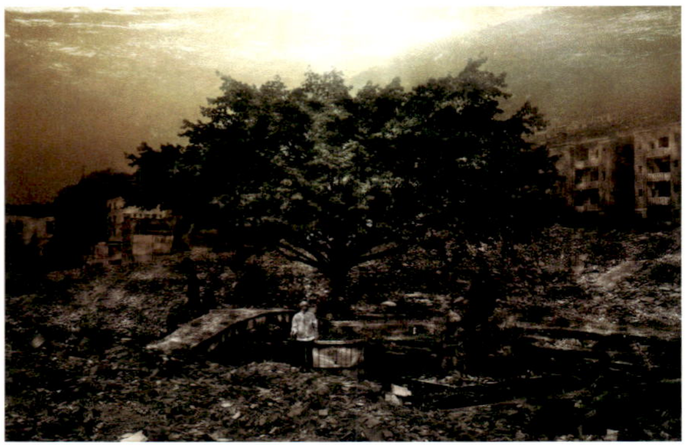

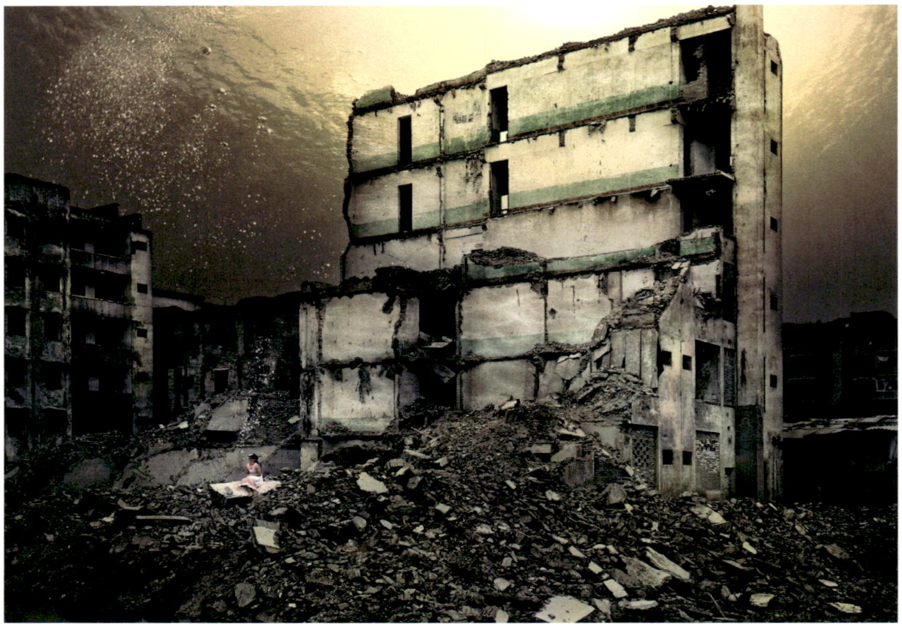

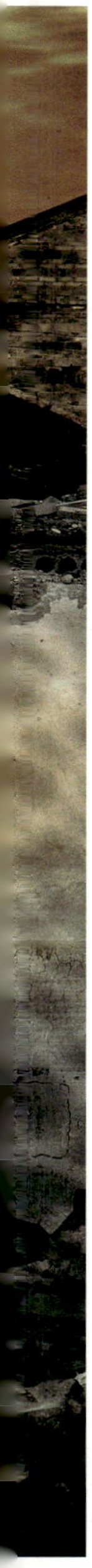

YANG YI

In his series *Uprooted,* 2007–2008, the Chinese artist Yang Yi (* 1971) addresses a theme that is important to him personally: the construction of the Three Gorges Dam in China and its consequences. The government's argument for the necessity of this project rests on the urgent need to improve flood protection. But there is hardly any other major project of the past few years that has been so controversial. The artificial lake created by the dam extends over 600 kilometers, covering areas that were once densely populated; over two million people had to be relocated. Yang's hometown of Kaixian, Chongqing on the Yangtze River was one of the towns displaced by the water. All that was left were abandoned houses and empty streets, which gradually disappeared beneath the surface. Before the forced relocation was completed, the artist photographed the town's last remaining inhabitants situated in their normal surroundings. He uses digital manipulation to suggest that the whole landscape is already under water, and that only a few human beings patiently hold out in the ruins of the ghost town, complete with goggles. In one picture, two men are actually playing cards in the same spot where they had always played cards. Yang wants his hometown to be remembered, and so through his remarkable artworks, he creates testaments to the past: "I don't intend to dwell on the meaning to be found in my photography. What is important for me is that I came from that town. It is about all that we have in common there: our accent, our spicy coriander, the nod we give each other, a friendly signal to say hello when we pass one another on the street; these streets that we have traveled alongside our ancestors, that have herded us along together ... this series was created for all of that. It will be my personal memoir!"

Uprooted
2007, The old town of Kaixian, Chongqing, China
Courtesy Galerie Paris–Beijing

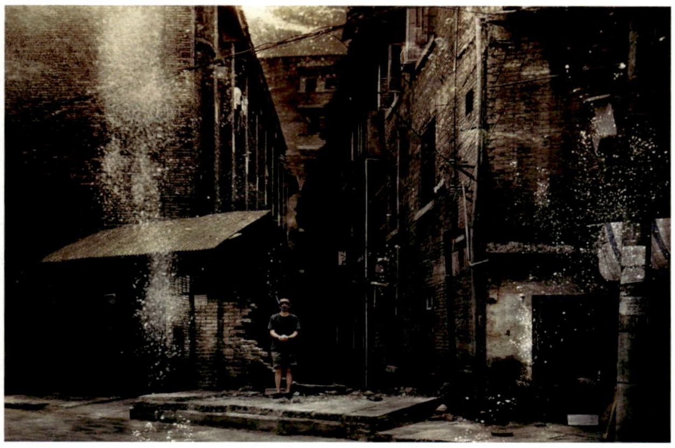

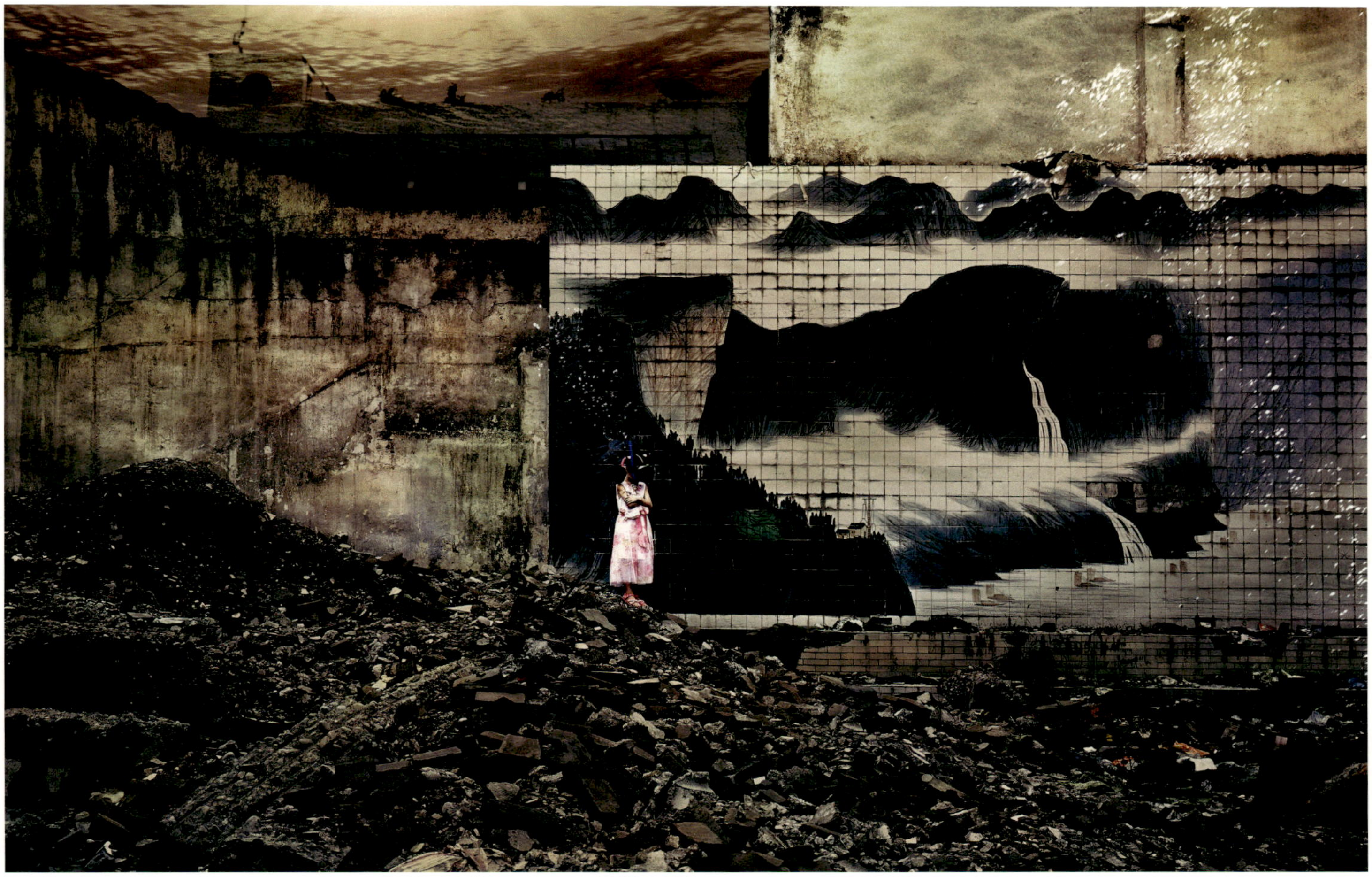

ZHANG HUAN

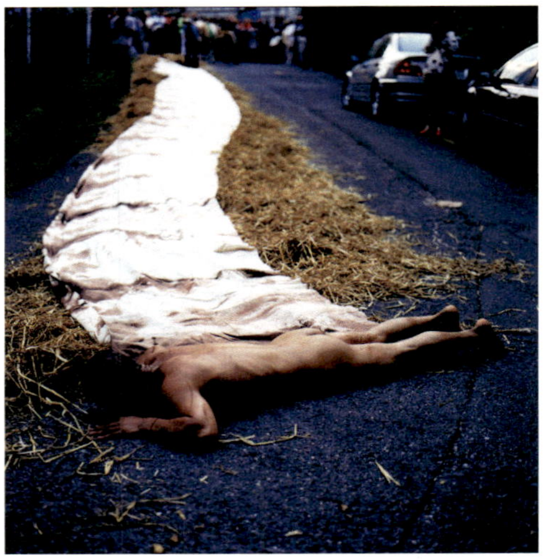

1

Zhang Huan (* 1965), who was born in Anyang, Henan province, works in a wide variety of media: performance, photography, painting, and sculpture. Much of the time, this Chinese artist's oeuvre casts a critical eye over politics and society in China. He is also interested in the cultural differences between East and West. In the 1990s, he became known for his body performances, which often took him to the limits of his own personal pain tolerance. At that time, in an unchanging state like China, his activities created unrest. His one-man performance *12 Square Meters,* in the summer of 1994, involved standing for an hour naked in a dirty public toilet on the edge of Peking—turning his body, which was specially covered with fish oil and honey, into a living fly trap. This performance has been considered a classic of recent Chinese art history ever since. At the time, Zhang was living in the rundown village of Dashancun (between Peking's third and fourth orbital motorways, and directly opposite Peking's giant municipal tip), with a number of other young artists. This collection of shacks soon became known as Peking's "East Village." Led by Zhang, the activists staged sinister projects and performances featuring pain, dirt, intimacy, and sexuality to reflect the artists' negative feelings about living in this inhospitable environment, and their restrained rage over the suppression of the Chinese reform movement in June 1989. However, as the East Village colony became more and more well-known, the state intervened, possibly at the behest of local farmers. In any case, in the summer of 1994, an order for breaking up the artist colony was issued, and subsequently implemented by the authorities. Four years later, Zhang took part in the highly regarded exhibition "Inside Out: New Chinese Art" in New York's P.S.1. He took the opportunity to settle in New York, where he spent the next eight years, creating ever more sophisticated performances across America and Europe. The artist created a series of performances for specific regions and cities, trying to imitate the everyday life there, and to continue it in ritualized form. The artist believes that it is the acts we perform every day that most clearly reveal what it is to be human, and what our relationship to the world is. For instance, in Seattle in 1999, he let himself be pelted with white bread for several minutes, by 60 naked Americans for the performance *My America (Hard to Acclimatize).* In 2002, he marched through New York in a massive bodybuilder's suit made from raw meat. In the same year, he covered himself with honey and sunflower seeds and locked himself in a cage with 28 doves in the Hamburger Kunstverein for *Seeds of Hamburg.* Zhang's series of photographs are rather less well-known, but are equally carefully thought out and compelling. For the artist, their creation is a performative act. These series tell of the importance of his family and others as vital elements in his life, and as sources of inspiration for his artwork. In the ten photographs that make up Zhang's *Foam* series, 1998, each image shows his head from the same angle. In each of the pictures, he has a snapshot of a member of his family, or of his wife in his open mouth, and his face is covered in foam. This could be seen as a symbol of birth, in the natural or mythological sense. For the series *Family Tree,* 2000, the artist underwent a painful process of having his face written on for a day by three calligraphers, until it was black all over. They wrote well-known names, stories, and fables they had heard, as well as any randomly occurring thoughts that they had onto his face. By the end of the day, a thick layer of black pigment completely covered his face, creating a mask or second skin, which consisted of what had been learned by individuals and transmitted down many generations. In his sculptures, which have recently occupied an important position in his oeuvre, he transfers the ideas explored in his performances into everyday studio practice. Zhang describes the effect of his 6-meter-high statue erected in 2008 in San Francisco, which is the partner city of Shanghai, by stating: "*Three Heads Six Arms* reflects the changing realities of Chinese people today, and also reflects the attitude that humankind has conquered nature, and even reflects deeds of volition and hope."

2

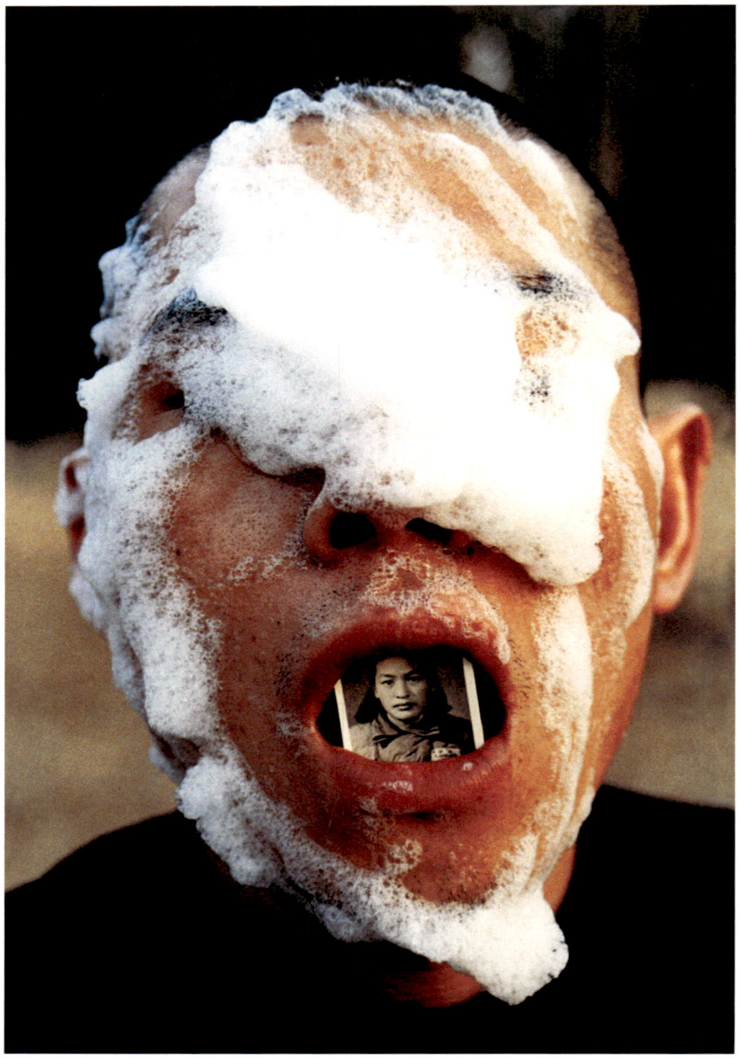

1
My Switzerland
2005, Kunstmuseum Bern, Bern, Switzerland
2
Foam
1998, Beijing, China
3
Three Heads Six Arms
2008, San Francisco Civic Center Plaza, San Francisco, USA, Steel and copper
Courtesy San Francisco Arts Commission and The Pace Gallery, New York
4
My New York
2002, Whitney Museum, New York, USA
5 (next spread)
Family Tree
2000, New York, USA

3

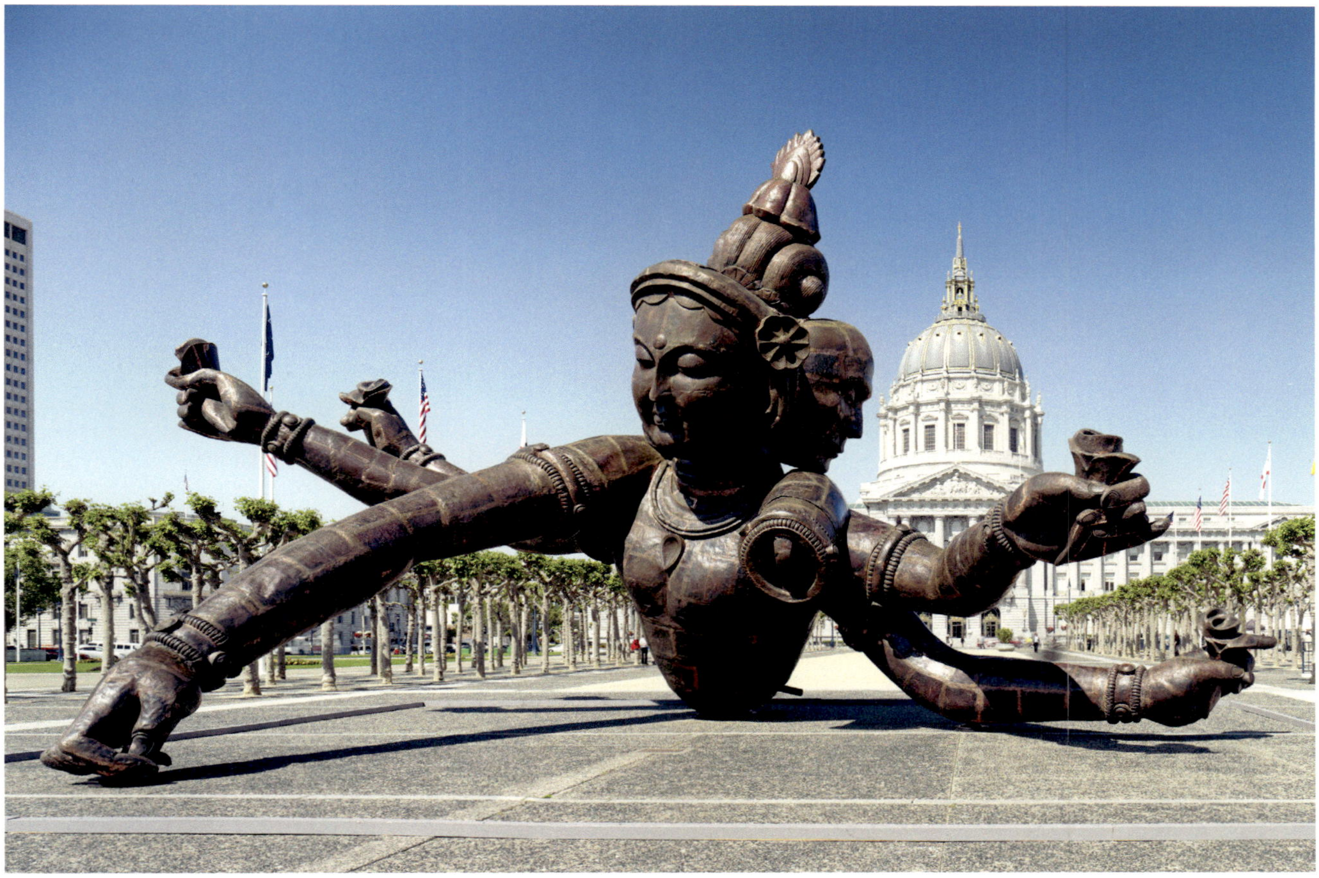

4

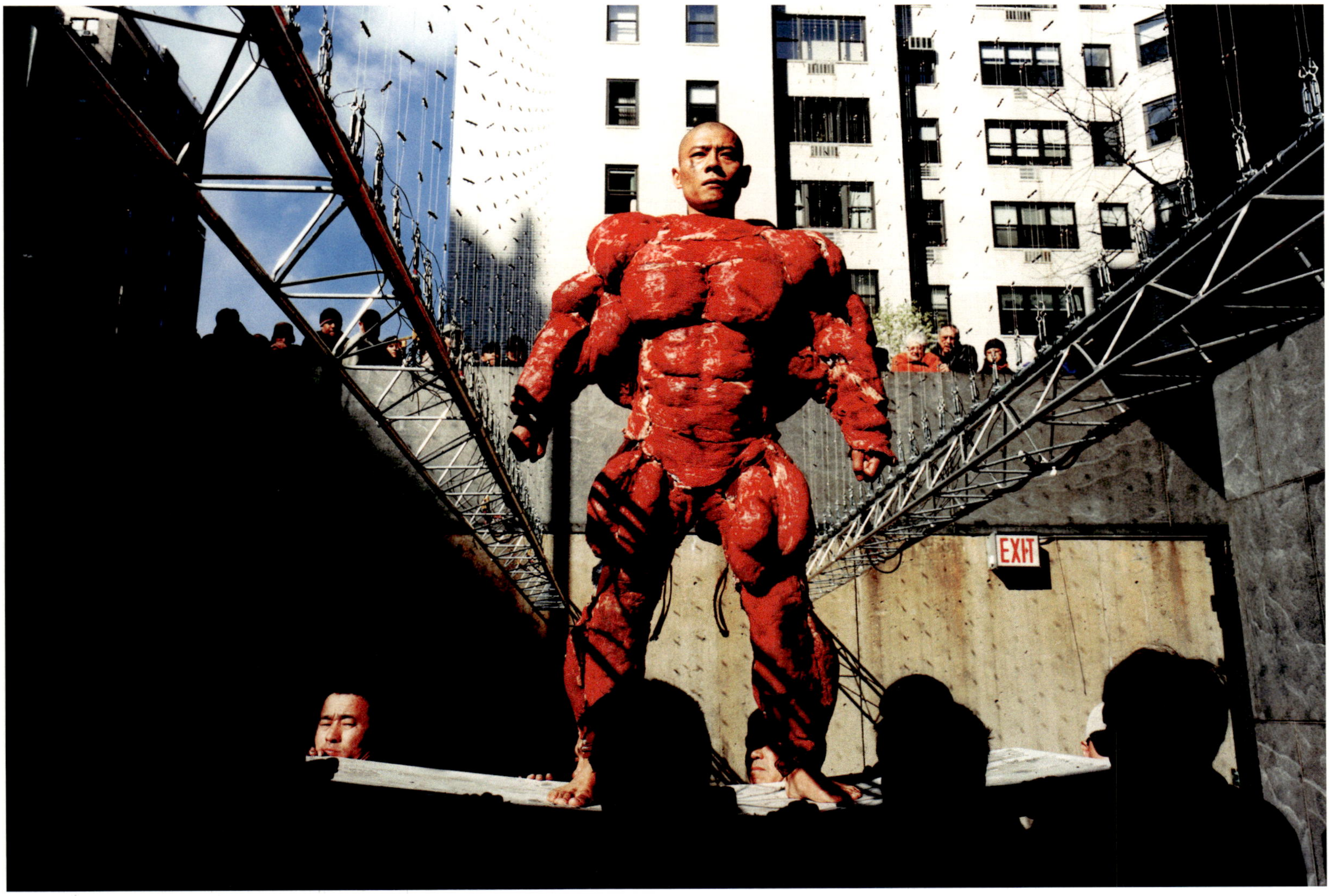

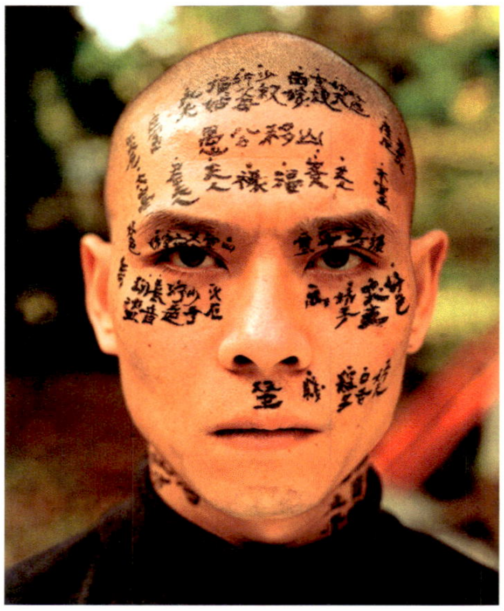
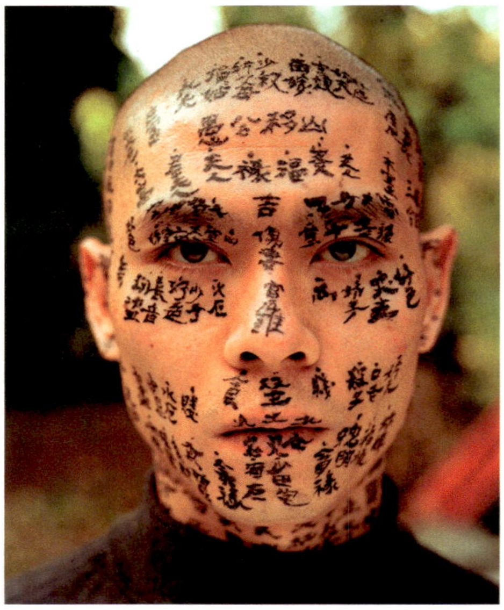
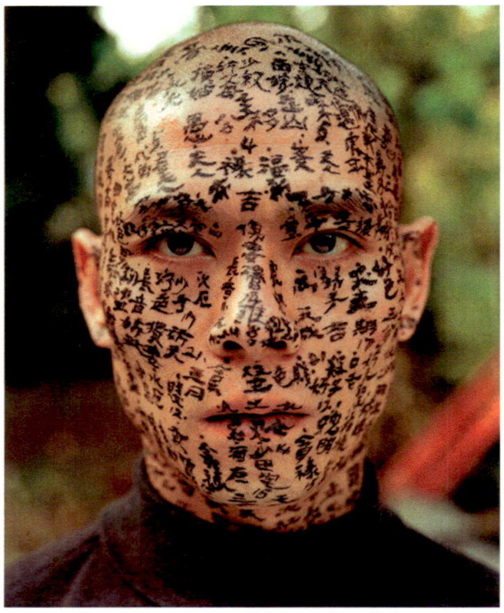
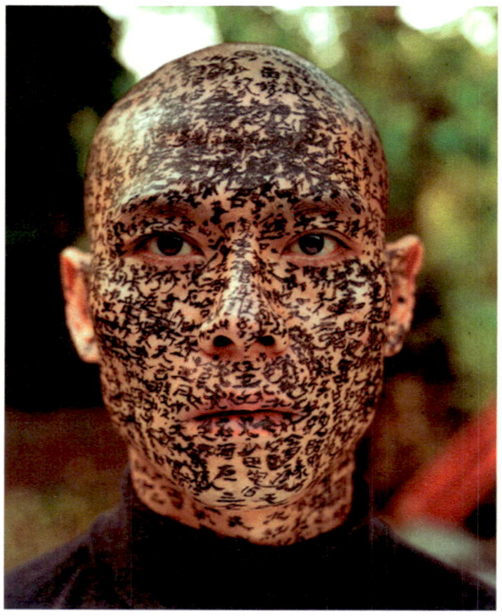
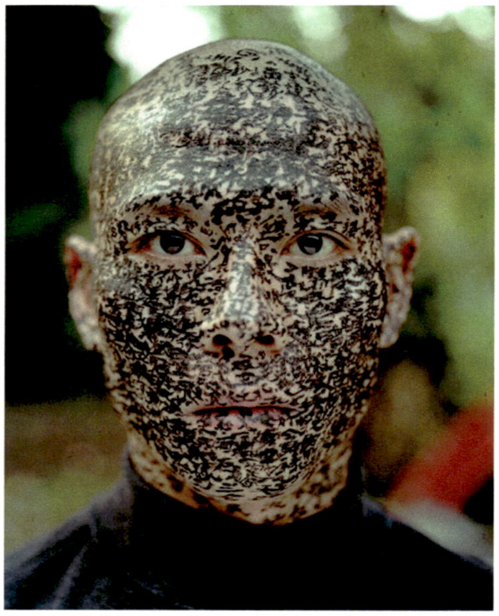
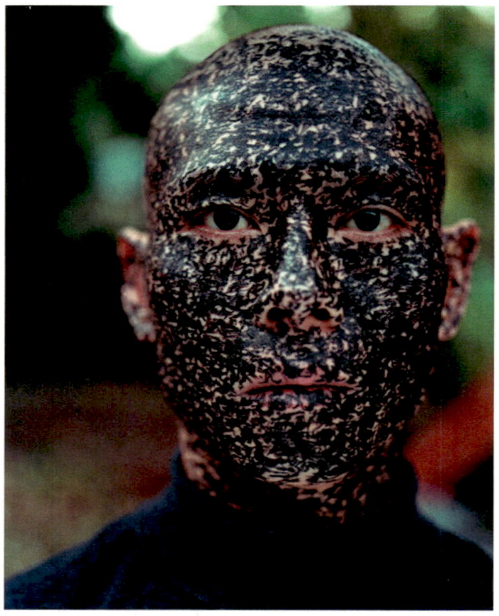
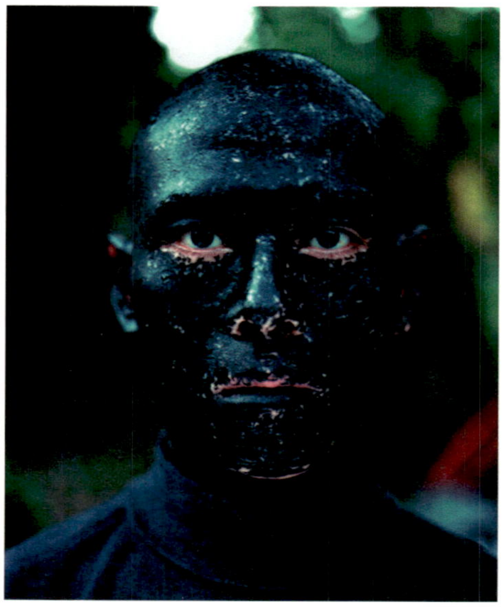
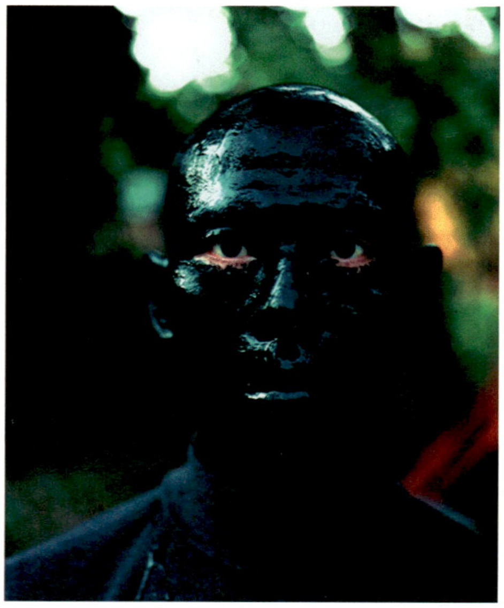
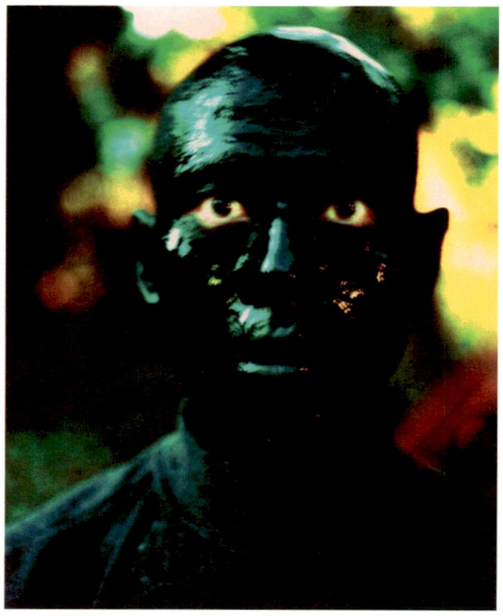

“WHEN I PERFORM, I’M ALWAYS VERY QUIET. VERY QUIET, UNLIKE A LOT OF AMERICAN OR EUROPEAN PERFORMANCE ARTISTS, WHO USE A LOT OF ACTION AND NOISE IN THEIR WORKS. WHEN I HAVE A PERFORMANCE, I ALWAYS SHAVE MY HEAD. I SHAVE IT BEFORE EVERY PERFORMANCE. I GUESS IT’S A RITUAL. FOR ME, PERFORMING IS ABOUT NOT PERFORMING”

1

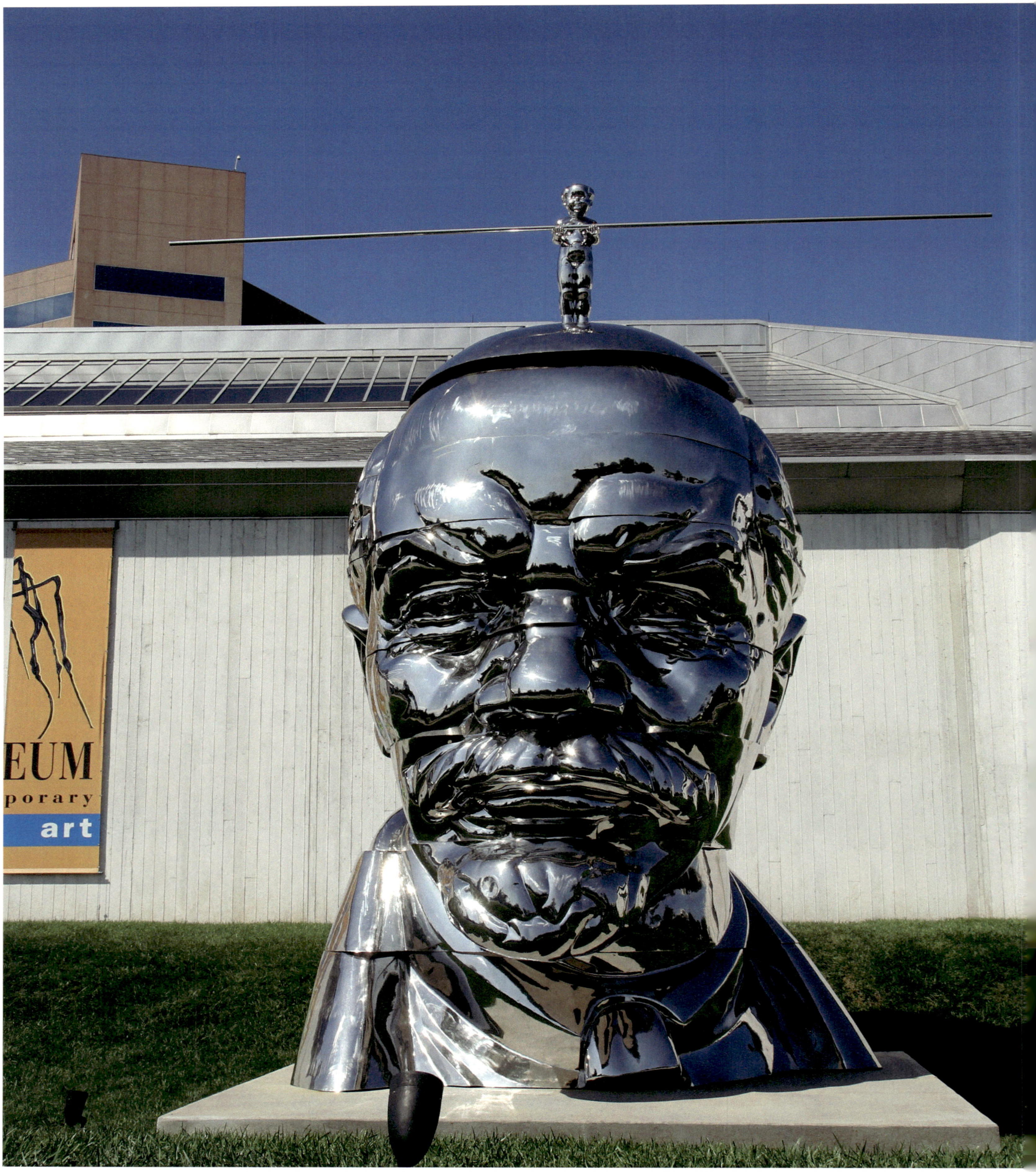

GAO BROTHERS

They are considered the enfants terribles of the Chinese art scene. At home, the Gao Brothers—Zhen (* 1956) and Qiang (* 1962)—make headlines with their sculptures, photographs, and performances, which criticize the Chinese system. In Europe and the United States, their artworks create a furor. The duo were unable to leave China for 14 years due to a travel ban issued by the Chinese authorities in 1989, but this has not stopped their reputation abroad from steadily growing. The travel ban was still in place in 2001, which prevented the Gao Brothers from accepting an invitation to the 49th Venice Biennale to perform their artwork *Hug on a Human Plateau.* Instead, the exhibition had to take place in Jinan, China, with people from all over the world taking part via the internet. Since then, they have organized mass embraces of a similar kind—as a step toward collective reconciliation—that have taken place in several locations, including New York, Moscow, and Berlin. The theme that runs through their oeuvre is that of coming to terms with Chinese history, and the brothers use satire and very black humor in their work as their way to put across their point of view. They endeavor to understand events whose destructive impact was felt within their own family: the Gao Brothers' father was one of the 1.5 million casualties of the Cultural Revolution, which also razed much of China's cultural inheritance to the ground (both literally and figuratively). In particular, their sculptural artworks constantly feature China's former communist leader Mao Zedong. Mao is still venerated in China, while the art scene pays ironic tributes to the instigator of the devastating Cultural Revolution as a form of self-liberation. *The Execution of Christ,* 2009, shows several life-size figures depicting Mao's face aiming bayonets at a figure of Christ. One of these Mao figures is turning away, perhaps because he regrets his actions and wants to reconsider. The historical artistic source is unambiguous: the scene is inspired by Édouard Manet's famous painting *Execution of Maximilian,* which, in turn, was inspired by Goya's *The 3rd of May 1808: The Executions on Principe Pio Hill.* The historical context of the Gao Brothers' sculpture is equally clear: when the communist party in China took power, it imposed atheism on the Chinese people. Beliefs such as Christianity could only be practiced in secret. In another series, the brothers present us with a bare breasted bust of *Miss Mao,* with a long nose to symbolize the many lies that permeated Mao's leadership. A series of large, stainless-steel sculptures show a tiny Miss Mao atop the head of Vladimir Lenin, whose conception of communism had a profound influence on the history of China. All of their sculptures also reference the present mood of nostalgia connected with Mao. This has had consequences for the artists, as in 2008, when the Chinese authorities ordered the covering up of the Mao sculptures. They also put the artists' studio under surveillance for a time, making note of all those who entered and left the building.

1
Miss Mao Trying to Poise Herself at the Top of Lenin's Head
2009

2
Miss Mao No. 2
2006

2

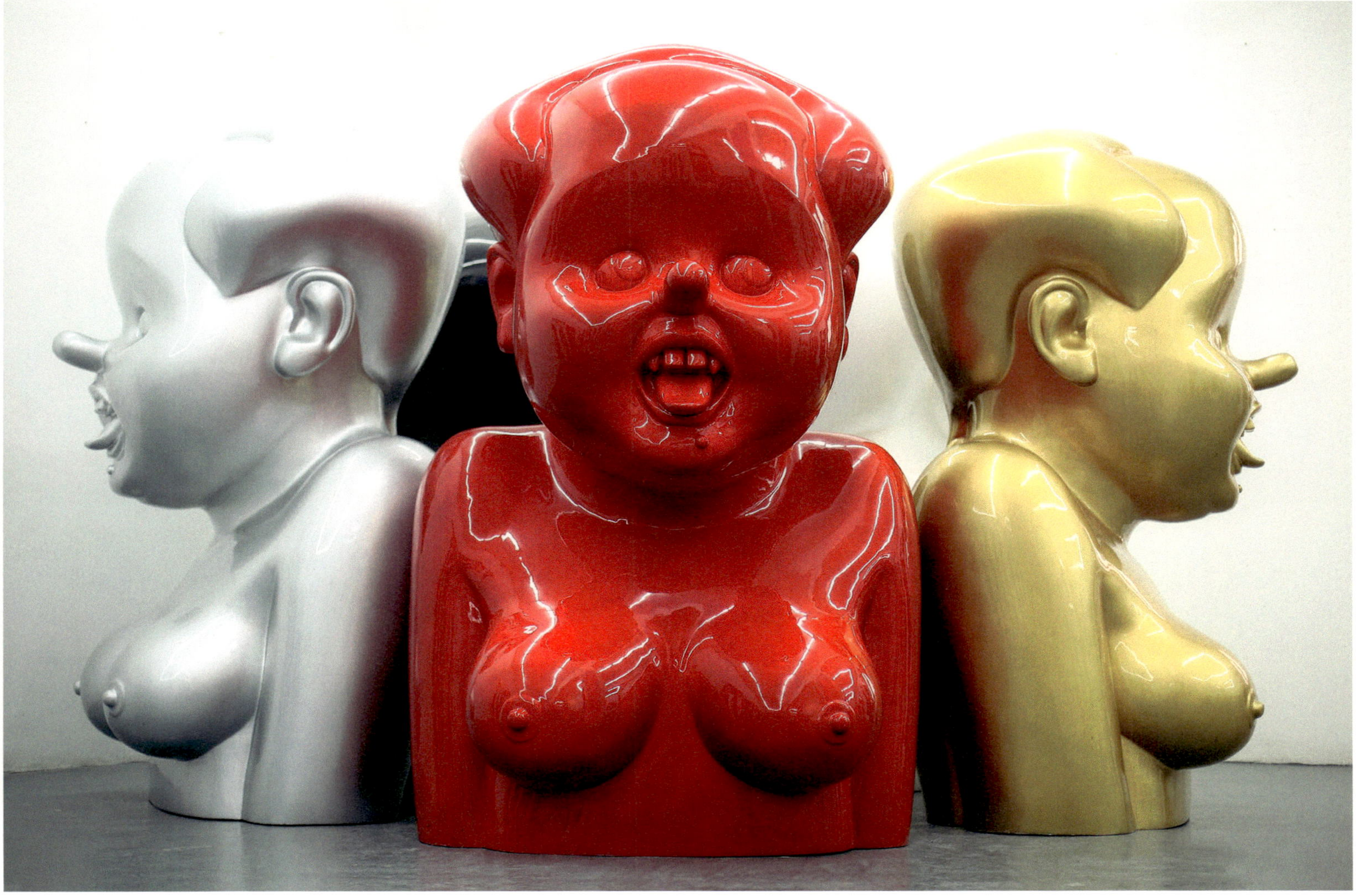

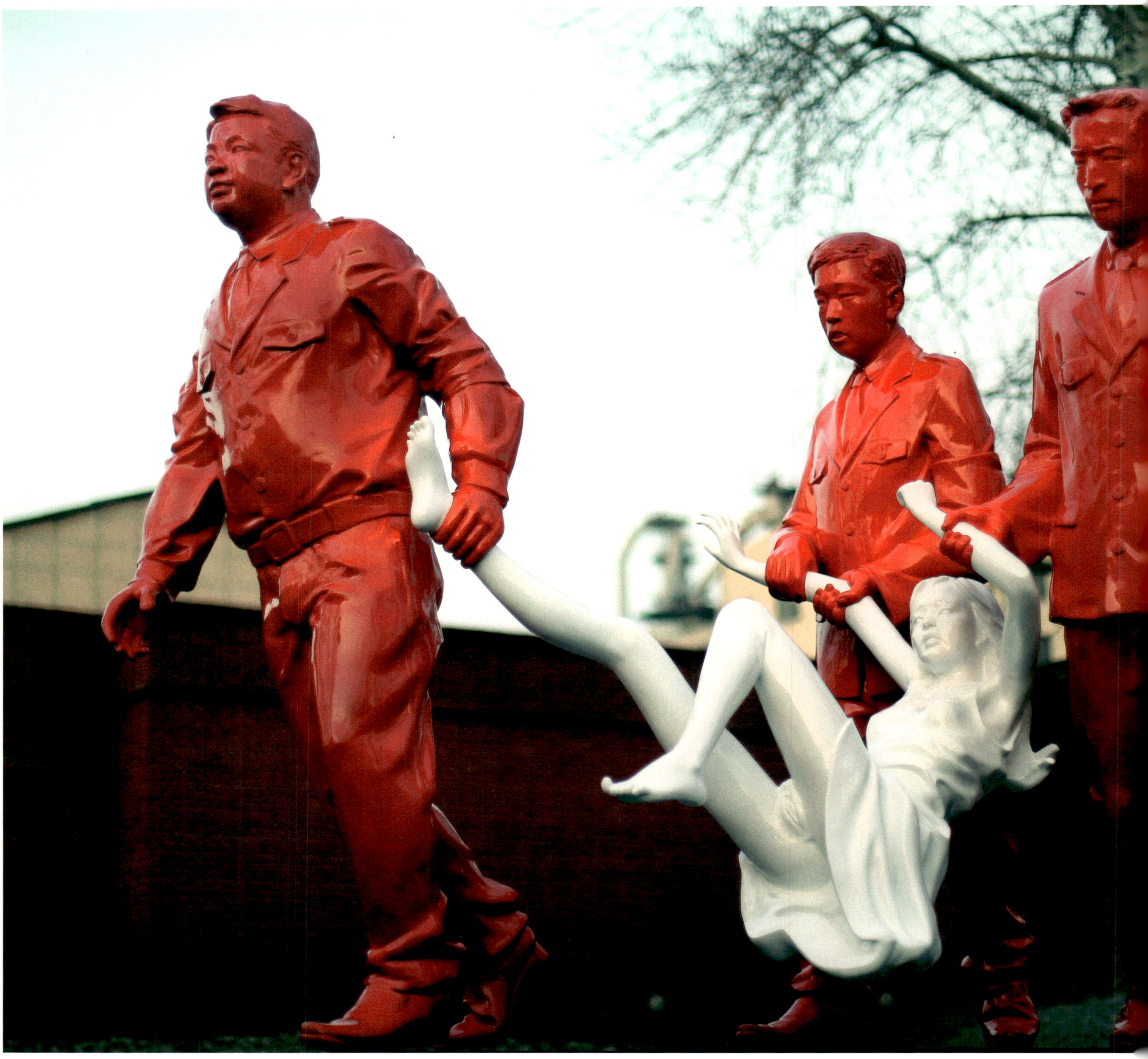

3

"CHINA IS LIKE A HUGE CONSTRUCTION SITE. ITS POLITICAL IDEOLOGY OR ECONOMIC STATUS, SOCIAL SYSTEM, AND URBAN DESIGN ARE ALL IN AN UNFINISHED STATE."

3
Arresting Prostitute
2007
4
Mao's Guilt
2009
5
The Execution of Christ
2009

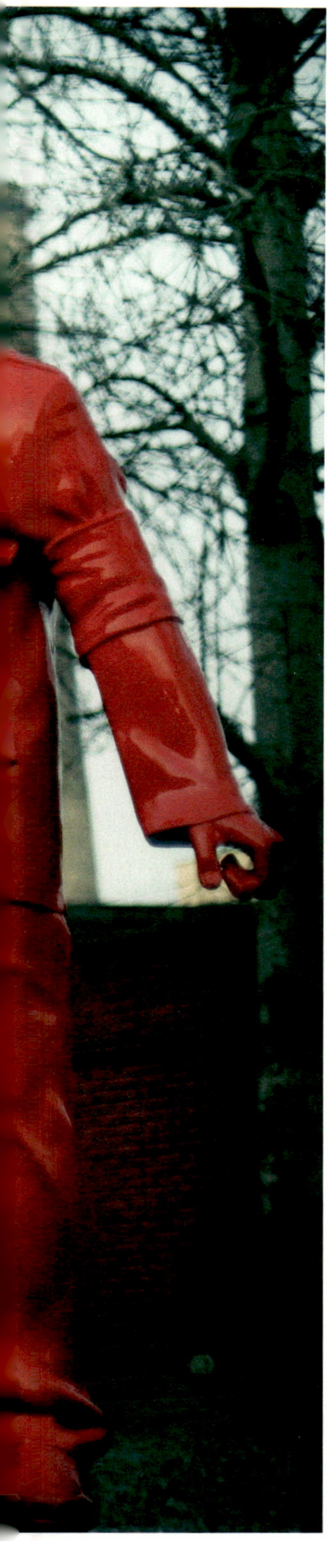

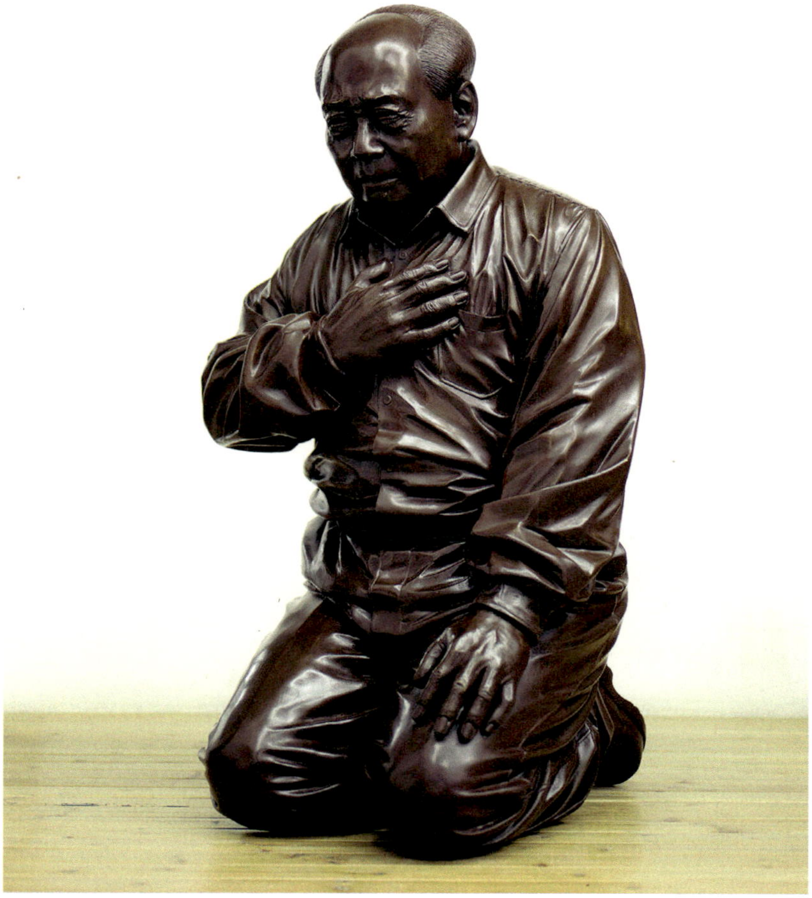

4

5

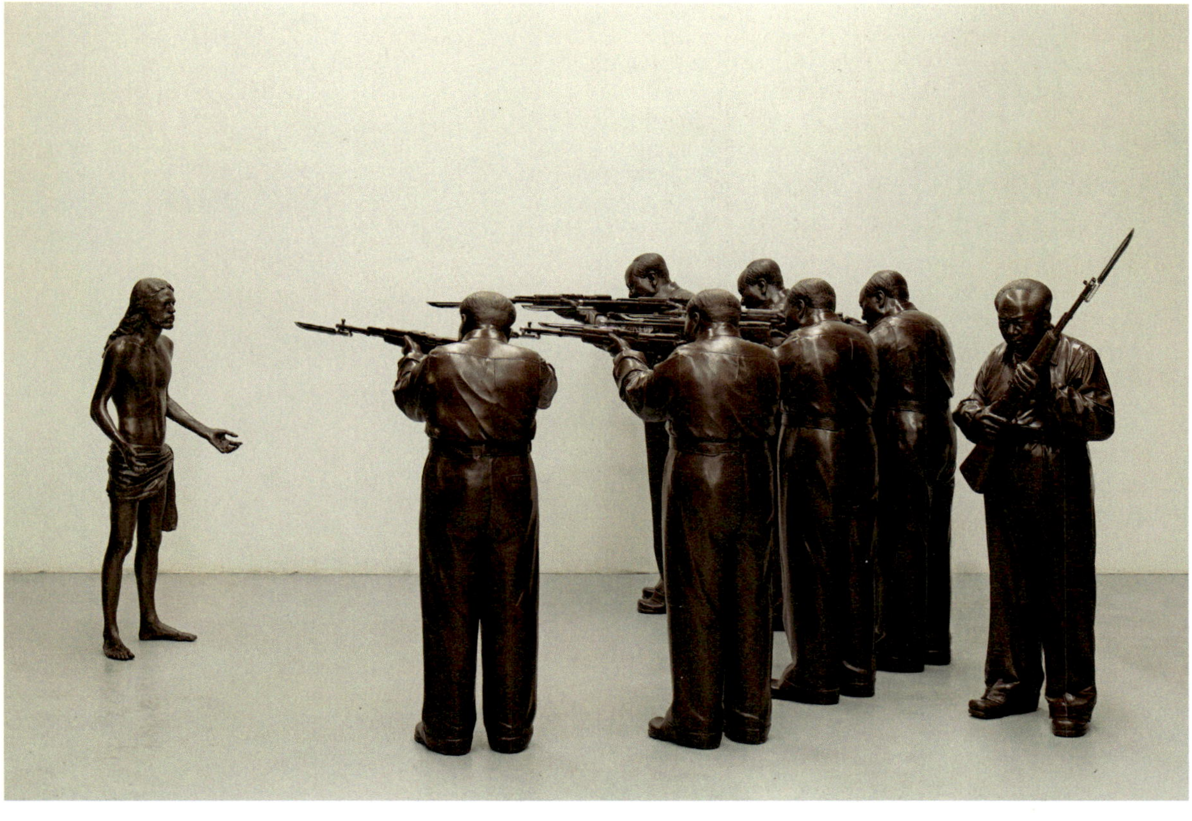

JR

Through his global effort of recognizing the "other," the Paris-based artist JR brings the inhabitants of marginal communities to the attention of those living in urban centers. JR uses portraiture and recorded oral histories to document the lives of individuals living in extreme poverty, violence, and social conflict. The images are the product of an immersion in the community, and a process involving an intensive communication with the resident subjects. The photographs themselves are often charming, humorous, and fun. They tend to defy or exaggerate the preconceived notions portrayed of those inhabiting the periphery by the mainstream media. JR blows up his pictures into large-scale photo murals which are pasted onto buildings in public space. His practice is inherently populist, in that he creates images that are visually appealing and often funny, which are then placed where everyone can see them, and are meant to establish a discourse or dialogue between opposing forces—the center and the periphery.

His first project, titled, *Portrait of a Generation,* took place as a response to the riots in Paris in 2006. JR ventured to the *banlieue,* the densely packed immigrant communities in the outskirts of Paris, and photographed the urban youth causing the unrest. The images were then pasted overnight in the center of Paris, calling attention to the fact that the rioters were young Parisians hungry for recognition and equality, citizens who in fact were harming themselves by burning their own cars and destroying parts of their own neighborhood. JR often picks the sites for his interventions based on what he sees on the news. In 2007 media coverage led him to Israel and Palestine where he initiated the *Face 2 Face* exhibition. The project consisted of photographing Jews and Palestinians in the same trade and placing their gigantic images next to each other on the sides of buildings and on the wall dividing the two territories. The artist had many intentions with this endeavor: First he wanted to establish a dialogue by showing that the inhabitants of both sides of the wall are not so different. He then made it clear that both sides are suspicious of each other, living in fear and isolation of the "other," to the degree that the artist was warned by inhabitants of both sides not to cross into the neighboring country. When confronted with the images, most viewers could not distinguish the nationality of those portrayed. JR explains that only a nonresident artist, free from the constraints of producing concrete results in promoting peace in the region, could have carried out these actions. JR's interventions have continued throughout the world. In order to maintain a presence and a link to the communities he works in, he has established nonprofit organizations in the Middle East, Kenya, and Brazil. These organizations do not have a functional agenda; success is not measured by traditional metrics. And his activities are not meant to be practical or useful. In the end, JR is taking art to communities that are struggling for survival. His greatest contribution is recognizing those who have no voice, and who are misrepresented by global media. For this he was granted privileged access by drug lords to a Brazilian favela—one of the most dangerous communities on Earth—and was able to tell their story on the condition that he take their portrait—their oral history—and confront the world with it. Through this process, JR is simply dignifying the "other."

1

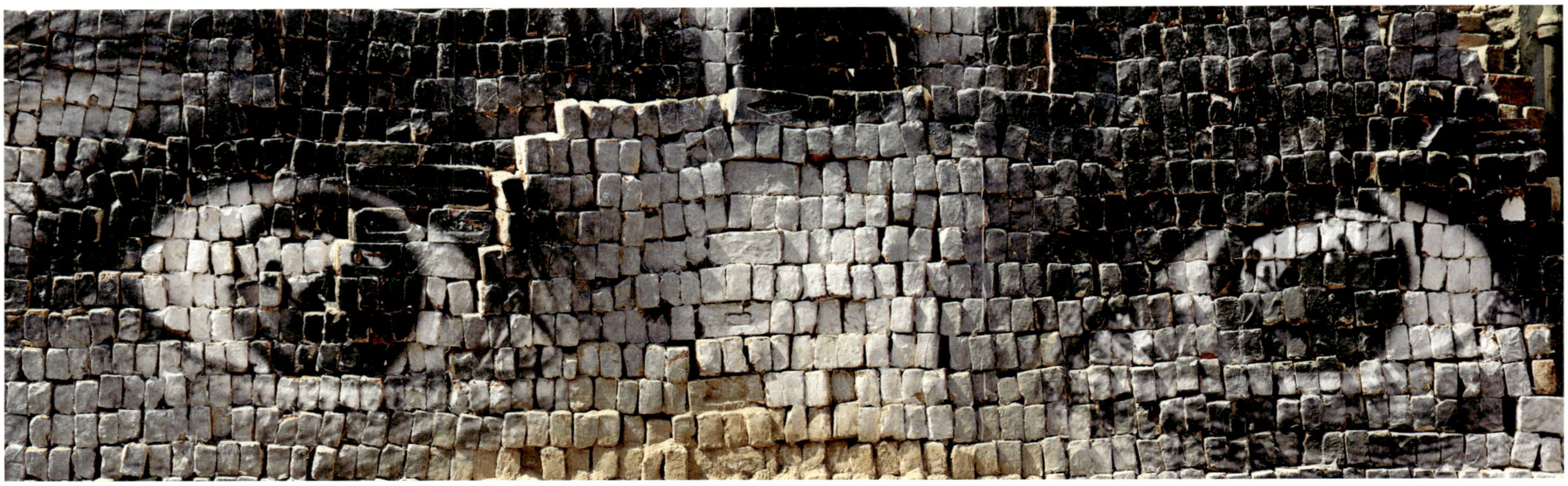

1
28 Millimetres
Women Are Heroes
2009, New Delhi, India

2–4
The Wrinkles of the City
2010, Shanghaï, China

2
Cao Minja

3
Jiang Qizen

5
28 Millimetres
Women Are Heroes
2009, Kibera Slum, Kenya

6 (next spread)
28 Millimetres
Women Are Heroes
2009, Favela Morro da Providencia, Rio de Janeiro, Brazil

2

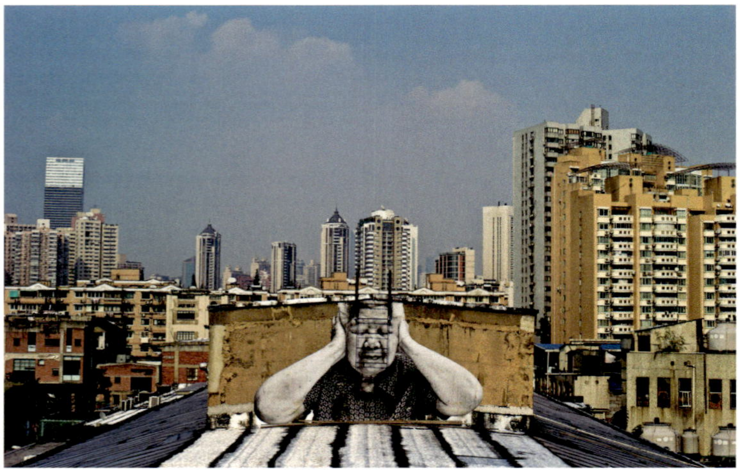

3

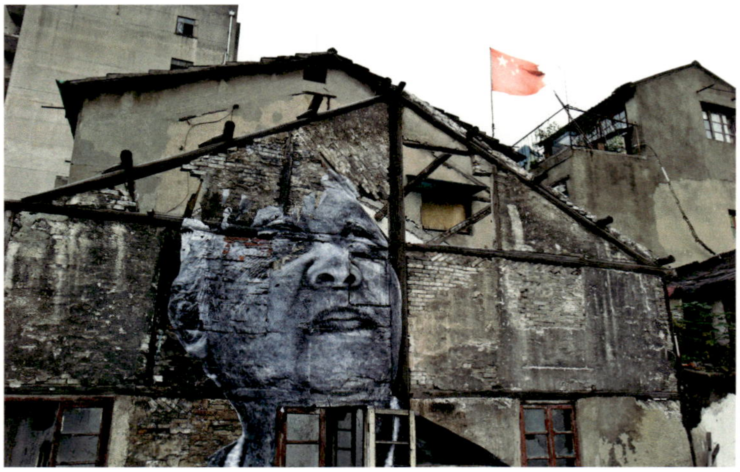

4

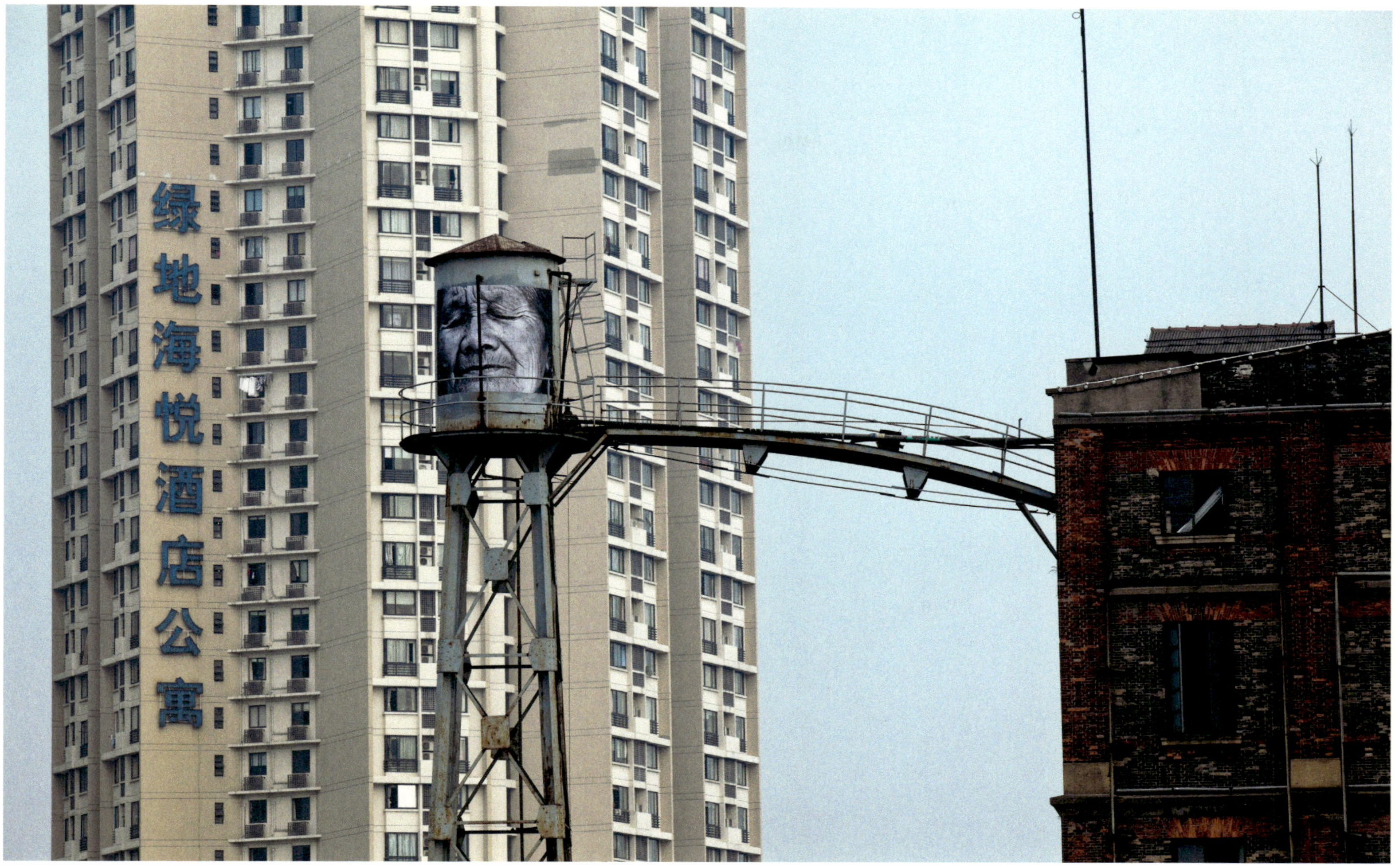

5

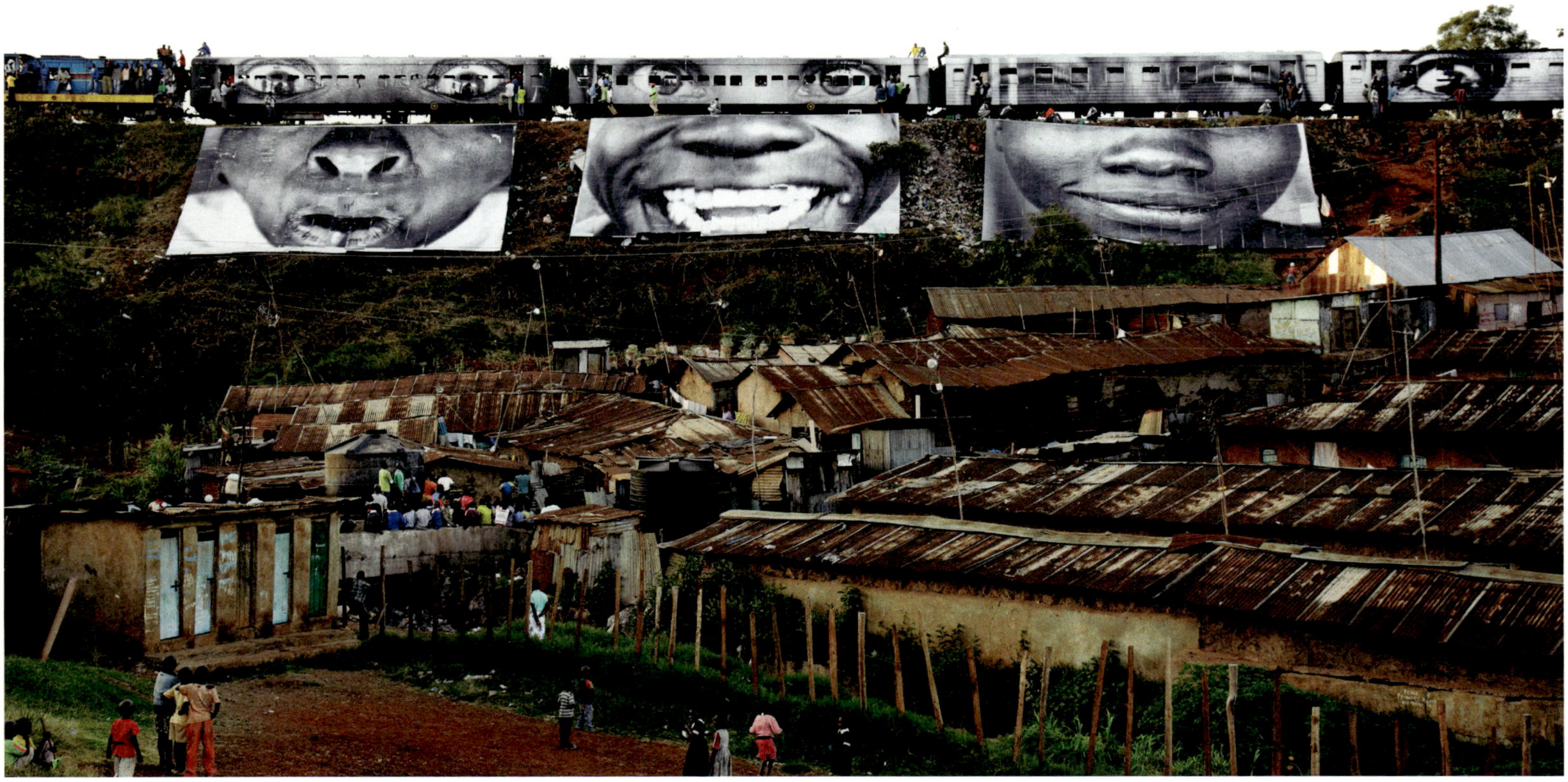

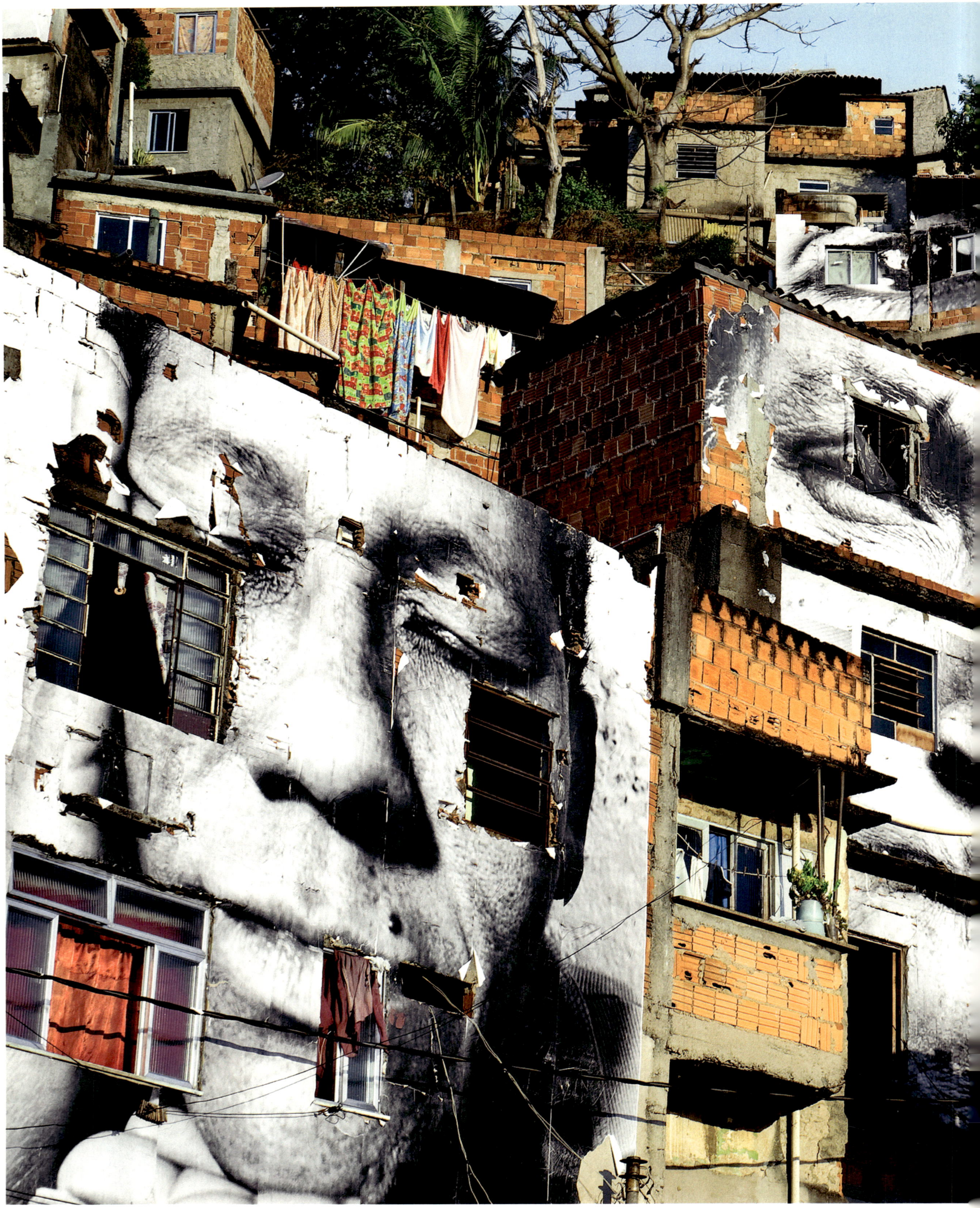

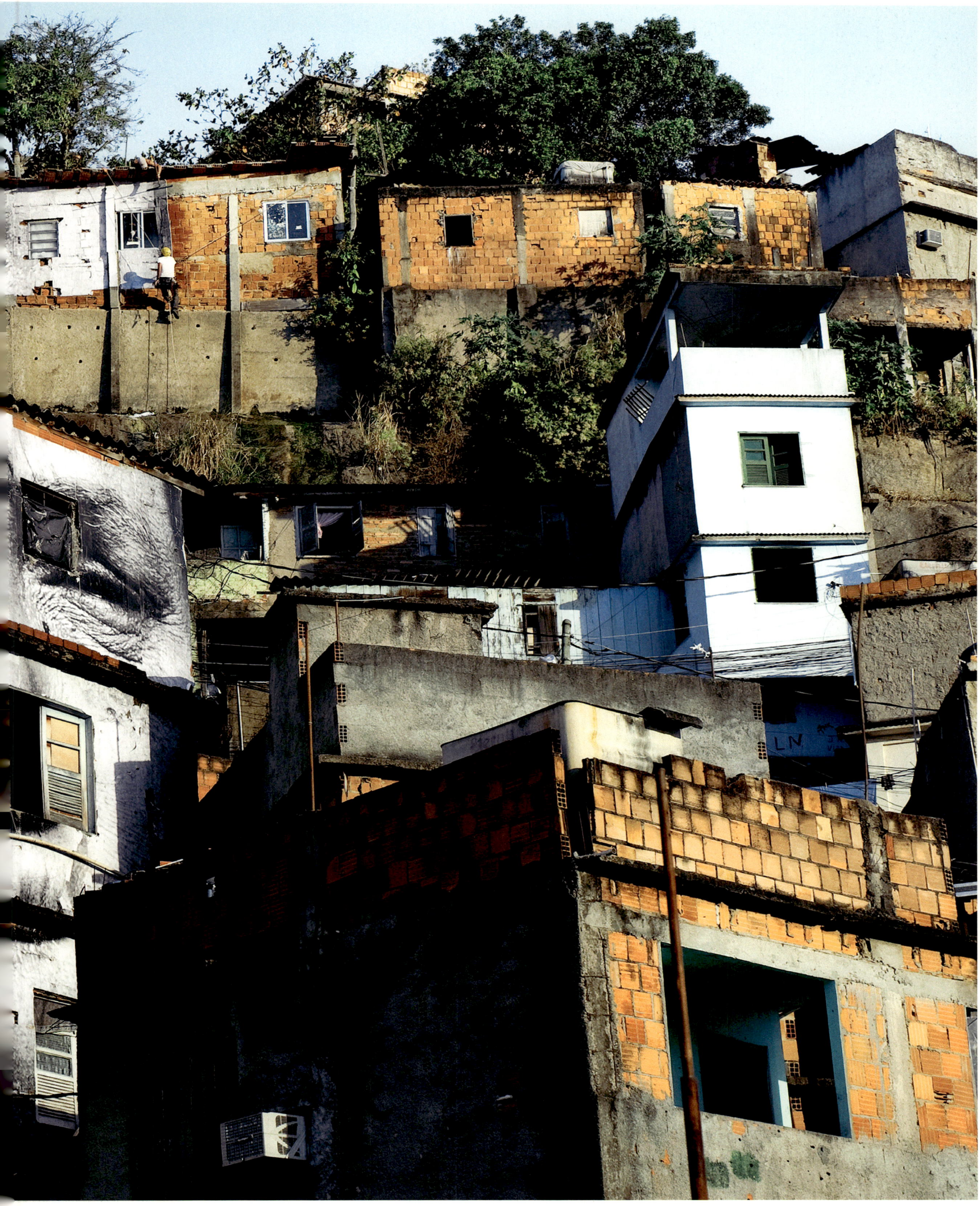

ALEXANDRE FARTO - VHILS

1-2
To Have or to Be
2010, San Diego, USA, Photo by Geoff Hargadon
3
Scratching the Surface
2009, Porto, Portugal
4
Scratching the Surface
2010, Medellin, Colombia
Scratched Plaster

Alexandre Farto (* 1987), born in Lisbon and lives in London, is better known as "Vhils," his artistic pseudonym. He creates his own special kind of street art using the methods of vandalism and a variety of often innovative processes, which he researches on an experimental basis. He is interested in the environment he is working in. Vhils tries to work with what he finds when he gets there, engaging in more ways than one with the layers of history in each location. In the series *To Have or to Be,* 2010, for instance, he creates portraits from layers of posters stuck on top of each other. He creates the shapes and colors by tearing off the various layers in different places. For the artwork in his *Scratching the Surface* series, 2010, the artist makes direct use of the building façade by applying to it a combination of quick-drying ink (Quink) and standard household bleach. He then removed layers of the façade piece by piece, creating portraits of unknown people that penetrate, so to speak, directly into the façade. These likenesses cannot simply be removed; they are now a fixed part of the house. Vhils's working methods bring the act of destruction and natural decay into contact with a creative, constructive process. In doing so, he finds inspired ways of incorporating exposed brickwork and other architectonic elements.

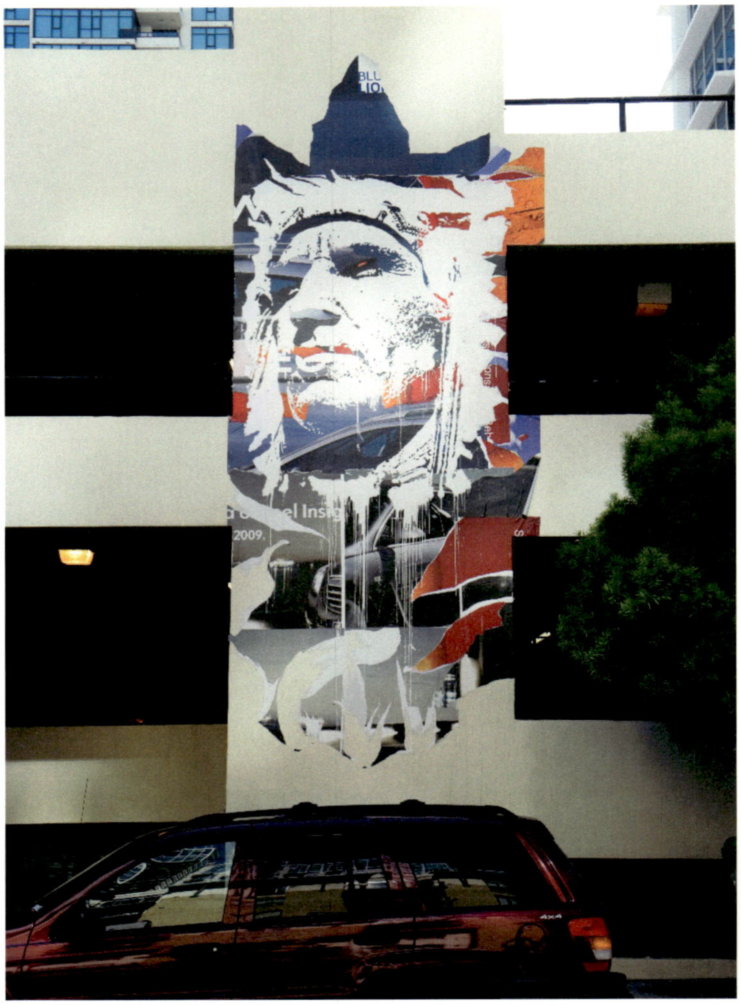

1

3

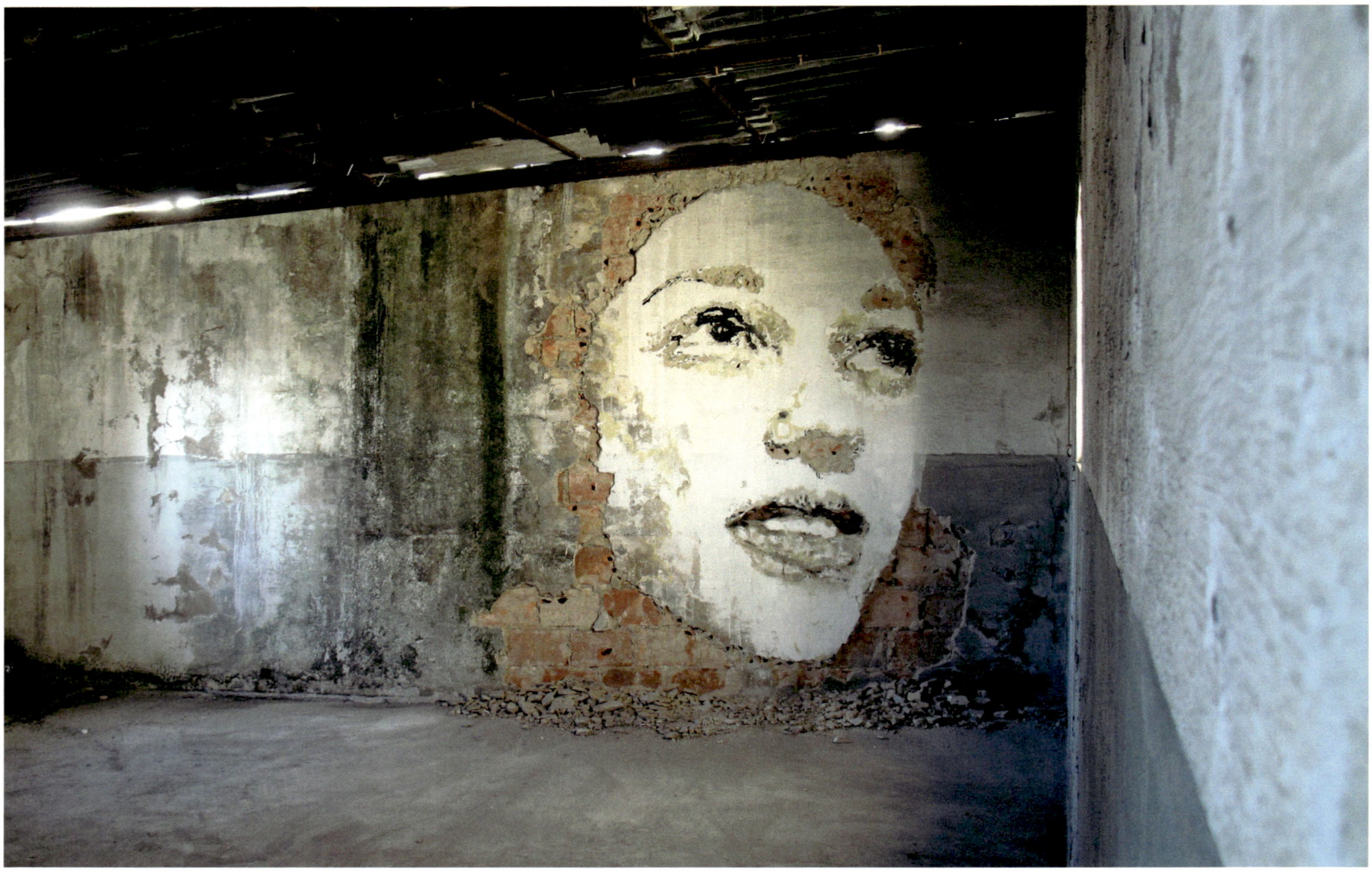

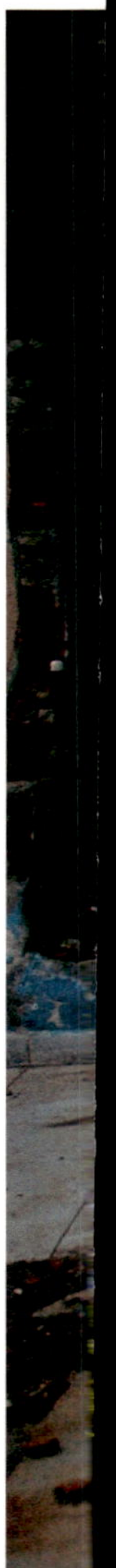

2

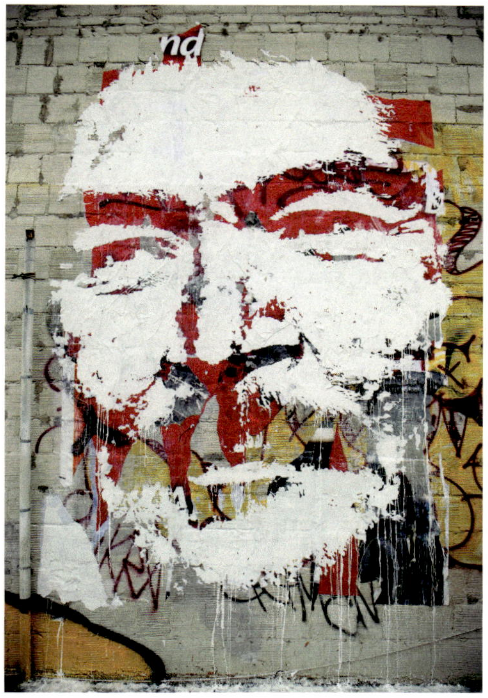

"ALL THIS CONFRONTATION BETWEEN DIFFERENT LAYERS, DIFFERENT MEDIA, GENERATES NEW THINGS. IT'S LIKE SAMPLING IN MUSIC; OUR GENERATION IS QUINTESSENTIALLY CUT AND PASTE, DIY."

4

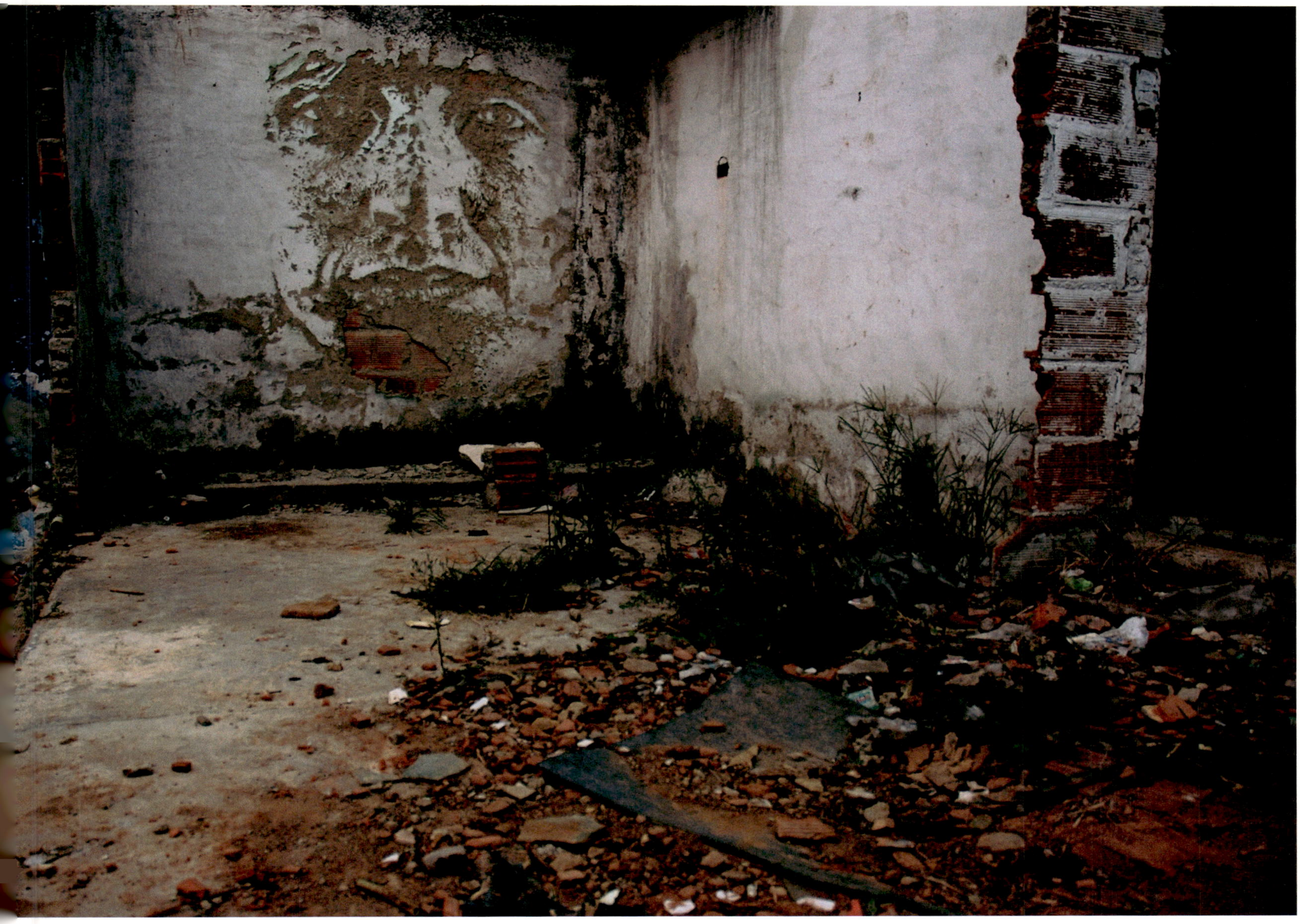

BLIUMIS

1
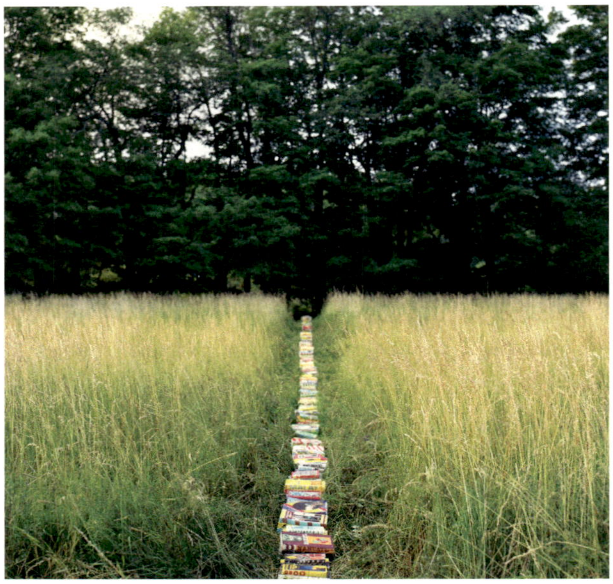

1–2
Language Barrier
2008, Andes, New York, USA
3–4
Language Barrier
2008, Lower Manhattan, New York, USA
3
Patel News Stand
September 30, 8–11 A.M., NE corner of Church Street and Park Place

Bliumis is an artist duo: Alina (* 1972) and Jeff (* 1958) Bliumis. Both were born in the former Soviet Union, and currently live and work in New York. They have been a team since 2000. For the artists, the country where they have made their new home provides the subject matter for many shared projects: how one integrates into a foreign cultural sphere, and the way that this cultural sphere is constantly influenced by new incoming cultures. In several projects, the duo use “dictionaries” made from foam, and have erected barriers made from these dictionaries, placing them in rural and urban spaces. The books' covers reproduce multilingual titles in print embellished with acrylic paint, suggesting the multifarious possibilities of communication, but also the many difficulties it involves. The fact that these books cannot be opened, and that they are often incorporated into the installations in such a way that the titles can only be guessed at, at best draws attention to language barriers, but also shows how they form bridges with other cultures. After all, through language and the way we express ourselves, we constantly transmit part of our own culture into another culture. In 2008, Bliumis installed the *Language Barrier* around their studio in Andes, New York. They wanted to create a visual representation of how the regional dialect spoken in the area defines a geographical area, as well as the cultural identity of local people. The wall of books created by the duo forms an almost continuous line that winds through and adapts itself to that landscape. For instance, it becomes an extension to an old stone wall, or takes on the shape of the hill. In this way, the artists define their own territory, and at the same time connect themselves with a country that they were not born into, but instead consciously chose as their home. The multicoloured book covers emphasize the cultural influences that they bring to their new home. The artist duo use foam for a very good reason: the *Language Barriers* they build are a kind of protective chain, but are easy to break into. For their urban space interventions in 2008, the artists chose Lower Manhattan—an area characterized by a unique mix of cultures, and by juxtapositions of past and present. They erected their *Language Barriers* in various public places, each of which represented a factor that had shaped the development of the community. Sometimes Bliumis blocked the main route (Duane Park), or obstructed an entrance (the Civitella Ranieri Foundation), thereby highlighting the differences between events that take place inside and those that take place outside, and what it means for the exchange between the two, to be disrupted.

2
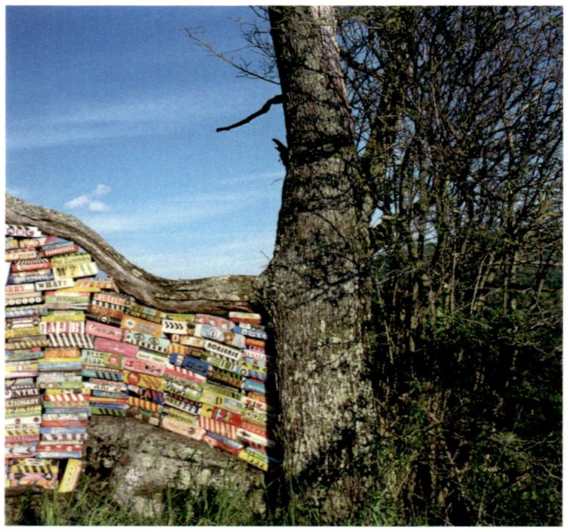

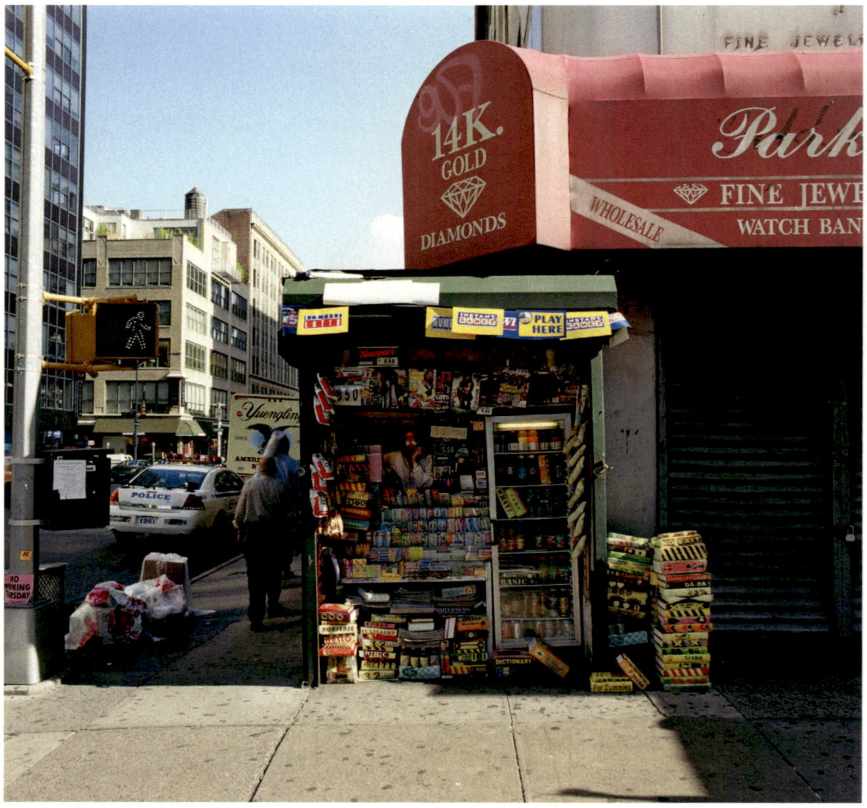

3

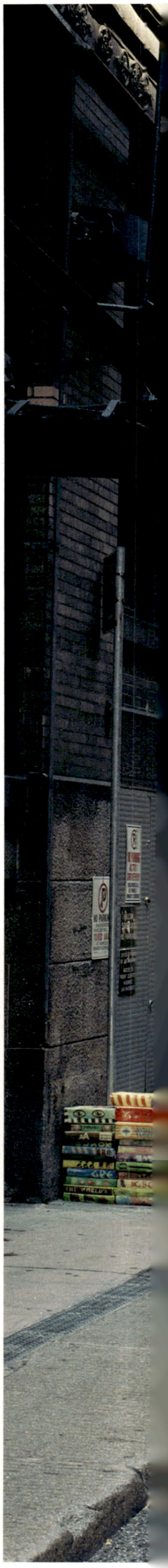

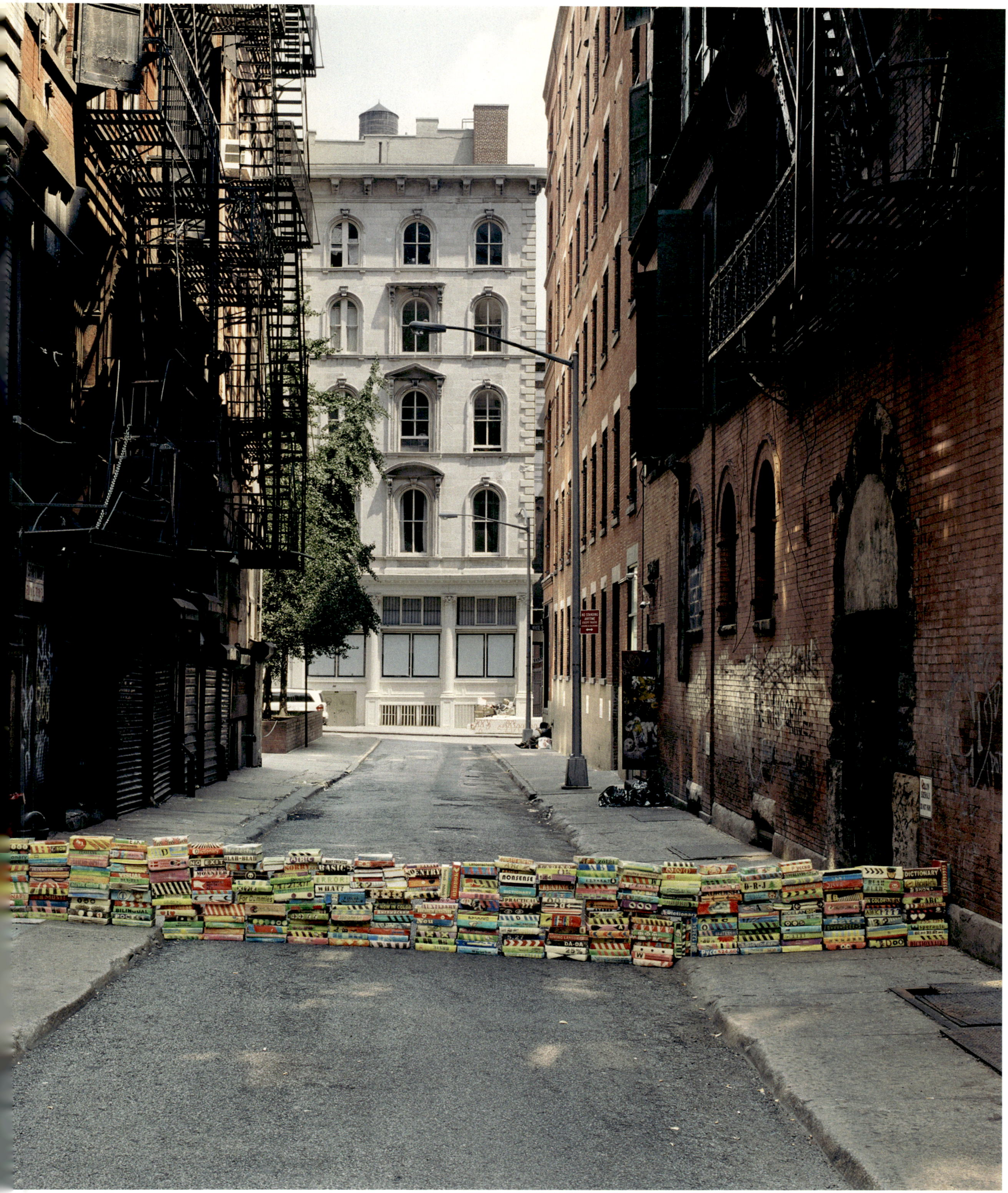
Dictionary
BLAH-BLAH
NO EXIT
MONSTER
VISUAL
BILINGUAL
POCKET
For Dummies
BASIC
ERROR!
WHAT?
NO ENTRY
NOW IN COLOR
NONSENSE
DICTIONARY
PRACTICAL
WARNING
DA-DA
DICTIONARY

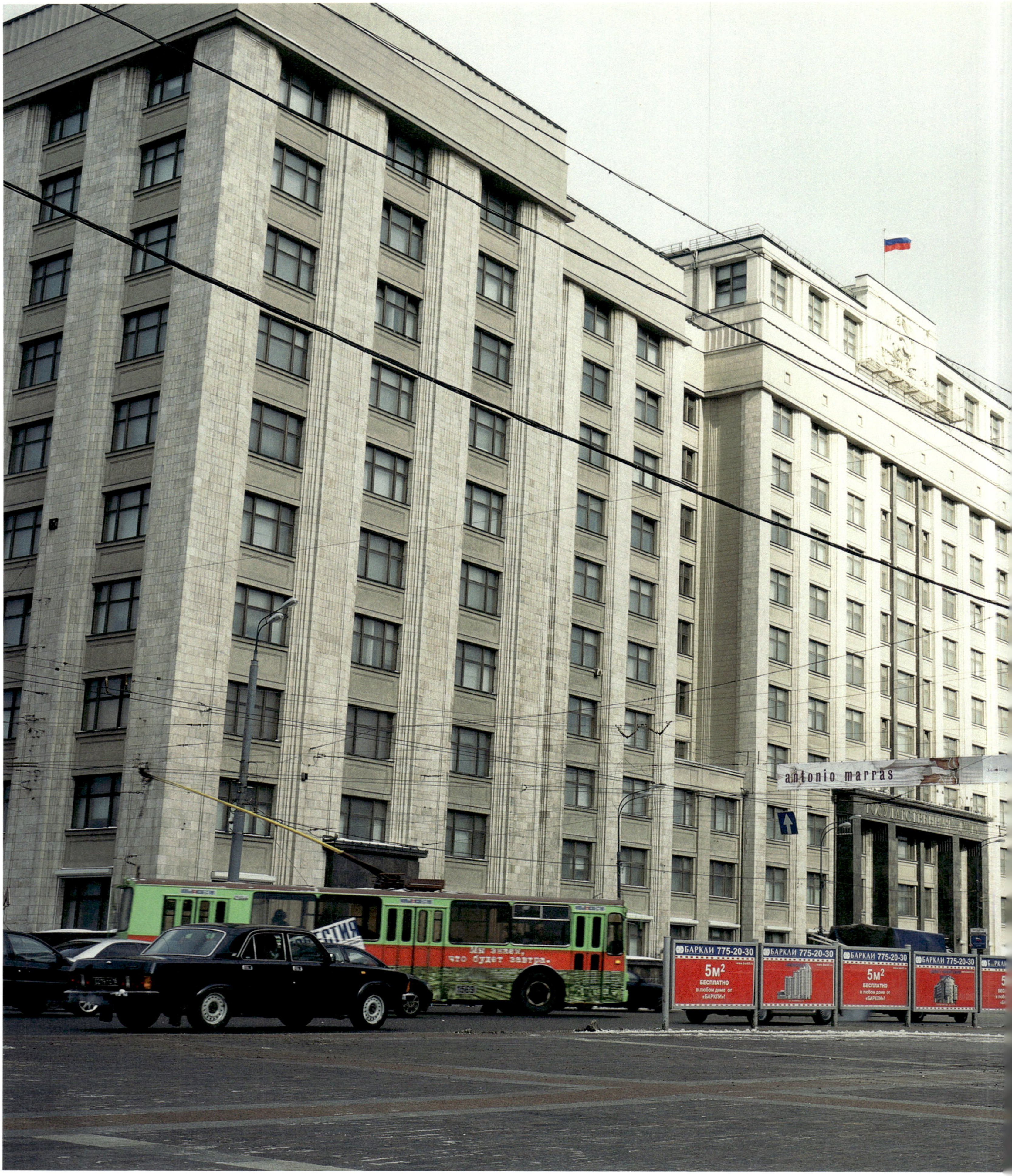
antonio marras
что будет завтра.
БАРКЛИ 775-20-30
5м2
БЕСПЛАТНО
в любом доме от
«БАРКЛИ»!

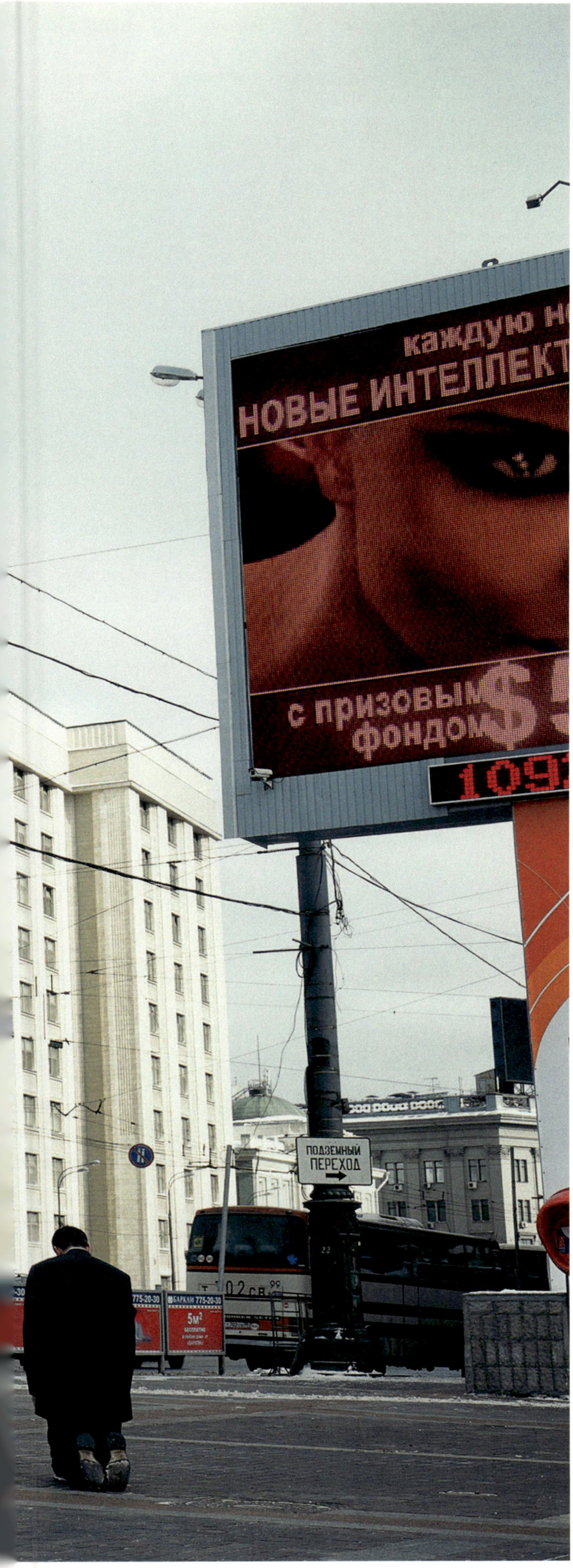

ZLATKO KOPLJAR

The Croatian artist Zlatko Kopljar (* 1962), who was born in Zenica, studied painting in Zagreb and Venice. Kopljar has been working on a cycle of artworks entitled *K* since the 1990s, with *K* standing for "konstruckcije" (constructions). In this cycle of artworks, Kopljar alternates between concept, construction, and feeling. He also relies on the conviction conveyed by strong images, and crosses materialism with metaphysics. In his photographic series *K9 Compassion,* 2003–2005, he kneels before the temples of economics, politics, and art: Wall Street and the Guggenheim Museum in New York, and the Duma in Moscow. His silent performance has religious connotations, but also suggests humility, sympathy, and submissiveness. For Kopljar, kneeling symbolizes a willingness to offer oneself—and as a sinner, one kneels in shame. In any case, Kopljar's series is a silent gesture without pomp or revolutionary aesthetics, but is strong enough to call into doubt the hegemony of power structures.

K9 Compassion
& K9 Compassion+
2005, Collection MSU Zagreb, Croatia, Photos by Christian Nguyen

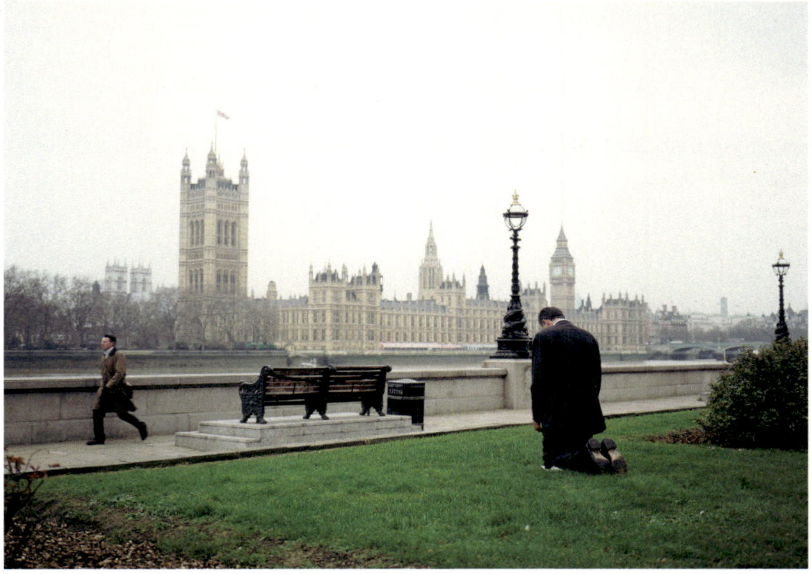

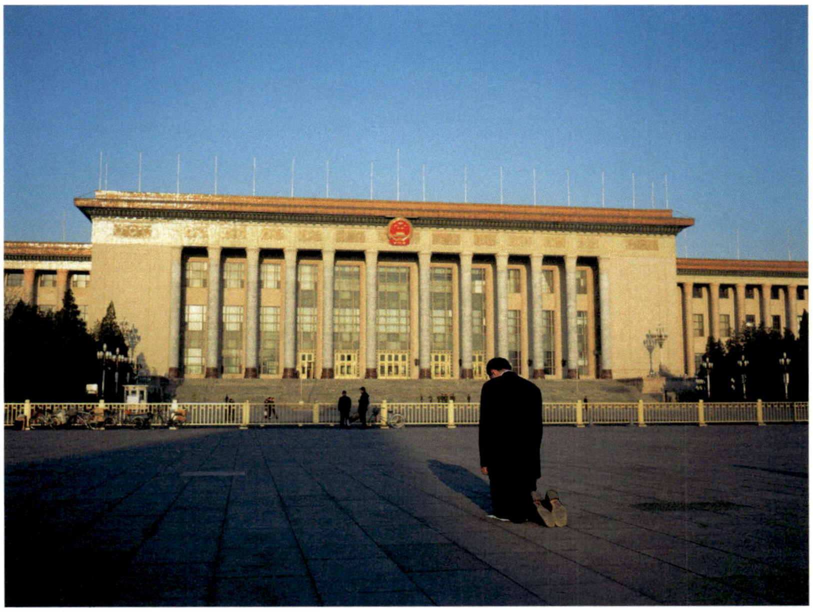

DULCE PINZÓN

1

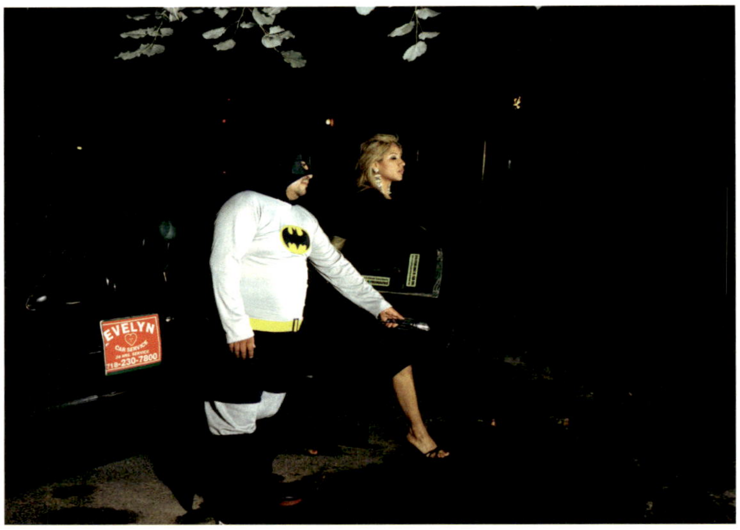

Superheroes perform incredible feats and save lives. Believing in them can help us to come to terms with dangers, and with our fears. In the wake of 9/11, it struck the Mexican artist Dulce Pinzón (* 1974), who was born in Mexico City and now lives in New York, that this concept had gained a particularly high currency in the United States. "The notion [of the American hero] served as a necessity in a time of national and global crisis to acknowledge those who showed extraordinary courage in the face of danger, sometimes even sacrificing their lives in an attempt to save others." However, people who perform superhuman feats every day—not risking their lives in the process, but who are often driven to the limits of their strength—are not described as superheroes, and this is how Pinzón sees Mexican immigrants. "It is common for a Mexican worker in New York to work extraordinary hours in extreme conditions," she says. They work "for very low wages, which are saved at great cost and sacrifice, then sent to families and communities in Mexico, who rely on them to survive." She illustrates this situation in her *Superheroes* series of photographs, which she started work on in 2005, by dressing Mexican immigrants as superheroes from American and Mexican comic series and films and photographing them in their workplaces in New York. For instance, a waiter appears as Mr. Elastic, who can easily reach the bar and the table at the same time; The Thing is able to operate a pneumatic hammer without any great effort thanks to his super strength; and the protector Batman makes a perfect driver. By transforming the immigrants into heroes whose powers match what the protagonists need to do in their daily work, the artist highlights the magnitude of their achievements. Each photographic portrait is accompanied by a caption giving the subject's name, their hometown in Mexico, workplace, and type of employment, plus the sum of money that the immigrants send home weekly to their families in Mexico. These bare facts connect Pinzón's heroes with reality, while at the same time stressing their heroic actions even more. Given the considerable amounts involved and the sender's comparatively low income, viewers quite rightly ask themselves how these heroes manage to get by in an expensive city like New York.

2

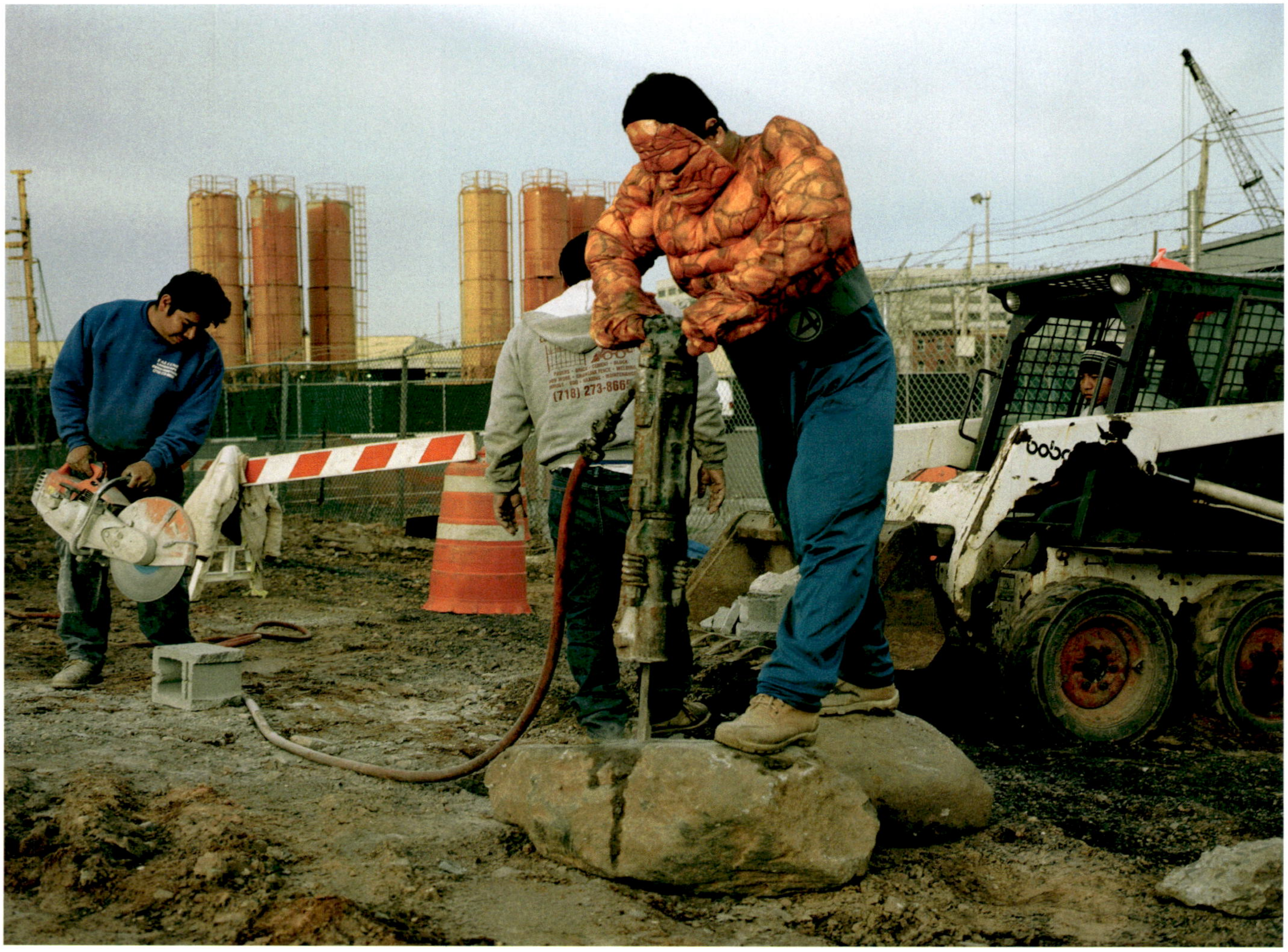

3

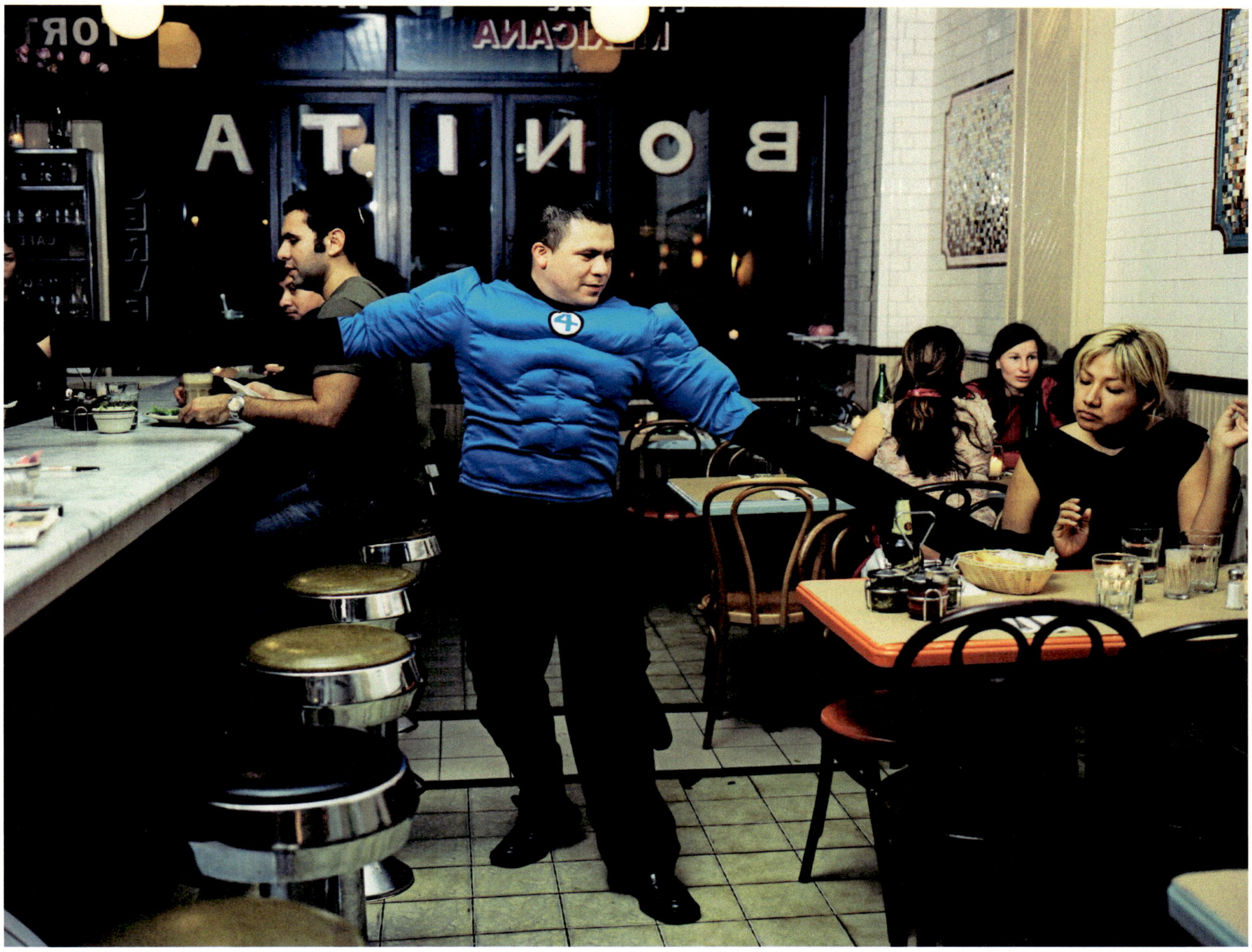

4

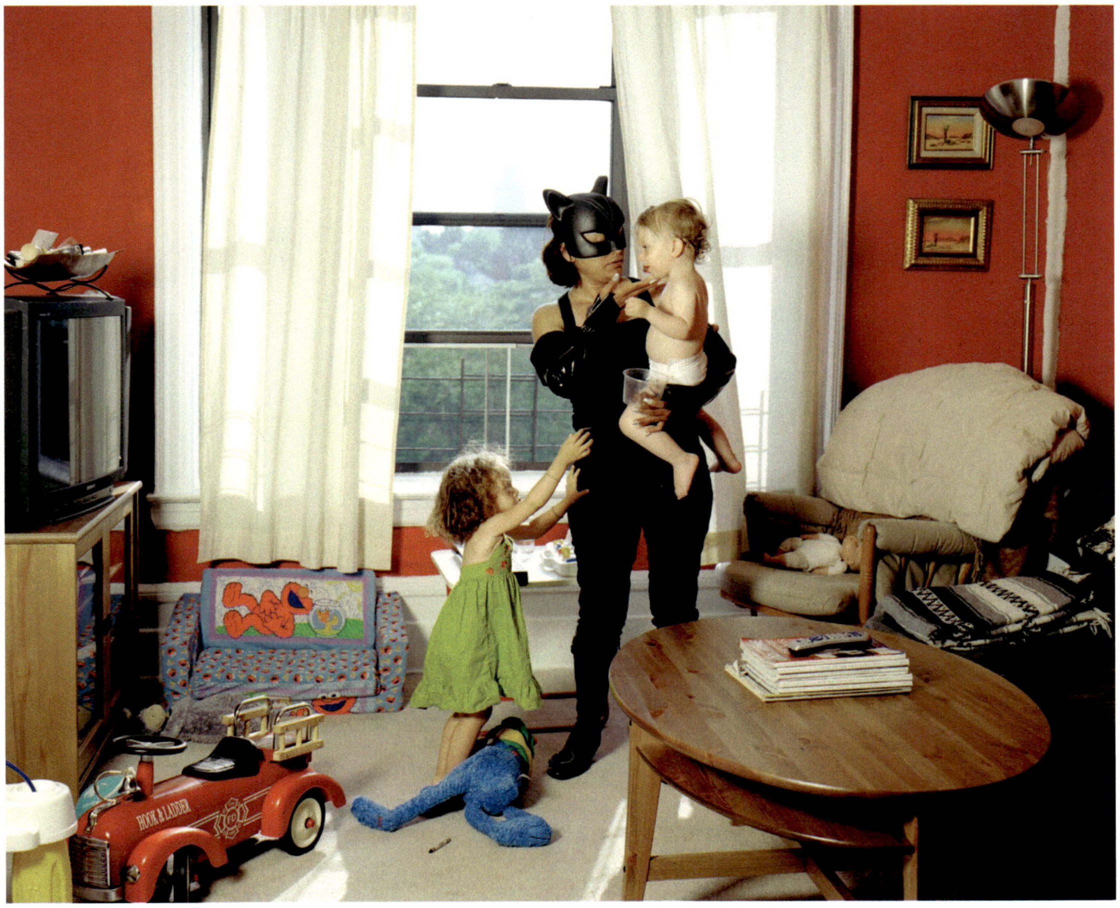

1–4
Superheroes
2005–2010, New York, USA

1
Batman 2
Federico Martinez from the State of Puebla works as a taxi driver in New York.
He sends 250 dollars a week.

2
The Thing
Luis Hernandez from the State of Veracruz works in demolition in New York.
He sends 200 dollars a week.

3
Catwoman
Minerva Valencia from Puebla works as a nanny in New York. She sends 400 dollars a week.

4
Mr. Elastic
Sergio García from the State of México works as a waiter in New York. He sends 350 dollars a week.

ELVIRA SANTAMARÍA

"I DON'T USE THINGS, I TRY TO HAVE A DIALOGUE WITH THEM."

1
48.480 White Ones
and a Red One
2007, Bogotá, Colombia
Photo by Eduardo del Corral
2
Stairs of the Paradise
2007, Bogotá, Colombia
Photo by Eduardo del Corral
3
Escala 1:1
2007, Bogotá, Colombia
Photo by Eduardo del Corral
4
Carmaquia with Rose
2009, Sweden
Photo by Giovanni Salaris

Elvira Santamaría's (* 1967) artworks combine rituals that are part of Indian culture with the political history of Mexico and the United States. Her performances are attempts to express the turbulent history of the two countries, which is full of tension and conflict. In *Escala 1:1,* 2007, for instance, she used her own body to measure the Plaza de Bolívar in Bogotá, while wearing a white garment to which the dirt—and by extension the place itself—clung to. She would stretch out on the ground, place a rose by her head, and then lie on her other side, repeating this process—continuing inspite of rain and physical exhaustion—until she had measured the whole plaza. Its surface area was 186 times the length of her body in total. The artist often receives spontaneous assistance in her performances, especially from children. Santamaría incorporates this intervention into her practice. The intentions can also change in the course of the performance, as the artist explains: "Action art is an amorphous form of art and existential practice of self-knowledge. Its poetry postulates self-creation through actions, and it is an endless process of learning. The symbolic act creates important reference points in the evolution of the consciousness of the artist, but the non-symbolic one is the true dimension of the present. I work with the things that life presents me in the moment. I don't use things, I try to have a dialogue with them. For me, the public context is the place where the creation of situations can deconstruct what we think about reality, human relationships, and ourselves. Following the ideas of the situationists—'The audience must not exist anymore, but les vivants (the living people), in their plural and diverse forms.'"

1
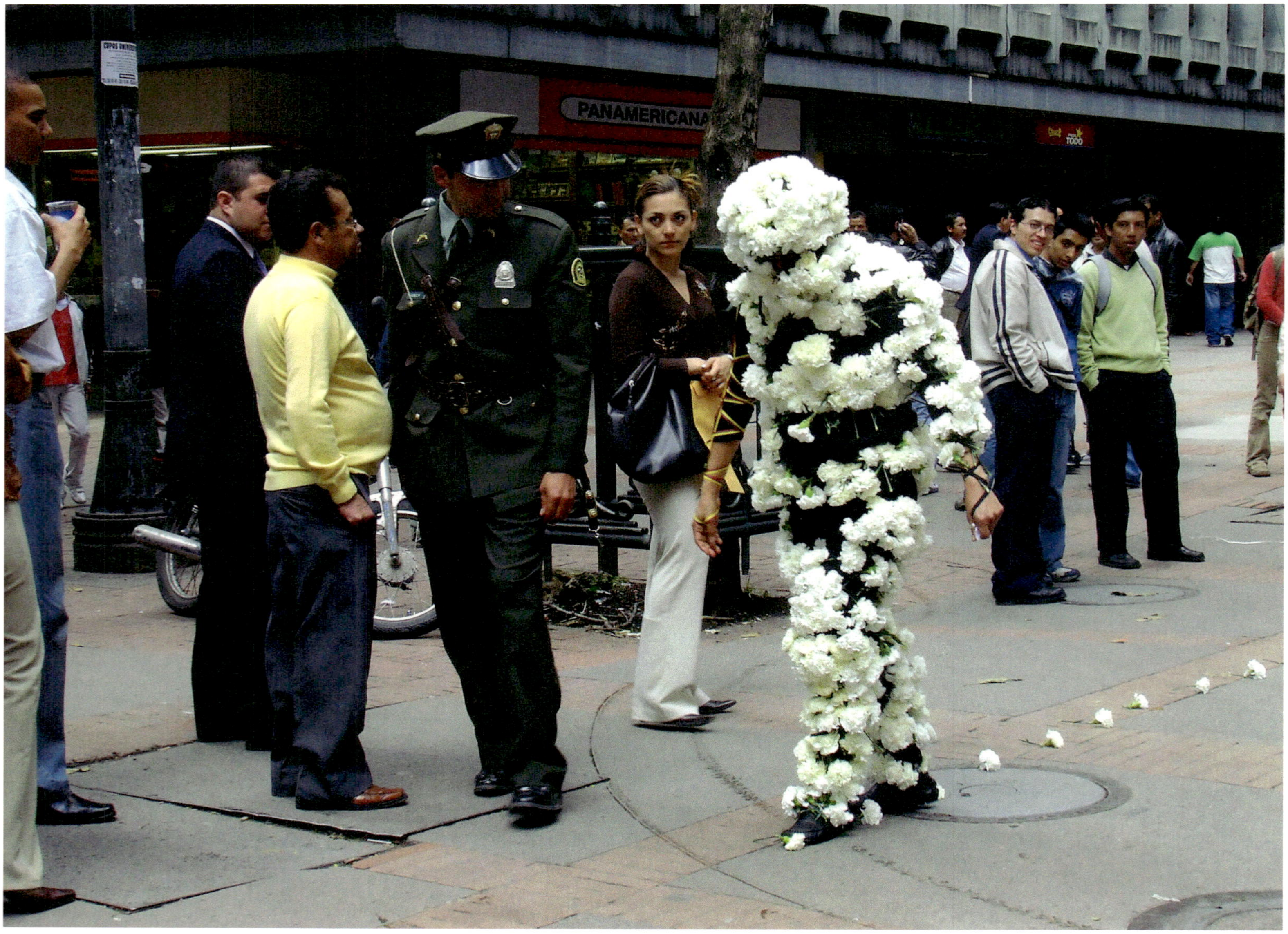

2

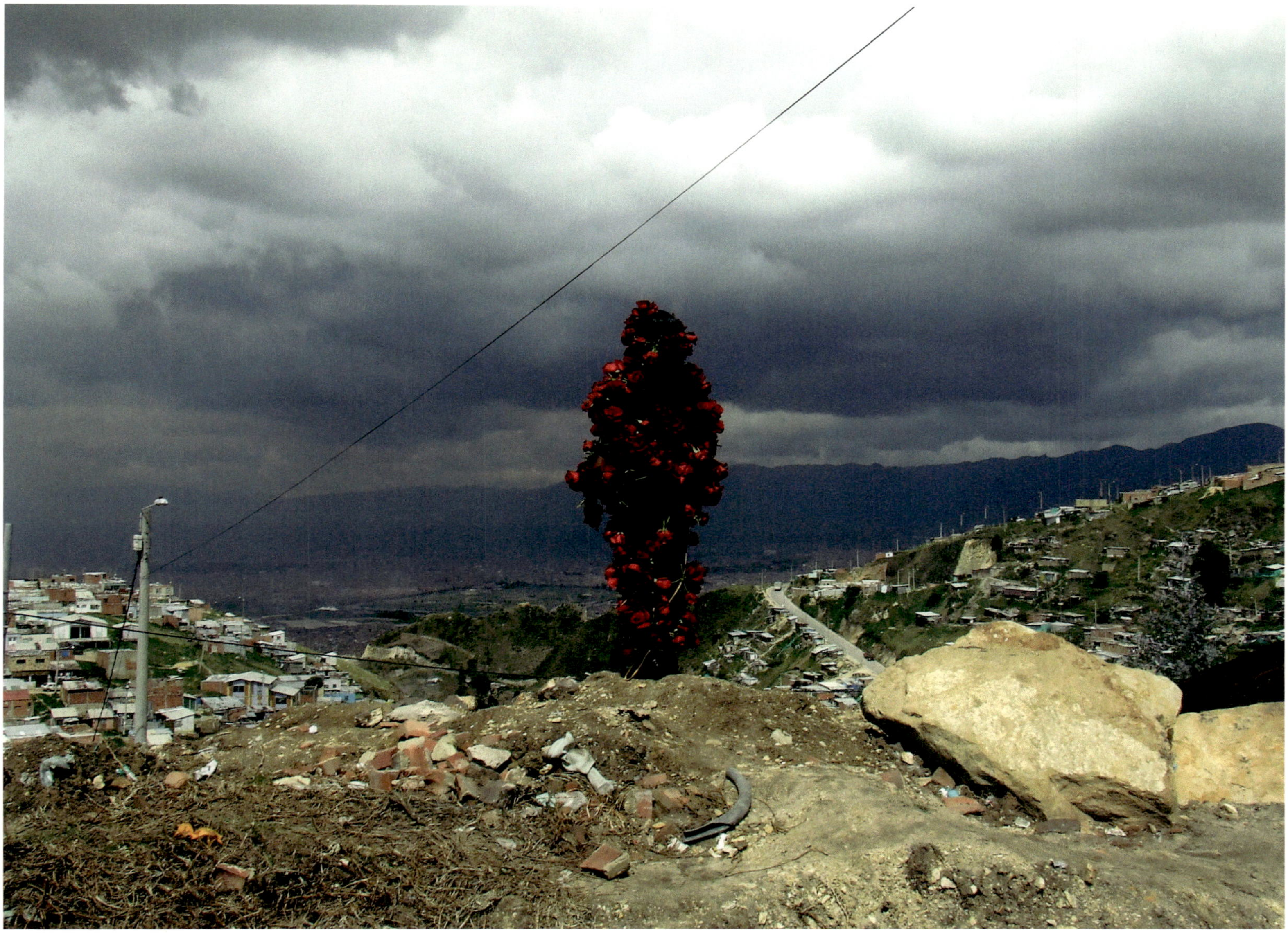

3

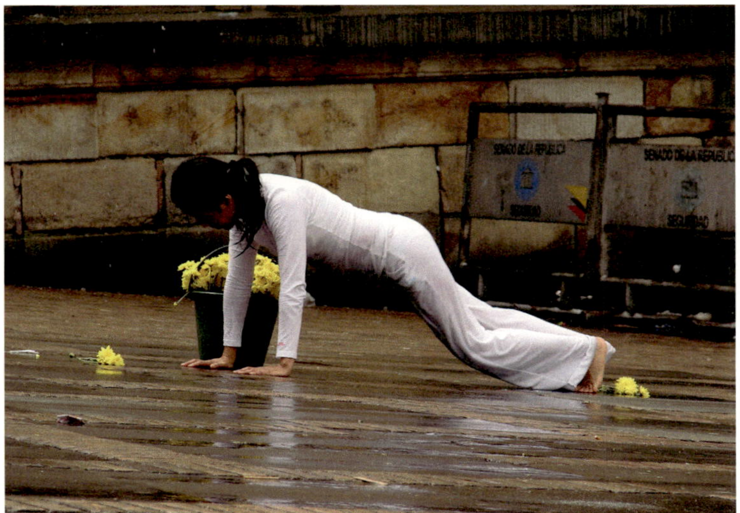

4

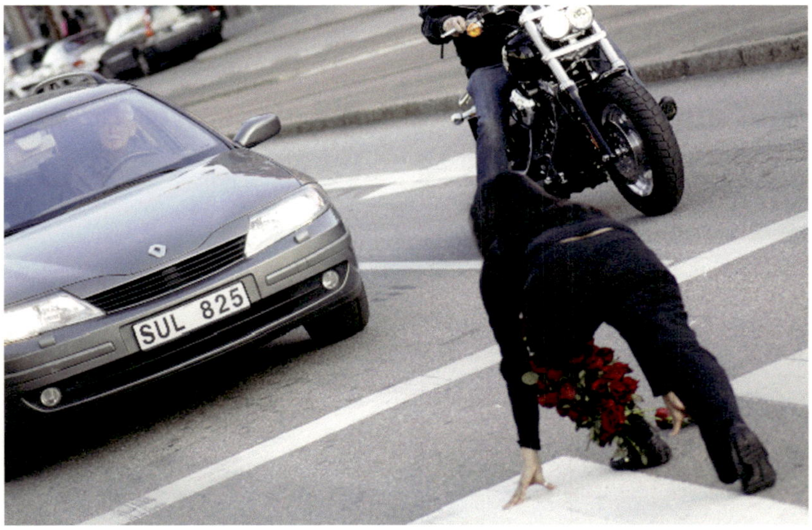

MORIS (ISRAEL MEZA MORENO)

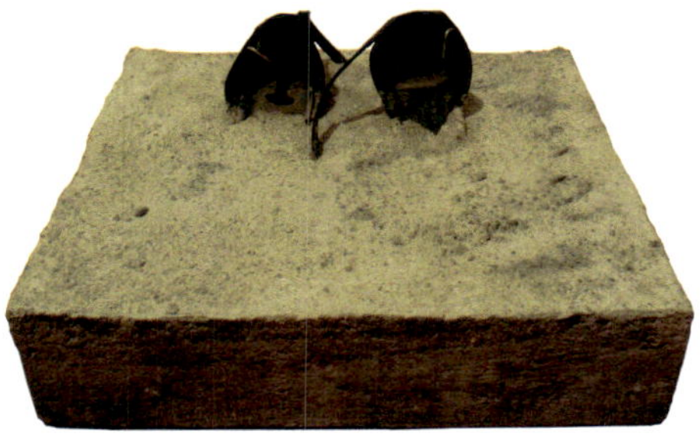
1

"THE WORKS DO NOT EXIST IN A MOMENT THAT ENDS WITH CENSURE OR THE EXIT OF THE VISITOR, THEY ARE ACTIVATED AFTER THE FACT IN THE FORM OF A RUMOR OR SHARED ANECDOTE, ENDOWING THE BEARER OF THE GIVEN EXPERIENCE WITH A NEW HABITUS THAT CAN BE USED OR FORGOTTEN."

1
Sembrar II
2009, Poured cement, found women's shoes
2
Paisaje Censurado 17
(Censored Landscape 17)
2010
3
Robar Invalido
(Rob invalid)
2007
4
Hermoso Paisaje 1
(Cartolandía)
Beautiful Landscape
(Cardboard City)
2007, Mexico, Collection Isabel and Agustín Coppel

Moris (Israel Meza Moreno) uses the dense urban jungle of Mexico City as an excavation site and laboratory for his artistic practice. For Moris, public space functions as the site for field exercises where the artist moves about the city observing, collecting data, and objects that will later be studied, processed, and transformed into art. Moris studies the survival strategies developed and adopted by the inhabitants of marginal communities in Mexico City. His art is a response to the adverse conditions that are dealt with on a daily basis by millions of people around the world. Rudimentary architectural techniques used to build shelters by the homeless, or basic housing for low-income families, homemade tools—including weapons—designed for specific needs, codes of conduct, signage, and secret ciphers used by burglars all form part of Moris's urban vocabulary. The artist is also tapping into the unbridled ingenuity and extreme resourcefulness of these communities—skills needed to survive in communities with limited resources and strict codes of conduct.

Moris is an insider; his level of engagement goes beyond observation and collecting data. The artist lives in one of the most dangerous neighborhoods in Mexico City, where his studio is in ground zero from which he ventures not as a tourist, but as a native. Working from within, he is granted privileged access to the city and its inhabitants. This familiarity allows for exchanges with the people who live there. Tools that have been used to commit violent acts such as bats, knives, and other weapons, are at first appropriated and then modified to make art. Moris has pasted text onto a club that read, *Solo yo tengo la razon* (Only I Am Right), 2010. In one of his most compelling series of works titled *Nido de malvivientes* (Delinquent's Nest), 2007, the artist deciphered the symbols used by burglars to mark homes before robbing them. The symbols were drawn onto three torn sheets of corrugated cardboard with phrases such as, *Woman Alone, Charitable House,* and *Can be Robbed.*

Homeless children inspired the large-scale installation titled, *Hermoso Paisaje 7: golpes, pan duro y banõs de agua fria* (Beautiful Landscape 7: beatings, stale bread, and cold showers), 2010. A tower resting on a bed of sand alludes to a playground. Four plaster statuettes of San Judas Tadeo support the base—the patron saint of miracles serves as the pillars. The top half of the tower, which was made of cardboard boxes inscribed with prayers, has collapsed, revealing a makeshift mattress covered in the toxic glue known in Mexico as Resistol 5000. Replicas of *bolillos,* loaves of Mexican white bread, are strewn around the tower. Three tarps used to cover loads on trucks hang from the ceiling bordering the sand. The tarps have been cleaned, with dirt and grime removed from the surface in order to draw an idyllic American-style home; a brick wall that symbolizes the lack of access to a normal life, with text painted onto canvas that reads: "We are here but we are not playing." The installation shares the same theme as Luis Buñuel's classic film, *Los Olvidados* (The Forgotten) in which bands of homeless children struggle for survival. The artist incorporates elements used by children to navigate the urban jungle. Children beg for money and steal in order to purchase *bolillos* and Resistol 5000. The former is the cheapest and least-nourishing food, the latter is a toxic substance desired for the fumes that stave off hunger, and whose intoxicating high gives a false sense of security to those forced to sleep on the streets.

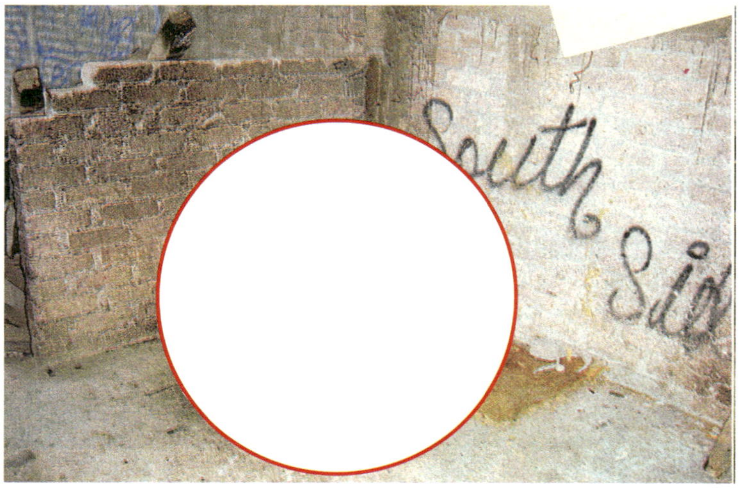

2

3

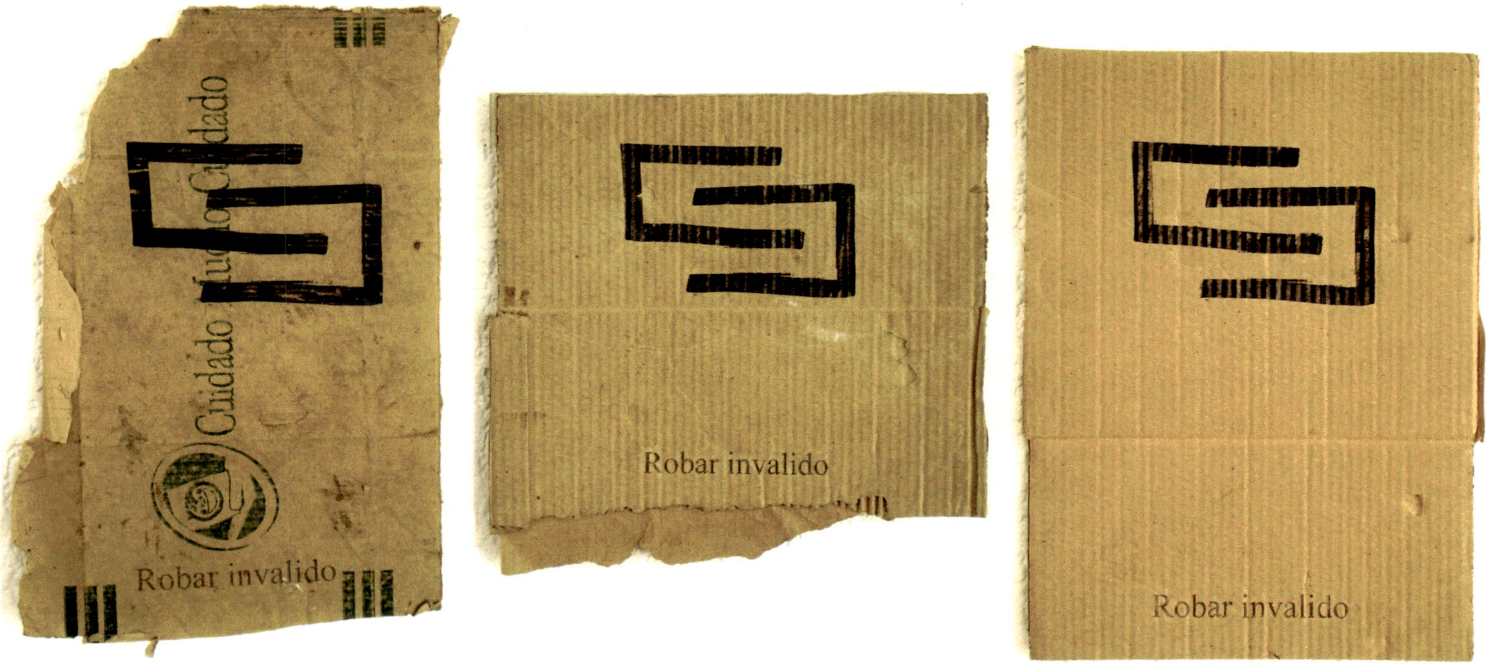

4

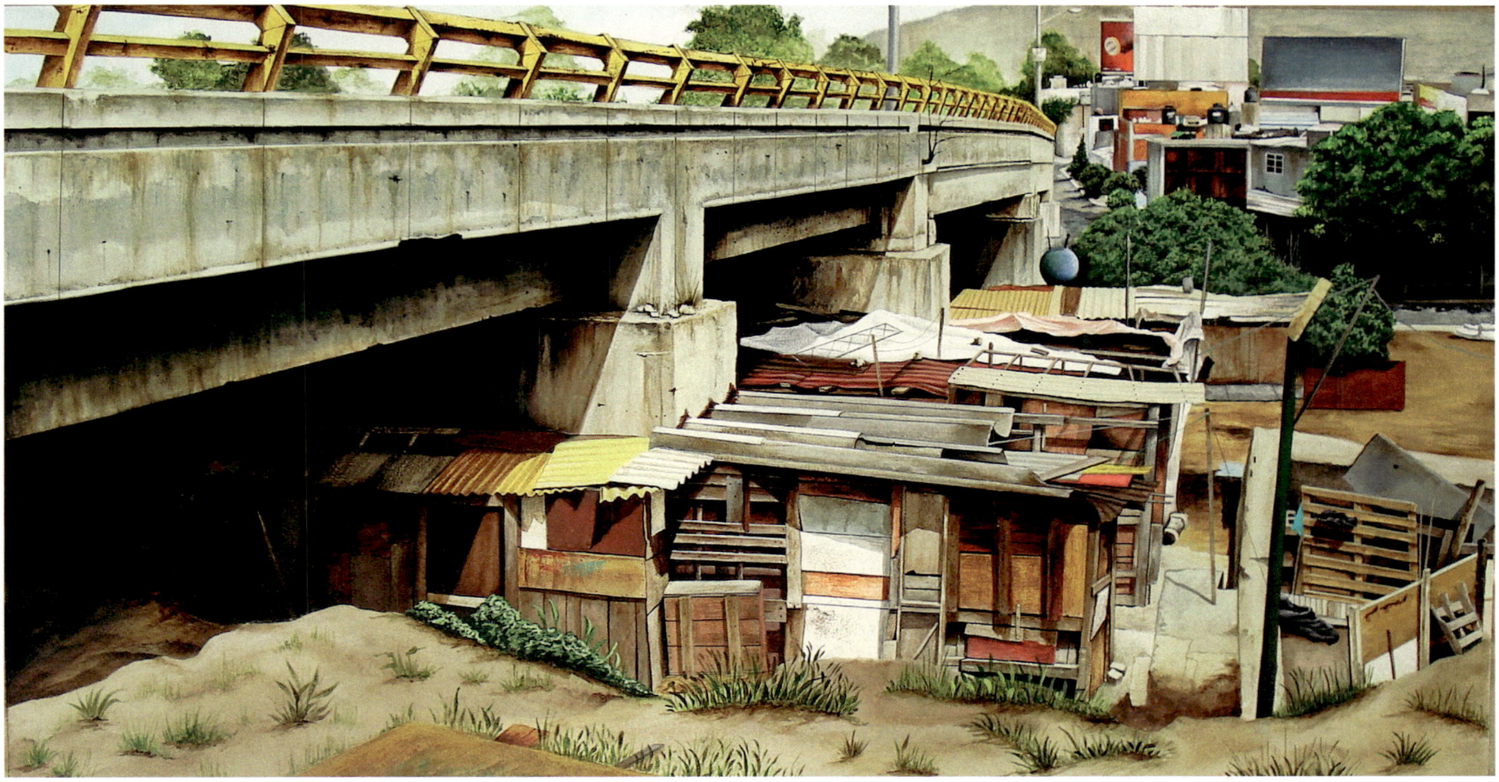

MARCOS RAMÍREZ "ERRE"

The economically lopsided relationship between the United States and Mexico shapes the work and practice of Marcos Ramírez "Erre" (* 1961). The artist, born and raised on the United States/Mexico border, resides in Tijuana, where the First and Third World meet. Although earning a law degree in Mexico, he chose to work building homes in San Diego for 17 years until he became an artist. In Tijuana, he waited in line for at least an hour a day to cross the busiest border in the world to work in the United States. There are few, more dramatic border-crossing experiences on earth. The chaos, dust, scarcity, and vitality of Tijuana functions in direct contrast to San Diego's gated communities, tree-lined streets, and military order. The abundance of resources found in California stands out against the shortages encountered across the border in Mexico. Ramírez's keen observation of economic disparity has led him on a quest to raise awareness of the systems of power that support corruption, and the concentration of wealth and resources. "Erre" combines his experience as a carpenter and his legal training to carry out a very public and site-specific practice. The former allows him to build beautifully crafted large-scale sculptural works, while the legal training infuses the work with critical arguments related to the theme he is pursuing. His work is most often found in public space, directly confronting the public with the issue at hand.

In 1994, as part of inSite, Ramírez addressed the issue of urban development and displacement by building a shantytown up against Tijuana's signature building, the Centro Cultural Tijuana (CECUT). The CECUT's emblematic spherical IMAX theater symbolizes the city's effort to transcend the image of the gritty border town full of cantinas and bordellos. Financed by the federal government, the CECUT is an integral part of the Rio Tijuana urban redevelopment project that transformed the shantytown into the cultural, financial, and commercial corridor that now exists there. The former inhabitants were pushed out. Three years later, again as part of inSite, Ramírez built a 10-meter-tall, two-headed Trojan horse that was placed on the border demarcation between Mexico and the United States. The horse sat in the middle of the busiest border on earth surrounded by thousands of cars that cross from Mexico into the United States every day. The Trojan horse was intentionally designed to be transparent, allowing the public to look inside the belly of the beast, revealing any hidden dangers. The two heads, one in each country, alludes to the complexities of the binational relationship between the bordering nations and the "gifts" exchanged between them. Two of Mexico's largest exports into the United States, labor and narcotics, are illegal. Both are fueled by a demand that is not officially recognized, and is primarily dealt with using strategies such as deterrence, or the militarization of the border—policies that enrich arms manufacturers and purveyors of military gear and vehicles. While the cheap labor from Mexico is needed to sustain a low-cost, high-standard of living enjoyed in the United States. In return, the United States unofficially exports weapons and cash for drugs that fuel a lethal combination of violence and corruption that is tearing Mexico apart.

1
The Prejudice Project
2006, Border San Diego, USA/Tijuana, Mexico

2
Century 21
1994, Tijuana, Mexico/San Diego, USA

Photos by Phillip Schultz Reitman

1

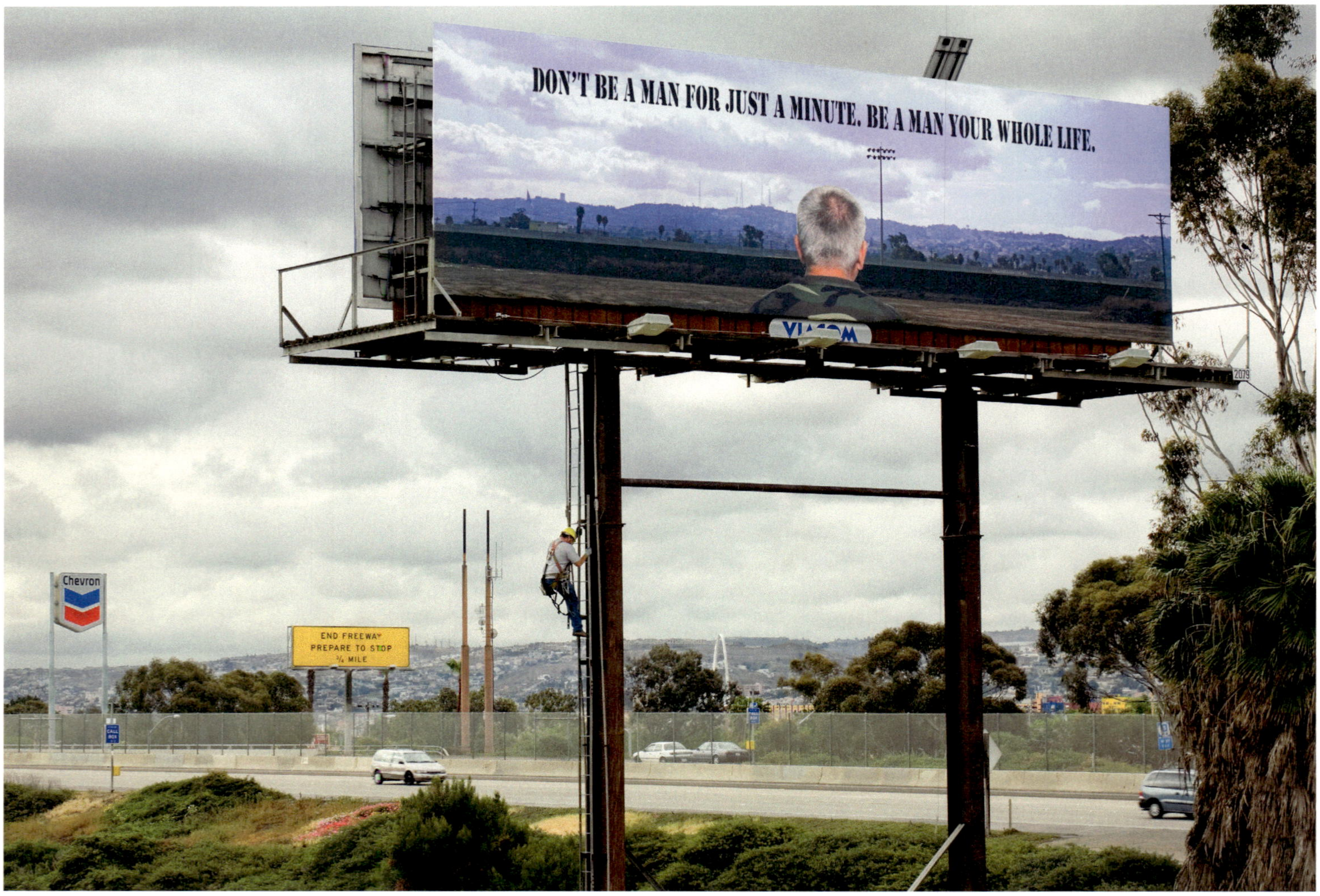

2

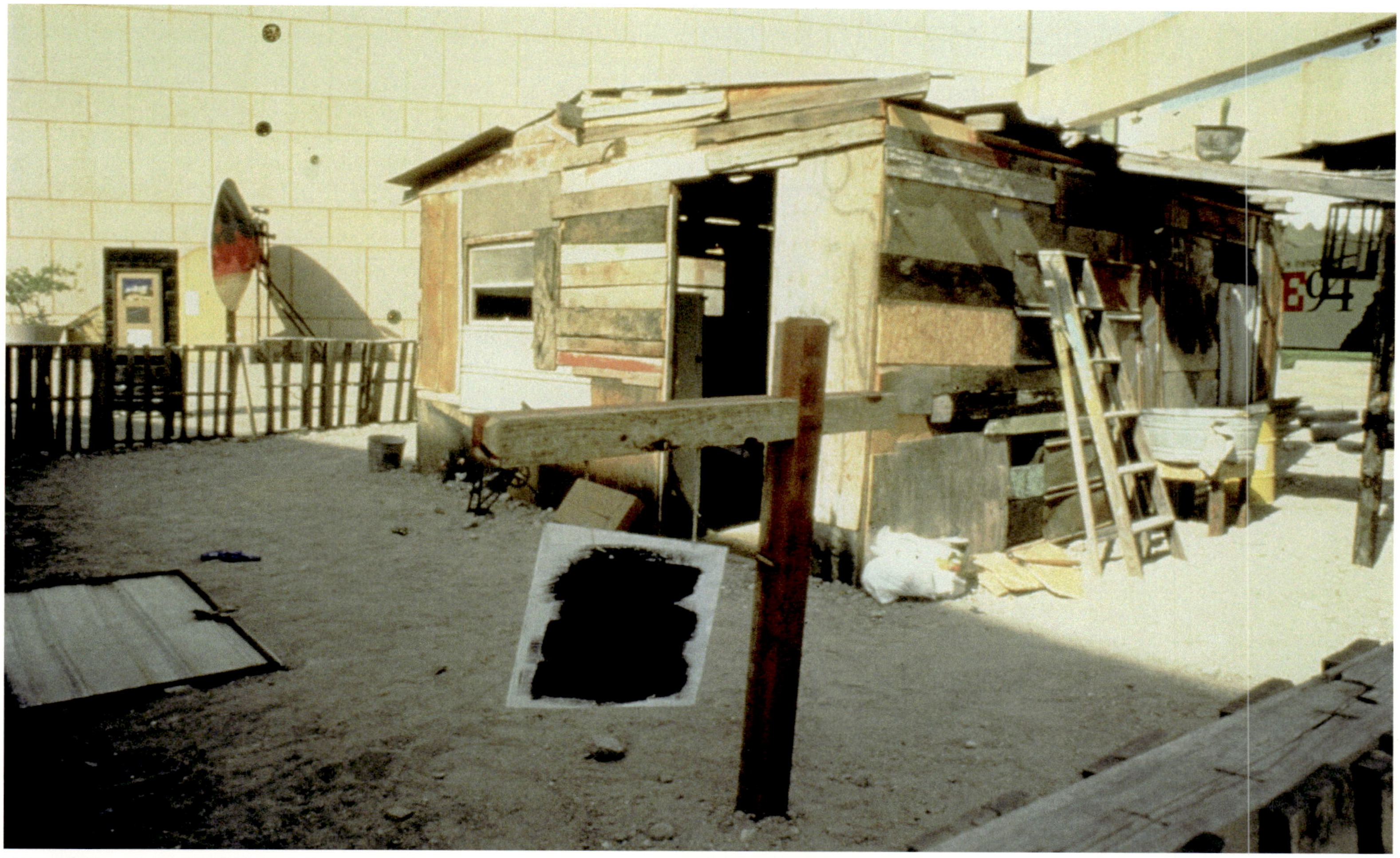

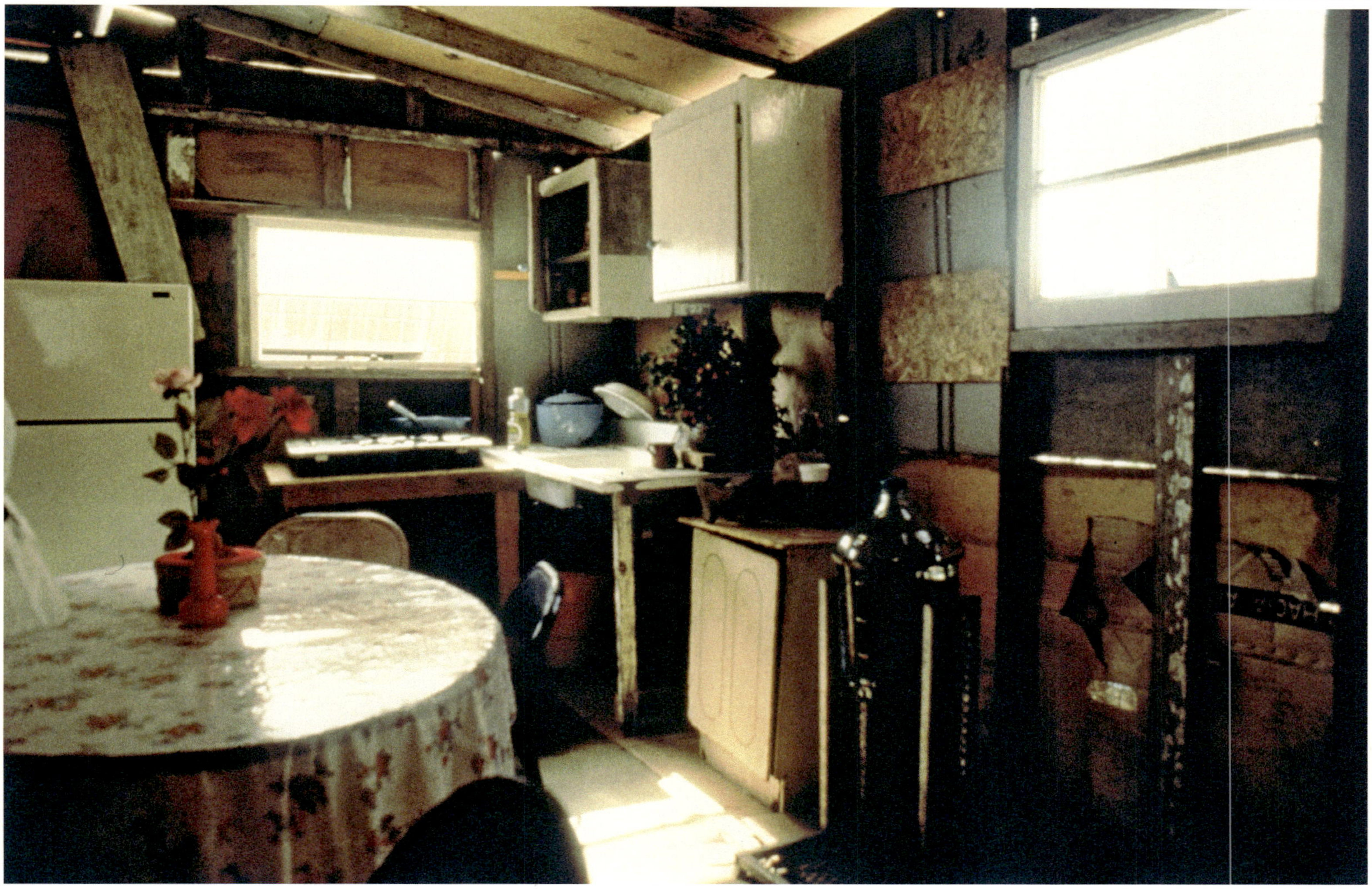

ESTUDIO TEDDY CRUZ

Tijuana/San Diego is the most crossed international land border on Earth. It is where the wealthiest nation on the planet meets the Third World. This area functions as one extremely complex community composed of two cities divided by an international demarcation, where by simply crossing the border the staggering differences between a *developed* and a *developing* nation are abundantly clear. Estudio Teddy Cruz (ETC) is an architectural firm that functions as a research team engaged in the exercise of simple observation of the dramatic contrast between Mexico and the United States, Baja California and California, Tijuana and San Diego, First World and Third World. ETC compares and contrasts the formal structures and systems of building, as well as real estate development in San Diego with the seemingly chaotic informal development in Tijuana. Where, for instance, homogenous communities are promoted; residential, industrial, and commercial use are strictly divided; density is controlled; and building codes enforced. While in Tijuana, which was one of the fastest-growing cities in Latin America, things just happen—the city grows and changes in many cases without the proper infrastructure. Mixed-use sites are not planned, they evolve; building materials are not fabricated, they materialize as urban waste from San Diego.

ETC created a chart combining text with images describing the exchange of materials and architectural influence between the two communities. The section entitled "South to North" describes the, "encroachment of Tijuana's land use patterns" on neighborhoods in San Diego using the example of immigrants transforming a single-family home into a Buddhist temple. In the other direction, discarded materials from San Diego head south and are used to build homes; old garage doors function as walls, and old tires are used to build retaining walls. This is not merely a relationship of excess versus scarcity where the excess materials flow across the border to be recycled and used; this is more about resourcefulness than resources, ingenuity and flexibility, versus codes and urban planning. The image in *Manufactured Sites* depicts steel elements that are designed and fabricated in Tijuana with the function of stitching together American waste to build a home. The homes rest on stilts, stationed above an area that will be used for commercial ventures.

ETC proposes an inverted model of urban planning and development that is not dictated by bureaucrats, businessmen, and politicians, but by learning from and employing the strategies developed by the inhabitants of informal communities—a bottom-up approach as opposed to the entrenched top-down model. "We argue that an alternative urbanism in our time will not be led by the buildings, but by the fundamental reorganization of the socioeconomic relationships."

1–4
Manufactured Sites
San Diego, USA/Tijuana, Mexico
Mexican factory produced frames used to stitch urban waste imported from the USA

5
North to South: Urbanism Made of Waste
South to North: Pixelating the Large With the Small
2010, San Diego, USA/Tijuana, Mexico
A video created by Estudio Teddy Cruz, as part of the studio's installation for "Spazio," an exhibition at the MAXXI Museum in Rome.

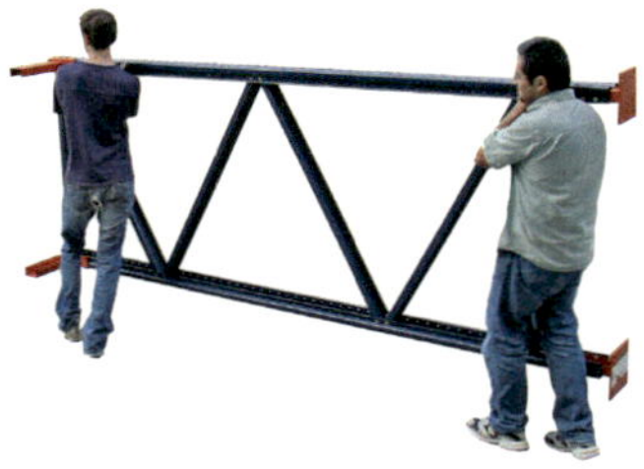
1

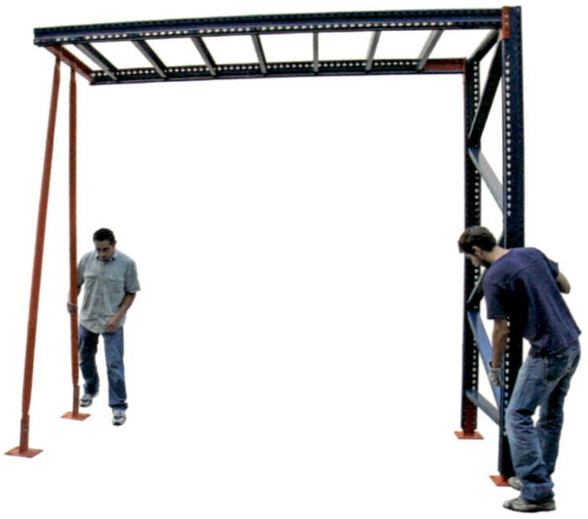
2

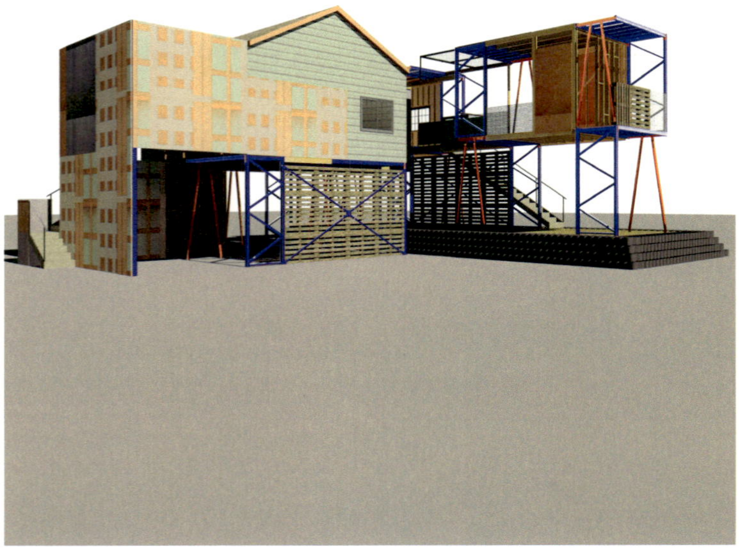
3

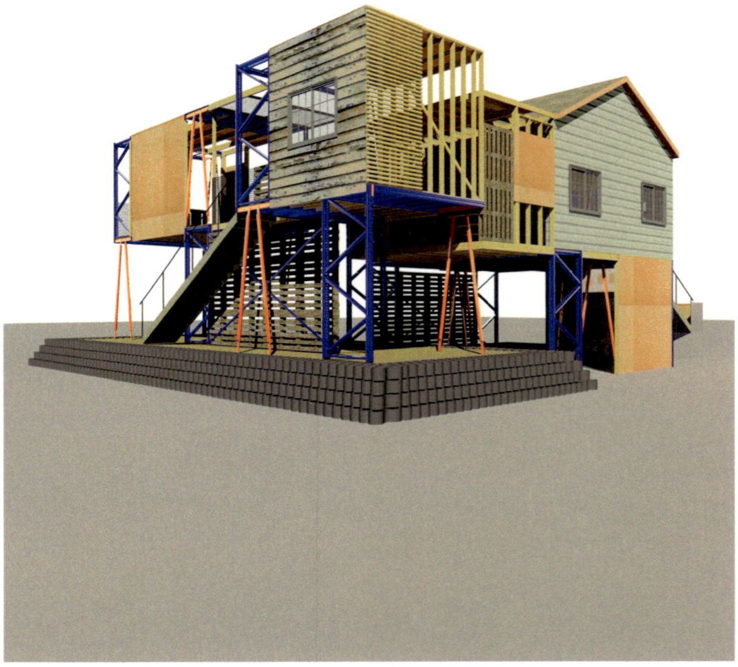
4

5

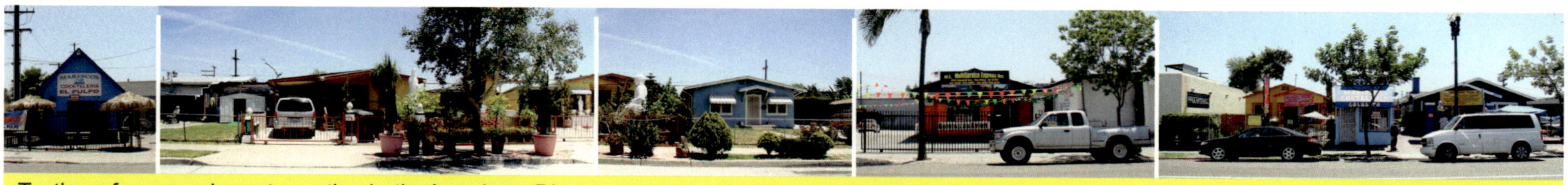

Tactics of encroachment: as the Latin American Diaspora travels Northbound, it inevitably alters and transforms the fabric of San Diego's older subdivisions, generating non-conforming mixed uses and high densities that retrofit Levittown with difference.

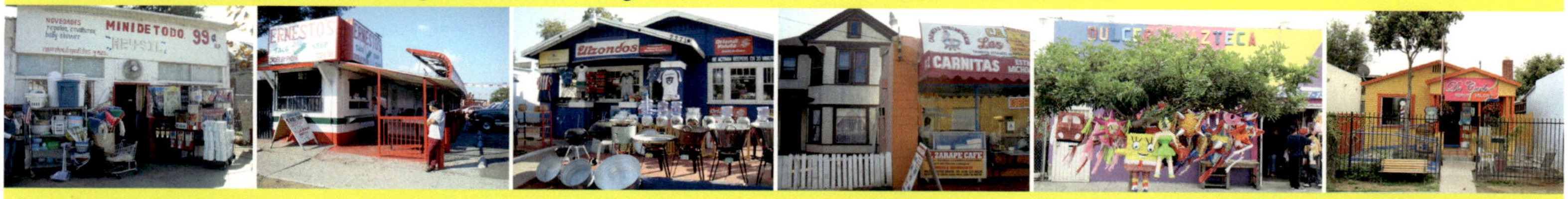

Non-Conforming Buddha: a tiny post-war bungalow in a San Diego mid-city nieghborhood has been transformed from a single-family residence into a Buddhist temple.

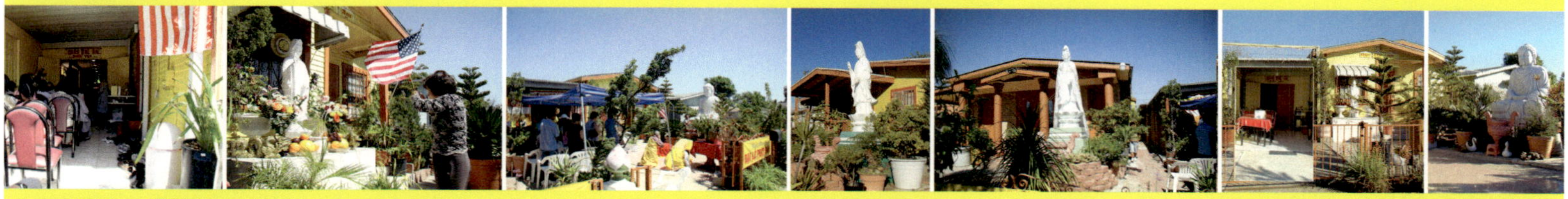

An urbanism 70' deep: thirty some tunnels have been dug beneath Homeland Security in the last eight years. One of the largest ones was discovered last year. It had retaining walls, water and air extraction systems and electricity. It connected a house in Tijuana and a factory in San Diego.

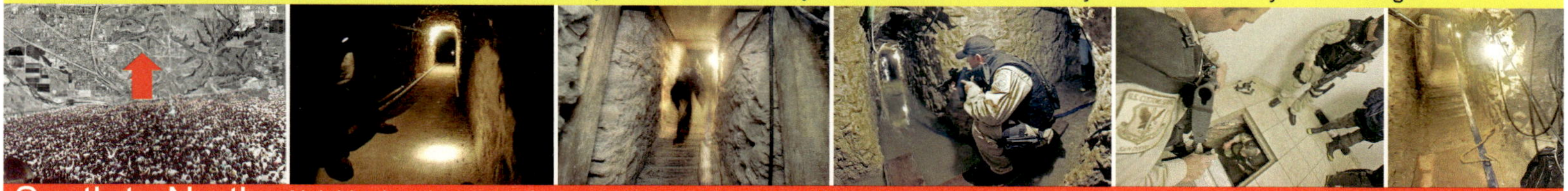

South to North: Neighborhoods made of non-conformity. Tijuana's informal land use patterns encroach into San Diego's sprawl.

North to South: Neighborhoods made of waste. San Diego's Housing waste is recycled into Tijuana's slums.

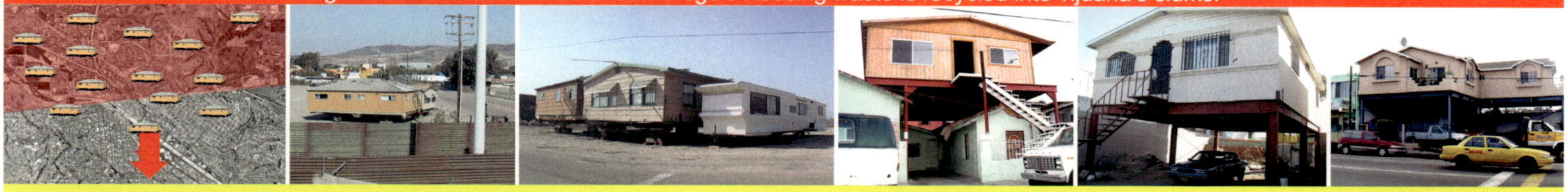

Migrant housing: Mexican builders recuperate post-war bungalows that are slated for demolition in San Diego, and bring them across the border. Once imported into Tijuana they are assembled above one story steel frames. These floating houses define a space of opportunity beneath them, that will be filled with other uses.

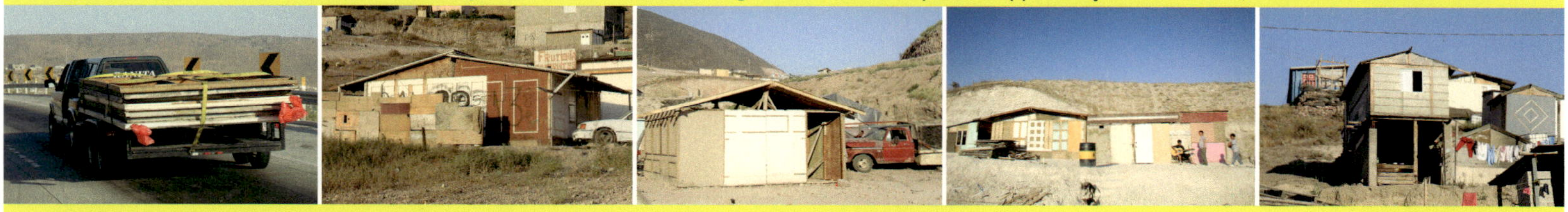

Housing urbanism made of waste: one city recycles the leftover of the other into a second hand urbanism. Used garage doors and wooden crates make wall systems.

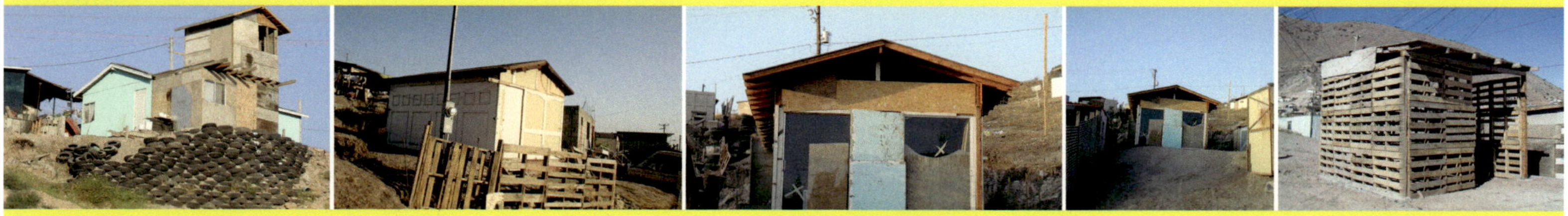

Recycled rubber tires are cut and dismantled into folded loops, creating a system that threads a stable retaining wall.

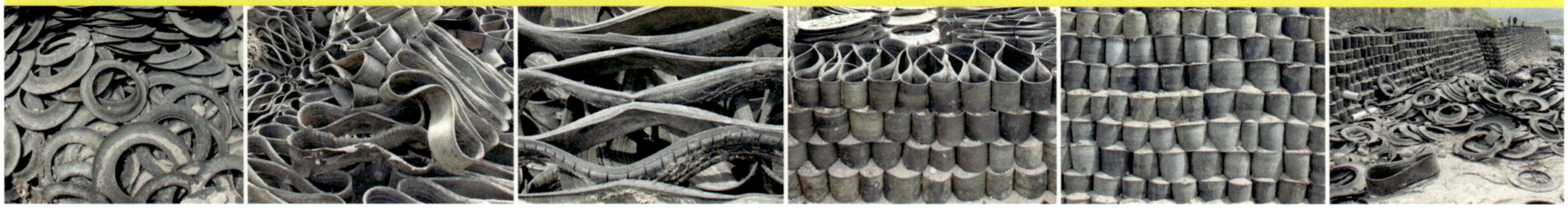

REGINA JOSÉ GALINDO

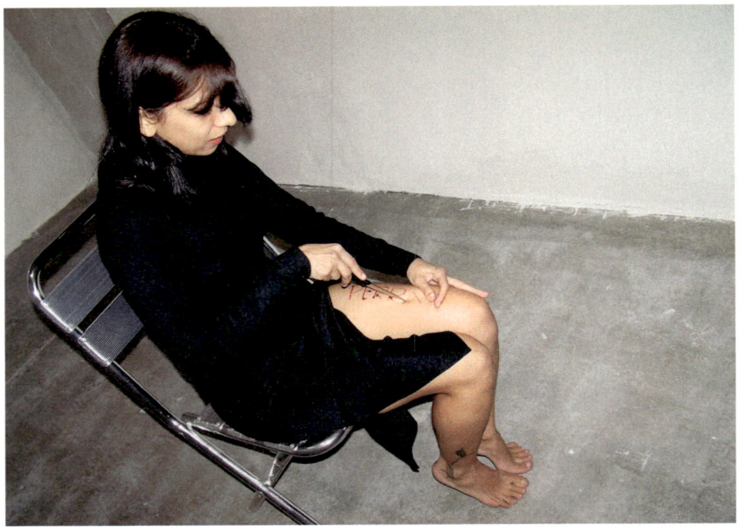

To understand the performances by artist Regina José Galindo (* 1974), one must first understand the grim history of Guatemala. For 36 years, the country was enveloped by a bloody civil war that cost more than 200,000 people their lives. For decades, the country was run by corrupt governments and brutal military regimes, with the situation exacerbated by CIA intervention, U.S. smear campaigns, and devastating natural catastrophes. When former dictator Efraín Ríos Montt, responsible for numerous massacres against the indigenous population, ran as a presidential candidate in 2003, Galindo went on to the street with a basin filled with blood. "I feel impotent, unable to change things, but this rage has sustained me, and I've watched it grow since I first became aware of what was happening. It's like an engine—a conflict inside me that never yields, never stops turning, ever," says Galindo. For one project, she dipped her feet in a basin and walked from the Constitutional Court to the National Palace—leaving behind her a trail of bloody footprints *(Who can erase the traces?)*. Montt lost the election. In her performances, Galindo typically adopts the pose of a martyr, using her own body to illustrate the harm that has been done, and thereby reliving it. For her performance *Himenoplastia,* 2004, she had her hymen reconstructed in a clinic. Her reason for this was that in many societies, it is still essential that a bride be a virgin, and human traffickers place a higher value on the body of a virgin. This makes the hymen the symbol of a male-dominated society. For another performance, *Angelina,* 2001, she went about her daily business for a month dressed as a maidservant, experiencing for herself the humiliations suffered by maids, who are one of the most discriminated against professions in Guatemala.
For *Confesión,* 2007, she experienced a waterboarding torture session, and for *No perdemos nada con nacer* (We Don't Lose Anything by Being Born), 2000, she had herself thrown onto a rubbish tip in a sack. "I cannot separate myself from what happens. It scares me, it enrages me, it hurts me, it depresses me. When I do what I do, I don't try to approach my own pain as a means of seeing myself and curing myself from that vantage[point]; in every action I try to channel my own pain, my own energy, to transform it into something more collective," says Galindo. This experienced pain is compelling. Watching her videos, one feels her pain and sees images one can never forget. This small and slight artist abuses her body to reflect the collective sins of humanity—but her rage also gives her strength. She says that: "Art does not save the world, but art saves me."

1
Perra
2005, Prometeogallery di Ida Pisani, Milano, Italy
Photo by Kika Karadi

2
Confesión
2007, Caja Blanca, Palma de Majorca, Spain
Photo by Julián Stallabrass

3
No Perdemos Nada con Nacer
2000, Mexico
Photo by Belia de Vico

4
Himenoplastia
2004, Guatemala City, Guatemala, Photo by Belia de Vico

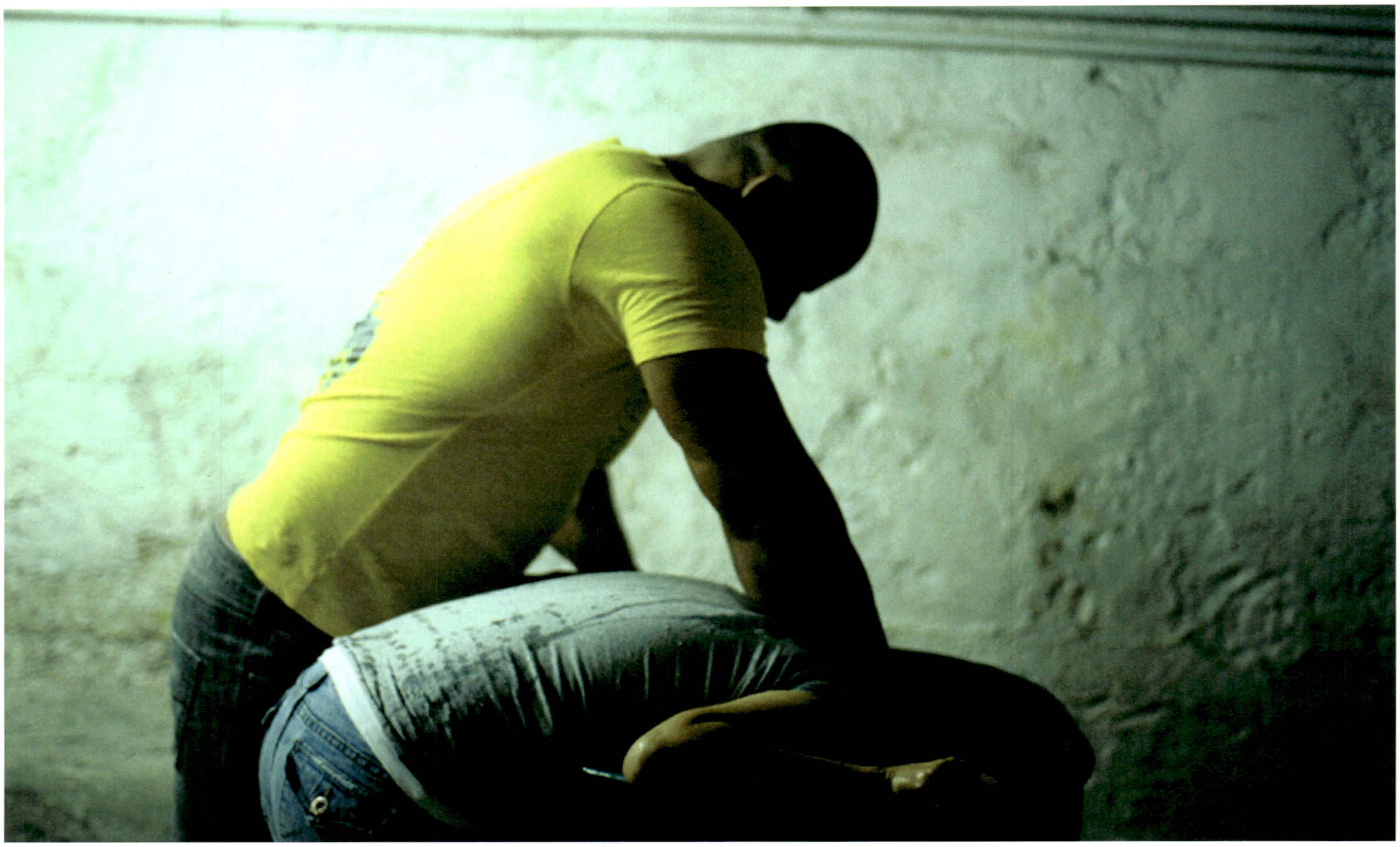

3

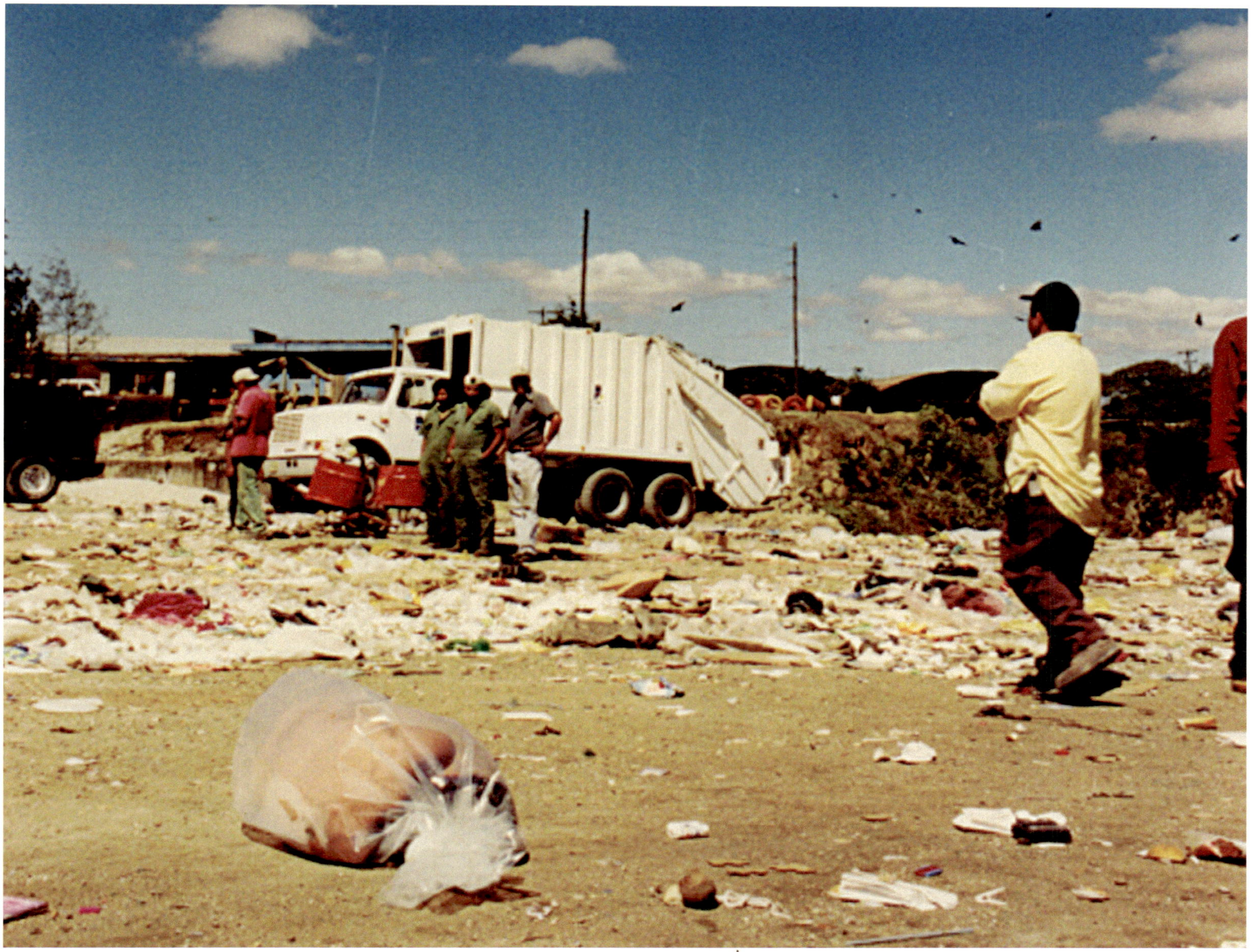

4

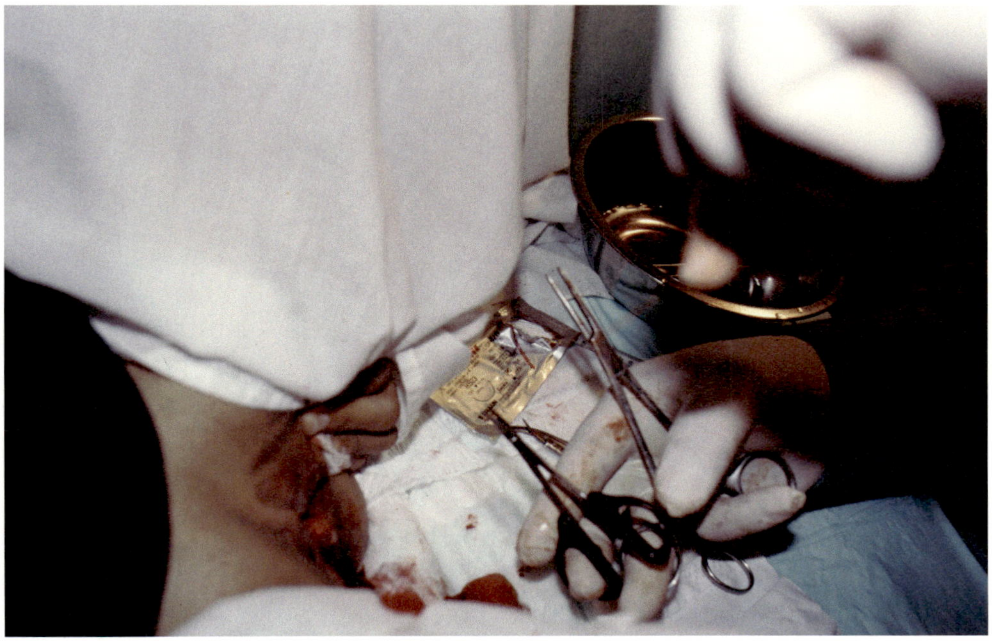

“ART DOES NOT SAVE THE WORLD, BUT ART SAVES ME”

SUSAN HEFUNA

Susan Hefuna (* 1962) from Cairo, is an artist of Egyptian and German heritage who works in a variety of media. Her artworks are created in Egypt, England, and Germany and have a central theme: the mashrabiya, a window structure made from lathed wood that is a feature of Islamic architecture, which helps to regulate the circulation of air and filters the light coming into a building. The artist's first use of this shape was entirely unintentional. When she exhibited her drawings in Egypt in the 1990s, viewers quickly recognized the familiar shape of the mashrabiya, while a German audience generally interpreted the drawings as abstract art.

Hefuna was initially surprised by this and the difference made by the context in which she exhibited her work, making her aware that "there is not one truth. Instead, there are layers of interpretations and perceptions." In the drawings, installations, and photographs that she subsequently created, she consciously thematized the mashrabiya, an item traditionally used to shield the inner world from the outer world. Once upon a time, it allowed women to see without being seen. The artist uses the sense of partition associated with the mashrabiya as a metaphor for separation and connection: between inside and outside, between women and men, between families and outsiders, between the forbidden and the permitted. In particular, Hefuna sees this traditional screen window as standing for the role of women within cultures. Originally, the mashrabiya only permitted the gaze to pass from the interior to the exterior, but Hefuna intentionally changes this in her artworks: "For me, the mashrabiya has become a symbol of a potential two-way dialogue, rather than a barrier to it."

This is why Hefuna embellishes her mashrabiyas with words and phrases in Arabic, English, and German. One's interpretation of these depends on which side of the mashrabiya one is reading them from, as well as whether one understands the relevant language. The text is hard to decipher—although not indecipherable—when viewed from the rear side. By incorporating foreign words into the traditional Arabic mashrabiya, the artist widens the dialogue she is initiating and adds an unknown quantity. She allows something foreign to penetrate the house's protective screen. In literally translating Arabic commonplaces like "patience is beautiful," and thereby causing them to deviate from the actual meaning, the artist is connecting with her own life experiences. She grew up between two homes and knows only too well how it feels to be trapped or entangled between two worlds. From a distance, the text in Hafuna's mashrabiya sculptures is easy to decipher, but it can be read at close quarters only with great difficulty. This is the artist's way of extending the metaphor; the distant home is idealized so much that the old homeland has no chance of living up to expectations. The artist knows this from living for many years in Egypt and in Germany: "Wherever I live or belong, a feeling of being a constant observer penetrates my work."

1
Woman Cairo
2008, Wood, ink
Private collection

2
Not for Sale—Enta Omri
2007, Wood, ink
Private collection
Photo by Graham Waite

3
Knowledge is Sweeter than Honey
2006, Wood, ink
Collection, British Museum, London, U.K.

2

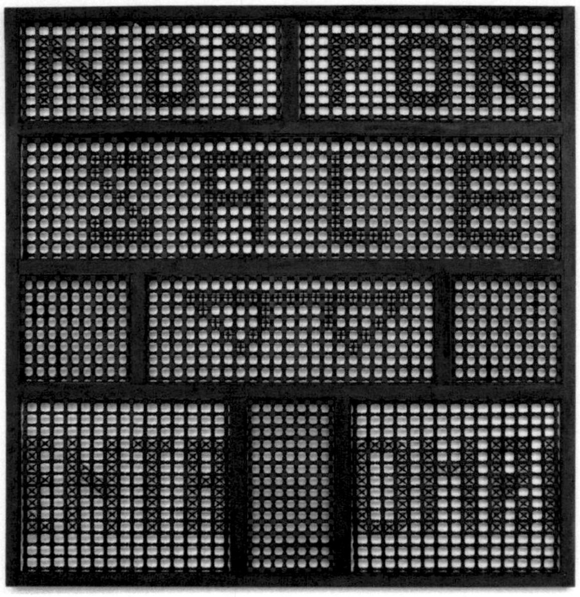

3

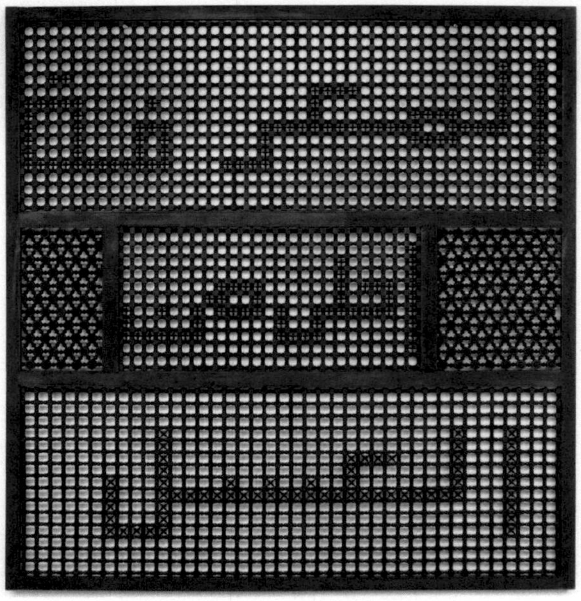

1

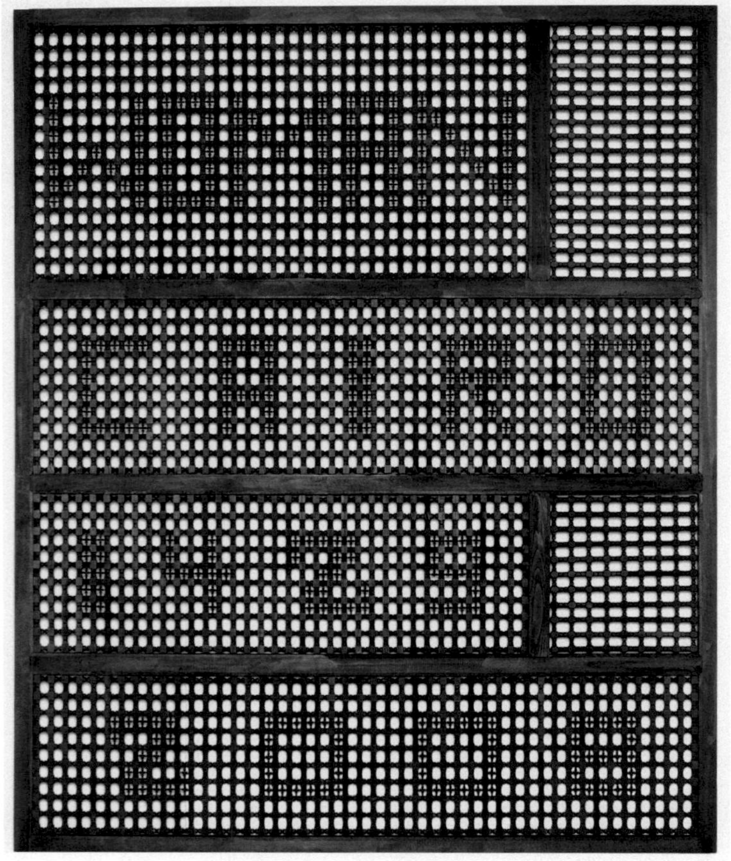

MAHMOUD KHALED

The sculptures, films, and installations of Egyptian artist Mahmoud Khaled (* 1982) from Alexandria, address the boundaries between the private and the public sphere, and in particular the importance of personal identity under particularly difficult political or social conditions. *Safety Zoom,* 2008/2009, was originally a scene filmed accidentally—and this is what makes it all the more impressive. It shows how the perceptions and fears that arose following 9/11 and the London bombings have turned into the current state of perpetual terrorism alerts. On the last day of his visit to London as a scholarship student, Khaled made a film of the Thames purely as a tourist, with no preexisting artistic intentions. While doing so, he saw a British family on a yacht in the river and, driven by a certain voyeurism, he zoomed his camera in on them. When the father of the family saw an Arabic-looking man intruding on this British family idyll with a camera, he reached for his own camera in an almost panicked fashion to film the observer. Adding a third observer—the film's viewer—extends the process of mutual observation ad absurdum, without losing any of its bitter subtext.

In his installation with the ambiguous title *Thanks 4 the Ad/d,* 2008, the artist looks at the difficult position of people infected with HIV in Egypt, who live in a society that marginalizes and frequently even criminalizes them. To seek advice and get in touch with others in the same position, they use the Internet—taking very personal issues into a seemingly anonymous but highly unpredictable public sphere.

The door to the installation opens into a tiny hallway that leads to a stifling room with light boxes on the wall showing fictional online profiles of HIV sufferers. These profiles give us an insight into the feelings and desires of the infected individuals, showing us their strengths and insecurities—and also revealing key information about their physical appearance and their lifestyle. The profiles are written in the language typically used in online communication—a forum in which we never know what is being concealed and what is made up. Khaled emphasizes the precarious and even absurd situations of those who depend on this kind of virtual communication because they receive no support in the real world by displaying showcases intended for the outdoors in a hospital room within his installation.

1
Safety Zoom
2008/2009, London, U.K./ Alexandria, Egypt, Video installation, 7:13 minutes, Wall paint, wallpaper, life jackets, painted plywood, photographic paper collage

2
Thanks 4 the Ad/d
2008, Cairo, Egypt
Installation

1

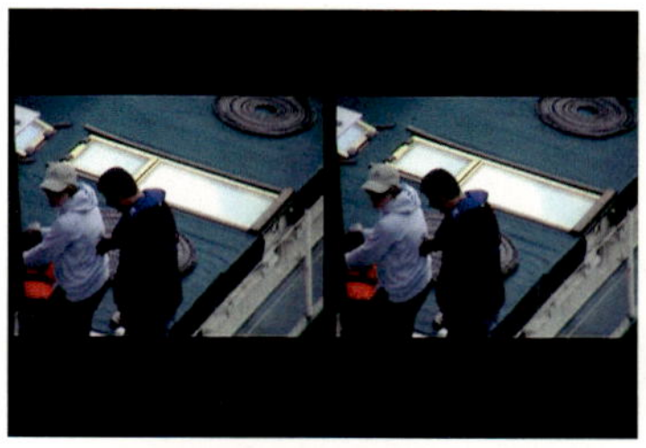
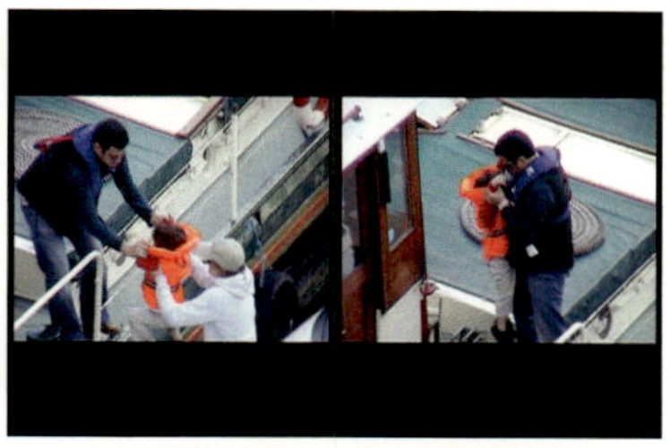
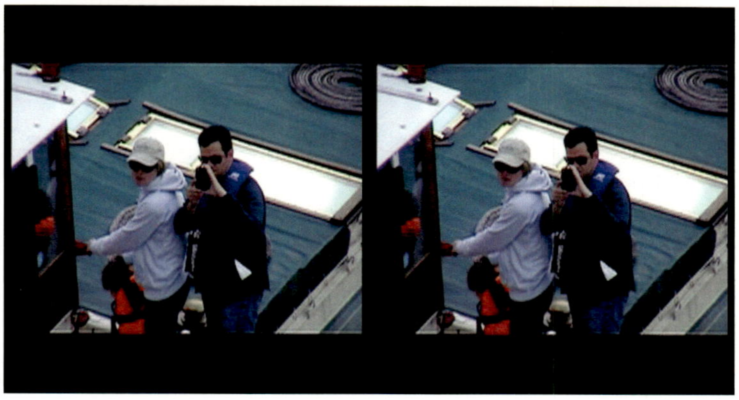
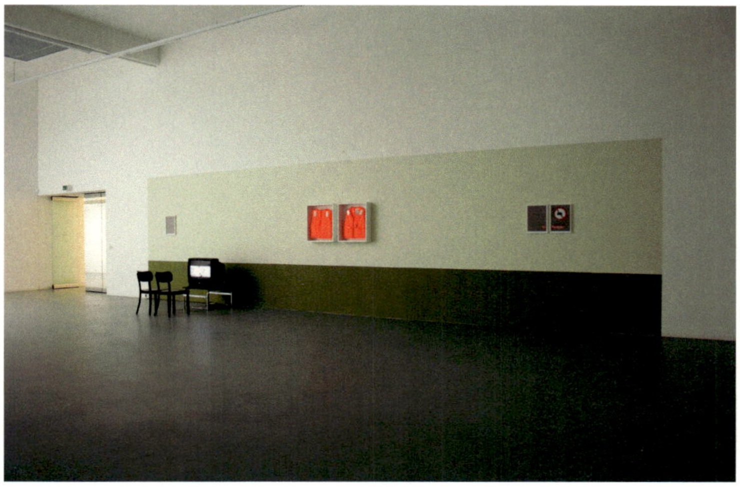
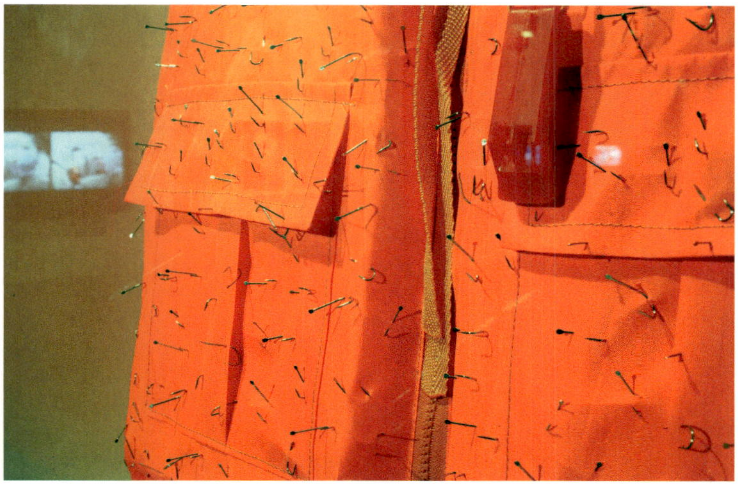

2

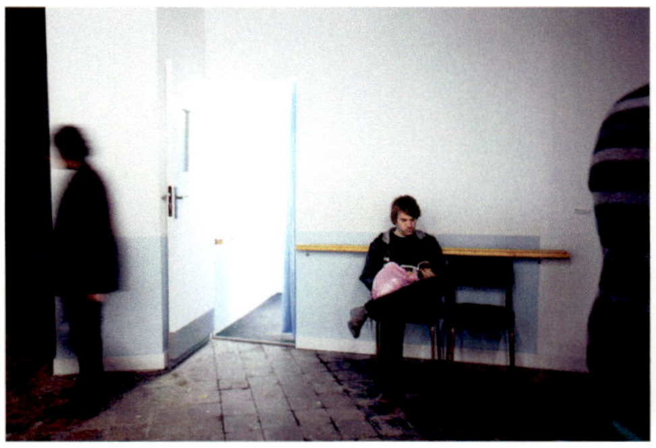
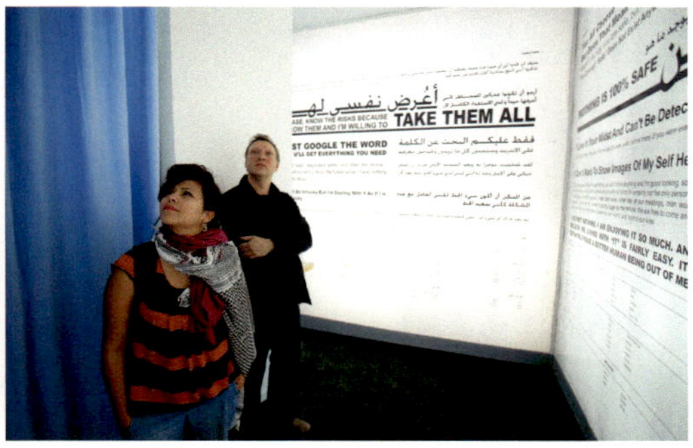

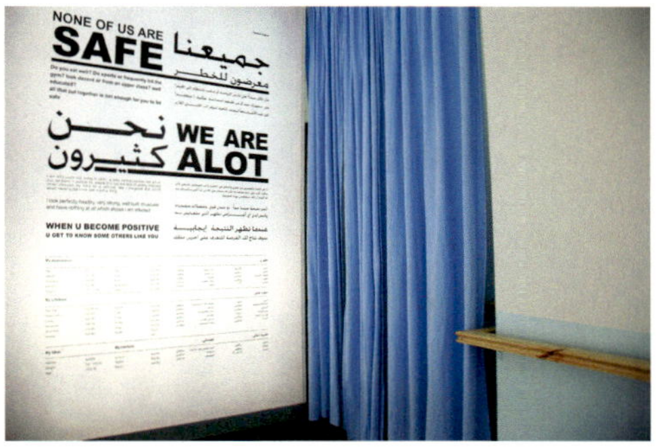

MONA HATOUM

1

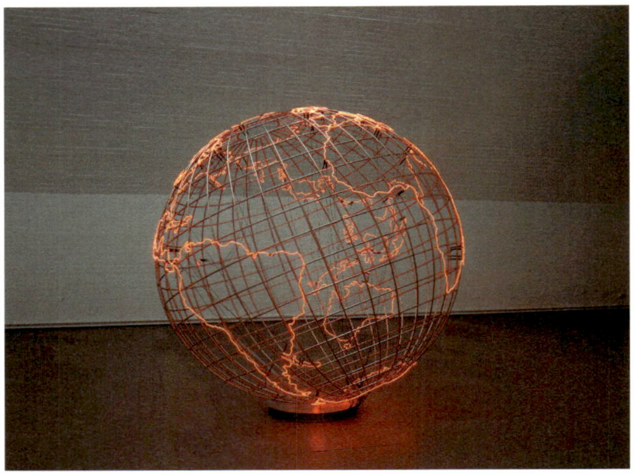

Mona Hatoum (*1952) from Beirut, creates artworks using commonplace materials such as glass, wool, electric cable, steel, light bulbs, and barbed wire, combining them to create unsettling sculptures and large installations.

In her installation *Mobile Home,* 2005, a group of furniture and other household objects strung together with thin wires are slowly pulled back and forth between two police barriers. The movement is activated by three electric motors housed inside one of the barriers therefore this endless and absurd journey from one impenetrable boundary to another is accompanied by an electrical hum that creates the unsettling impression that the wires are electrified. Clearly there is no way in or out of the system.

Bukhara (red and white), 2008, a Persian carpet similar to those Hatoum recalls from her childhood, looks as if it is in a state of disintegration. Large areas of the pile seem to have been eaten by moth or worn away. A closer look reveals that the seemingly random patches come together to form an atlas of the world. Like Arno Peters's world map, it depicts the continents in true proportions and corrects the distortions of the usual maps that show an enlarged Western Europe and North America. Another work entitled *Projection,* 2006, uses the same map in the form of a work on paper. Made of cotton pulp and abaca, there is here a reversal of the image as the continents seem to be sinking into the seas and oceans which are embossed and engulfing the land masses that seem to be etched or eroded. Her large illuminated globe ambiguously entitled *Hot Spot,* 2006, could also be seen to present the world as unreliable, dangerous, and mired in conflict and unrest.

Hatoum's work continually addresses the vulnerability of the individual, the violence inflicted by institutionalized power, and above all the feeling of being foreign. These issues have probably impacted on her own life experience. Her parents were Palestinian exiles that left their homeland for Lebanon four years before she was born. Many years later, Hatoum herself had a similar experience which led to an involuntary exile in London. In 1975, at the age of 23, during a visit to London she was unable to return home when the Civil War broke out in Lebanon. She stayed on in London, getting by with a variety of jobs and supported herself through six years of art studies graduating from the Slade School of Art in 1981. She now lives in London and Berlin.

1
Hot Spot
2006, Stainless steel and neon tube, Photo by Jörg von Bruchhausen, Courtesy Galerie Max Hetzler, Berlin

2
Mobile Home
2005, Furniture, household objects, suitcases, galvanized steel barriers, Photo by Jason Mandella, Courtesy Alexander and Bonin, New York

3
Witness
2009, Biscuit porcelain Photo by Kleinefenn Courtesy Galerie Chantal Crousel, Paris

4
Bukhara (red and white)
2008, Wool, Photo by Marc Domage, Courtesy Galerie Chantal Crousel, Paris

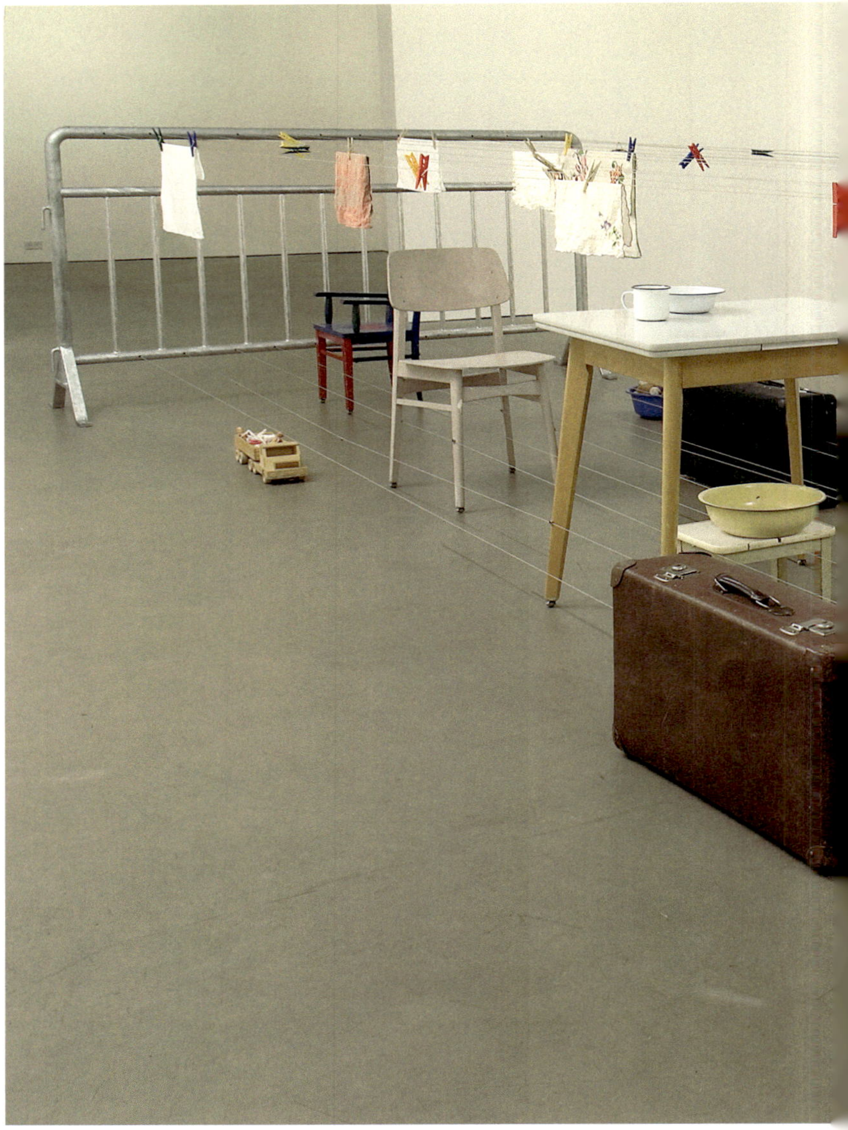

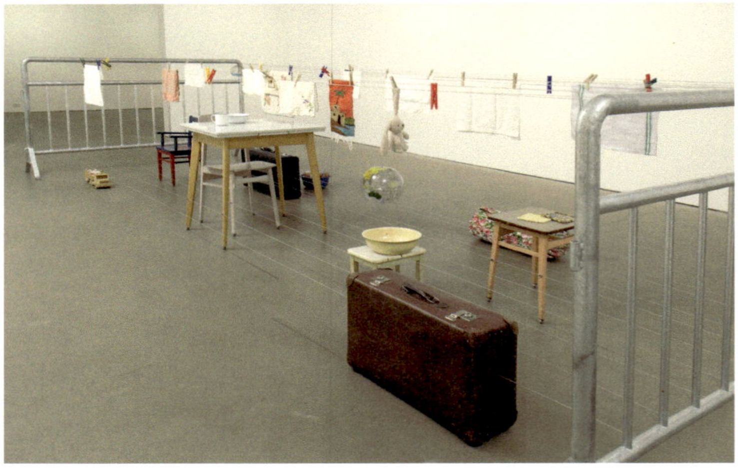

2

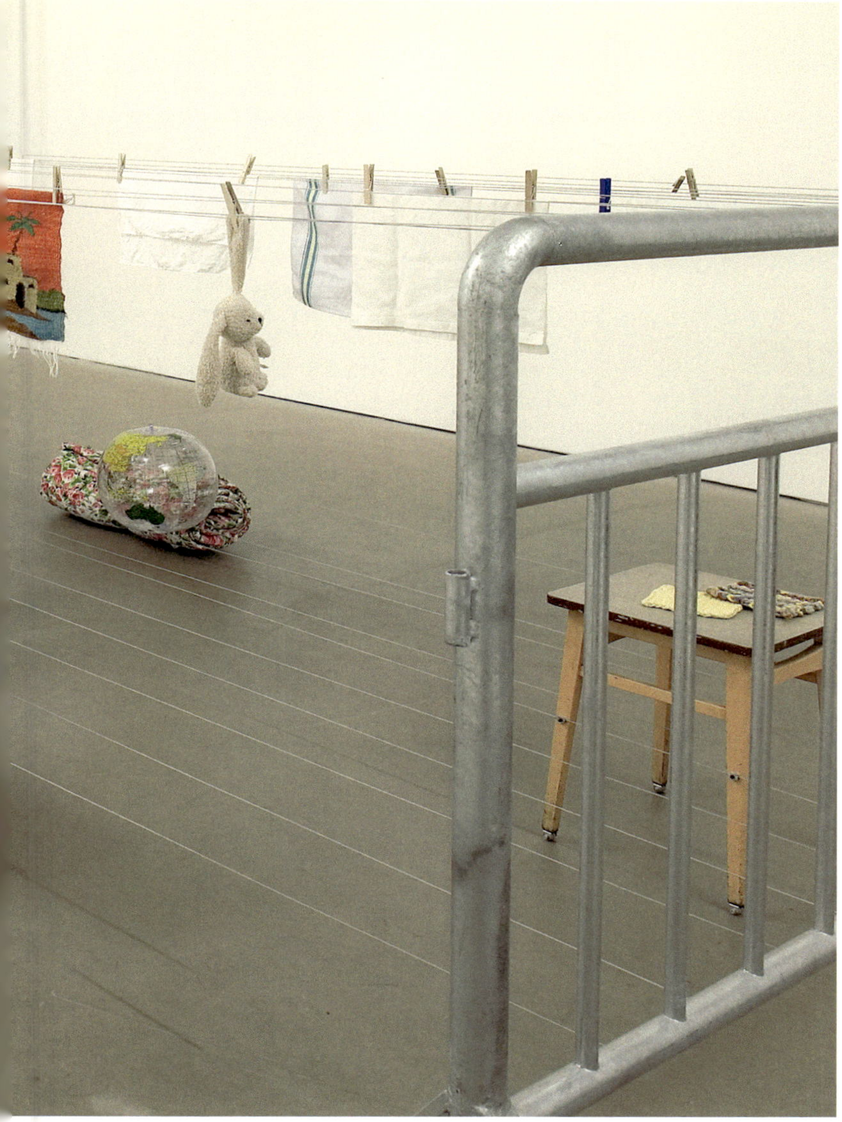

3

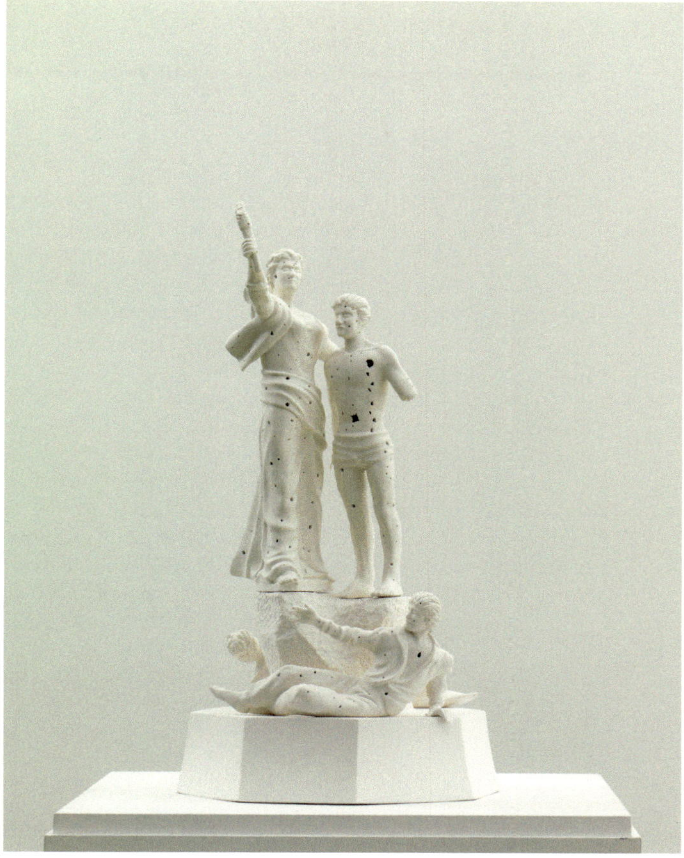

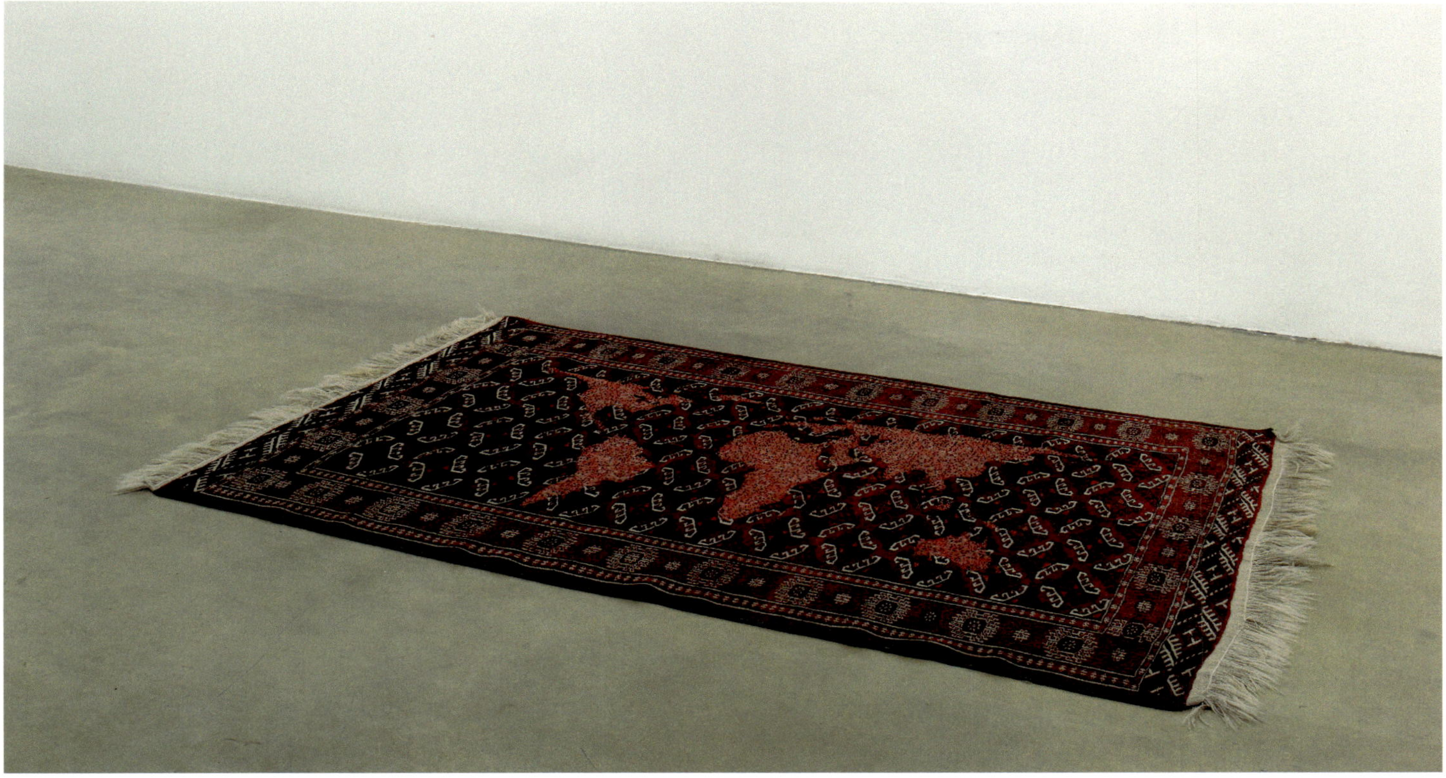

4

MILICA TOMIĆ

Milica Tomić (* 1960) from Belgrade, is one of the best-known artists in Serbia. She studied painting at Belgrade's University of Arts. Today she is primarily a performer and video artist. For her project *One Day*, 2009, she walked through Belgrade's inner city with a Kalashnikov and a white plastic bag, visiting places where key actions by the Yugoslavian resistance against the occupying German force took place during the Second World War. Tomić explains her project by stating that: "It is an attempt to proceed from the position of a rebel, assuming an active position, without referring to the position of a victim, moving from the position of a victim on to the streets, politically distanced from the politics of terror and anti-terror, without resentment, with a machine gun in hand, carrying it simply and necessarily, as if it were a supermarket carrier bag or an umbrella." The title is a reference to a poem by Serbian poet and partisan Oskar Davičo: "One day, instead of one night, a burst of machine gun fire will flash, if light cannot come otherwise." Many of Tomic's works derive thematically from the history of her homeland and are based on historic events—but usually events that have a connection with the present day. Tomić says that: "The fight against fascism has faded from the Serbian consciousness, and there is nothing to mark the historic sites where acts of resistance took place. Instead, new forms of fascism are gaining currency, and because it is institutionalized in laws and bureaucratic processes, we can barely see it." In her video artwork *I am Milica Tomić*, 1999, Tomić, wearing a white dress, turns round and round and introduces herself in various languages, giving different nationalities each time. With every rotation, new stigmata, new cuts, and wounds appear. The artwork's theme is the problem of national, religious, social, or gender based collective identities—our identities instantly make us the enemies of others, resulting in physical and spiritual wounds. Tomić says that: "I cannot help but deal with what I see in a critical way."

1
Remembering
2000, Photo by Herbert Fiedler

2
I Am Milica Tomić
1998/99

3
One Day
2009, Photo by Stasha Tomic

4
One Day, Instead of One Night, a Burst of Machine Gun Fire Will Flash, If Light Cannot Come Otherwise (Oskar Davičo, fragment of a poem)
2009, Belgrade, Serbia, Intervention in public space, Photo by Srđjan Veljović

Courtesy Charim Galerie, Vienna

1

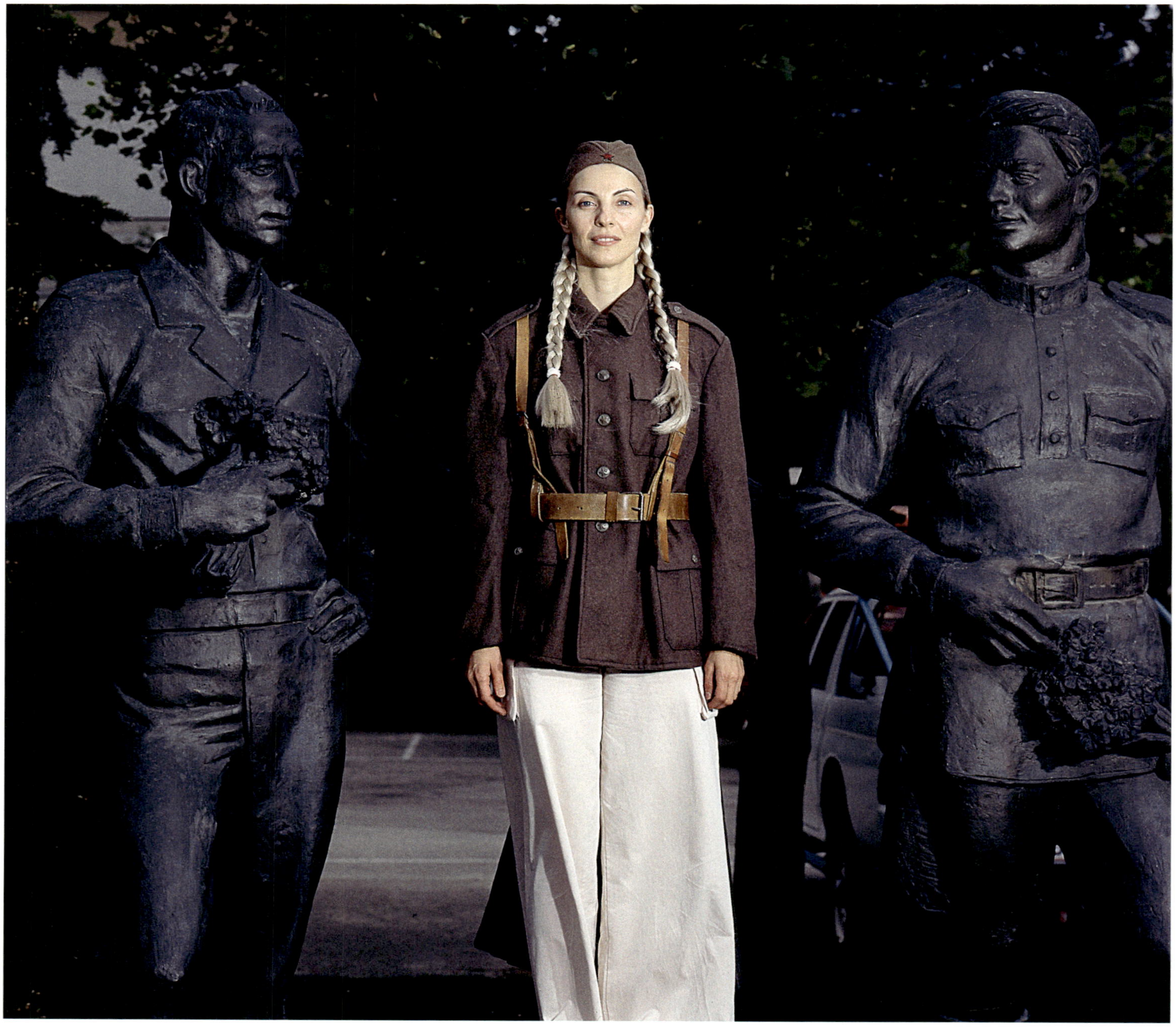

2

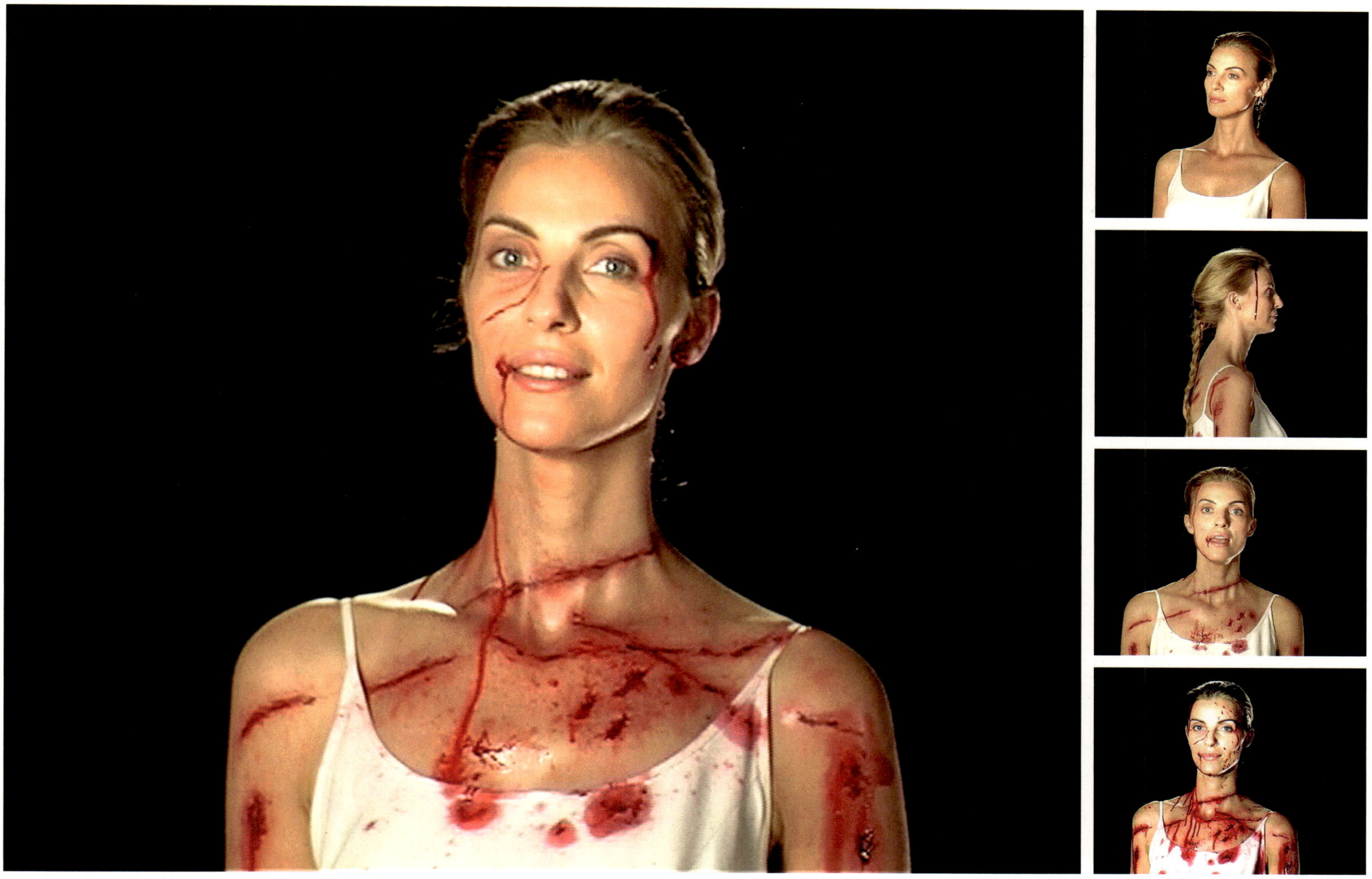

3

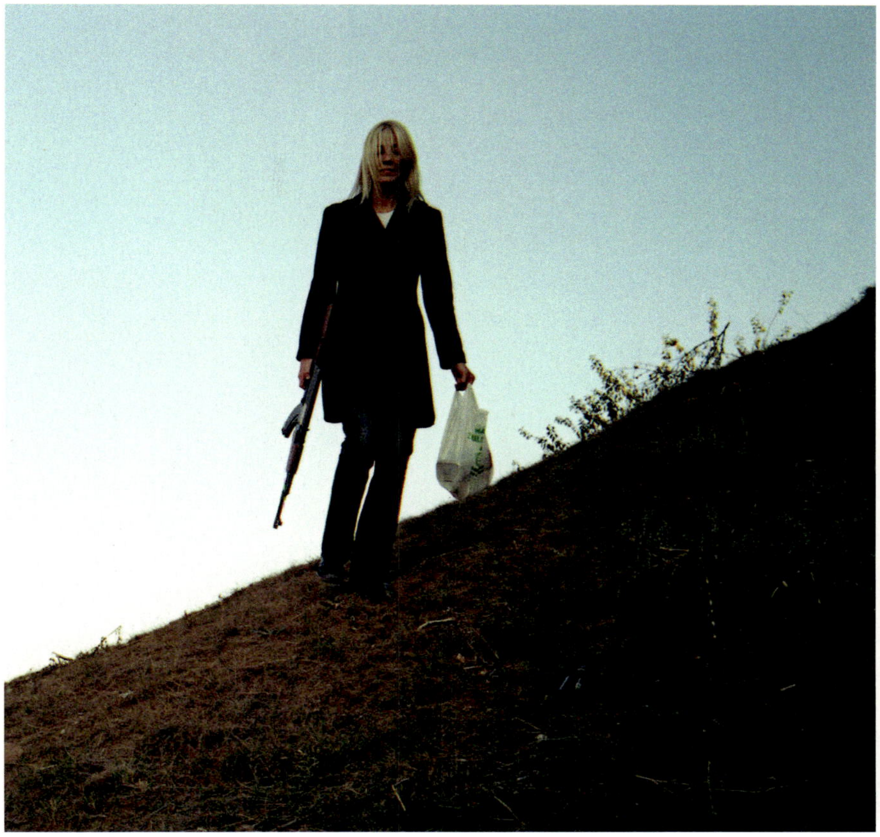

4

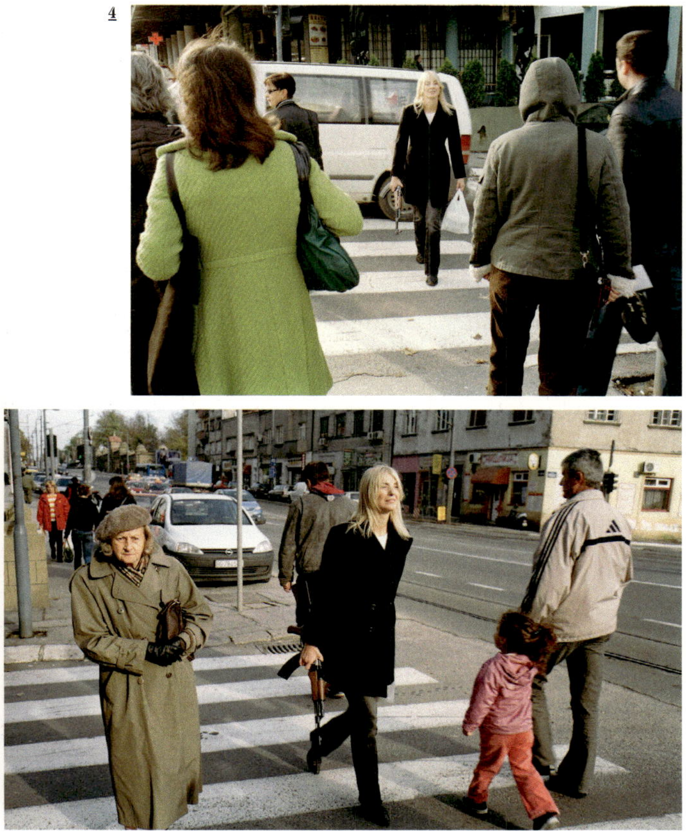

ARTUR ŻMIJEWSKI

In his essay "Applied Social Arts," Artur Żmijewski (* 1966) writes that "Art may be political as long as it stays away from politics—it can act politically in galleries but not in real-life debates unfolding in a different communal space, such as the media. It may be social as long as it does not produce social consequences." Żmijewski, as an artist, photographer, filmmaker, and art director for the Polish left-wing intellectual political magazine *Krytyka Polityczna,* he is one of Poland's most influential artists. In 2005, he represented Poland at the Venice Biennale. In 2007, he took part in documenta in Kassel, Germany, and he has been appointed to curate the Berlin Biennale in 2012. He began as a sculptor, but later moved on to photography and film, recognizing at an early stage that: "The world is too complicated to sculpt." He also had no wish to take part in the production of absurd objects, the "overproduction of meaninglessness"—commenting once that the world was overstuffed with art already. Eventually, he chose the documentary format for his art: Żmijewski sets up situations and shows them as they are, seemingly as an uninvolved bystander, without cynicism, pathos, or sympathy. He is known for his *An Eye for an Eye,* 1998, series of photographs, in which he photographed disabled people without an arm or a leg, naked. In some of the pictures, intact human beings stand in for the missing limbs, like a kind of "spare parts depot." The bodies that appear in Żmijewski's work are often disabled, crippled, sick, or old—the kind of bodies that rarely appear in art, or in the mass media. "I most often answer to questions I am 'not asked.' Practicing in the field of art I answer the questions 'not asked' by the art world: the curators, the gallerists, the critics," Żmijewski says. "This is what I see as the artist's responsibility, one who directly answers questions which others are even afraid to pose. And this is what I see as the artist's illusory freedom, which is nothing more than society's refusal to admit that it expects very specific things on the part of artists—specific actions, addressing certain themes, ideological activity." Many of his documentaries are concerned with social group experiments. He gets young, deaf people together to sing in a choir (*Singing Lesson,* 2001), persuades a Holocaust survivor to have the concentration camp number tattooed on his forearm renewed (*80064,* 2004), and films a group of naked men and women playing tag in what used to be the gas chamber of a concentration camp (*The Game of Tag,* 1999). In the film *Them,* 2007, he documents the outcome of a staged meeting of three antagonistic social groups—in his studio, he initiated an art workshop in which Polish Jews, patriotic Catholics, and members of left-wing groups took part. This playful experiment and its opening dialogue were rapidly followed by violence, and with each group destroying the other groups' pictures. Żmijewski explains his experiments by saying that: "I am simply attracted to the political mechanism that consists of conflict and resolution, conformism and resistance, denunciation and revolt. I am interested in how the political is tackled by individuals who are not professional politicians, and whether our nonprofessional political abilities could be used to protect us from being deprived of politics, and evicted from the field of the political."

1
Singing Lesson I
2001
2
An Eye for an Eye
1998, 20 photographs

Courtesy Foksal Gallery Foundation

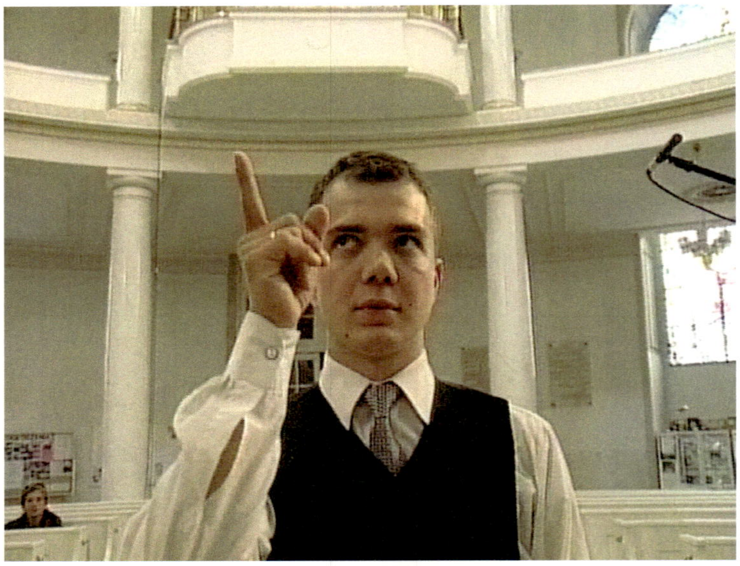

1

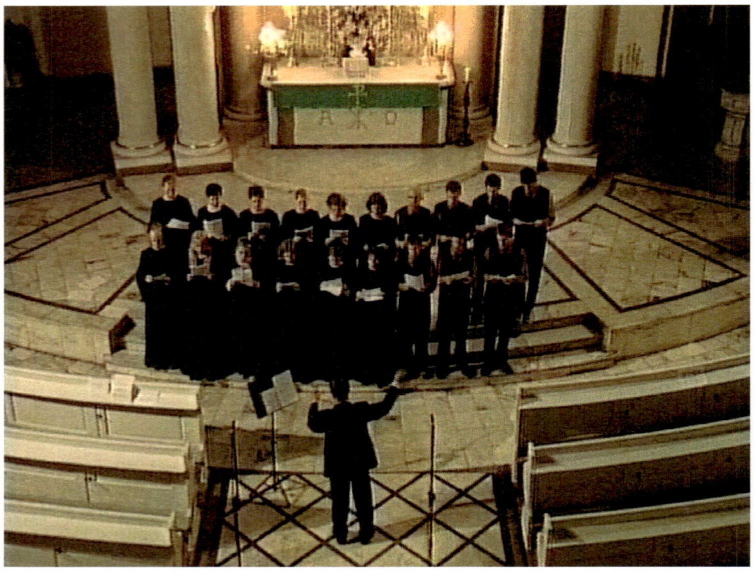

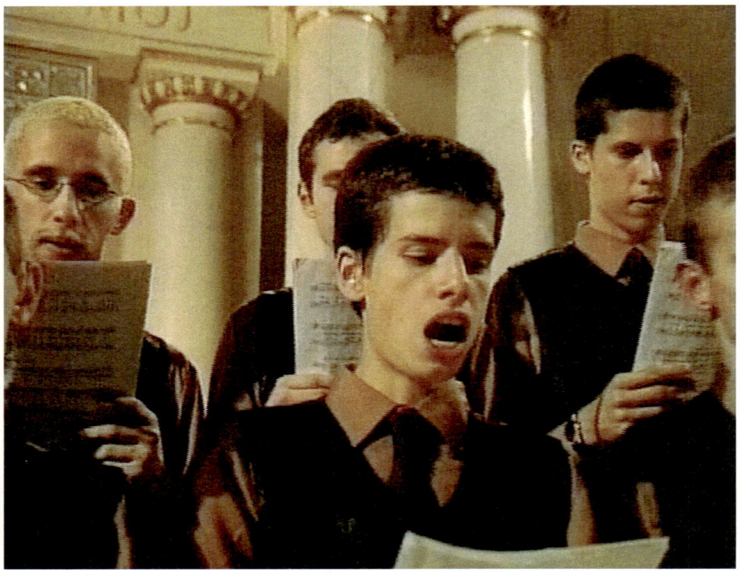

2

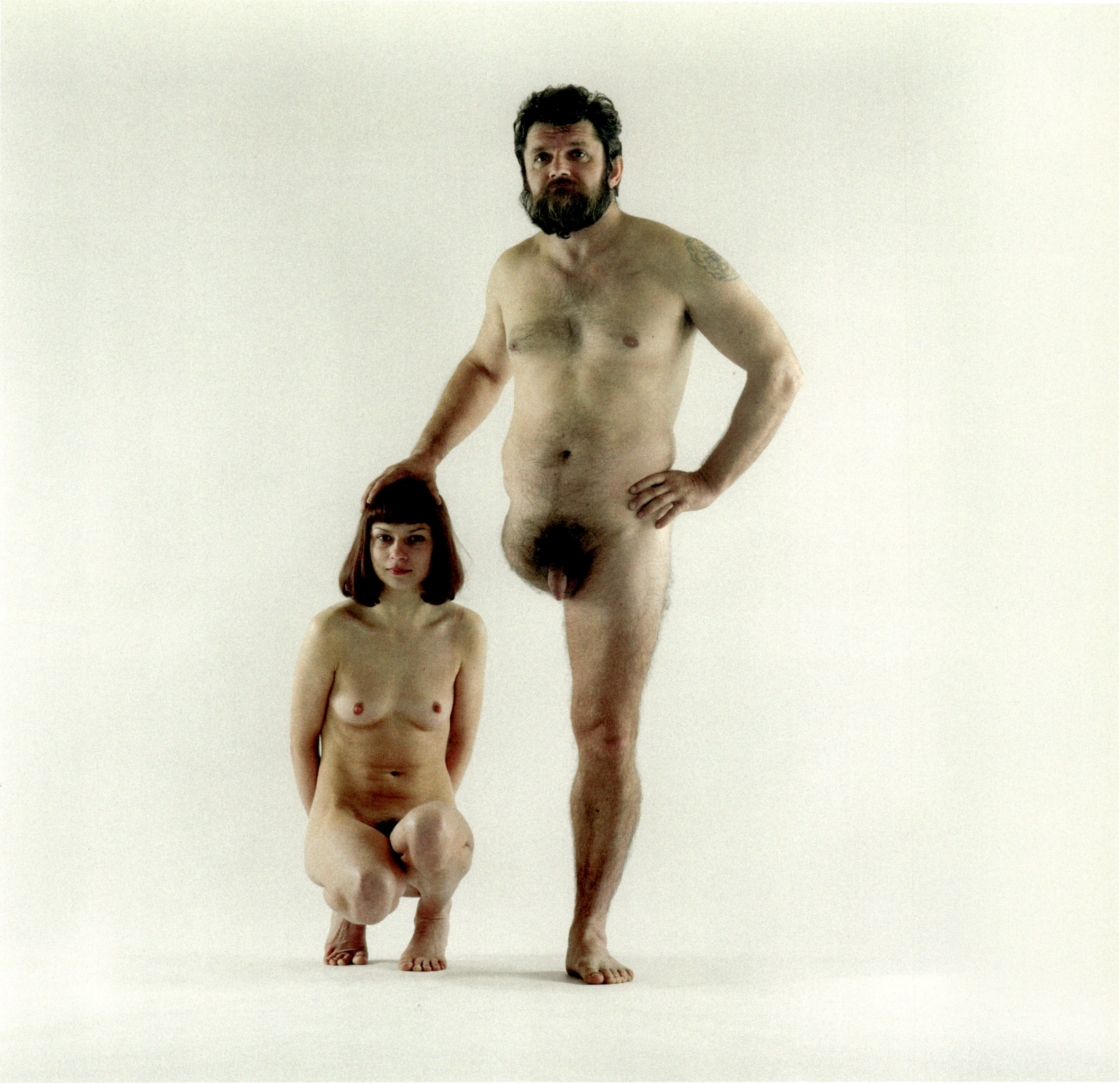

“THE WORLD IS TOO COMPLICATED TO SCULPT”

3
The Game of Tag
1999
4
Them
2007
5
KR WP, 2000
2000

Courtesy Foksal Gallery
Foundation

3

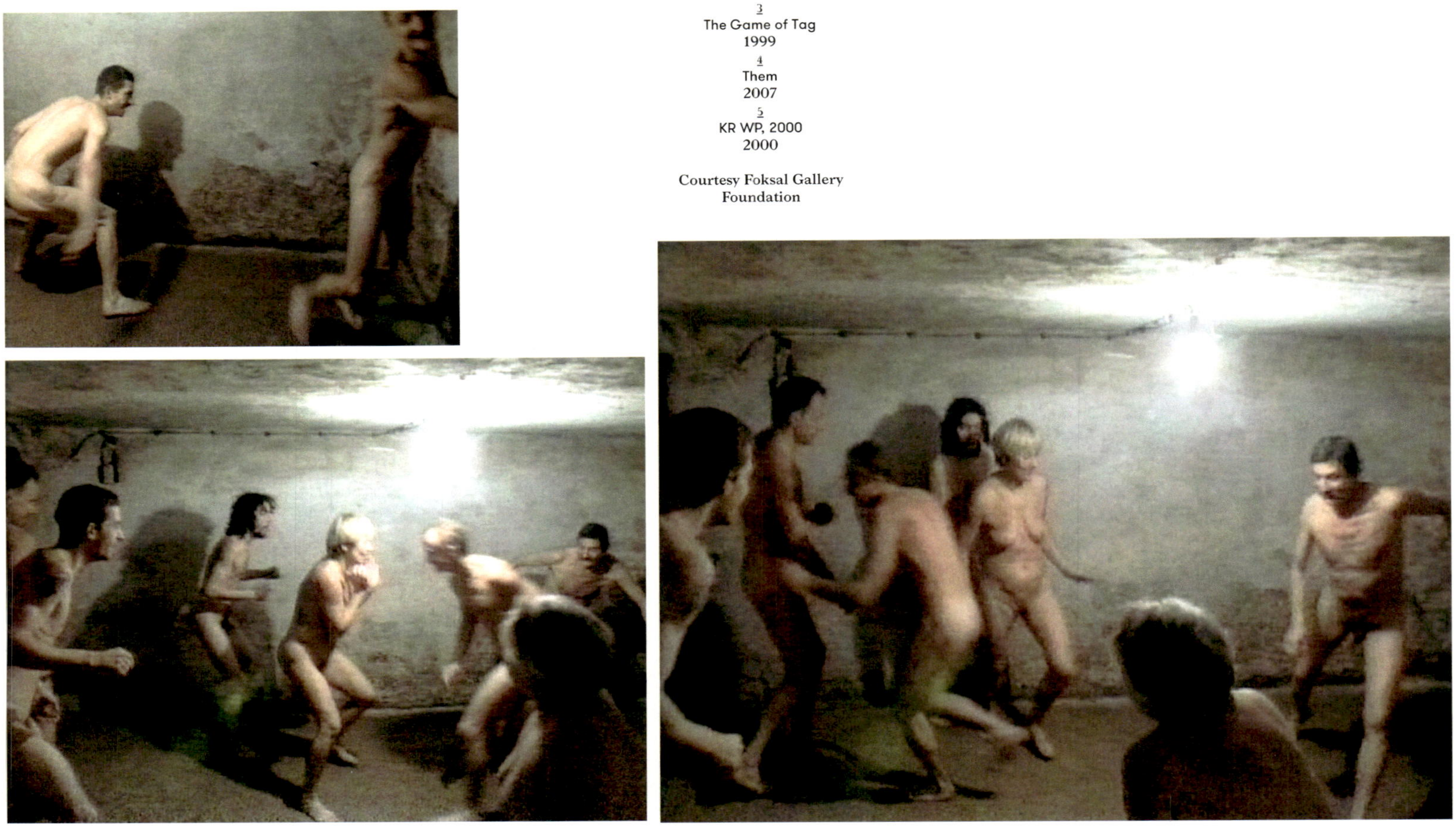

4

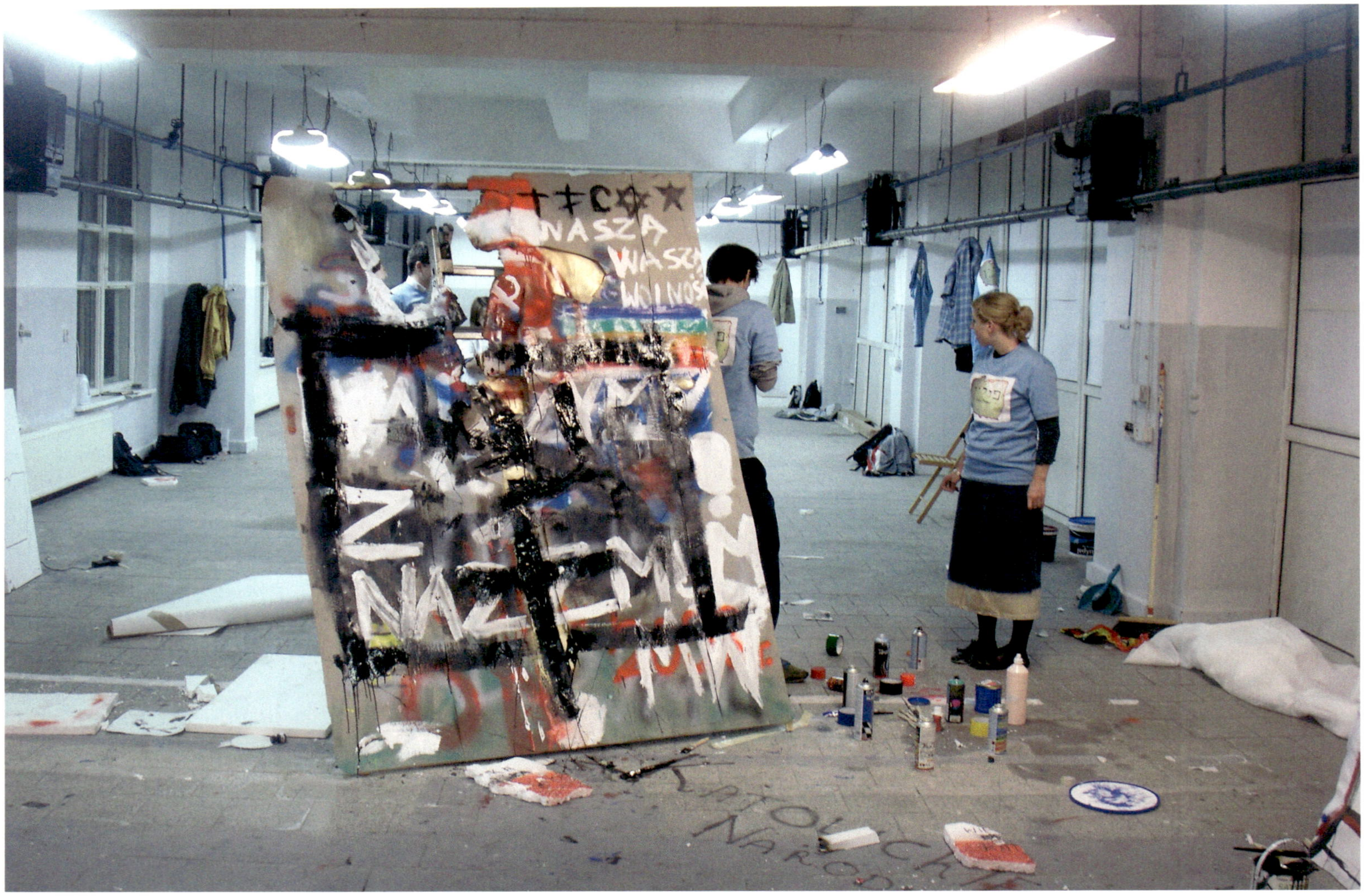

5

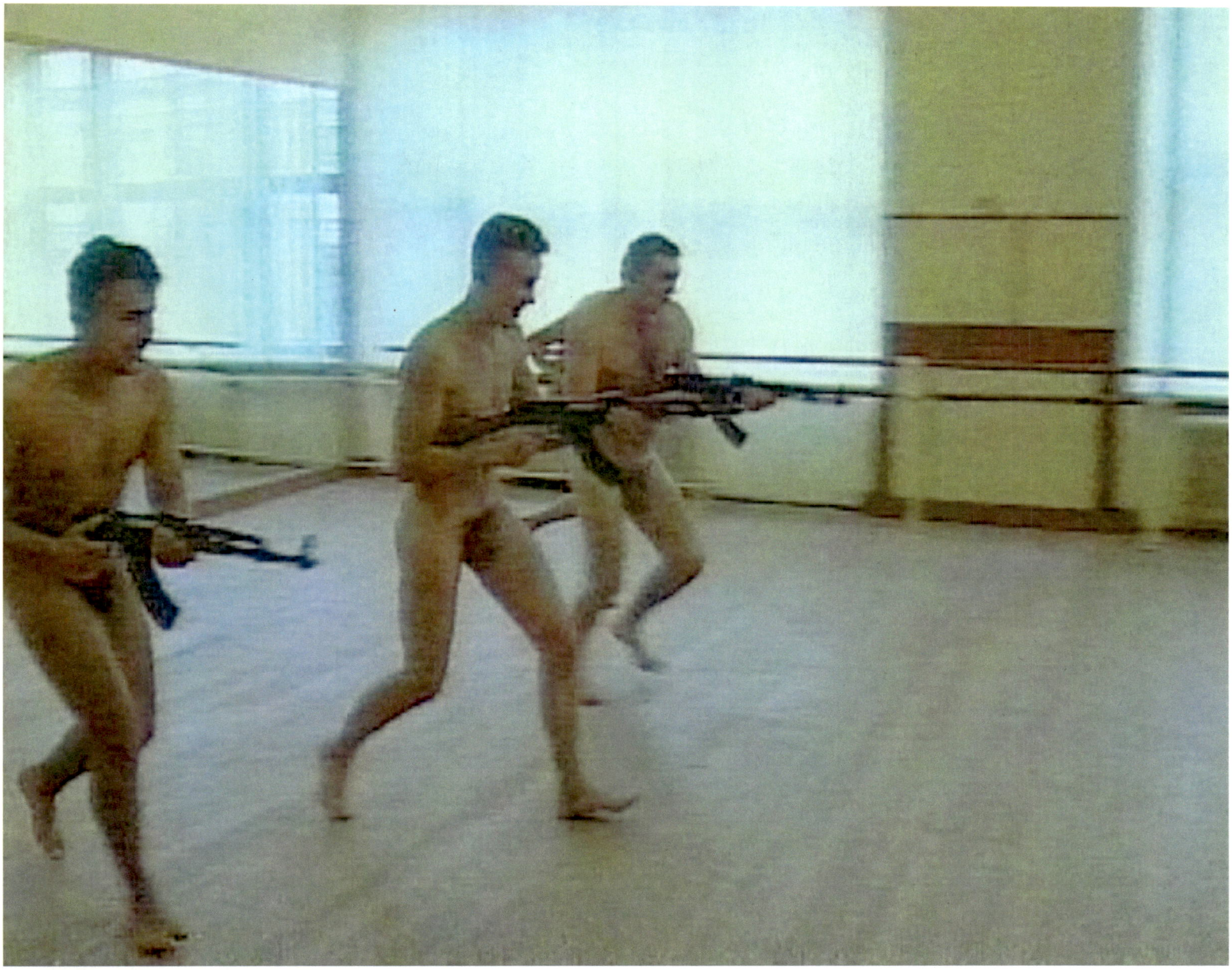

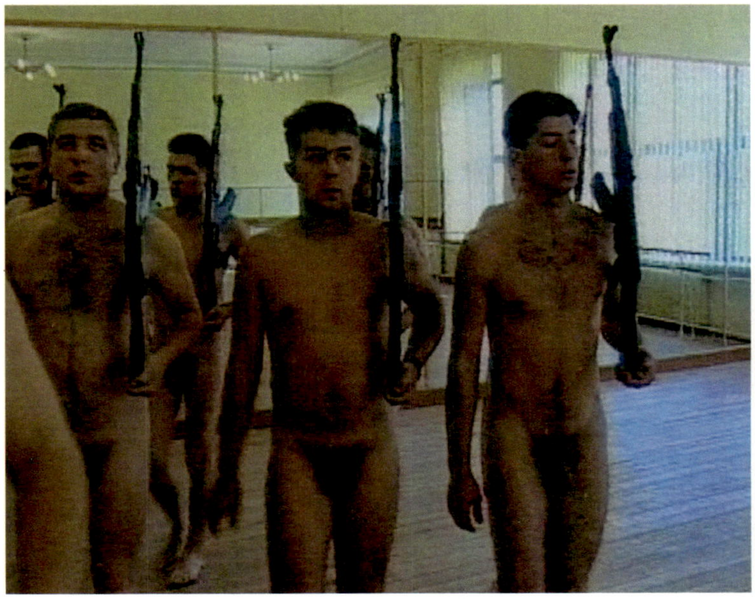

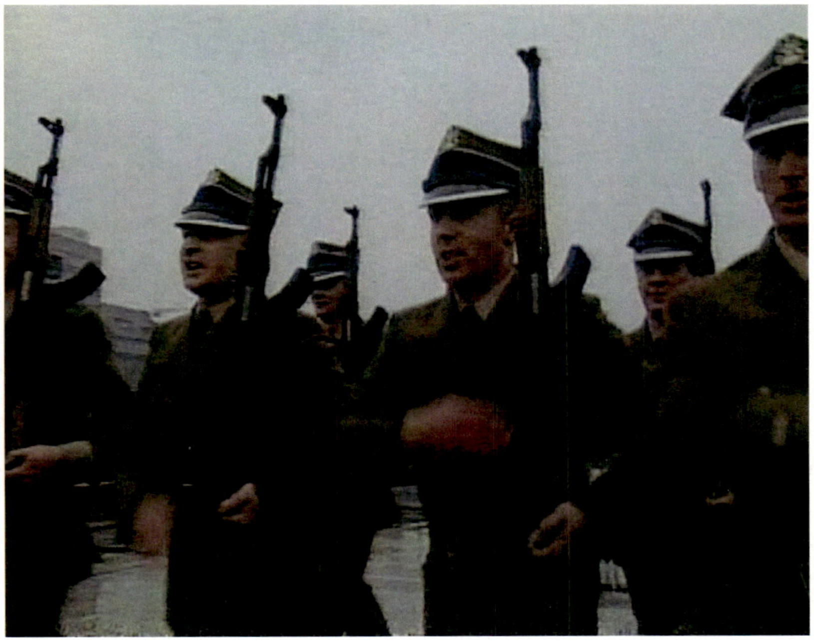

MARINA ABRAMOVIĆ

1
Lips of Thomas,
2005
2
Count on Us
2003, Belgrade, Serbia
Video/Photo Installation
3
8 Lessons on Emptiness
with a Happy End:
The Family VI
2008, Laos

"AN ARTWORK SHOULD NEVER BE JUST BEAUTIFUL, BUT IT SHOULD ALSO NEVER BE JUST POLITICAL, OR JUST PAINFUL"

Marina Abramović states that: "The body is a cosmos. To understand it is to understand the universe. For me, performance is a tool. I show the audience: if I can go through this pain, then so can you. That is the message I want to give." Abramović (* 1946), who was born in Belgrade, is probably the best-known performance artist in the world; and is an inspiration to many younger artists, such as Regina José Galindo. Since Abramović embarked on her first performances in 1973, her central theme has been rejection—initially the rejection of her parents, and later the rejection of social structures and of the art establishment. She has repeatedly exposed herself and her body to pain and torture—her artworks are always concerned with the limits of physical endurance and altered consciousness. Her major themes are discipline, violence, impermanence, sex, totalitarianism, and pain—the goal in her performances is often to overcome either physical or spiritual pain. Abramović crosses every line for the sake of her art, and was once almost critically injured during a performance. In *Rhythm 0,* 1974, she placed herself at the audience's disposal as an object, and provided exhibition visitors with 72 different items to choose from, including knives, sulphur, whips, and razor blades—but also grapes, lipstick, and perfume. For six hours, she allowed the audience to do whatever they wished with her, using the items at their disposal. She was painted, undressed, but also dangerously injured. The public separated into two camps: vandals and protectors, and many became sadists. "An artwork should never be just beautiful, but it should also never be just political, or just painful," she says. "It should have multiple facets." For *Lips of Thomas,* which premiered in 1975 in Innsbruck, Austria, and was reperformed at the Guggenheim Museum, New York, in 2005, she used a razor blade to carve a communist star around her navel. In *Nude with Skeleton,* 2002 and re-created in 2005, she lay naked beneath a skeleton, waking it to life by means of her breathing; and for *Imponderabilia,* 1977, two naked bodies—Abramović and her then-partner, the German artist Uwe "Ulay" Laysiepen—blocked the entrance to the exhibition space so that visitors would have to push past them to get in. Her performance *Balkan Baroque,* 1997 and 2010, with which she won the Golden Lion at the Venice Biennale, related to the conflicts in the Balkans. Every day, Abramović sang death songs from her native country while using a brush to clean a pile of cattle bones, amid an intolerable stench of decay. And in her art film *Balkan Erotic Epic,* 2005, she gives her own take on sexual and fertility rituals, by showing men penetrating the ground, and with women raising their bare breasts to the sun. Abramović says that: "Human beings are afraid of two things: of their own mortality and of pain. Only when you free yourself of both these fears can you enjoy your life."

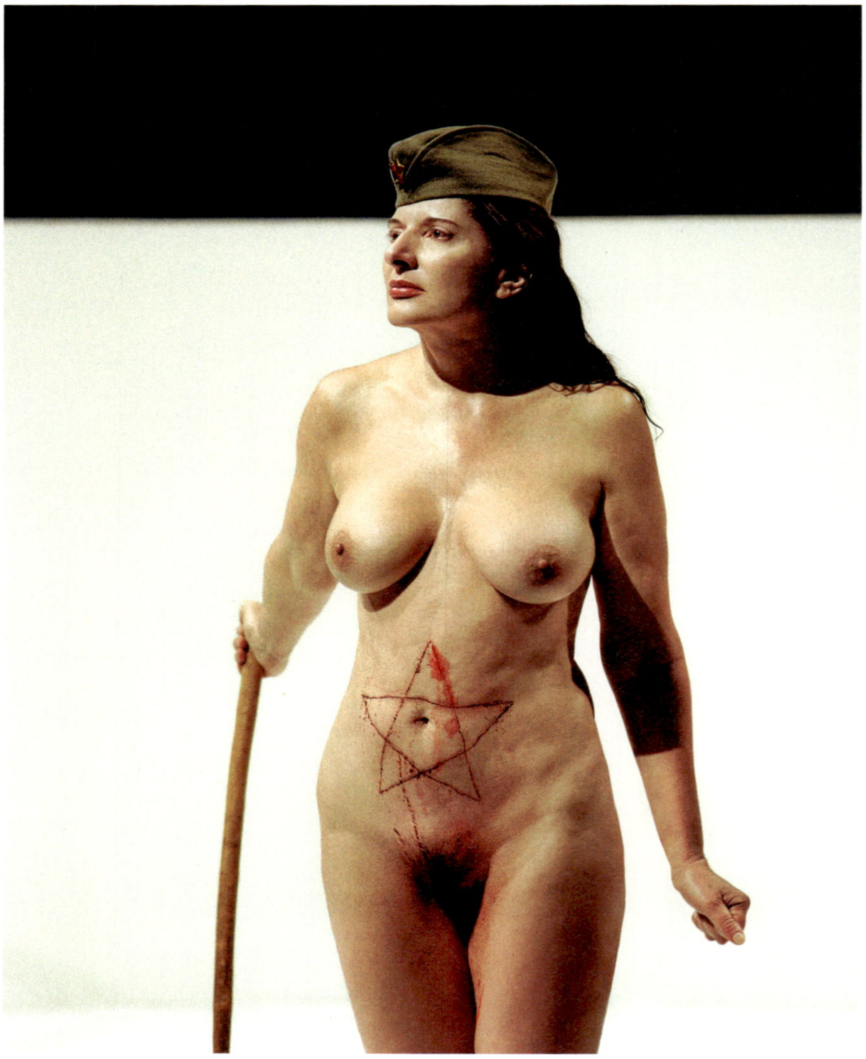
1

2

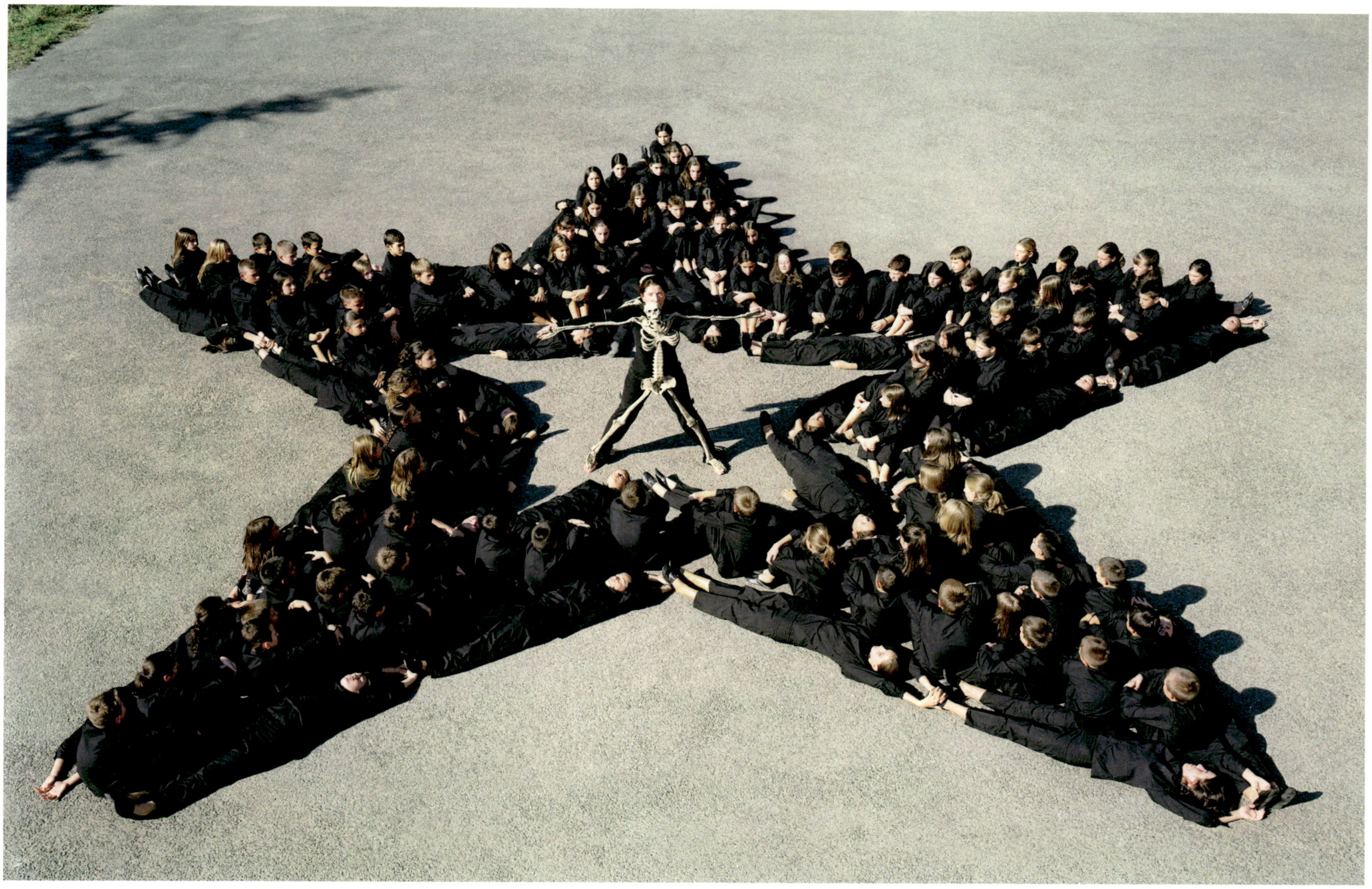

3

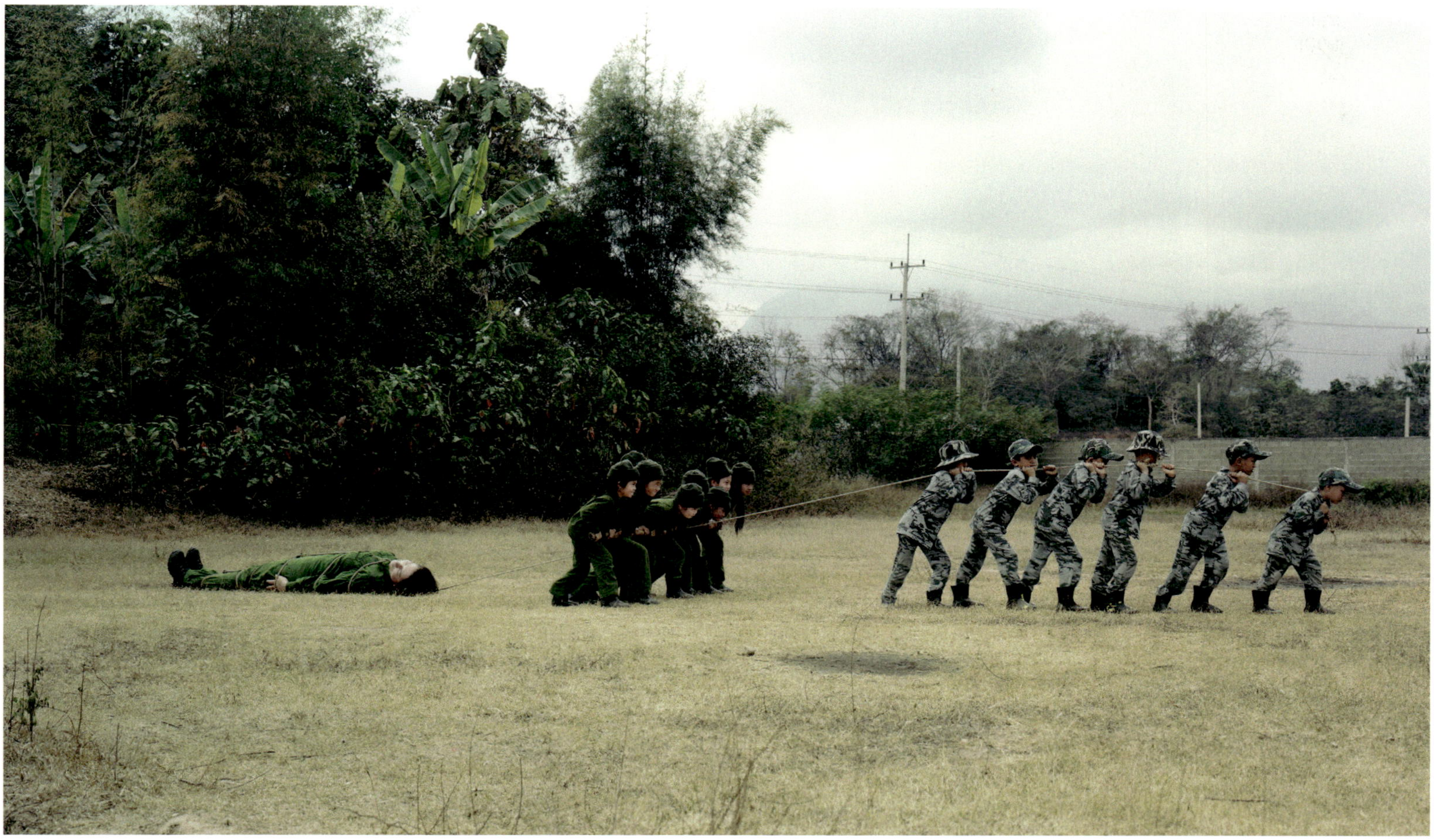

MARINA ABRAMOVIĆ

4
Balkan Erotic Epic
2005
5
8 Lessons on Emptiness
with a Happy End:
The Family III
2008, Laos
6 (next spread)
Balkan Baroque
1997

5

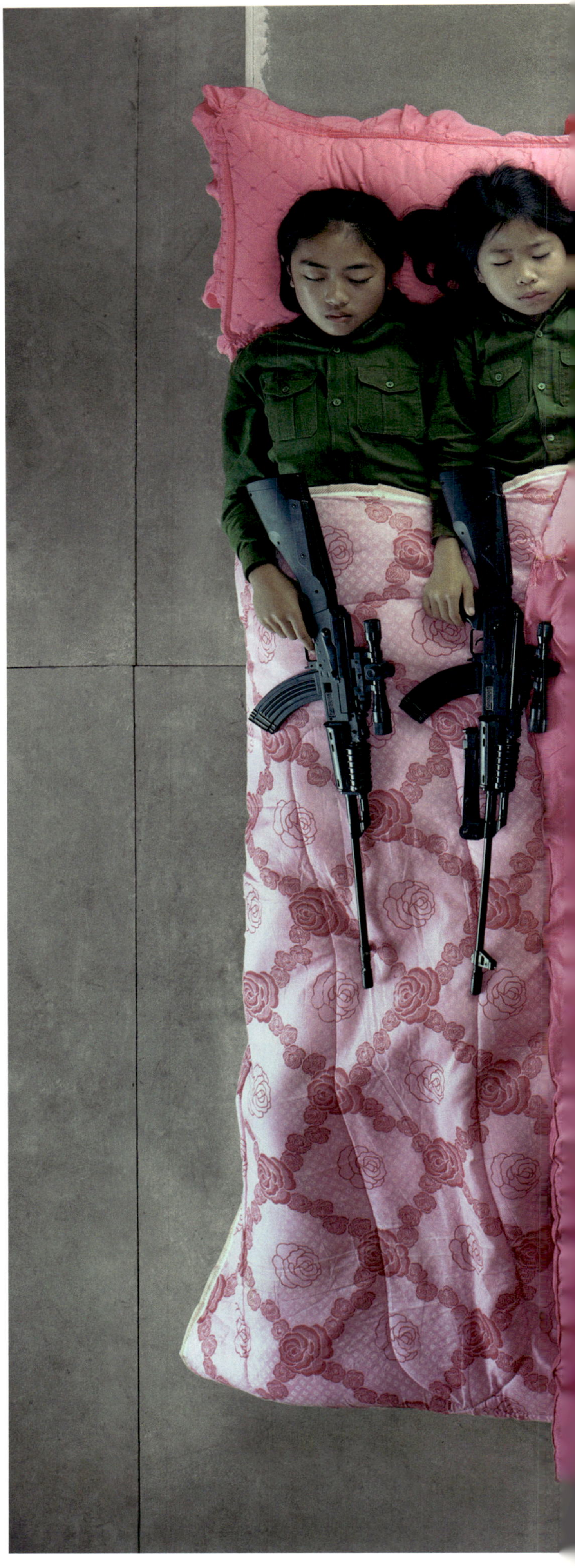

4

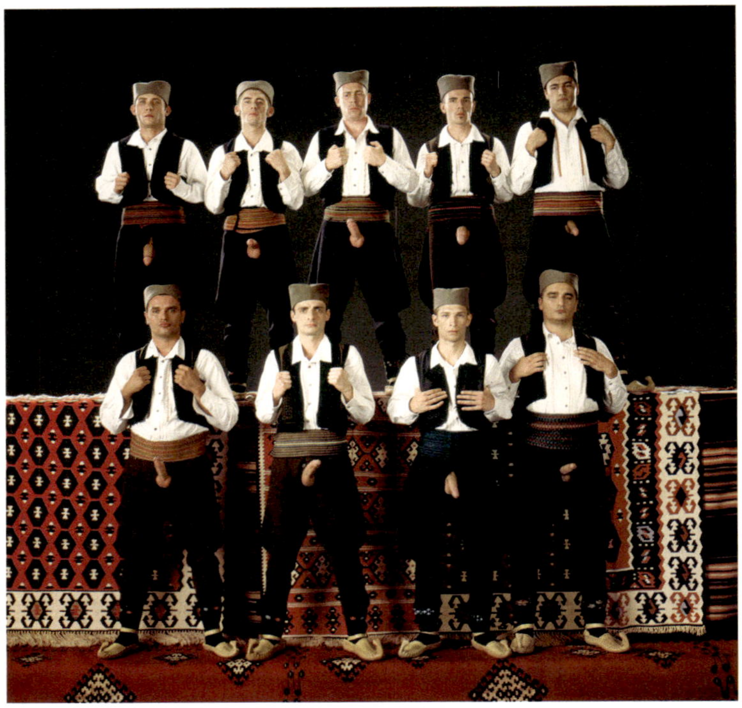

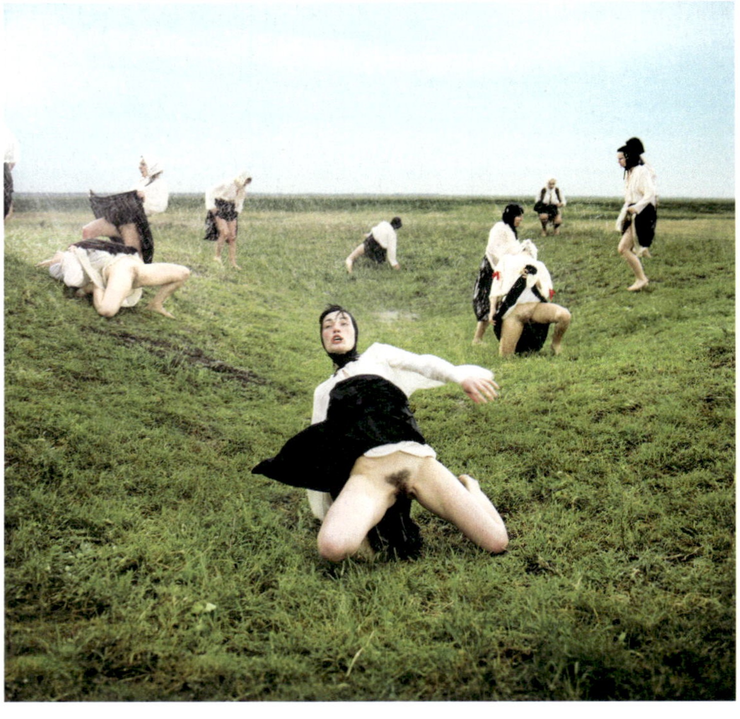

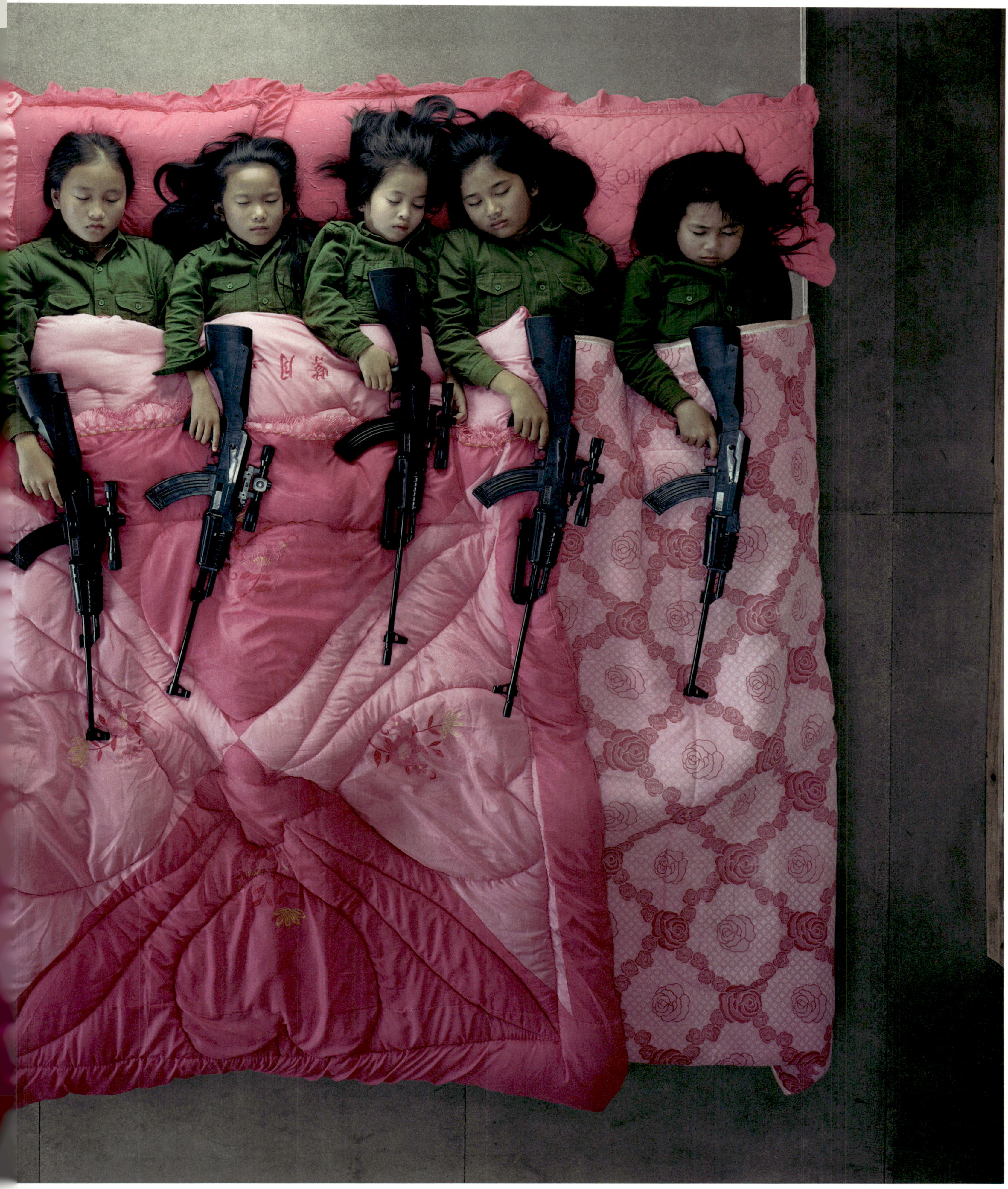

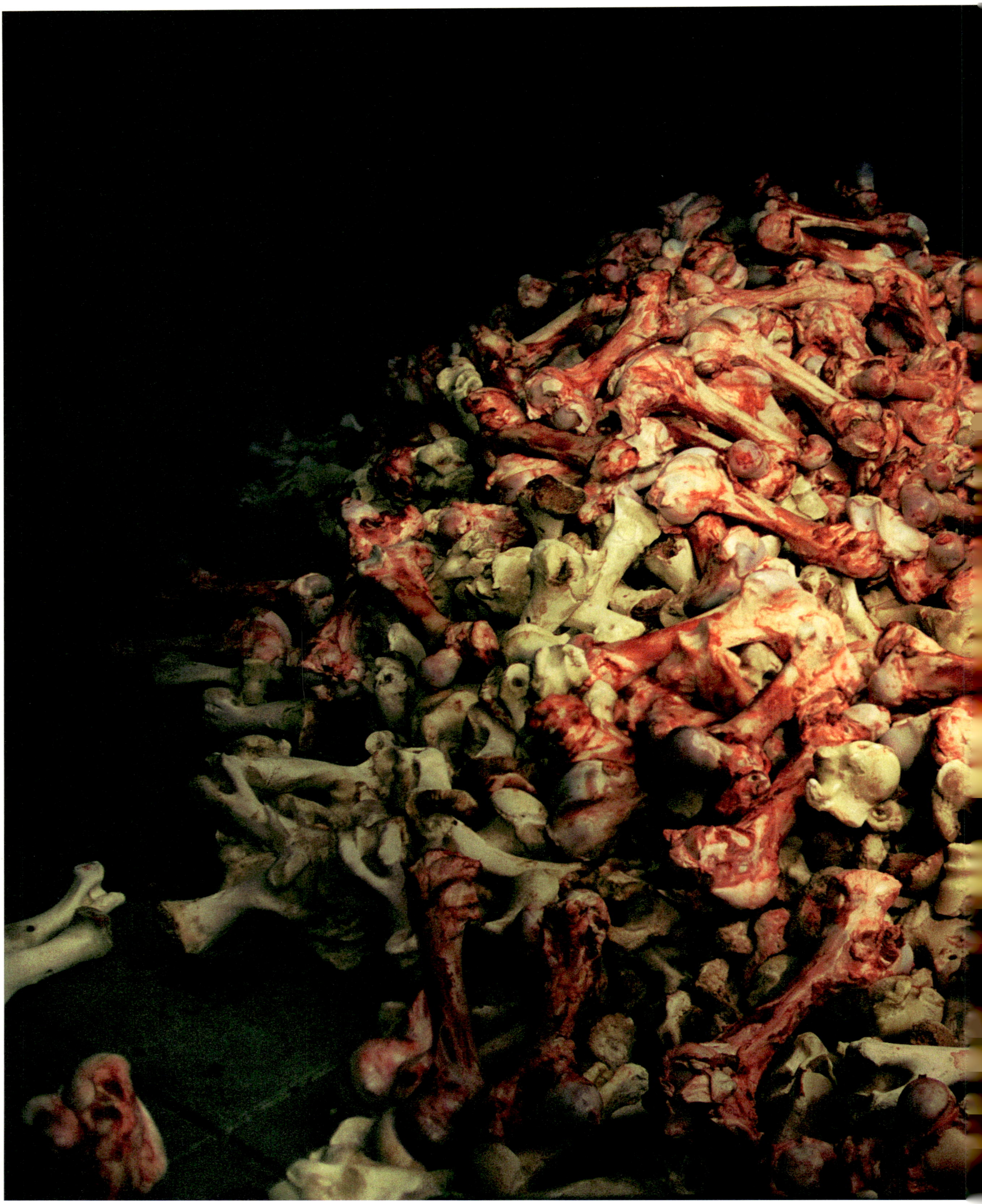

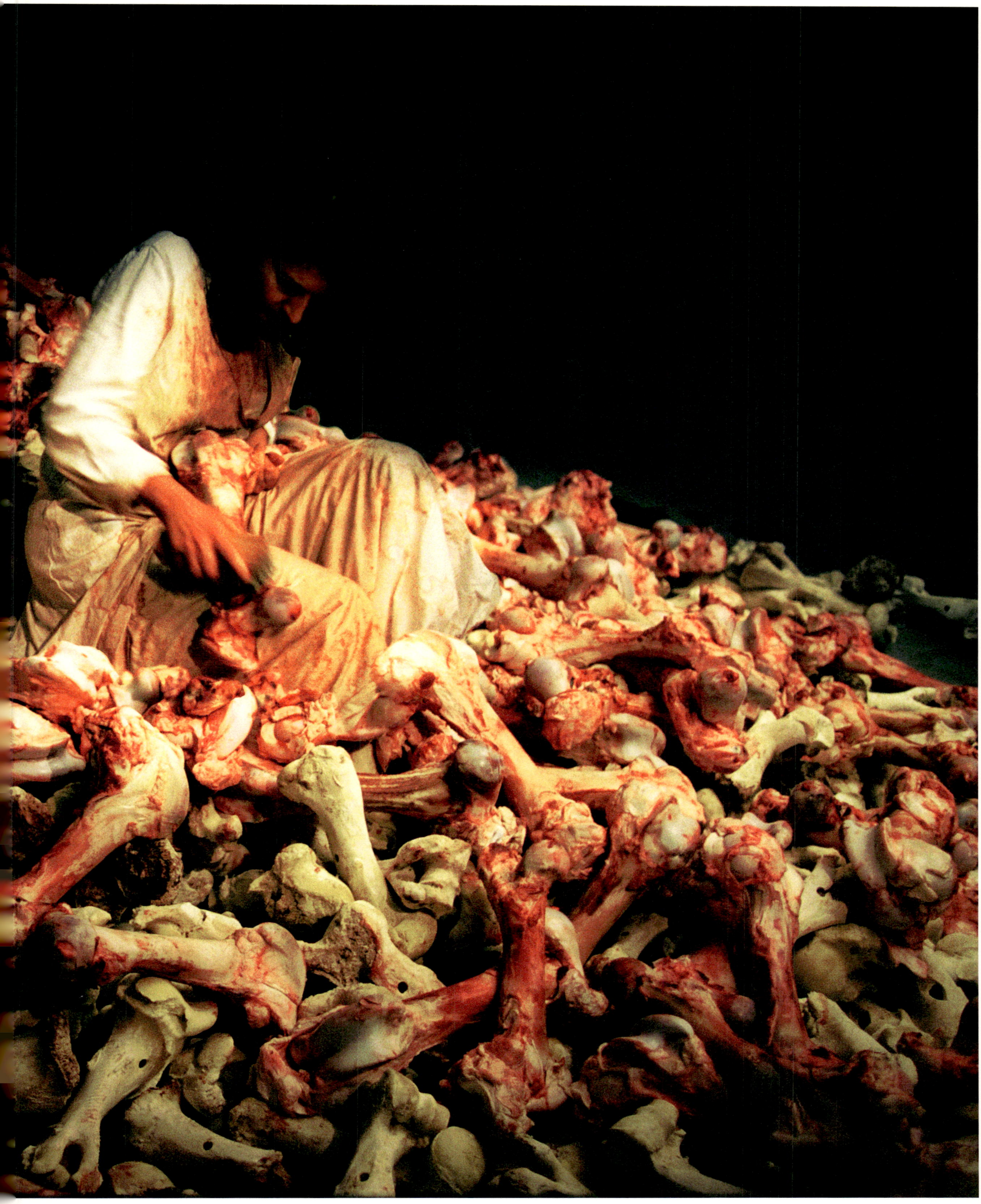

PEDRO ALONZO

ANGER IS AN ENERGY

Political themes, social awareness, and activism in the visual arts are thriving in the first decade of the twenty-first century. The hold of the formal aesthetic and the "art for art's sake" mentality has loosened, allowing for a divergence in the making of art where contemporary artists, street artists, and collectives not only address but take on issues that, for several decades after the Second World War, were left largely to civic organizations, radical groups, activists, journalists, and relief efforts.

The effect of global interconnectivity, which was made available through the internet, allows for an international sense of awareness. Themes such as race, civil rights, the environment, political issues, inequality, and corporate scandal are prevalent in the artistic practice of a significant group of artists. In addition, these issues have risen to the surface, no longer hidden behind the veil of a formal or conceptual aesthetic that only an informed elite is granted the information or education to understand. The traditional venues for art have expanded to incorporate public space, mass media, the internet, and artists and collectives working with distressed communities suffering from disasters, such as from New Orleans to Haiti, and with ongoing, unresolved political issues from Israel and Palestine to the Balkans.

In order to convey their message, artists mimic the style and forms of dissemination used in advertising and propaganda, making explicit works or staging interventions that raise awareness and call for action. Some artists, such as JR see p. 178 and Swoon see p. 90, have crossed the line that divides art and activism in establishing nonprofit organizations in order to have a direct impact on communities around the globe. The strategies used today, while not new, have a new register and impact. Through engaging in a postmodern practice, artists pick and choose from aesthetic approaches and economic models, from within the art world and without, combining these in order to achieve their goals. The historical development of political art and artistic activism provides artists today with a rich tradition from which they draw inspiration and artistic strategies.

Political art today is the product of the fundamental changes in western society that transpired at the end of the nineteenth century. The dramatic shifts in patronage, political systems, industrial production, and technological advances had a profound affect on the role of art. The tradition of patronage carried out by the monarchy and church, epitomized during the Renaissance, fundamentally changed during the Industrial Revolution. The invention of film and photography not only questioned the role of representation or the ability to capture reality in art, but the ease, speed, and efficiency of mechanical reproduction made obsolete many of the genres traditionally explored by artists, such as portraiture, landscapes, and historical depictions. These advances compelled artists to think beyond representation, as well as raising the need for a distinction between "high" and "low" art and culture, and between cheap mechanical reproduction versus fine art. Politically, the shift from kingdoms to formal states with elected governing bodies during the early stages of modern democracy, helped spread power from an aristocracy to a newly forming political and business elite. The dissolving patronage of the monarchy, and the rise of capitalists, created the early stages of an art market. The industrial revolution concentrated wealth into the hands of the capitalist owners, and created a slave-like dependence and extreme poverty for the workers, giving rise to labor movements across Europe. The observations of this phenomenon by the philosopher Karl Marx, led to the publishing of his book, *Capital*. This Marxist theoretical framework supplied ruthless dictators, namely Lenin, Stalin, and Mao Zedong, with the arguments to foment a revolution and take control, as well as providing their fascist counterparts, Hitler, Mussolini, and Franco, with a concept of the enemy.

The sociopolitical upheaval and technological advances that followed the industrial revolution had a fundamental impact on artistic practice in the twentieth century. These events led to the apparent stylistic and often ideological struggle of two seemingly distinct and ostensibly opposing tendencies, referred to here as modern and political art, represented by abstraction and realism, respectively. Modern art is primarily characterized through the rejection of academic traditions; the embracing of various forms of abstraction; and the use of formal values to achieve esthetic purity, which is free of representational elements. Realism is characterized as figurative and representational; encompassing work that contains a clear narrative; work which often deals with social justice or historical achievements, and is therefore considered political. A look at the manifestations of political and modern art in reference to the sociopolitical conditions art responded to in the twentieth century demonstrates that in the hands of artists, these apparently opposing concepts and artistic strategies are not in opposition to one another, but are part of an aesthetic repertoire that functions in relation to the social context they inhabit, and the political forces they struggle with.

Political art thrived in Germany as a response to the upheavals and uncertainty that led up to the First World War, the brief period of Weimar rule, and the onset of the Second World War. In anticipation of the Second

SWOON

"I'M ALWAYS ASKING MYSELF HOW I CAN REALLY BE A PART OF THE WORLD AS IT'S HAPPENING; AS IT'S BEING LIVED? SO LIKE EVEN THIS THING OF MAKING BOATS AND GOING DOWN THESE RIVERS, WE'RE STOPPING IN TOWNS. WE'RE COMMUNICATING WITH PEOPLE. WE'RE INVITING THEM TO BE A PART OF THIS EXPERIENCE. WE'RE SHOWING UP TOTALLY OUT OF NOWHERE FOR THEM, AND THEY'RE LIKE, "WHO ARE YOU? WHERE ARE YOU COMING FROM? WHAT IS THIS?" AND WE'RE MAKING SOMETHING WHICH IS A PART OF PEOPLE'S DAILY LIVES IN A PLACE THAT THEY'RE NOT EXPECTING TO FIND IT IN A REALLY DIFFERENT WAY. AND IT SOUNDS VERY DIFFERENT, BUT FOR ME IT'S ACTUALLY REALLY SIMILAR—A REALLY SIMILAR APPROACH OF THAT THING OF INTERACTING WITH AND UPON CULTURE, AND NOT JUST SORT OF COMMENTING ON CULTURE IN THIS MORE KIND OF RARIFIED AND PROTECTED SPACE."

World War, many European artists and intellectuals, such as the Italian, Fillipo Marinetti in his *Futurist Manifesto* of 1909, looked forward to the obviously inevitable war as a means to regenerate society. It was a case of "out with the old, in with the new." The armed conflict and the corresponding social and political upheavals were viewed as benefiting society by ushering in a new civilization. These beliefs led German artists such as George Grosz and Otto Dix to a Max Beckmann, to enlist into the army and serve in the Second World War trenches. Their stark experiences with modern warfare left them disillusioned and depressed. However, the war also had intensified a sense of brotherhood among artists and intellectuals, promoting political activism and extremism.

DIEGO RIVERA

"THE SOCIAL STRUGGLE IS THE RICHEST, THE MOST INTENSE AND THE MOST PLASTIC SUBJECT WHICH AN ARTIST CAN CHOOSE. THEREFORE, ONE WHO IS BORN TO BE AN ARTIST CAN CERTAINLY NOT BE INSENSIBLE TO SUCH DEVELOPMENTS."

After the Second World War, artists expressed their disillusionment with the Weimar democracy during a period of extreme poverty, unemployment, and hyperinflation. The latest version of expressionism campaigned to denounce the corrupt upper class, and to depict the despair and struggle of the common man. Max Beckmann portrayed mutilated veterans begging for food; George Grosz and Otto Dix caricatured the industrial and military elite; and John Heartfield used photomontage and graphic design to create searing satires of the establishment. Grosz in particular—a member of the left along with Heartfield—used art as a weapon for society. He actively defended workers' rights, and deflated German greatness. Expressionism had changed from a movement that used color and the distorted figure to express feelings and states of being, into a way of advancing political confrontation, which showed the establishment and urban life as being sinister, and something not to be trusted.

Amid the sociopolitical and economic chaos following Second World War, nothing appeared to have changed. The power structure composed of the industrial elite and the militarists remained the same in spite of them having lost the war. Some things were worse; during the period after the war, Weimar Germany was being punished and humiliated by the allied powers. The signing of the Treaty of Versailles in 1919 at the end of the First World War, where Germany had lost significant territory to Poland and Czechoslovakia, on top of the enormous reparations to be paid to the allies, severely impacted on the economy and the newly formed, democratically elected Weimar Republic's ability to rule. The extreme left did not recognize the legitimacy of the government, and were promoting the ideas of the Soviet Revolution of 1917; the right wanted to abolish Weimar and reinstall a conservative, authoritative regime. Contradictions abounded; the extreme left and right fought against each other for power, but worked together to debilitate the Weimar government. The political struggle and the promotion of a "strong Germany" to the masses by the militarists, created a sense that democracy was an experiment that could not work. As such, the despair and anger over the appalling living conditions, and a sense of anger and defeat in a demoralized Germany, allowed for a messianic leader to rise.

Once in power, the Third Reich organized the infamous "Degenerate Art" exhibition in 1937 in Munich, exhibiting a selection of 650 works labeled as un-German. This was an unparalleled attack on modernity and its avant-garde forms of expression. The work of sanctioned artists who supported Nazi rule was considered a valid art form, while the latest trend toward abstraction was considered a marker of inferiority. This, of course, changed immediately after the defeat of Nazi Germany. The once "degenerate" artists have recuperated their position in society, while the Nazi artists, such as the sculptor Arno Breker, and others, like the filmmaker Leni Riefenstahl, have long been discredited, or are considered puppets of the Nazi propaganda machine.

The Russian avant-garde, which formed toward the end of the Russian Empire, began with a rejection of academic traditions and bourgeois taste. The movement promoted an end to an academic art-historical continuum, by embracing abstraction, new visual forms, and media, all of which were considered part of a revolutionary spirit geared to the advancement of a new society. These artists wanted to forget the past and create something new. In 1915, two years before the revolution, Kasimir Malevich presented his theory of suprematism—a new type of pure geometric abstraction, which was unrelated to natural forms. After the October Revolution of 1917, artists believed that they were playing a role in the creation of a new society: The Great Utopia. For many artists of this period, their intention was to create art that would contribute to the uplifting of the working class. Education became a priority in a country were it had virtually not existed before. Educational reform consisted of building schools, developing new curriculums, and the widespread publishing of books, posters, and newspapers. El Lissitzky, who was committed to the idea of creating art with a purpose, specifically an art that would foster change in society, was deeply involved in designing books for children.

Constructivism became the official artistic language to express the views of soviet society. The principals were applied to a variety of disciplines with the intention of addressing and servicing the masses. El Lissitzky, Rodchenko, and Stepanova among many others, were involved in designing propaganda for the state. Rodchenko and Stepanova gave up painting in order to work in more populist mediums, such as photography and graphic design, in order to communicate more effectively with the masses. Among the most important and accomplished works is El Lissitzky's *Beat the White with the Red Wedge,* 1919. This poster was created during the Russian Civil War in support of the Red Bolshevik army, and shows a red wedge piercing a white circle representing the monarchists. As of the mid 1920s, avant-garde ideas were put to work in the service of government directives. The period of unprecedented artistic innovation and freedom in Russia concluded in 1934, when Stalin prohibited all forms of art except Socialist Realism. Ironically, authoritarian control stifled artistic production that had supported and exalted the state.

Mexico's muralist movement, while not exactly direct government propaganda, had a very close relationship with the newly formed postrevolution ruling party. The Mexican muralist movement was born at the end of the bloody Mexican Revolution as a means to unite a broken country. As early as 1920, large public murals were commissioned by the Mexican Ministry of Education in Mexico City, in order to create a sense of national identity in a country where a large portion of the population was illiterate and lived in rural communities. This was a truly populist artistic movement with a defined social and political agenda. The message was sent in a representational and narrative form of art, which was easily understood by the masses. The colorful, large-scale works often featured historic figures, exalting Mexico's pre-Columbian heritage and prosperity through national unity, as well as promoting Mexico's industrial and scientific achievements. The murals were strategically placed in public buildings, such as schools, government offices, and at the Palace of Fine Arts, making them accessible to almost everyone. Part of the funding for the public art program came from the people; Mexico's national lottery was established as a means to finance the program, producing a series of visually stunning lottery tickets and advertisements, which were created by some of the country's most important and influential artists.

During the Great Depression, the United States adopted the idea of public art based on the work of the Mexican muralists. The Works Progress Administration (WPA) was established in 1935 as part of President Franklin Delano Roosevelt's New Deal. The WPA was to inject capital back into society by putting people to work erecting public buildings, such as post offices, and building roads. At a later stage, the WPA hired thousands of artists to paint public murals around the country. Los Tres Grandes—the three most important muralists Diego Rivera, José Clemente Orozco, and David Alfaro Siqueiros—were invited to the United States to paint large-scale works; these artists were also of great influence stylistically and thematically to artists in the United States. Most of the murals they created, including *Detroit Industry*, 1932, at the Detroit Institute of Arts by Rivera, or Orozco's mural, *Prometheu,s* in Pomona, California, are still in public view. The WPA adopted the Mexican model in spite of the fact that the Mexican muralists' humanist and communist views presented a direct conflict with American capitalist values. The success of the program in Mexico influenced the WPA's national aspirations of using public art as a catalyst to get labor working in order to elevate the people's spirits and to glorify the New Deal policies in hopes that the artistic representation of national unity would get the country through economic hardship.

Unlike Mexico, government support of the arts was unheard of in the United States, a country whose arts establishment had traditionally depended on commercial galleries and wealthy clientele. Most of the artists were happy to have work, and practiced their trade within the guidelines established by the WPA. However, at a time when the disparity between the rich and poor in the United States was at a historical extreme, artists could not ignore the poverty and hardship faced by most of the population, which was in direct contrast to the relatively extravagant lifestyles of the wealthy. These socioeconomic factors, combined with the work of the Mexican muralists, ignited a trend of social realism among artists in the United States—among them, Thomas Hart Benton, Jacob Lawrence, and Ben Shahn. These painters depicted the stark reality of social inequality, as well as the struggles faced by workers and immigrants. Their work also presented the nation's history, heritage, and the utopian spirit of democracy. The American version of social realism was not limited to painting. Photographers, most notably Walker Evans and Dorothea Lange (who were both employed by the WPA), documented the stark images of rural poverty and urban soup kitchens, exposing the harsh living and working conditions faced by the nation's poor. Through literature, John Steinbeck also depicted these hardships in his classic novel of 1939, *The Grapes of Wrath.*

In 1934, Nelson Rockefeller ordered the destruction of a mural he had commissioned by Diego Rivera inside Rockefeller Center. The mural was destroyed because the artist would not remove a portrait of Lenin it depicted. This event symbolizes a key moment in art history, when the support of representational art begins to decline among the artworld elite. Instead, collectors, critics, and museum professionals began to favor the nonrepresentational variety of art, namely abstract expressionism and the European avant-garde. The Rivera vs. Rockefeller conflict also signals the early stages of hibernation of political art around the world. A series of factors over several decades, including the Red Scare and the two world wars, shifted the capital of the art world from European centers such as Paris, Moscow, and Berlin to New York.

SAM DURANT

"HISTORY IS A SUBJECTIVE AND A SORT OF CONSTANTLY FLUCTUATING THING BUT THE INTERESTING THING ABOUT IT IS THAT HISTORY IS ALWAYS AND ONLY TAKING PLACE IN THE PRESENT AND WE'RE SORT OF TRYING TO GET SOME SENSE OF IT AT ANY GIVEN MOMENT. MY WORK IS NOT TRYING TO BE AUTHORITATIVE, IT'S TRYING TO CHALLENGE THE IDEA OF HISTORICAL AUTHENTICITY OR HISTORICAL AUTHORITY TO AT LEAST PAUSE AT THE IDEA THAT THINGS MAY NOT BE ALWAYS THE WAY THEY WERE PORTRAYED TO BE."

Europe was busy rebuilding after the war, visual art was not a priority, or as in the Soviet Union, it was dictated by the state. Many of the European protagonists such as Max Ernst, Wassily Kandinsky, Walter Gropius, and George Grosz had moved to the United States fleeing persecution. The United States had become a super power and was hungry for culture. In the 1950s the United States accounted for 7percent of the world's population, but produced 50percent of the goods being traded worldwide. As consumer culture and mass media developed in North America, visual culture and consumer goods became synonymous with each other, widening the gap between "high" and "low" culture. From abroad, the perception of American consumerism became associated with the appealing imagery produced in Hollywood, and through advertising mass-market products like Coca-Cola. The United States used its brand of New York-based abstract expressionism, cultural criticism through the words of Clement Greenberg, and the economic might of an industrial elite to crown New York—its greatest city—as the capital of the art world. These factors led to a stifling of political and representational forms of art, and the thriving of nonrepresentational, apolitical, conceptual, and formal aesthetics—the echoes of which we deal with to this day.

Political art did not disappear completely; it lived a marginal existence after the Second World War. Greenberg's model of modernism, which favored formal abstraction and critical discourse surrounding formal values, had taken hold. The illusion of a clear distinction between high art and low art was cemented; references to popular culture or personal experiences were not in favor. Art was supposed to be about itself. It was reasoned that those who did not understand high art were not worthy. The emergence of the two Super Powers, the Soviet Union and the United States, after the Second World War pitted the former allies' diametrically opposed social, political, and economic ideologies—capitalism and communism—against each other in the Cold War. The conflict was also fought on a cultural front: abstract expressionism representing the United States versus the Soviet's socialist realism. The former genre was argued to represent individuality and self-expression and was epitomized by the work of Jackson Pollock's action painting. Ironically, Pollock had trained with the Mexican muralist Siqueiros in New York, and was well aware of the work of Orozco. Pollock's abstract form of painting was born of the artist's psyche, fears, inner struggles, and their manifestation onto the canvas through his manipulation of paint. The work was completely removed of figurative representation, history, or narrative. Pollock and his contemporaries, including his wife, Lee Krasner, Helen Frankenthaler, Willem de Kooning, and Mark Rothko, all of whom were engaged in varying styles of formal abstraction, were supported by an intellectual and economic elite including the art critic Clement Greenberg, collector Peggy Guggenheim, Alfred H. Barr, the founding director of the Museum of Modern Art in New York and of the Central Intelligence Agency (CIA). Many artists, particularly Rothko, Adolph Gottlieb, and Barnett Newman, disagreed with Greenberg's purely formalist views of their work. Although their work was abstract and nonrepresentational, these artists were politically active and vocal about their ideas; they formed groups and issued manifestos, which countered Greenberg's views of their work.

In spite of the abstract expressionist artist's intentions or left-leaning political beliefs, their works were used to promote "American" capitalist values. Exhibitions of this genre were financed by the CIA and toured around the world. Ironically, less enlightened political leaders, including the President, Harry S. Truman, and George Dondero, a senator from Michigan, attacked abstraction as un-American, declaring that it was "a weapon of communism," and questioned artists, such as Wassily Kandinsky, for their Russian origins and political inclinations (it should be pointed out that during the Cold War, painters were spared the brunt of the attacks that were directed toward the film industry). Barr was compelled to decry these assaults and defend the avant-garde artists by demonstrating the intolerance and persecution of abstraction and the promotion of state-sanctioned realism in Nazi Germany and the Soviet Union. This type of contradictory debate, and conflicting policies within the American political establishment and intelligence services, illustrates the clash between the country's rural conservatism and socially liberal urban elite. It is no coincidence that the CIA adopted this promotional strategy considering the agency's practice of enlisting privileged young men from Ivy League universities into its ranks. This type of open clash can take place within a democracy. It cannot take place in a totalitarian state.

In 1927, after exiling Leon Trotsky, Stalin claimed power in Russia and took complete control of culture. Stalin developed a centralized idea of mass culture. It was part of his overarching plan to industrialize a nation, force the collectivization of agriculture, modernize the army, and control all social classes. The atrocities committed, such as mass killing, forced labor, and displacement, in order to further the goals of the regime, required a massive propaganda machine. In 1932, the Union of Soviet Writers was established as an organization that controlled all cultural output. Socialist Realism was the artistic law of the land; all independent art groups and forms of expression were abolished. The Russian avant-garde and their groundbreaking innovations in art and visual culture were a thing of the past. Social Realist art had to support and glorify the communist party, as well as represent socialist ideologies. In this situation there was no room for debate. The art of the state was a form of involuntary propaganda, a clear message for artworks was obligatory, and in a country with a large, illiterate rural population, figurative, representational, and narrative forms of art were deemed compulsory. In many ways Soviet social realism completely opposed abstract expressionism. From the work itself, figurative versus abstract; to the intended audience: art made for the masses versus art made for the elite; to the form of patronage: state support or commercial enterprise. Regardless of whether the artist's intention of making work was political or apolitical, both forms of expression are a product of the context from which they emerged, and were subjected to social, economic, and political manipulations. It was not until 1991 that the Soviet state's firm hold on culture was released.

During the late 1960s and early 1970s, when the world was in political and social upheaval, popular forms of culture, such as the music of Bob Dylan, fashion, and graphic arts, commonly expressed dissent and called for change; at this time, the mainstream visual arts were largely silent on the political front. The contemporary art world's gaze had largely turned in upon itself, fostering an insular dialogue between artists, critics, and museum professionals. The dissent posed by artists working within the art world circuit at this time was primarily directed toward their predecessors and the art world establishment. Although a few art groups, such as the Guerrilla Art Action Group (GAAAG), staged nonviolent protests against the war in Vietnam, relatively little was done within the core of the art world to address political issues outside it.

GUY DEBORD AND GIL J. WOLMAN

"DETOURNEMENT NOT ONLY LEADS TO THE DISCOVERY OF NEW ASPECTS OF TALENT: IN ADDITION, CLASHING HEAD-ON WITH ALL SOCIAL AND LEGAL CONVENTIONS, IT CANNOT FAIL TO BE A POWERFUL CULTURAL WEAPON IN THE SERVICE OF A REAL CLASS STRUGGLE."

Ironically, the protest culture of the late 1960s embraced "art actions," the radical new forms of artistic expression commonly know as "happenings" and "performance." Political activists of the era, such as Abbie Hoffman, learned from art actions and turned them into "political actions" in order to stage media events that drew attention to social and political issues. Although "political" and "art" actions are virtually identical, both are site-specific, take place in public space, and demand spontaneous interaction between the protagonist and the public, there was a clear differentiation between the two types of actions. The role and activities of the artist and the activist were separate and clearly defined.

Groups fighting for civil rights such as the Black Panthers, student organizations, Chicano activists, and feminist groups, employed artists working outside the establishment. Graphic designers, among them Emory Douglas and Rupert García, were used to create posters, cartoons, and signage to protest issues ranging from social inequality and police brutality, to the war in Vietnam. These images were often reproduced as posters, and were used to drive traffic to rallies for public protest. It was during this period, in 1968, that Jim Fitzpatrick created the iconic image of Che Guevara, based on a photograph by Alberto Korda.

The most radical changes within the established art world were seen in the development of pop art in the United States and Britain, and the Situationist International on the European continent. Pop art presented a controversial return to figurative painting and the use of common references such as signage, commercial products, comic books, and advertising to make art. Although incorporating aspects of consumer society and popular culture, the work of pop artists such as Andy Warhol and Roy Lichtenstein, was primarily intended for and consumed by the elite, not the masses. Guy Debord and a small group of colleagues including the artists Asger Jorn and Pinot-Gallizio, formed the Situationist International in 1957. Based on Marxist theory, the Situationist International rejected organized government and the corresponding ideologies of capitalism and Soviet socialism. Their criticism of the establishment included the art world system, in which artists created goods to be commodified and sold through galleries and exhibited in museums, which, in their view, supported the establishment's dominance over culture in society. Furthermore, the situationists believed that art must be political, committed to undermining the elite's hold on the working class, and able to free the working class from the boredom of everyday life. The apex of the situationists' strategies presented itself in 1968 through their direct involvement in student uprisings in the University in Strasbourg, France. Although the situationists' goal was to incite a revolution where autonomous workers' councils would be engaged in direct political control of society, the complexities of their ideas and writings as well as the selective nature of the organization, limited their exposure beyond a small group of radicals, students, and artists. The complexity of the Situationist International movement is due in part to the efforts of its leaders to avoid being co-opted by the system. The group dissolved in 1972 in a definitive effort to maintain its integrity.

Through seemingly distant means, both pop art and the situationists critiqued the flashy surface of consumer culture and its artificial nature, as well as the art world establishment. Warhol, for instance, addressed this through representational paintings of products and celebrities, while the situationists launched a direct attack defacing the public mediums of communication through techniques such as "détournement" and the "dérive." Détournement, involved utilizing aspects of existing infrastructure, such as advertising or street signs, and modifying it to subvert the original meaning. The dérive involved prolonged spontaneous movement through a city in order to capture its essence. Both of these subversive strategies reflect a desire to reclaim public space and challenge the system. For how can society function if the intended labor force is roaming around the city defacing signage and writing on walls? These actions predate the guerrilla tactics used by the youth culture movement of the late twentieth and early twenty-first centuries, among them punk, graffiti, and street art. Pop, through its use of visually and intellectually accessible imagery, and the situationists' defiant strategies, are a tremendous influence on many of the artists engaged in political and social activism in the early twenty-first century.

Artists continued to struggle with the modernist mantra of, "art for art's sake," and an attempt to bring about social change through art. In his book, *Art Since 1960,* Michael Archer poses the question that arose in the 1970s: "Could art communicate and be understood politically, or would the perception that it was performing a political function necessarily undermine its aesthetic purpose?" The late sixties and the seventies were the high point of minimalism and conceptual art. The exploration of new materials and mediums reflected an effort by certain artists to defy the market and the gallery system, a process that led to the dematerialization of art. Dan Graham's film and video work, and more importantly, his making art by paying to insert text and images into magazines, made it intentionally difficult to sell his work. Donald Judd's use of industrial materials was also an effort to defy the precious nature of the art object symbolized by academic painting and sculpture. The minimalist aesthetic allowed no references to anything other than the materials themselves, and their innate formal values. Artists' efforts to fight the commodification of their creations, and their harsh critique of art institutions, posed a tricky situation: how were artists to survive if they did not sell their work, and to what end did it benefit them to refuse to work with museums whose mission it was to function as the archive or repository of their life's work? The brave struggle of conceptual, performance, Land, and Minimal artists ultimately liberated the tyranny of painting and sculpture as the consecrated mediums of choice. Looking at a Fibonacci series piece by Judd in a museum in the twenty-first century, or at an image of an untitled work made of, red fluorescent Plexiglas and stainless steel in an auction catalog, it is difficult not to think of his work as a precious art object. This attitude against the market was directly opposed to Warhol's position, which was to embrace the market. Painting was his medium of choice, and elevating elements of popular culture or "kitsch" was a central theme of his version of high art. Warhol's use of an industrial process to make art in his studio, known as the Factory, and the volume of work and repetition of images taken from mass media and popular culture, challenged the notion of originality, uniqueness, as well as the preciousness of a work of art made under these conditions.

SAM DURANT

"I THINK ALL ART IS POLITICAL. BASICALLY, SOME WORK IS EXPLICIT IN ITS POLITICS AND SOME IS IMPLICIT. THAT'S THE GREAT DEFINITION THAT ADRIAN PIPER CAME UP WITH THAT I REALLY AGREE WITH. IF WE MAKE THE POLITICS OF THE WORK MORE EXPLICIT, IT WOULD ATTRACT A MUCH BROADER, WIDER SCOPE OF PRACTITIONERS AND THERE WOULD BE MANY MORE POINTS OF VIEW REFLECTED."

The true dematerialization and decommodification of the art object did not come from artists working within the art world establishment, but sprouted in poor working-class neighborhoods in the form of graffiti: an art form that literally exploded across the face of New York City in the early 1970s. Anonymous youth, often in their late teens, took to the streets to make their mark on city walls, in the ultimate attack on public space. These artists had no relationship with the elite; their actions were completely illegal; their work was not intended to be sold; their art was born and functioned completely outside the art-world establishment. These artists did not have the conflicted relationship with the art world that formally trained artists faced; that would come later. Initially, they were just having fun, making their mark on society, challenging each other in terms of repetition, audacity, visibility of the work, and stylistic development. Although graffiti art took place in public space, it was not intended to be consumed by the elites or the masses. Graffiti artists were, and are still today, primarily making art for each other. Yet, even the history and evolution of graffiti is as complex and insular as that of art history. Although not strictly a political art form, as there was no agenda behind the work, the fact that poor, working-class teens found a voice through the medium of spray paint and imposed it upon society is a truly political act and cultural phenomenon. In the early 1980s, the artists and their work were co-opted by savvy art dealers eager to make a profit on a new movement. Sadly the artists and their genre were not properly cultivated, and they were dropped by the art world almost as fast as they were picked up. It is not until today that there is a renewed interest in this work as well as the genre, which is being looked at seriously by some institutions; and although most of the original work has been destroyed it has not been forgotten.

The art-historical archive, as narrated by the establishment, has not been kind to much of the community-based art projects and social activism that took place in the 1970s and early 1980s. Artist collectives such as Collaborative Projects (COLAB) were active in working outside the institutions and galleries. COLAB consisted of a union of artists grouped together in order to pool and share funding, equipment, and to organize exhibitions. COLAB's activities and exhibitions served as a template for the formation of alternative spaces around the country. One such exhibition, "The Real Estate Show," which took place on January 1, 1980, exemplifies the political and activist nature of art during this period. The artist collective known as the Committee for the Real Estate Show (CRES), took over an abandoned city-owned building in lower Manhattan on New Year's Eve in order to house an exhibition about gentrification and the city's arbitrary real estate development laws, which were causing the eviction of families from their homes. CRES had previously attempted to rent the building located at 123 Delancey Street from the Department of Housing Preservation and Development (HPD) in order to use it as an exhibition space. On January 2, one day after the exhibit opened, the police shut the exhibition down. The artists experienced being thrown out of their space in much the same way that many New Yorkers had experienced eviction from their homes. In spite of the artists having entered the building illegally, their mistreatment by city officials led to the granting of space for the collective and their exhibition in another building. Ironically, it has been artists, followed by their dealers, who settle in once unattractive neighborhoods such as SoHo and the warehouse section of Chelsea, transforming them into some of the most desirable neighborhoods in the city. Clearly the HPD lacked vision.

The challenge remained in reconciling formal aesthetics with the desire to communicate with a wider audience. Conceptual art's ambiguous, and in many cases inaccessible, political message was in direct opposition to making art with a clear message and intention, which was what was needed for it to have any hope of effecting social change, and so it remained on the art world periphery. In the 1980s, two social movements, feminism and the activism born from the AIDS epidemic, served as a catalyst to unite art and activism. Although the tyranny of the artistic medium had been done away with, as painting and sculpture were now sharing space with video, installations, and other nontraditional forms of art, the creators themselves were less egalitarian: they were still primarily white men. The stark inequality of resources dedicated to women in the arts, which included the lack of museum and gallery exhibitions for women artists, was brought to the attention of the general public and the art world. Most notably, the Guerrilla Girls, a group of women working anonymously, wearing gorilla masks and short skirts, ridiculed the arts establishment using guerilla tactics, humor, and wit in publicizing these differences—through the use of posters in public space and other methods—in order to expose the embarrassing statistics concerning women in the arts. Museums and galleries that were publicly criticized for not exhibiting women strove to better their ratings. It is important to point out that in order to communicate and activate change, the Guerrilla Girls were compelled to use strategies that completely disregarded formal and conceptual trends. Feminist art's struggle for equality, before and after the Guerrilla Girls, inspired a rich tradition of women artists who found a voice, and used it to communicate their political and social views. Among them, Martha Rosler and her use of imagery found in media and advertising to condemn war and the representation of U.S. armed conflict abroad by the mainstream media. Jenny Holzer started wheatpasting truisms in public space in 1977, and later used multiple forms of media including LED lights, billboards, T-shirts, and baseball caps to convey her messages, which questioned dominant forms of power through the use of language. In an effort to address controversial issues, such as domestic violence and legalized abortion, the conceptual artist Barbara Kruger subversively mimiced the graphic and conceptual strategies used in advertising.

When the AIDS epidemic first started, it was not recognized by the United States government or by organized religion. As the disease spread across the world, initially killing millions of gay men and drug addicts, before it spread widely among other groups, the global heath crisis was ignored in the United States. The lack of action prevented funding for medical research and education; it perpetuated misinformation, gay stereotypes, and inspired fear and intolerance. It was through the combined efforts of nongovernmental organizations and artist collectives that awareness was raised and action demanded. As of 1987, a group of artists and activists joined forces to take on the AIDS issue, forming the AIDS Coalition to Unleash Power (ACT UP). The group held events and demonstrations to raise awareness and call attention to the epidemic and the U. S. government's lack of attention to the matter. As a means to promote social justice, ACT UP carried out savvy acts of civil disobedience employed to draw the attention of media and the masses. Artist collectives such as Gran Fury and the Silence = Death Project worked in conjunction with ACT UP to disseminate the message by launching a street art campaign that covered New York City with posters and stickers. The artists combined sexually charged imagery with humor, wit, and searing satire to create provocative works designed to confront the public with the government's inaction. Gran Fury's, *Read My Lips* poster series from 1988, featured images of same-sex couples kissing. While stickers were emblazoned with, "Men, use condoms or beat it." The outcome of the joint collaboration between ACT UP and the artist collectives resulted in changing public perception of gays and lesbians, dispelled myths about AIDS, and changed public policy that resulted in lowering the cost of AIDS treatment, and a governmental campaign to promote safe sex.

SHEPARD FAIREY

"THOUGH MY ART MAY MAKE SOME PEOPLE UNCOMFORTABLE, I'VE ALWAYS FELT THAT PROVOCATION, STIMULATING DEBATE, IS MUCH MORE DESIRABLE THAN IGNORING SENSITIVE ISSUES TO AVOID HURTING ANYONE'S FEELINGS."

The feminist and gay rights movements found a voice for their respective causes in art. Art functioned as a creative channel for their outrage and frustration, creating an impressive body of work and pushing society to recognize them. Their success provided a model for other minority groups to follow. Artists of African-American, Native American, and Hispanic origins began to take a more prominent role in the arts establishment. Unlike most of the white male counterparts, people of color were not as encumbered by a formalist doctrine, and were able to freely insert issues of race, social justice, and sexual orientation, into their work. As a result, a multicultural discourse ensued. One the most successful artists of this period is Félix González-Torres, who was also dealing with AIDS, as well as homosexuality, and racial issues. He is best known for a reductive body of work represented by common objects, text, images, and artistic gestures, that represented various aspects of his life. The work is extremely personal and biographic. As a gay, Hispanic artist, who lost his lover and later died of AIDS himself, González-Torres's work was intrinsically political, but wrapped in a conceptual esthetic. In an interview with the artist Tim Rollins he stated: "Formal strategies are there for your use." His mixing of formal strategies with a personal narrative and emotions goes against the basic tenets of early conceptual art, which was devoid of personal experience and emotion. However, his work was not overtly political because the message was difficult to decipher without key information about the work. In 1991, as part of a project room exhibition at the Museum of Modern Art, New York, he took his message to the streets with a famous billboard project in over 20 sites around Manhattan. The image consisted of two pillows on an empty bed. This work is about the

SWOON

"I WAS BORN FEELING LIKE THE ART WORLD HAD ALREADY TURNED INTO THE OPERA AND THAT IT WAS NEVER GONNA MATTER TO MY LIFE OR TO ANYONE THAT I CARE ABOUT. AND FEELING LIKE HOW—HOW DO I DO THE THING THAT I LOVE AND NOT LET IT DIE?"

passing of his lover, Ross Laycock, who had recently died of AIDS. By inserting his personal experience into a formal aesthetic, he defied the early notions of conceptual art by pioneering a postconceptual model that others would follow but, at the time, compared to the clearly stated message of Gran Fury, this work looks like a bad advertisement for Bed, Bath, and Beyond. The strategy of infusing personal experience and sentiment into a conceptual or formalist vehicle was to continue. Artists such as David Hammons, Lorna Simpson, Daniel Martinez, and Iñigo Manglano-Ovalle take a similar approach to confronting issues of identity, race, social justice, and the abuse of power.

In contrast to the reductive conceptual style employed by González-Torres, Keith Haring used a complex figurative language of characters and shapes to address gay rights. His inherently populist practice, employing humor and cartoon-like illustrations, projected a clear message intended to raise awareness of the AIDS epidemic and promote safe sex. The colorful, unambiguous style combined with his strategy of placing work in public space and on to all sorts of products, provided an effective vehicle for the cause. The accessible nature of Haring's practice serves as a model for the genre of street art.

The work of Hans Haacke and Leon Golub epitomizes the idea of contemporary political art. Haacke's practice rejects the modernist approach to art and criticism. He is highly critical of arts institutions, but works within the system to express his condemnation through exhibitions in museums and galleries. Haacke is famous for revealing the dirty secrets of corporations and individuals who support the arts. He has, for instance, publicized the questionable practices of leading art collectors, such as Peter Ludwig, the German chocolatier (who is the founder of two prominent German museums), and corporations such as Exxon. Haacke is very careful about who acquires his work in order to prevent it being purchased and hidden away by the collectors or corporations he is criticizing. In some cases, his formal approach is similar to that of González-Torres in that he uses objects that are representative of the political issues he is questioning. However, with Haacke the political message supersedes the formal qualities. Text and documentation based on researching pubic records are employed, making the message direct and unambiguous. Haacke has paid the consequences for his highly critical practice. In 1971 his solo exhibition at the Guggenheim Museum in New York was cancelled because of his revealing profile of Harry Shapolsky's real estate holdings and his questionable business practice. Leon Golub's paintings are also direct and unambiguous, depicting scenes of torture and the abuse of power. His images condemn U.S. military involvement in foreign countries, and support the civil rights struggle at home. Although not directly involved in activism and protests, Golub strives to send a clear message against American imperialism and abuse of power through his figurative images as they travel through society via museums, art galleries, and collectors' homes. There is no room for abstraction or modernist strategies in his work.

The artistic strategies, concepts, styles, and references in art of the twentieth century are present in today's artistic expression. Society has continued to open up culturally, allowing for a plurality of ideas, lifestyles, and forms expression to thrive. The internet and inexpensive video equipment have lowered the barrier to entry in order to produce and disseminate alternative ideas through independent platforms and media outlets. The election of George Bush in the year 2000 was a tremendous impetus to create political art. Artists around the globe joined forces to condemn the Bush administration's policies. The growing disparity of wealth between the rich and poor, corporate abuse and scandal, the lack of an effective environmental strategy, as well as decaying infrastructure and social services in developing nations are some of the key issues taken up by artists dealing with politics and activism in the twenty-first century. The spirit of the situationists is still alive today. Corporate greed and ineffective political process inspired The Yes Men see p. 72 to employ guerrilla tactics and misinformation to discredit governmental organizations and big business. The Yes Men use the internet and manipulate mass media in order to reach an audience outside the art world with their message. The anonymous U.K.-based artist Banksy is famous for his interventions. In the summer of 2006, he placed a blow-up doll dressed as a Guantánamo Bay prisoner next to the Big Thunder Mountain ride in Disneyland, going to great risk in order to draw attention to the Muslim prisoners held without trial by the U. S. government on a military base in Cuba.

The street art campaigns carried out in the 1980s by artists such as Jenny Holzer, Gran Fury, Jean-Michel Basquiat, and Keith Haring served as a model and inspiration for the genre now known as street art. Shepard Fairey see p. 266 began the *Obey* campaign in 1989, at the age of 19, while still in school. Fairey produced and distributed homemade stickers featuring the wrestler André the Giant for free by advertising in skateboard magazines. Twenty years later, he has distributed over 10 million stickers around the world. His use of the word "obey" is meant to assert a sense of defiance and inspire those who see his art to question it and all of the messages from the government and corporations that flood public space. The viral nature of his practice and the business model he developed in order to carry out the campaign predate online viral distribution and the web 2.0 business model. Fairey's most influential contribution to political art is the portrait he designed of the then Democratic presidential candidate, Barack Obama. The image, often referred to as the *Hope Poster*, not only helped to elect the president of the United States, but the style of the image has been the subject of many imitations and appropriations by the Right in an apparent effort to harness the image's power.

Although influenced by art-historical movements and ideas, the genre of street art goes against the fundamentals of the art world establishment in that it is intentionally populist, accessible, and, in some forms, inexpensive. Taking a cue from the Mexican muralists, the artworks address the general population with figurative imagery and a clear message. Similar to graffiti, the genre is best known for illegal works of art placed in highly visible sites. The references to popular culture and the use of industrial methods to create and disseminate work are reminiscent of pop art. One of the greatest and most controversial achievements of this genre is that these artists managed to circumvent the gallery system and art world establishment by creating their own conditions in order to promote, sell, and distribute their work. Many of these artists embraced capitalism, and developed strategies to sell less expensive versions of their work, primarily prints, through their own websites. This allowed them to survive and carry out their illegal street art campaigns while they achieved enough prominence to land a gallery and sell more expensive versions of their art to collectors. Although the political messages vary, one of the main motivations behind street art is to reclaim public space from corporate and government advertisements. The genre is also promoting the empowerment of others to have their say on public space by using simple and inexpensive techniques such as stenciling, wheatpasting, and spray painting. Although some within the genre consider working with museums and obtaining permission to place work in public a form of selling out, many have begun to work within the establishment.

In 1999, Rosa Martinez, the curator of the Third International Biennial Exhibition, organized by SITE Santa Fe, included images of protest interventions carried out by Greenpeace. Including Greenpeace's actions in a biennial of contemporary art begged the question: is it art or merely artistic? Like Abbie Hoffman, Greenpeace's intention was not to make art nor to become part of the art system, but to draw attention to the dangers of nuclear power by staging a dramatic intervention in placing multiple white crosses in front of a nuclear reactor. The images of these interventions are powerful, clear, and very similar to the strategies used by artists. Whether or not this intervention is in fact art, is secondary; Rosa Martinez was addressing the issue of how the boundaries between art and activism have blurred. The Slovenian artist, Marjetica Potrč see p. 139 has focused her career as an artist on studying the survival strategies developed by different impoverished communities, and by working with them to solve problems and help raise their standard of living. After a six-month stay in a shantytown in Caracas, Venezuela, Potrč worked in collaboration with the Israeli architect Liyat Esakov and the local neighborhood association to develop the *Caracas Dry Toilet*, a dry, ecologically safe commode that collects fertilizer for an area with a limited water supply. Potrč also creates adaptations of instruments used for survival, and exhibits them as fine art in galleries and museums.

Unhampered by protocols and regulations that relief organizations must adhere to, artists are free to work on desired projects in the manner they determine is most beneficial. Although certain hot spots, such as New Orleans, have become destinations for artists, the level of engagement tends to be temporary and the final product or work of art is then exported into the art world circuit. New York based Swoon and the Parisian artist JR have taken art and activism to a new level. Swoon and JR are best known as street artists. Swoon has wheatpasted her intricately cut images of "forgotten" people and friends from many nations on city walls around the world. She has also formed collectives in order to build boats out of trash and reclaimed materials in order to float them down the Mississippi and Hudson rivers, as well as across the Adriatic Sea from Slovenia to Venice and into the Grand Canal. Most recently she has formed a nonprofit organization to rebuild homes and a community center in a small town outside Port-au-Prince in Haiti. JR has formed three nonprofits as a way to continue his activities, and to support the communities where he has carried out his interventions. These organizations reside in Rio de Janeiro, Brazil, rural Kenya, and Israel/Palestine. JR uses large-scale photo murals in an effort to recognize, dignify, collect, and disseminate the stories of individuals who live in conditions of extreme poverty and social conflict.

In spite of the postwar modernist trend to establish formal values in art and criticism as the only valid model of artistic expression and discourse, political and activist art is thriving today. From preaching to the choir within the art world, to a public call to action and new levels of direct engagement with communities in need, artistic practice is fueled by outrage at the status quo and a desire for change. Outrage and frustration have helped artists to find a voice and develop strategies in order to address a myriad of issues and themes that affect our global community. Their work has been instrumental in establishing identities, liberating women, raising AIDS awareness, exploring the contradictions and atrocities of apartheid, and fighting oppression. Anger is harnessed into a creative force, utilizing realist imagery and formal strategies alike in order to address issues of global concern. And, to quote the immortal words of Johnny Rotten, the lead singer of the punk band the Sex Pistols: "Anger is an energy."

SHEPARD FAIREY

"I THINK AWARENESS, IN AND OF ITSELF, PROMOTES ACTIVISM, ACTION. YOU CAN JUST PROCEED MORE POWERFULLY IN LIFE IF YOU'RE PAYING ATTENTION. SO WHILE SOME OF MY WORK IS ABOUT SPECIFIC ISSUES, SOME OF IT IS JUST ABOUT ENCOURAGING PEOPLE TO QUESTION EVERYTHING THEY ENCOUNTER."

HISTORY REPEAT-ING

TABLE OF CONTENTS

INTRODUCTION

For a long time, representing historical events was the sole reserve of painting. Monumental historic images, which over the centuries oscillated between allegorical and antique styles, were chiefly intended to glorify specific happenings and statesmen, and to strengthen contemporary history by capturing these moments and individuals on canvas. In the nineteenth century, history painting was regarded throughout Europe and the United States as the greatest of all genres. In the twentieth century, artists began using history painting in a new way—to cast a critical eye on very recent events. Thus, Otto Dix drew on his own experiences to depict the horrors of war, while Picasso's monumental painting Guernica, in which he denounces the atrocities of the Spanish Civil War, is perhaps the most famous piece of anti-war art in the world. Unlike their predecessors, today's artists rarely employ conventional tools such as brushes and paint. Their chosen media are as varied as their motifs and, most importantly, the motivating factors that drive their work. Although traditional history painting has become obsolete, many modern-day artists work within an awareness of the genre. Russia's ASF+F Group [see p. 236] produces allegorical pictures inspired by antique literature, while Korean artist JoSeub [see p. 234] reconstructs famous Christian paintings to reflect Korean history. The unique commemorative works of American photographer Jennifer Karady [see p. 260] do more than allow viewers to contemplate and reflect on what they see; they also allow the protagonists to process their own personal experiences.

Yet contemporary works of art that reflect history do not necessarily present a specific scene; rather, they infiltrate the techniques that history painting used to depict its subjects. Some artists use sounds and music while others choose to go beyond simply showing historically relevant places by turning them into settings for their videos and campaigns. While history paintings of centuries past had clear messages that aimed to strengthen national identity, today's works often call this approach into question. It is not unusual for artists to express their criticism with crystal clarity, tearing apart heads of state like Bush and Blair instead of glorifying them. The kennardphillipps [see p. 232] artist collective, for example, uses photo montages created from press materials and other images to cast Bush and Blair's role in the Iraq war in a new light.

Works dealing with history in relation to the present day are dominated by issues that address the co-existence of different ethnic groups and the hierarchies between them that, despite crumbling long ago, continue to make themselves felt to this day. These include slavery, apartheid, the colonization of Native American land, discrimination and delinquency among young African-Americans, and cultural differences between East and West. Artists frequently avoid adopting a clear position, choosing instead to encourage viewers to unravel the structures, whose roots are often buried deep in the past.

SEBASTIÁN ERRÁZURIZ

For his artwork *Memorial of a Concentration Camp*, 2006, Chilean designer and artist Sebastián Errázuriz (* 1977) planted a 10-meter-high magnolia tree in the center of a football pitch. It was placed directly on the spot where, in 1973, the Chilean dictator Augusto Pinochet tortured and then executed thousands of political prisoners in the national stadium in Santiago, Chile. In this week-long project, he transformed the arena into a public park where people could stop and reflect. On the final day of the project, the artist arranged for Chile's two top football teams to play a match around the huge tree, in front of 20,000 spectators. Both Errázuriz's artwork and his design work are characterized by absurd ideas that often have a serious foundation. His designs also often use elements from nature, and have a certain morbid character. For instance, he uses a tree dug up and varnished in Chile as the foot for an elongated glass table; he turns a twig into a bookshelf; and uses a stuffed duck as a macabre table lamp. His design items are very limited-edition pieces; for example, his motorboat coffin for stylish suicides was initially presented at trade fairs only as a sketch. Works like these illustrate the fluid distinction between art and design in his work. "I invest what I earn from my designs in my art objects," says Errázuriz, who is something of a local celebrity in his home region. He writes a column on design in the daily paper, and has his own radio series and television show. His is also a well-known name, as his family has produced three presidents—which is why it only took a few telephone calls to get permission to plant a tree in the national stadium, and to organize a high-profile football game. In New York, where the artist lives today, things are a little more difficult, but he can still fulfill his objectives even without the cooperation of the municipal authorities. He is currently planning a guerrilla project that involves erecting 4,000 white crosses in Central Park—the number of crosses represents the number of people who die in a month in New York. In 2009, he implemented a similar project at the foot of the Brooklyn Bridge.

Memorial of a
Concentration Camp
2006, Santiago de Chile, Chile

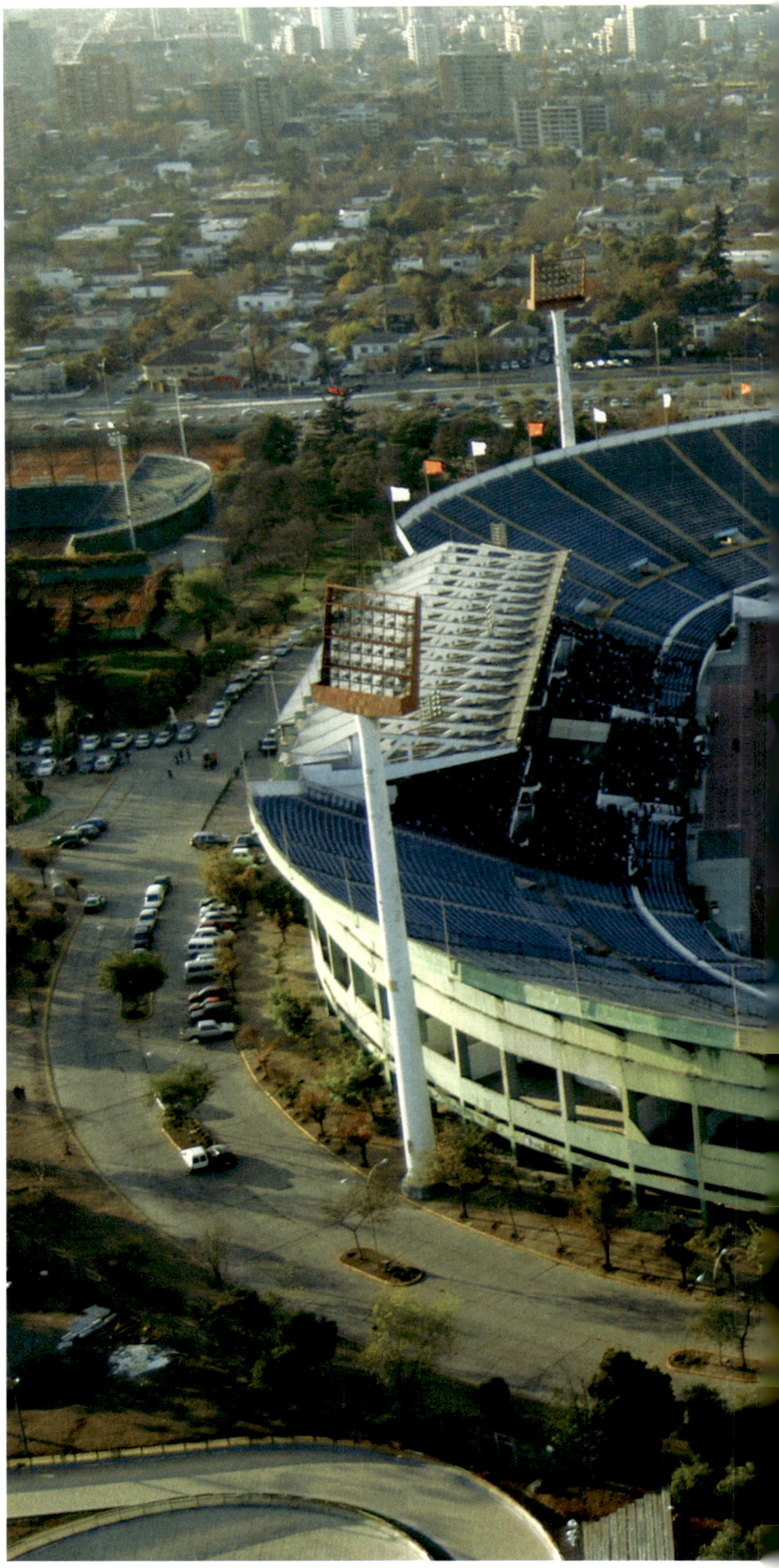

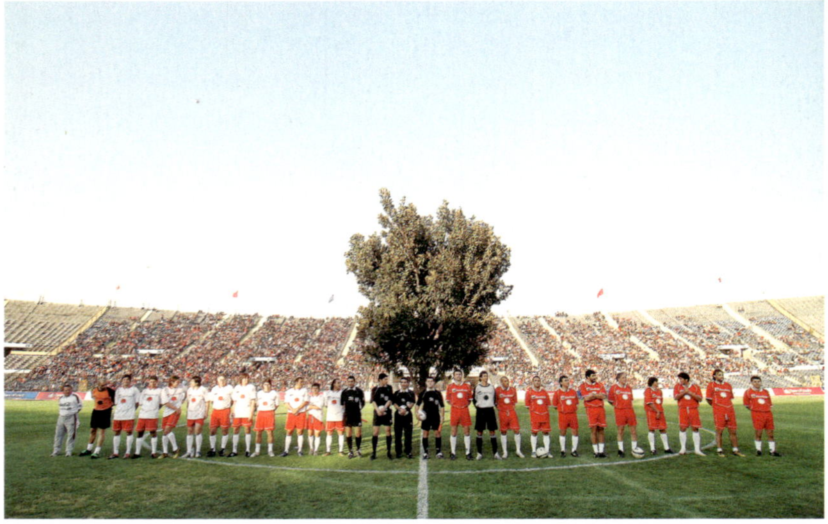

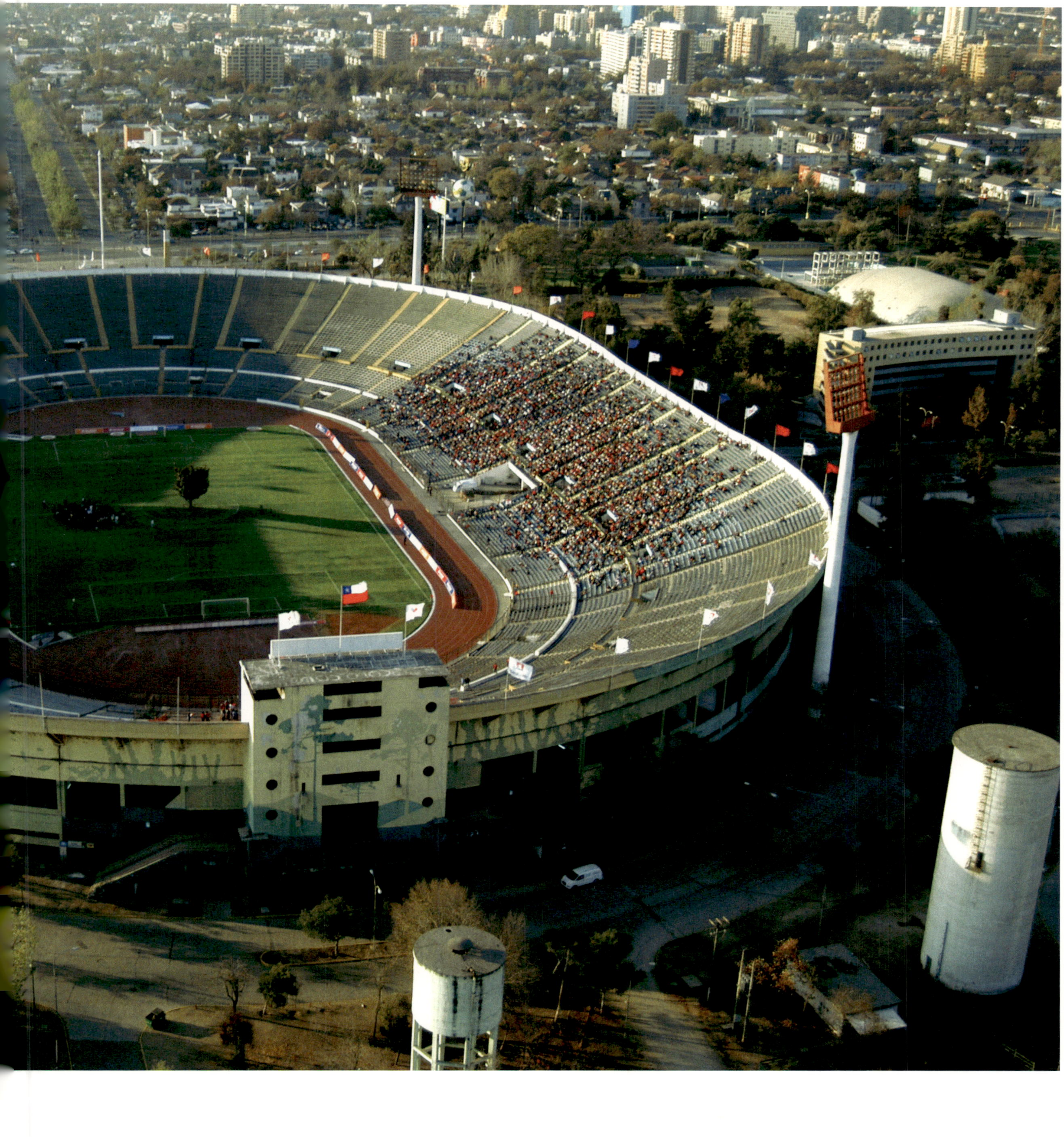

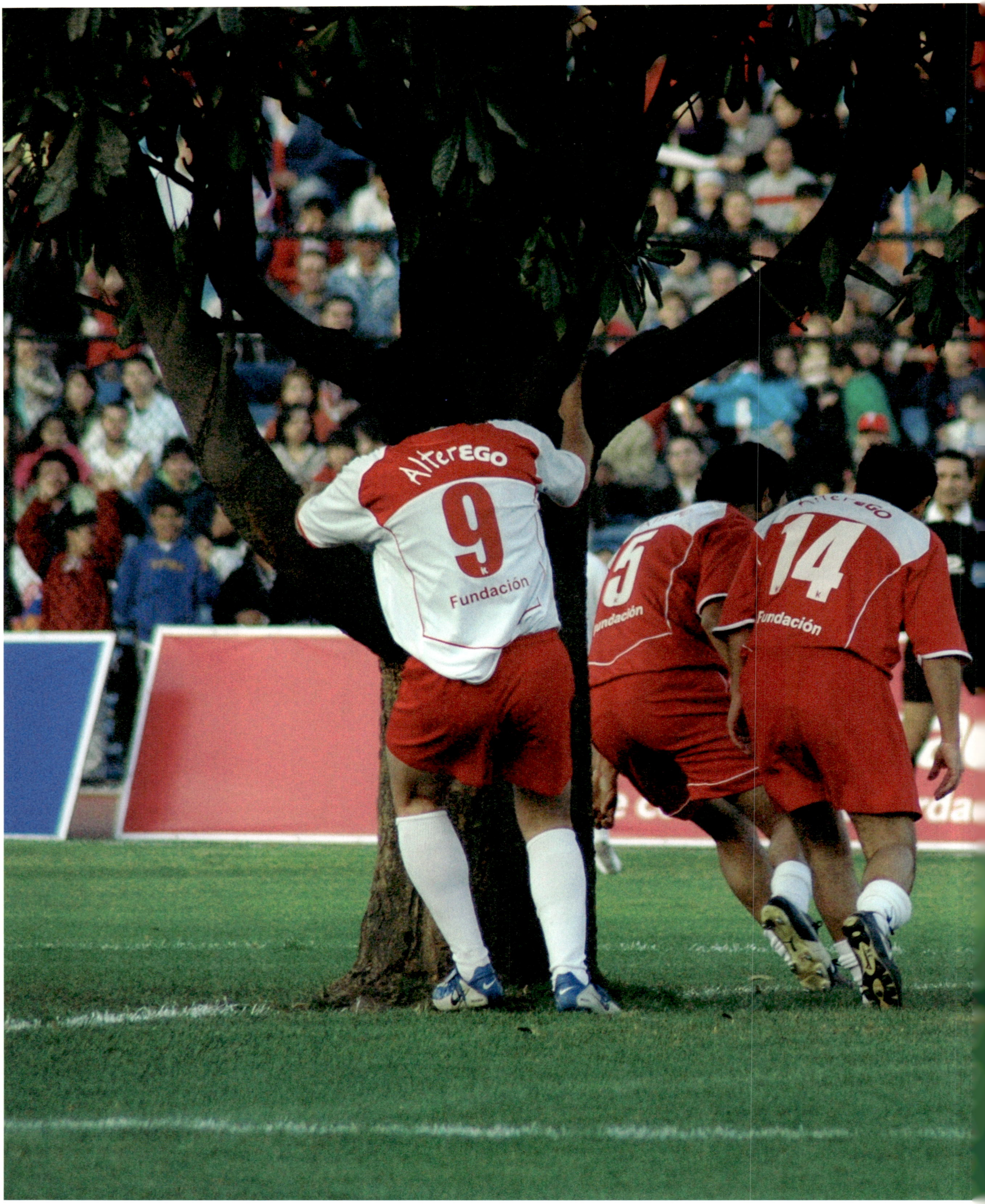
AlterEGO
9
Fundación
5
Fundación
14
Fundación

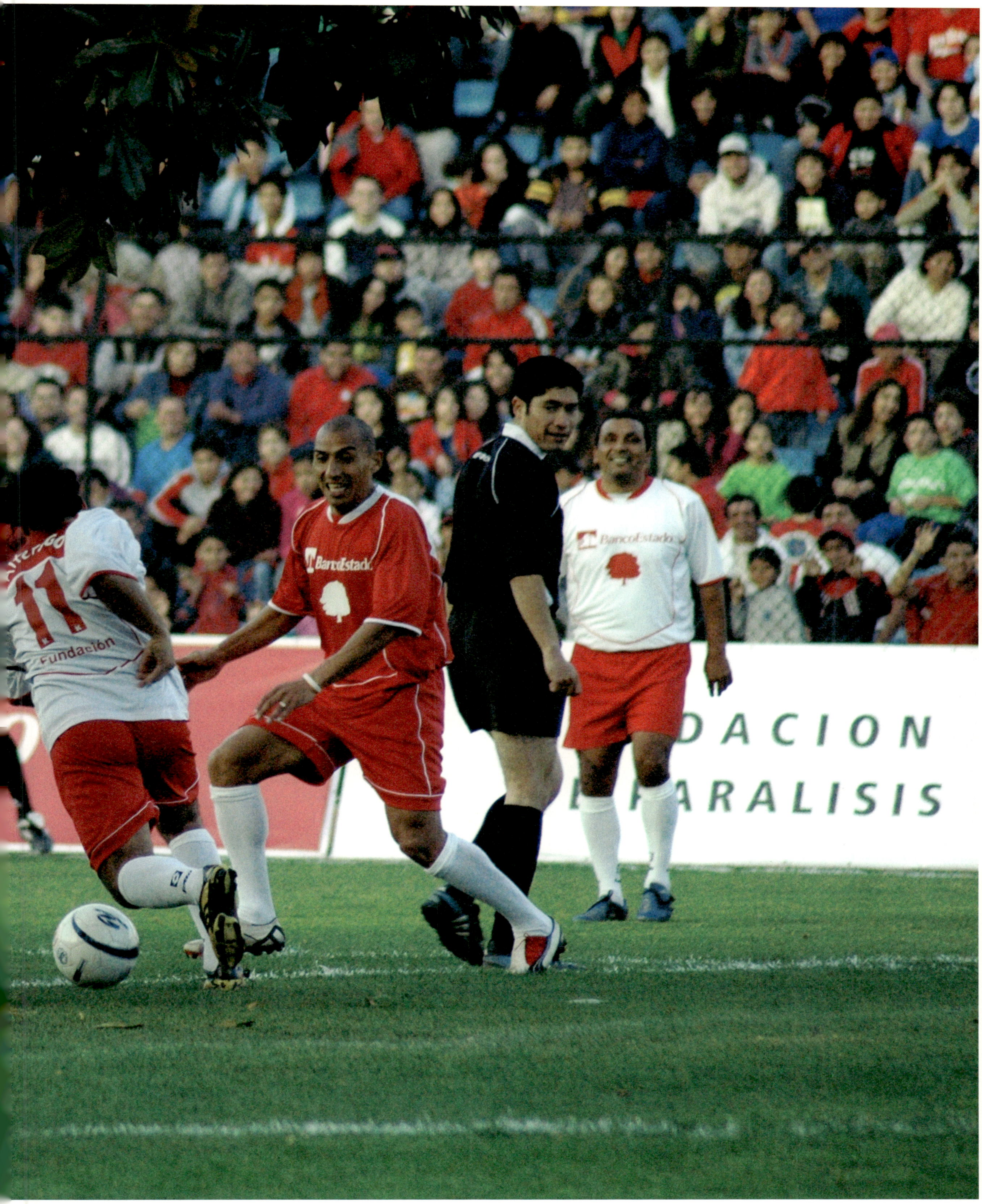
BancoEstado
11
Fundación
BancoEstado
DACION
ARALISIS

KENNARDPHILLIPPS

1
Know Your Enemy
2005
2
Photo Op
2005
1&2
Newsprint poster (inkjet print), Part of the poster series *STOP,* which were given out for free to the audience for use in antiwar protest activities during the eight-week installation, *War on War Room,* at EASTinternational 05, curated by Gustav Metzger
3
Soldier #1
2007
4
No Third Runway
2008, Photomontage

The kennardphillipps artist duo came into being in 2002 for quite concrete political reasons. Peter Kennard and Cat Phillips started to work together to express their outrage about the illegal invasion and occupation of Iraq, above all to call for protests. Their collages and montages are intended to open people's eyes, to direct their thoughts towards what is happening in the world. They use press photographs and place these in a new context in order to unmask political strategies such as the American and British governments' assertions about Iraq's weapons of mass destruction. Peter Kennard is by no means unknown; his politically charged works have been on show since the 1960s—not just in the Tate and the Victoria and Albert Museum, but also in the Imperial War Museum and the Science Museum. Part of the concept he shares with Phillips is to publicize their images across as wide a range as possible—as posters, on the internet, in newspapers, and in magazines. They also offer poster production workshops. Their posters are often used in demonstrations, which entirely suits the two artists: "We don't see the work as separate to social and political movements that are confronting established political and economic systems. We see it as part of those movements, the visual arm of protest. We want it to be used by people as a part of their own activism, not just as pictures on the wall to contemplate. To facilitate this, as well as selling our limited edition prints on the site, enabling us to fund the making of the work, there is a free download page of images with a voluntary contribution to the International Solidarity Movement."

Their work speaks a clear language and they make pointed statements ironically. Many of their photomontages feature the former Prime Minister Tony Blair. They include an image in which former President George Bush is patting him on the shoulder while their backs are turned on a torture scene from Iraq. Their best-known picture of Blair shows him taking a photograph on his mobile phone against a background of burning Iraqi oil fields. He is wearing his "trust-me" smile.

1
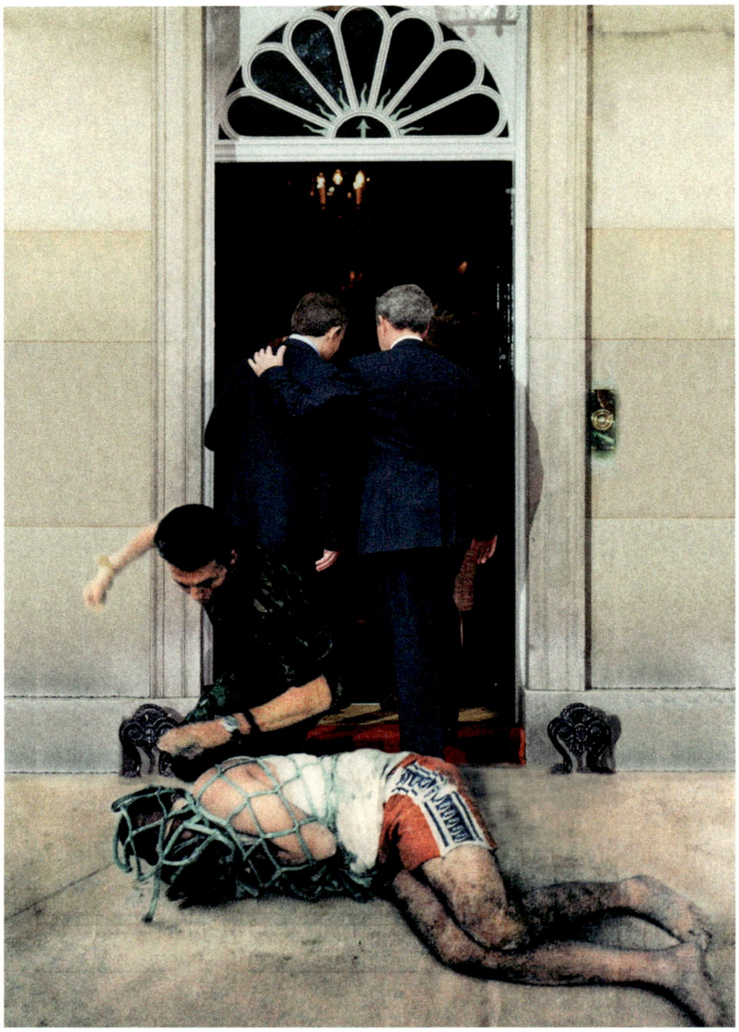

No Third Runway, 2008, shows former Prime Minister Gordon Brown stepping briskly out of 10 Downing Street onto a runway. Here kennardphillipps are supporting the Greenpeace campaign in its resistance to expanding London's Heathrow Airport, which Brown and his party were trying to push ahead. The planned third runway would make Heathrow the biggest CO_2 emissions producer in Great Britain. According to Greenpeace, the airport would emit 27 tons of CO_2 per year—in other words, as much as that emitted by the 57 countries in the world that produce the least CO_2. In order to prevent this, Greenpeace bought land in the middle of the future runway and then resold it to about 4.000 further purchasers, including many celebrities, in order to make the circle of people whose land would have to be appropriated considerably larger.

2
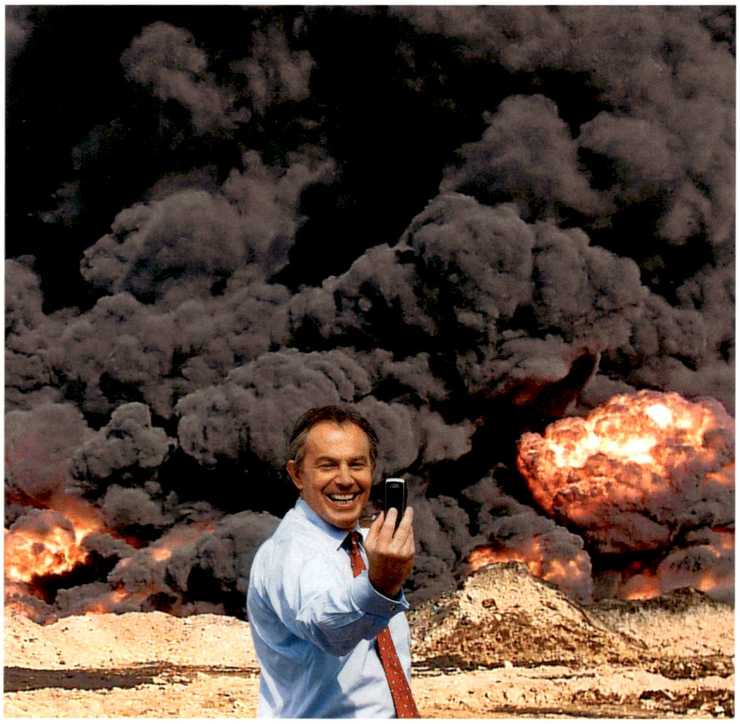

3
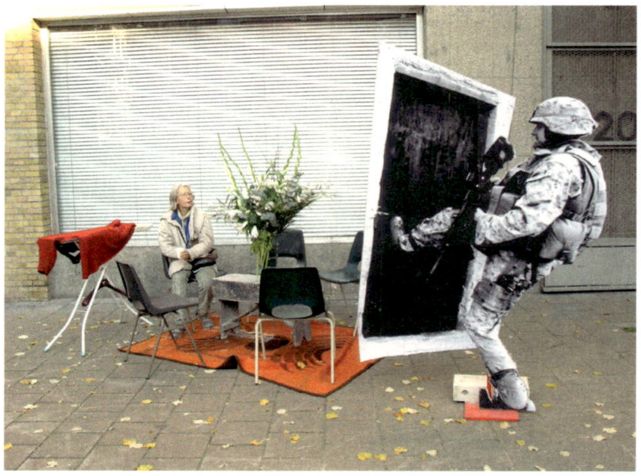

4

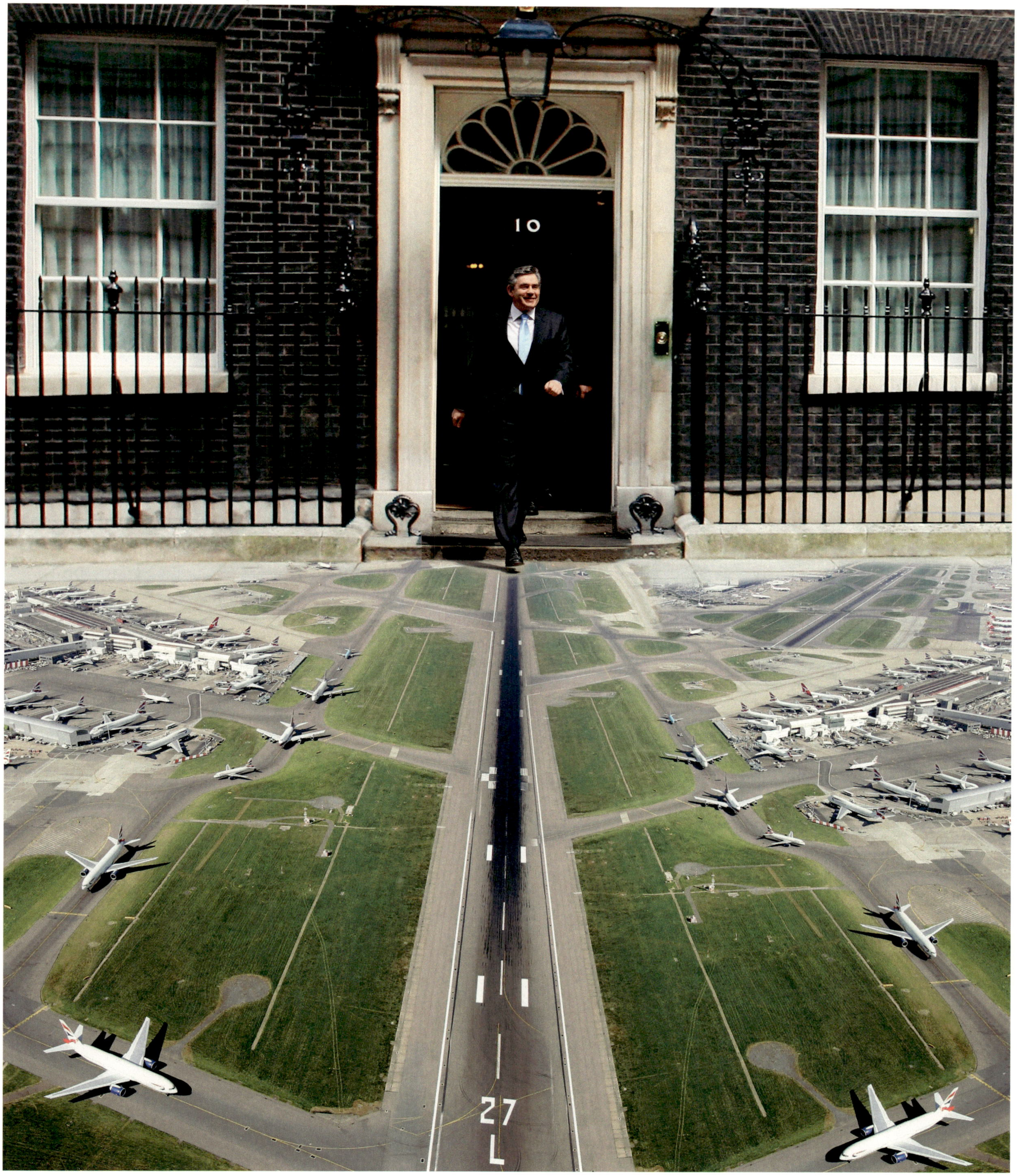

JOSEUB

1

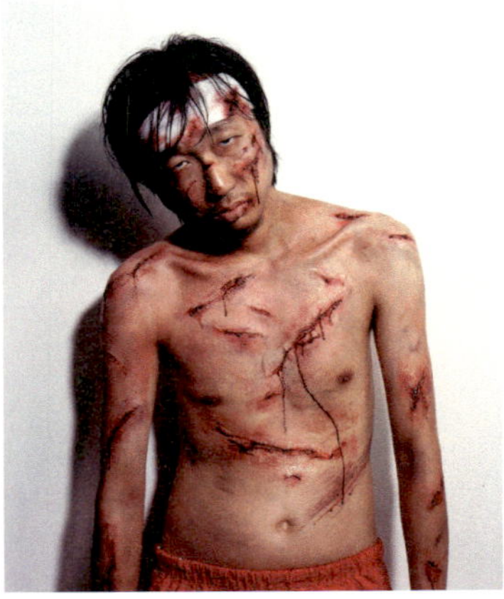

2

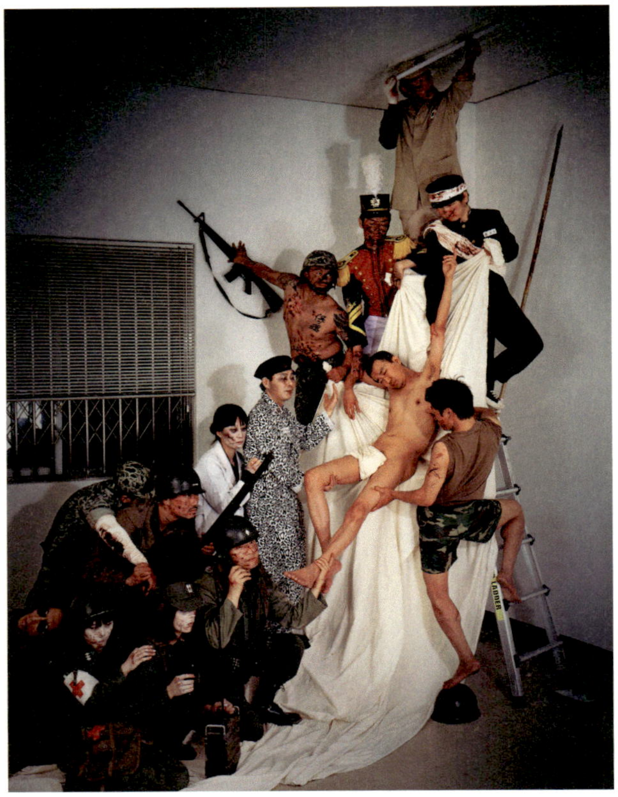

1–3
Who Wants to Live Forever
2008
4
Water Torture
2005
5
Subjugate
2005
6
I Hate Red Peanut
1999, Color print and scratch on the color print

The artist JoSeub (* 1975) lives in Seoul, the capital city of South Korea. His art is a response to the authoritarian democracy that surrounds him. Within his artworks he has the audacity to show soldiers in less than heroic situations, such as singing karaoke or even visiting a brothel. In the 1990s, Jo was actively involved in student protests. His art criticizes the system and targets South Korean patriotism. It also shines a spotlight on the collective memory of his generation, which grew up under the military regime. In the series *Who Wants to Live Forever,* Jo references art history by recreating famous paintings with the aid of fellow South Koreans, taking religious scenes and turning them into critical images of his own reality. He has copied Peter Paul Rubens's painting *Descent from the Cross* twice, creating two absurd scenes with civilian and military protagonists respectively. In both scenes, a caretaker is standing at the top of the ladder replacing a spent neon tube—a symbol for everyday happenings, which, in the artist's real-life experience, are frequently incomprehensible. His protagonists are often shown in exaggerated poses reminiscent of comic book figures, and the artist deliberately creates caricatures with his camera. The real-life background to his pictures, however, should not be forgotten; for instance, in photographs like *Water Torture,* 2005, he references the events and atrocities that have taken place in his country.

3

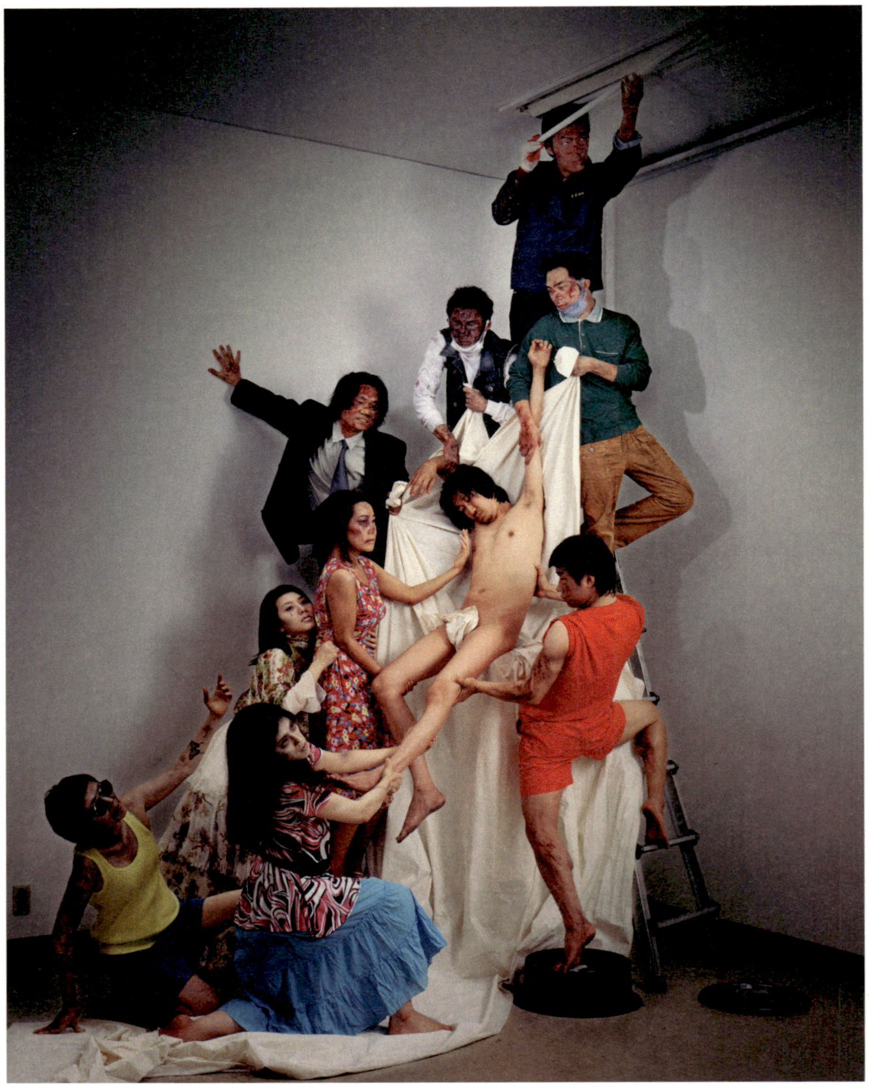

4

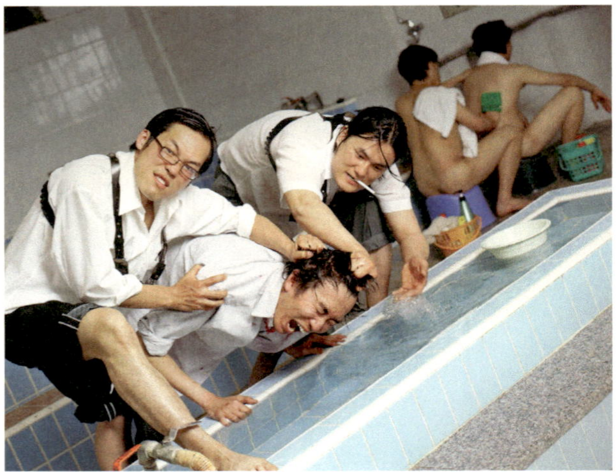

5

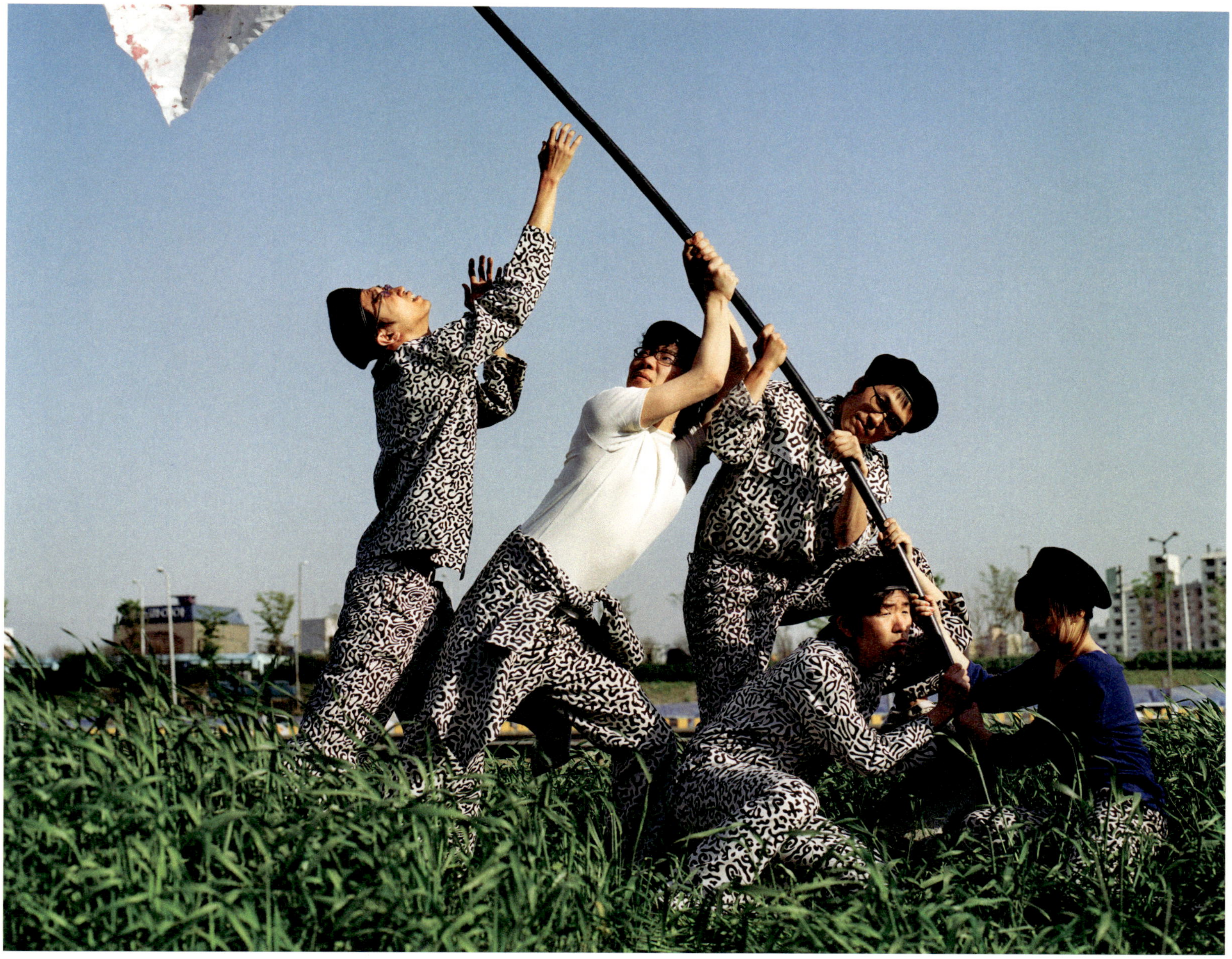

6

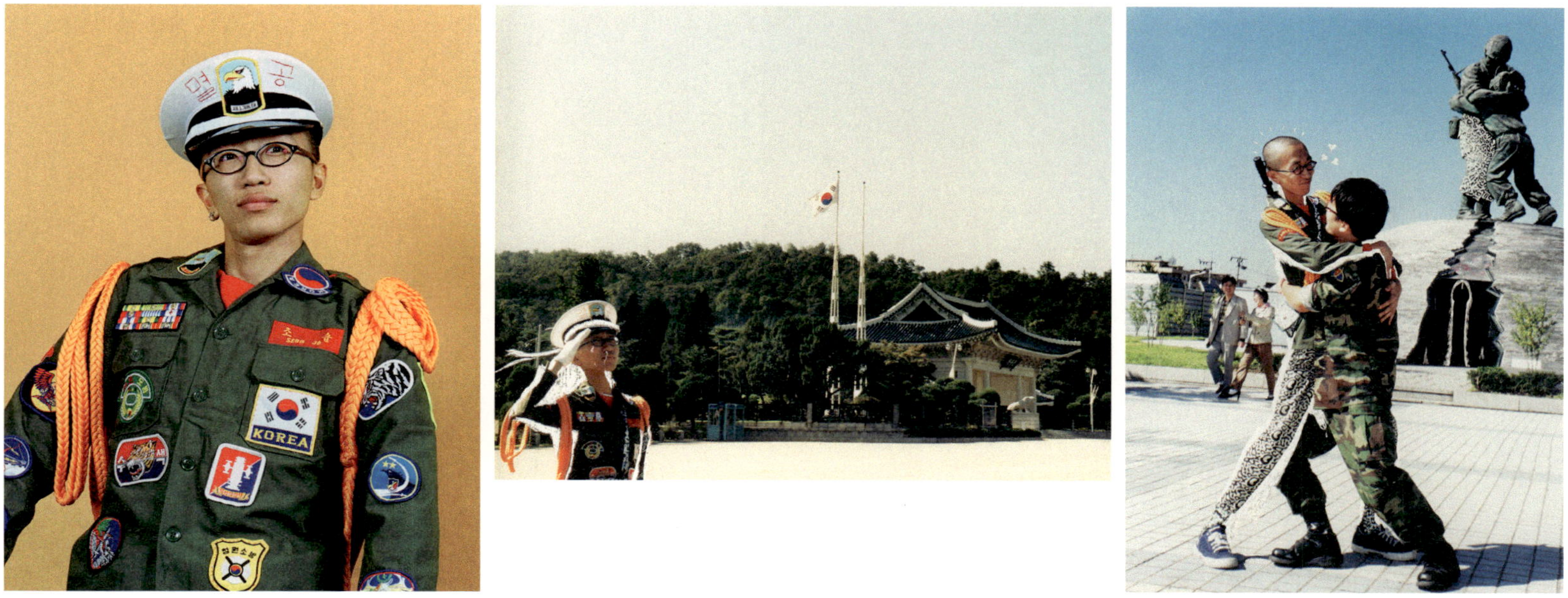

AES+F GROUP

1
AES – Witnesses of the Future. Islamic Project
1996–2003, Digital collages
© 1996–2003 AES Group, Courtesy Triumph Gallery, Moscow
2
The Feast of Trimalchio Allegory #3
(The Triumph of Africa)
2010, Digital collage,
© 2010 AES+F, Courtesy Triumph Gallery, Moscow

Tatiana Arzamasova (* 1955), Lev Evzovich (* 1958), and Evgeny Svyatsky (* 1957)—whose backgrounds are in architecture and graphics—have been working together as AES since the 1980s. In 1995, they were joined by photographer Vladimir Fridkes (* 1956), who represents the "+F." This Russian artist group's artworks address social phenomena through taking a critical perspective. In *The Feast of Trimalchio,* 2010, for instance, they address the subject of the nouveau riche. In a reference to the "feast of Trimalchio," from the satirical novel *Satyricon* by the classical author Titus Petronius (of which only an incomplete version survives), the group went in search of modern-day "former slaves," and found what they were looking for in a luxury hotel. According to AES+F, "they (the servants) are participants in an orgy, bringing to life any fantasy of the 'masters,' from gastronomic to erotic. At times the 'masters' unexpectedly end up in the role of 'servants.' Both become participants in an orgiastic gala reception, a dinner in the style of Roman Saturnalia, in which slaves, dressed as patricians, reclined at table and their masters, dressed in slaves' tunics, served them." In the ancient source text, the nouveau riche social climber

"WE FEEL THAT CONTEMPORARY VISUAL CULTURE IS VERY SIMILAR TO THAT OF THE BAROQUE: EVERYTHING IS EXTREMELY EXPRESSIVE, FIGURATIVE, AND VERY VISUAL AND FOUNDED ON IMAGES AND AT THE SAME TIME VERY DECADENT."

Trimalchio tries to impress his guests with rare dishes, with performances, and with his erudition. As it turns out, all he succeeds in proving is that money does not automatically buy education or good taste. Based on this central concept, the artists photographed their protagonists, dressed as people from different social classes, within a luxury hotel, creating allegorical scenes in homage to *Satyricon.* In these totally overdone staged images, the group placed their collective finger on a glaring fault: the mutual dependence within this colorful illusory world that is so distant from reality.

Other artworks by this artist group examine the western world's attitude to Islam. In 1996, the artists started their *Islamic Project,* which involved a fictional travel agency and a questionnaire to the public asking their views about the future; these results were later presented in visual form. This revealed westerners' negative images of Islamic world cities, prompting us to reflect on western society's fears about Islam. Criticism of the media is a recurring theme in the artists' photographs, projects, and video artworks. In 1998, for instance, they created a photographic series, *Who Wants to Live Forever,* showing "Princess Diana" covered with blood and sitting on a detached car seat. In *Last Riot,* 2005, AES+F tackle video games—the panoramic photographs reference the video game aesthetic, as does the video they later created. The protagonists are involved in apocalyptic battle scenes—or are they dance scenes? Everyone seems to be acting in opposition to everyone else, but there are no decisive acts. AES+F see the virtual world as a "life-form created in a test tube," which constantly expands and engulfs its founders. "We can see the processes of glorifying violence and death in film, video games, and throughout global media culture. Not a single drop of blood can be seen in our *Last Riot* project—a metaphor for video games, where you can kill a hundred people without being responsible for rivers of virtual blood."

1

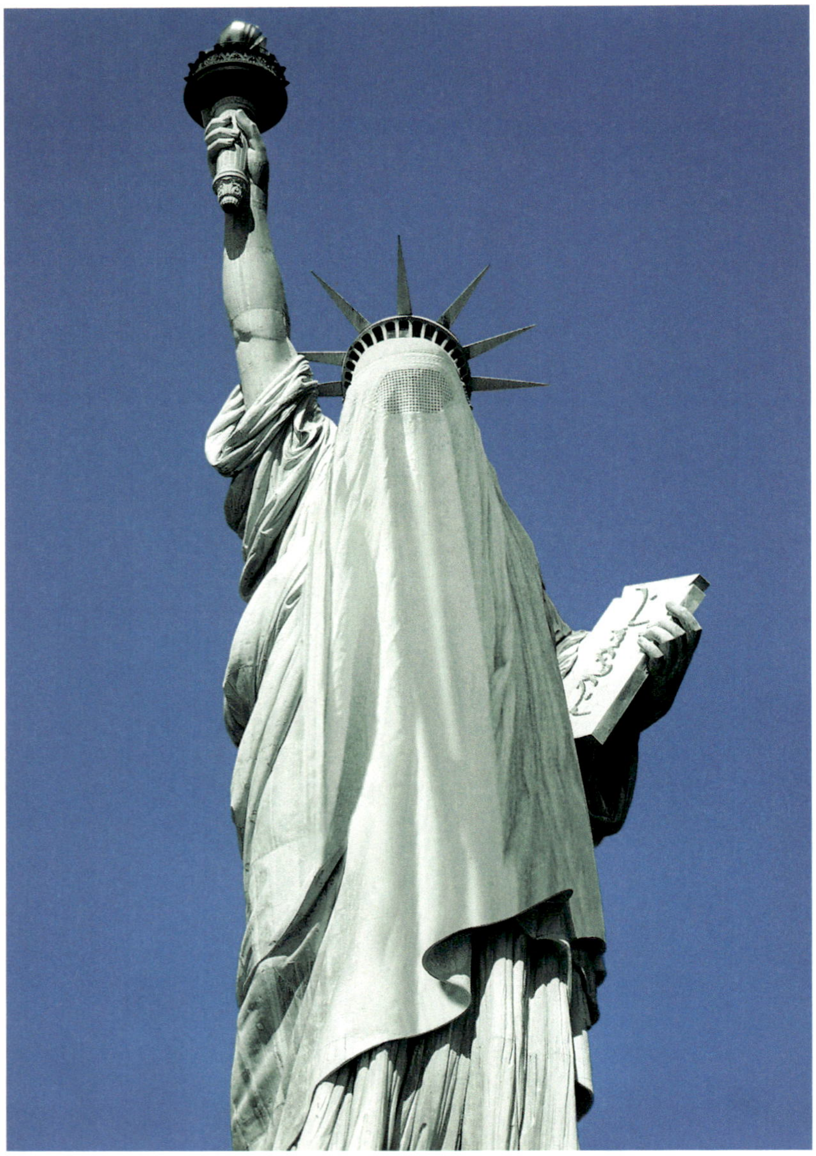

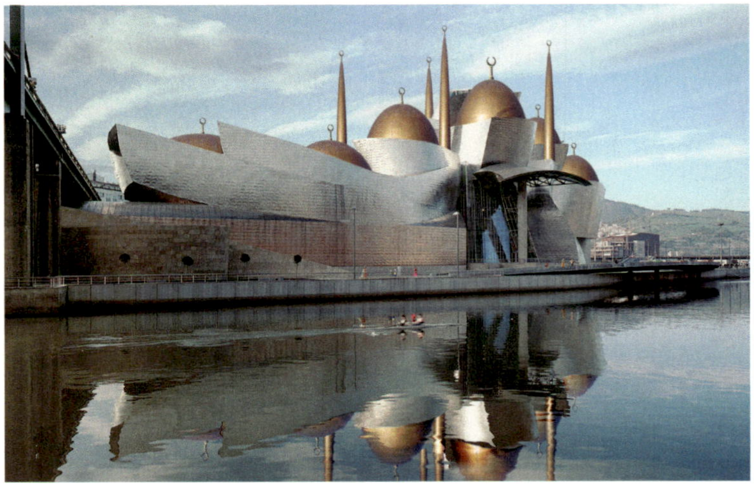

2

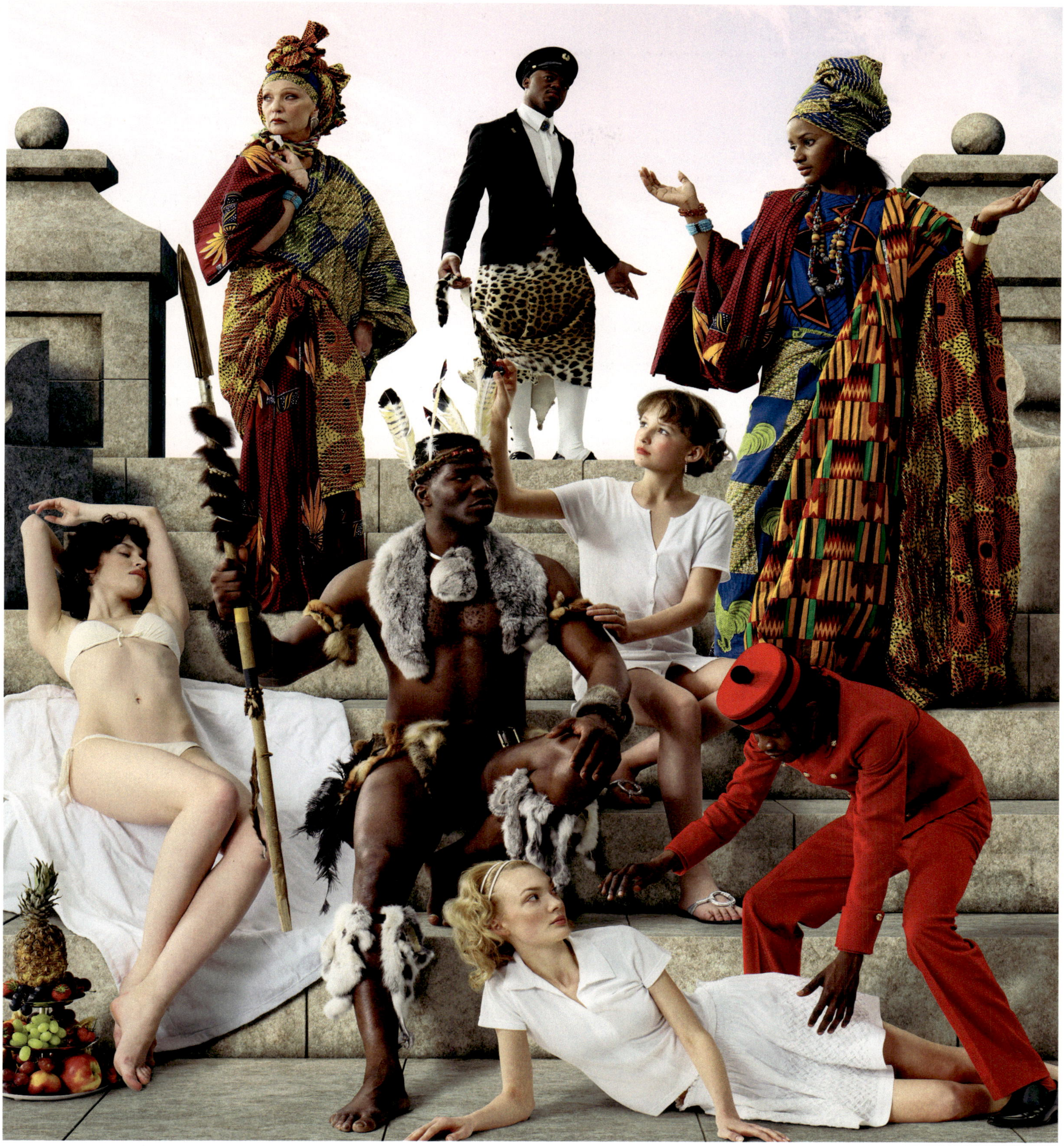

PAOLO CANEVARI

The work of Italian artist Paolo Canevari (* 1963), who became well-known in the 1990s for using rubber to create arte povera–style artworks, shows a desire to abolish the classical canon of shapes and materials. The influences on Canevari's art are highly diverse. For instance, he comments that when he was looking at prayer wheels in a Buddhist temple in India: "... it suddenly seemed to me that the wheels of cars were the modern equivalent. This is not to say that cars have literally taken the place of God and religion in our society—I think that would be a hackneyed, banal interpretation. I was thinking in the context of India, where 95 percent of transport is by truck. These trucks are decorated with folklore motifs, and have a place in the popular cults that are part of people's lives. Each truck has its own characteristics, and there is a kind of contest as to whose truck is best decorated. When I wrote one of the oldest and shortest mantras, namely Om Mani Padme Hum on the wheels of a truck, it seemed a logical thing to do: a modern prayer wheel that rolls along the road and repeats the prayer kilometer by kilometer. Also, just like a prayer wheel, a tire has a direction." A few years later he returned to the theme and made it more personal by writing the names of the 12 apostles on truck tires. What he is interested in is the movement; he sees the 12 apostles as an association of individuals that come together and then set off to every corner of the globe. The invention of the wheel is a kind of highly condensed signal for the beginning of a new culture—just like the apostles traveling to every part of the world. This is a thought that Canevari extends in later artworks, charging it with more associations. Fundamentally, his artworks center on political suggestions—an example of this is the artwork *Jesus-Buddha-Mohammed,* 2001. In Egypt, he had noticed black protective car covers and bought three. He was intrigued by the type of cover with little bulges in the sides for the wing mirrors, which looked as if they had ears. He took the covers from Cairo to Amsterdam, and finally traveled to Thailand, where he created the installation. "On the journey, the names of the three prophets of the three cultural spaces I was traveling through rang in my ears like a tune: Jesus, Buddha, Mohammed... so, I rented three cars. I thought it was important for the cars to be driven there on their own wheels, so to speak; to use scrap cars or mock-ups would have undermined the artwork. It was an absurd place, outside of Bangkok, an abandoned road next to the freeway. By the time I had installed everything there—the black covers with Jesus, Buddha, and Mohammed written on them in white—I barely had enough time to photograph the 'Monument' before a deluge started. All morning, the sky had been like a grey bell dropped over the world, and all at once it unleashed a wall of rain with furious torrents. As we drove back, a street sign crashed into one of the cars. There is power in the invoking of names. I felt that my artwork had been noticed." The significance of place also plays an immense role in his video *Bouncing Skull,* 2007, which was shown at the 52nd Venice Biennale, in which Canevari illustrates how death can become part of everyday life for children growing up during a war. The video shows a boy playing football in front of bombed-out buildings. However, the boy is not playing with a ball, he is playing with a skull. Canevari shot the video around Slobodan Milošević's former headquarters, which had been bombed by NATO.

1
Home Sweet Home
2003, Spain
Installation, acrilyc paint on bunker

2
J.M.B.
2001, Bangkok, Thailand
Installation on the outskirts of Bangkok, Photo by the artist

3
Seed
2004, New York, USA
Performance/Photo
Courtesy the artist

4
J.M.B.
2002, Rome, Italy
Photo by Claudio Abate

5 (next spread)
Bouncing Skull
2007, Belgrade, Serbia
Video HD 10', video still,
Courtesy the artist

1

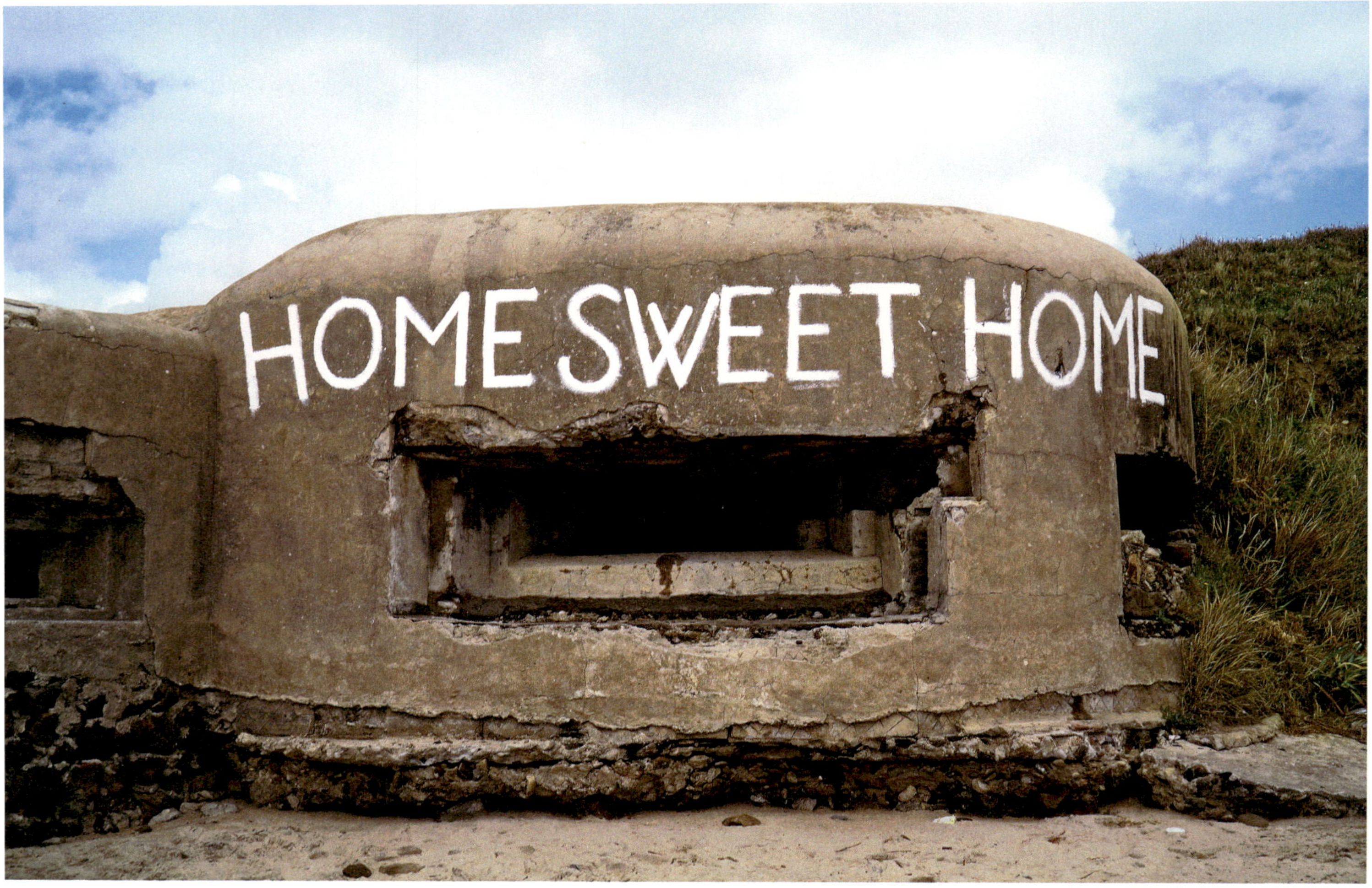

2

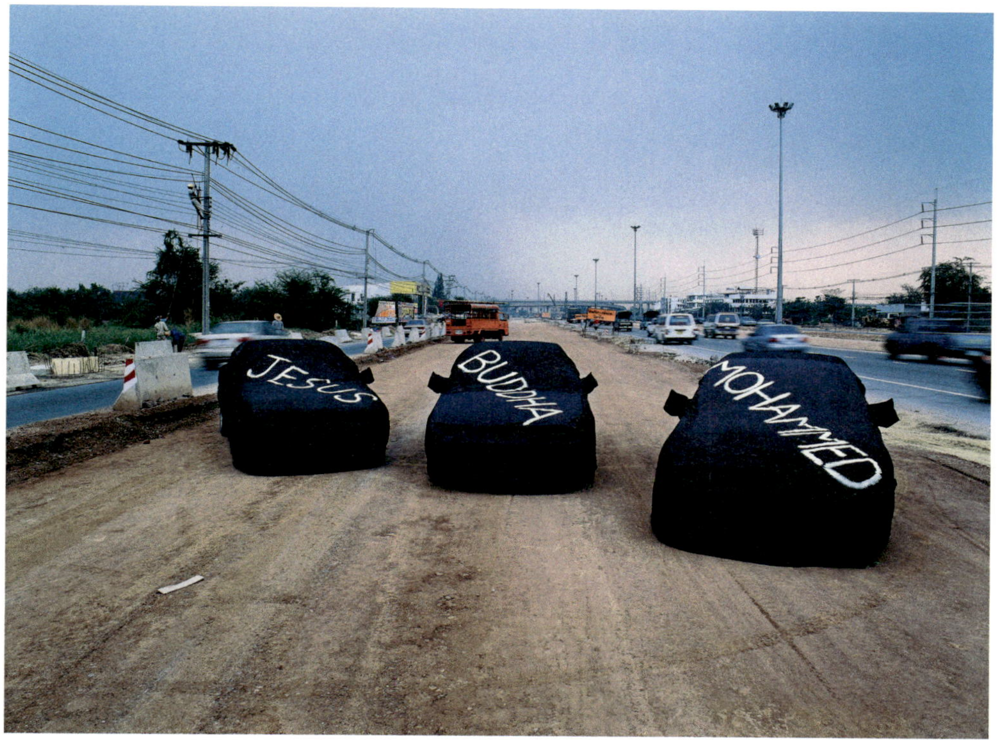

3

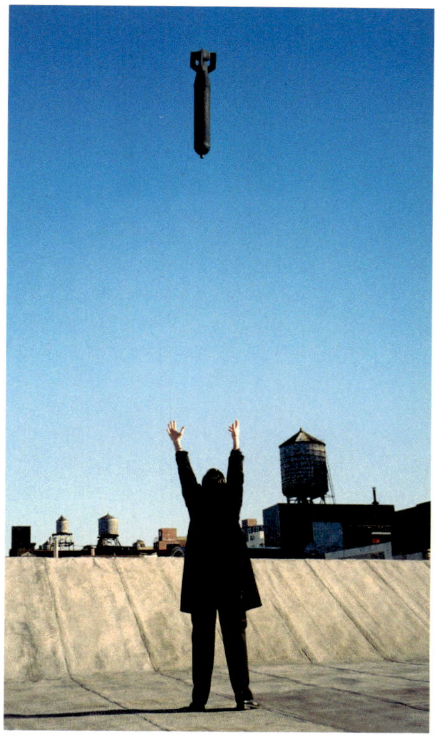

4

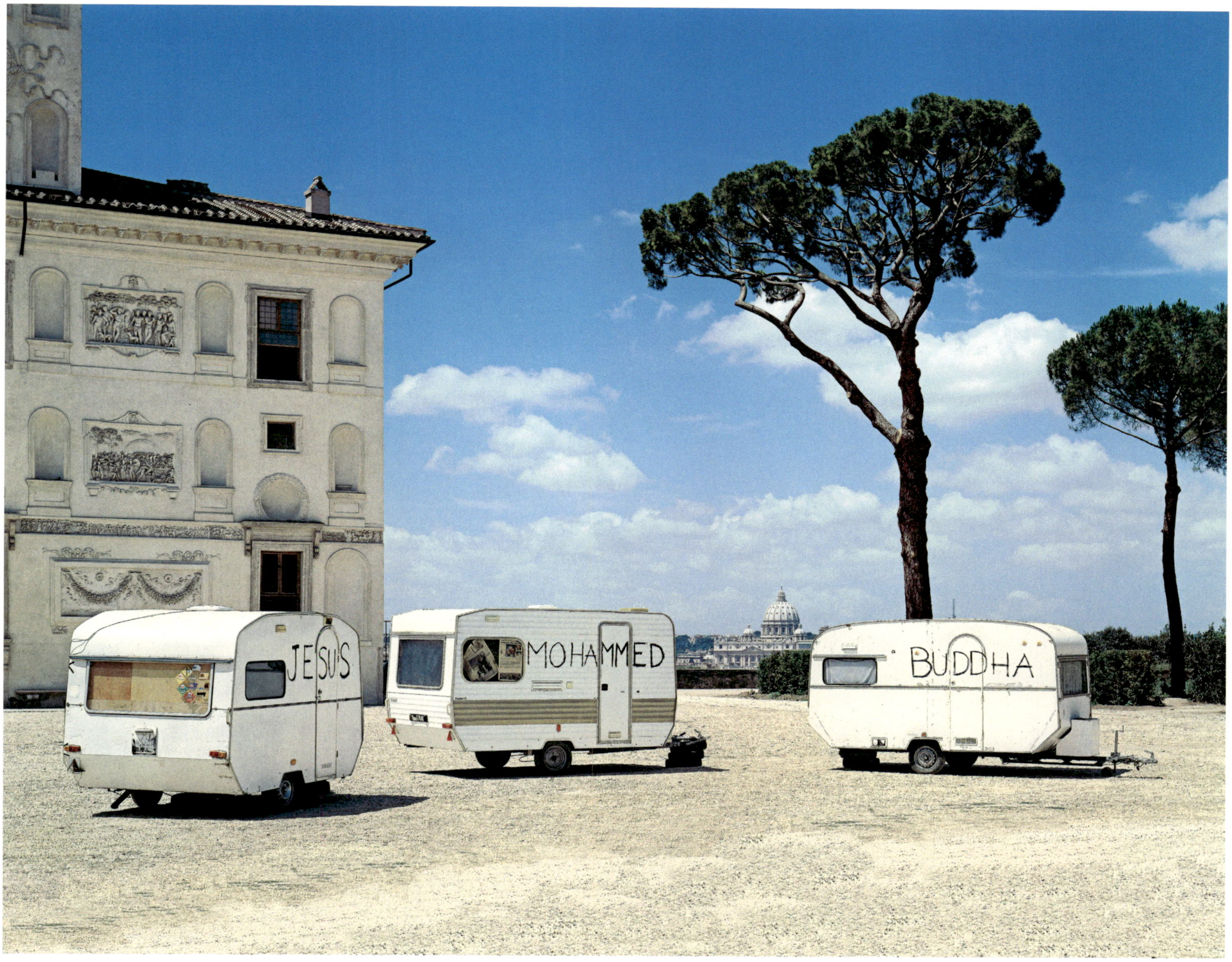

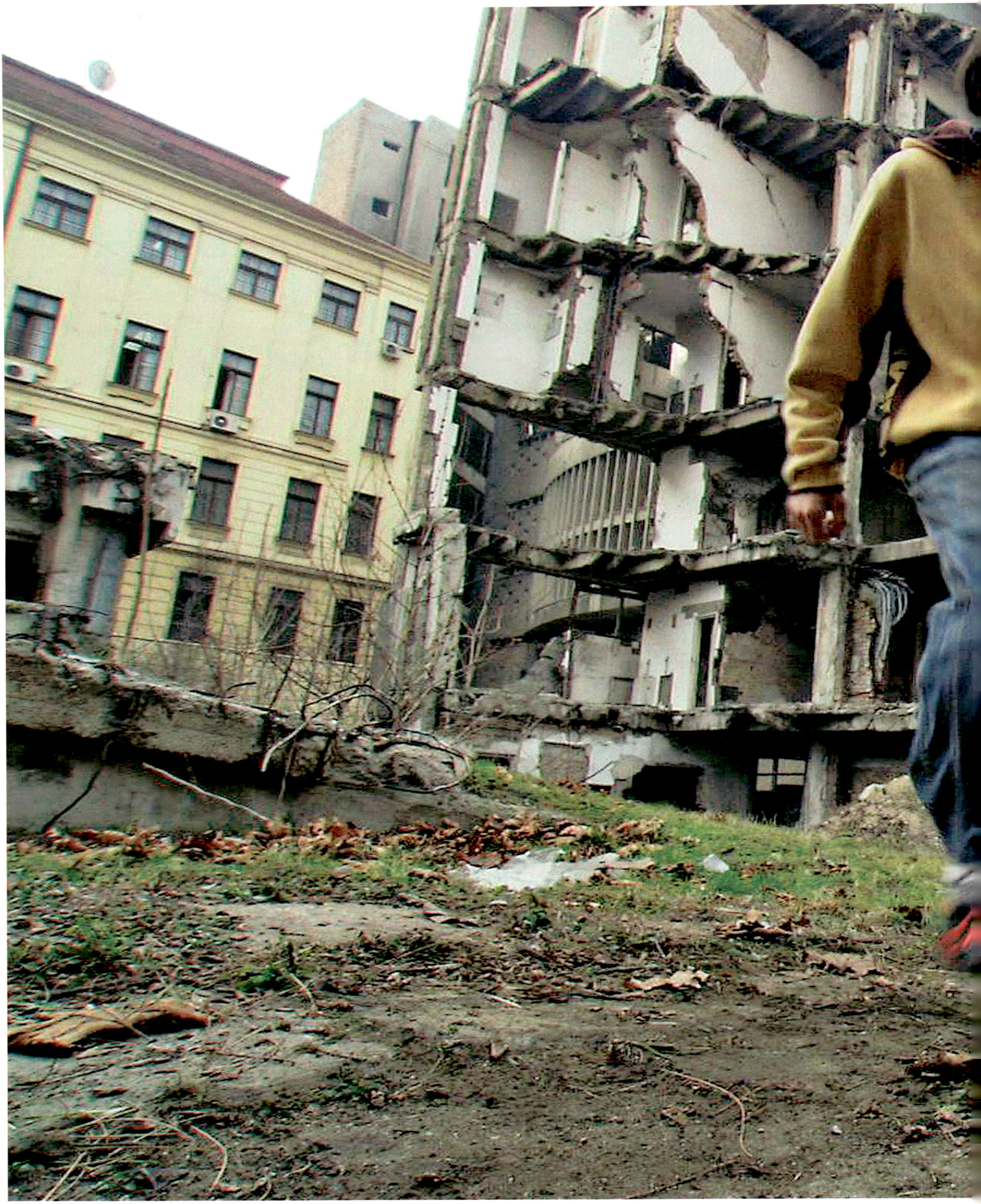

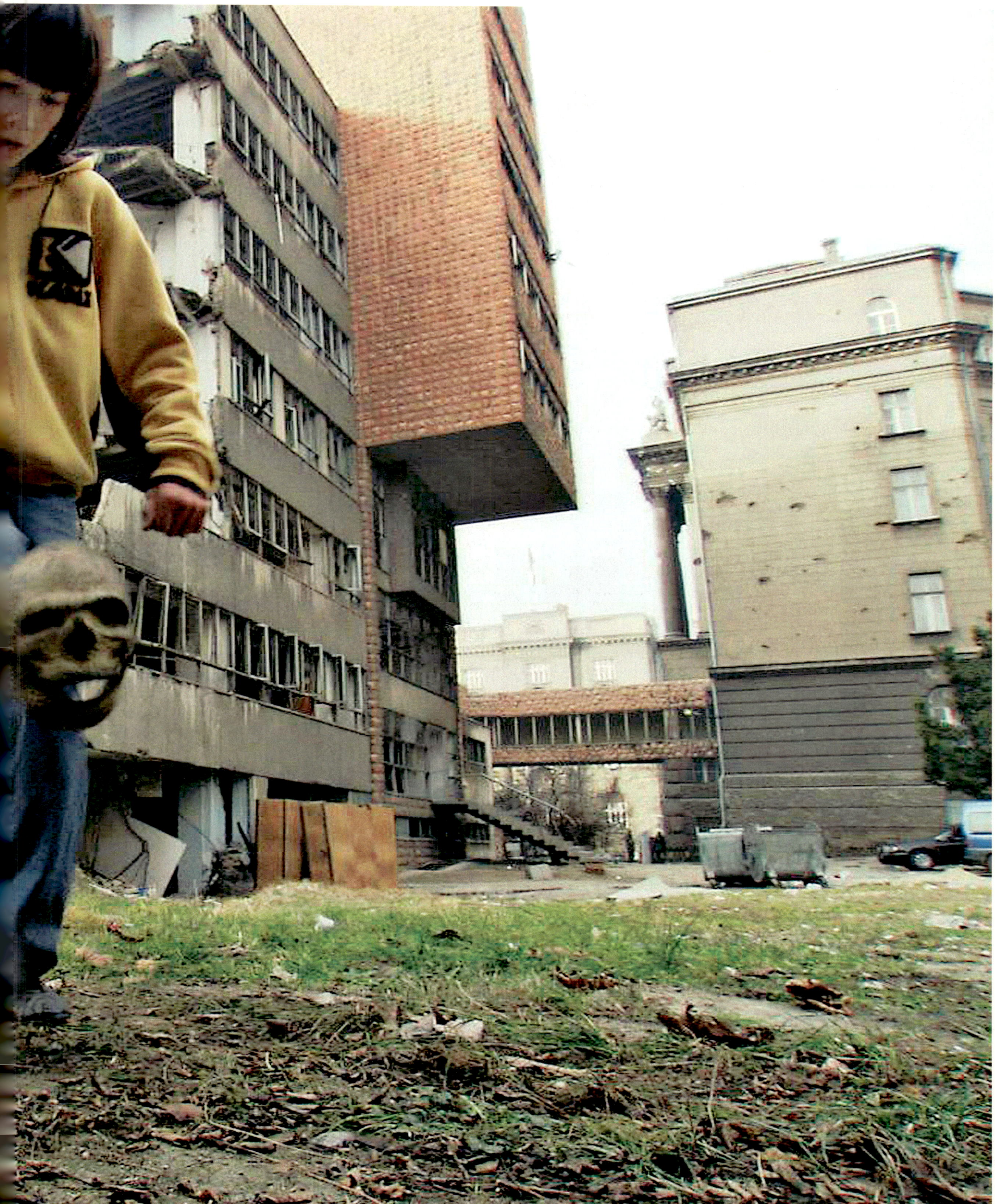

ADALBERTO ABBATE

1–4
Rivolta Series
2009
1
Interval
2
Antagonist Family Portrait
3
For Politicians Only
4
Hierarchical Demonstration
5
Erziehungs-Entwicklungs-prozess
2003
6–7
Microscultpures
6
Retreat, Genova G8
2005, Scultpure/painted model, mixed-media
7
Big Game Hunting
2004

"THE PROBLEM IN ITALY IS THAT THE ART BUSINESS IS JUST AS CORRUPT AS THE POLITICAL SYSTEM"

"We live in a society in which the balance between Dada and Da-da-um-pa is becoming increasingly marked," says the Italian artist Adalberto Abbate (* 1975) from Palermo, Sicily, meaning by this that the omnipresent spectacle and devouring mass culture often has artistic traits within its absurdity. Abbate's *Microsculptures*, 2004, provide evidence of this absurdity: he shapes everyday tragedies, which he has taken from the mass media, into little miniature worlds. Traffic accidents, suicide, corrupt policemen, grave robberies, the G8 riots, and the Madrid train bombing are all recreated in miniature, as if this is the only way possible to grasp the horror properly, and yet the bird's-eye view renders it small and trivial again. Abbate, inspired by artists such as Piero Manzoni, the Chapman brothers, and Bertrand Lavier, by writers such as Charles Bukowski and John Fante, and by filmmakers such as Federico Fellini, Martin Scorsese, or Russ Meyer, does not think in terms of artistic formats, but rather thinks about about how he can capture reality from a variety of angles. In his photographic series called *Processo Evolutivo Educativo* (Education Development Process), 2003–2004, all the images are dominated by a swastika, sometimes subtly, sometimes boldly. This cycle of artworks was censored, and could not be shown for a long time because it seemed to glorify the swastika. In reality these images are playing with clichés, showing that the swastika is still slumbering in the smallest of corners, and offered a successful resistance to the symbolism by ridiculing it. Who can treat a grandmother seriously when she is just taking her swastika biscuits out of the oven? In his *Rivolta* series, 2009, Abbate took on the subject of the political coup and analyzed it. He painted ski masks on family photographs, decorated baseball bats, and recorded protest slogan graffiti onto the walls of buildings in Palermo. Is this art or politics? "The problem in Italy is that the art business is just as corrupt as the political system," says Abbate.

1
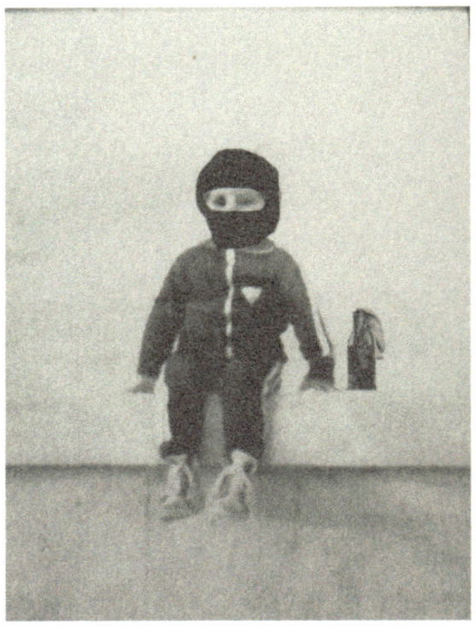
2
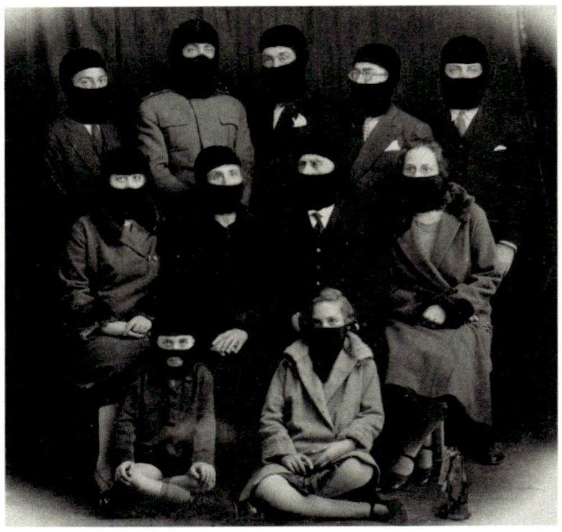
3
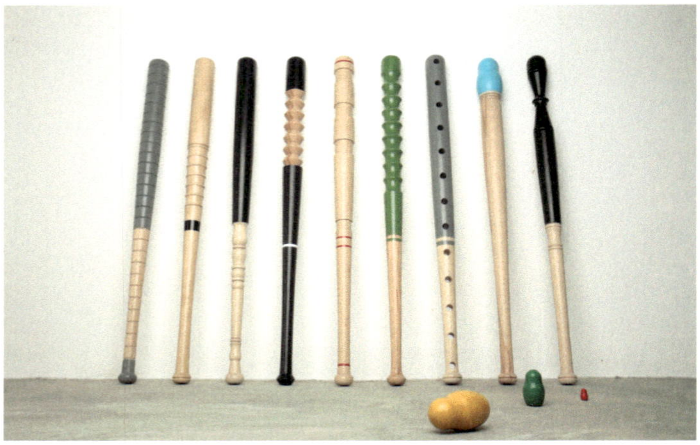
4
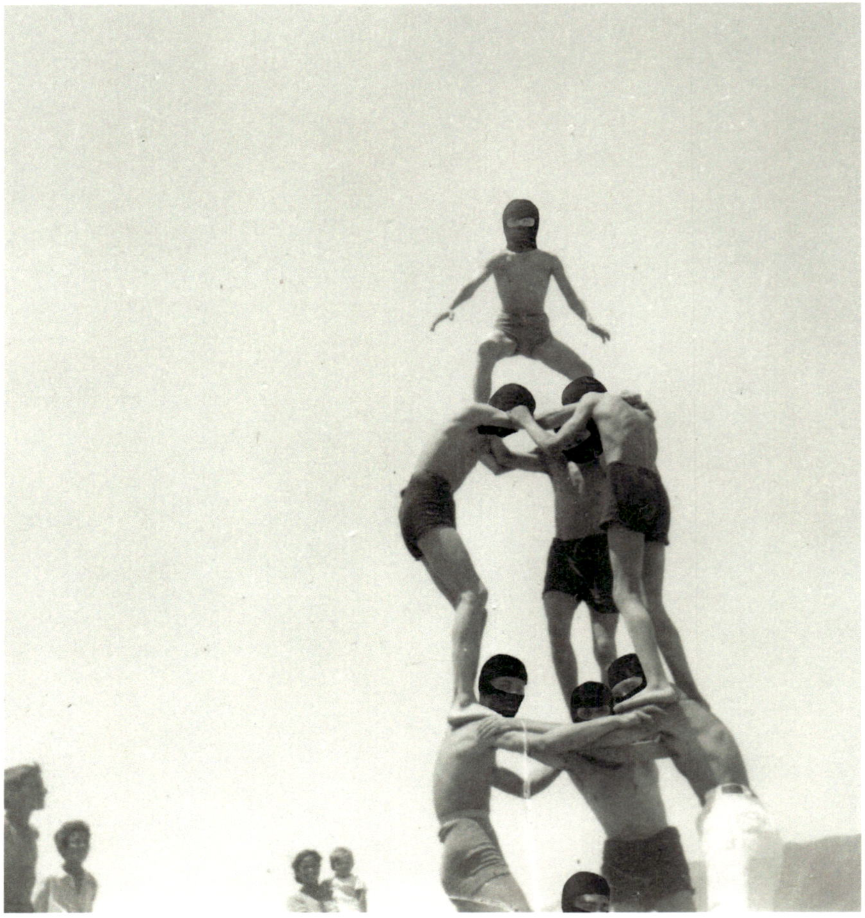

5

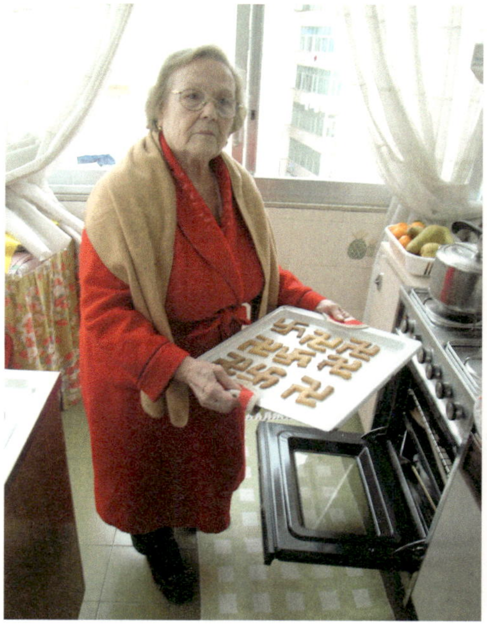

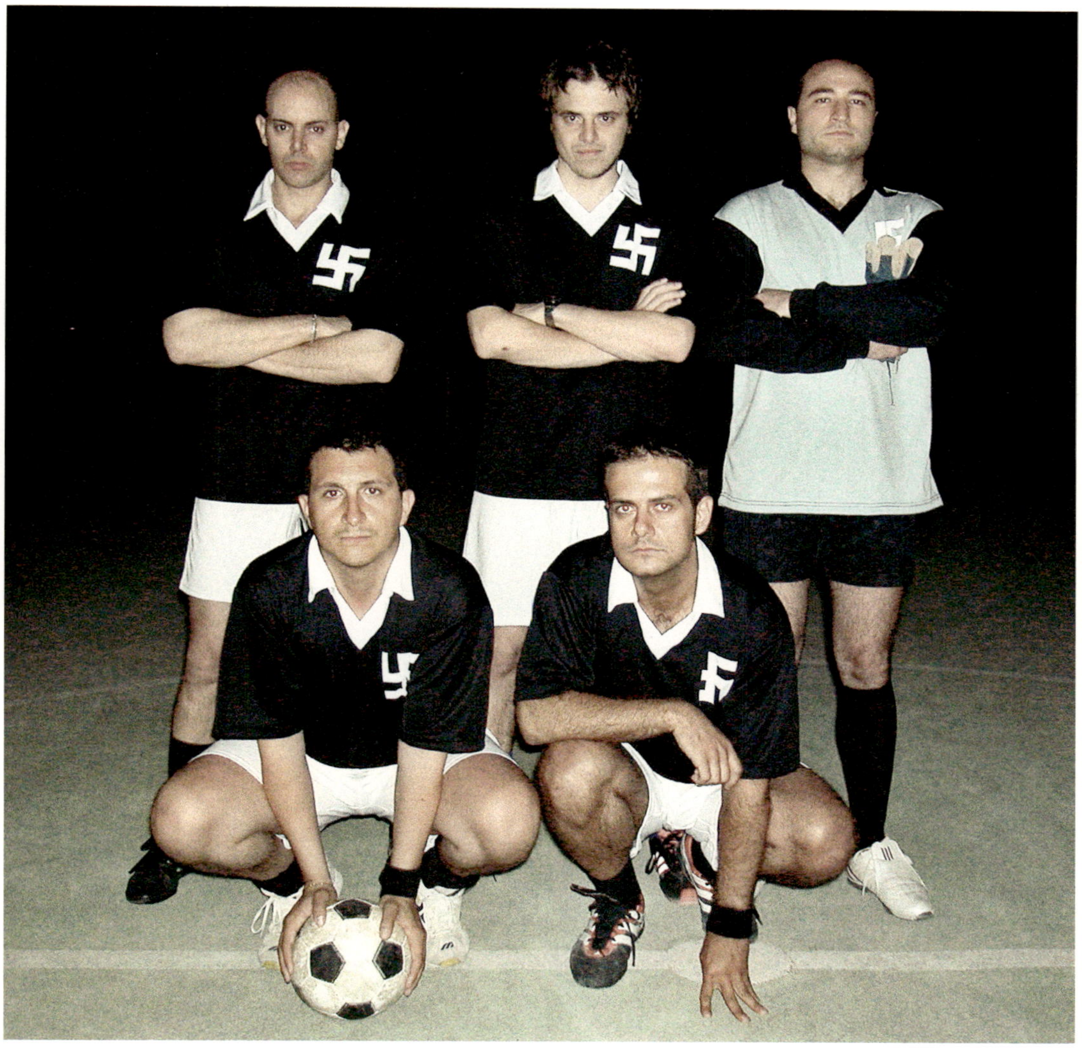

6

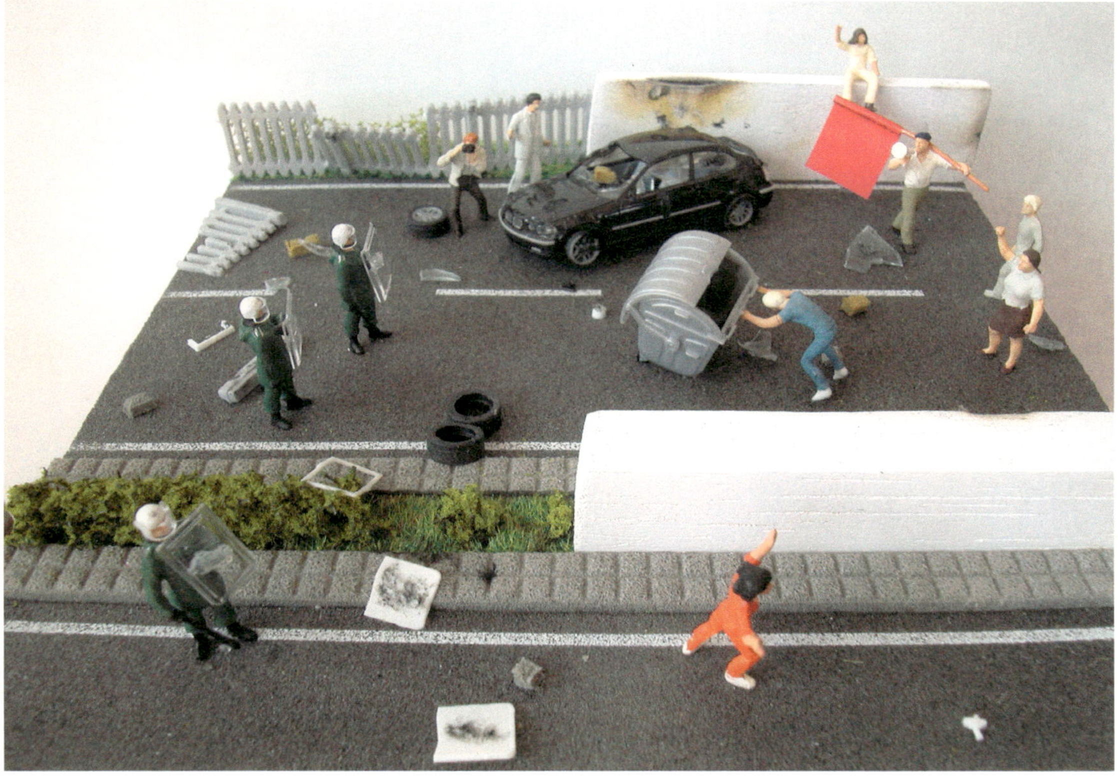

7

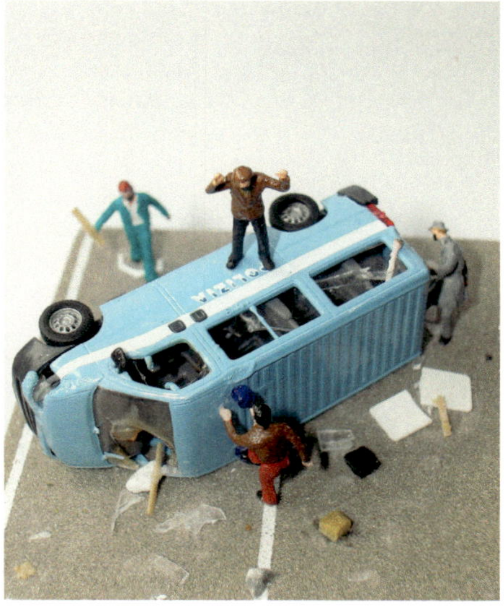

PAUL MCCARTHY

1

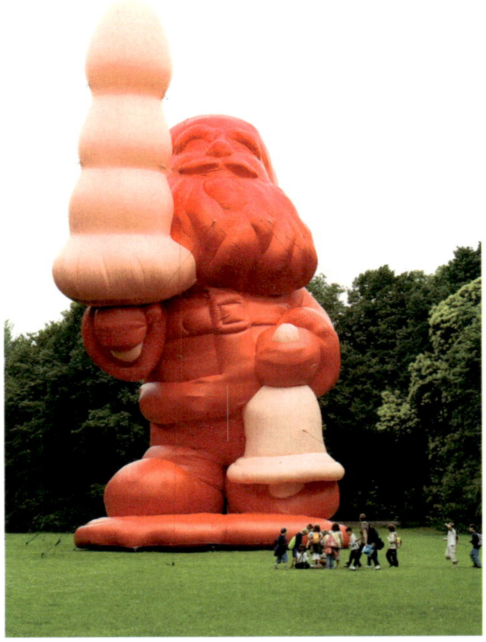

2

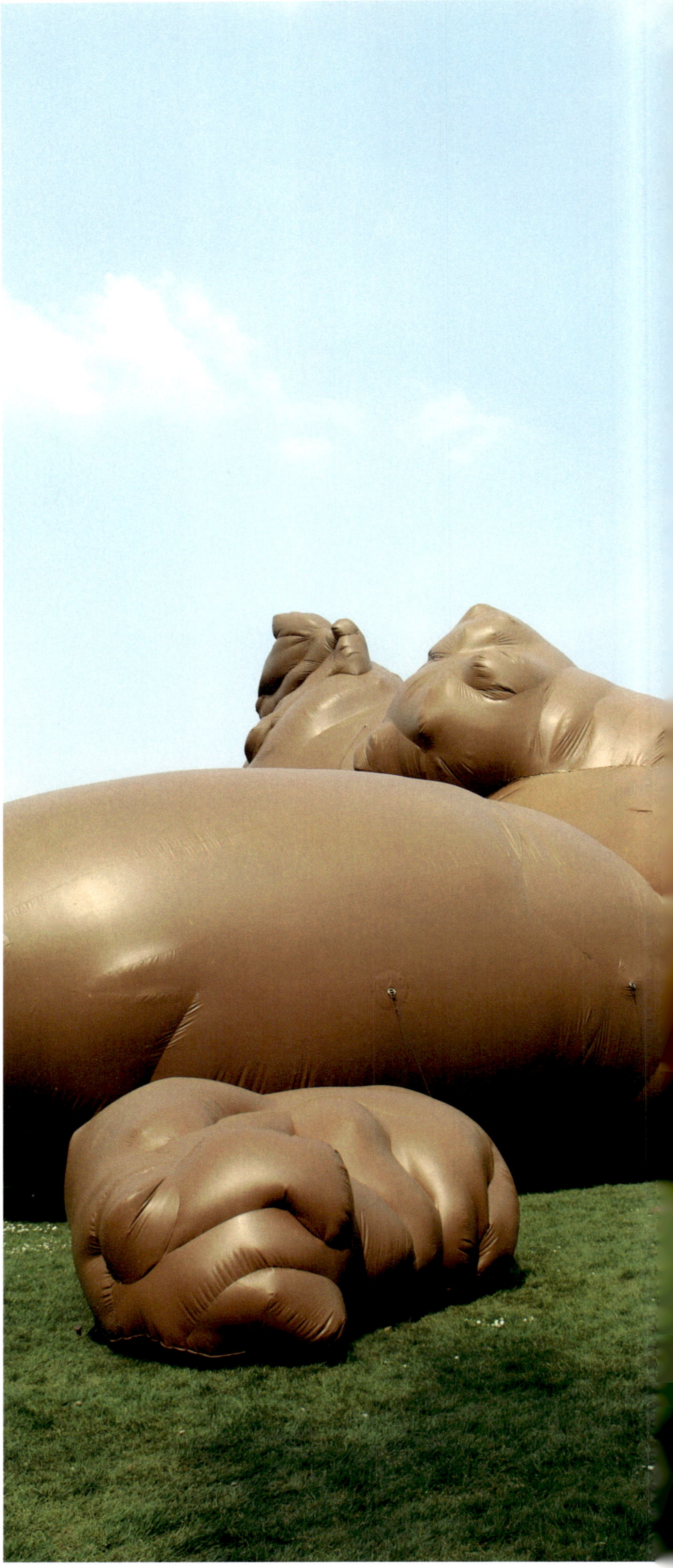

1
Santa Claus with a Butt Plug
2007, Vinyl-coated nylon, four fans, rigging, Installation view at "Air Born | Air Borne | Air Pressure", Middelheim Museum, Antwerp, Belgium
Photo by Philippe de Gobert
2
Complex Pile
2007, Vinyl-coated nylon fabric, six fans, rigging
Installation view at "Paul McCarthy – Air Pressure," De Uithof, Utrecht, Netherlands,
Photo by Philippe de Gobert
3
Bush Head White Head
2007, Vinyl-coated nylon fabric, fans, rigging, Installation view at Den Haag Sculptuur, Den Haag, Netherlands

Courtesy the artist and Hauser & Wirth

For 40 years now, Paul McCarthy (* 1945) has been using unashamedly adolescent humor, obscene installations, and gigantic nightmarish visions to attack American icons and value systems. George Bush, Osama Bin Laden, and Walt Disney are some of his favorite targets; for example, in his White Snow cycle of drawings, Snow White has erotic dreams and masturbates, watched by the Seven Dwarfs with sad, limp, phallic noses. His drawings are also decorated with all sorts of trash sourced from the media: porn magazine collages, advertisements, and pictures of models and stars. For McCarthy, the Walt Disney Company is the epitome of conventionality, puritan prudery, and insatiable consumerist culture. McCarthy states that: "I research how we react to the absurdity of our existence, how we have constructed reality and our world—and especially the significance we accord to consumption, and the way we condition perceptions. My art work, then, is an attempt to talk about this absurdity. I think that waking up to an awareness of the absurdity of our situation often triggers fears or a certain sense of shock." In the 1970s, McCarthy began holding art performances, with him painting his genitals, climbing into absurd costumes, and flinging himself naked into chocolate sauce, ketchup, or mayonnaise—a kind of slapstick equivalent of the Vienna actionists. His 24-meter-high inflatable sculpture *Santa Claus with a Butt Plug,* 2007, shows Santa Claus holding a Christmas tree in one hand that on further inspection turns out to be an anal dildo. McCarthy later actually reproduced this popular sculpture as a multiple in chocolate—in a humorous parody of American mass consumption and of himself. McCarthy is like a naughty child out of control, whose videos, photographs, sculptures, and installations are full of anal imagery and which center on the body, sexuality, lust, and aggression. They also gleefully puncture the American "perfect family," hypocritical moral messages, and the squeaky-clean image of the American church and politics.

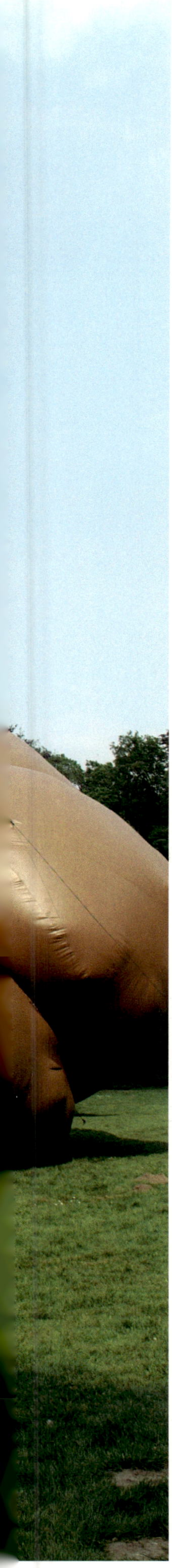

3

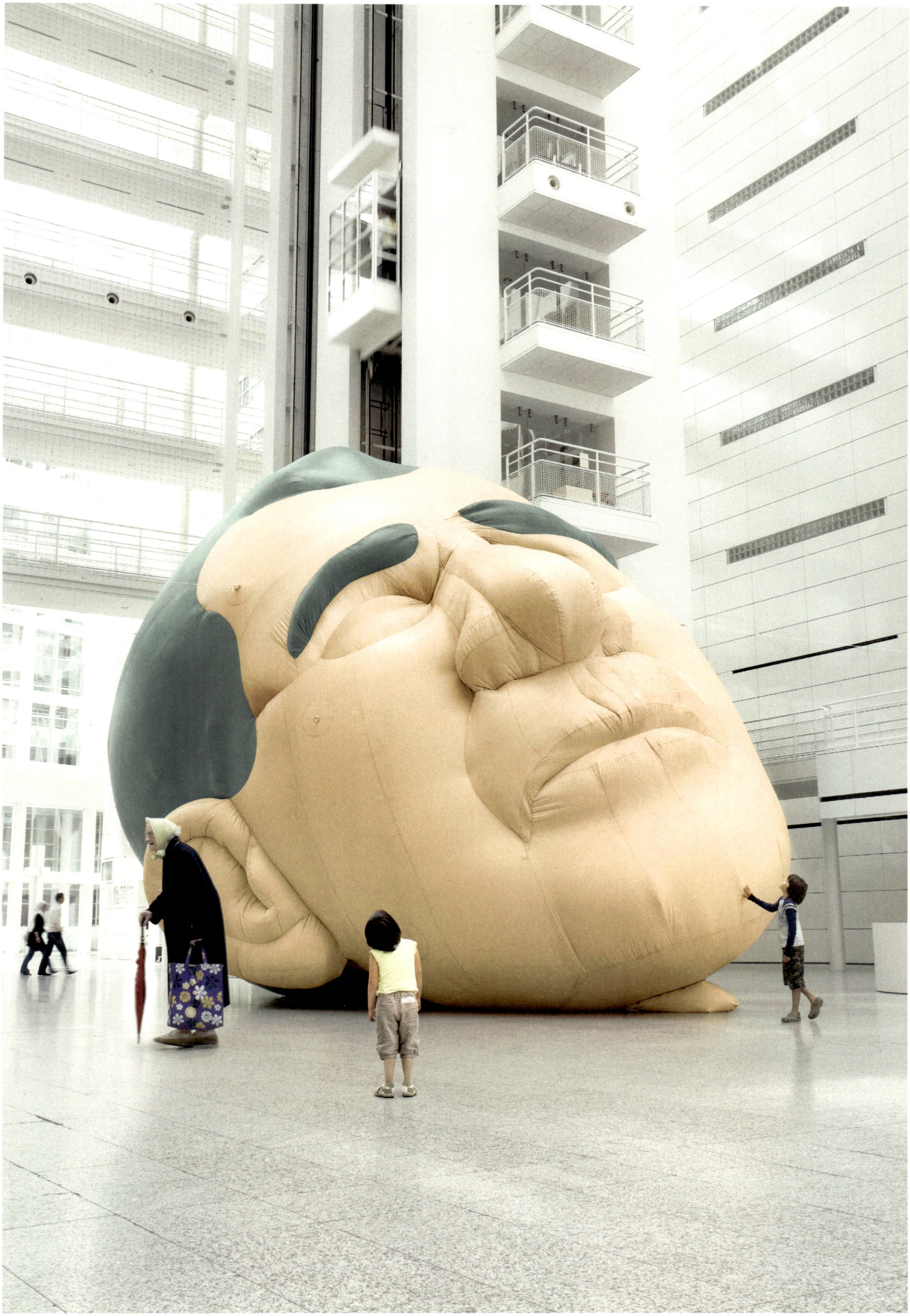

4

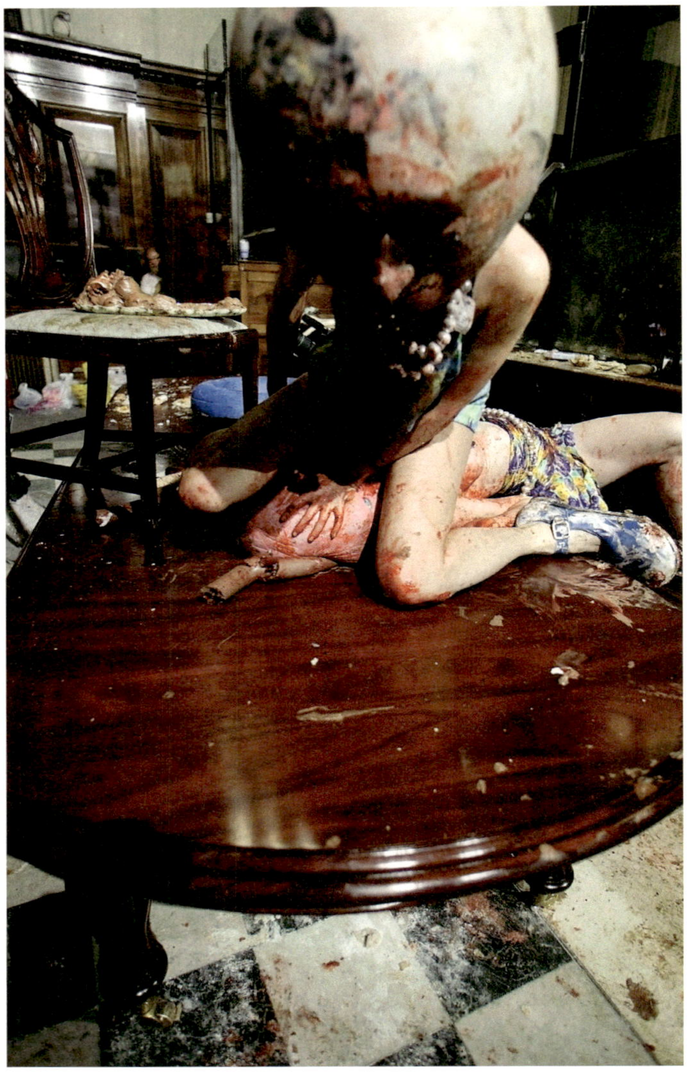

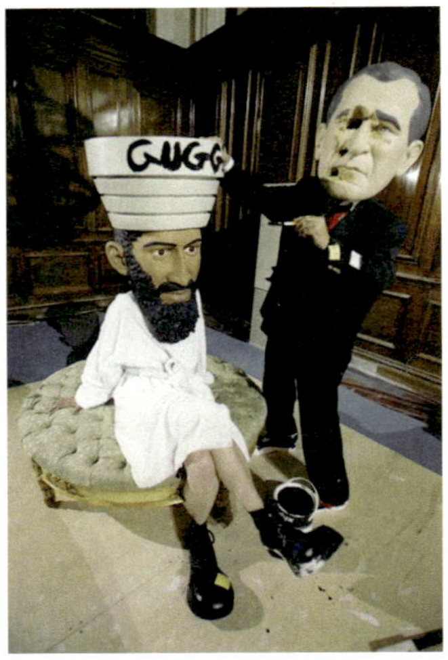

PAUL MCCARTHY

4
Piccadilly Circus
(In collaboration with
Damon McCarthy)
2003, Performance, video,
installation, photographs
Photos by Ann-Marie Rounkle
Courtesy the artist and
Hauser & Wirth

5
Pig Island
2003–2010, Mixed-media
Installation view "Pig Island,"
Fondazione Nicola Trus-
sardi, Milan, Italy, Photos by
Roberto Marossi, Courtesy
the artist, Fondazione Nicola
Trussardi, Hauser & Wirth

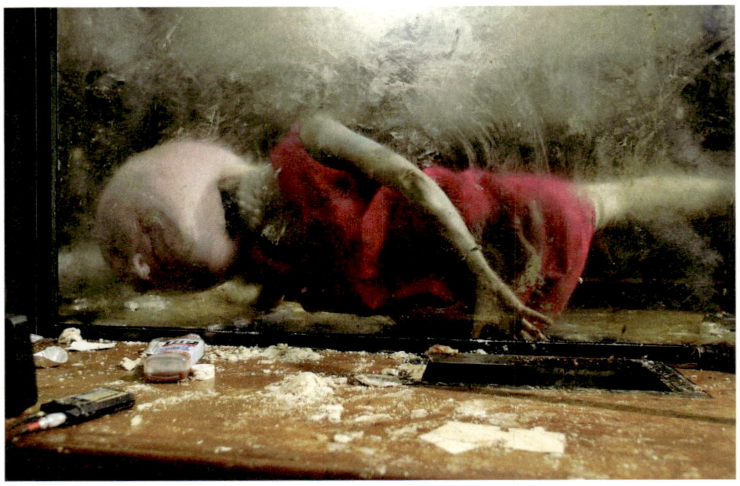

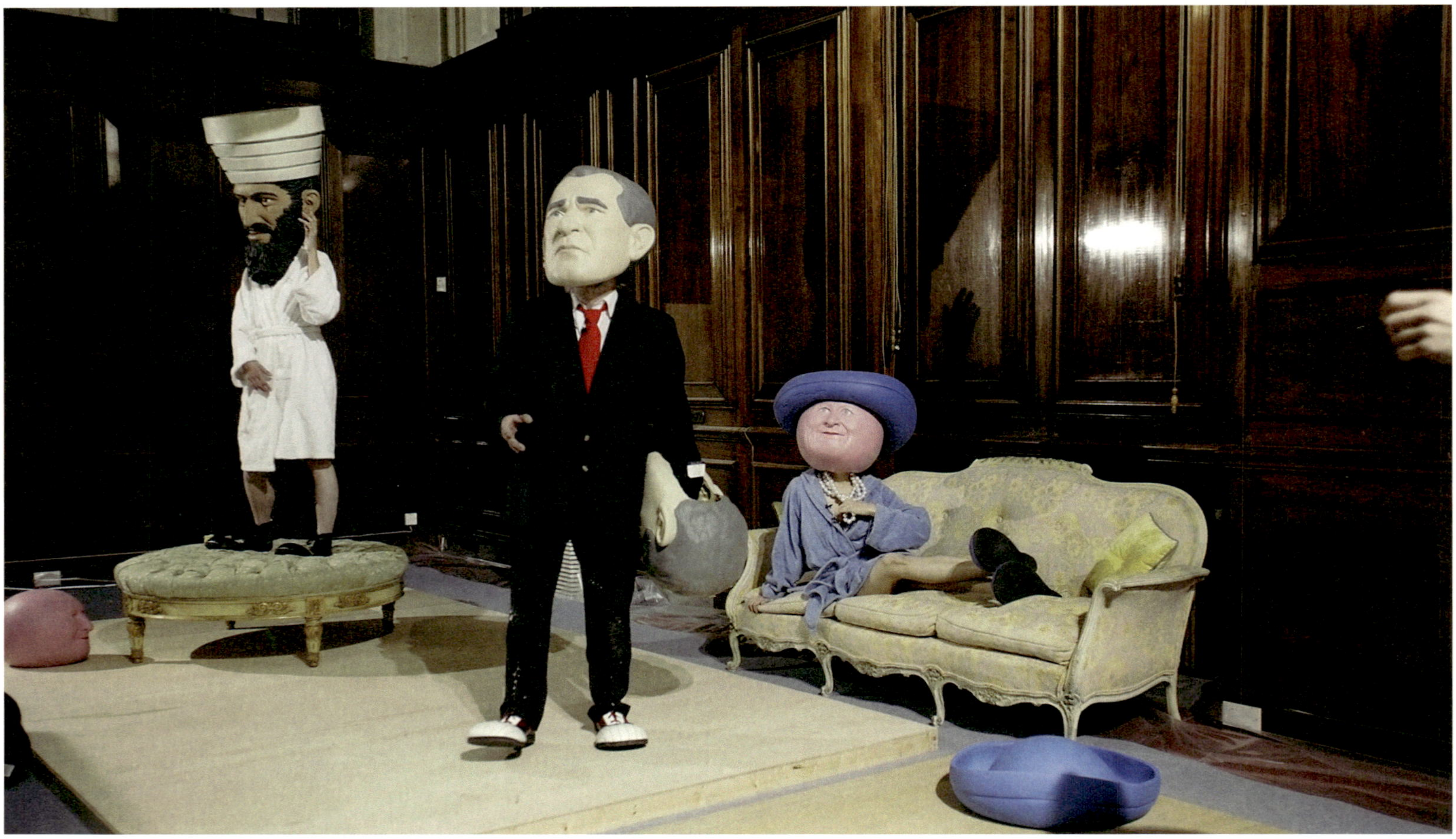

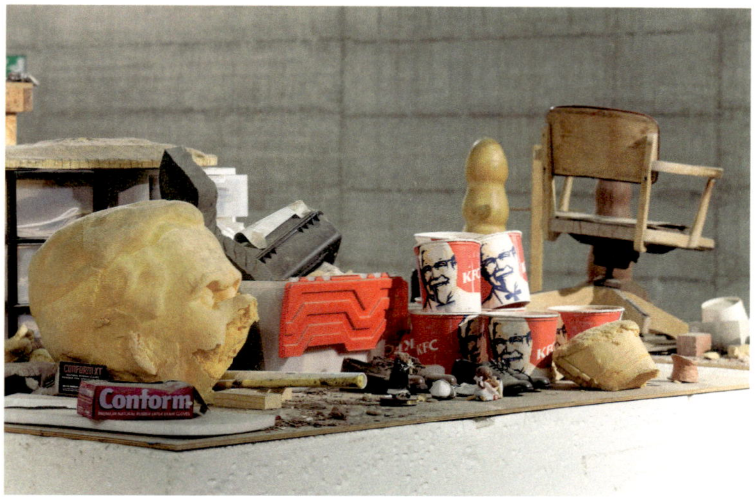

5

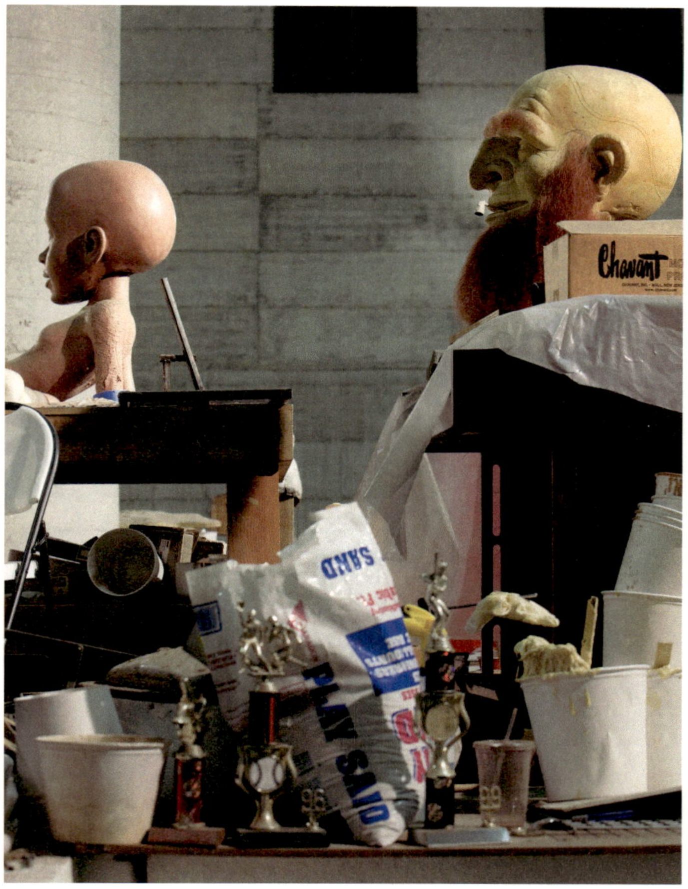

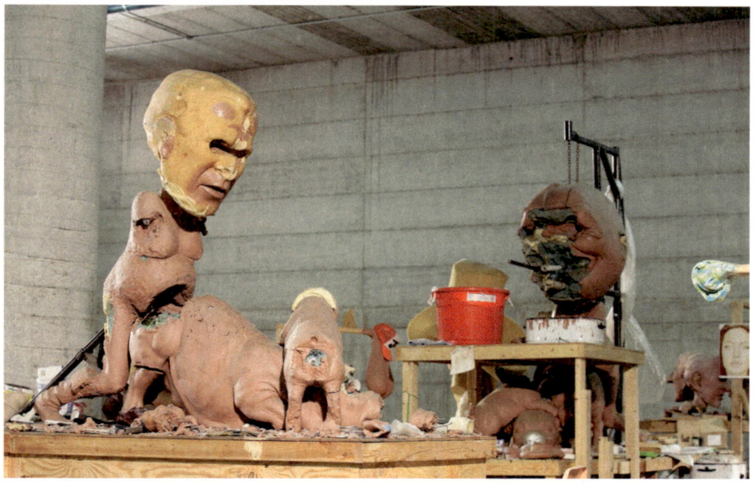

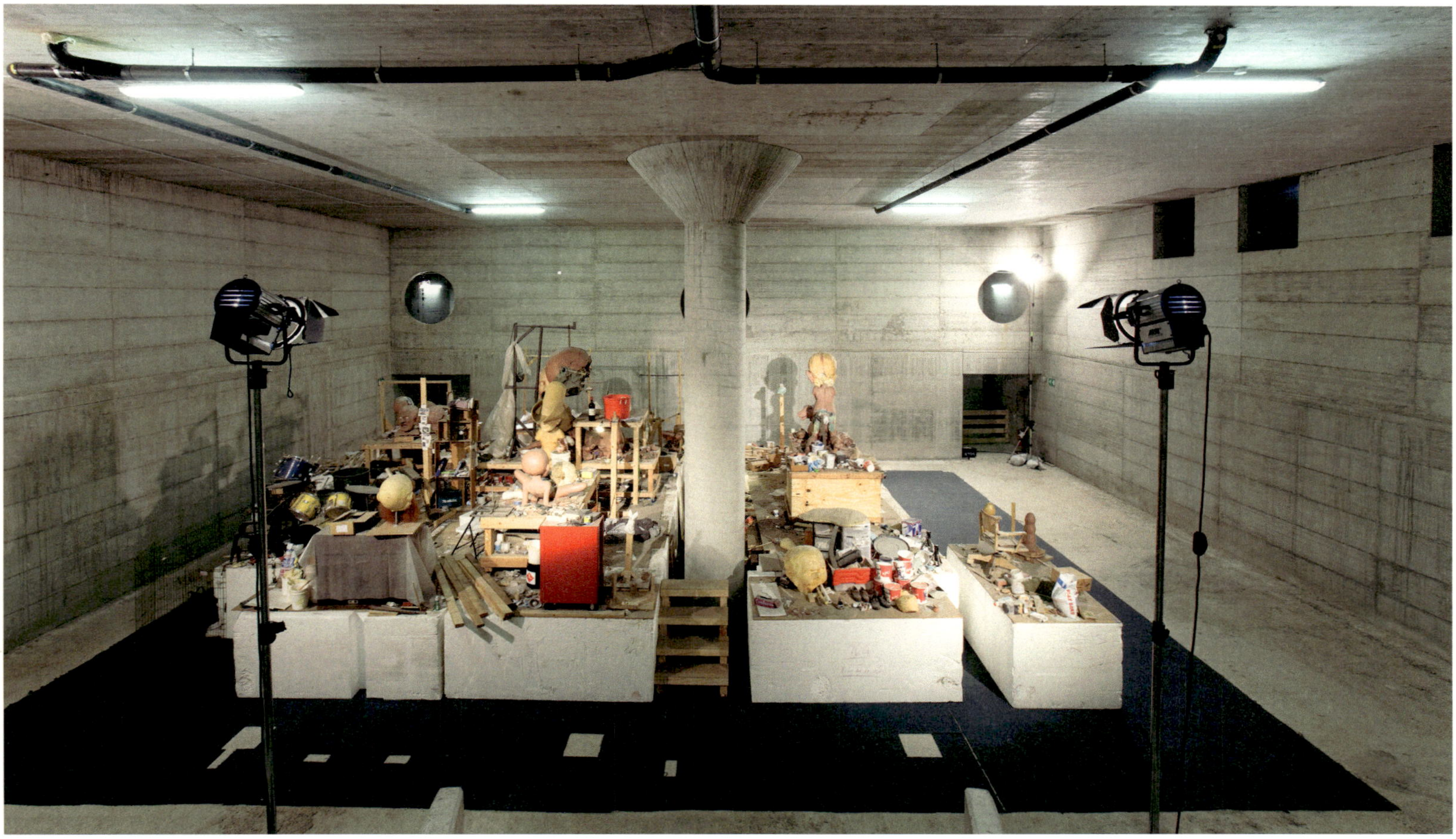

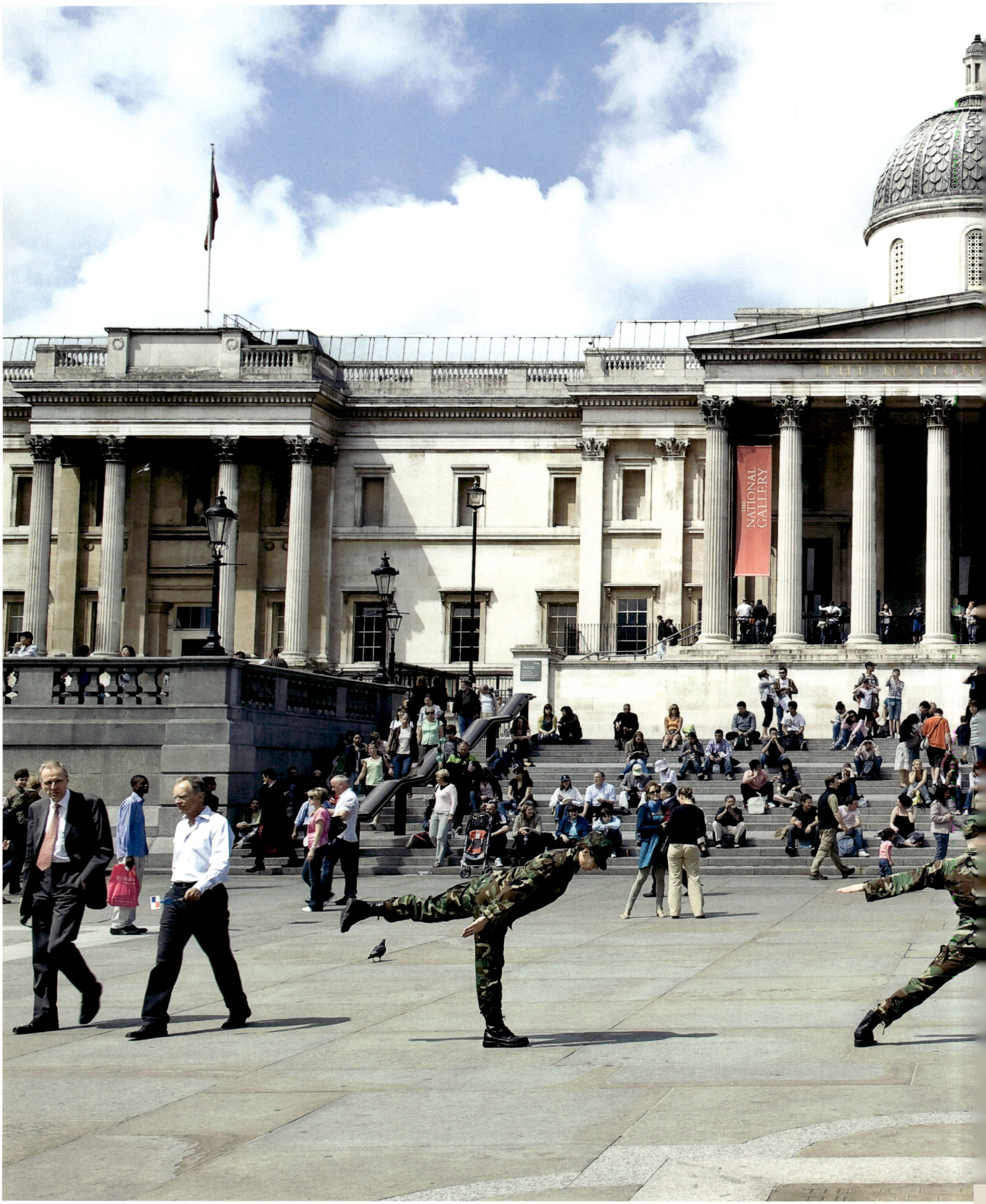
THE NATIONAL GALLERY

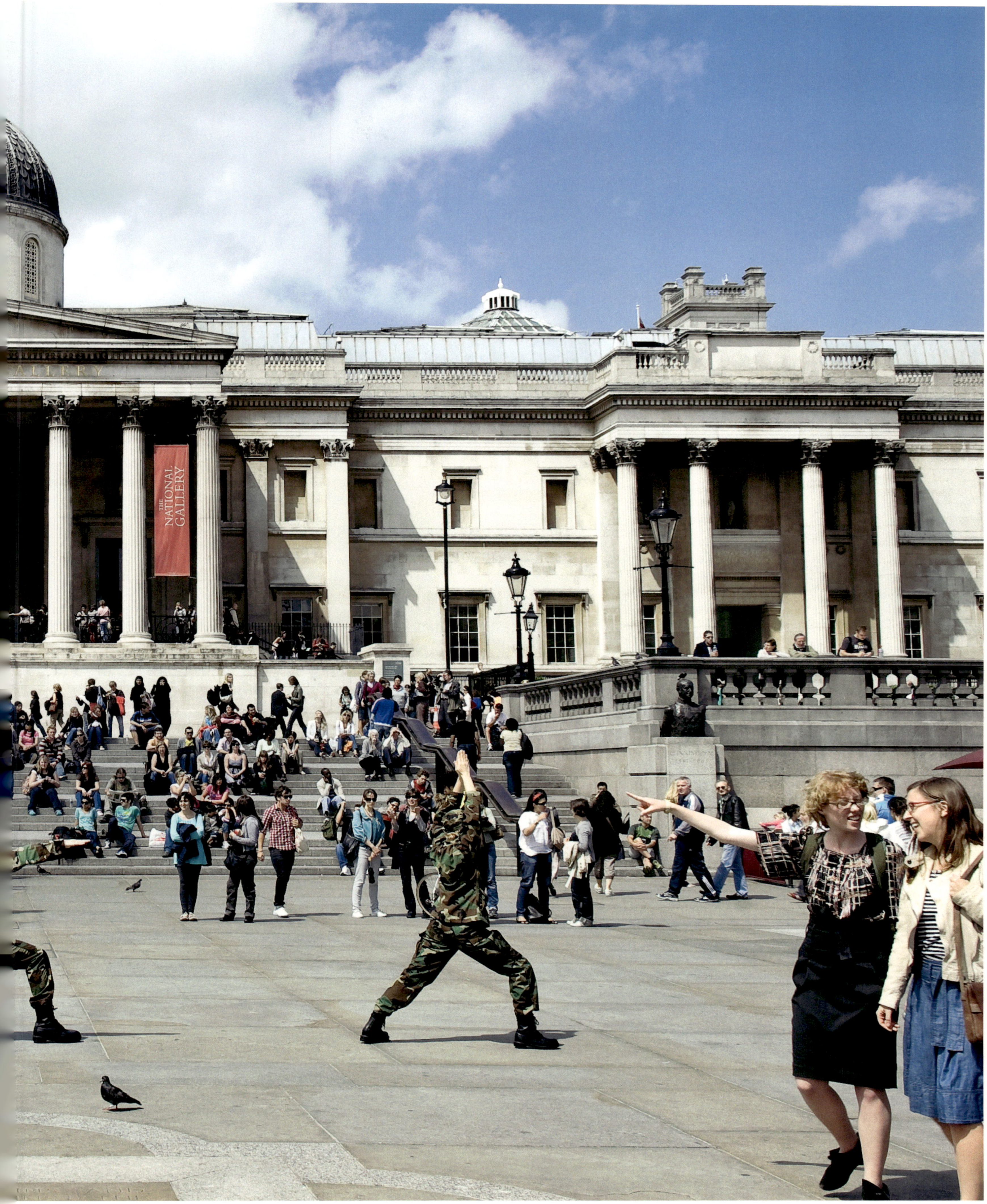

THE NATIONAL GALLERY

ALLORA & CALZADILLA

"THE IDEA OF CONFLICT AS AN AESTHETIC FORCE IS TROUBLING FOR US, AS IT ASKS HOW SOCIAL VIOLENCE IN THE FORM OF CONFLICT AFFECTS SENSORY VALUES AND TASTE."

2

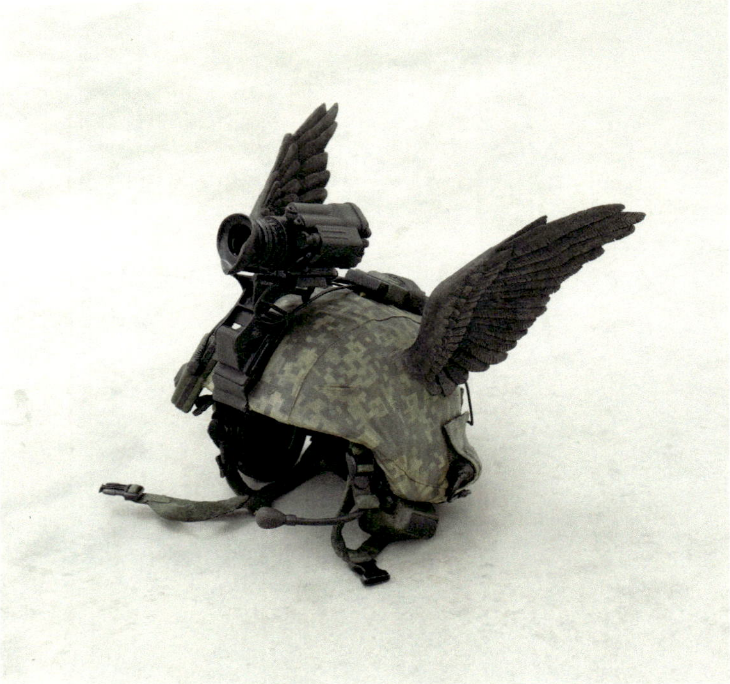

Jennifer Allora (* 1974) and Guillermo Calzadilla (* 1971) have been working as a team since 1995. Their artworks combine sculpture, photography, sound, performance art, and video art. Allora studied at the University of Richmond and at the Massachusetts Institute of Technology, whereas Calzadilla studied at the Escuela de Artes Plásticas in San Juan, Puerto Rico, and Bard College in New York. The duo's conceptual artworks focus on specific historical events, and their social implications. They use artistic techniques to analyze complex systems such as militarism, state architecture, and natural phenomena. Their artworks are subtle and poetic, but this does nothing to diminish their political power. Allora says that: "The idea of conflict as an aesthetic force is troubling for us, as it asks how social violence in the form of conflict affects sensory values and taste." For their sculpture *Clamor,* 2006, a combination of a bunker and a mountain landscape, they placed brass instruments in the arrow slits instead of guns and cannons. Inside the sculpture is a live band, playing military music from different eras and different parts of the world at deafening volume. Their video artwork *Returning a Sound,* 2003, was created on the Puerta Rican island of Vieques, which was used as a military training ground by the United States and NATO in the 1960s. Opposition by the civilian population led to the troops being withdrawn. As well as showing the Vieques landscape, the video brings us the sounds of the island. For the island's inhabitants, this soundscape will forever be marked by the memory of the massive acoustic force of the bombardment. Allora & Calzadilla's artworks generally have a critical and playful political dimension. They often treat their subjects metaphorically. Allora says that: "We see metaphors as both aesthetic—shaping form to create new sensibilities and perceptions—and political—making possible new meanings which can influence someone's choices in how they relate to a given subject." The duo is to represent the United States at the 2011 Venice Biennale.

1 (previous spread)
Balance of Power
2007, Courtesy the artist and Lisson Gallery, London

2
The Bird of Hermes is My Name, Eating My Wings to Make Me Tame
2010, Courtesy the artist and Lisson Gallery, London

3
Land Mark (Foot Prints)
2000–2002
24 color photographs

4
Clamor
2006, Courtesy the artist and Kunsthalle Zurich, Photo by A. Burger

5
Returning a Sound
2004

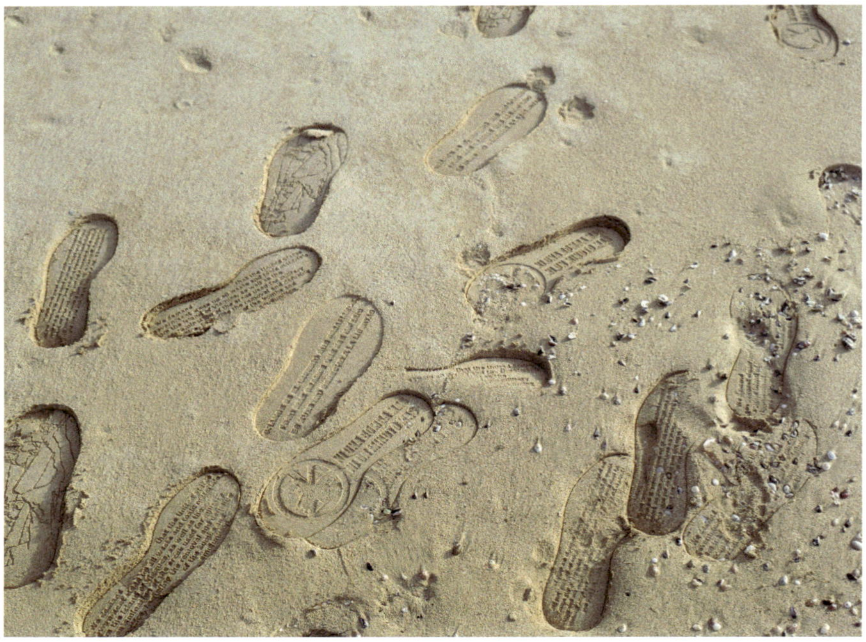

3
The photographs are an extension of a series of actions that took place in Vieques, Puerto Rico, from 2000 to 2002. The artists collaborated with various activist groups involved with protest actions in the disputed U.S. Navy Bombing Range. The project consisted of designing custom soles, which were attached to the shoes of people seeking to reclaim the land. As a result of wearing these shoes while walking on the range, the participants marked their presence in the form of a stamp on the landscape. The images on the bottom of the shoes, chosen by each individual participant, depicted territories (geographical, bodily, linguistic) that functioned as counter-representations of the site's current and future functions.

4

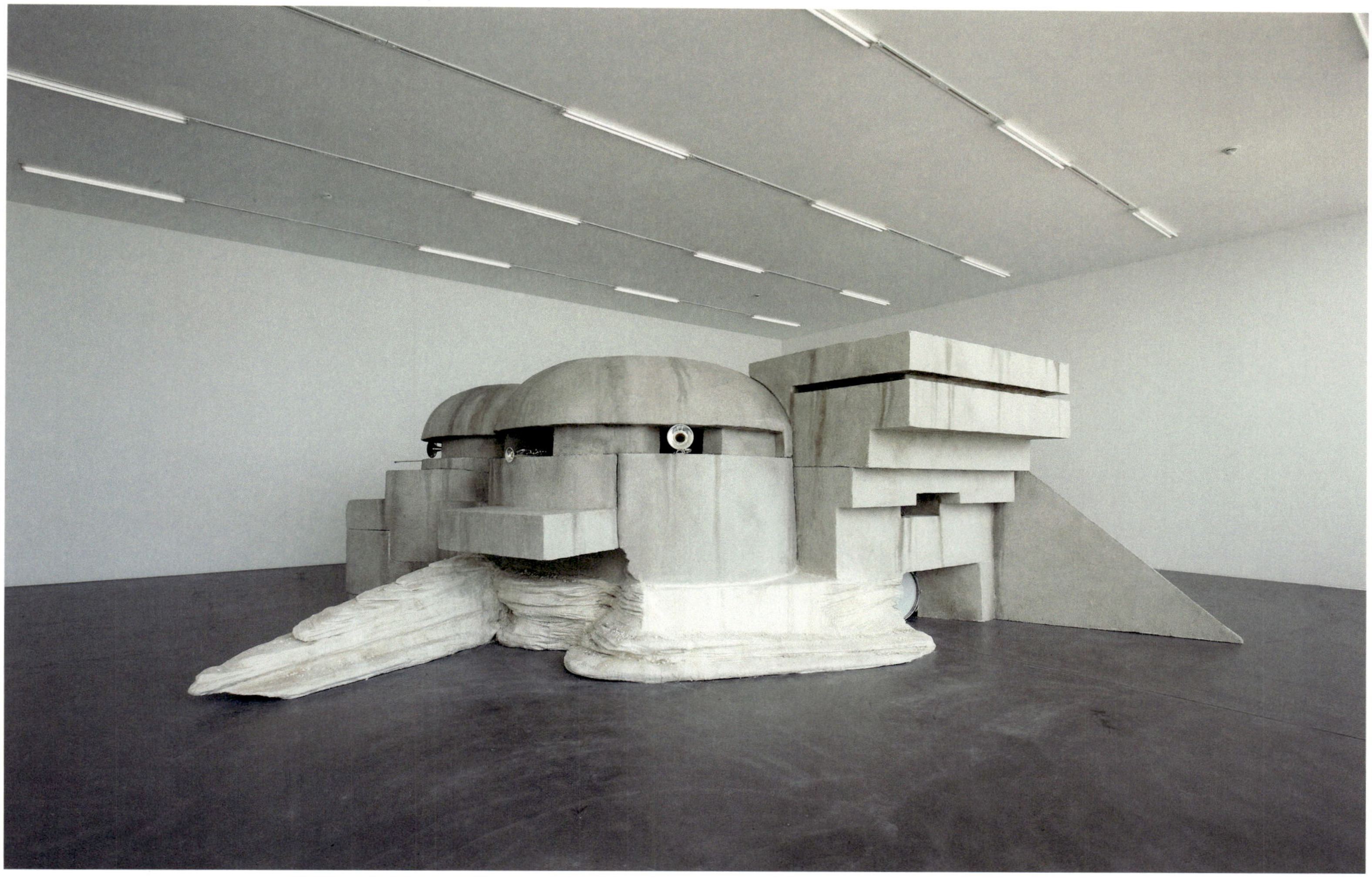

5

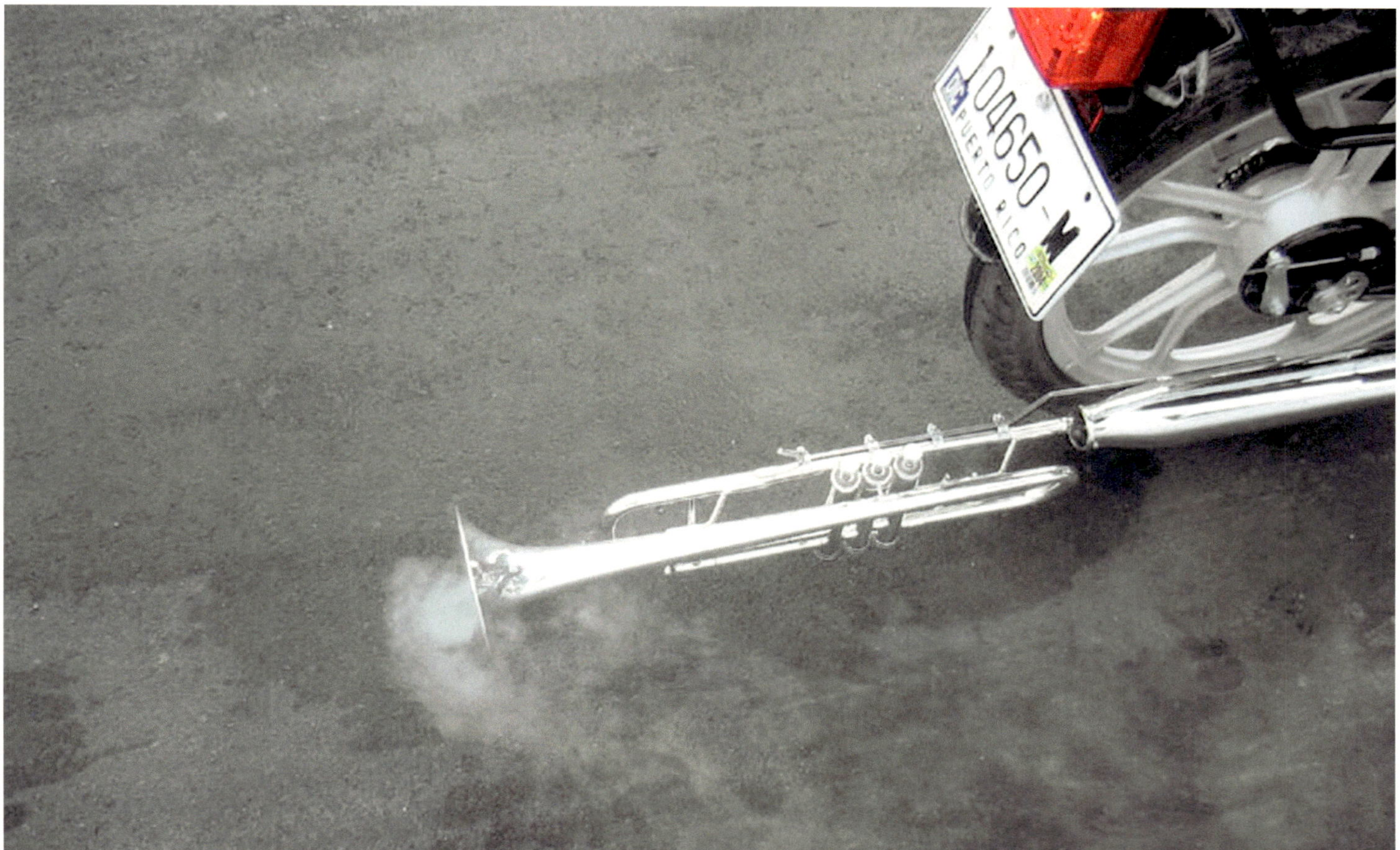

LARS Ø. RAMBERG

1

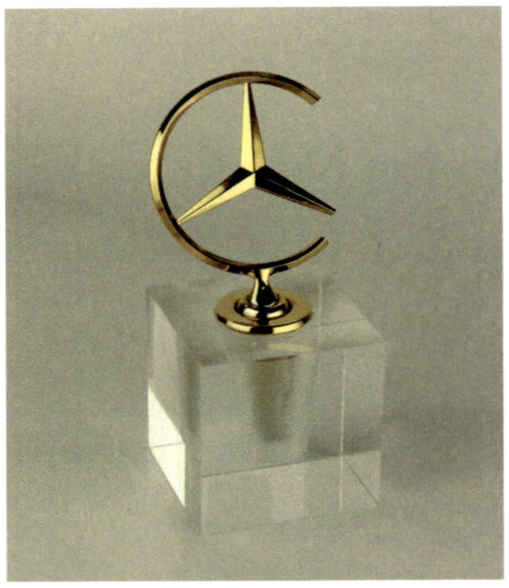

1
Made in Turkey
2005, Martin-Gropius-Bau, Berlin, Germany
Gold, steel

2
La Distinction
2009, Munch Museum, Oslo, Norway, 22 steel containers, each 1×1×2 m, 4.500 kg
© Lars Ø. Ramberg/ Virre Dahl

3
Palast des Zweifels
2005, Palast der Republik, Berlin, Germany
Steel, aluminum, neon

Goethe once said that as knowledge grows, so does doubt. The Norwegian artist Lars Ø. Ramberg (*1964) who was born in Oslo, believes that doubt is a fundamental part of Germany and of the German mentality—and he means this as a compliment. After all, doubt is also essential to democracy, as it stands in the way of totalitarianism. In the 2005, the artist expressed this belief by installing neon letters more than six meters high on the roof of Berlin's Palast der Republik that read "Zweifel" (doubt). His *Palast des Zweifels* (Palace of Doubt) was a geographical, social, and political commentary on our times. This ideological statement called for a new way of living; for an awareness of identity and globalization; for new perspectives; and for a historical transformation. "Doubt is the ideal logo for our times," says Ramberg. At the Venice Biennale in 2007, he created a scandal by installing three French public toilet buildings in front of the Norwegian pavilion. They were painted in the French national colors, which are also the colors of the United States and of Norway, and were entitled *Liberté, Egalité, Fraternité*. People who used the toilets could hear recordings of historic speeches by Charles de Gaulle, King Haakon VII, and Franklin Roosevelt; in addition to the recordings, the national anthems of France, Norway, and the United States were playing. When plans were mooted to improve the new financial district in Oslo by adding cultural features, Ramberg responded with the temporary installation *La Distinction*, 2009. He exhibited 22 bank vaults from local banks, with their backs facing east and their doors facing west. "I am hoping that I am starting a process, and not finishing one," says Ramberg. "A piece of art is like a ship that is completed and setting sail, going through storms, being rebuilt, etc."

2

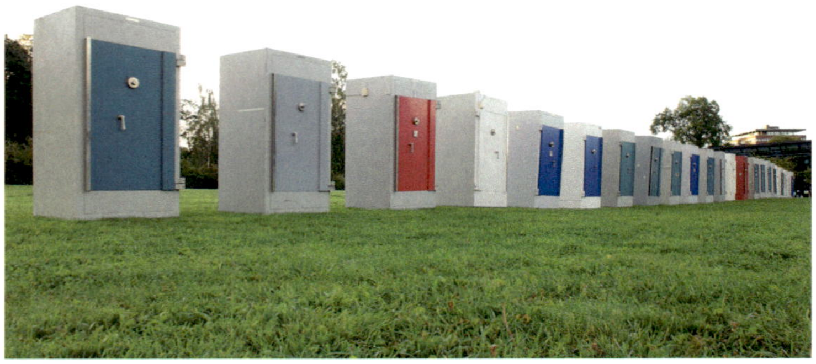

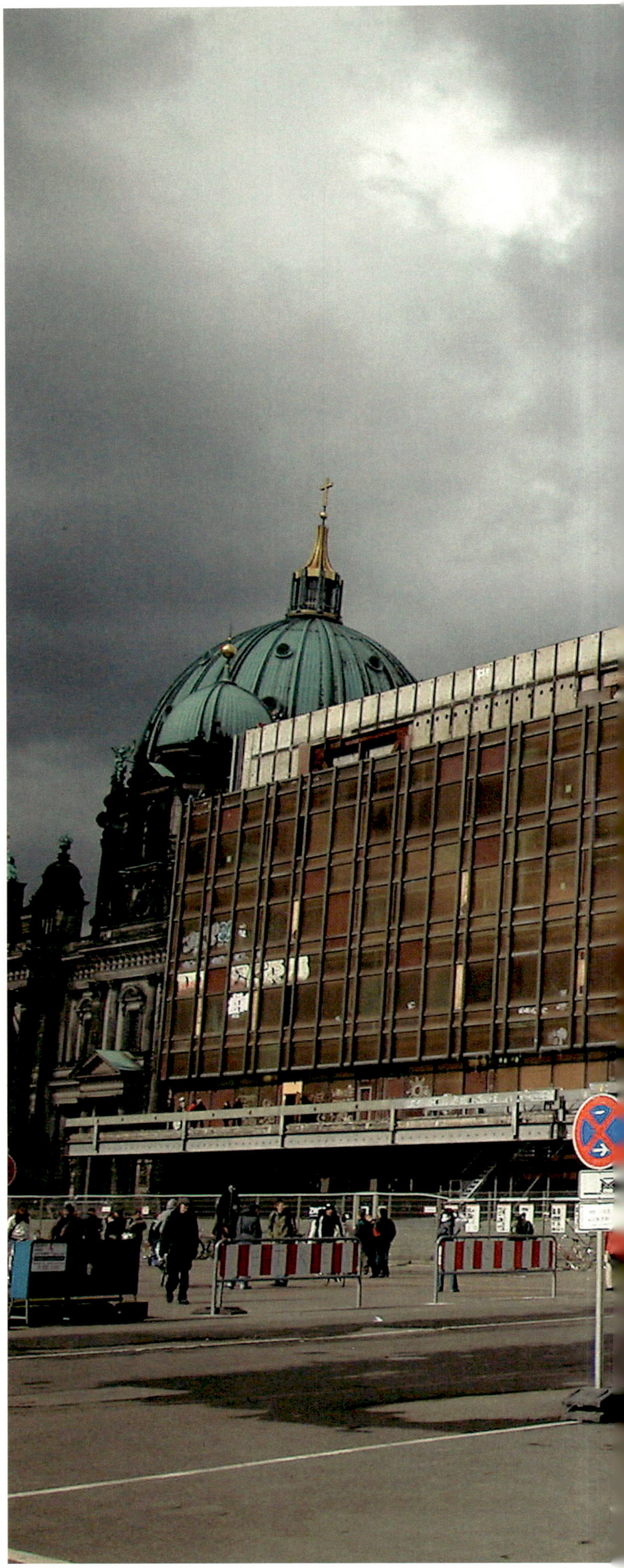

3

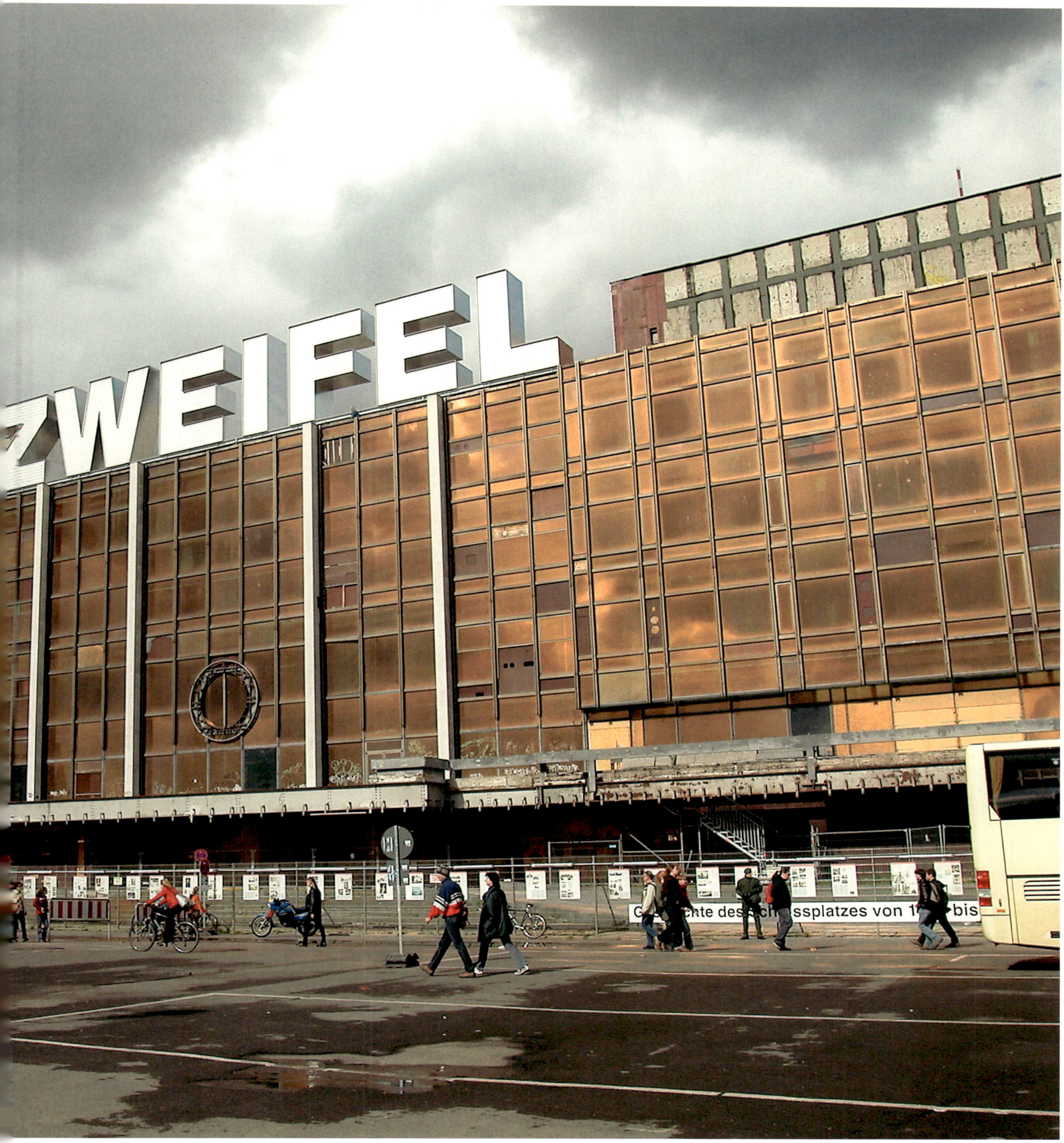

VLAD NANCĂ

In many of his works, the Romanian artist Vlad Nancă (* 1979), who was born in Bucharest, looks at the cultural identity of his country, which, following the revolution of 1989, went from being a people's republic and a socialist republic to being a semi-presidential republic. The title of his artwork *I Do Not Know What Union I Want to Belong to Anymore,* 2003, makes it clear that it is concerned with national identity. By combining the Soviet Union flag and the European Union flag, together with incorporating the colors of the Romanian tricolor, the artist creates a visualization of the questions that many Romanians are asking themselves. For instance, questions such as: is European Union membership really the only realistic option for Romania, a country that has not finished coming to terms with the trauma of the past?; or are the measures that have been imposed to reformat the country really any different from imposed communist precepts? The references to Romania's history that appear in Nancă's work are often highly humorous, but with an underlying seriousness. *Original Adidas,* 2003, for example, plays on the fact that in the 1980s meat was hard to come by in Romania, and when it was available it was likely to be pigs' heads or feet. Romanian citizens attempted to respond to this depressing situation by calling the pigs' legs "Adidas." Here, the artist shows us pig forelegs together with the Adidas stripe logo, partly, as he says himself, to remind people what it was like when food was scarce, and to thereby make them think about their newly brand-conscious lifestyles. In his project *Ideal,* 2007, which consists of the Hungarian, German, and Romanian flags with the communist symbol cut out of the middle of each, Nancă is trying to draw attention to the similarities between the three "revolutions." He phrases it like this: "In 1956, during the Hungarian Revolution, the communist symbols were torn out of the flags, leaving a hole in the middle. The same liberating gesture was repeated in 1989: first in Germany, then again in Hungary and later in Romania. For a few days, in each of these countries, the national flag was not only without an emblem, but had a hole in the middle. To me this is a symbol of pure freedom, something that could only happen in times of such strong spiritual engagement and idealistic vows. By putting the three flags together, I am aiming to realize a spiritual union that transcends time, history, and borders. The three countries—and their flags—are connected by the emptiness of the middle of the flag, a union of genuine revolutionary freedom, where no symbols spoil the essence of those days of liberty."

1
I Do Not Know What Union I Want to Belong to Anymore
2003, Screen print on textile/ installation

2
Original Adidas
2003, Leather stripes on pork feet

3
Ideal
2007

Courtesy the artist and Sabot

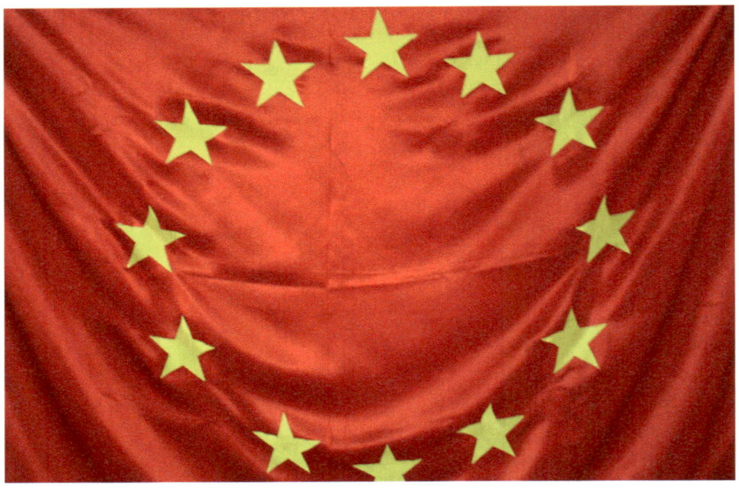

1

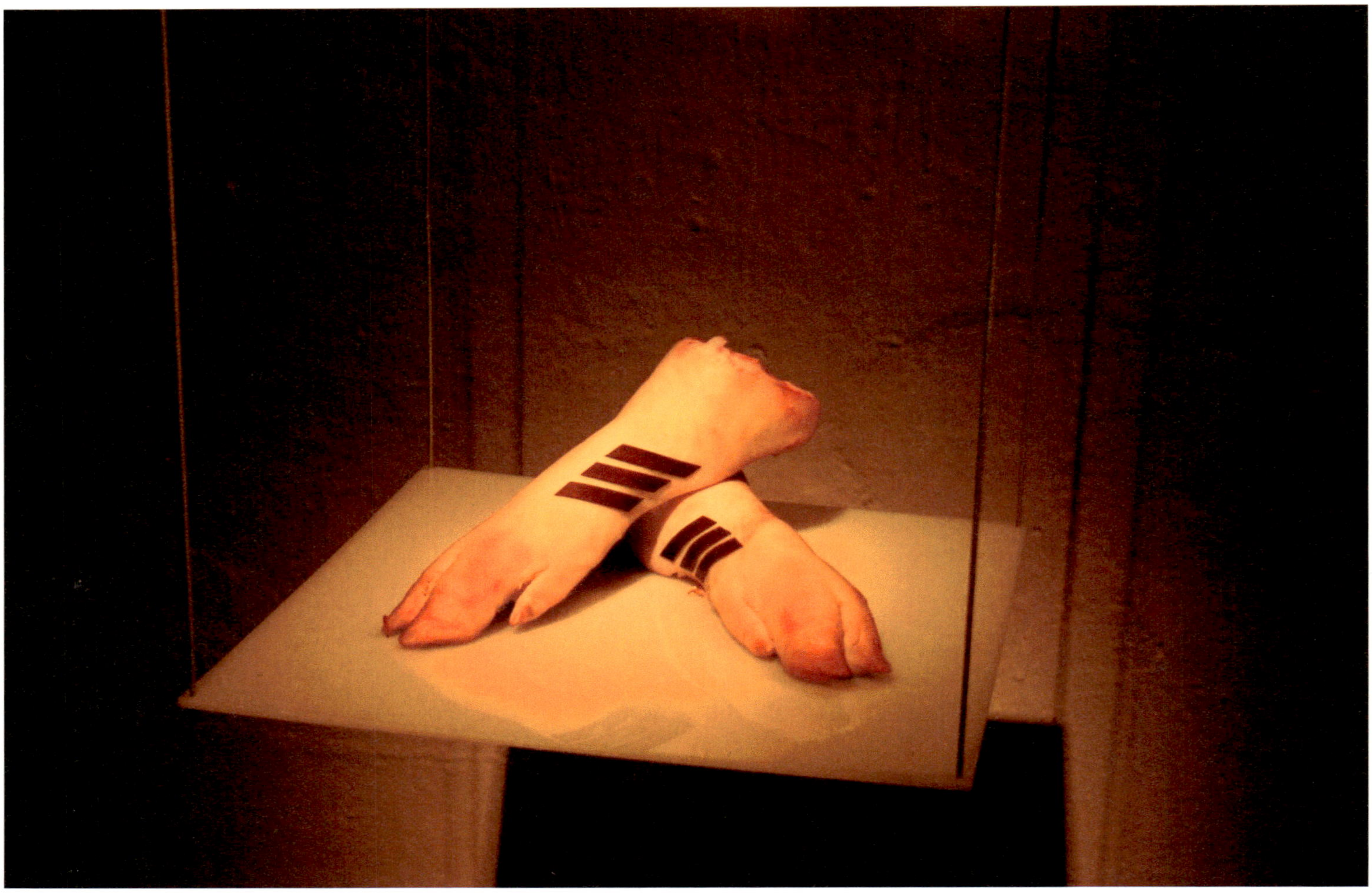

2

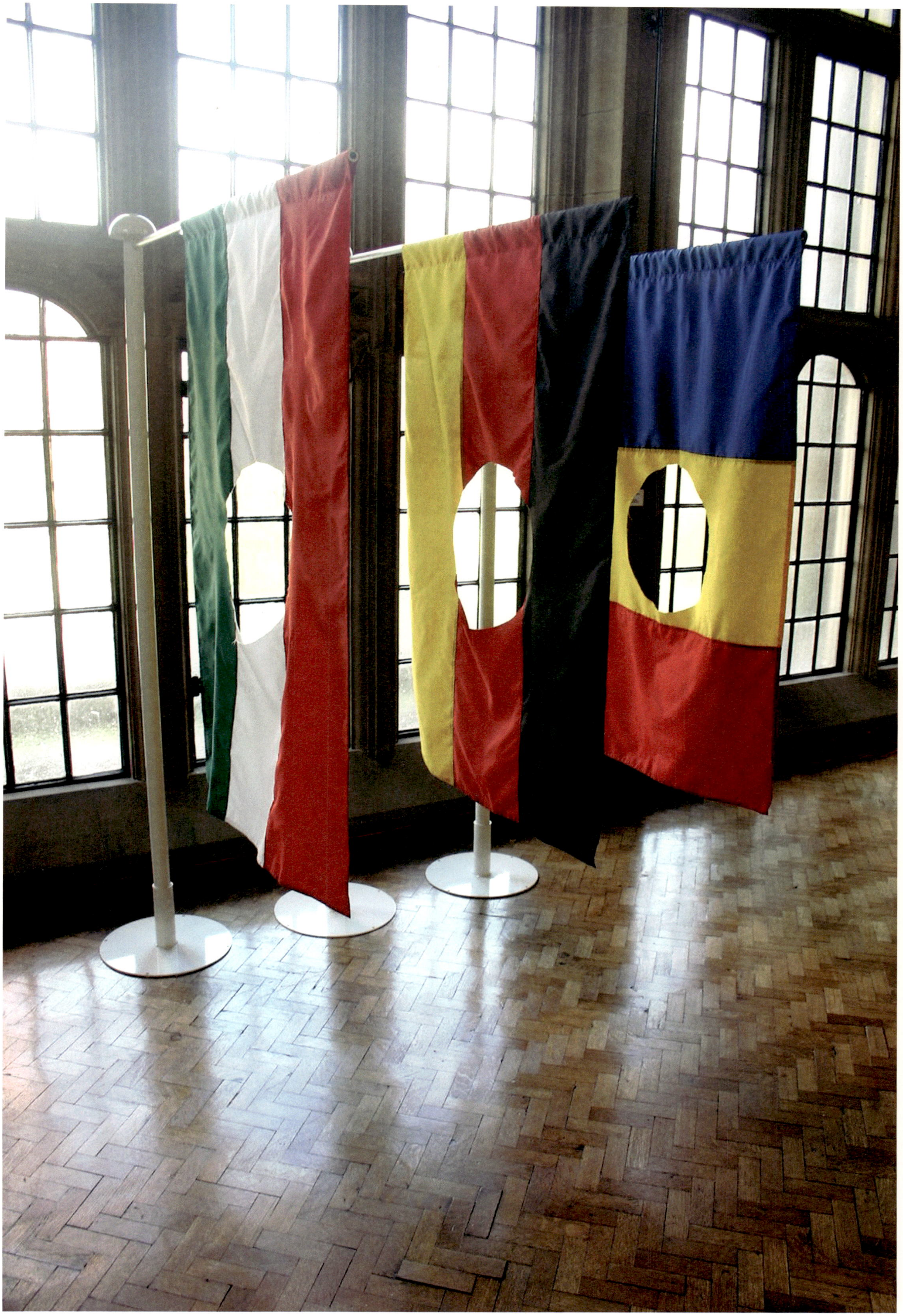

JAMES POWDERLY & UBERMORGEN.COM

1

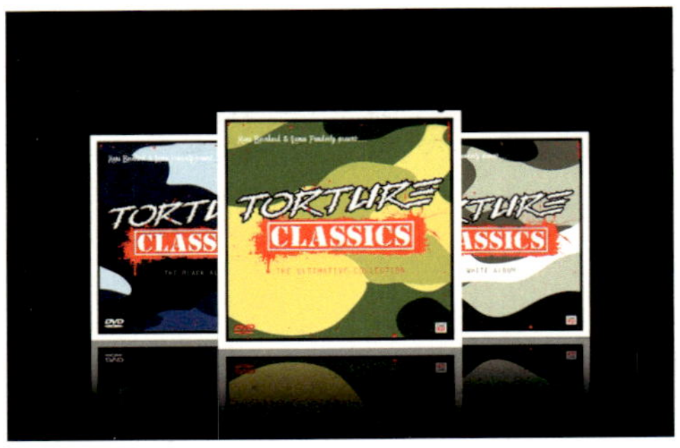

1
Torture Classics
2010, Seoul, South Korea/ Vienna, Austria
© Ubermorgen.com, James Powderly
Artwork by Philipp Teister

2
Powderly in Israeli "banana" position at Daebudo

3
Powderly handcuffed, hooded, and subjected to sonic interrogation via headphones

4
Powderly hooded and in the "Palestinian chair" stress position, subject to 24-hour Justin Bieber's "Baby"

Photos by Hans Bernhard

The American artist James Powderly (* 1976), who was born in Chattanooga, Tennessee, created the CD *Torture Music* in collaboration with artist duo Ubermorgen.com. The music project had its own website, on which its release was announced as follows: "TIME LIFE announces the release of the TORTURE CLASSICS COLLECTION. *Torture Music* is the kind of music that's perfect for sitting in the Afghan or Iraqi desert, sharing a prisoner for a night, or relaxing in a military barracks or a CIA black site in some godforsaken country on a lazy afternoon. It's music that just makes you feel free, and drives others crazy. But the artists included in the TORTURE CLASSICS COLLECTION have taken the *Torture Music* sound and given it a psychotic and everlasting quality. This *Torture Music* compilation includes 60 songs, tons of images, uncensored videos, PDFs, and extra bonus material. The Ultimate Collection DOWNLOAD-DVD includes both *The White Site Album* and *The Black Site Album*." *The Black Site Album* contains blasted-out tracks by Metallica, Rage Against the Machine, Eminem, and Nancy Sinatra. *The White Site Album* contains catchy tunes by Bob Marley, Justin Bieber, Johnny Cash, and Hanson. With this CD, whose cover has a military uniform camouflage-style design, the artists react in their customary absurd and apt way to events in Iraq and Afghanistan—taking a sideswipe at the music industry and its high-profile and not-so-high-profile stars while suggesting that those who committed the acts of torture share a certain musical taste. The seriousness with which the artists announce the project makes us aware of the disturbing nature of the facts that suggested this idea to them, without them actually having to name names or dates. In the performance that goes with it, Powderly is unrecognizable due to the cloth bag over his head. We see him with shackles on his hands and feet, with large headphones over his ears, and in various uncomfortable positions, sometimes convulsing in pain as he is exposed to the music. On the website, the artists praise the CD in the language deployed so successfully by the advertising industry. For instance, there is a quote from Hans Bernhard, one of the members of Ubermorgen.com: "With TORTURE CLASSICS and the 24-hour TORTURE GALA PERFORMANCE, we create a spectacular media event and a s(e)oul-penetrating product. We shine a single spotlight on this dark world of sonic military interrogation." James Powderly adds to this: "Now, you too can own the TORTURE CLASSICS COLLECTION, America's Red-Hot and Dark-Blue Torture Hits. The DOWNLOAD-DVD is designed to enhance U.S. security, keep Americans safe, and preserve freedom at home and in the rest of this festering, sad, and unstable world. I could listen to these magical tunes over and over and over and over and over and over and over and over and over..."

3

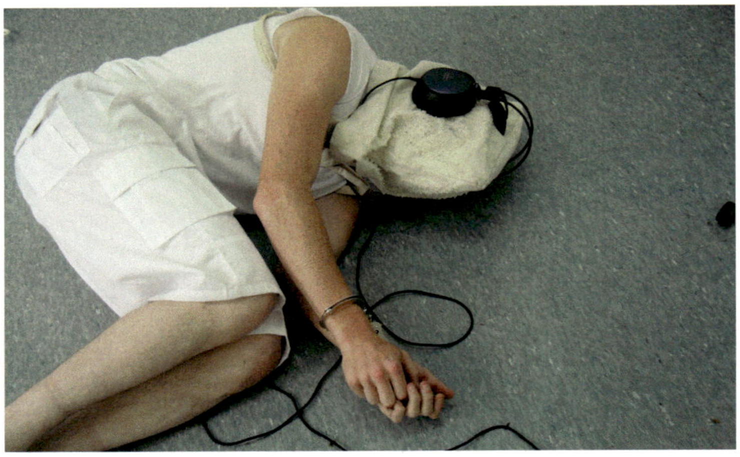

2

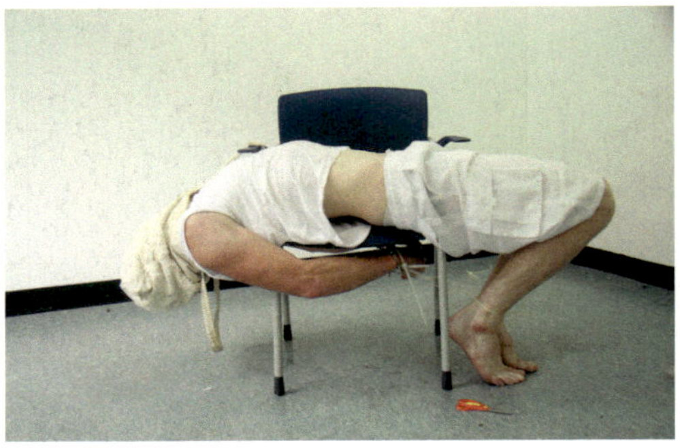

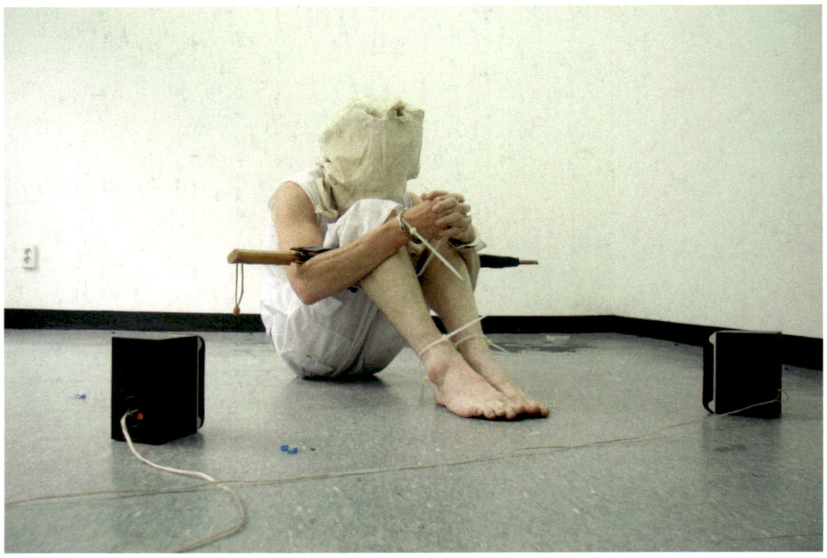

4

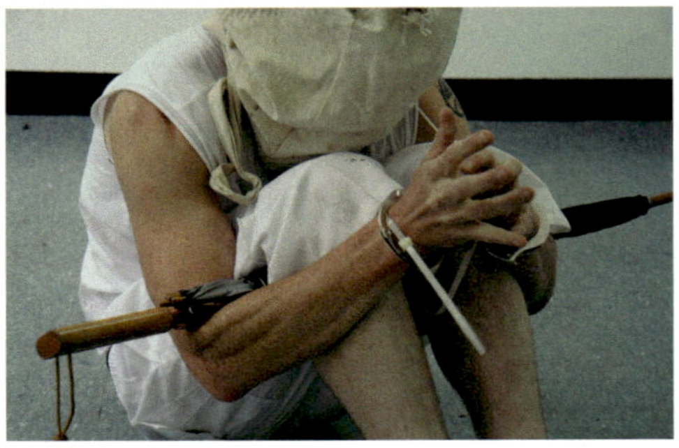

KHALED HAFEZ

Khaled Hafez (* 1963) from Cairo, Egypt, has been addressing the cultural oppositions between East and West for over 20 years. He often directly references his native Egypt as well as France—where he lived for many years—taking them as his examples of East and West. His artwork reflects the seemingly unstoppable blending of Western and Eastern concepts, the merging of which, however, constantly encounters barriers and obstacles. For instance, Hafez's video artwork *Revolution: Every Revolution Comes with a Bag of Unfulfilled Promises* references the different political forces in modern Egypt. The video is in three parts, which are shown at the same time in parallel. The left-hand screen shows the military, which promises social justice, but the pistol in the hand of the protagonist and his obsessive actions reveal the true objectives behind military politics and its promises. The second screen stands for the free market, which promises profit, prosperity, and economic freedom, but the hammer in the hand of the protagonist and his rhythmical striking of the nail, represent what is truly being promised: neoslavery in the guise of middle management. Finally, the third screen shows rising fundamentalism, with the beheading of the blond Barbie dolls by an Islamist representing cultural conflict and intolerance.

1
Revolution
2006, Video, Mini-DV
Photo by the artist
Courtesy the artist and
Singapore Biennale

2
Visions of
Contaminated Memories
2007, Mini-DV, stock images/
footage and text, Three-
channel video, 5 minutes

3
The Third Vision:
Around 1:00 pm
2008, Video, Mini-DV, stock
images/footage, Photo by
the artist

1

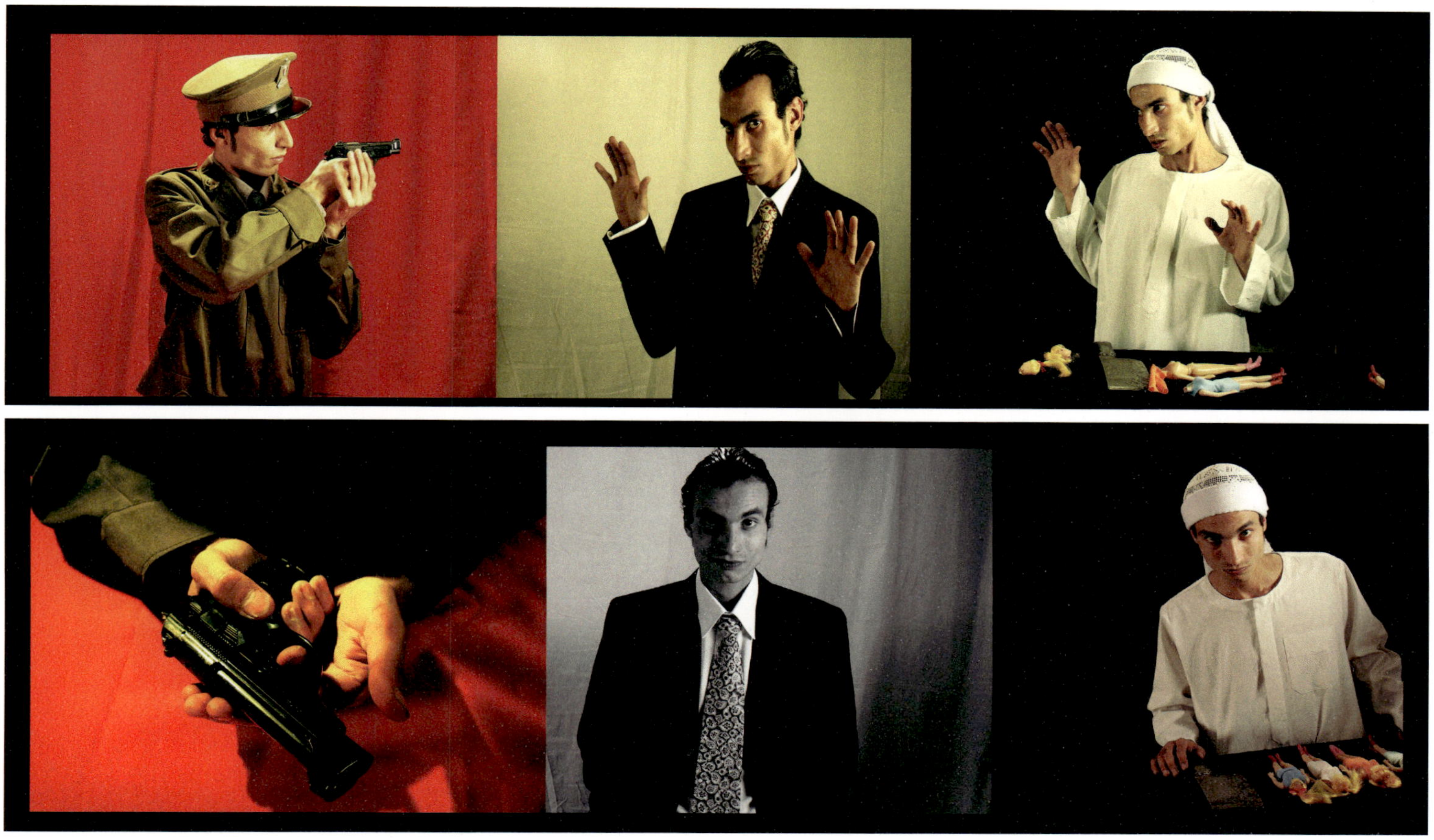

2

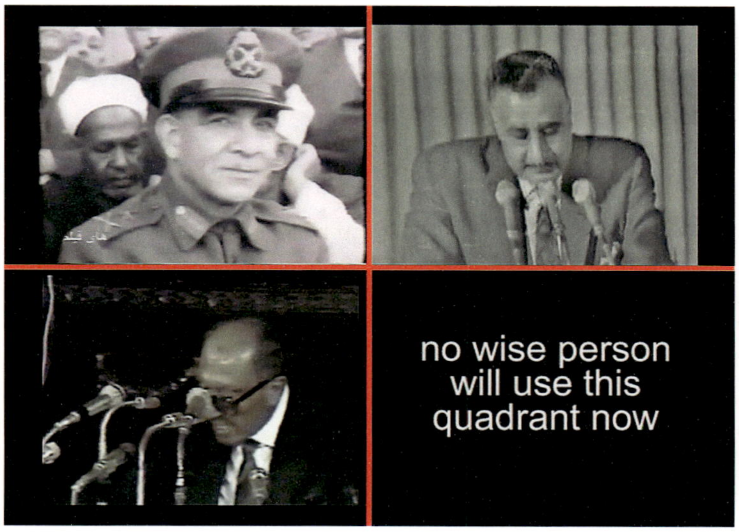

3

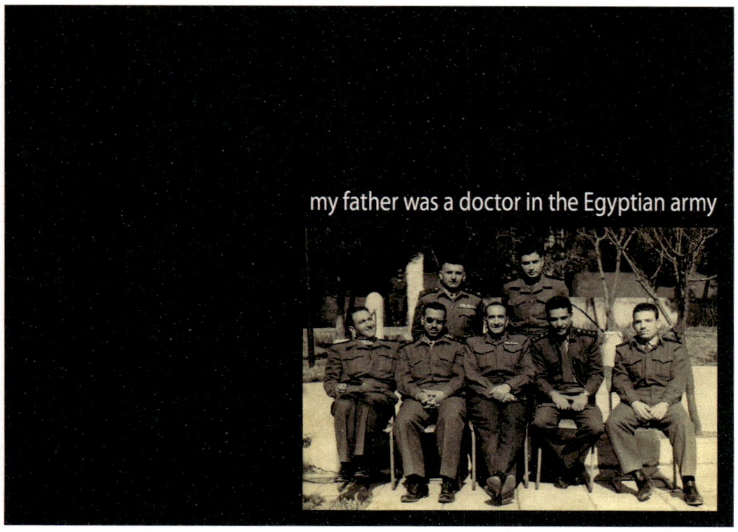

KORPYS/LÖFFLER

Artists André Korpys (* 1966) and Markus Löffler (* 1963) both born in Bremen, Germany, have been working together since 1989, investigating the structures and locations of power. Their films, photographs, and drawings generally have political events on the edge of public consciousness and places with a checkered history as their starting points. For instance, the artist duo observe the collision of state power and protest movements in two of their films, *Gorleben* and *Heiligendamm,* respectively. The film *Atom,* 2008, is set in the Wendland forest, a tract of land in immediate proximity to the nuclear waste dump at Gorleben, which was occupied by environmental activists during the regular transports of casks of nuclear waste. For three days and nights in the winter of 2008, the woods were once again a temporary habitat for the activists and police. The film alternates between a documentary and a staged presentation. In addition to the protests by the antinuclear activists and the police attacks, the artist duo show the mine shaft that is the final repository for the nuclear waste, though the major setting for the film is the forest. The superimposed images, the play of light, and the linear appearance of the trees give the individual details a graphical appearance. The artists have inserted sequences between the images of real events in which they act out oblique, grotesque commentaries on what is happening. For instance, two police officers in the forest begin to think about the meaning of life without really communicating with each other. One police officer quotes arguments from high energy physics, while another recites East Asian aphorisms, loosely based on Fritjof Capra's *The Tao of Physics.*

In their film *Villa Feltrinelli,* 2008, Korpys/Löffler investigate a location with many different faces and histories: the Villa Feltrinelli, built in 1892 in Gargnano on Lake Garda. This outstanding building, which is an elegant luxury hotel today, is loaded with images of the past—and of very different circumstances. The film begins with the artists racing on motorbikes through a winding mountain tunnel towards the Villa Feltrinelli. Initially the camera captures the idyllic landscape, the immaculate villa complex, and the luxurious furnishings, but the film does not stop there. The camera goes hunting for—and finds—suspicious traces. For instance, it discovers the name "Feltrinelli" written in blood on a bath. Intentionally laid clues like this point to the difficult history of the property and its owners, overshadowing its romantic fairytale palace image. The villa was the summer residence of the prominent Feltrinelli family until its confiscation and was later appropriated as a residence by Mussolini, dictator of Italy from 1943 to 1945. Pier Paolo Pasolini shot his film *The 120 Days of Sodom* here, making the villa the site of the four libertines' orgiastic pact. The artists book Mussolini's former bedroom for a night. They dismantle the original bed—still to be found in the room—and make a cooking area between the parts of the bed, where they warm a can of ravioli. To the pasta they add torn pieces of posters depicting the mutilated corpse of Mussolini, leaving a historical stew to be digested. During this absurd ceremony, soft and relaxing music plays. Now—if not before—it is clear that the artists are making an ironic commentary about the banalization of brutality in the biographies of Feltrinelli, Mussolini, *and* Pasolini.

1
Atom
2010, DV, 31 minutes

2
Villa Feltrinelli
2008

© VG Bild-Kunst, Bonn 2011

1

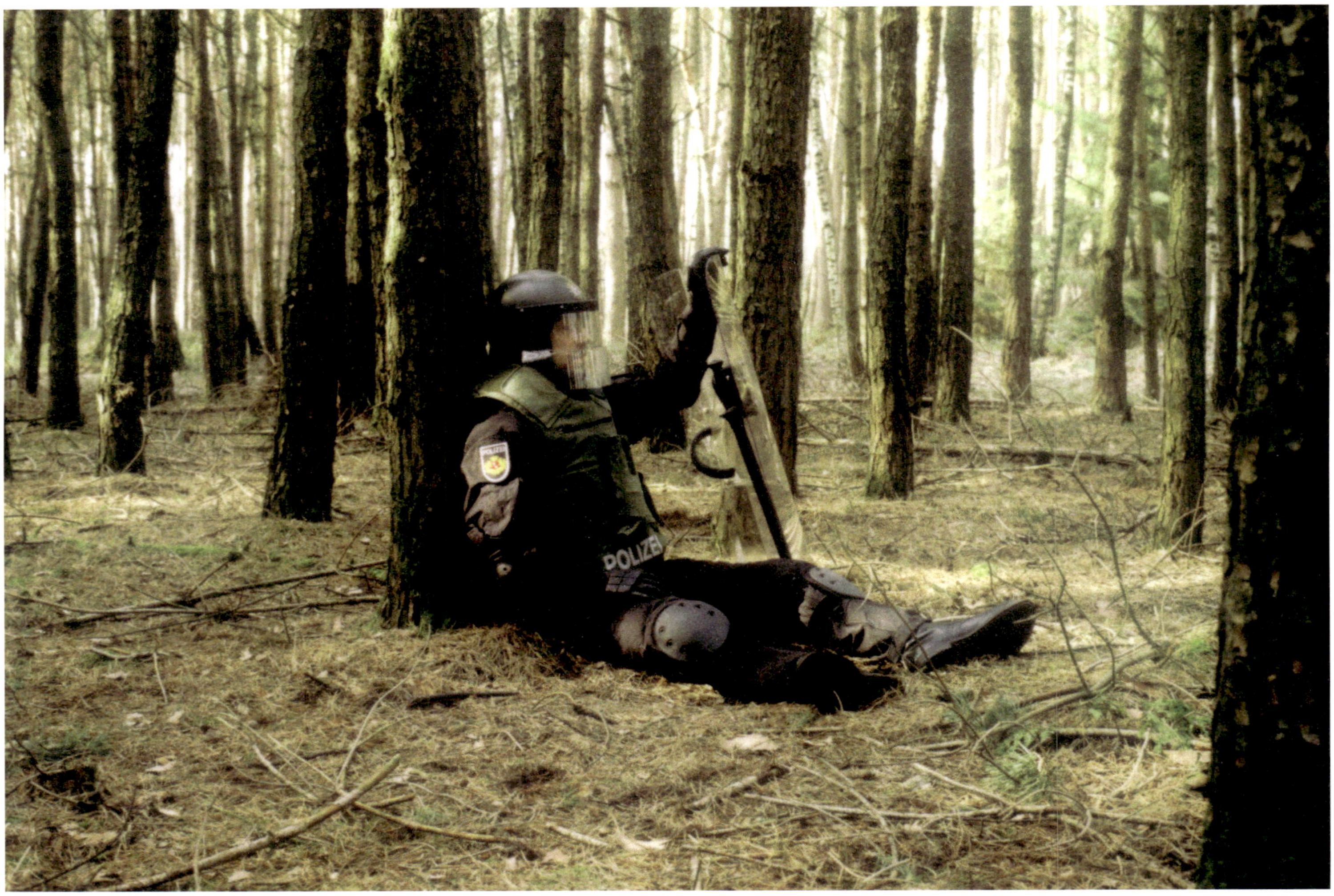

2

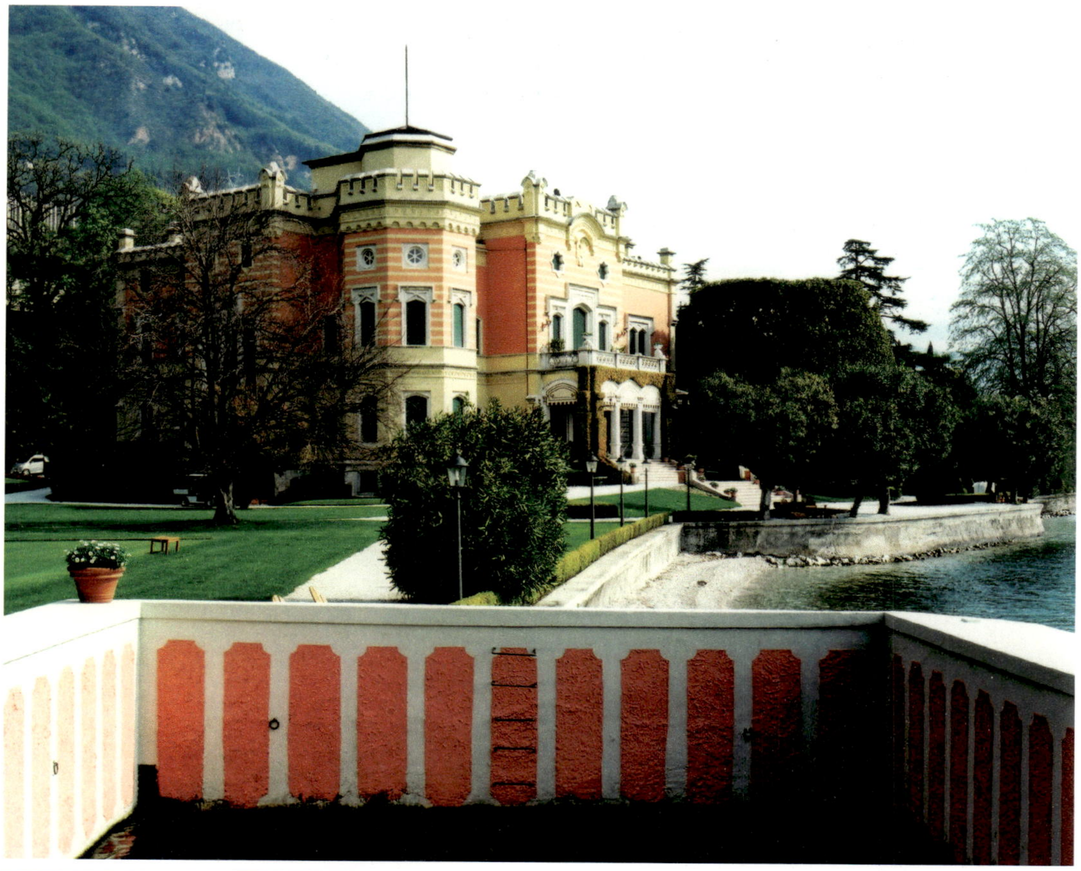

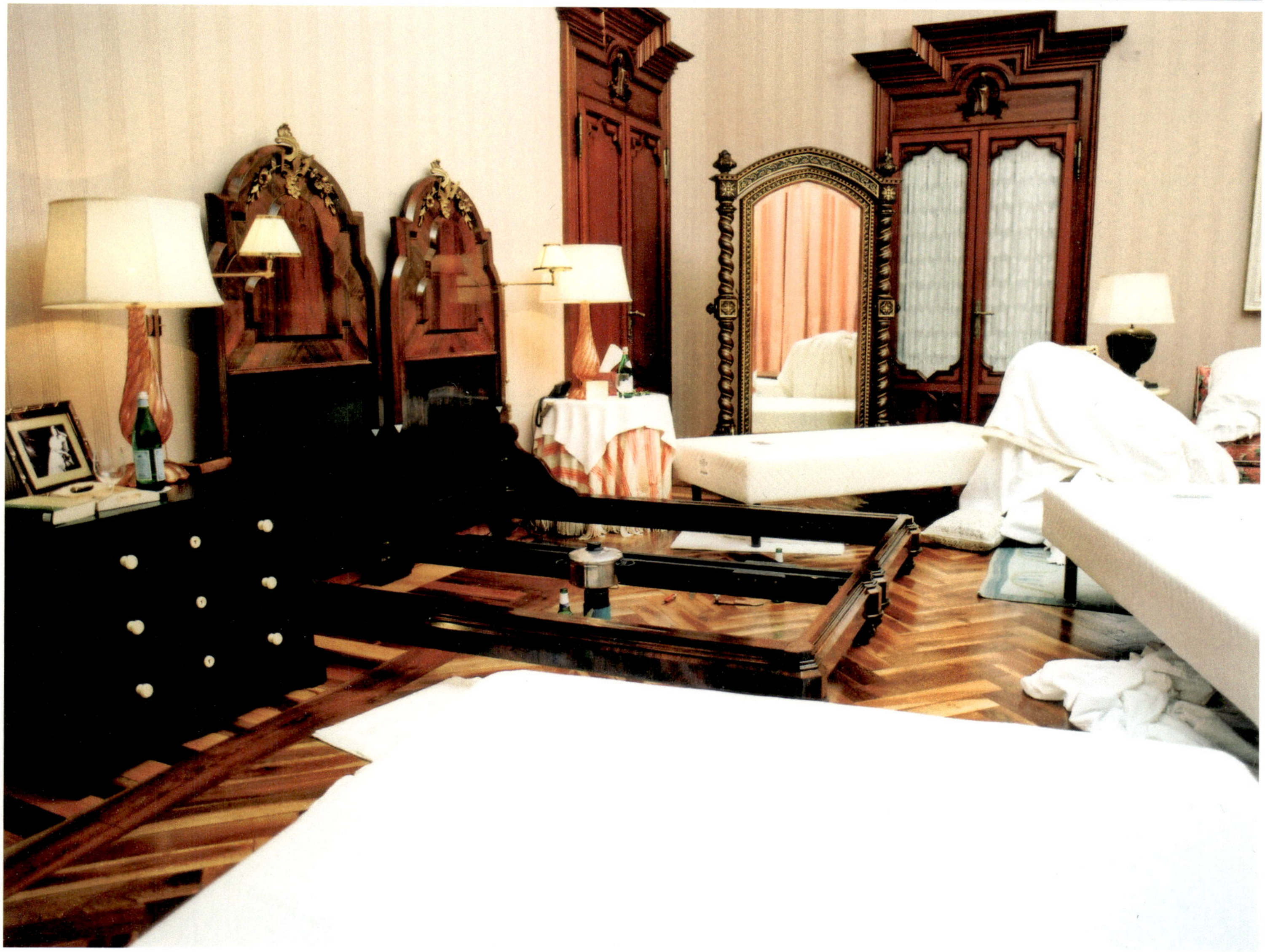

JENNIFER KARADY

“THE IDEA, CONCEPTUALLY, OF TAKING THAT MOMENT AND RECONTEXTUALIZING IT, AND PLACING IT IN THE CIVILIAN WORLD, IS BASED ON A THERAPEUTIC MODEL.”

1–5
Soldiers' Stories from Iraq and Afghanistan

All following texts were transcribed and edited from interviews conducted by Jennifer Karady between 2007 and 2010

In her series *Soldiers' Stories from Iraq and Afghanistan*, which she started work on in 2006, the American photographer Jennifer Karady (*1967) impressively addresses the fate of soldiers returning to various states and regions of the United States, from the war zones in Iraq and Afghanistan. The photographs tell soldiers' individual stories, capturing the impressions and memories that will never leave them, in pictorial form. Unlike other photographers who stage narrative scenes by taking pictures of actors, Karady works with the veterans themselves. After an extensive interview with the veteran and his or her family, the veteran will collaborate with Karady on an image or a memory of war, which is then restaged in an elaborate process, similar to creating a film set of the incident. Every single detail is significant, and the setting is analyzed several times before the final shooting, with the veterans given as much time as they need. In total, one photograph can take more than a month to conceive and shoot. The veterans reenact the memories chosen by them in uniform, and in the safe environment of their normal everyday surroundings, often surrounded by their family and friends. Karady describes this sensitive process as part journalistic and part therapeutic. “This thing is replaying visually in the person's head, and we really have no idea what is going on,” she says. “But the idea, conceptually, of taking that moment and recontextualizing it, and placing it in the civilian world, is based on a therapeutic model.”

Karady's pictures reveal the memories and nightmares that can intrude into and perpetuate themselves within the soldiers' everyday lives even in seemingly war-free zones. For the audience, these staged photographs make the persistent difficulties soldiers have in adapting back to civilian life after war much more real and evident than any documentation could.

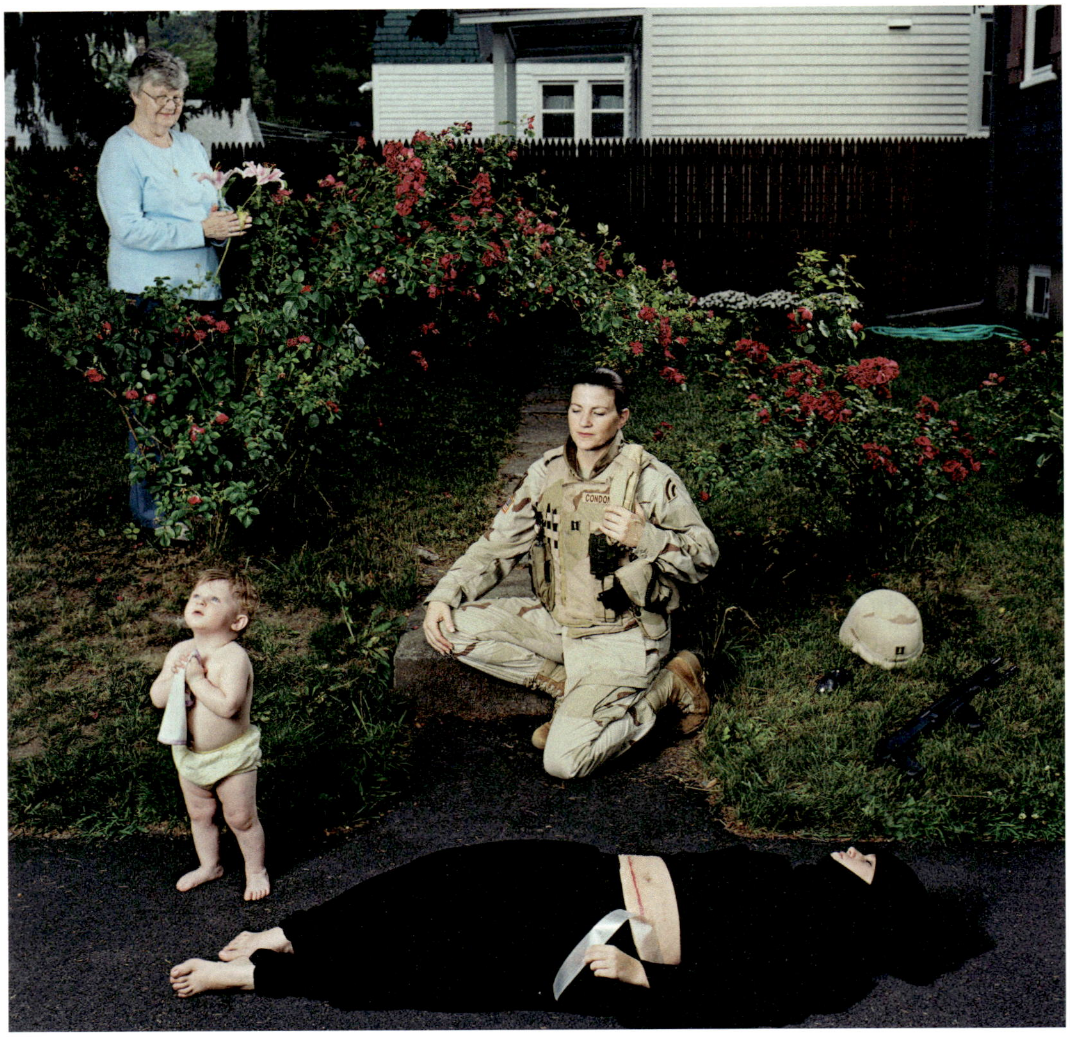

1
Captain Elizabeth A. Condon, New York Army National Guard, veteran of Operation Iraqi Freedom, with daughter, Kate, and mother, Elizabeth; Troy, NY
USA, 2008

One of my missions in Iraq was to check the water levels in remote areas, because the underground water infrastructure had been destroyed by Saddam Hussein. We were curious to find out how the locals were getting water to sustain themselves and what we could do to help them. An Iraqi man approached us and asked if somebody could take a look at his wife or daughter or whoever she was. She was just a girl, maybe sixteen years old. We had a doctor with us, but they didn't want the male doctor to examine her. They looked to me because I was the senior ranking female person.

I went into this room, and the girl was lying on a runner-like rug on the dirt floor. She lifted her black burka to show me her stomach. She recently had a caesarian. She was cut from hipbone to hipbone, like somebody just took a knife, cut her open, and took the baby out. The wound was held together by thin, one-inch-wide box tape, the kind with little strings in it. It was obviously infected, so I just kind of cleaned up her wound with rubbing alcohol, antibiotic cream, and sterile dressings. It was healing but it was nasty. She was very thankful. No one responded until the eldest woman did. There must have been eight women and twenty kids all watching me. The eldest woman came over and started kissing my cheek and thanking me. One by one, she introduced me to her whole family, never saying a word.

When I came back I couldn't deal with the welcome home—everyone glad to see me, trying to give me hugs—because I had been so cold, isolated, and nonemotional. A lot of people had died, and I'd been to too many memorial services. I said to myself, “Okay, the Muslims have Mecca, where's my Mecca?” I'm a Catholic, so it's the Vatican. So I went to Italy.

I volunteered to go to Iraq when I was told I couldn't have children. I was 36 or 37 at that time and was engaged and wanted kids. Having a family was always very important to me, but my career in the military and my goals had always gotten in the way because I wanted to be educated. I wanted to be a commander.

In Italy, I went into the Sistine Chapel. It was like the place where it was OK to release my emotions. I walked up the steps to the altar and bawled my eyes out. I don't know how long I was there. I remember that before I left for Italy, my mother told me, “Sometimes men don't listen, you need to speak to their mothers. Moth- ers have a way with their sons. So if you have any special requests while you're there, talk to Jesus' mother.” So I did. I went to the Basilica and just prayed, “Mary, I've always wanted to have a family, but it's totally up to you. Maybe I could adopt or whatever, I've got my money saved.” That was in December. Four months later in April I was pregnant. I got this wonderful gift out of all that tragedy. I really attribute my daughter to the Iraqi woman with the caesarian.

Elizabeth Condon has been promoted to major and is currently pursuing studies that could make her eligible for further promotion to lieutenant colonel, colonel, and perhaps someday general.

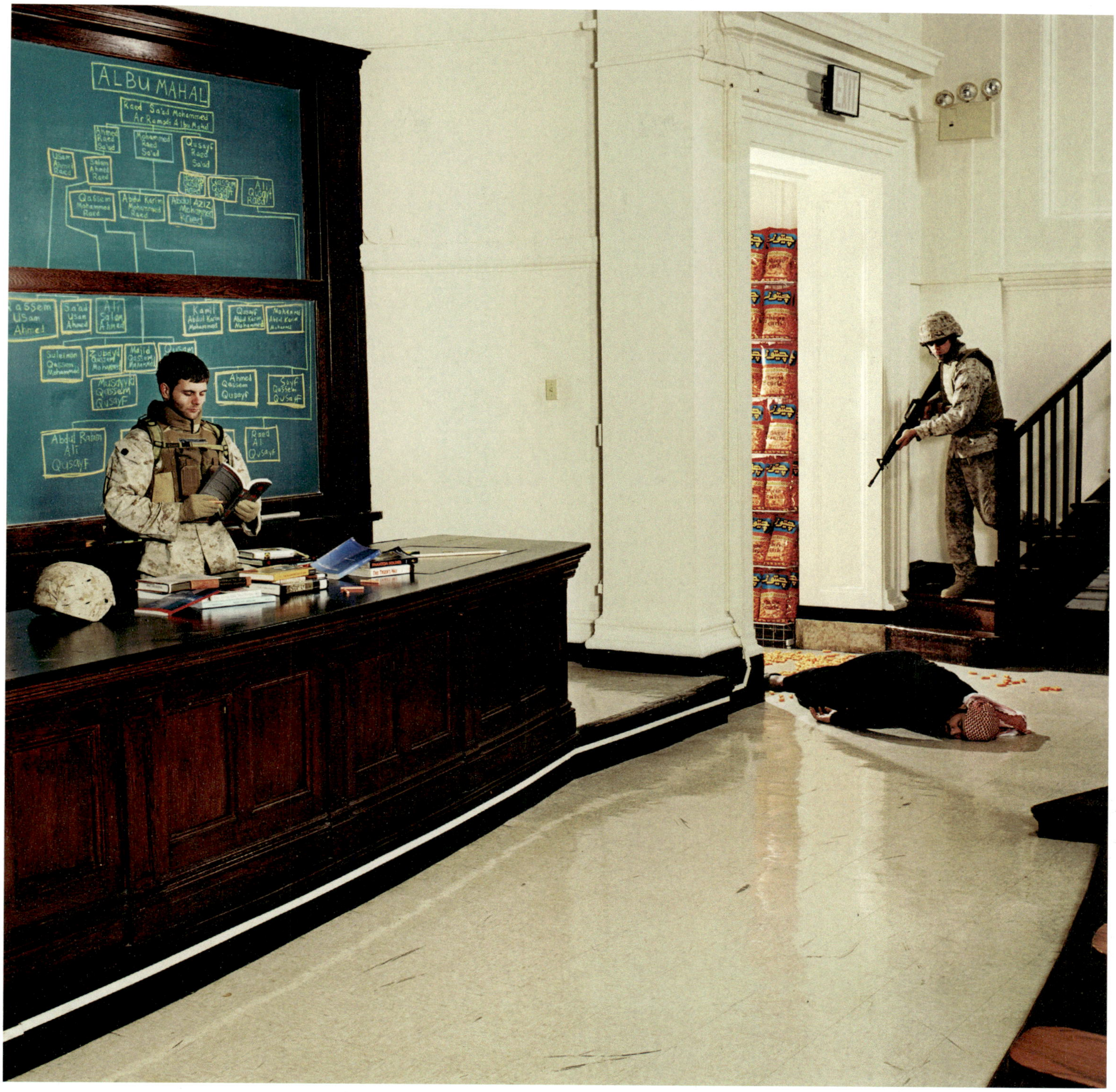

2

Former Sergeant Jason Lemieux, U.S. Marine Corps Infantry, 3/7 Lima Company, veteran of Operation Iraqi Freedom and member of Iraq Veterans Against the War; Columbia University, New York City USA, 2008

On April 17, 2004, Lima Company was in a twelve-hour firefight in Husaybah. Four marines in my platoon and our company commander were killed in the first half of the day, with more marines wounded. Shortly after the four marines in my platoon were killed, our lieutenant passed the word that the new rules of engagement [ROE] from Lieutenant Colonel Lopez were that any military-aged male wearing a black dishdashah and a red headdress, even if unarmed, was an enemy combatant and was to be shot on sight. The rationale for this was that the resistance fighters were wearing similar outfits, even though such outfits were common in Husaybah. Lima marines eagerly embraced the new ROEs and began shooting at anyone within eyesight wearing the aforementioned outfit.

I remember turning a corner and witnessing the marine in front of me raise his rifle at a civilian man who stepped out of a doorway. The man was wearing a black dishdashah and a red headdress. He was unarmed and appeared to be around 50 years old, with gray hair. I cannot remember the marine actually shooting the man. I have discussed this incident with a VA psychological counselor, and she informed me that it is possible my brain blocked the memory of the shooting because it was so traumatic. The next part of that incident I remember is stepping over the dead man's body to clear the room he came out of. The room was a small storage room full of an Arabic brand of cheesy puffs (like Cheetos). There were no weapons in the room, nor were there any weapons on or around the deceased man.

After this incident, I actually extended my contract by ten months to redeploy to Ramadi for my third tour. My agreement with my commanding officer for extending was that I was going to lead this little experimental intelligence section. This assignment allowed me to read all the intelligence reports that came in every day, from everywhere. There was one report of an army unit that got in a firefight with a bunch of insurgents somewhere in the middle of town. There was this local traffic cop who, according to the report, was apparently pro-American, and he was accidentally killed in the crossfire between the insurgents and the army. His family knew that he was pro-American and they generally leaned that way too, but the day he died, his brother and two cousins joined the insurgency.

Later I read about this sort of tribal culture where they're socially obligated to get revenge. When someone is killed, that's initiating a blood feud. You're socially obligated to get revenge and you would be stigmatized if you didn't. So this traffic cop was our friend, and by accidentally killing him we created three more enemies.

That was the first real proof that trying to win the way we are is mathematically impossible. We're trying to win by killing, and the simple math is that we're multiplying our enemies every time we kill someone.

That report talked about his whole family with the same last name, who was the son of whom, and who was pro-American and who was anti- American. So we made a flow chart of the whole family and we circled all their names in green, and then those three that were insurgents, we circled in orange. A couple of months later I got another report talking about the exact same family and almost every one of them was an insurgent. I just went through circling all of these names in orange. You just had this big flow chart on the wall and everything was orange.

Jason Lemieux is currently studying political science at Columbia University. Descriptions of the Husaybah firefight are from Jason Lemieux's testimony to the Congressional Progressive Caucus as part of the "Winter Soldier on the Hill," event in Washington, DC, where members of Iraq Veterans Against the War gave eyewitness accounts of their experiences in Iraq, May 15, 2008.

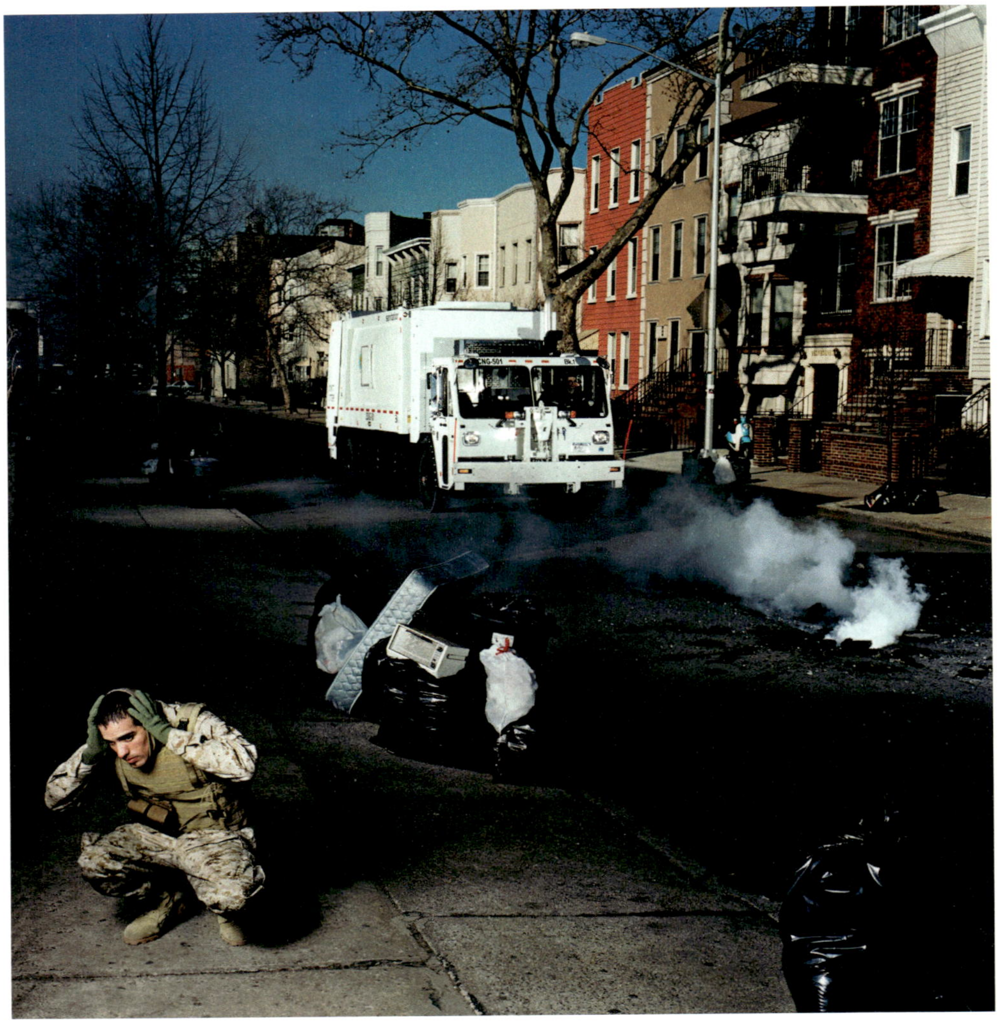

3

Former Sergeant Jose Adames, U.S. Marine Corps Recon, Stinger Gunner, 1st Platoon, Alpha Company,
Veteran of Operation Iraqi Freedom; Brooklyn, NY
USA, 2009

I got hit by a mortar while on a convoy, which was not a typical mission for us. Three pieces of shrapnel went through my leg. It pretty much swept me sideways, and I was knocked out cold. I was immediately helivacked over to Baghdad Hospital, and from there to Frankfurt, Germany. Eighteen marines in my platoon were wounded. When I heard the stat reports a couple of weeks later, I found out we were hit by 40 mortars and two machine gun assaults. It was in a canyon, so there was no way to go forward or back. When mortars are coming in, it's pretty much hard to cover yourself from that. That's the scariest thing I've ever been through. That's the bad part; I'll never forget it.

I am terrified of trucks, garbage trucks in particular, and it has to do with the fact that New York has so many potholes. When they hit one they make this deep echoing sound that sounds similar to a mortar exploding. I see a dump truck rolling down the street and I just try to go to the other end as fast as possible. I black out, not in a bad way. I just tune out. Everything gets dark, and these images keep fluttering through my mind of the night we got hit. It just replays in my mind.

When I returned I was homeless for a total of five months. I spent two months in a shelter and I couldn't take it. It was just this thin line of frustration, and then my PTSD wasn't helping. So I really needed to come up with other ideas. I was stuck in a vicious circle from boarding house to a shelter at Bellevue. It was ridiculous what they did to me. I had a better chance sleeping on the A train. I felt more comfortable, actually. In New York, 85 percent of the homeless are veterans. I see a lot of veterans feeling very, very angry.

Jose Adames works with homeless veterans at Black Veterans for Social Justice in Brooklyn, NY, and is studying accounting at Long Island University.

4

Former Staff Sergeant Starlyn Lara, C Detachment, 38th Personnel Services Battalion, 1st Infantry Division, U.S. Army, veteran of Operation Iraqi Freedom; Treasure Island, San Francisco, CA
USA, 2010

We were in a convoy between my camp at Kirkush Military Training Base and Camp Anaconda in Balad, which is where everything happens—that's the hub. At the time I was the FOO [field ordering officer] and I was responsible for all of the money that came in and out of the installa- tion. I would convoy very frequently in order to transport money—like $100,000 in cash—under my vest.

I was in a Humvee, but our unit isn't a tactical unit, so we didn't have armored Humvees. What we had were Kevlar plates that lined the seats but not the vehicle. They were designed to keep you from dying but not designed to protect you. When the bomb went off, it actually shot pieces of the engine up. I was in the passenger seat.

As soon as the vehicle exploded, my first thoughts were about the safety of the money. Then there was just all this blood, and I didn't know where it was coming from. My ears were ringing from this huge concussion blast. I couldn't hear, and my vision was blurred. And so many things were happening. I couldn't make out the sounds around me—I was disoriented. I was looking... the windows were shattered and my arms were cut, I was bleeding, and I just couldn't figure out where all of the blood was coming from. It seemed like forever but it probably took place in the blink of an eye.

There are many things that connect me back to that moment. It's usually only when I can't sleep or when I am sleeping. I had a really weird dream that I was chasing a pink rabbit. I was trying to catch the damn pink rabbit and it was huge. I think it's funny—I'm laughing in the dream, going, "I can't believe this pink bunny!" And then, the pink bunny runs into the street, and I'm wondering, "Why is the pink bunny in the street?" And I stop, and the pink bunny gets hit by my Humvee. I see myself in the vehicle and I realize that the pink bunny is the bomb.

So sometimes my dreams aren't necessarily reliving the experience. They're some kind of distortion, how I find ways to cope with the things that are really uncopable. There's really no easy way to get around them.

Starlyn Lara currently works as a human resources/accounts payable assistant at Swords to Plowshares, a nonprofit veterans organization that provides numerous services for veterans in need, and as a part-time emergency medical technician.

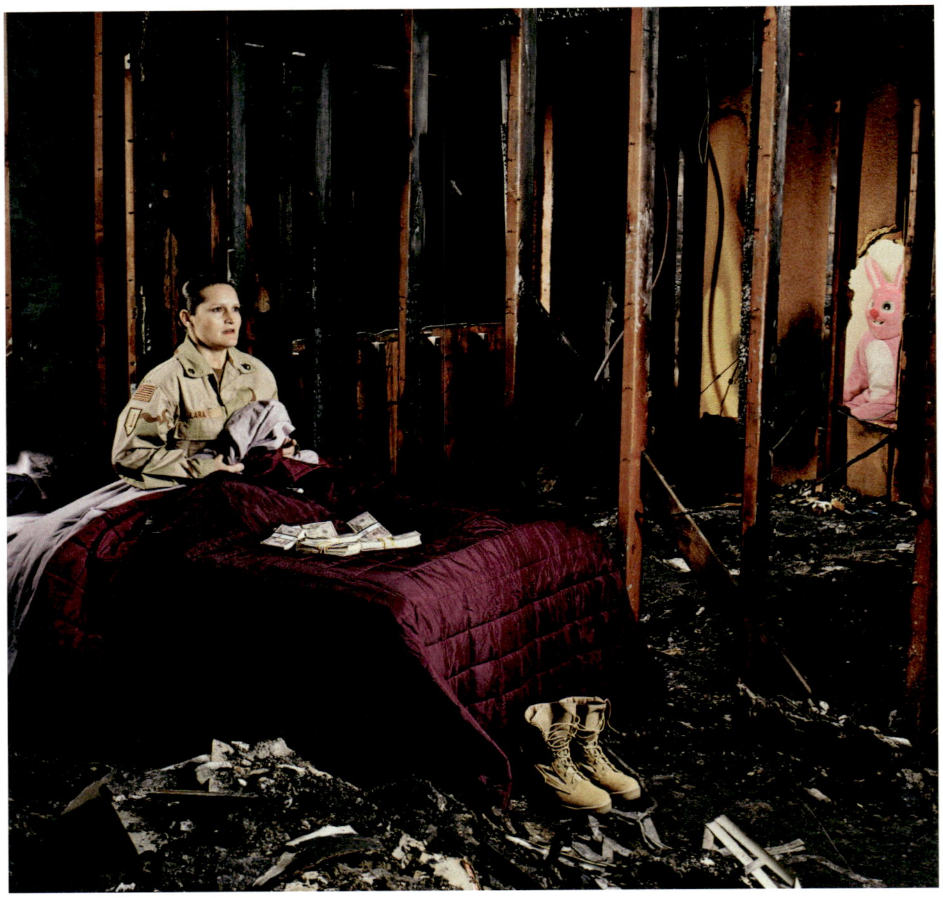

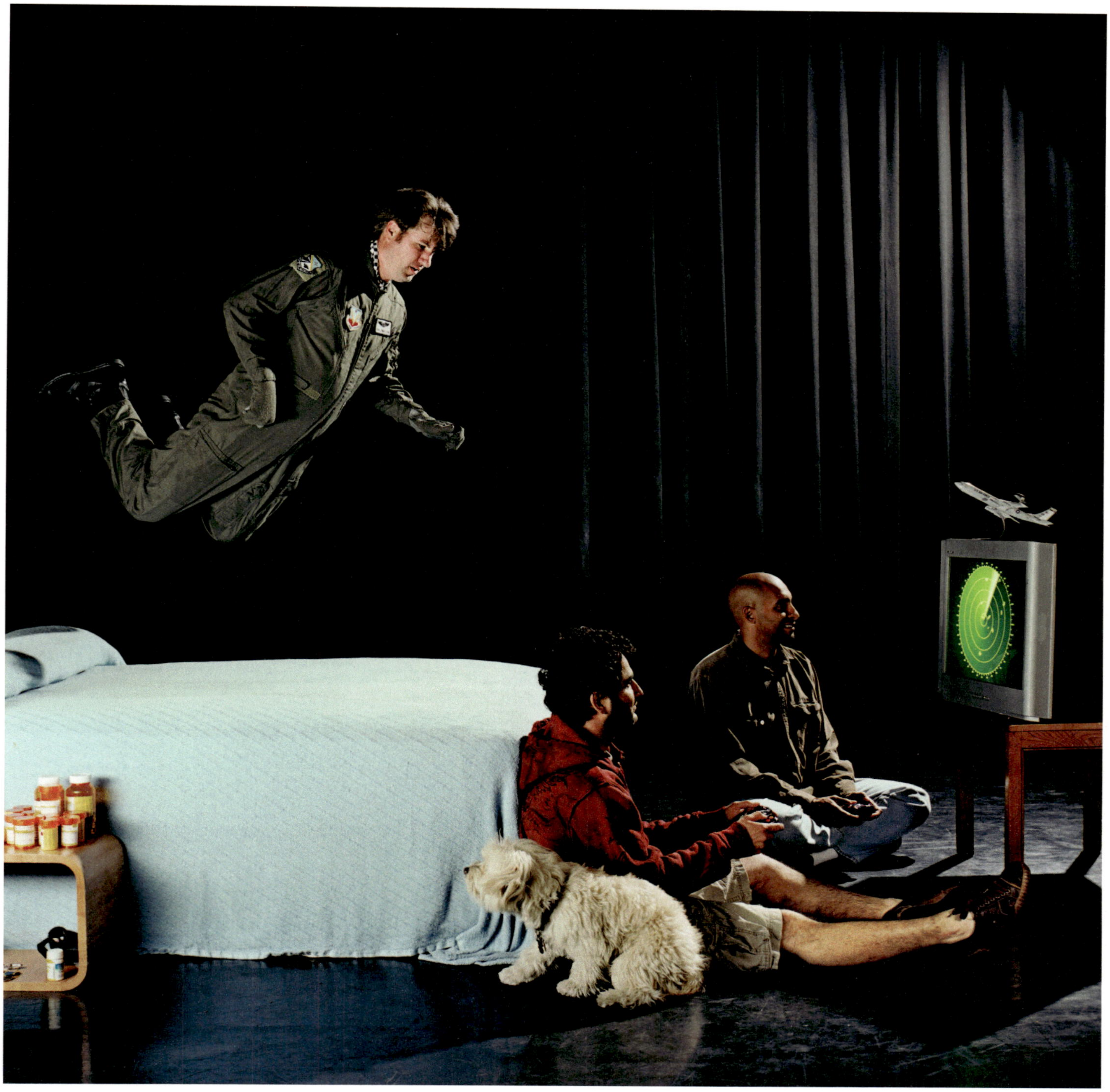

5
Former Senior Airman John Tingley, U.S. Air Force, airborne radar technician/firefighter for AWACS, veteran of Operation Enduring Freedom and Operation Iraqi Freedom, with Manuel and Sid; Highways Theater, Santa Monica, CA
USA, 2008

I was an airborne radar technician/firefighter. I ran the radar on the Airborne Warning and Control System (AWACS). It's a secret, so I'm not going to tell the specifics, but the AWACS can see a certain range around the aircraft. If we see on the radar that there's a little camp of bad guys over here, then we call up the good guys and say, "Hey, there's some bad guys over here, go take care of it." So they fly over, drop some bombs, kill everybody, and then fly off. So we were the first ones there, the last ones out, and we were always one of the main targets, because we basically ran the war from the aircraft.

A lot of people say, "You can't have PTSD [posttraumatic stress disorder], because you were in the Air Force." I think to myself, "Are you kidding me?" First of all, flying is in itself inherently dangerous. We were shot at all the time; we had missiles launched at us. We had to drop from 30,000 feet to 10,000 feet without any warning. I was the only guy standing up because I needed to be able to walk around the jet while everyone else was sitting in their seats strapped in. When you have to drop suddenly, the pilot doesn't have time to let you know he's dropping. I hit my head on the top of the plane, landed in somebody's lap, and almost broke my arm on a chair. It was rough. That's how they think I got my TBI [traumatic brain injury].

Once on a night combat mission a buddy of mine says, "Hey man, you've got to check this out." I walk up to the flight deck (there are no windows in the back of the AWACS), and he hands me some night vision goggles. I look out the window and it was like a laser light show, and I'm like, "Hey, what's that?" I thought it was really cool looking. He said, "That's the enemy shooting at us." I went to the back of the jet and I never went up front again, not once.

For me, that was the first time I realized that every single time we went up, we were in danger of being shot. I haven't been able to put on night vision goggles since and I can't play video games where you have to switch to night vision.

Here at the VA, we have a support group for OEF/OIF [Operation Enduring Freedom/Operation Iraqi Freedom] soldiers to talk about the stuff that you dealt with. Last week, the topic was how you were able to integrate back into society after you got out. I told them that I wasn't sure if it was really happening because it felt so bizarre to me. Even a simple thing like taking a trip to the store and being around society in general—around people doing normal things again—I just wasn't positive if it was real or not. Somebody coming up and hugging your mom, saying hi, or something felt like it was way over here and it's right next to you. It's hard to describe, but that's what it felt like. It felt like I wasn't there. Like I was in a dream when, you know, you're outside of the dream, so you can watch yourself.

Karady met John at the Highways Theater in Santa Monica, CA, where he and other veterans residing in the "Dom" (Domiciliary) were participating in a performance. The Dom is a residential rehabilitation treatment program on the West Los Angeles VA campus that provides comprehensive healthcare in a therapeutic environment and aims to prepare veterans for reentry into the community.

IÑIGO MANGLANO-OVALLE

1

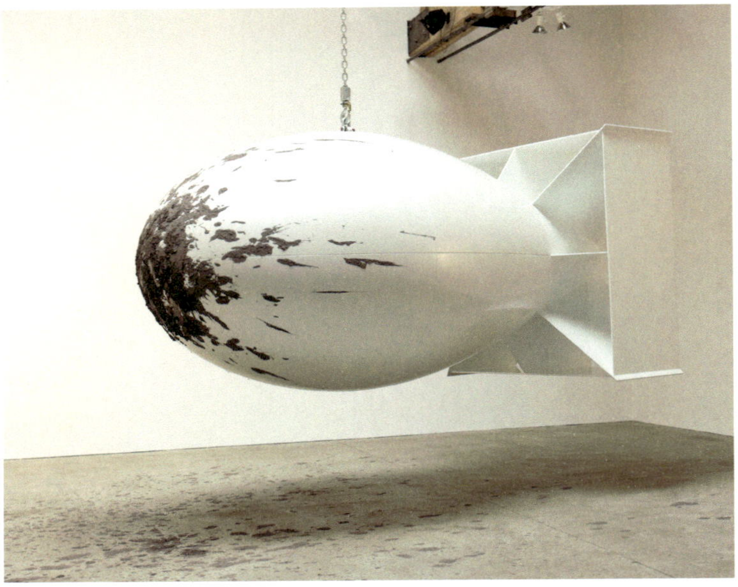

1
Dirty Bomb
2008
Installation view
2
Phantom Truck
2007, Installation view, Commissioned for documenta 12
Photo by Barbara Sax/AFT/Getty Images
3
The Garden of Delights
1997, Installation view

Iñigo Manglano-Ovalle (* 1961) believes that making apolitical art is a political statement. He uses minimalist aesthetics and formal values—infused with personal and political significance—as vehicles to challenge art history, modernist principles, and dominant social structures. Manglano-Ovalle has a complicated relationship with modernism. Although he was inspired by minimalist forms and the spare use of materials, in particular the architecture of Mies van der Rohe, he is troubled by the classist and elitist ideologies that lie within modernism. In his first work dealing with Mies van der Rohe, *Le Baiser/The Kiss,* 1999, the artist projects a video of himself cleaning Farnsworth House, Van der Rohe's legendary glass house, which is located in Plano, Illinois. The artist, who is dressed in a worker's jumpsuit, stands outside the house washing the windows with soap, water, and a squeegee. Inside the house, a woman stands behind some audio equipment mixing music. However, the music can only be heard when the camera is inside the building. The artist is pointing out that when dealing with modernity, not everyone is invited to the party.

The artist is the product of a multicultural home and upbringing. Born in Madrid to a Spanish father and Colombian mother, he lived between Madrid and Bogotá until his family moved to Chicago. It was as a child in Madrid that his paternal uncle used a Spanish colonial castas painting to illustrate Manglano-Ovalle's racial classification. *Pinturas de castas* or caste paintings, is an eighteenth-century genre of paintings, which were commissioned by the Spanish crown in order to categorize the racial miscegenation as it was labeled at the time—Spanish, Indian, and Negro—when these different races inhabiting the New World began to breed. These artistic renderings are in effect a taxonomic chart depicting the race of a man, woman, and child, each clearly labeled in the painting. The combination of Spaniard and Indian woman produce a mestizo as an offspring. This experience made the artist keenly aware of the labels applied to minorities by those in power and prompted a career that explores issues of race and identity as in his series of genetic portraits titled, *The Garden of Delights.*

Manglano-Ovalle's practice is the product of intense research into a specific subject, and the reapplication of technology for a nonutilitarian purpose. In the case of *The Garden of Delights,* he used genetic technology that produces abstract organic forms to create DNA portraits of friends and family. In *Nocturne (White Poppies),* 2002, the artist employs a state-of-the-art night vision camera to capture an image of the white poppy cultivated for heroin production in Afghanistan. The flower that finances terrorist groups and Muslim extremists in a protracted war against the United States, sits in a darkened room. Its image is captured by the night-vision camera and projected onto a wall in the room. The blurry, pixilated image resembles the television footage of the first Gulf War in 1990–1991. The light from the projection illuminates the flower, making it possible for the image to be captured; the camera cannot work in absolute darkness. This light is recycled from illuminating the poppy into the camera and when it is projected onto the wall, serves as a metaphor for the ongoing war and international drug trade that fuels it. The consumption of drugs in the United States finances the insurgency, extending the war as well as the endless demand for weapons.

In 2007 for documenta 12, Manglano-Ovalle presented *Phantom Truck.* This work is a response to Colin Powell's address to the United Nations Security Council in February 2003, which was intended to justify the invasion of Iraq by U.S. military forces. Powell, armed with grainy photographs of the alleged mobile units stationed across Iraq fabricating weapons of mass destruction, was able to substantiate the attack on Iraq. However, the mobile units were never found, and furthermore it was later proven that the information given to Powell was false. For documenta 12, a scale model of the infamous truck was hidden within a building in the city of Kassel, Germany. Unlike most artists' works which were listed on maps, and had signage directing visitors to the art projects, the phantom truck was truly hidden; visitors had to find it for themselves.

2

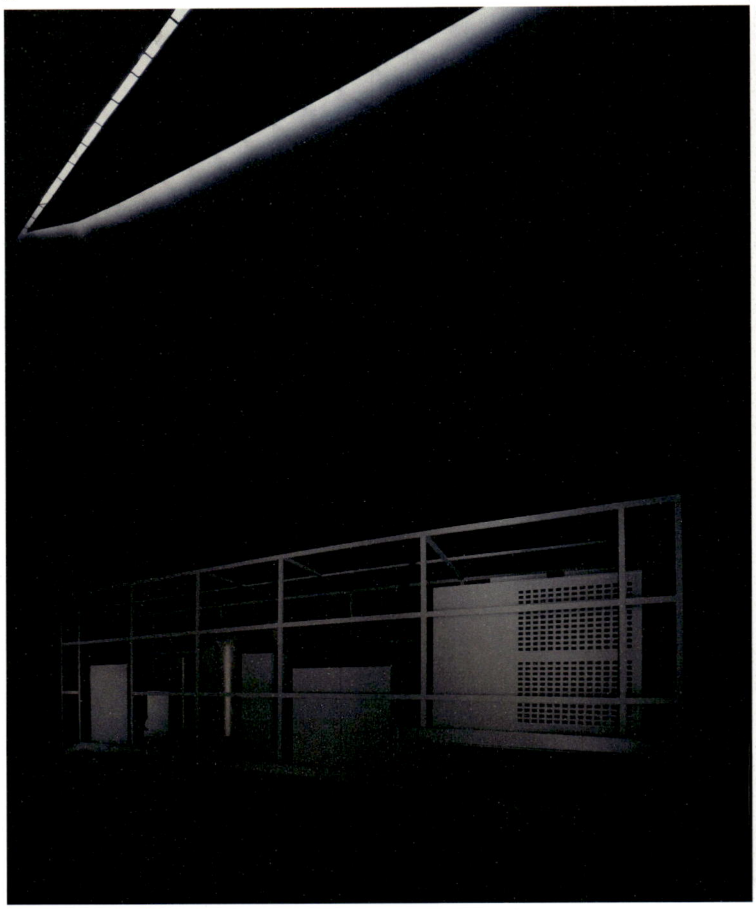

3

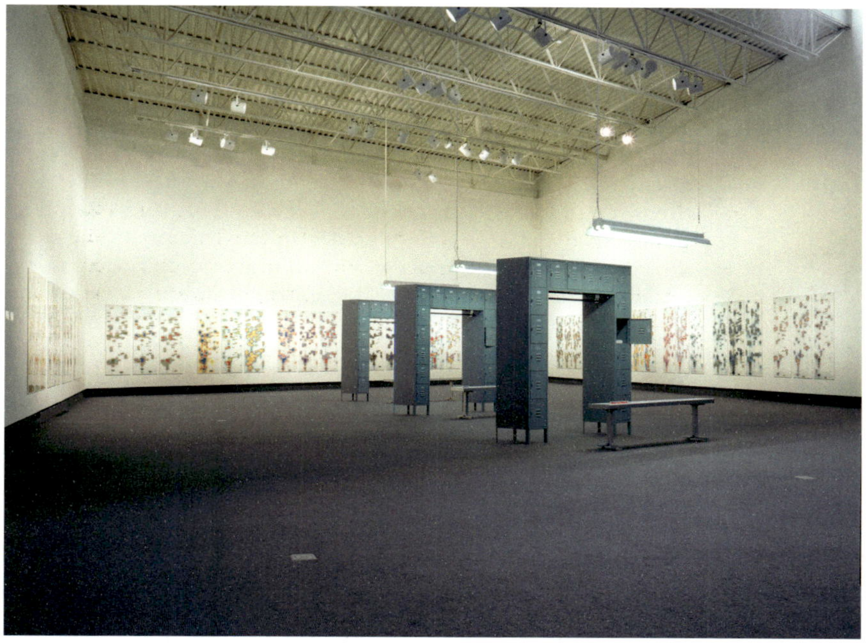

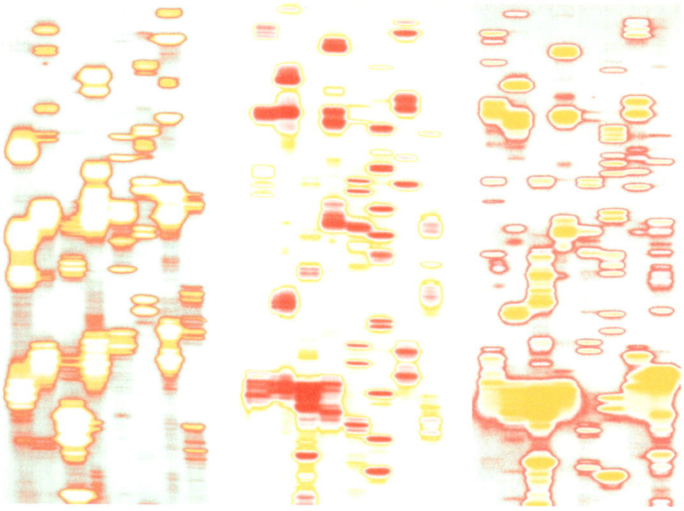

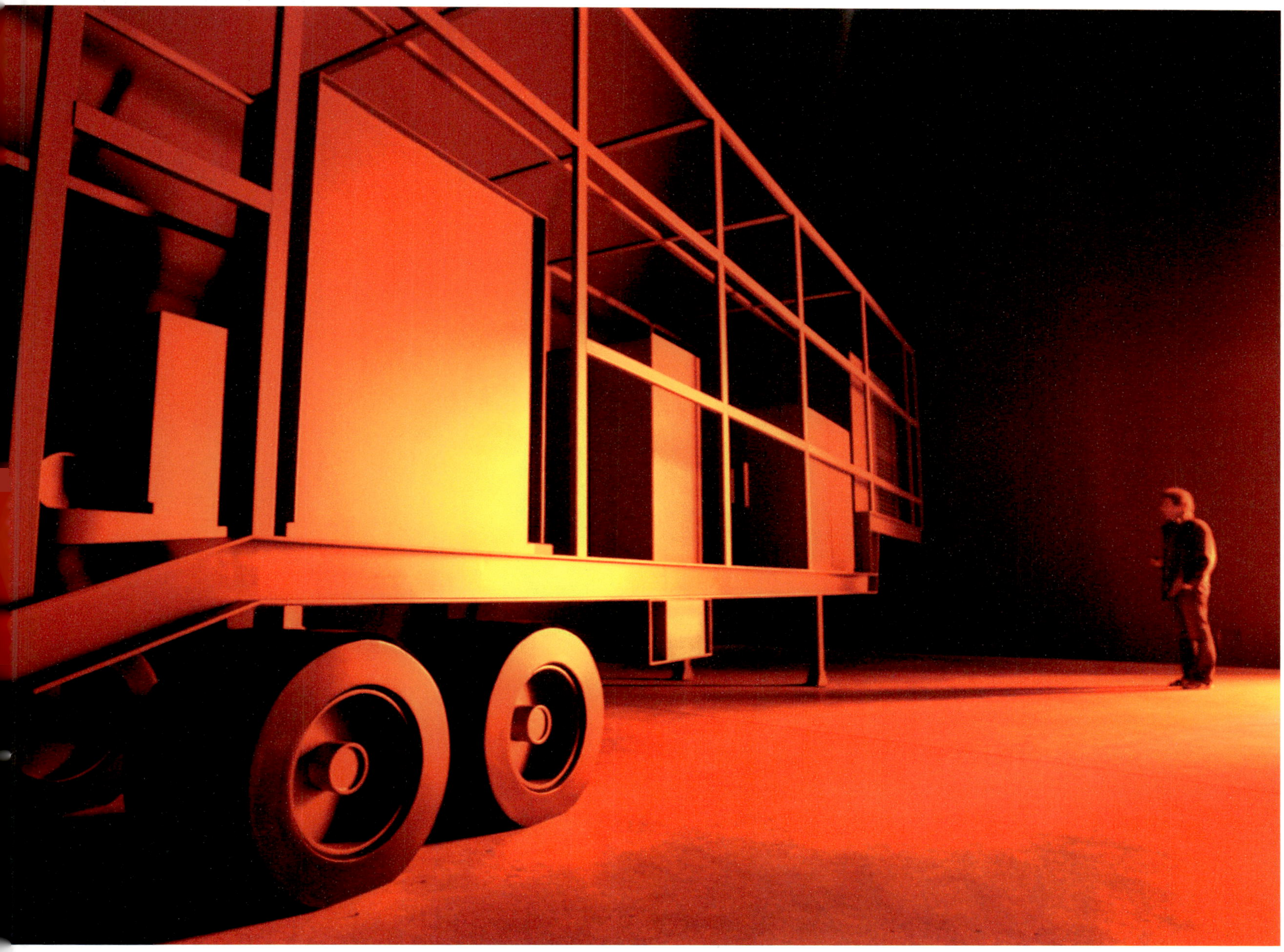

HANK WILLIS THOMAS

1

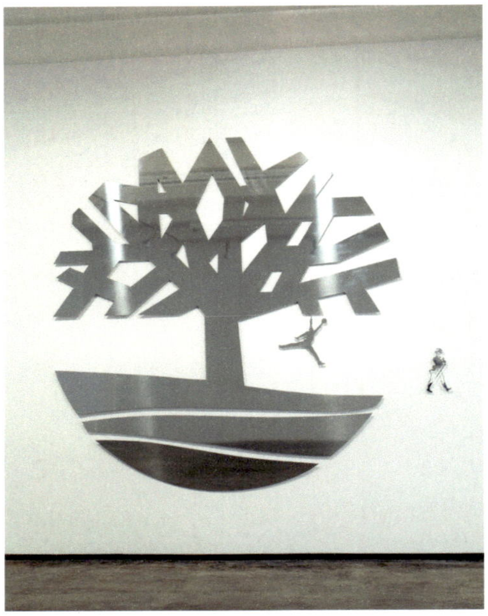

1
Jordan and Johnny Walker in Timberland Circa 1923
2009, Polished aluminum
2
Black Is Beautiful
2009, Installation view, Roberts & Tilton, Los Angeles, USA, Archival Inkjet print on adhesive paper
3
Afro-American Express
2004
4
The Chase MasterCard
2004, Mixed-media
Made in collaboration with Ryan Alexiev

Courtesy the artist and Jack Shainman Gallery, New York

The African-American role model is African-American artist Hank Willis Thomas's (* 1976) central theme. The artist states that his art is motivated by the murder of his 27-year-old cousin, best friend, and housemate, Songha Willis, in the year 2000: "Almost all of my work of maturity came after my cousin was murdered, and after years of trying to find out creative ways to talk about issues that were related to that for myself." He attempts to come to terms with, and do justice to, this tragic event in very personal, very complex artworks. His photographic series *Winter in America,* 2006, is particularly impressive. In collaboration with Kambui Olujimi, Thomas used the GI Joe figures he had played with as a child to recreate the event. After all, for the artist, the death of his cousin also represented the end of their shared childhood. At the same time, using the toy figures is the artist's way of highlighting the absurdity of this senseless act. Two dark-skinned youths shot Songha to steal a gold chain necklace—which Songha was not even wearing. In hip-hop culture, socially disadvantaged young people of color are particularly strongly influenced by status symbols and the branding culture. Under the motto "Get Rich or Die Trying," they try to realize their version of the American Dream, resulting in a high potential for violence in the black community. Thomas presents this situation in his now-legendary artwork *Priceless,* 2004. Through referencing the well-known advertising campaign by MasterCard, he shows us a photograph of the grieving family at his cousin's funeral, with the price of the father's suit and socks, the value of the nonexistent gold chain, the cost of the weapon, and the type of ammunition written above the MasterCard logo. Below the list of items and their cost are the words: "Picking the Perfect Casket for Your Son: Priceless." This work is part of the *Branded* series, in which Thomas examines the image of African-Americans in advertising, by placing logos in new contexts. In another series entitled *Unbranded,* he removes logos. Several of his artworks also feature the Timberland brand label transformed into the biblical tree of knowledge. Michael Jordan, the quintessential African-American advertising icon, is leaping up to its branches as if they were a basketball hoop, perhaps reaching for the fruit of knowledge. This picture shows the fine, dark humor that shines through in all Thomas's works despite his bitter and difficult subject matter. The observer is invited to a position of self-conscious reflection by being reflected in the tree. Thomas's monograph was published in 2009 and was awarded the Aperture West Book Prize. The book was entitled (like several of his artworks) *Pitch Blackness,* partly because of the way he had to recover his sense of purpose after the death of his cousin, and partly because advertising and its representations of black males are among his most important themes. The artist once explained that: "Blackness is pitched as a way to cash in on street cool, or urban icon—this idea of cool, hip blackness. Lastly, pitch blackness as in, 'pitch blackness, off-whiteness, coffee is the colour of my skin,' which is to say although I will always be black, maybe at some point, in some part of my evolution, I have to get rid of this idea of blackness to really get to my humanity. We have this definition, especially in America, this conversation of White vs. Black. [...] There are all these connotations in our language that kind of imply whiteness is good, blackness is bad, but there are black people who are your complexion, and there's all these kinds of things about blackness that don't describe a single black person, since there are no black people. And there's nothing to describe a white person."

2

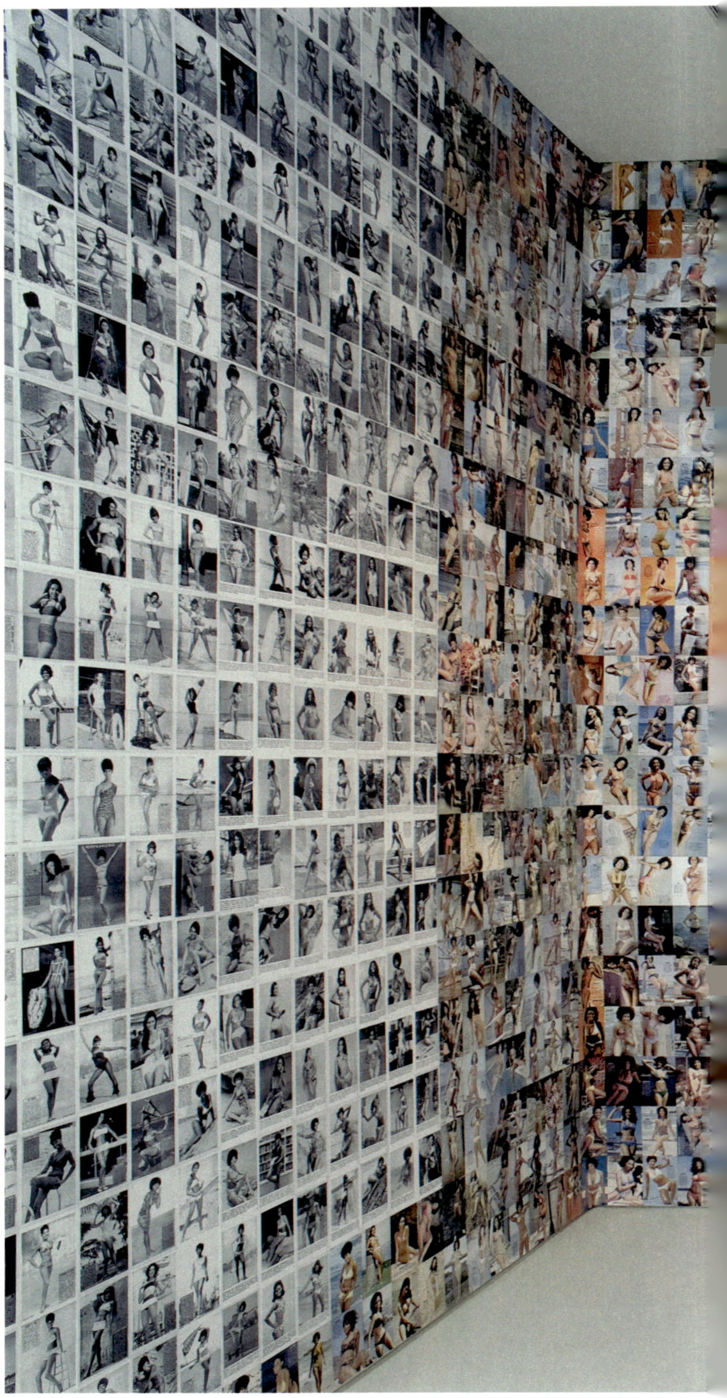

3

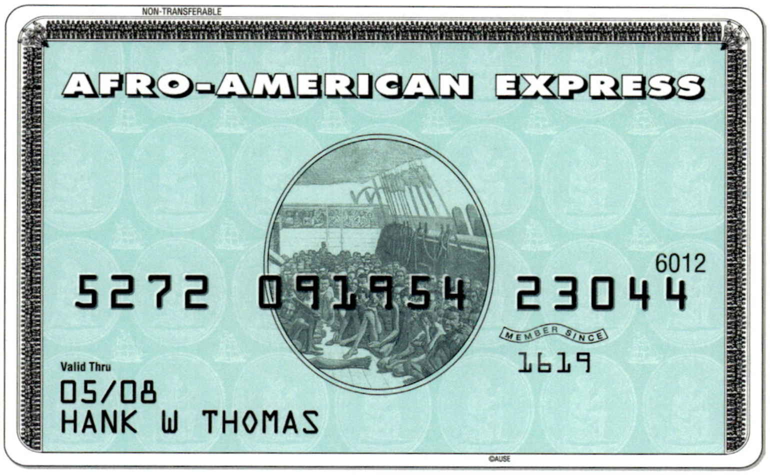
NON-TRANSFERABLE
AFRO-AMERICAN EXPRESS
6012
5272 091954 23044
MEMBER SINCE
1619
Valid Thru
05/08
HANK W THOMAS

4

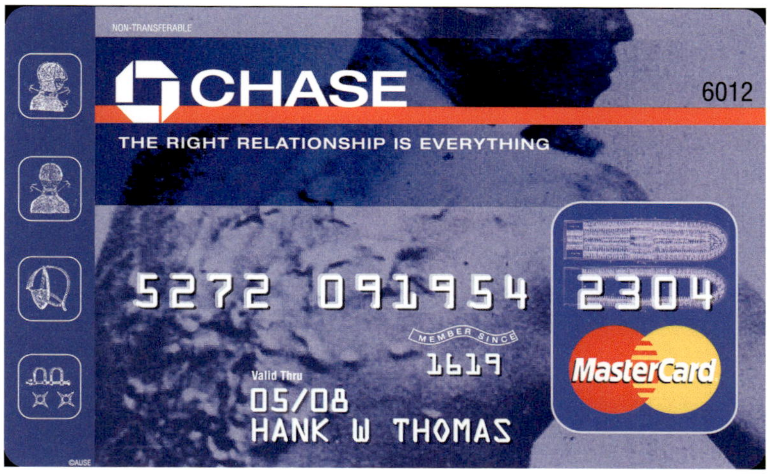
NON-TRANSFERABLE
CHASE
6012
THE RIGHT RELATIONSHIP IS EVERYTHING
5272 091954 2304
MEMBER SINCE
1619
Valid Thru
05/08
HANK W THOMAS
MasterCard

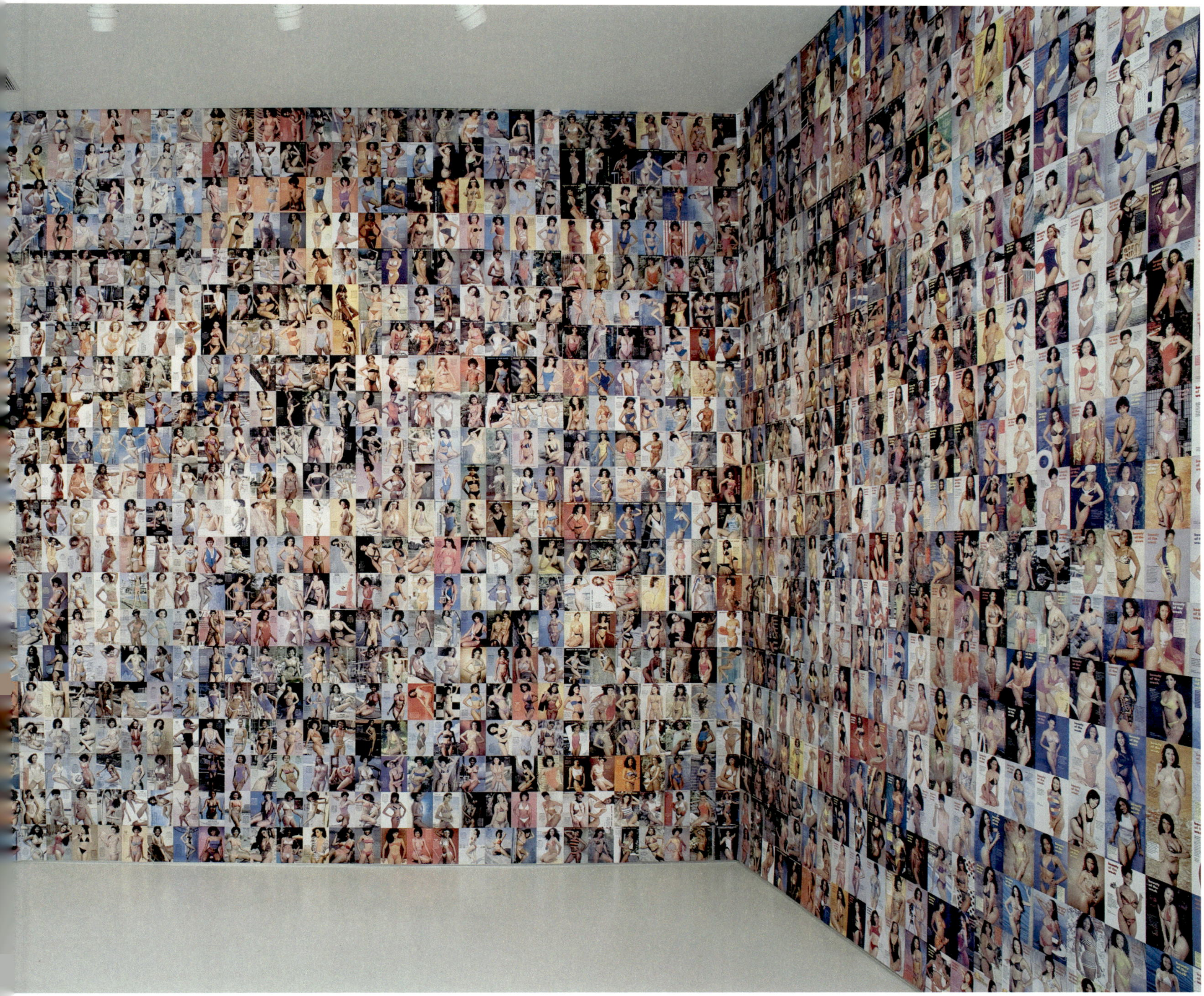

SAM DURANT

In drawing from various periods in the history of the United States, Sam Durant (* 1961) questions how collective memories and historical inaccuracies are formed. His work is based on a process of intense historical investigation, collecting information that is then used to address social and racial inequality. Durant employs conceptual strategies to deal with politically charged issues that are present today. He uses history as a means for us to look back as a society and understand where we are now. The artist states that: "History is always and only taking place in the present; we are trying to get a sense of it at any given moment." Durant uses a variety of mediums and formal strategies to address difficult issues. He sees no separation between politics and form in art. For Durant, biographical elements are scattered throughout his work. Growing up near Plymouth Rock, Massachusetts in the 1960s, he attended anti-Vietnam War rallies. The rhetoric of the revolution, and the attitude of the counter culture inspired an interest in the use of language and hand-painted protest signs, as well as a profound interest in the Black Panthers and other revolutionaries.

Durant engages history by looking at the other side or at both sides of the story. His version of history is similar to that of the late Howard Zinn's, where the official narrative as told by the conqueror is compared to the less-flattering history of the conquered. In *Pilgrims and Indians, Planting and Reaping, Learning and Teaching,* 2006, the artist used a didactic strategy common in historical museums to tell the story. Durant bisected a circular spinning platform, and placed two scenes back-to-back, using wax figures from the now-closed historical museum in Plymouth Rock. One side of the platform tells the favored story of the reason for the beloved American holiday, Thanksgiving, in which the friendly Indian teaches the Pilgrims how to grow corn in the new world by planting the seed with a fish in order to fertilize the crop. The collaboration and resulting abundance of crops leads to the now famous yearly feast. The dark side of the story depicts Myles Standish standing over a prostrate Pequot Indian with a knife in the Indian's chest. In this alternative view, Durant is suggesting that Thanksgiving may have been instated by the governor of the settlement to celebrate the eradication of the hostile Pequot Nation. Ample evidence supports both narratives, although only one possibility has official support.

The binary model of the conquering white man versus the conquered Indian presented the possibility of Thanksgiving as a day of mourning. The Indian as victim surfaces again in the work dealing with western expansion, titled *Proposal for White and Indian Dead Monuments Transposition, Washington DC,* 2005, the white settlers in this work are victims alongside the Native American. Durant proposes moving the monuments commemorating Indian and white massacres to the Mall in Washington DC This work, composed of replicas of the monuments, addresses the fact that poor whites were used to settle and take over Indian territories, and provoke a war for land and resources. The poor settlers were used as cannon fodder for expansion. In this situation both sides were victimized. In this work, Durant once again presents a nuanced account of the situation.

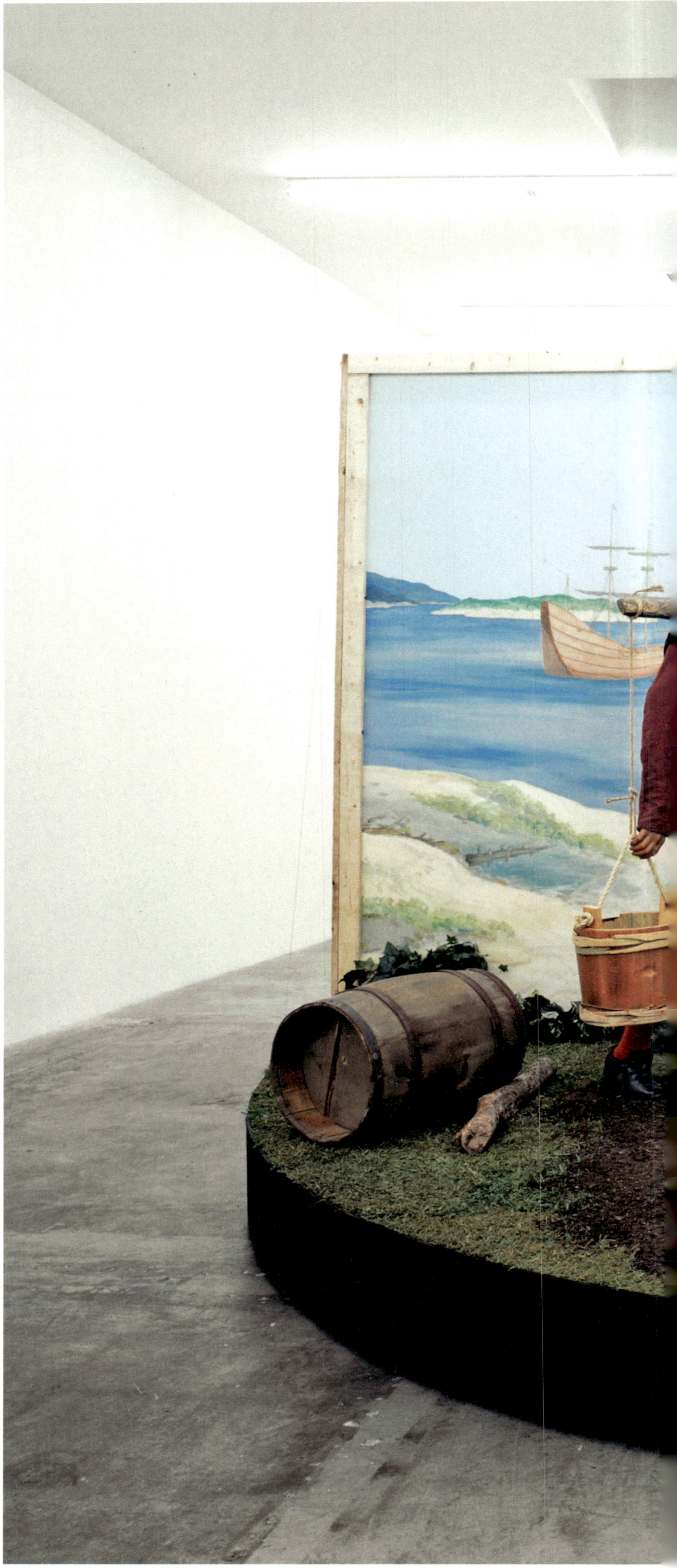

1
Pilgrims and Indians, Planting and Reaping, Learning and Teaching
2006, Mixed-media, motorized platform
Courtesy the artist and Blum & Poe, Los Angeles
Photo by Joshua White

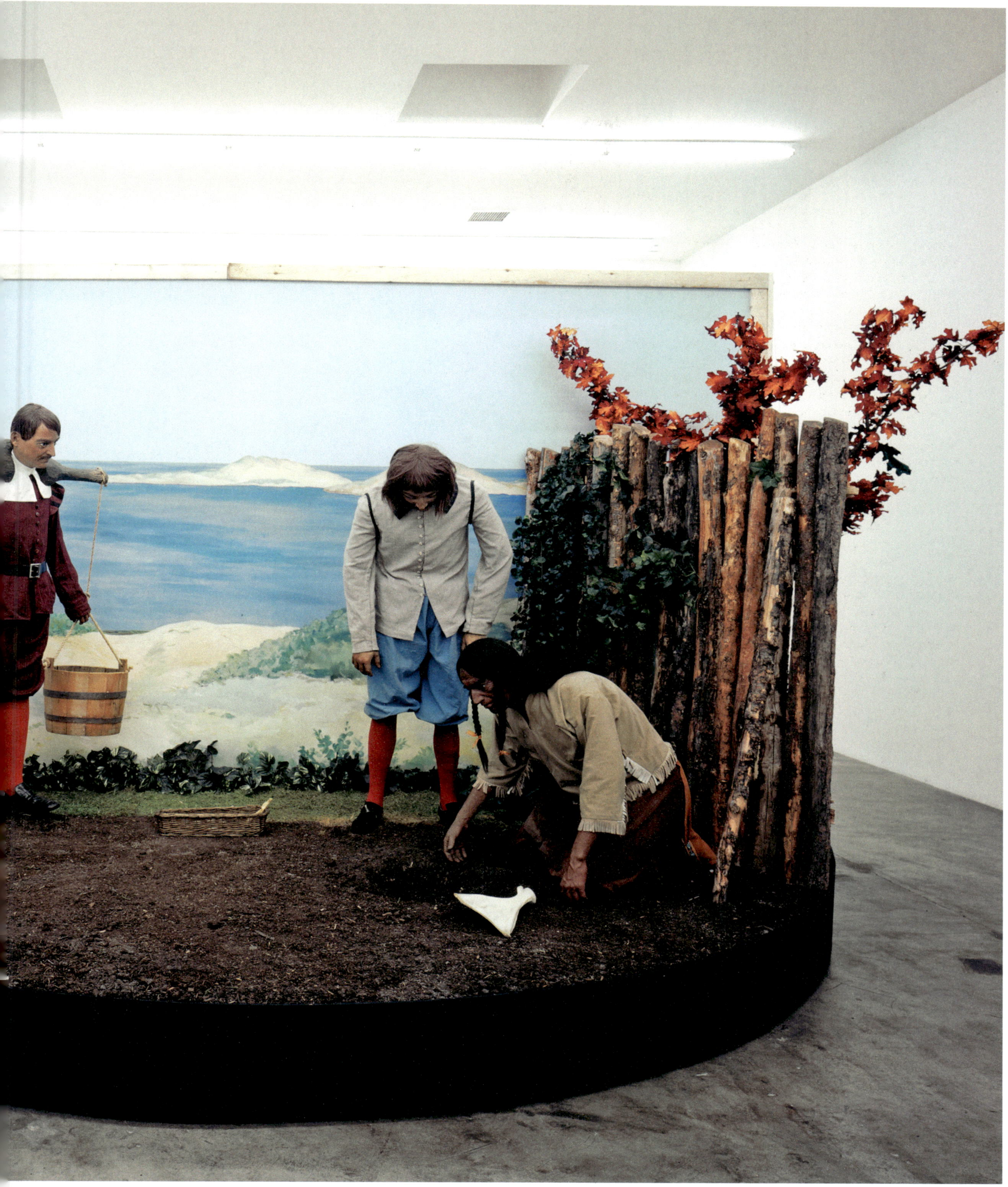

4

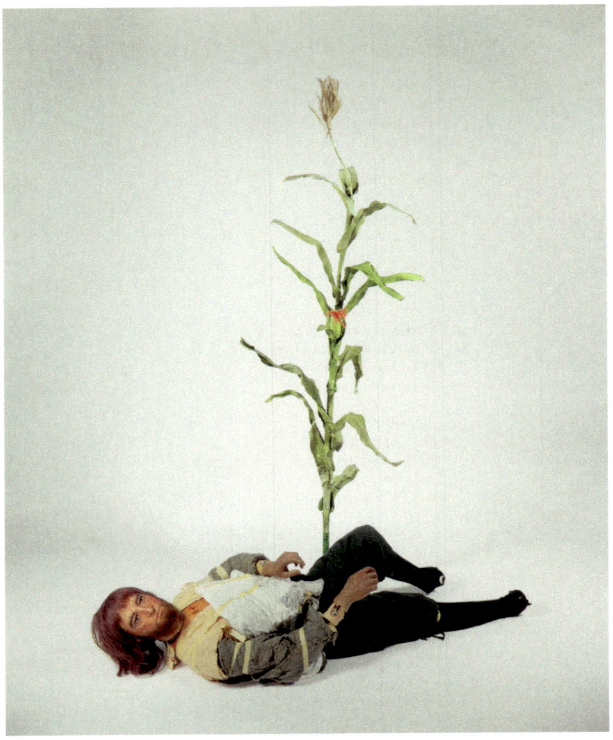

2

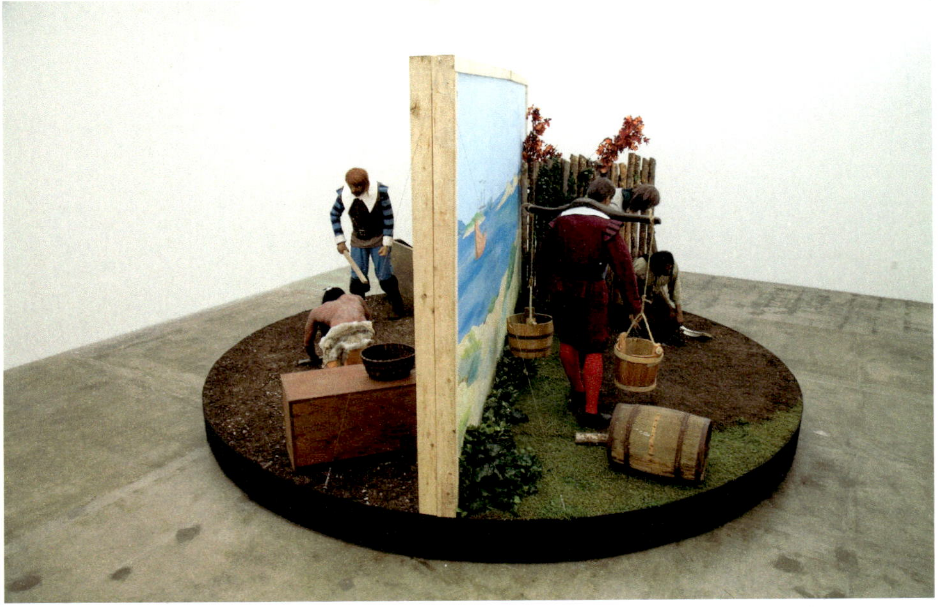

3

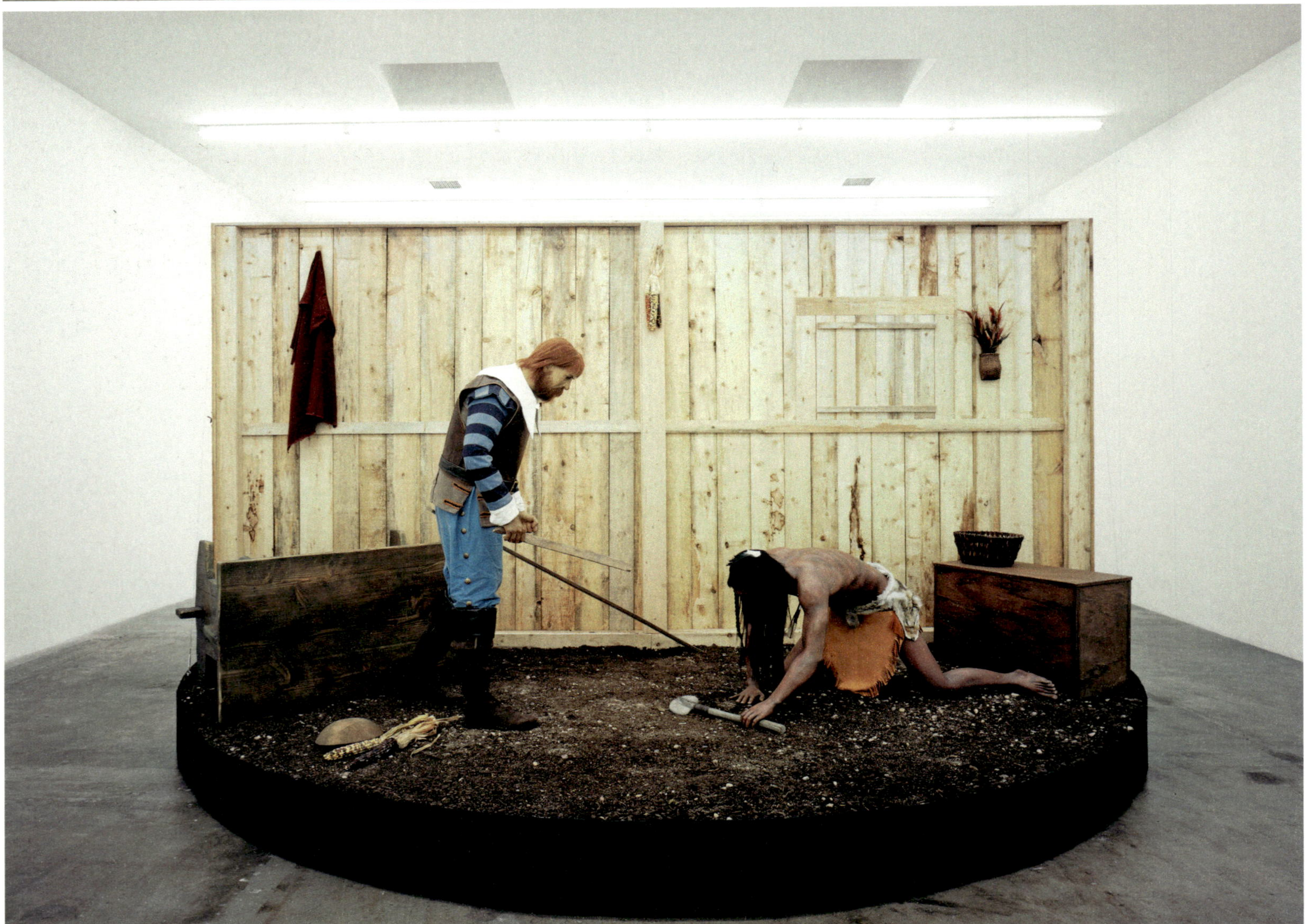

SAM DURANT

2 & 3
Pilgrims and Indians, Planting and Reaping, Learning and Teaching
2006, Mixed-media, motorized platform
Courtesy the artist and Blum & Poe, Los Angeles
Photo by Joshua White

4
Male Colonist (With Cornstalk)
2006, © Sam Durant, Courtesy Paula Cooper Gallery, New York

5
White Mirrors
2006, Inkjet print, 42×36 in., Courtesy the artist and Blum & Poe, Los Angeles
Photo by Joshua White

6
Forefather's Rock
2006, Inkjet print, 42×36 in.
Courtesy the artist and Blum & Poe, Los Angeles
Photo by Joshua White

7
Proposal for White and Indian Dead Monuments Transposition
Installation view, © Sam Durant, Courtesy Paula Cooper Gallery, New York

8
End White Supremacy
2008, Electric sign with vinyl text, © Sam Durant, Courtesy Paula Cooper Gallery, New York

7
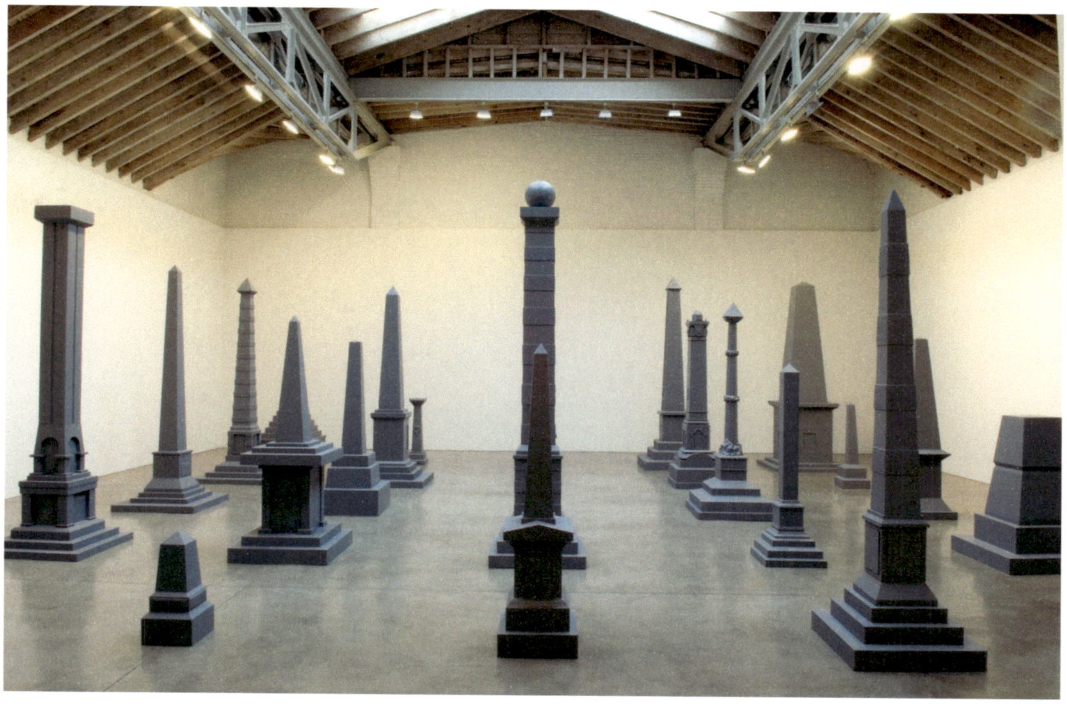

8
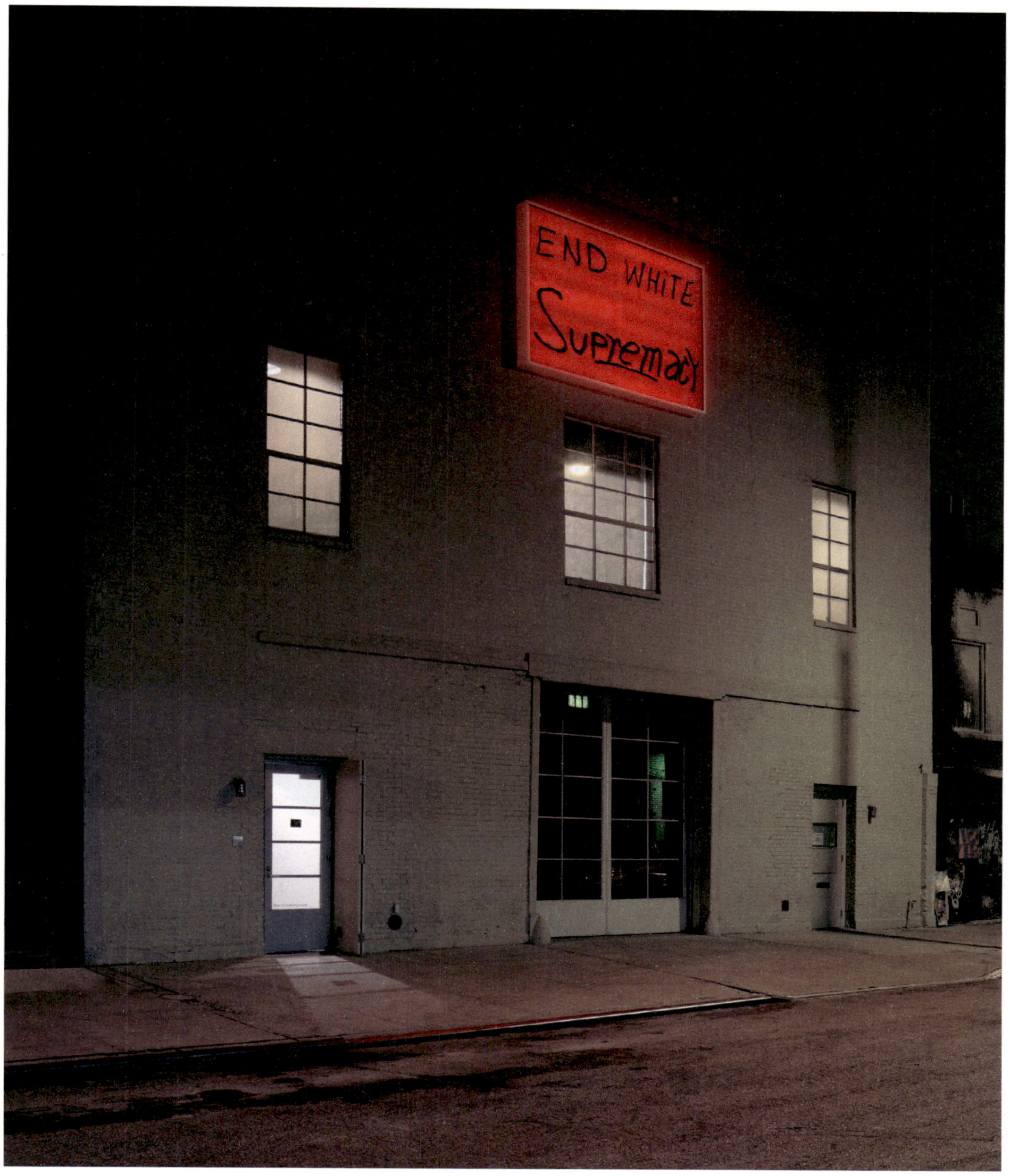

5
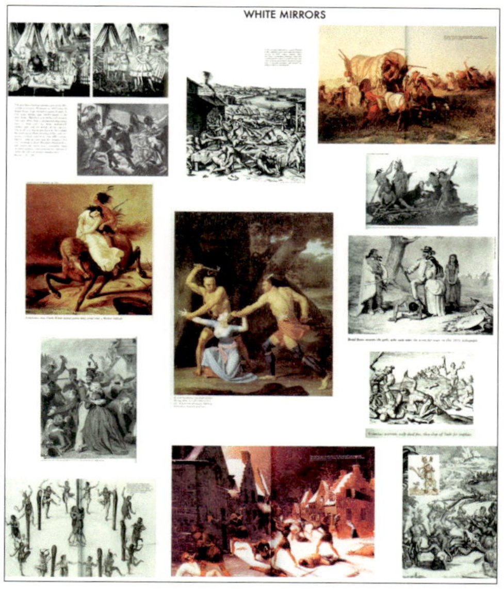

6
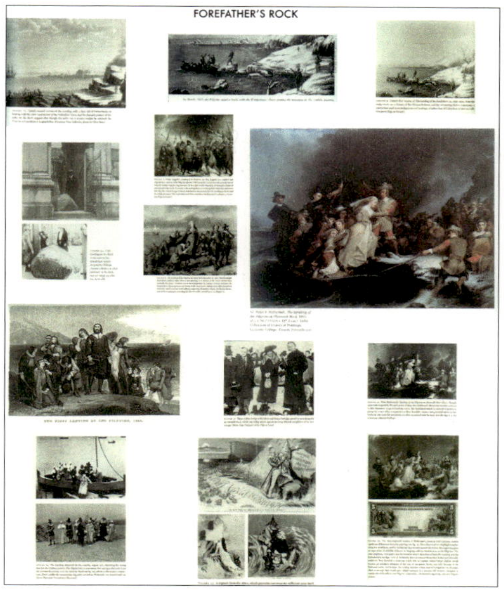

WILLIAM KENTRIDGE

The South African artist William Kentridge (* 1955) dives deeply into specific themes as an integral part of his process. Tremendous research and investigation go into the multiple layers of production and mediums he uses to address the contradictions, moral ambiguity, and disillusionment of a broken political system. His early work is deeply rooted in his native South Africa, the atrocities committed there, and the feeling of entrapment of living under those conditions. Kentridge has spent most of his life living and working in South Africa. The statement by the South African Prime Minister, B.J. Vorster, who in 1969 while defending the reasoning behind Apartheid, serves to illustrate the absurdities the artist was faced with: "The policy of separate development is not intended and must not be seen as a denial of anyone's human dignity. It is aimed at protecting the whites." Kentridge's later body of work continues to engage the contradictions and distorted realities inherent in a repressive regime.

The work itself takes multiple forms, all of which are centered around the chosen theme, and can encompass dreamlike animations, expressive charcoal drawings, paper cutouts, collage, prints, sculpture, tapestries, as well as theatrical productions. It is as if the artist cannot get enough work out and therefore uses a variety of methods to reach as diverse and as wide an audience as possible. Kentridge is engaged in a multidisciplinary practice. Before becoming an artist, he worked in graphic design, printmaking, theater, film, and television. The skill sets he developed early on in his career were later incorporated into his work as an artist. First in animation, and later in the staging and directing of Mozart's opera, *The Magic Flute* in 2005, and for Dmitri Shostakovich's, *The Nose* in 2010.

Much of the early work that deals with Apartheid in South Africa revolves around a character called Soho Eckstein, the greedy industrialist. In his films and drawings, Soho is depicted as a cruel figure who keeps the heads of black African workers in his bookcase as if they were trophies. In the drawing, *Johannesburg 2nd Greatest City after Paris* (Soho with Cigar), 1989, Soho leans back smiling at his desk, wearing a pinstriped suit and smoking a cigar. Soho looks satisfied with himself and the glory of his success. In a later work, *History of the Main Complaint,* 1996, Soho's success takes a turn for the worst, as he lies in bed, sick with an unknown disease. Kentridge is not providing answers as part of a search for utopia, nor is his work an overt condemnation; he is instead subtly pointing out the uncertainties of life and the constant struggles we all face. His most recent body of work is based on Shostakovich's opera, *The Nose,* which is based on a short story by Nikolai Gogol. Kentridge is no longer directly referencing South Africa. He is using an absurdist story—where a low-level bureaucrat in postrevolutionary Soviet Union wakes up without his nose—to highlight the contradictions of another broken social and political promise.

1
History of the Main Complaint
1996, 35 mm film transferred to video and laser disc

2 & 3
Johannesburg, 2nd Greatest City after Paris
1989, 16 mm film, video and laser disc transfer

4
Preparing the Flute
2005, Model theater, two 35 mm animated films transferred to DVD
Photo by John Berens

Courtesy Marian Goodman Gallery, New York/Paris

1

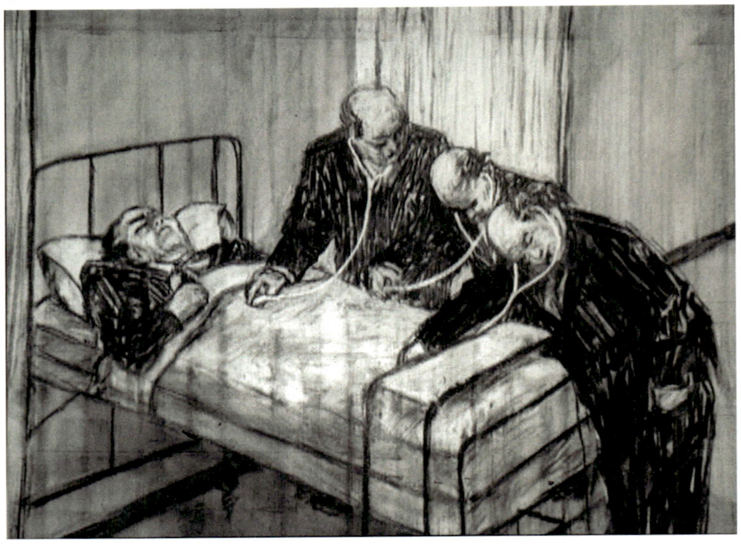

2

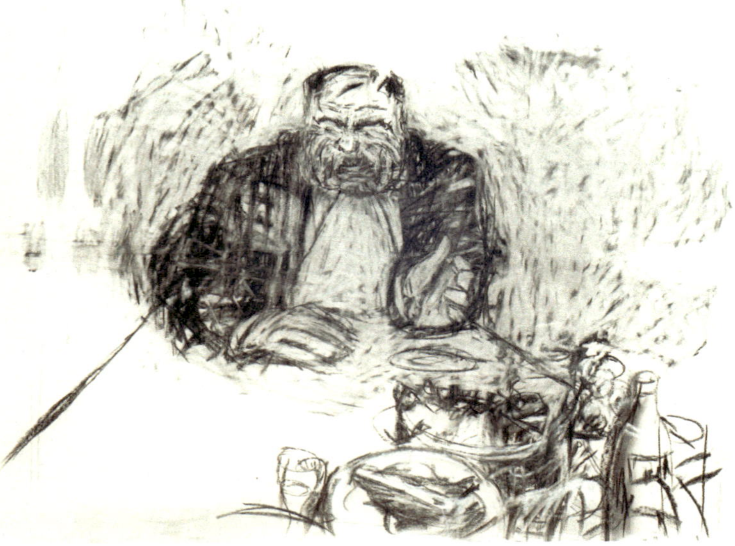

3

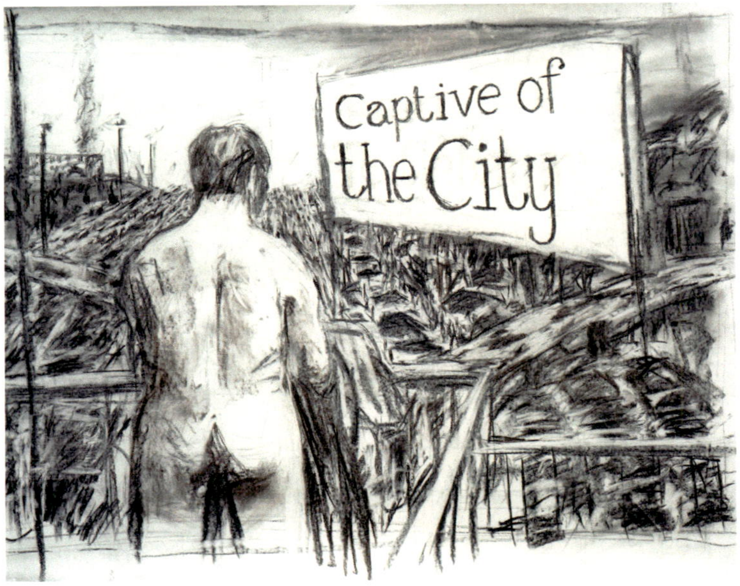

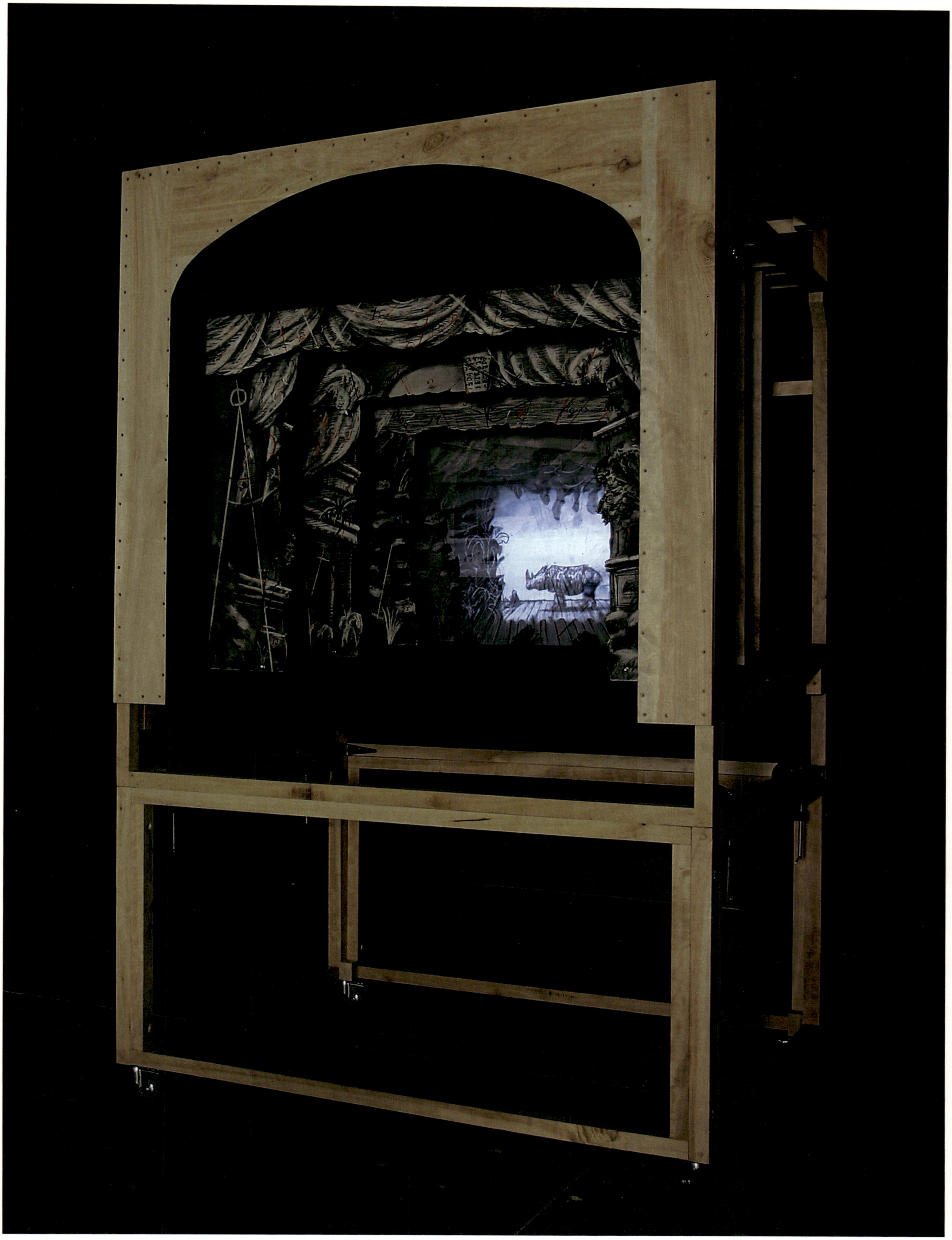

FERNANDO BRYCE

1
Die Welt
2008, Installation view Galerie Barbara Thumm, Berlin, Germany, Courtesy Galerie Barbara Thumm, Berlin
2–5
Südsee
2007, Series of 89 drawings
Ink on paper, Courtesy of Michael Krichman and Carmen Cuenca
6–10
Revolución
2004, Series of 219 drawings
Ink on paper, Courtesy Private Collection, Spain, and Galerie Barbara Thumm, Berlin

Fernando Bryce (* 1965) looks at world history, power relationships, and their representation through studying and reproducing primary documents. Each he embarks on undergoes a process of intense archaeological research during which the artist spends years searching for and reviewing archival materials to develop each body of work. He has referred to this process as an archaeological exhumation. The documents he scours include newspapers, business correspondence, images, pamphlets, portraits, travel brochures, and posters, to name a few. Bryce is looking for ideological representations in the documents. He refers to this process as "mimetic analysis." Once studied and selected, the primary documents are simultaneously reproduced and reinterpreted as the artist's copies by drawing the contents of each onto a cream-colored paper using ink. The entire body of work may consist of several hundred drawings, which are often exhibited together. In doing so, he is creating his own version of history, through a satirical look at representations of power, revolutionary or political struggle, and national identity. The artist uses drawings to reproduce the images as a means to homogenize the information, and allow for comparisons through a recontextualization of the documents. Only through removing the information from the context of its original design and intent can it be reinterpreted, allowing for a variety of historical narratives and a new, nonlinear view of the present.

A series of works titled, *Revolución*, 2004, consists of 219 drawings. The name of the series was taken from the first official Cuban newspaper of the Castro regime. Several of the drawings consist of the front page of the newspaper, *Revolución*. The series provides a critical view of power relationships between the United States and Latin America, as well as an account of 1960s revolutionary politics. One of the drawings depicts Che Guevara walking next to his Peruvian brother in arms, Juan Pablo Chang. The work is dated, "Bolivia 1967." The original image must have been taken shortly before both men were assassinated. In another work, the headline reads in Spanish: "We will not betray the trust of the people." When placed together and in retrospect, the broken promises and rhetoric of the Castro regime are evident, as is the illusion that was created of hope and commitment to a better future.

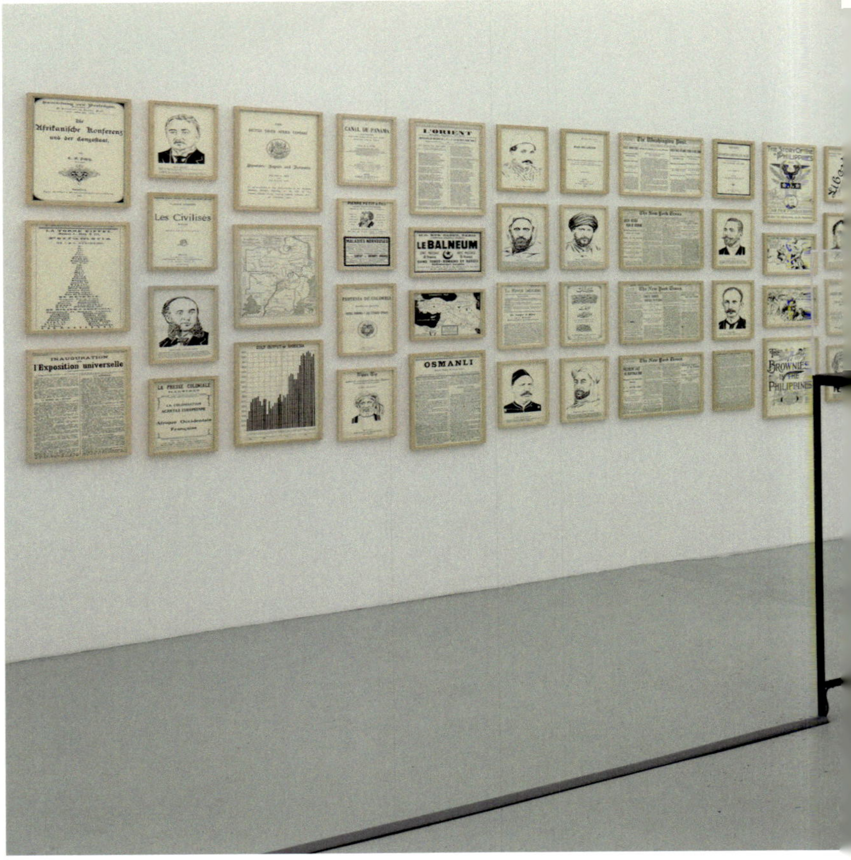
1

2
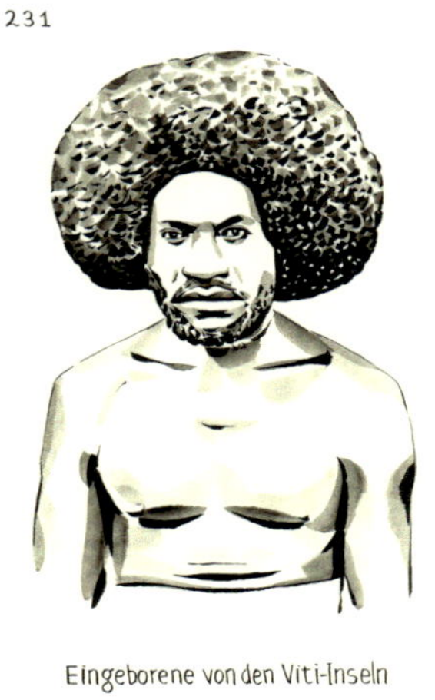

3
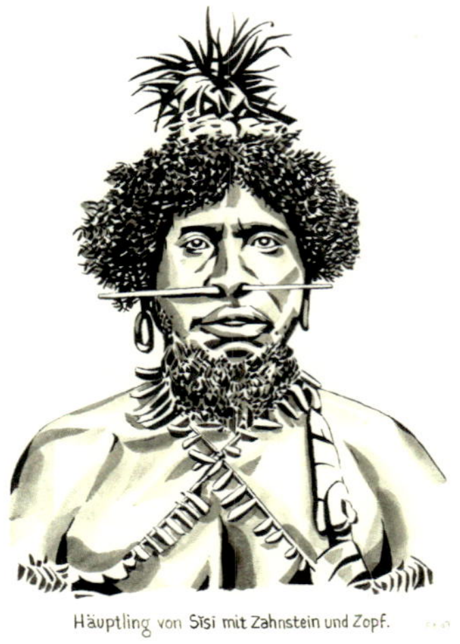

4
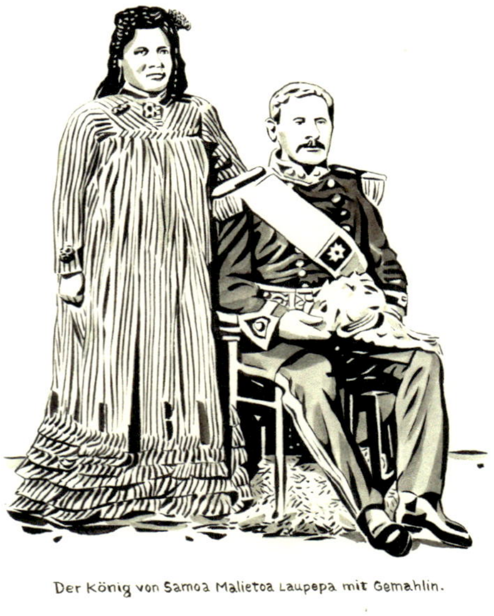

5
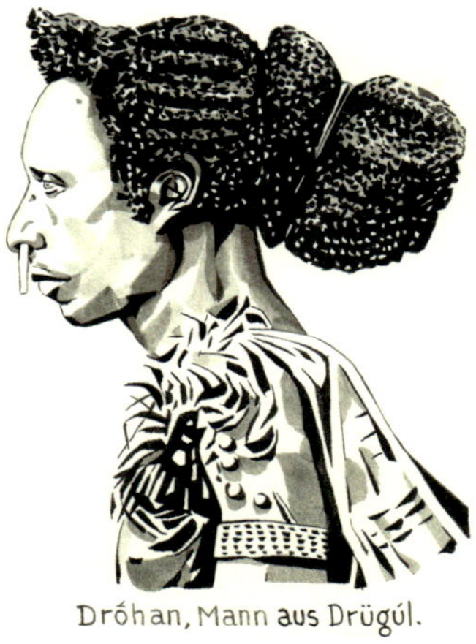

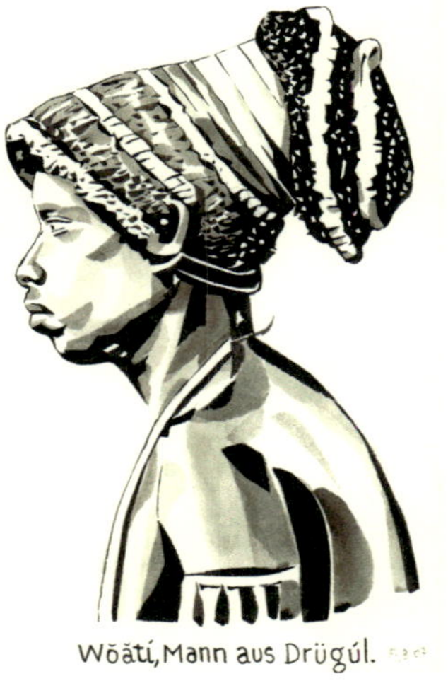

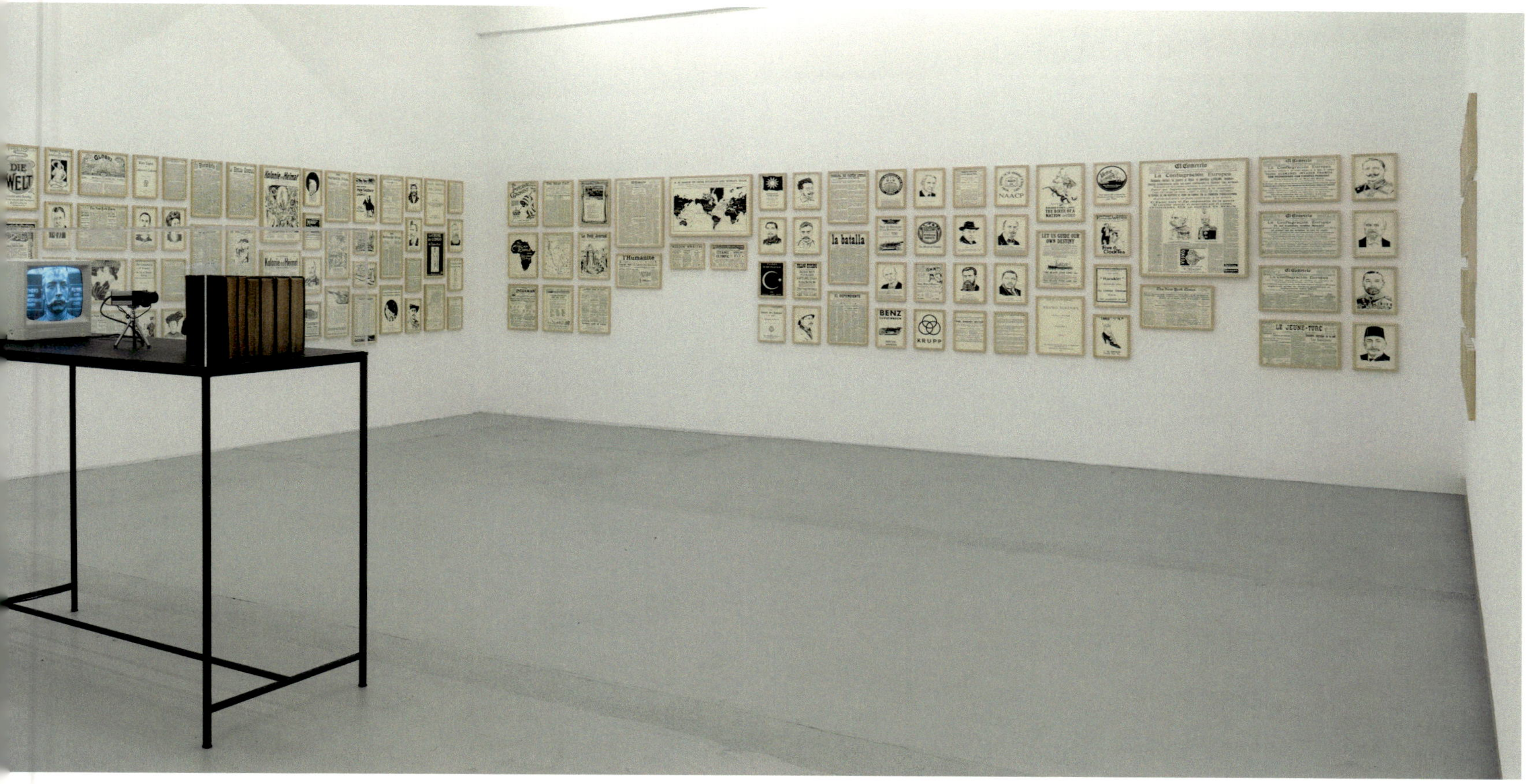
DIE WELT
la batalla
BENZ
KRUPP
NAACP
LE JEUNE-TURC

6

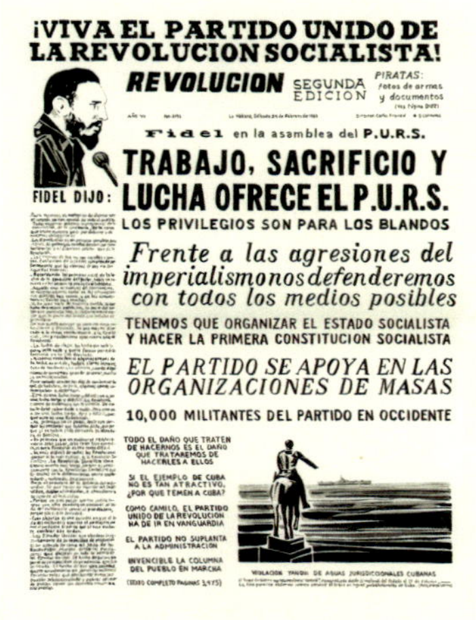
¡VIVA EL PARTIDO UNIDO DE LA REVOLUCION SOCIALISTA!
REVOLUCION SEGUNDA EDICION
PIRATAS: rotos de armes y documentos
Fidel en la asamblea del P.U.R.S.
FIDEL DIJO:
TRABAJO, SACRIFICIO Y LUCHA OFRECE EL P.U.R.S.
LOS PRIVILEGIOS SON PARA LOS BLANDOS
Frente a las agresiones del imperialismo nos defenderemos con todos los medios posibles
TENEMOS QUE ORGANIZAR EL ESTADO SOCIALISTA Y HACER LA PRIMERA CONSTITUCION SOCIALISTA
EL PARTIDO SE APOYA EN LAS ORGANIZACIONES DE MASAS
10,000 MILITANTES DEL PARTIDO EN OCCIDENTE

7

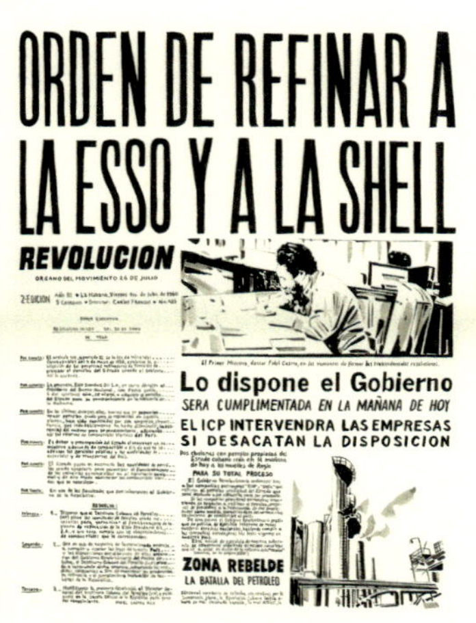
ORDEN DE REFINAR A LA ESSO Y A LA SHELL
REVOLUCION
Lo dispone el Gobierno
SERA CUMPLIMENTADA EN LA MAÑANA DE HOY
EL ICP INTERVENDRA LAS EMPRESAS SI DESACATAN LA DISPOSICION
ZONA REBELDE
LA BATALLA DEL PETROLEO

10

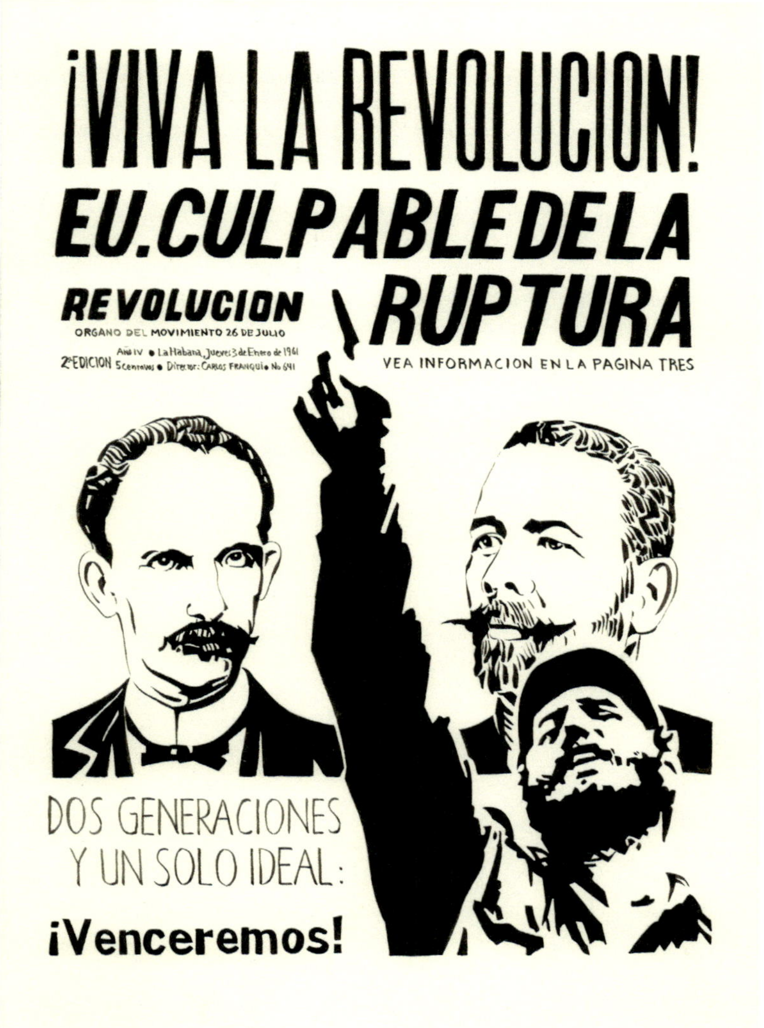
¡VIVA LA REVOLUCION!
EU. CULPABLE DE LA RUPTURA
REVOLUCION
ORGANO DEL MOVIMIENTO 26 DE JULIO
2a EDICION
Año IV • La Habana, Jueves 5 de Enero de 1961
5 centavos • Director: Carlos Franqui • No 641
VEA INFORMACION EN LA PAGINA TRES
DOS GENERACIONES Y UN SOLO IDEAL:
¡Venceremos!

8

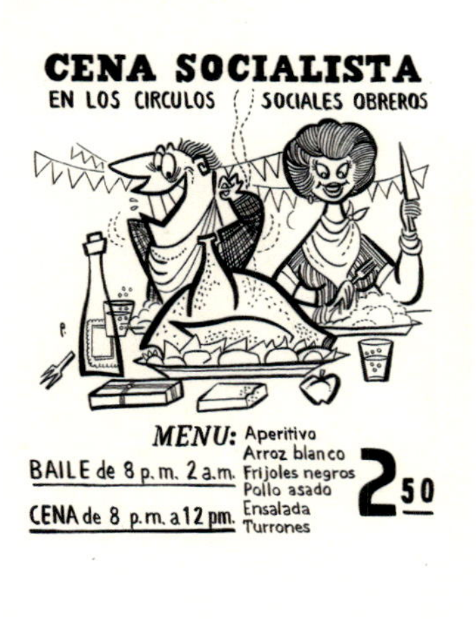
CENA SOCIALISTA
EN LOS CIRCULOS SOCIALES OBREROS
MENU: Aperitivo
Arroz blanco
Frijoles negros
Pollo asado
Ensalada
Turrones
BAILE de 8 p.m. 2 a.m.
CENA de 8 p.m. a 12 pm.
2 50

9

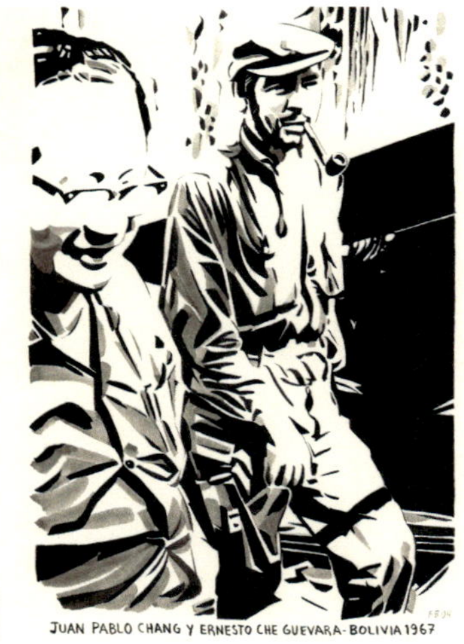
JUAN PABLO CHANG Y ERNESTO CHE GUEVARA - BOLIVIA 1967

SHEPARD FAIREY

The U.S. artist Shepard Fairey (* 1970) is a leader in the global street art movement. In 1989, he initiated a street art campaign that has now distributed over 10 million stickers. His images, reproduced onto paper, cover city walls around the world. At these industrial levels, street art is an expensive practice; not only is a great deal of time spent out on the street risking arrest, the cost of materials, fabrication, and distribution soon add up. In order to continue to expand his practice, Fairey has developed a business model that incorporates selling editions of prints through his website, gallery exhibitions, books, products, and a line of clothing. These ancillary activities have led to him receiving criticism about his integrity as an artist, and the so-called "purity" of his work. Fairey has dedicated his life to making art that almost everyone can understand, purchase, and see. The images he creates and the references he uses are very common and well known, making the work intellectually accessible. Fairey sells his limited edition prints online directly to consumers through his website for 45–100 dollars. That is as cheap as art will get and the buyer does not have to go through a gatekeeper or gallery to buy it, anyone can buy a print as long as they are attentive online and quick with a mouse. Fairey's commitment to placing his images in public space allows anyone to see his work. The public is not limited to seeing the art in a gallery or museum.

The populist imagery and practice, confronted with a capitalist approach to production and dissemination of his work, presents a contradiction that is difficult for some people to accept. Fairey explains his work as a social experiment that is based on Martin Heidegger's ideas of phenomenology. The images on stickers and wheatpasted paper prints were intended to awaken the passerby who encountered them from their daily routine. In this awakened state, the aim was for the public was to question the nature of all other visual messages in public space. Up until the year 2000, Fairey's work did not have an overtly political message. His use of a socialist realist style, borrowed from Soviet-era propaganda posters, was intended to steal the public's attention and arouse suspicion. With the election of George Bush, Fairey was outraged at the American government's new direction. This gave him a political cause to pursue, and an abundance of material to work with. The war in Iraq and the policies that surrounded the build up to the war and the later conflict, inspired a dramatic shift in the artist's intention. The work itself and the method of dissemination on city walls had gone from being a subversive act intended to raise questions and reclaim public space from corporate advertisements and the government, to a direct assault on the war in Iraq and the Bush administration. Fairey once stated that he had taken the Clinton years for granted: "I had no idea how good we had it until Bush stepped in." The work that had always been about raising awareness and empowerment now contains a call to action, and addresses many topics such as the environment, alternative fuels, and gay rights. During the 2004 presidential election campaign, Fairey created one of his most famous works, the Obama *Hope* poster. In this work, the artist was able to articulate what millions of voters were feeling about the young candidate. The image became central to the campaign and helped get Obama elected.

Although Fairey clearly states that he is not an activist, he has taken his political involvement beyond a call to action by creating prints and donating a percentage of the proceeds to support specific causes such as gay marriage and immigration reform among many others. In most cases the artist sells the prints through his own distribution channels, providing the beneficiary organization with funding and images that supporters can rally around. In the same way that many great musicians are able to speak to the masses through their music, Fairey is able to articulate visually what many people are feeling. His art speaks directly to a very wide audience, who are inspired by his aesthetic, images, and ideas. As is the case with the Obama image, the visual articulation of the cause is often more valuable than the funds received.

1
Duality of Humanity 3
2008, screen print and collage on canvas
Photo by Al Rockoff

2
Afrocentric
2007, Screen print and collage on paper

3
Two Sides of Capitalism: Good
2007, Mixed-media on canvas

4
No…I'm Vegetarian
2007, Spray paint and stencil on canvas

5
Duality of Humanity 5
2010, Screen print on paper
Reference photographer: Al Rockoff

© Shepard Fairey/ObeyGiant.com

2

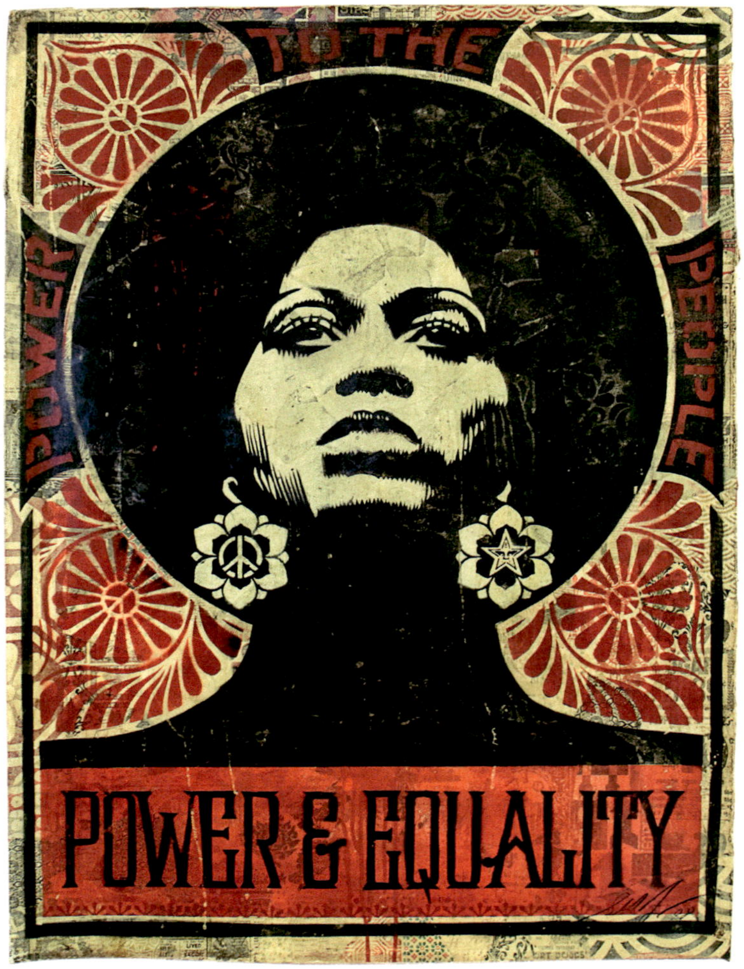

1

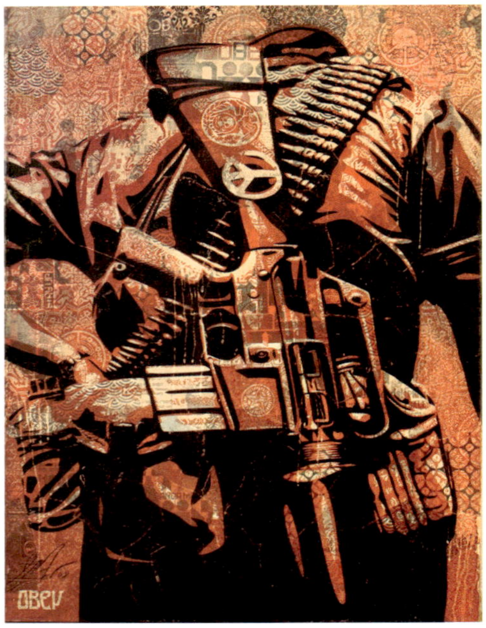

3

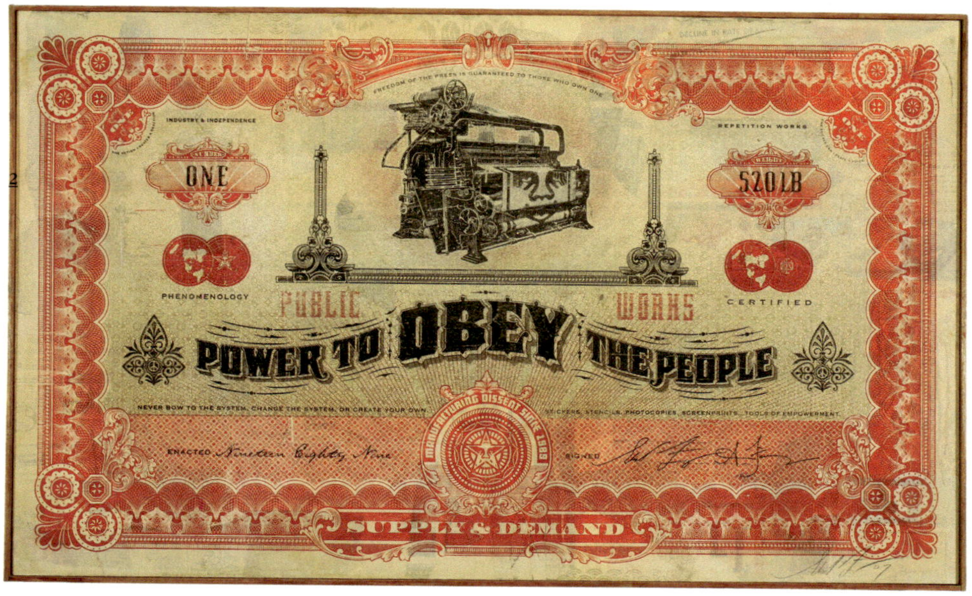
INDUSTRY & INDEPENDENCE
REPETITION WORKS
ONE
5201B
PHENOMENOLOGY
CERTIFIED
PUBLIC
WORKS
POWER TO OBEY THE PEOPLE
SUPPLY & DEMAND

4

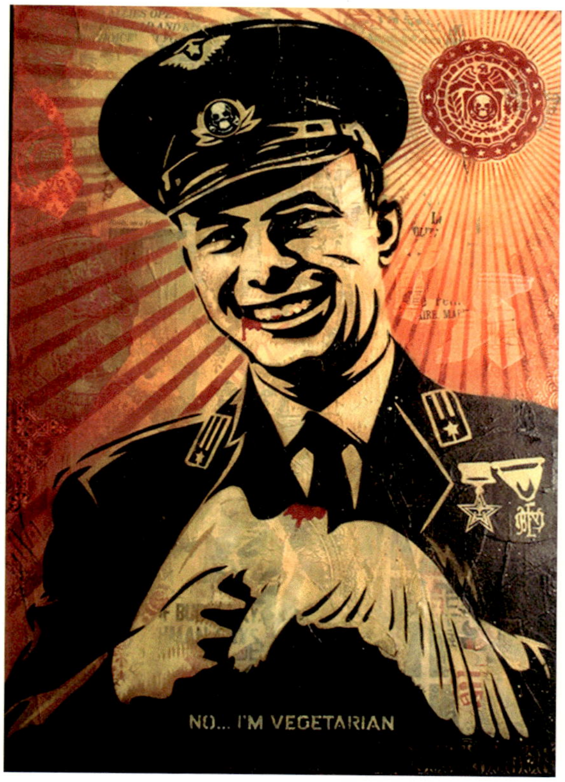
NO... I'M VEGETARIAN

5

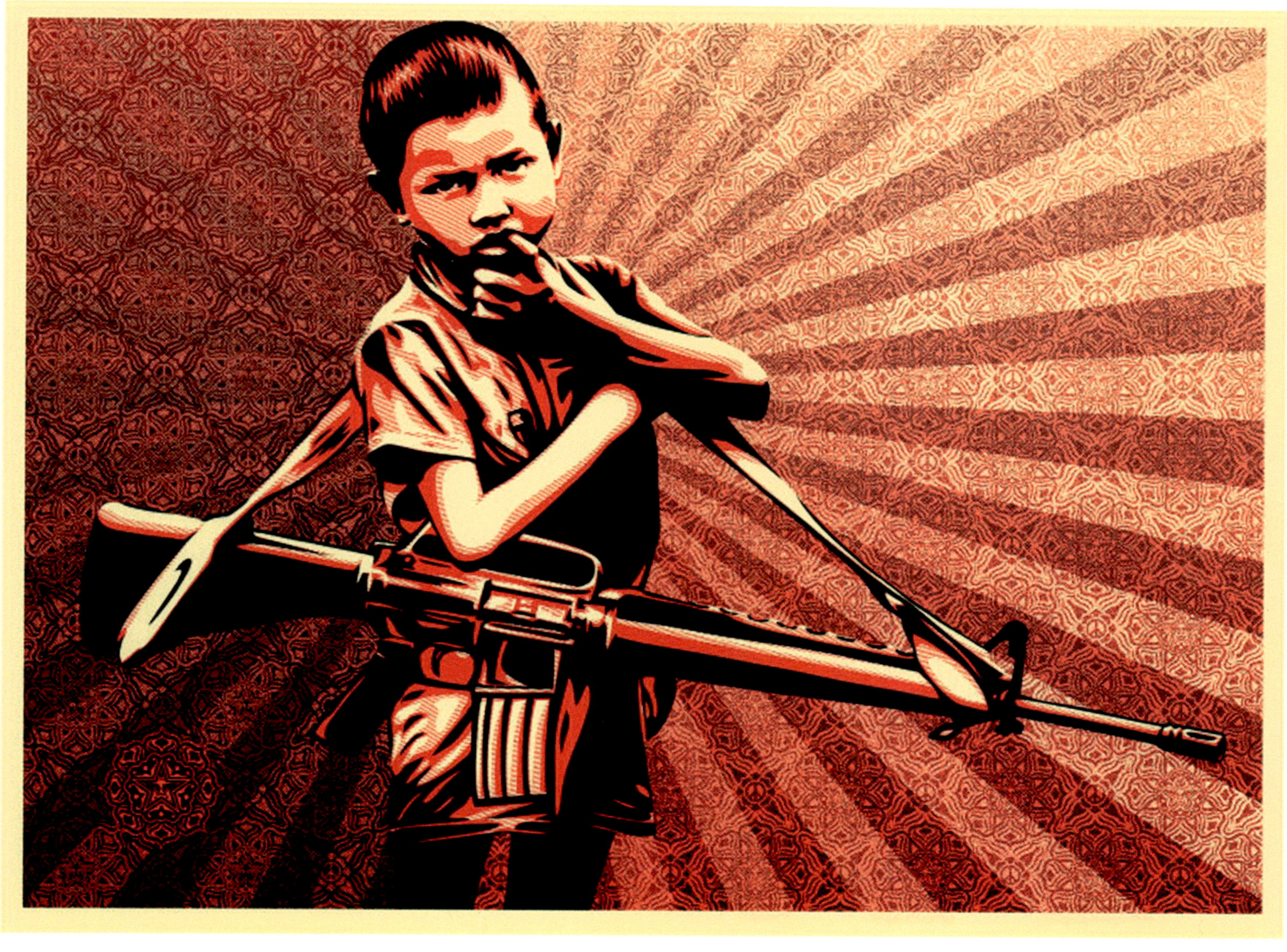

KARA WALKER

The American artist Kara Walker (* 1969) has established a signature style and unique visual language through the use of paper cutouts or silhouettes, a method that was developed in the nineteenth century. She has also made films using animation and shadow puppets. These mediums are reminiscent of cartoons; they have a quality that appears as if designed for children. Even though the caricature-like forms and shapes carry a connotation of innocence, the content deals with mature subject matter. The images are created after a process of gathering information in notebooks, developing ideas, and collecting objects related to African American history. The black cutout images are assembled to create large-scale narratives that depict the myths and stereotypes associated with African-Americans. Women are often portrayed naked, with large backsides, and placed in sexually demeaning positions. The white man or master is aroused, looking for sex and other forms of exploitation. Although the stories are often set in the old South, the scenes are not meant to be historical. They are fantasy wrapped in the specific historical period that is best-suited for exploring issues of race in the United States. The various narratives reveal the complicated and abusive history of race, identity, and power. The antebellum imagery serves as a reminder of the wounds inflicted by slavery, and the legacy of issues that are still being dealt with today.

Walker addresses the forbidden passion and desire associated with black identity. The scenes in her work are often lurid and scatological; her work alludes to the contradictions of the slave/master relationship in an era of supposed Victorian propriety, where sexual debauchery and violence were commonplace. The artist's use of an antiquated medium is meant to simplify the complexities of the history and the complex relationships between people. Walker is not concerned with ambiguous formal strategies; the work is meant to tell a brutal story. In contrast to the elegantly cut paper shapes, the images are cruel and intentionally disturbing, as rape and other abuses are commonplace in the work. In a multipart mural titled *Endless Conundrum, an African Anonymous Adventuress,* several characters are engaged in sadistic sexual acts: a slave woman is up against a tree, where a small man is driving a nail into her pubis with a mallet. In another vignette, a bearded, white man wearing a pith helmet shoots a well-endowed slave in the midsection. This work, which appears to be set in Africa, also contains several references to outrages committed during the exploration of the so-called Dark Continent and the native cultures from which the slaves were torn—for example, an explorer runs with a newborn from an African idol that waves goodbye. Walker incorporates visual elements and objects from native African cultures; an idol chained to a ball stands inside a serving platter, alluding to the chaining and restraining of a culture through displacement and slavery.

1
Jockey
1995, Cut paper on canvas
Courtesy Sikkema Jenkins & Co., New York

2
National Archives Microfilm Publication M999 Roll 34: Bureau of Refugees, Freedmen and Abandoned Lands: Lucy of Pulaski
2009, Video on DVD (color, audio), Original music by Alicia and Jason Moran

3
Untitled
2009, Cut paper and collage on paper, Courtesy Sikkema Jenkins & Co., New York

4
Somebody Call an Ambivalence
2007, Paper collage, gouache on wood panel
Courtesy of Sikkema Jenkins & Co., New York

5 (next spread)
Danse de la Nubienne Nouveaux [detail]
1998, Cut paper and adhesive on wall, Courtesy Sikkema Jenkins & Co., New York

1

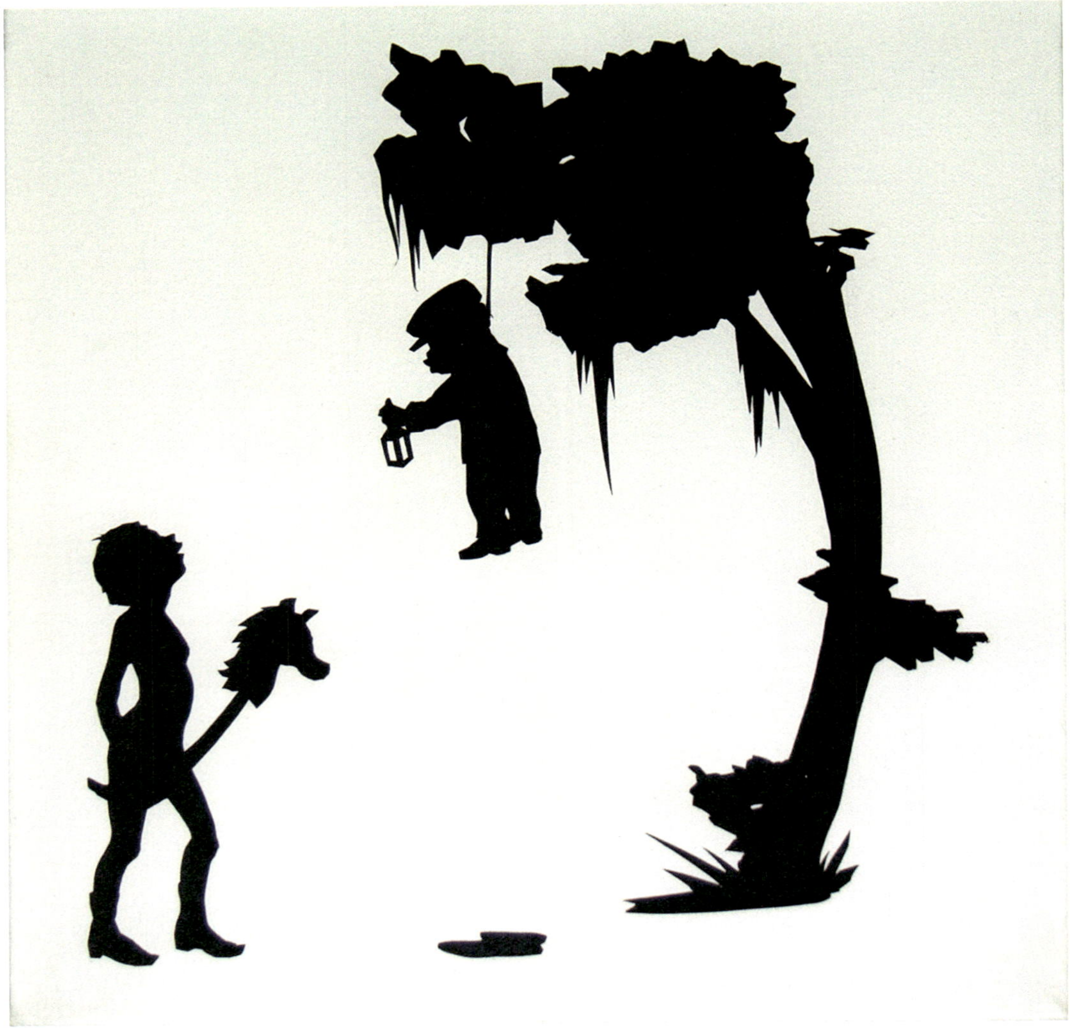

2

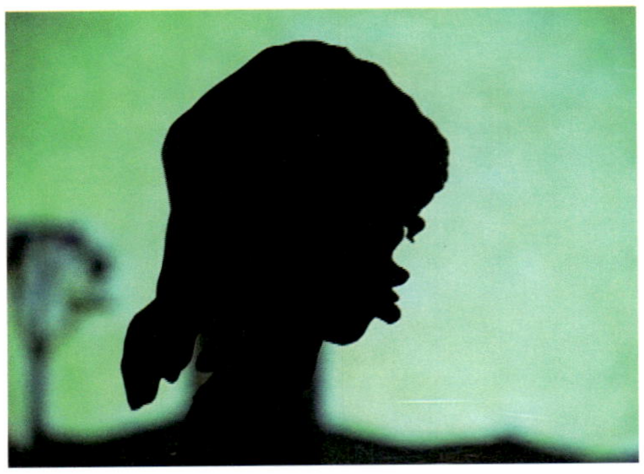

3

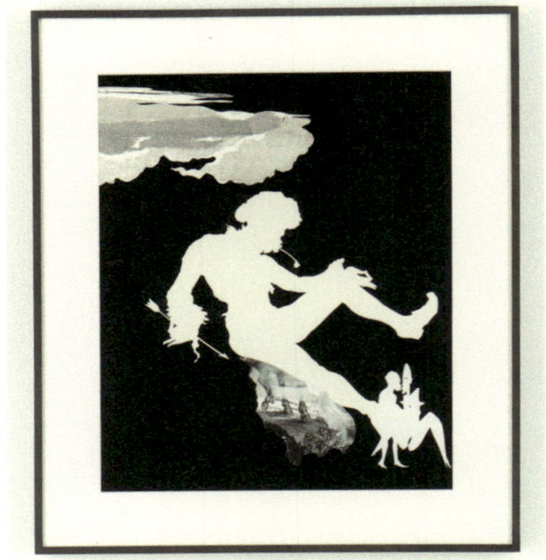

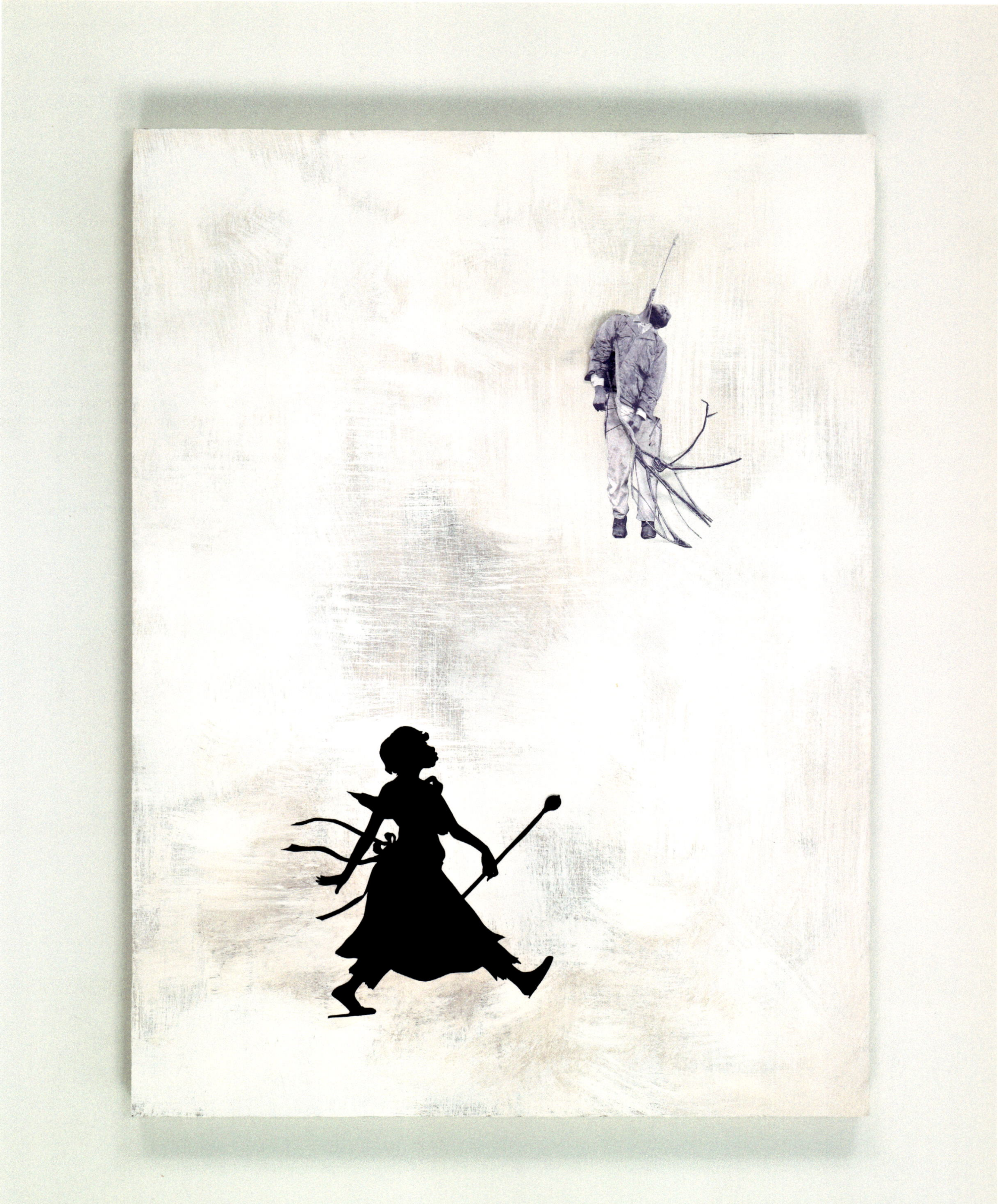

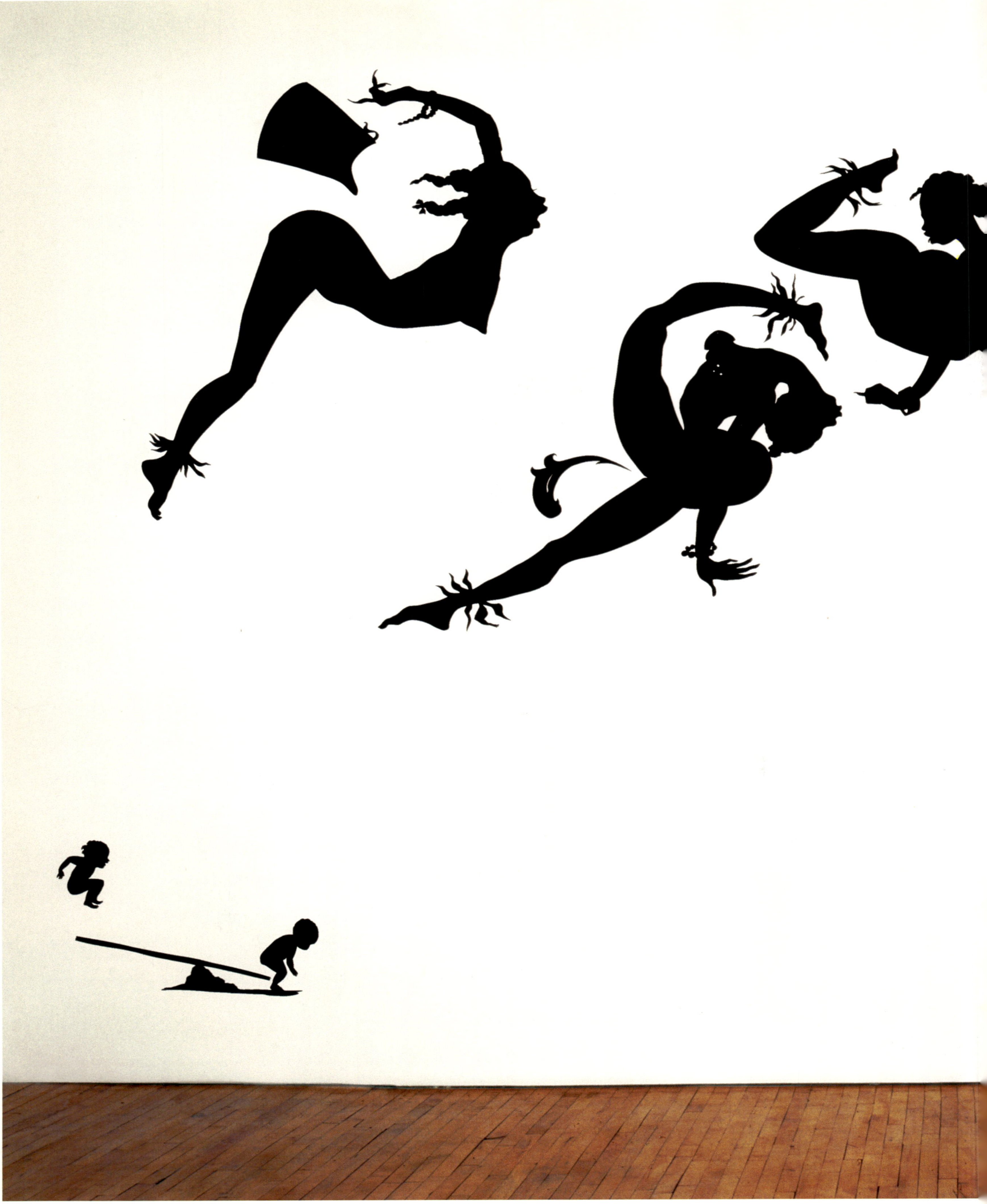

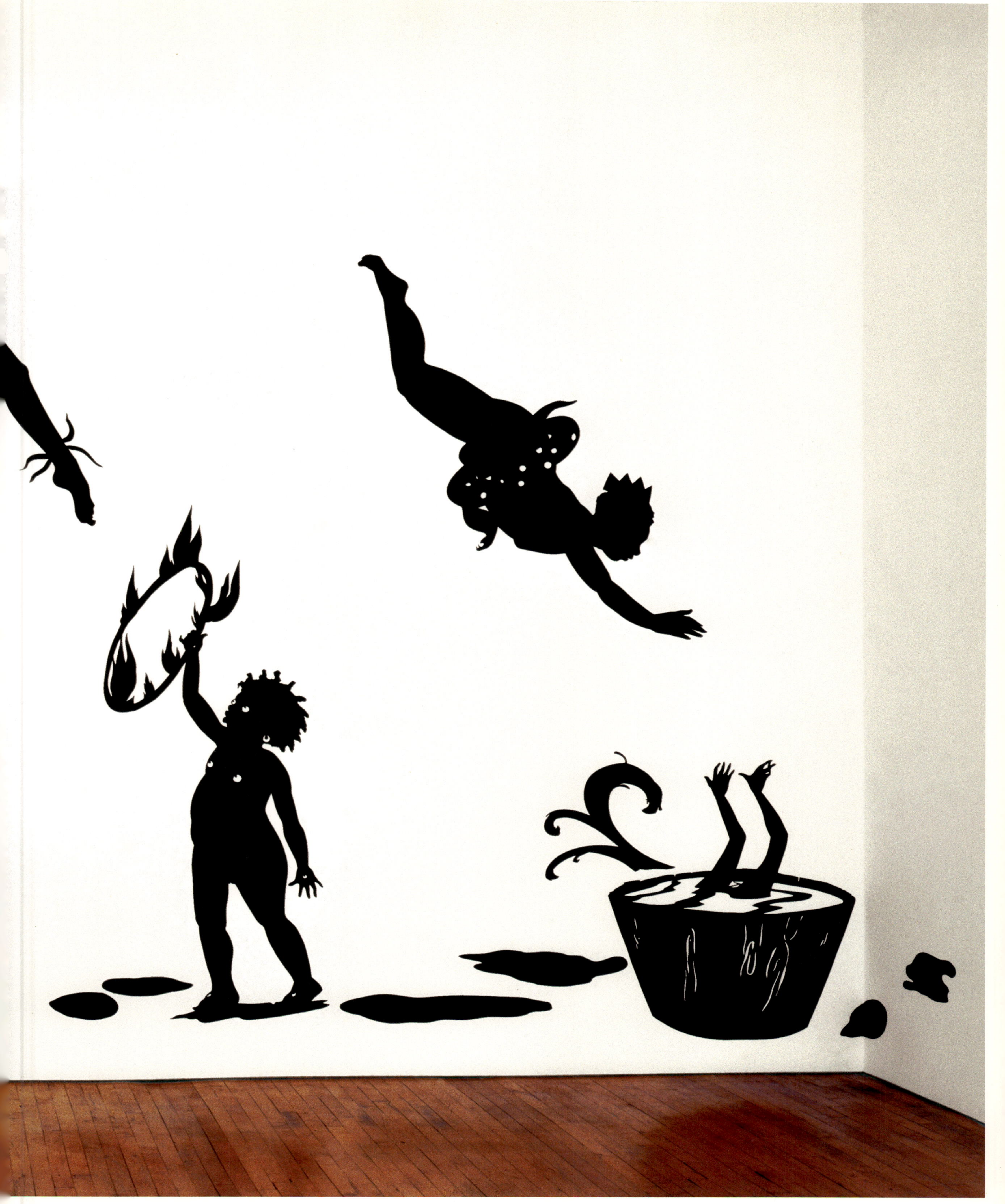

ARTIST INDEX

A

B

C

D–E

SEBASTIÁN ERRÁZURIZ
Chile/USA
www.meetsebastian.com
pp. 228–231

ESTUDIO TEDDY CRUZ
USA
www.estudioteddycruz.com
pp. 196–197

MARCO EVARISTTI
Denmark
www.evaristti.com
pp. 128–129

F–G

SHEPARD FAIREY
USA
www.obeygiant.com
pp. 276–277

ALEXANDRE FARTO - VHILS
Portugal
www.alexandrefarto.com
pp. 182–183

CHRISTOPH FAULHABER
Germany
www.christophfaulhaber.de
pp. 116–117

REGINA JOSÉ GALINDO
Guatemala
www.reginajosegalindo.com
pp. 198–199

GAO BROTHERS
China
www.gaobrothers.net
pp. 174–177

MURRAY GAYLARD
Germany
www.murraygaylard.com
p. 33

KENDELL GEERS
South Africa
www.stephenfriedman.com
pp. 108–109

OLIVER GOODHALL
United Kingdom
www.olivergoodhall.com
p. 84

WIEBKE GRÖSCH/ FRANK METZGER
Germany
www.groeschmetzger.de
pp. 120–121

H

HERMANN JOSEF HACK
Germany
www.hermann-josef-hack.de
p. 82

KHALED HAFEZ
Egypt
www.khaledhafez.net
p. 257

MONA HATOUM
Lebanon
www.whitecube.com
pp. 202–203

SUSAN HEFUNA
Egypt
www.susanhefuna.com
p. 200

HARMEN DE HOOP
Netherlands
www.harmendehoop.com
p. 70

ZHANG HUAN
China
www.zhanghuan.com
pp. 170–173

J–K

MARK JENKINS
USA
www.xmarkjenkinsx.com
pp. 98–99

PACKARD JENNINGS
USA
www.centennialsociety.com/durham.html
pp. 30–31

JOSEUB
South Korea
www.joseub.com
pp. 234–235

JR
France
www.jr-art.net
pp. 178–181

JENNIFER KARADY
USA
www.jenniferkarady.com
pp. 260–263

LAURA KEEBLE
United Kingdom
www.laurakeeble.com
p. 37

KENNARDPHILLIPPS
United Kingdom
www.kennardphillipps.com
pp. 232–233

WILLIAM KENTRIDGE
South Africa
www.gregkucera.com
pp. 272–273

MAHMOUD KHALED
Egypt
www.mahmoudkhaled.com
p. 201

L–N

O–P

R

S

TOM SACHS
USA
www.speronewestwater.com
pp. 38–39

ZOË SHEEHAN SALDAÑA
USA
www.zoesheehan.com
p. 36

ELVIRA SANTAMARÍA
Mexico
www.elvirasantamaria.com
pp. 190–191

GREGOR SCHNEIDER
Germany
www.gregorschneider.de
pp. 140–141

SANTIAGO SIERRA
Mexico
www.santiago-sierra.com
pp. 122–125

HELMUT SMITS
Netherlands
www.helmutsmits.nl
pp. 126–127

SUPERFLEX
Denmark
www.superflex.dk
pp. 76–77

SWOON
USA
www.swimmingcities.org
pp. 90–93

T

HANK WILLIS THOMAS
USA
www.hankwillisthomas.com
pp. 266–267

THYLACINE
Switzerland
www.thylacine.ws
p. 138

MILICA TOMIĆ
Serbia
www.charimgalerie.at
pp. 204–205

NAVID TSCHOPP-SADROSSADAT
Switzerland
www.navid.ch
p. 71

NASAN TUR
Germany
www.nasantur.com
pp. 68–69

U–W

UBERMORGEN.COM
Austria
www.ubermorgen.com
p. 256

VOINA GROUP
Russia
www.en.free-voina.org,
www.plucer.livejournal.com
pp. 146–151

THE WA
France
www.the-wabsite.com
pp. 136–137

KARA WALKER
USA
www.sikkemajenkinsco.com
pp. 278–281

WASTE
United Kingdom
pp. 20–21

LI WEI
China
www.liweiart.com
pp. 158–159

AI WEIWEI
China
www.aiweiwei.com
pp. 160–163

WOCHENKLAUSUR
Austria
www.wochenklausur.at
pp. 61–65

Y–Z

THE YES MEN
USA
www.theyesmen.org
pp. 72–75

YANG YI
China
www.galerieparisbeijing.com
pp. 168–169

ARTUR ŻMIJEWSKI
Poland
www.berlinbiennale.de
pp. 206–209

ZTOHOVEN
Czech Republic
www.ztohoven.com
pp. 112–115

ALAIN BIEBER

Alain Bieber (*1978) studied rhetoric, sociology, literature, and political science in Tübingen (Germany) and Paris. He works as an art critic (for artnet, *ARTE, ART Magazin, Neural*, etc.), blogger, project manager, and curator in Strasbourg. In 2004, he founded the rebel:art media foundation, a platform for art, culture, and politics (www.rebelart.net). Past projects include *Pillowfight Klub* and the *OH!* video magazine. Ongoing projects are: GuteSeiten, a curated kiosk and magazine club; the International Sticker Awards; and PARASITES, an illegal exhibition series. Bieber co-curated the Subversiv Messe in Linz and the Dockville Festival in Hamburg. He was a jury member at the DokFest Kassel, the Viral Video Award, and the Backup Media Festival, and he has given lectures about street art, subversive strategies, fanzines, and illegal interventions in Berlin, Leipzig, Hamburg, Frankfurt, and Eindhoven. For three years Bieber worked as a journalist for the German *ART Magazine* in Hamburg. He's currently the project manager for ARTE Creative in Strasbourg.

PEDRO ALONZO

Pedro Alonzo, a Boston-based freelance curator, was recently appointed as an Adjunct Curator at the Institute of Contemporary Art (ICA) Boston. Alonzo was formerly an adjunct curator at the Institute of Visual Arts, University of Wisconsin, Milwaukee from 1996–2002. He has organized exhibitions in public museums and private collections internationally including: Estacion Tijuana, Tijuana, Mexico, and the Museo Rufino Tamayo, Mexico City, Mexico; the Baltic Centre for Contemporary Art, Newcastle, England; Pinchuk Art Centre, Kiev, Ukraine; Van Moerkerke Collection, Oostende, Belgium; and the ICA Boston and the Museum of Contemporary Art (MCA) San Diego. Alonzo has worked with many artists including: Miguel Calderon, Maurizio Cattelan, Banksy, Quisqueya Henriquez, Rineke Dijkstra, FAILE, Meschac Gaba, Dan Graham, Ryan McGinness, Rivane Neuenschwander, Iñigo Manglano-Ovalle, Paula Santiago, and Marcos Ramírez "Erre." Pedro has conducted a series of interviews with artists such as Swoon, Mark Ryden, William Cordova, Jeff Soto, and Os Gêmeos for the book *The Upset: Young Contemporary Art.* For the ICA Boston he recently curated Shepard Fairey's 20-year survey titled "Supply and Demand," and a solo exhibition with Dr. Lakra in 2010. For the MCA San Diego he organized the group exhibition "Viva la Revolucion: A Dialogue with the Urban Landscape." He is currently working on the first solo exhibition for Swoon at the ICA Boston.

GREGOR JANSEN

Dr. Gregor Jansen has been artistic director at the Kunsthalle Düsseldorf since 2010 and has curated exhibitions there by Hans-Peter Feldmann and Ferdinand Kriwet. From 2005 to the end of 2009 he was head of ZKM | Museum of Contemporary Art in Karlsruhe, Germany, where he curated exhibitions such as "Light Art from Artificial Light" (with Peter Weibel), "Totalstadt. Beijing Case", and "Vertrautes Terrain: Contemporary Art in/about Germany" (with Thomas Thiel). Gregor Jansen studied art history, architectural history, and philosophy at RWTH Aachen University and completed his PhD thesis, *Eugen Schönebeck, a German Legend*, in 1998. Since 1991 he has worked as a curator, an art historian, an author, and a lecturer in visual studies and media theory at several universities in Germany and the Netherlands.

SILKE KROHN

Silke Krohn trained as a bookseller; studied art history, media, and romance languages and literature in Kiel, Germany; worked in Paris; and completed a PhD thesis entitled *Der Hirsch: Popularisierung und Individualisierung eines Motivs* (The Stag: Popularization and Individualization of a Motif) in 2006. She worked at the Kunsthalle zu Kiel and the Stadtgalerie Kiel from 2000 to 2007, in the dean's office and the PR department (designing events and exhibitions) at the Muthesius Academy of Fine Arts and Design from 2004 to 2007, and as a research assistant at the National Museums in Berlin from 2007 to 2009. She has been part of the National Gallery's art education department since 2007. In 2009/2010 she curated the exhibition "Hans Bellmer – Louise Bourgeois: Double Sexus" for the New National Gallery's Scharf-Gerstenberg Collection. Since 2010 she has been a research assistant in the museum pedagogy and PR department at Berlin's Museum of Communication and a teaching assistant in Piotr Nathan's drawing and graphic art class at the Muthesius Academy of Fine Arts and Design. She is the author of various written works and audio guides on the art of the twentieth and twenty-first centuries.

MATTHIAS HÜBNER

Matthias Hübner graduated in 2006 with a degree in visual communication from the Kunsthochschule Berlin-Weißensee with a focus on book design. Since then, he has published and designed numerous books for Die Gestalten Verlag, including *Writing: Urban Calligraphy and Beyond* and *Urban Interventions*. Hübner continues to work with local and international artists on publications such as *Writing the Memory of the City, Das Prinzip Zast Real Estate*, and *Arrow Pieces*. In 2008, while working for onlab, he was involved in the presentation of the German Pavilion at the 11th International Architecture Exhibition at the Venice Biennale.

ROBERT KLANTEN

Robert Klanten works as a publisher, editor, and curator in the fields of visual culture, art, and design.

FOOTNOTES

Page 6: Pevsner, Nicolaus. *Die Geschichte der Kunstakademien*, Munich: Mäander: page 195.
Page 5: Latour, Bruno. From his speech at the opening of the 2005 exhibit "Making Things Public" at ZKM, which can be found at http://on1.zkm.de/zkm/stories/storyReader$4581.
Page 9: Duchamp, Marcel. From his lecture at the Museum of Modern Art, October 19, 1961. which can be found at http://radicalart.info/things/readymade/duchamp/text.html.
Page 51: Camus, Albert. "Art and Revolt." *The New Partisan Reader* (1945–1953).
Page 52: Heath, Joseph and Potter, Andrew. *The Rebel Sell: How the Counter Culture Became Consumer Culture.* John Wiley & Sons, 2006.
Page 53: Bruguera, Tania. *Political Art Statement*, 2010, http://www.taniabruguera.com/cms/388-0-Political+Art+Statement.htm.
Page 55: Camus, Albert. *The Rebel, An Essay on Man in Revolt.* page 255.
Page 218: Rivera, Diego. "The Revolutionary Spirit in Modern Art." *Modern Quarterly*. Vol. 6, No. 3, 1932.
Page 221: Debord, Guy and Wolman, Gil J. "A User's Guide to Détournement." in *Guy Debord: Complete Cinematic Works.* 2003.
Page 223: Fairey, Shepard. "Education or Exploitation" *Obey: Supply & Demand, The Art of Shepard Fairey.* Gingko Press.
Page 225: Shepard Fairey. Interview, on *These Days.* KPBS San Diego.

Art& Agenda

POLITICAL ART AND ACTIVISM

Edited by Robert Klanten, Matthias Hübner,
Alain Bieber, Pedro Alonzo, and Gregor Jansen

Texts by Pedro Alonzo, Alain Bieber, and Silke Krohn
Preface by Gregor Jansen and Robert Klanten

Cover image by kennardphillipps
Layout & cover by Matthias Hübner for Gestalten

Quote on the back cover from Joseph Heath and Andrew Potter, *The Rebel Sell: How the Counter Culture Became Consumer Culture*, John Wiley & Sons, 2006

Project management by Elisabeth Honerla for Gestalten
Project management assistance by Rebekka Wangler for Gestalten
Production management by Vinzenz Geppert for Gestalten
Proofreading by Eileen Daly and Rebecca Silus
Printed by Optimal Media Production GmbH, Röbel
Made in Germany

Published by Gestalten, Berlin 2011
ISBN 978-3-89955-342-0

For more information, please visit www.gestalten.com

Bibliographic information published by the Deutsche Nationalbibliothek.
The Deutsche Nationalbibliothek lists this publication in the Deutsche Nationalbibliografie; detailed bibliographic data is available online at http://dnb.d-nb.de.

None of the content in this book was published in exchange for payment by commercial parties or designers; Gestalten selected all included work based solely on its artistic merit.

This book has been printed on FSC certified paper which ensures responsible paper sources with sustainable forest management.

Gestalten is a climate-neutral company and so are our products. We collaborate with the non-profit carbon offset provider myclimate (www.myclimate.org) to neutralize the company's carbon footprint produced through our worldwide business activities by investing in projects that reduce CO_2 emissions (www.gestalten.com/myclimate).

myclimate
Protect our planet